Management Information Systems

Effy Oz

The Pennsylvania State University, Great Valley

COURSE TECHNOLOGY

ONE MAIN STREET, CAMBRIDGE, MA 02142

an International Thomson Publishing company I(T)P®

Cambridge • Albany • Bonn • Boston • Cincinnati • London • Madrid • Melbourne • Mexico City
New York • Paris • San Francisco • Singapore • Tokyo • Toronto • Washington

*To Narda, my wife and only
addiction and to my children:
Ron, Noam, Adi, and Sahar*

Management Information Systems is published by Course Technology.

Managing Editor	Kristin Duerr
Editorial Assistant	Lisa Ayers
Product Manager	Jennifer Normandin
Developmental Editor	Janet M. Weinrib
Production Editor	Debbie Masi
Composition and Art	GEX, Inc.
Photo Researcher	Abby Reip
Book Design	Books by Design
Cover Designers	Books by Design and Efrat Reis

© 1998 by Course Technology —I T P®
A Division of International Thomson Publishing, Inc.

For more information contact:

Course Technology
One Main Street
Cambridge, MA 02142

International Thomson Publishing Europe
Berkshire House 168-173
High Holborn
London WCIV 7AA
England

Thomas Nelson Australia
102 Dodds Street
South Melbourne, 3205
Victoria, Australia

Nelson Canada
1120 Birchmount Road
Scarborough, Ontario
Canada, M1K 5G4

International Thomson Editores
Campos Eliseos 385, Piso 7
Col. Polanco
11560 Mexico D.F. Mexico

International Thomson Publishing GmbH
Königswinterer Strasse 418
53227 Bonn
Germany

International Thomson Publishing Asia
211 Henderson Road
#05-10 Henderson Building
Singapore 0315

International Thomson Publishing Japan
Hirakawacho Kyowa Building, 3F
2-2-1 Hirakawacho
Chiyoda-ku, Tokyo 102
Japan

Disclaimer
Course Technology reserves the right to revise this publication and make changes from time to time in its content without notice.
ISBN 0-7600-4946-7 (Student Edition)
ISBN 0-7600-4983-1 (Annotated Student Edition)
Printed in the United States of America
10 9 8 7 6 5 4 3 2 1

Brief Contents

Contents

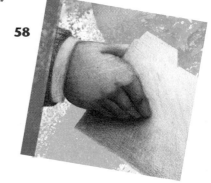

PART III INFORMATION TECHNOLOGY IN MANAGEMENT 241

Preface

Management Information Systems was written to provide a real-world understanding of information systems (ISs) for business and computer science students. This text establishes a firm foundation in information systems on which students can build successful careers—whether they find themselves formulating strategic plans in executive suites, optimizing operations in businesses or on factory floors, fine-tuning plans for their own entrepreneurial ventures, designing information systems to optimize their organization's needs, or creating valuable new information products in any number of industries.

The essence of this book is that ISs are everywhere in business. They are pervasive because information is the single most powerful resource in every business function in every industry. *Management Information Systems* provides students with exactly the right balance of technical information and real-world applications. No matter what field they undertake, students will enter the business world knowing how to get information to work for them. They will know enough about information technology (IT) to work productively with IS specialists, and they will know enough about business applications to get information systems to support their work in the best way possible.

Management Information Systems uses a combination of strong pedagogical writing, special focus features, illustrations and photographs for visual reinforcement, and plenty of real-world cases and anecdotes to cover the full range of essential IS topics. Just as business practices are ever changing, so is the IS discipline itself. To remain current, the book is committed to addressing each IS topic with a constant view toward emerging business trends, including:

◆ The transformation of business by the combination of online electronic commerce and increasingly powerful database and telecommunications technologies

◆ The trend toward having every person in business "own" the IS that serves him or her, either by participating with IS specialists in enterprise-wide IS development, or by using end-user IS development tools to create specialized ISs

◆ The increasing use of ISs to create leading-edge strategic advantages in competitive markets

◆ The increasing use of ISs to support decision making from the operational to the executive levels

◆ The growing impact of ISs on the reorganization of businesses, including moves such as downsizing, right-sizing, and merging

◆ The increasing use of interorganizational and international alliances in the drive to succeed in a globalized economy

◆ The increasing use of ISs to create new information products that become strong revenue sources in a variety of industries, sometimes forming the foundation of successful new companies

◆ The increasing use of outsourcing to develop and operate information systems

◆ The increasing integration of state-of-the-art technologies, such as virtual reality and data mining, into business strategies and operations

◆ The increasing use of advanced information technology by industries that have traditionally "lagged behind," such as manufacturing

The book was reviewed by more than 30 professors at various stages. It was encouraging to see that they agreed with the philosophy reflected in the pedagogy of this text, which can be summarized as follows:

Maintaining a proper balance between the technical and the practical. The text provides students with enough technical background to build a strong business foundation, but not so much as to cloud the important themes of real-world IS applications. Real-world lessons are used throughout the book to provide a business context, even in the most technical discussions. Special highlighted case studies and features open and close each chapter and, along with margin-note anecdotes, reinforce topics throughout the text. In its balance between technology and business, the book includes chapters dedicated to providing the technical foundations of ISs, as well as a chapter dedicated to explaining the uses of ISs in a full range of business functions—from accounting and manufacturing to marketing, inventory management, and strategic planning—which are a part of virtually every industry.

Presenting all material in an easy-to-read and easy-to-follow manner. Using clear writing, strong visual tools, and carefully designed features to reinforce concepts, the text teaches every topic, no matter how technical or complicated, in a way that allows students to use the text for self-study. The text establishes a strong framework by placing every topic in a big-picture context.

Emphasizing the latest trends throughout the book. The only way to teach a subject that changes as quickly as information systems in business is to look beyond the present. The book does not confine this view to a few boxes or a single chapter. The text provides constant reminders of how the business trends discussed above will affect ISs in the future. These trends include the growing importance of ISs in strategic planning and in gaining a competitive advantage, the growing use of the Internet as a key business tool, the increasing need for interorganizational and international information systems, the increasing involvement of end users in IS planning and development, the increasing prominence of ethical and societal issues in IS decision making, and the increasing challenge of managing ISs themselves.

This book puts in professors' hands a tool to motivate and inspire their students to see that (1) information systems are not only a technology but also an indispensable managerial tool, (2) knowing more about the technology and mastering it will help them in their careers, and (3) learning information technology *can* be fun. I believe that this book can help professors make their classes so interesting that many students will choose MIS as a career.

PEDAGOGICAL APPROACH

The purpose of a college textbook is to make teaching easier for professors, and learning more enjoyable for students. There are several features that distinguish this text from other introductory MIS texts.

EMPHASIS ON THE REAL WORLD

This is the *only* MIS book committed to portraying the world *as it is, not as we wish it to be. Management Information Systems* is not afraid to address the effect that interoffice politics might have on a particular type of project, or to include, in the discussion of the great potential of ISs in business, warnings about their limitations. Of course, this book includes chapters and features that provide a thorough, concise—and refreshingly clear—grounding in the technology of information systems, because all managers in successful organizations are involved in making decisions about hardware, software, and telecommunications. But, through current, detail-rich, real-world case studies throughout the book, and a dedication to qualifying each presentation with the real-world factors that may affect business, this book stays close to the workplace in its presentation. *Management Information Systems* also dedicates a highlighted place for cases at the beginning and end of each chapter. All cases are written to help professors illustrate concepts, and to help students understand the main body of the chapters. The real-world focus is reinforced in the "Points of Interest" in the margins of the text, featuring business anecdotes and news stories. In addition, an entire chapter (Chapter 10, "Information Systems in Business Functions") describes the types and uses of ISs in a variety of business functions, from accounting to marketing, from human resources to engineering.

THOROUGH PRESENTATION OF ONLINE BUSINESS PRACTICES

Perhaps the most fundamental new development in the way business is conducted today is the increasing use of telecommunications. Many important business phenomena—from electronic commerce to telecommuting to virtual organizations—are products of the enthusiastic adoption of this technology. How online commerce is changing business and how the impact will continue to grow are subjects addressed in the context of virtually every topic in the book. And, of course, *Management Information Systems* presents a sound technological foundation for understanding telecommunications, with separate chapters on both telecommunications (Chapter 5, "Information Technology in Business: Telecommunications and Networks") and the Internet (Chapter 6, "The Internet and Intranets"), devoted to the Internet, the Web, and the fast-spreading organizational intranets. While both chapters provide clear explanations of the technical infrastructure, the ultimate emphasis is on its contemporary business use. The entire text is also sprinkled with *Net Notes* that encourage the students to log on to interesting, entertaining, and useful Web sites, and each chapter includes an Internet assignment.

ATTENTION TO NEW BUSINESS PRACTICES AND TRENDS

Large parts of the text are devoted to discussing innovative uses of information technology and its benefits and risks. Contemporary concepts such as re-engineering, downsizing, the increasing demands of international ISs, and outsourcing—and how modern information technology relates to these trends— are explained in plain, easy-to-understand language. The latest technological developments and the most recent management concepts are also addressed, including client/server architecture, electronic commerce, intranets, firewalls, data warehousing and data mining, object-oriented software, outsourcing and end-user application development. About 80% of the examples, case studies, and anecdotes are from 1996 and later. In addition, the *A Look into the Future* boxes project how each chapter's specific area of MIS might change in the next 5 to 20 years.

ILLUSTRATION OF THE IMPORTANCE OF EACH SUBJECT TO THE STUDENT'S CAREER

Business students often do not understand why they have to learn about information technology. The reason many students are frustrated with introductory MIS courses is that they do not fully understand how information technology works or why it is important for them to understand it. One of the primary goals of this book is for its entire presentation to make the answers to these questions apparent. First, all subjects are explained so clearly that even the least technically oriented student can understand them. For instance, databases, telecommunications techniques, and the Internet (Chapters 5 through 7), which are often confusing to students, are presented with clear, concise, and vivid descriptions to paint a picture of technology at work. In addition, each chapter includes a feature titled *Why Should Managers...*, which explains to students how being well-versed in that chapter's aspect of IT, its benefits and risks, and its management, is extremely important to their careers.

A COMMITMENT TO CLEAR WRITING AND ILLUSTRATING

This textbook was written to support professors, however they wish to teach their courses. While chapters build upon each other, they were nevertheless written with a sensitivity to the fact that different professors teach topics in different sequences, and that some professors may wish to skip some topics altogether. For example, if students are already well-versed in hardware and software, the instructor can skip the two chapters (Chapters 3, and 4, "Information Technology in Business: Hardware," and "Information Technology in Business: Software," respectively) that cover these topics, while still achieving his or her instructive goals. With clear pedagogical writing, the use of graphics to emphasize concepts in dimensions beyond words, and thorough cross-referencing, *Management Information Systems* uses sound and creative pedagogy to make learning fun and inspiring. A full range of features (described below) punctuates the strengths of the text with anecdotes and news items related to each chapter.

EMPHASIS ON STRATEGIC THINKING

While there is a separate chapter on Strategic Information Systems, the topic is not relegated to those pages alone. Discussions throughout the text emphasize how businesses are increasingly using ISs to plot and implement strategic moves and to create new products (mostly unheard-of until the recent harnessing of IS power) of strategic importance to organizations. In addition, the end-of-chapter discussion questions and assignments encourage students to develop ideas about the use of information technology to gain a competitive advantage.

EMPHASIS ON ETHICAL THINKING

The book puts a great emphasis on some of the questionable and controversial uses of information technology, with special treatment provided in the *Ethics and Society* boxes. The students are required to weigh the positive and negative impacts of technology, and to convincingly argue their own positions on important issues such as privacy, free speech, and professional conduct.

EMPHASIS ON CRITICAL THINKING

Critical thinking is used throughout the text as well as in the book's many features. For instance, critical thinking questions are included at the end of each chapter's *A Look into the Future* feature, which focuses on the impact specific aspects of IT might have in the next 5 to 20 years. [The questions motivate students to evaluate many aspects of each situation and to repeatedly consider how quickly IT evolves.] *Think Critically* questions require the student to look beyond the marvel of a new technology or management technique and to consider its full impact on society, the economy, employees, and consumers.

THE ORGANIZATION OF THIS BOOK

Management Information Systems is organized into five parts, followed by a glossary, reference table of measurement units, and index.

PART I: THE INFORMATION AGE

Part I of the book includes two chapters. Chapter 1 provides an overview of information technology (IT) and information systems (ISs) and a framework for discussions in subsequent chapters. Chapter 2 discusses the strategic uses of information systems. Together, these two chapters address the essence of all overarching ideas that are discussed at greater depth in subsequent chapters.

PART II: INFORMATION TECHNOLOGY

To understand how information systems enhance managerial practices one must be well versed in the technical principles of information technology, which are covered in *Part II*. Chapters 3 and 4 provide a concise treatment of state-of-the-art hardware and software technology in business. Chapter 5 discusses data communications and telecommunications, which constitute the most important infrastructure of modern ISs. This provides the technical foundation for Chapter 6, which is fully devoted to a thorough discussion of the Internet and its most popular segment: the World Wide Web. Chapter 7 covers database management systems and their impact on business.

PART III: INFORMATION TECHNOLOGY IN MANAGEMENT

Part III is devoted to managerial issues as they relate to information systems. Chapter 8 is a review of the managerial pyramid and the information needs of managers at the different levels of responsibility. Chapter 9 describes the organization of the information systems unit in corporations and the responsibilities of information systems professionals in organizations. It also reviews different approaches to arranging systems in business organizations. Chapter 10 discusses the uses of information systems in different business activities. And Chapter 11 discusses interorganizational and international information systems, which are the foundation of many successful alliances.

PART IV: INFORMATION SYSTEMS IN DECISION MAKING

Part IV provides a view of state-of-the-art decision support and expert systems, including the use of artificial intelligence in business. Chapter 12 opens with a general discussion of decision making and moves on to discuss types of decision support systems. Taking the approach that expert systems are an advanced version of decision aids, Chapter 13 provides an extensive discussion of artificial intelligence in the context of decision making and expert systems.

PART V: PLANNING, ACQUISITION, AND CONTROLS

Without careful planning and development, ISs may fail. *Part V* is devoted to planning, acquisition, and controls of information systems to ensure their successful and timely development and implementation. Chapter 14 discusses how professionals plan information systems. Chapter 15 details the phases of systems analysis, design, and construction, as an ideal and as it works in the real world. Chapter 16 presents alternative acquisition methods to development: outsourcing and end-user systems development, which are growing in popularity. Controls and security measures, covered in Chapter 17, have to be incorporated into systems to ensure the integrity of business operations. In this chapter, we discuss the risks that information systems face and ways to minimize them.

GLOSSARY

Often, an instructor or a student may run into a term and not be sure about its meaning. The glossary at the end of the book is an alphabetical list of terms mentioned throughout the text, with their meanings.

MEASUREMENT UNITS

Information technology has its own set of units to measure anything from the speed of a computer to the capacity of a communications line. Both professors and students can turn to this list at the end of the book for help with measurement conventions.

FEATURES

The book includes several unique pedagogical features that were designed to help the professor anchor concepts in real-world experience. Each chapter includes the following features:

OPPORTUNITY/SOLUTION

Each chapter opens with a case study that embodies the issues raised in the chapter, prepares the students for the material discussed in the chapter, and encourages them to read on. Each *Opportunity/Solution* segment illustrates how an organization solved a problem, met a challenge, or created an opportunity related to the chapter's subject.

LEARNING OBJECTIVES

Each chapter also opens with a succinct statement of the thesis of the chapter, followed by a statement of the chapter's learning objectives. This helps students focus on the chapter'(s) overarching issues. The instructor can measure the extent to which the students have accomplished the objectives through the *Review and Discussion Questions* provided at the end of the chapter.

WHY SHOULD MANAGERS...

This feature explains why students must understand and appreciate the concepts, terminology, and issues presented in the chapter in order to be successful. *Why Should Managers...* is unique to this book, and was designed to help MIS professors create a compelling case that studying MIS is important to students' careers.

ETHICS AND SOCIETY

With information systems increasingly invading every aspect of our lives, ethical and societal concerns related to IT have become extremely important, often showing the price society pays to enjoy certain benefits of technology. The case of violating privacy through the inappropriate distribution of personal data, the security risks created by the increasing use of electronic commerce and the Internet in business, the disastrous loss of business due to computer viruses, the pervasive crime of software piracy, the challenges to free speech presented by certain laws, the financial losses due to the incompetence and unprofessional conduct of some IT specialists, the risks of overreliance on computers, and other similar risks must be addressed to ensure the well-being of businesses, individuals, and society as a whole. Each chapter includes an *Ethics and Society* box that provokes students to examine both sides of a particular issue, formulate their own opinions, and argue their views in class. At least one review question at the end of each chapter refers to this feature.

A LOOK INTO THE FUTURE

Information technology develops extremely fast. Today's innovative equipment or application may be obsolete in 12 to 18 months. *A Look into the Future* gives the students a glimpse into what they can expect to see in three, ten, or twenty years: billions of bytes of information stored on a dot-sized chip, light-based computers, virtual reality tools for daily business activities, brain-activated computer input, and other developments. The purpose of this feature is to intrigue the students with relevant and often entertaining information and to provide a glimpse into the research topics that captivate today's IS professionals.

REAL WORLD CASES

As in other fields of business, case studies are an effective way for students to integrate and internalize concepts. The cases in *Management Information Systems* were carefully chosen to reflect each chapter's discussion and to illustrate specific problems and solutions in the planning and use of information systems. Each case ends with questions that test the students' understanding of the material and challenge them to think in terms of real business situations.

SUMMARY

The purpose of the summary is to help highlight the most important points of each chapter. It's an excellent tool to review what has already been studied.

MARGIN NOTES

POINTS OF INTEREST The margins of each chapter are peppered with news items and small anecdotes that punctuate the subject matter covered in the chapter. These information capsules may be used to illustrate a principle, give a unique perspective on a particular managerial practice, or present interesting statistics on the subject of the chapter.

NET NOTES Students much recognize the Internet as an information resource. Each chapter contains several *Net Notes* that provide short backgrounds and the addresses of interesting Web sites where students can find additional information about the subject matter, do research, widen their general knowledge, download useful software, or enjoy a little entertainment. While some site addresses will have changed by the time you use this book, most are expected to remain the same.

END-OF-CHAPTER MATERIAL

REVIEW AND DISCUSSION QUESTIONS The review and discussion questions help students determine if they have absorbed the material in the chapter, and can be used by professors to lead discussion in the classroom. At least one of the questions refers to ethical and societal concerns.

CONCEPT ACTIVITY All chapters include concept activities requiring students to delve further into a concept presented in the chapter. Often, students are asked to approach executives with questions about methods of problem solving and decision making in their organizations. The purpose of the activity is to illustrate to students that what they have learned in the chapter reaches far beyond the classroom. The assignments encourage students to think, analyze, and propose solutions to practical problems.

HANDS-ON ACTIVITY Learning by doing is an important element in the teaching of any subject. The *Hands-On Activity* at the end of each chapter requires students to use software to learn or enhance a computer skill, or to use a skill they have already mastered to prepare a paper or to analyze data. The activities involve the use of word processors, spreadsheets, and database applications.

TEAM ACTIVITY The purpose of the *Team Activity* is twofold: to enrich students by both the content of the assignment and by the manner in which it is carried out. The team assignments teach students to carry out small-scale research projects, usually interacting with executives and IT professionals. Accomplishing the assignment with other students teaches the students to work as part of a team. This is an important aspect of work in organizations in general and in the area of information systems in particular. Many MIS professors have emphasized the importance of teamwork exercises, in which students break assignments into smaller, individual tasks; negotiate work load; integrate individual accomplishments into a coherent result; and present the result either in writing or orally. The purpose of this feature is to respond to this pedagogical method.

EXPLORE THE WEB This assignment, presented in each chapter, requires students to carry out a task on the Web. Usually this is a small research project, whereby students are asked to look for relevant information to answer a question, to evaluate IS services and products, or to evaluate Web sites themselves as a means of electronic commerce.

TEACHING SUPPLEMENTS

Management Information Systems includes teaching supplements to support professors in the classroom. In addition to a Web site for the text, three ancillaries accompany the textbook: an Instructor's Manual, a Test Bank, and a PowerPoint presentation, Course Presenter. This is one of the few textbooks whose Instructor's Manual and Test Bank are written by the author, ensuring compatibility with the textbook in content, pedagogy, and philosophy.

THE INSTRUCTOR'S MANUAL

The purpose of this manual is to provide materials to help instructors make their classes informative and interesting. The manual offers several approaches to teaching the material, with a sample syllabus and comments on different components. It also suggests alternative course outlines and ideas for term projects. For each chapter, the Manual includes a chapter outline, learning objectives, lecture notes (including discussion topics) teaching tips, and solutions to Review and Discussion Questions and the questions following each case study.

THE TEST BANK

Course Test Manager is a powerful testing and assessment package that enables instructors to create and print tests from test banks designed specifically for Course Technology titles. In addition, instructors with access to a networked computer lab (LAN) can administer, grade, and track tests online. Students can also take online practice tests, which generate customized study guides that indicate where in the text students can find more information on each question.

COURSE PRESENTER

A CD-ROM-based presentation tool developed in Microsoft PowerPoint, Course Presenter offers a wealth of resources for use in the classroom. Instead of using traditional overhead transparencies, Course Presenter puts together impressive computer-generated screen shows including graphics and videos. All of the graphics from the book (not including photos) have been included.

WEB PAGE

There will be a dedicated Web site for the text that will provide a dynamic ongoing update to the book and an online supplement to learning. The site includes an overview of the book as well as hyperlinks to sites students can use to increase their exposure to technical, managerial, and ethical issues regarding information technology and ISs in business.

ACKNOWLEDGMENTS

This book is the fruit of a great concerted effort. A project such as this could not be successful without the contribution of many people. I would first like to thank my colleagues in the IS area whose ideas and opinions over all these years have helped me understand the real educational needs of our students. I also recognize the indirect contribution of the many students I have taught. Their comments helped me understand the points that need extra emphasis or a different presentation to make subjects that are potentially overwhelming more interesting.

Many thanks to Kristen Duerr, Jennifer Normandin, and Lisa Ayers for being so enthusiastic about this project and for their absolute faith in my ability to complete it in time and up to their high standards. All three were always there for me with advice and encouragement. Debbie Masi shepherded the book through the production process, constantly contributing her own valuable expertise. The designer, Dianne Schaefer, and GEX skillfully rendered our ideas in vivid pictures. The copyeditors at Foxxe Editorial Services went beyond the call of proper grammar to suggest clearer communication of ideas. I applaud all of them.

It is extremely difficult to convince a marathon runner to run another ten miles when he reaches the finish line. Janet Weinrib, the developmental editor of this book, did it. When I was sure there was no more air in my lungs to continue the run, Janet managed to make me run many more miles. I thank her for her excellent and relentless help. Our work together produced rare synergy.

Reviewers are the most important aides to any writer, let alone one who prepares a text for college students. I would like to thank the following reviewers for their candid and detailed feedback:

GARY ARMSTRONG, Shippensburg University
KARIN BAST, University of Wisconsin/La Crosse
SIDDHARTHA BHATTACHARYA, Southern
   Illinois University/Carbondale
DOUGLAS BOCK, Southern
   Illinois University/Edwardsville
GEORGE BOHLEN, University of Dayton
JANE CAREY, Arizona State University
JUDITH CARLISLE, Georgia Institute
   of Technology
JASON CHEN, Gonzaga University
PAUL CHENEY, University of South Florida
JIM DANOWSKI, University of Illinois/Chicago
SERGIO DAVALOS, University of Portland
GLENN DIETRICH, University of
   Texas/San Antonio
JAMES DIVOKY, University of Akron
CHARLES DOWNING, Boston College
KAREN FORCHT, James Madison University
JEFF GUAN, University of Louisville
CONSTANZA HAGMANN, Kansas
   State University

CHARLOTTE HIATT, California
   State University/Fresno
ELLEN HOADLEY, Loyola College
JOAN HOOPES, Marist College
ANTHONY KEYS, Wichita State University
AL LEDERER, University of Kentucky
JO MAE MARIS, Arizona State University
KENNETH MARR, Hofstra University
JOHN MELROSE, University of
   Wisconsin/Eau Claire
LEAH PIETRON, University
   of Nebraska/Omaha
JACK POWELL, University of South Dakota
RAGHAV RAO, State University of
   New York/Buffalo
LORA ROBINSON, St. Cloud State University
SUBHASHISH SAMADDAR, Western
   Illinois University
WILLIAM SCHIANO, Bentley College
SHANNON TAYLOR, Montana State University

Lastly, I would like to thank the members of my family. Narda, my wife of a quarter century, gracefully accepted my long hours in the office and the days at home when she could see only my back. My children, Sahar, Adi, Noam, and Ron, spent a long period of their lives with this project in the background. Thank you for your patience, guys. Here is the product.

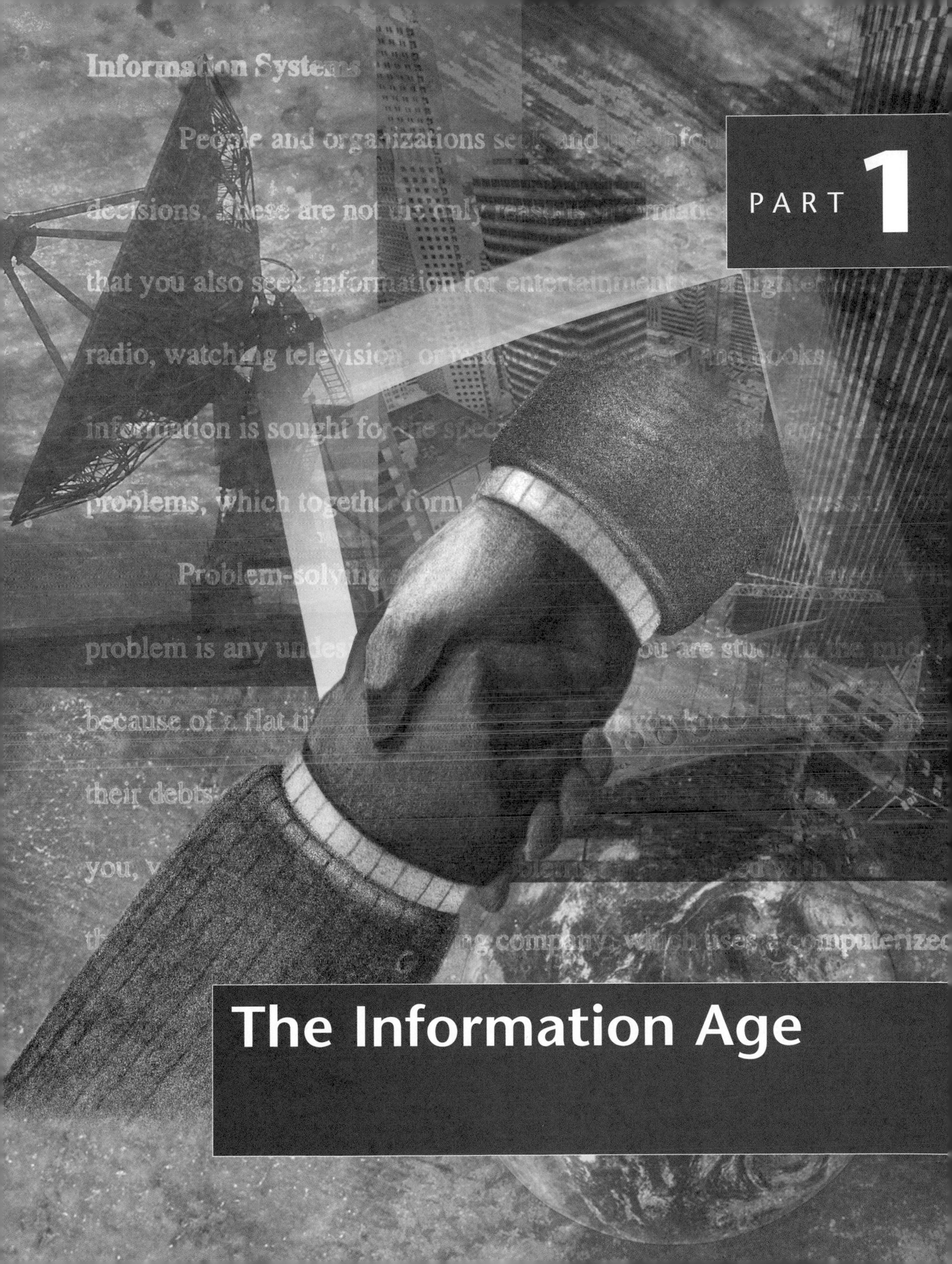

PART 1

The Information Age

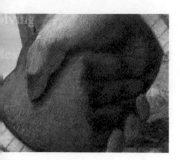

Chapter 1

Business Information Systems: An Introduction

A Mover Moves Up

Blake Miller worked for a moving company seven days a week, to pay for college, and Brad Armstrong was one of his clients. They both lived in Austin during a recession when the market was saturated with well-established moving firms that were offering deep discounts to attract customers. Nonetheless, Miller, 23 years old and fresh out of college with a psychology degree, and Armstrong, a lawyer five years his senior, decided to start Blue Whale Moving Co., Inc. in 1988.

The moving business has a reputation for sloppy service. On the premise that one mover is as bad as the next, customers usually choose on a lowest-price basis. Customers also want to receive a price quote immediately after a company representative visits their home to review the household contents to be moved.

Blue Whale Moving Co. decided to take advantage of customer desire for quick estimates. The two entrepreneurs commissioned a consulting firm to custom-design a computer-based information system that allows Blue Whale to make estimates without taking the time to inspect each site. A Yellow Pages™ ad lists typical household and office items. The customer fills in the list and phones or faxes it to the company. The estimator enters the data, and the program produces price figures on the screen, with a total for a quote. The quote can be given within minutes after the data are entered. The estimator gives an exact price over the phone and sends written confirmation.

Blue Whale's customers are reassured every step of the way. Customers receive a confirmation phone call a day before the move and a follow-up call the day after the move. Miller and Armstrong give their customers peace of mind for a fair price. The new information system and the courteous service helped the company grow in a highly competitive industry. The owners opened an office in Houston and another one in Dallas. From an initial investment of $10,000, Blue Whale's annual revenues have reached $1.7 million. As the owners plan further expansion, they will continue to rely on information systems to provide top-of-the-line service. Blake and Brad believe Blue Whale will continue to make waves.

Source: "Blue Whale Moving," Real World Lessons for America's Small Business, *Nation's Business*, 1994, pp. 182–183.

Information systems pervade almost every aspect of our lives. Whether we are withdrawing money from a bank's automatic teller machine or ordering a magazine using a toll-free phone number, hardly a day goes by without our feeding data into, or using information generated by, an information system. In business especially, most of the information we use is generated by computer-based information systems, which have become essential to successful business operations.

When you finish this chapter you will:

◆ Understand how and why information systems are essential to business

◆ Know how computers are used to process data into useful information for problem solving and decision making

◆ Understand the functions of different types of information systems and how different levels within an organization are served by different information systems

◆ Understand how telecommunications and database technology are used to implement the goals of information systems

◆ Know how to evaluate information systems and their role in organizations

◆ Be able to identify and discuss the ethical and social conflicts created by the widespread use of information systems

Katherine Barchetti of K. Barchetti Shops, a multi-million dollar business built on the strength of information systems, has a motto she has lived by: "If you're not using the data you're collecting, don't ask for it," Barchetti advises.

A number of years ago, Barchetti wrote letters to 3,000 people asking why they no longer shopped at her stores; 290 people wrote back. Although it took her a year and a half to reply to each person, she quickly acted on the feedback by saying good-bye to an unfriendly manager and modifying her prices. For the past 26 years she has been gathering client information and using it to squeeze out a profitable $3 million in annual revenues from two tiny clothing stores.

In the mid-1980s, Barchetti's late husband developed a database and pumped 20 years of handwritten customer information into it. Then Barchetti and her staff started analyzing data, such as buying habits and buying preferences. Paying attention to that information has meant an eight percent increase in gross profits in the last seven years, faster inventory turnover, and more focused direct-mail campaigns.

Source: "Capitalizing on Customer Data," *Inc.*, April 1996, p. 107. Reprinted with permission, *Inc.* magazine. Copyright © 1996 by Goldhirsh Group, 38 Commercial Wharf, Boston, MA 02110.

INFORMATION SYSTEMS

People require information for many and varied reasons. For instance, it is likely that you seek information for entertainment and enlightenment, by listening to the radio, watching television, and reading newspapers, magazines, and books. In business, however, people and organizations seek and use information specifically for the purposes of sound decision making and creative problem solving—two closely related practices that form the foundation of every successful company.

What is a problem? A **problem** is any undesirable situation. When you are stuck in the middle of nowhere because of a flat tire, you have a problem. If you know that some customers are not paying their debts on time, but you don't know which ones they are or how much each owes, you have a problem. Both problems can be solved with the aid of information. In the first case, you can call a towing company, which can use a computerized tracking system to send the tow truck closest to your location; in the second case, a simple accounting program on a computer can help.

Whenever an organization or individual is faced with more than one way to solve a problem, a **decision** must be made. Therefore, "2+2=?" is a problem, but it does not require decision making because there is only one solution. However, as a manager, you may face this sort of dilemma: "Which is the best way to promote the company's new car?" There are many potential ways to promote the new car—television advertising, radio advertising, newspaper advertising, auto shows, direct mail, or any combination of these methods. This is a case that calls for decision making.

Both problem solving and decision making require information. Gathering the right information in an efficient fashion, storing it so that it can be used and manipulated as necessary, and using it to help an organization achieve its business goals—all topics covered in this book—are the keys to success in business today. As a future manager, you will need to understand and apply these information fundamentals.

DATA, INFORMATION, AND SYSTEMS

We use the words "data," "information," and "system" almost daily. Understanding what these terms mean, both generally and in the context of business, is necessary if you are to use information effectively in your business practices.

DATA VS. INFORMATION

The terms "data" and "information" do not mean the same thing. **Data** is the plural of the Latin *datum*, literally a "given," or fact, which may be in the form of a number, a statement, or a picture. Though it may be singular in meaning, the word is commonly used in the plural form. Data are the raw materials in the production of information. **Information**, on the other hand, is data that have meaning within a context. Information can be raw data or it can be data that has been manipulated through addition, subtraction, division, or any other operation that leads to a greater understanding of a situation.

DATA MANIPULATION

Here is a simple example that demonstrates the difference between data and information. Assume that you work for a car manufacturer. Last year, the company introduced a new vehicle to the market. Because management realizes that keeping a loyal customer base requires continuous improvement of products and services, it conducts periodic surveys of large samples of buyers. The questionnaires sent out include 30 questions in several categories, including demographic data (such as gender, age, and annual income), complaints about different areas of performance (such as ease of handling, braking, and the quality of the sound system), features with which buyers are most satisfied, and courtesy of the dealer's personnel.

Reading through all these data would be extremely time-consuming and not very helpful. However, if the data are manipulated, they may provide highly useful information. For example, if the complaints are categorized by topic, and the numbers of complaints are totaled for each type of complaint and each car, the company may be able to pinpoint a weakness in a car. The *information* can then be passed along to the appropriate engineering or manufacturing unit.

The company may already have sufficient data on the dealers who sold cars to the surveyed customers, the car models, and the way each purchase was financed. By calculating the average age and income of current buyers, the marketing executives can better target advertising to groups who are most likely to purchase each car. If it is found that the majority of buyers do not ask for financing, the company may wish to drop this service option and divert more loan money to financing the purchase of other cars. In this way, accumulated data become useful information.

GENERATING INFORMATION

In the example above, the calculations of totals, averages, and trends associated with buyers and their input are processes. In fact, a **process** is *any* manipulation of data, usually with the goal of producing information, although some processes produce yet another set of interim data (see Figure 1.1). Hence, while data are the raw material, information is the output.

Sometimes, what is data in one context is considered information in another context. For example, if an organization needs to know the ages of everyone attending a basketball game, then a list of that data is actually information. But if that organization wants to know the average price of the tickets purchased by each age group, the list of ages is only data.

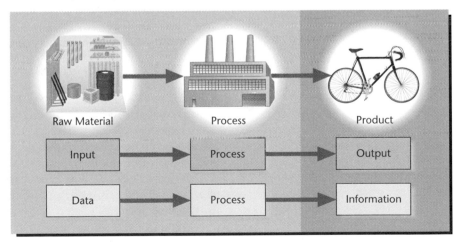

Figure 1.1 *Input-process-output*

Relevant:	Information has to pertain to the problem at hand. For example, the total number of years of education may not be relevant to a person's qualifications for a new job. The relevant information might be that the person has so many years of education in mechanical engineering, and so many years of experience.
Complete:	Partial information is often worse than no information at all. For example, marketing data about household incomes may lead to bad decisions if not accompanied by vital information on the consumption habits of the targeted population.
Accurate:	Erroneous information may lead to disastrous decisions. For example, an inaccurate record of a patient's reaction to penicillin may lead a doctor to harm the patient while believing that she is helping him.
Current:	Decisions are often based upon the latest information available, but what was a fact yesterday may no longer be one today. For example, a short-term investment decision to purchase a stock today based on yesterday's stock prices may be a costly mistake if the price of the stock has risen in the interim.
Economical:	In a business setting, the cost of obtaining information must be considered as one of the cost elements involved in any decision. For example, the demand for a new product must be researched to reduce risk of marketing failure, but if the market research is too expensive, the cost of obtaining the information may diminish the profit from sales.

Figure 1.2 *Characteristics of useful information*

INFORMATION IN A CONTEXT

Information is an extremely important resource for both individuals and organizations—but not all information is useful. Consider the following story. Two people took a tour in a hot-air balloon, but they encountered unexpected wind and were soon blown off course. When they managed to lower their altitude, they saw a farmer on the ground and shouted to him, "Where are we?" "You are right above a corn field!" he answered. The balloonists looked at each other, and one of them groaned, "Some information! Highly accurate and totally useless!" To be useful, information must be relevant, complete, accurate, current, and economical. The characteristics of useful information are listed in Figure 1.2.

WHAT IS A SYSTEM?

Before we discuss what are called **information systems**, it is important to explain what the two words mean. You have probably used the word "system" many times. Simply put, a **system** is an array of components that work together to achieve a common goal, or multiple goals, by accepting input, processing input, and producing output in an organized manner. Consider the following examples:

A sound system consists of many electronic and mechanical parts, such as a laser head, a turntable, an amplifier, an equalizer, and so on. This system uses input in the form of electrical power to reproduce music and other sounds.

You have heard the words "to beat the system." Here, the term system refers to an organization of humans beings—a government agency, a commercial company, or any other bureaucracy. Organizations, too, are systems; they consist of

For decades, visionaries have predicted that the office of the future would be paperless. The "future" has come and gone. Not only are our offices not paperless, several studies have found that in the decade between 1980 and 1990, the use of paper in America's offices doubled. Managers who use information systems efficiently use very little paper, because they realize that a report does not have to be printed on paper. It can take the form of magnetic or optical code, and be retrieved whenever and wherever it is needed.

The main reason offices consume so much paper is that the increased accessibility of word processing and spreadsheet programs leads people to produce many different versions of paper output (reports, letters, drawings, and the like). In addition, improved worker efficiency due to the increased use of information systems means that each worker simply produces more than he or she did years ago.

Maybe the future is coming. Technologies such as electronic data interchange (EDI) (which allows organizations to exchange data and conduct operations purely electronically) and digital imaging are designed specifically to eliminate paper from offices.

components—divisions, departments, and people—that work together to achieve common goals.

SYSTEMS AND SUBSYSTEMS Needless to say, not every system has just one goal. Often, a system consists of several **subsystems**—components of a larger system—with subgoals, all of which contribute to the main goal (see Figure 1.3). Subsystems can receive input from and transfer output to other systems or subsystems.

Consider the different departments of a manufacturing business. The marketing department tries to promote sales of the organization's products; the engineering department tries to design new products and improve the existing ones; the finance department tries to plan a clear budget and earn interest on every penny that is left unused at the end of the day. Each department is a subsystem with its own goal, which is a subgoal of a larger system (the company), whose goal is to maximize profit.

Now consider the goals of a manufacturing organization's information system, which stores and processes operational data, and produces information about all aspects of the company's operations. The purpose of its inventory control subsystem is to let managers know what quantities of which items are available; the purpose of its production subsystem is to keep track of the status of parts manufactured; and the assembly control subsystem presents the bill of material, a list of all the parts that make up a product, and the status of assembled products. The goal of the entire system is to deliver finished goods at the lowest possible cost within the shortest possible time.

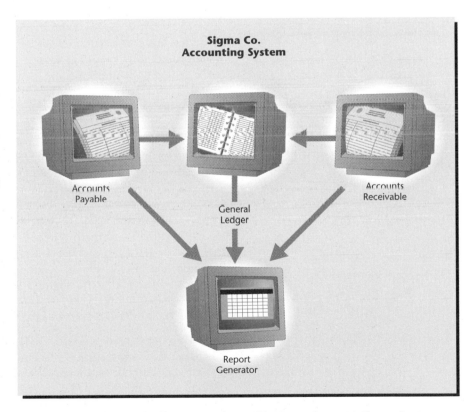

Figure 1.3 *Several subsystems make up this corporate accounting system.*

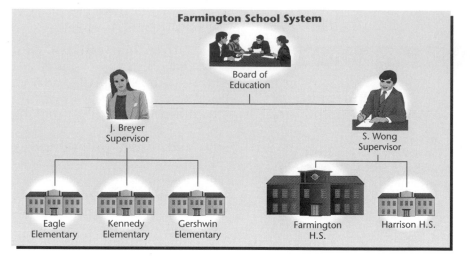

Figure 1.4 *The Farmington High School is a subsystem within the Farmington school system.*

POINT OF INTEREST

Productivity on the Rise

In recent years, some economists have argued that the $750 billion invested by industry in the acquisition of information technology (IT) has yielded only a small increase in productivity. But IT researchers claim that the ways productivity has been traditionally measured, such as reduction in head counts, are inappropriate. A study by the University of California at Irvine's Center for Research on Information Technology and Organizations supports the positive relationship between IT and productivity. Among the 11 Asian countries studied, productivity was the highest in countries where the investment in IT exceeded other investments, such as plants and equipment.

Figure 1.4 illustrates another example of the relationship between a system and its subsystems. Each high school in the Farmington School district is trying to provide interesting and useful teaching and sports activities. Supervisors provide guidance and enforce the decisions of the board, the board creates policies and the overall budget, and all work toward one goal: providing the best education at the least expense to the local taxpayer.

CLOSED VS. OPEN SYSTEMS Systems are referred to as closed or open, depending upon the nature of information that flow within an organization. A system is said to be **closed** if it stands alone, with no connection to another system: nothing flows in from another system, nothing flows out to another system. A system is said to be **open** when it has an interface with and interacts with other systems. For example, an accounting system that records accounts receivable, accounts payable, and cash flows is considered open if it receives its payroll figures from the payroll system. Subsystems, by definition, are always open, because they are components of a bigger system and therefore must receive and give information from and to other subsystems.

FORMING INFORMATION INTO SYSTEMS With an understanding of the words "information" and "system," the definition of an information system is almost intuitive: an **information system (IS)** is the aggregate of components that work together to process data and produce information. Almost all business information systems are made up of many subsystems with subgoals, all of which contribute to the organization's main goal.

INFORMATION AND MANAGERS

Thinking of an organization in terms of its suborganizations or subsystems—referred to as **systems thinking**—is a powerful management tool because it creates a framework for both excellent problem solving and excellent decision making. In order to solve a problem, a manager needs to isolate it, which is done by recognizing the subsystem in which the problem occurs and solving the problem within the constraints and strengths of that subsystem.

The Computer-Aided Manager

It is 9 a.m. Joan Spivak has just entered her office at Mow, Inc., one of America's largest manufacturers of lawn mowers. She turns her computer on and clicks on the Production Schedule item.

Joan knows that a problem occurred yesterday on one of her assembly lines. A supplier failed to ship parts that are essential to manufacturing Mow, Inc.'s mowers. Joan checks the status of those semi-assembled mowers and finds that the parts have not arrived.

An idle assembly line means idle workers and unrecovered costs. Joan decides to explore the possibility of using the line to assemble another model of mower. She selects an item from the menu and asks the computer, "Should we assemble an alternate model on line B?" The computer "hears" the question and, for verification, displays it in type on the bottom of the screen, asking, "Is this what you mean?" Joan says, "Yes." The computer engages the plant's MRP II system and an expert system.

The computer displays the question: "How long do you expect to wait for part SR-102?" Joan is not surprised. The computer detected that this is the missing part, because according to the schedule it was supposed to be either in the warehouse or on the line. She says, "Eight hours." The computer now figures out if it would be economical to remove the partially assembled Model A mowers, and use the line to assemble Model B mowers until the SR-102 units for Model A arrive.

Retooling the line for the assembly of another model takes time and incurs cost. Obviously, Joan wants to know whether this cost would be greater or smaller than leaving the line idle. After ten seconds a message appears on the screen: "Use the line to assemble Model B. You will save approximately $6,779.45 in total cost."

Joan brings up another menu. She says, "Retool line nine for assembly of Model B until further notice." The foreman on the floor receives the message a second later and gives the appropriate orders.

This scenario may sound as if it is taken from a science fiction movie, but it is not. To some extent, many of the features described here—speech recognition by the computer, speed-of-light analyses of data—already exist. The actual implementation of systems that combine manufacturing resource planning systems and expert systems has not yet taken place in a real-world setting. But when it does, it will minimize cost in production facilities.

THINK CRITICALLY

Do you think ISs will eventually replace managers completely? Why or why not?

In addition, systems thinking can help keep successful managers focused on the overall goals and operations of a business. It encourages them to consider the entire system, not only their specific subsystem, when solving problems and making decisions. The solution to a problem may be satisfactory in one subsystem, but inadequate for the business as a whole. Figuratively, effective managers view their areas of responsibility as puzzle pieces. Each piece is important and should fit in well with the adjacent pieces, but the entire picture should always be kept in mind.

One of an information system's most important contributions to the sound workings of an organization is the automation of information exchange among business subsystems (such as departments and divisions). In fact, such exchanges of information make up a major portion of all the interactions among business subsystems.

In the ideal "information map" of a business—that is the description of the flow of data and information within an organization—there is a chain, or a network, of information subsystems that exchange information with each other and with the world outside the system. In an ideal organization, there would be no need for any human being to retrieve information from one IS and transfer it to another. Only new raw data would be captured, usually from outside the organization or from its operations, and data captured at any point in the system would automatically become available to any other subsystem. Thus, "systems thinking" is served well by **information technology (IT)** a term that refers in general to all technologies that facilitate the construction and maintenance of Information systems.

ETHICS AND SOCIETY

The Power of Information

The advent of information technology and the quick pace at which it advances have created many unresolved ethical and societal issues. Three of the most important issues are introduced here and discussed at greater length in the book.

Challenges to Privacy. Information technology allows fast and inexpensive communication of information, and the collection and storage of vast amounts of data. On one hand, these capabilities allow individuals and organizations access to useful information. On the other hand, information is power, and misplaced information can grant unjustified power. So, while organizations can become more efficient with better information about consumers, consumer privacy may be violated. All types of organizations collect vast amounts of personal data. However, what most governments can do with the personal data is restricted, while what most commercial operations can do with their personal data—especially in the U.S.—is relatively unrestricted. Sometimes we reveal details about ourselves freely: We might answer a questionnaire identifying the products we use or how much money we make in exchange for discounts, coupons or free products. On the other hand, we don't always have the choice about what information we give away. For instance, anyone who wants to be considered for a mortgage must provide detailed personal financial information about bank accounts and the like. What we often don't consider is that once the information is in the hands of a commercial organization it is likely to be sold to other organizations and individuals, and our treasured privacy can quickly be violated.

Should society ban the collection of personal data? If we do, organizations will not be able to market their products directly to the consumers who are interested in them; they will have to spend more resources on marketing, and consumers will eventually pay more for products. If the sale of personal data is banned, more affluent companies will gain a significant market advantage. With their financial resources, they will be able to collect personal information directly from consumers. Smaller start-up companies, however, will not have the financial resources to collect data from the public.

Software Piracy. Information technology has created a situation where it is extremely easy and cheap to duplicate computer programs. As an

(continued)

It is important to remember that computers can only carry out instructions that are given to them by human beings. Computers can process data accurately at speeds far greater than people can, yet they are limited in many respects—the most prominent of which is lack of common sense. Why, then, do we use computers? Because of the synergy between human beings and computers.

Synergy occurs when a combination of resources produces output that is better than the sum of the outputs of the same resources when they are employed separately. Some people call synergy the 2+2=5 rule. A computer works fast and accurately; human beings work relatively slowly and make mistakes. A computer cannot make decisions, however, or formulate steps for solving problems. Thus, a human-computer combination allows the results of human thought to be translated into efficient processing of large amounts of

increasing number of business and other activities are performed on computers, programs have become an important class of intellectual property. However, millions of people the world over unthinkingly engage in illegal copying of programs, which is a violation of intellectual property rights.

To run computers we must employ software, the sets of instructions that control computer operations. Illegal copying of software, popularly called software piracy, causes tremendous losses of revenues to software companies that spend billions of dollars annually to develop programs for businesses, education, entertainment, and many other purposes. It is extremely difficult to find and prosecute people who engage in piracy. Software developers prod business executives to take measures against software piracy, and the U.S. government has been successful in pressuring other governments into passing appropriate laws, but the criminal activity continues. Ultimately, those of us who purchase software are the ones who pay the price.

Ethical Codes for IS Professionals. However, unlike other professionals, IS professionals are not bound under the law to adhere to any ethical and professional standards. Those who engage in the development and maintenance of ISs are generally recognized as members of an emerging profession, the IS profession. These are people who plan ISs, suggest methods to develop them, develop the systems, and maintain them. Many organizations depend on these specialists, who collect large sums of money for their services. And as more and more businesses have come to depend on IT, we are hearing more about incidents where IS projects are abandoned to fail because these "professionals" have miscalculated time and money resources, or because they simply lacked the expertise to develop the systems.

If a lawyer fails to represent you in court, you have an avenue for recourse based on an established code of professional standards under the law. Doctors are licensed by the state and bound by the Hippocratic oath. And certified public accountants know exactly what the rules of their profession are. But what professional rules bind IS "professionals"? Currently, none. Several professional organizations have issued their own codes of ethics, but none is enforceable under the law. It may take years for a standard code of ethics to be adopted by this emerging profession. It may take even longer for certification and other measures to be mandated by law.

If railroad freight cars could talk, what would they say? Well, for one thing, they could tell you their location. More than one million railroad freight cars, locomotives, and other pieces of equipment are now equipped with transponder tags. These tags make it possible to identify the car, locomotive, or equipment that the tag is attached to and its location. Strategically placed tag readers (there are 1,200 in all) collect the information as the tagged equipment rolls past them; the information is routed to computer systems, where it is used for route management. The primary benefit of the tagging system is fewer delays, according to the Association of American Railroads.

Humans	Computers
Think	Calculate and perform programmed logical operations extremely rapidly
Have common sense	Store and retrieve data and information extremely rapidly
Can make decisions	Perform complex logical and arithmetical functions accurately
Can instruct the computer what to do	Execute long, tedious operations
Can learn new methods and techniques	Perform routine tasks less expensively than humans
Can accumulate expertise	Are adaptable (can be programmed and reprogrammed)

Figure 1.5 *Qualities of humans and computers that contribute to synergy*

data. Figure 1.5 presents the qualities of humans and computers that result in synergy. It is important to notice not only the potential benefits of synergy but also what computers should not be trusted to do on their own.

INFORMATION SYSTEMS

In an organization, an information system consists of data, hardware, software, people, and procedures, all with their strengths and weaknesses, which are summarized in Figure 1.6. In the general sense of the term, an information system does not have to include electronic equipment. However, "information system" has become synonymous with **computer-based information system**, a system with a computer at its center to which peripheral equipment is connected. That is how we use the term in this book. In a computer-based information system, computers collect, store, and process or manipulate data into information, in accordance with instructions provided by people via computer programs.

Several trends have taken place that make the use of ISs so important: the power of computers has grown tremendously, while their prices have dropped; the variety and ingenuity of computer programs have increased; quick and reliable communication lines have become widely available and affordable; and an increasing ratio of the workforce is computer-literate. In this environment, organizations would quickly lag behind if they did not take advantage of this progress and use these technologies and skills to meet their goals.

Data:	The input that the system takes to produce information.
Hardware:	The computer and its peripheral equipment: input-, output-, and storage-devices. Hardware also includes data communication equipment.
Software:	Sets of instructions that tell the computer how to take the data in, how to process the data, how to display the information, and how to store data and information.
Telecommunications:	Hardware and software that facilitate fast transmission and reception of text, pictures, sound, and animation in the form of electronic data.
People:	Information systems professionals and users who analyze organizational information needs, design and construct information systems, write computer programs, operate the hardware, and maintain software.
Procedures:	Rules for achieving optimal and secure operations in data processing. Procedures include priorities in running different applications on the computer, and security measures.

Figure 1.6 *Components of an information system*

Remember that in a broad sense, an information system consists of physical and nonphysical components working together. A computer by itself is not an information system. A computer in combination with a software program may constitute an information system, but only if the program has been designed to produce information to assist an organization or person to achieve a specific goal. For instance, the purpose of a climate control system is to regulate the temperature and humidity in a room; it does not produce information. However, today most types of hardware and software are used to produce some kind of information.

THE FOUR STAGES OF PROCESSING

Information systems operate in the same basic fashion whether or not they include a computer. However, the computer provides a convenient means to execute the four main operations of an information system: entering data into the IS (**input**), changing and manipulating the data in the IS (data processing), getting information out of the IS (**output**), and storing data and information (**storage**). A computer-based IS also uses a logical process to decide which data to capture and how it should be processed. This will be discussed later.

INPUT AND TRANSACTION PROCESSING The first step in the production of information is the collection and introduction of data into the IS, known as *input*. Most of the data an organization uses as input to its IS are generated and collected within the organization. These data are the results of transactions undertaken in the course of business. A transaction is a business event: a sale, a purchase, the hiring of a new employee, etc. These transactions can be recorded on paper and later entered into a computer system, or they may be directly recorded through the terminals of transaction processing systems (TPSs), such as cash registers and order entry terminals. A TPS is any system, usually including a computer, that records transactions.

An input device is the tool used to enter data into an IS. Input devices include the keyboard (currently the most widely used input device), infrared devices that sense bar codes, and voice recognition systems. Other means to input data are described in Chapter 3, "Information Technology in Business: Hardware." The trend has been to shorten the time and ease the effort of input by using devices that allow visual or auditory data entry.

PROCESSING The computer's greatest contribution to ISs is in the efficient processing of data, which is essential to a robust IS. The computer's speed and accuracy allow organizations to process millions of pieces of data in several seconds; in the past, such quantities of data could not have been processed in time to be meaningful. It is the astronomic growth in the speed and affordability of computing that has made information the essential ingredient for an organization's success.

While computers are essential tools for the input, processing, and output of most companies' ISs, they also introduce another component to information systems: the need to translate instructions from natural—or human—languages into computer languages. Computer programs, which are lists of instructions understandable to computers, give computers directions on how to interpret and manipulate data, and in what form (whether visual, aural, or otherwise) to provide information to the organization. There are thousands of programming languages in use today, and their fundamental operation and function are discussed in Chapter 4, "Information Technology in Business: Software."

OUTPUT Output is the information produced by an IS and displayed on an output device in the format most useful to an organization. The most widely used output device is the video display, or video monitor, which displays output visually. However, computer output can be communicated through speakers in the form of music or speech, and can also be transmitted to another computer or electronic device in computer-coded form, for later interpretation.

STORAGE One of the greatest benefits of using computers is the ability to store vast amounts of data and information. As you will learn in Chapter 3, computers store information both on devices that are internal to the machine and on external devices. The computer's internal memory is used to store data and programs for the duration of the processing. For longer periods of storage, the computer transmits data to external storage devices such as magnetic tapes and magnetic disks, where it is stored in a form that allows the computer to retrieve and process it. Whole encyclopedias are now stored on optical disks. Technically, it is not inconceivable to store a library of millions of volumes on such disks.

COMPUTER EQUIPMENT FOR INFORMATION SYSTEMS

Figure 1.7 illustrates the four basic components of the computer system within an IS: input devices are used to introduce data into the IS; the computer itself is used to process data through the IS; output devices are used to display information; and storage devices are used to store data and information. In addition to communication between computer components, communication takes place between computers over great distances (called telecommunications).

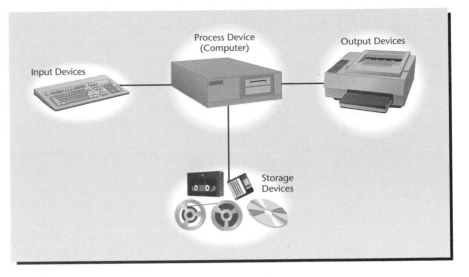

Figure 1.7 *Input-process-output-storage devices*

Communication technology not only allows users to access multiple input, output, and storage devices with a single computer, but to access the data and resources of more than one computer as well.

ISS: FROM RECORDING TRANSACTIONS TO PROVIDING EXPERTISE

There are many different types of information systems for different types of organizations, for different functions within organizations, and for different business needs. Business enterprises differ in their objectives, structure, interests, and approaches, and therefore no two can use exactly the same IS. However, ISs can be generally categorized according to the level of complexity and the type of function they serve. They range from the transaction processing system, or TPS, which records events such as sales, to expert systems, which provide expert advice.

TRANSACTION PROCESSING SYSTEMS

The earliest electronic information systems in business consisted of computers and programs that recorded and reported transactions. Such systems are called **transaction processing systems**, or **TPSs**, and are the most widely used information systems. TPSs are used predominantly to record data collected at the boundaries of organizations, in other words, at the point where the organization interfaces with the parties with which it does business. TPSs include cash registers recording sales, automatic teller machines recording cash withdrawals, purchase orders recording purchases, and the like. Once these data are collected, the IS either automatically processes the data into information, or stores it for later processing on demand.

MANAGEMENT INFORMATION SYSTEMS

In the 1970s, managers realized that they could use computer-based information systems for the purposes of planning, control, decision making, and problem solving, rather than just for reporting transactions. These new types of information systems came to be known as **management information systems**, or **MISs**. In this book, any information system that helps managers and other professionals in planning, control, and decision-making activities comes under the umbrella of management information systems. (Transaction processing systems on their own do not serve managers in their daily work; therefore, while they are ISs, they are not considered *management* information systems.) MISs have varying levels of complexity. To some degree, the type of MIS one uses depends on one's level of management.

DECISION SUPPORT SYSTEMS Middle and senior managers often need to select one course of action among many alternatives. Because managers have neither the time nor the resources to study and absorb long, detailed reports of data and information, organizations started to build information systems specifically designed to help managers make decisions. These have come to be called **decision support systems (DSSs)**. *Executive support* and *expert systems* are specific types of DSSs, serving the highest level of decision making, and the most knowledge-intensive decision making, respectively.

Decision support systems help answer "What if?" questions. What if we purchased raw goods overseas? What if we merged our warehouses? What if we doubled our shifts and cut our staff? DSSs were programmed to process raw data, make comparisons, and generate reports to help managers glean the best alternatives for financial investment, marketing strategy, credit approval, and the like. It is important to understand that a DSS is not an alternative to human decision making, however.

Often, managers must make decisions as a group, rather than make individual decisions. To reach consensus, they may use a **group decision support system (GDSSs)**. GDSSs help managers brainstorm, generate ideas, prioritize various suggested actions, and reach a decision acceptable to all, or to the majority of the decision-makers.

Executive Information Systems. Information systems designed to help high-ranking officers direct an organization are called **executive information systems (EISs)** or **executive support systems (ESSs)**. These systems, which are often programmed to integrate thousands of pieces of data and produce summary reports, evolved in the mid 1970s to help executives focus on long-range strategic planning within the organization. For example, executives in a hospital chain may receive bed-occupancy rates each quarter, month, or day. When they notice a persistently low occupancy for a certain hospital, they may start asking questions of the hospital's management in order to pinpoint the problem.

Expert Systems. Although they are powerful tools in decision making, DSSs and ESSs only include formulas, or models, that process data. Often, however, there is need for more than just formulas. Managers, or other workers, may need expertise to make certain decisions. In the past, only human experts in a specific line of work could provide advice to decision-makers. Now, ISs can be developed that embody human expertise. These systems are called **expert systems (ESs)**. When decision making is highly structured, it is easy to choose the one alternative out of many that would yield the best results, thanks to a previously proven set of steps. Expert systems, on the other hand are used when the decision being made is *not* structured. One example of structured decision making might be determining how to spend television advertising dollars during Super Bowl week. In this case, data will show that every dollar spent on television advertising during the Super Bowl increases sales ten times as much as advertising during regular prime time programming. Where to spend advertising dollars during Super Bowl week is an easy decision.

However, many environments are not sufficiently structured to allow an IS to use data to provide the one best answer. For instance, stock portfolio management is not a structured environment. There is no single method to decide which is the best securities portfolio, that is, the one that would yield the highest return. Medicine is another unstructured environment. There may be more than a single method of diagnosing a patient on the basis of symptoms. Indeed, given a particular set of symptoms, a patient may receive as many different diagnoses as the number of doctors he or she visits.

Using expert systems saves a company the high cost of employing human experts. Once the expertise is garnered from experts and built into a program, it can be distributed and used repeatedly. The expertise resides in the program in the form of a knowledge base consisting of facts and the relationships among the facts.

KNOWLEDGE WORKER The proliferation of ISs has helped knowledge workers do their work better. **Knowledge workers** are people whose main function is to generate information based on knowledge in their respective fields. These include people such as budget planners, project leaders, and marketing directors. As the number and importance of knowledge workers grew within corporate and other organizations, MISs became a topic taught in universities, not only as part of computer science, but as a specialty in business schools as well.

ON-DEMAND OUTPUT Probably one of the greatest changes in the use of MISs is in the reporting—or output—part of the system. Early management information systems were programmed to automatically produce only periodic reports (weekly, monthly, bimonthly, and so on). Additional reporting could be quite expensive. Now managers can obtain current standings online, with on-screen readouts and often no need for printouts. Today, MISs require simpler instructions to generate prescribed reports. Managers can instruct computers to produce reports tailored to their needs at virtually any time, giving them tighter control of processes, and the ability to react to problems quickly and seize opportunities.

There is still a place for the periodic reporting of information, to allow an organization to coordinate the analysis of its operations. Periodic reports are automatically generated by information systems weekly, monthly, quarterly, and the like. Sometimes managers request unplanned, special reports to help solve specific problems. These are called on-demand, or **ad hoc reports**. Reports that flag facts or numbers that deviate from preset standards are called **exception reports**. They allow managers to focus on the exceptions, and take care of the situation that caused something unplanned to happen.

INFORMATION SYSTEMS IN BUSINESS

Without exception, information systems are used in every business function in every business sector. From government agencies to manufacturing, from accounting to marketing, information systems are key tools in the transaction processing, decision making, problem solving, and operations of all organizations.

Managers can use online systems to generate ad hoc reports, which can then be examined on a computer monitor or printed out on paper. Exception reports are particularly helpful to managers in pinpointing areas of unsatisfactory performance.

Used by permission from ADP

INFORMATION SYSTEMS IN FUNCTIONAL BUSINESS AREAS

Different types of ISs are used for different purposes throughout the organization in what are known as "functional business areas,"—the in-house services that support the main business of an organization. Functional business areas include, but are not limited to, accounting, finance, marketing, and human resources, and they exist in most companies in one form or another.

ACCOUNTING In accounting, information systems help record business transactions, produce periodic financial statements, and create reports required by law, such as balance sheets and profit-and-loss statements. Accounting systems verify proper double entry and ascertain the accuracy of the organizational assets and liabilities.

FINANCE In finance, information systems are used to organize budgets, manage the flow of cash, analyze investments, and make decisions that could reduce interest payments and increase revenues from financial transactions.

MARKETING Marketing information systems help analyze demand for various products in different regions and population groups, to more accurately market the right product to target consumers. MISs provide information that helps management decide how many sales representatives to assign to specific products in specific geographical areas. The systems are used to identify trends in the demand for the company's products and services. They also aid in answering questions such as, "What would the effect of an advertisement campaign be?"

HUMAN RESOURCES Human resource management systems help mainly in record keeping and employee evaluation. Every organization must maintain accurate records of its employees. Human resource management systems maintain such records, including employees' pictures and details that serve other systems, such as payroll.

Evaluation systems provide essential check lists for managers for evaluating their subordinates. These systems also provide a scoring utility to quantify the strengths and weaknesses of workers' performance.

INFORMATION SYSTEMS IN DIFFERENT BUSINESS SECTORS

Information systems of all types are used in different business sectors.

MANUFACTURING Information systems are used throughout a manufacturing operation, from inventory control to paying suppliers. ISs help allocate resources such as personnel, raw material, and time to optimize productivity. Inventory control systems help in planning the optimal reorder quantities of raw materials, so that the company does not pay too much for materials that will not be used for a long time, while ensuring that the materials will be available when required. Information systems are used to process customer orders, prepare production schedules, perform quality assurance, and prepare shipping documents.

In an environment of fierce global competition, keeping costs low may make the difference between the success or failure of a manufacturing organization. Resource planning information systems play a vital role in determining which resource should be used at what place and time. When a machine stands idle even for just a few minutes, the company incurs costs that do not contribute to revenue. The problem is even worse if the machine is just one station in a production line performing a sequence of operations; an entire production line may then be idled. Information systems can help minimize the rate of such mishaps.

Warehouses are now managed through computers. Specialized information systems automatically report every item whose quantity reaches a reorder level and that item's economic order quantity (EOQ). The item is then immediately ordered, to avoid stoppage. The more sophisticated systems are directly connected to the suppliers' systems, so that suppliers keep an eye on inventory, and will ship low-level items without much effort on your employees' part.

GOVERNMENT Over the past four decades governmental and commercial organizations have installed computer-based ISs to automate processes and replace human labor. Tax authorities keep millions of taxpayers' records and use sophisticated programs to cross-reference filings. National insurance and welfare agencies keep track of payments from taxpayers and fund transfers to eligible recipients. Defense departments plan equipment procurement and training activities using ISs. Economic organizations, such as departments of commerce and labor, and central banks, use ISs for planning so they can advise decision-makers on economic policy. Immigration authorities keep track of people who cross national borders. All of these activities and many more are facilitated by the use of ISs.

SERVICE In the service sector, information systems play a central role. Actually, they are often the backbone of service organizations. Imagine an airline without an information system—it would not be able to reserve seats for passengers, and it could not schedule flights. Think for a moment of what banks would do without ISs. We could argue that the only thing they "manufacture" is information. Their information systems are fed with the type of account and with deposits and withdrawals; their output consists of statements, which show interest paid or owed, balances, and other information. Even cash withdrawals are done, in most cases, through information systems called automated teller machines (ATMs). Less and less information is given to customers in paper form. Clients can now use their phones to receive information about their accounts directly from information systems. Some banks allow their clients to do so through their computers, from home.

RETAIL Retail chains have invested millions of dollars in information systems in the past decade. For example, Wal-Mart and Kmart stores are now linked to communication networks by satellite. Management can promptly determine which items move quickly and which do not. The information is available on a regional and national basis. Slow-moving items may then be removed from inventory, and popular items will be stocked in greater quantities to improve profit. Because of the online availability of information, the manager of a store that has run out of a certain item can quickly restock it with the help of a nearby store that has plenty of that item on its shelves.

NEW BUSINESSES Beyond mere automation, many firms have implemented ISs to provide new products and services that became economical only with the development of information technology. Credit history firms, such as

TRW, Equifax, and TransUnion, use ISs to record important credit information on millions of credit card holders and borrowers. They sell the information to banks and other financial institutions. Some airlines sell the services of reservation systems to travel agencies. Shipping companies provide tracking services to their clients to track parcels on the way to their destinations. These are just three examples of services that would not be available without ISs.

SHARED DATA RESOURCES

As described above, most organizations depend on many information systems, many of which share data. The TPS collects information about sales, or inventory levels, or cash withdrawals; the MISs take and manipulate that same data to help managers and executives make decisions and run the organization.

ISs are often used to create large pools of data, called **databases**. A company's database is one of the most powerful resources it has to run its organization. If all the data—sales, returns, inventory values, interest payments, and so on—were just recorded in one long list, its power could not be harnessed by the organization. But when categorized and structured, the data can be manipulated and can produce useful information (see Figure 1.8).

Ideally, an organization would hold its data in one integrated database from which different ISs could draw the data they need. However, having one integrated database is not always possible; in fact, when decentralized use of data increases within an organization, getting databases to communicate with each other within a company becomes an important challenge. To the user, these databases must seem to interface seamlessly, so as to enable access to as much data as is needed to produce the required information.

Figure 1.9 illustrates this concept. The organization's database receives data from transaction recording and processing systems, such as cash registers or ATMs. The company's DSSs, GDSSs, ESSs, ESs, and Operations ISs draw data from the pool to make decisions, solve problems, and run daily operations.

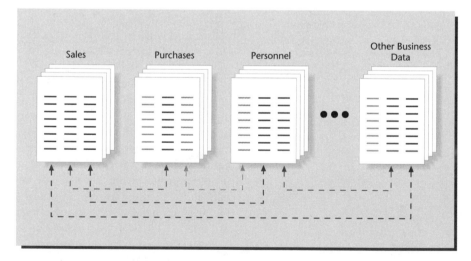

Figure 1.8 *Computer-based databases are an important resource for any organization.*

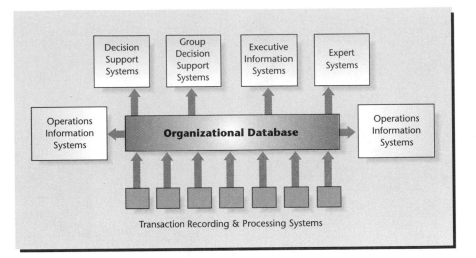

Figure 1.9 *A generalized concept of organization information systems*

Be Well-Versed in Information Systems?

Information is the life blood of any organization, commercial or not-for-profit; it is essential to sound problem solving and decision making, upon which business success is built. In fact, the main factor limiting the services and information computers can provide within an organization is the budget. The amount of money a company can afford to spend on its computer system has a limit. Knowing the practical limitations of the type and volume of information your organization's systems can provide is an essential component to being an effective manager.

Unlike many other components of business, information systems are quickly changing in form and content. A computer that is considered fast now will be an outdated machine in 18 months. A computer program that is considered innovative now will be surpassed by a better program in two years. The dynamic nature of information technology is like a moving target. If a manager does not stay informed, he or she will not be able to guide a company appropriately.

Managers must at all times maintain a clear picture of their organizations and the outside business environment, including a knowledge of the resources available to them and to their competitors. Computer-based information systems are excellent tools in the collection, storage, and presentation of such facts. But to be truly effective, those facts must be manipulated into useful information that can indicate the best allocation of different resources, including personnel, time, money, equipment, and other assets. Regardless of what operations are being managed, ISs will be an important tool. Successful managers must know which ISs are available to their organizations, and what ISs may be developed in the future.

Used by permission from Michael Rosenfeld/Tony Stone Images *(a)*

Used by permission from IBM Corporation *(b)*

Used by permission from Chris Sorenson/The Stock Market *(c)*

Information systems have affected almost all industries, including (a) manufacturing; (b) the service sector; and (c) retail business.

WHY STUDY INFORMATION SYSTEMS?

If you find the subject of information systems interesting, there are many ways to build a career on that interest, from conceptualizing IS operations, to programming code, to running IS systems. Even if you do not want to be an IS professional, information systems will be important to your career. The view that managers should specialize in their own domains, such as finance or marketing, and that information systems are the domain only of IS specialists is no longer a valid one. Controllers, financial analysts, marketing professionals, and managers in virtually every other field use information systems daily, to improve their performance.

To take advantage of information technology, you must be familiar with different types of information systems and know how to use them. Without knowledge of information systems you will lag behind your peers who can make their work more efficient. Increasingly, organizations expect their personnel to solve many of their efficiency problems on their own, using user-friendly IS software. Software packages provide easy-to-learn features that help users tailor computer programs to their specific needs. You do not have to be an IS professional to understand and operate these systems, but your chances of finding a rewarding position are slim if you are not familiar with the technology.

Furthermore, studies have shown that workers who use computers earn an average of 10–15% more than those who don't, even for the same job. Secretaries who use computers enjoy a salary premium of up to 30%. The differential has held up despite a big increase in the number of workers with computer skills. The demand for computer literacy is especially great among knowledge workers, that is professionals and managers. In the near future, it is unlikely that a college graduate in any field will be able to find a rewarding position without minimal knowledge of information systems. Chapter 8, "Managers and Their Information Needs," provides details of different specializations in MIS, for students who are interested in pursuing careers in this fast-paced field.

BUSINESS, THE INTERNET, THE WEB, AND DATABASES

More and more successful businesses are turning to database and online technologies to help make their ISs as productive as possible. Growth in telecommunications has given birth to a new information industry: business on the Internet and its World Wide Web. The Internet is the vast network of computers, connected across the globe, that can share both information and processing. The World Wide Web is that part of the Internet that displays graphics and moving images; the Web has enticed thousands of businesses to become involved in the Internet. Chapter 6, "The Internet and Intranets," is dedicated to providing a primer on the Internet, its basic technology, its promise and its limitations.

In order to be successful in business, You must also have a clear understanding of the concept and technology of databases (discussed in Chapter 7, "Data Management"). Databases allow systems to store huge pools of data to be used repeatedly by many different parts of an organization for different purposes, without expending any effort to re-enter and maintain separate data. The marriage of database technology with online sources has created a uniquely powerful business tool.

DEGREES IN IS

To keep up with industry demand, colleges and universities offer degrees in computer science or management information systems. The latter programs are offered in business schools. Compared to computer science programs, MIS curricula tend to put less emphasis on technical issues. In these programs, students learn how to be managers. They also learn about different information technologies, such as database management and telecommunications. The

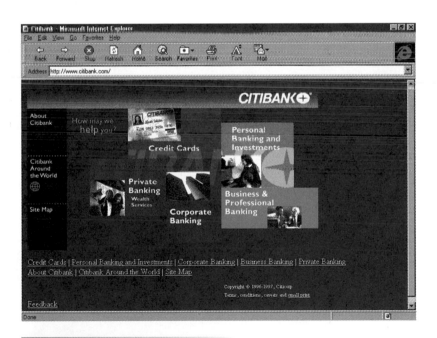

The World Wide Web is changing the face of information systems in business.

combination of technical and managerial skills prepares them to be the link between information technology and other managers in the organization. Many graduates accept positions in firms that specialize in providing information systems services. Their careers revolve around advising other organizations how to efficiently and effectively use the technology.

INFORMATION SYSTEMS CAREERS

There are many exciting career choices in the area of information systems. The demand for professionals in this field will continue to grow, because development in the field is moving fast, and the need for information systems in organizations is increasing.

Graduates of MIS programs usually start their careers as systems analysts, who participate in the analysis of business needs that can be satisfied with information technology (IT), and then help design and construct ISs. From here, they can then choose from various career paths: functional systems developer (financial or marketing systems), telecommunications specialist, database administrator, and so on. Some graduates spend several years in commercial companies or government agencies, and then leave and start their own consulting businesses.

A career in information systems is rewarding in two ways. First, daily work is challenging because you are always creating new systems, or a new module for existing systems, that help people do their jobs better. Second, the financial rewards are well above those of graduates in many other disciplines. Figure 1.10 presents starting salaries of graduates of a typical business school.

The U.S. Department of Labor predicts that the overall need for computer systems analysts will near 700,000 by the year 2000. Many of the holders of these positions will come from business schools.

The career of an IS professional is no longer limited to the IS field. Often, IS managers advance to high positions in other fields. Some have become the presidents of their organizations.

	Mean	Percentiles	
	1995	90th	10th
All Business	28,613	40,000	19,000
All Accounting	27,017	34,000	22,000
All Accounting/Finance	27,172	22,000	35,000
Accounting/Public	25,000	30,000	20,000
Accounting/Govt. & Bus.	27,689	36,000	22,000
Finance/Bus. Economics	27,260	35,000	20,000
Management	33,208	50,000	21,000
MIS	29,360	31,800	19,000
Marketing	27,595	40,000	20,000

Source: Wayne State University Office of University Counseling & Placement Services, 1996.

Figure 1.10 *Starting salaries of business graduates of a typical university ($)*

Cutting the Paper Chase

GTE, the giant telephone carrier, has a division whose business it is to serve customers. The organization, Data Systems Services Organization (DSSO), employs 200 field service representatives. The vans of these representatives serve not only as a means of transportation, but also as their offices. In 1994, several years of 15% growth rate per year had buried GTE's on-call field service representatives in a growing amount of paper that included customer documents and service records, time cards, travel expense forms, and part order and receipt forms. They were spending too much time processing paper-based documents associated with each on-site service call.

The division faced a daunting task: curtail rising costs and inefficiencies. It particularly wanted to shorten the lag time in the customer billing cycle and gain control over inventory management. Other goals included reducing the number of service dispatchers, reducing data entry errors, minimizing voice mail communications costs, and controlling escalating overnight mail charges incurred by sending "must have" procedure changes to field representatives.

"Because of the volume, a lot of things fell through the cracks and were never billed," said one manager. "We also needed tighter inventory control. We have parts in the back of cars across the country, and two depots that we ship parts from. Trying to keep track of them was a real nightmare." Also, 45% of the service records turned in from the field were filled out incorrectly. As a result, the billing department personnel had to correct the errors and manually input the changes into the company's database. The manager added, "Our field representatives hate paperwork. They just want to fix the equipment and get on to the next call."

Now, they do exactly that. They are armed with laptop computers and special software, RemoteWare. When customers call the central dispatch facility in Chantilly, Virginia, pertinent information is logged into a database that houses information on field service representative availability, qualifications, and proximity to the customer service site. Once assigned, the on-call representative is paged via standard pager. A representative who is driving simply pulls over and dials via cellular phone into the server located at

GTE Services' Colorado Springs, Colorado, facility. The system automatically downloads the customer ticket describing the location and nature of the service call.

At the same time, the technician also receives high priority e-mail, parts shipment status, and graphical documents such as hand-sketched maps, schematics, and equipment disassembly instructions. The entire communications session lasts about a minute. The representative replies with an estimated time of arrival at the customer site, logs the time spent and the parts requested, checks the status of parts being sent for other service calls, and lets dispatch know his or her present location. At night, at home, the representative connects the laptop computer to the telephone network. The computer automatically connects to the office database to receive new customer service orders and inventory updates. Billing information is communicated to the office, which later bills the customer.

The mobile service representatives have drastically reduced the amount of paperwork required for on-site service calls. This has increased productivity by more than 50%. The new system solves two big problems: getting data back from the field reliably so customers can be billed, and keeping inventory up to date. While each document used to travel to five different people before the services it detailed could be billed, it now involves only two employees.

With each RemoteWare connection, time cards, customer service records, expense reports, and other documents are routed electronically to the company's corporate database for processing. As a result, errors have been reduced, bills are no longer lost in the shuffle, and billing turnaround is less than 30 days.

Source: "Cutting the Mobile Paper Chase," Communcations News. March 1997. Reprinted by permission.

Questions

1. Refer back to the business functions discussed in the chapter. Which business functions are supported by the new system?

2. Which technologies (hardware, software, or telecommunications) have had the greatest contribution to the new system?

3. Explain how the new system supports the "office on the move" idea.

Cold Weather, Warm Service

Fargo, North Dakota, becomes very cold in the winter. Wind chills of –80 degrees Fahrenheit are not uncommon. When the temperature drops that low, people stay home, and businesses are closed. But some are using information technology to overcome the weather-enforced slowdown.

Fargo-based Great Plains Software, which develops and supports financial management applications, was shut down (by winter weather) four times in 1997. But Great Plains' employees and clients weren't left out in the cold, thanks to the hottest in software and hardware. Christina Bertsch, a sales executive based in the Fargo office, lives only eight miles from company headquarters, but went six weeks without being able to spend five consecutive days in the office.

"I work [with sales partners] in the Southeast... and I tell them it's like a three-day hurricane, only instead of being 60 or 70 degrees out, it's -30," Bertsch explains. "They find people in their cars out there frozen to death. I value my job and the people I work with, but I'm not going to risk life and limb." Stranded at home, Bertsch took advantage of Great Plains' communications network to keep business cooking. She could easily check her voice mail because phone and power lines were relatively unaffected by the storms. From her laptop, she worked via modem with her out-of-state partners. She could also access company databases to retrieve and download client information, technical help, or product specifications. If a client wanted to place an order, she simply jumped to Great Plains' Lotus Notes-based e-mail network and sent the order directly to sales operations.

"I don't think the clients see the difference, whether I'm sitting at home or at my desk, because I have access to all the information," Bertsch says. That's exactly the way it should be, explains David Knorr, a Great Plains sales manager. He encourages his staff of 17 to work in whatever environment makes them feel comfortable, safe, and productive. "Would you rather have them get stuck in a ditch for four hours, or mak[ing] sales calls?" Knorr says.

Meanwhile, Great Plains' customers weren't frozen out, even while company headquarters was turning into an igloo. Unable to reach a live human, customers with trouble had two options: log onto a secure area of Great Plains' Web site to get answers to technical questions, or call the automated phone system and leave a message in the emergency voice mailbox, which prompted support supervisors to respond quickly. "Customers appreciate the fact that we made a way for them to get the information, even though we were technically closed," says Pam Kram, a Great Plains spokesperson. "Our customers understand we're not going to go outside when the wind chill is –100 and there's zero visibility."

Source: Purdue, M., "Fargo: Chilling Tale of Sales Gone Good," Sales & Field Force Management, March 1997, p. 16. Reprinted by permission from Sales & Field Force Automation magazine. Copyright © 1997 Curtco Freedom Group.

Questions:

1. Enumerate the technologies that enable Great Plains Software to continue to serve customers while the office is closed.

2. Could Great Plains Software totally eliminate the use of its office? Why, or why not?

18 Wheels and a Satellite Dish

The image of the long-haul trucker, barreling down the highway with only his CB radio for company, is largely a thing of the past. Today's truckers rely on computers and satellite communications as much as on diesel engines and 18-speed gearboxes. Their vehicles are now equipped with satellite dishes and state-of-the-art mobile information systems. At the dispatch center, companies link to their customers with electronic document interchange and Web sites, all with the goal of giving the shipper a constant stream of accurate information on the status of every load.

"Our drivers are increasingly becoming the managers of their trucks," says Patrick E. Quinn, co-chairman of U.S. Xpress, based in Chattanooga, Tennessee, "and one of their key roles is providing timely service information." Precise information on load status is available because U.S. Xpress made an early investment in satellite communications, which enables drivers to stay in constant touch with the company's customer service, operations, and maintenance departments. But it wasn't easy.

Satellite communications vendors in the 1980s didn't understand how to apply their product to the transportation industry. Implementation took anywhere from 18 to 20 months because U.S. Xpress had to build most of the interfaces and connectivity capabilities itself. But for the company, the payback has made it all worthwhile. "Satellite tracking changed the way we do business," one manager said. "It gives us the ability to provide service for customers we used to just dream about. It's changed the industry."

With a sophisticated satellite communications system, U.S. Xpress truckers never lose touch with the home office. A trucker can send and receive e-mail and access information about payroll right from his cab. The system also allows home office operations staff to get precise data on every load in the field.

The company has also established an active presence on the World Wide Web. Its Xpress Connect service lets customers track shipments by logging onto the company's Web site. Shippers can check time and date of pickup, stops in transit, and destination of any shipment, as well as the all-important current location and on-time status. Customers can also use the Web site to make arrangements to have a load shipped.

As of 1997, customers have been able to log onto the Web site to download proof-of-delivery documentation directly from the company's document imaging system. Other services include online rating, which allows the customer to enter detailed information about the shipment and receive an instant price quote, and a feature that automatically sends a notice to the customer's pager if a load is delayed; not welcome news, perhaps, but crucial information if your business depends on timely arrival of that shipment.

Source: Whistler, D. "18 Wheels and a Satellite Dish," Sales & Field Force Management, March 1997, pp. 67–70. Reprinted by permission from Sales & Field Force Automation magazine. Copyright © 1997 Curtco Freedom Group.

Questions:

1. What was the only role of a truck driver a decade ago? In addition to this role, what is the driver's role nowadays?

2. Why is it important for a trucker to be in constant touch with the home office?

3. What are the benefits of giving U.S. Xpress's customers access to the company's information systems via the Web?

••• Computer-based information systems pervade almost every aspect of our lives. Their ability to help with problem solving and decision making makes them indispensable in business and management. Businesses continually face **problems**, which are undesirable situations. **Decisions** are called for when a course of action must be chosen from among many possible alternatives.

Computer-based information systems take **data** as their raw material, process the data, and produce **information** as output. While data can sometimes be useful as information, it usually must be manipulated in order to produce information.

A **system** is a set of components that work together to achieve a common goal. An **information system** consists of several components: **hardware** (the computer and its peripheral equipment), **software** (the programs that run the computer), data, **people**, and **procedures**. The common goal of these components is to produce the best information from available data.

Often, a system performs a limited task whose product is combined with the products of other systems to reach an ultimate goal. The system is then called a **subsystem**. Several subsystems may make up a system. Sometimes, systems are also classified as **closed** or **open**. When a system stands alone and has no contact with other systems, it is referred to as a closed system; when it has interfaces with other systems, it is an open system.

There are four basic stages in data processing. In the **input** stage, data are collected and entered into the computer. The computer then performs the next stage, **data processing**. In the following stage, **output**, the information is displayed or otherwise presented. We often also want to maintain data and information for later use. This activity is called **storage**.

There are several different types of information systems. **Transaction processing systems (TPSs)**, such as cash registers, ATMs, and other systems that record data and perform basic processing, the results of which may be simple reports. **Management information systems (MISs)** use recorded transactions and other data to produce information for problem solving and decision making. MISs include **decision support systems (DSSs)**, **executive information systems (EISs)**, and **expert systems (ESs)**.

DSSs contain **models**, or formulas, that manipulate data into information. They often answer "What if?" questions, in other words, "By how much will sales increase *if* we increase advertising expenses by 10%?"

Often, a group of managers, rather than an individual manager, has to reach a decision. **Group decision support systems (GDSSs)** help groups generate ideas, establish priorities, and reach decisions through concensus or a majority of votes.

EISs can glean information for high-level executives from vast amounts of data in the organization's databases. This information helps pinpoint problems in a specific organizational unit. EISs are highly useful in control and planning.

Often, there are no sure steps for reaching the best decision. Such situations require expertise. Computer programs that contain expertise gleaned from human experts are called expert systems. Once the knowledge is organized as part of the program, it can be replicated and distributed, thus saving companies the high cost of employing human experts.

ISs are used in many business functions, the most common of which are accounting, finance, marketing, and human resources. These systems aid in the daily operations of organizations by maintaining proper accounting information and producing reports, assisting in managing cash and investments, helping marketing professionals find the most likely buyers of their products and services, and keeping accurate employee records and assisting with the evaluations of their performance.

ISs have been employed in many different sectors of the economy. In manufacturing, they help keep inventories to a minimum while ensuring smooth operations of production and assembly lines. Government agencies use ISs for tax collection, economic planning, immigration control, and procurement from the private sector. Service organizations reduce cost by letting their customers use ISs instead of human servers, such as bank tellers. And some organizations market entirely new services that would not be possible without ISs, such as credit reports and shipment tracking.

One of the greatest assets of today's organizations is database technology. **Databases** allow organizations to collect, store, and manipulate large amounts of data from which useful information can be derived. The data are usually collected at the time a transaction takes place, and stored in databases, then used by the different MISs as needed. More and more, successful businesses are turning to the powerful combination of database and online Internet technologies to improve their operations.

Even if you do not intend to pursue an IS career, you must learn about the technology and how it is used.

Employers seek professionals who are computer-literate and know how **information technology (IT)** can be used for more efficient and effective business processes.

The rapid development and widespread use of IT have created many ethical and societal concerns. Three of them are **privacy, software piracy,** and **IS professionalism.** Privacy poses a dilemma because we wish to protect individual privacy at the same time allow commercial organizations to collect personal data for the efficient practice of activities such as targeted marketing.

These are conflicting ideals. Software piracy, the illegal copying and distribution of software, costs vendors billions of dollars in lost revenues, and also raises prices for those who pay for their software. Although businesses spend billions of dollars on development and maintenance of ISs, the IS profession is unregulated. Perhaps failed development projects and unused systems could be avoided, if IS specialists had a code of professional conduct such as physicians, lawyers, and public accountants.

REVIEW, DISCUSS, AND EXPLORE

REVIEW AND DISCUSSION QUESTIONS

1. Information systems are no longer the domain of technically-oriented personnel, but the business of every manager. Comment.

2. Assume that computers can easily recognize voices and detect exactly what their users mean when talking. Will the necessity for written language be reduced to zero? Why, or why not?

3. What is the difference between a TPS and a DSS?

4. What is a problem? Give an example of a business problem, and how it could be solved with a computer-based information system.

5. When does a manager need to make a decision? How can a DSS help make decisions? Why is this type of information system called a decision support system, and not a decision system?

6. An increasing number of knowledge workers must know how to use information systems. Why?

7. Give an example in which raw data also serve as useful information. Give three business examples (not mentioned in the text) of data that must be processed to provide useful information.

8. *Ethics and Society:* Give three examples of phenomena that were not of concern until a decade ago, and are now of concern because of information technology. Articulate your arguments.

CONCEPT ACTIVITY

Contact a business organization and ask for permission to observe a business process. Pinpoint the segments in the process that could be aided by a computer-based information system. Write a report detailing your observations and suggestions.

HANDS-ON ACTIVITY

Use the resume feature in your word-processing program to type up your resume. If you don't have a lot of work experience, remember to include all types of work, whether it's baby-sitting, camp counseling, mowing the lawn or whatever you've done.

TEAM ACTIVITY

Form a team with two or three students. Each team member should use the school's e-mail system to send to the other members, and to your instructor, a short message that contains the following items: name, major, personal interests, and what you expect to know by the end of this course.

EXPLORE THE WEB

If you do not have an Internet account, ask your teacher how to get one. If you are already on the Web, log onto a commercial site that offers products (such as compact discs) for sale. Record how many layers you had to go through to find a product to your taste. That is, how many times did you have to click marked text? Prepare a short report on the good and bad features of the site. Your report should include evaluations of the length of time it takes to navigate the site, how intuitive the icons are, and the overall appearance of the site.

Chapter 2

Strategic Uses of Information Systems

If the Shoe Fits

Thanks to software made by Trilogy Development, a Westport, Conn.-based company called the Custom Foot can give you a pair of custom-made shoes for the same amount of money you paid for off-the-shelf ones.

Here's how it works: In a Custom Foot store, the customer places her foot on an electronic scanner, which measures the foot in 14 different ways. She completes the shoe configuration with a salesperson, pointing and clicking on a computer screen to choose a shoe style, type and grade of leather, a color, an outsole, a lining, and so on. Trilogy's software translates the customer's set of choices into a specification order and transmits it—in Italian—to subcontractors in Milan, Florence, and Ancona. The shoemakers cobble the shoes and ship them back to the U.S., usually two to three weeks after the order is placed. The shoes sell from $99 to $250, the same range offered by most Manhattan shoe stores…

"We don't have any inventory, and there is no middleman," says Custom Foot founder and Chief Executive Jeffrey Silverman, 34, explaining how he can sell custom shoes at ready-made prices. Silverman has been selling shoes since he was 16 years old. "As a salesman, you're trained to sell the customer what you have, not what they want." Silverman says he was fed up with pushing not-quite-right shoes and decided to customize the process.

He contacted Joseph Pine, author of *Mass Customization*, and asked Pine to sit on Custom Foot's board of directors. Pine asked Silverman what configuration software he planned to use, and when Silverman replied, "What's that?" Pine told him to contact Trilogy…

His Westport store should do between $4 million and $7 million in its first year. He has venture backing and is moving to expand his concept before others can beat him to it. He plans to open six more Custom Foot stores by the end of this year and says he would like to have 100 stores nationwide by the end of next year.

Source: McHugh, J., "A shoe that really fits," *Forbes*, June 3, 1996, p. 126–127. Reprinted by permission of Forbes Magazine. Copyright © 1996 by Forbes, Inc.

LEARNING OBJECTIVES

During the 1990s, corporations changed their perception of information. Information was no longer exclusively seen as an operational resource supporting the immediate needs of the day-to-day running of a company. Now, information can significantly change an organization's long-term strategic position in national and global markets. Often, information systems applied to long-term planning completely change the way a firm conducts its business. Some systems even change the product or service that a firm provides.

When you finish this chapter, you will:

◆ Understand business strategy and strategic moves

◆ Understand how information systems can give businesses a competitive advantage

◆ Know the basic initiatives for gaining a competitive advantage

◆ Know what makes an information system a *strategic* information system

◆ Understand the fundamental requirements for developing strategic information systems

◆ Understand what makes one SIS a success and another a failure.

STRATEGY AND STRATEGIC MOVES

Although many information systems are built to solve problems, many others are built to seize opportunities. And, as anyone in business can tell you, it is easier to identify a problem than to create an opportunity. Why? Because a problem already exists; it is an obstacle to a desired mode of operation, and, as such, it calls attention to itself. An opportunity, on the other hand, is less tangible. It takes a certain amount of vision to identify or create an opportunity and seize it. Information systems that help seize opportunities are called **strategic information systems**. They can be developed from scratch, or they can evolve from existing ISs within an organization.

The word "strategy" originated in the Greek word *strategos*, meaning "general." In war, a strategy is a plan to gain an advantage over the enemy. The term has been borrowed by other disciplines, especially business. As you know from media coverage of business, corporate executives often discuss actions in a way that makes business sound like war. In business, as in war, one must devise decisive courses of action to win. In business, a strategy is a plan designed to help an organization outperform its competitors.

In a free market economy, it is difficult for a business to do well without some strategy. Although strategies vary, they tend to fall into some basic categories, such as developing a new product, identifying an unserved consumer need, changing a service to entice more customers or retain existing clients, or taking any other action that increases the organization's value through improved performance.

Many strategies do not, and cannot, involve information systems. But increasingly, corporations are able to implement certain strategies—such as maximizing sales and lowering costs—thanks to the innovative use of information systems. In other words, better information gives corporations a competitive advantage in the marketplace. **Strategic advantage** is achieved when a company uses strategy to make the most of its strengths, resulting in a **competitive advantage**. In this book, we will use "competitive advantage" and "strategic advantage" interchangeably.

ACHIEVING A COMPETITIVE ADVANTAGE

Let's consider competitive advantage in terms of a for-profit company, whose major goal is to maximize profits by lowering costs and increasing revenue.

A competitive advantage is achieved by a for-profit company when its profits are significantly increased, which is most commonly achieved through an increase of market share. Figure 2.1 lists the eight basic initiatives that can be used to win a competitive advantage, including having a product or service that competitors cannot provide, or providing the same product or service in a manner more attractive to customers. As Figure 2.2 indicates, many strategies can be used together to help a company gain a competitive advantage.

INITIATIVE #1: REDUCE COSTS

Customers like to pay as little as possible, while still receiving the quality of service or product they need. One way to increase market share is to lower prices, and the best way to lower prices is to lower costs.

For instance, if carried out successfully, massive automation of any business process will give an organization a competitive advantage. The reason is

INITIATIVE	BENEFIT
Reduce costs	A company can gain an advantage if it can sell more units at a lower price while providing quality and maintaining or increasing its profit margin.
Raise barriers to entrants market	A company can gain an advantage if it deters potential entrants into the market, leaving less competition and more market potential.
Establish high switching cost	A company can gain an advantage if it creates high switching costs, making it economically infeasible for customers to buy from competitors.
Create new products or services	A company can gain an advantage if it offers a unique product or service.
Differentiate products or services	A company can gain an advantage if it can attract customers by convincing them its product is different from the competition's.
Enhance products or services	A company can gain an advantage if its product or service is better than anyone else's.
Establish alliance	Companies from different industries can help each other gain an advantage by offering combined packages of goods or services at special prices.
Lock in suppliers or buyers	A company can gain an advantage if it can lock in either suppliers or buyers, making it economically impractical for suppliers or buyers to deal with competitors.

Figure 2.1 *Eight basic ways to gain a competitive advantage*

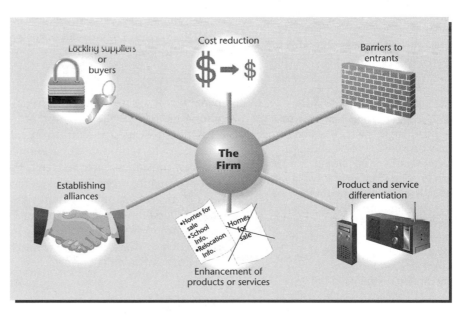

Figure 2.2 *Many strategic moves can work together to achieve a competitive advantage.*

simple: automation makes an organization more productive, and any savings in cost can be transferred to customers through lower prices. We saw this happen in the auto industry. In the 1970s, Japanese auto makers brought robots into their production and assembly lines and were able to reduce costs—and subsequently prices—quickly and dramatically. The robots weld, paint, and assemble parts at a far lower cost than manual labor. Until their foreign competitors began to employ robots, the Japanese had a clear competitive advantage because they were able to sell high-quality cars for less than their competitors.

INITIATIVE #2: RAISE BARRIERS TO ENTRANTS

The smaller the number of companies that compete within an industry, the better off each company is. Therefore, an organization may gain a competitive advantage by making it difficult, or impossible, for other organizations to produce the product or service it provides. This is done by using expertise or technology that is unavailable to competitors or prohibitively expensive for competitors to use.

Barriers may be raised in a number of ways. Patenting can keep a particular technology from competitors for a certain period of time. Another barrier that can keep potential new entrants out of a market is the high expense of entering the industry. An example of this is the pension fund management business, a field in which the most successful competitor is State Street, Inc. In the 1980s, State Street committed massive amounts of money to an IS that helped make the company a leader in managing pension funds and international bank accounts. Building a system to successfully compete with State Street's would require huge allocations of capital, which keeps new entrants out of the market. Instead, other pension management corporations actually buy the services of State Street's IS expertise. In fact, State Street derives most of its revenues (about 70%) from selling its IS services.

INITIATIVE #3: ESTABLISH HIGH SWITCHING COSTS

Switching costs are the expenses incurred by a customer who stops buying a product or service from one business and starts buying it from another. Switching costs can be explicit (such as charges explicitly levied on a customer for switching) or implicit (such as the indirect costs in time and money of adjusting to a new product that does the same job as the old).

Often, explicit switching costs are fixed, nonrecurring costs, such as a penalty that a buyer may have to pay for terminating a deal early. In the telephone industry, while long-distance companies mostly compete by trying to provide the deepest discounts on calls, some phone companies charge their customers to terminate their service. When evaluating new long-distance services, consumers have to weigh their gain in discounted calls against their cost of switching from one provider to another.

A perfect example of implicit switching expenses are those involved in the time and money required to adjust to any new software. Once a company has trained its personnel to use one word-processing or spreadsheet program, a competing software company would have to offer a very enticing deal to make switching worthwhile.

INITIATIVE #4: CREATE NEW PRODUCTS AND SERVICES

Clearly, creating a new and unique product or service that many people need gives an organization a great competitive advantage. Unfortunately, the

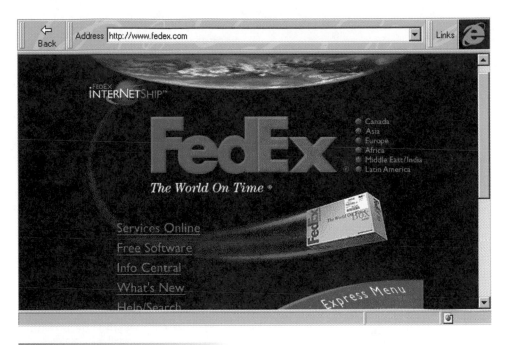

FedEx's clever use of ISs and the Web attracted many clients from competitors.

advantage lasts only until other organizations in the industry start offering an identical or similar product or service for a comparable or lower price.

Examples of this scenario are abundant in the software industry. For instance, Lotus Development Corporation was the major player in the electronic spreadsheet market after it introduced its Lotus 1-2-3 program. When two competitors tried to market similar products, the company sued for copyright infringement and won the case in court, sustaining its market dominance for several years. However, with time, other products gained a competitive advantage by including new features and providing the flexibility to integrate spreadsheet information into other programs.

Another example is Federal Express, which basically created a market when it started providing overnight service for the first time. FedEx market share slipped when the U.S. Postal Service, UPS, and other companies entered the same market, providing virtually the same service at the same or lower prices. However, FedEx regained market share by providing the means for clients to log onto FedEx's IS to track their own packages, a service now offered through the World Wide Web. Clients can connect to the system and receive real-time information about any item they have sent or are scheduled to receive. The extra service has been credited for attracting clients back to FedEx.

INITIATIVE #5: DIFFERENTIATE PRODUCTS AND SERVICES

A company can achieve a competitive advantage by persuading consumers that its product or service is better than the competitors', even if only in terms of public perception. This is called **product differentiation** and is usually achieved through advertising. The success of brand names is a perfect example of product differentiation. Think of Levi's Jeans, Chanel perfumes, Calvin Klein clothes. The customer buys the brand name because it is perceived to be superior to that of other similar products.

Like products, services, too, can achieve a reputation through brand-name recognition. For instance, MCI keeps advertising the merits of its Friends and Family calling program, claiming that it is superior to similar programs offered by competitors. The company succeeded in retaining subscribers in the program even when other telephone companies emulated its idea.

INITIATIVE #6: ENHANCE PRODUCTS OR SERVICES

Instead of differentiating a product or service, an organization may actually add something to it to make it more valuable to the consumer. This is referred to as product or service enhancement. For example, car manufacturers may entice customers by attaching a longer warranty to their cars; real estate agents may attract more business by providing useful financing information to potential buyers.

INITIATIVE #7: ESTABLISH ALLIANCES

Companies can gain a competitive advantage by making their combined service more attractive (which usually means less expensive) than purchasing services separately. These alliances provide two draws for customers: the combined service is cheaper and, by providing one-stop shopping, more convenient. The travel industry has become very aggressive in this area. For example, airlines collaborate with hotel chains to offer travel and lodging packages; credit card companies offer to discount purchases of tickets from particular airlines or the products of particular manufacturers. It is fairly common for credit cards to offer frequent flier miles for every dollar spent. In all these cases, alliances were established to create competitive advantages.

As Figure 2.3 indicates, by creating an alliance, the organizations enjoy synergy, whereby the combined profit for the allies from the sales of a "package" of goods or services is greater than the profits earned when each acts individually.

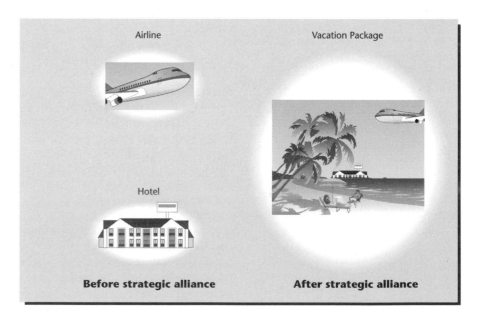

Figure 2.3 *Strategic alliances combine services to create synergies*

Used by permission from TWA and European American Bank

Strategic alliances of financial institutions and airlines use information systems to track the purchases made and mileage earned by credit card users.

Organizations can achieve a competitive advantage if they are powerful enough to lock either suppliers into their mode of operation or buyers to their product. Possessing bargaining power—the leverage to influence buyers and suppliers—is the key to this approach. As such, this competitive advantage is almost exclusively the resource of companies so large that suppliers and buyers must listen to their demands.

A firm has bargaining power with a supplier either when the firm has few competitors or when the firm is a major competitor in the industry. In the former case, the fewer the companies that make up a customer base for a supplier, the more important each company is to the supplier; in the latter case, the more important a specific company is to a supplier's success, the greater the bargaining power that company has over that supplier.

The most common leverage in bargaining is purchase volume; companies that spend millions of dollars purchasing parts and services have the power to force their suppliers to conform to their methods of operation, and even to shift some of their costs onto suppliers as part of the business arrangement. Let's look at the big auto makers as an example.

The big auto makers have used their bargaining power to get suppliers to adopt their particular standards of electronic data interchange (EDI). (EDI is the basic concept of using electronic rather than paper communication in business transactions.) EDI is implemented with a number of different standards, and companies can only participate in EDI if they use the same standards. A supplier who subscribes to one auto maker's standards is locked into that auto maker, because changing the standards would be too costly. That automaker can then use its bargaining leverage with the supplier to obtain lower-cost parts, cut costs, and thus improve its competitive position.

The same auto companies involved with EDI (General Motors, Ford, and Chrysler) have also adopted just-in-time (JIT) methods of manufacturing, whereby inventory costs are drastically cut by receiving parts just a short time before they are needed in the assembly line. The auto companies have used their bargaining power to shift the burden of maintaining inventory to the supplier. The suppliers are willing to modify the way they do business because they need the business of the auto makers.

Remember, once a supplier subscribes to one auto maker's standards, it may not be able to serve other companies' standards. In other words, that supplier is essentially locked in with that purchaser.

To lock in *buyers* in a free market, an organization must create the impression that its product is significantly better than the competitors', or enjoy a situation in which the customers fear high switching costs. For instance, IBM maintained a competitive edge for almost three decades because data processing managers subscribed to the notion that they could secure their own jobs by purchasing IBM equipment. The thinking was that once a company owned IBM machines, it would stay with IBM machines because the expense of replacing expensive IBM software and retraining personnel to use new systems would be prohibitive.

STRATEGIC INFORMATION AS A COMPETITIVE WEAPON

A strategic information system (SIS) is any information system that can help an organization achieve a long-term competitive advantage, based on the techniques discussed in the previous section. An SIS can be created from scratch, developed by modifying an existing system, or "found" by realizing that a system already in place can be used to strategic advantage. Strategic information systems embody two types of ideas: an idea of a potentially winning business move, and an idea of how to harness information technology to implement the move.

For an information system to be an SIS, two conditions must exist. First, the information system must be serving an organizational goal, rather than simply providing information; second, the IS unit must be working with the managers of the other functional units (including marketing, finance, purchasing, human resources, and so on) to pursue the organizational goal.

CREATING AN SIS

For an SIS to be developed, top management must be involved from initial consideration through development and implementation. In other words, the SIS must be a part of the overall organizational strategic plan. There is always the danger that a new SIS will be looked upon as a product exclusively of the IS unit; in order to succeed, however, the project must be a corporate effort, including the involvement of all managers who will make use of the system.

Figure 2.4 presents the questions that management needs to ask to determine if a new SIS should be developed. Executives meet to try to identify the areas in which information can support a strategic goal. Only when the activities outlined in Figure 2.4 have been completed will management be able to conceptualize a strategic information system that seizes opportunity.

---

1. What would be the most effective way to gain an advantage?

2. Would better (more accessible, accurate, timely) information help establish an advantage?

3. Can an information system be developed that will provide better information?

4. Will the development effort be economically justified?

◆ Can existing competitors afford to fund the development of similar systems?

◆ How long will it take the competitors to build their own, similar systems?

◆ Can we make our system a moving target to the competition by constantly enhancing it, so that it always retains its superiority?

5. What is the risk of *not* developing an SIS?

6. Are there alternative means of achieving the same goals and, if so, how do they compare with the advantages and disadvantages of a new SIS?

Figure 2.4 *Steps for considering a new SIS*

Step	Activity	Purpose
1	Present tutorial on competitive strategy and SIS.	Introduce the concepts of strategic targets and competitive strategy.
2	Apply SIS concepts to actual cases.	Raise consciousness about SIS possibilities, strategic thrusts, and targets.
3	Review company's competitive position.	Understand competitive position of the business and its strategies.
4	Brainstorm for SIS opportunities.	Generate SIS ideas in small groups.
5	Discuss SIS opportunities.	Eliminate duplication and condense SIS ideas.
6	Evaluate SIS opportunities.	Evaluate competitive significance of SIS ideas.
7	Detail SIS opportunities.	Detail each SIS blockbuster idea, its competitive advantage, and key implementation issues.

Source: Wiseman, C., *Strategic Information Systems,* Irwin, Homewood, IL 1988. p. 378

Figure 2.5 *Steps to take in an SIS idea generation meeting*

Figure 2.5 shows the steps involved in planning that SIS. As you can see, the activities involved in planning an SIS are devoted to education and brainstorming, not to discussion of technical details.

A word of caution regarding Question 4 in Figure 2.4, the issue of economic justification of an SIS. An increasing number of researchers and practitioners conclude that it is extremely difficult to estimate the financial benefits of information systems. This is especially true of SISs. These systems are not planned simply to reduce cost or increase output per employee; many of them create a whole new service or product. Some completely change the way an organization does business. Because there are so many fundamental business changes involved, the financial impact is difficult, if not impossible, to measure even after implementation, let alone before.

Re-engineering and Organizational Change

Sometimes, to implement an SIS and achieve a competitive advantage, organizations must rethink the entire way in which they operate. In the course of brainstorming about strategic plans, management should ask: "If we established this company again, from scratch, what processes would be implemented, and how?" The answer to this question often leads to the decision to eliminate one set of operations and build others from the ground up. Management consultants like to call changes such as these **re-engineering**. Re-engineering often involves the adoption of new machinery and the elimination of layers of managers. Frequently, information technology plays an important role in this process.

Re-engineering is not done to gain small incremental cost savings; it is done to achieve leaps of 100% and even 1000% in efficiency. With that degree of improvement, a company often gains a competitive advantage. Interestingly, a company that undergoes re-engineering along with implementation of a new SIS cannot always tell if an SIS was successful. The re-engineering process makes it impossible to determine how much each change contributed to the improved position of the organization.

The implementation of an SIS requires an organizational change when it is determined that business must be conducted differently in order to gain an advantage from the SIS. For example, when GM decided to manufacture a new car that would compete with Japanese cars, it chose a manner of production totally different from that of its other cars. As a result, Saturn was established as an independent company with a completely separate operation.

A part of this startup was the recognition by Saturn of the importance of the dealerships in gaining a competitive advantage. Through satellite communications, the new company gave dealers access to factory information so clients could find out if, and exactly when, different cars with different features would be available.

Another feature of Saturn's SIS improved customer service. Saturn embeds an electronic computer chip in the chassis of each car that has a record of the car's technical details and the owner's name. When the car is serviced after the sale, the new service information is added to the chip. Many Saturn owners were surprised to be greeted by name as they rolled down the window at their first service visit.

While the quality of the car itself has been important to Saturn's success, the new SIS also played an important contributing role.

COMPETITIVE ADVANTAGE AS MOVING TARGET

As you may have guessed, competitive advantage is not a long-lasting asset. In time, competitors imitate the leader, and the advantage diminishes. The quest for innovative strategies is dynamic. Corporations must continuously contemplate new ways of utilizing information technology to their advantage. In a way, companies jockeying for the latest competitive advantage is a lot like an arms race. Side A develops an advanced weapon, then side B develops a similar weapon that terminates the advantage of side A, and so on.

In an environment where information technology is available to all, SISs originally developed to create a strategic advantage quickly become an expected part of standard business practice. This is especially true in the banking industry, where surveys indicate that IS costs have increased without yielding long-range strategic advantages. Services such as ATMs and banking by phone once provided a powerful strategic advantage to the few banks that provided them, but they are now available from almost any bank.

A system can only help a company sustain a competitive advantage if the company continuously modifies and enhances the system, making it a moving target to competitors. American Airlines' SABRE—the online reservation system available to travel agents—is a classic example of this. The innovative IS was designed to expedite airline reservations and sell travel agencies a new service. But over the years, the company spun off an office automation package for travel agencies called Agency Data Systems. The reservation system now encompasses hotel reservations, car rentals, train schedules, theater tickets, and limousine rentals. It also provides a feature that allows travelers to use Sabre from their own computers. The system has been so successful that in some years American earned more from it than from its airline operations.

Scientific publishers used to make their money on primary publishing, that is, the publication of original documents such as research papers and review articles. At the same time, there were secondary publishers who sold comprehensive bibliographies of various publications in a particular discipline. Recently, publishers discovered that with the ease of access to photocopying technology, secondary publishers were starting to distribute photocopied versions of primary publishers' materials. With new technology, a business shift took place. Quickly, the value of the secondary, bibliographic information rose. Researchers became more interested in obtaining comprehensive bibliographic information and less interested in obtaining the primary publications. Once they found what they wanted in the bibliography, the researchers could purchase individual papers from the secondary publisher. Where did the primary market go? The primary publishers started selling their lists and abstracts to the secondary publishers, and collecting licensing income from the resale of the papers. Those primary publishers who foresaw this change started formatting their bibliographic and abstract information digitally in a database format that made it valuable to the secondary publisher. A new technology provided a new source of revenue.

Most strategic information systems are not the fruit of any calculated plan or forethought. Usually, they evolve because managers recognize that an existing system can be used to create a strategic competitive advantage. Strategic information systems have evolved from systems designed for automation, or from systems designed to provide a new service or enhance an existing service. SISs have also evolved from the profitable use of excess information being collected by a company's existing IS, or from the use of customer data to expand an existing business into complementary businesses.

While many SISs are based on existing technology, sometimes it is an advance in technology that creates an opportunity for an SIS. Technological advances in themselves do not guarantee strategic advantage, but the smart use of technology can make the difference between leading the industry and lagging behind. It is often the new idea that gives the organization the competitive advantage.

FROM AUTOMATION TO SISs Many SISs were originally developed to automate a manual process. Such is the case of ASAP, the information system that now allows Baxter International Inc.'s customers to place orders electronically and receive products more quickly than they ever have before.

In 1978, American Hospital Supply Corporation (AHS), now part of Baxter and one of America's largest providers of medical supplies, decided that shortening the lead time between receiving and shipping an order would give them a competitive advantage. That year, the company installed ASAP, a new information system, to help the company achieve its goal. The system integrates shipping, billing, invoicing, and inventory data and information, allowing the company to improve its service.

In an innovative step to facilitate communication with customers, AHS offered to pay for and install terminals and software in their customer hospitals' offices, so that orders could be entered by hospital personnel and transmitted electronically. No more paperwork for the hospital, and immediate useful data for AHS. Pretty soon, the hospitals realized that they were not only receiving their orders more quickly, but also spending much less time placing the orders. The hospitals came to prefer working only with AHS for all the items that AHS could sell them. AHS enjoyed a 17% compound annual growth rate in sales. With accurate up-to-date data regarding orders available to them at any time, AHS was able to reduce inventory and lower sales costs, allowing the company to enjoy a profit four times the industry's average.

In time, other sellers of hospital supplies adopted similar systems, but the hospitals that were hooked into ASAP had every reason to stay with AHS. They already had the hardware and software installed, and their personnel were trained to use the system. To switch to another purchase system would have been too costly.

What started as an automation system turned into an SIS. AHS gained a competitive advantage by providing enhanced services and incidentally creating high switching costs for their customers.

SISs FROM A NEW SERVICE Another famous example of an SIS is Merrill Lynch's Cash Management Account® or CMA account, which for the first time allowed clients to withdraw cash from their investments directly, rather than having to execute sales and wait for checks to clear before having access to their money. Merrill Lynch made this possible by establishing an alliance with a bank and providing a combined service of investment and banking that was much more efficient for the customer. In the late 1970s, the concept of a central asset account (also called an asset management account) was revolutionary and could only be provided by means of a computer-based information system that could promptly keep track of every investment and withdrawal of millions of client dollars promptly, efficiently, and effectively.

Before Merrill Lynch's CMA account, a customer had to have two separate accounts to access the cash value of his or her stocks or mutual funds: one account with a stockbroker (to invest money in stock and other securities) and another with a bank (to maintain a checking account). The customer could access the cash value of the stock only by first selling some of the stocks through the stockbrokerage account, then depositing the sales proceeds into a checking account, and finally waiting for the deposit to clear to write a check against the checking account. The process was time-consuming and inefficient.

With Merrill Lynch's new service, every dollar that a customer deposits is used to buy shares in a money market fund. All the customer has to do to liquidate some of his or her account is write a check. The shares of the mutual fund are automatically redeemed. The customer does not have to wait to receive the money from the broker and then deposit the money into a checking account.

At the time, this service was so revolutionary that Merrill Lynch registered it as a patent. Many corporations and individuals and small businesses subscribed to the service, and by the time other organizations followed suit, Merrill Lynch had captured the lion's share of the market.

Used by permission from Merrill Lynch

CMA gave Merrill Lynch a strategic advantage that the company still enjoys, thanks to great market share in the money market industry.

SISs From New Technology Often, the technology involved in an SIS has been around for some time, just waiting to be used for strategic purposes. Sometimes, however, it's a *new* technology that sparks a major change in the way a firm does business. For instance, progress in telecommunications technology now allows organizations to connect their branches across continents into one large network of offices. And sophisticated ISs provide American Express Travel-Related Services (TRS) with tools essential to its business. But one of the greatest examples of new technology that created a competitive advantage is the use of scanning technology by credit card companies to eliminate an entire industry of paper-handling.

American Express charge cards increased some 80% in number during the period 1985–1990. With that increase came the challenge of dealing with massive numbers of charge slips from retail businesses and a significant increase in the cost of doing business. This ultimately motivated the company to harness new scanning technology as an SIS.

In the past, the paper receipts from retailers were microfilmed for permanent storage and scanned for account and invoice amount by special devices called optical character readers. They were then imprinted with a code that contained this information, and stored. A mainframe computer generated combined bills to customers. The receipts and bills were joined and mailed. The process was extremely labor-intensive.

In 1984, TRS adopted image processing devices that produce clear laser images of the receipts, reduced in size. With this equipment, TRS uses cameras to produce a digital image of the slips, and the paper is then *thrown away*. The digital images are scanned for accounts by a character reader. The charged amounts are keyed into a computer, by a human being, from the images displayed on a computer monitor. The images are reduced and printed, and then mailed to the cardholder, along with the bill. No paper is stored, just the electronic images, and there is no need to rejoin the bill with the paper slips originally collected from the retailer.

The use of this new technology saves TRS millions of dollars in the form of reduced labor costs. Such savings may allow the company to reduce customer fees and augment its market share. In addition, image processing is a significantly more accurate (99%) means of storing data than the old, more manual, method (82% accurate).

SISs From Excess Information Sometimes, the potential for a strategic move is in a firm's existing information system. In fact, many companies collect huge amounts of data that are not necessary for their own line of business, but which may be put to use in a new service or complementary product. For instance, Sears Roebuck and Company, the second largest retailer in the U.S., often taps its databases to target sectors of its clientele for businesses other than retail sales. With a data bank of more than 40 million customer records, the company provides valuable information to its subsidiaries in the insurance and real estate industries, Allstate and Coldwell-Banker, respectively.

Looking for strategic use of its information systems, a company should ask these three questions:

1. What information that we generate, or could generate, from our databases could be useful to another company? What would that company be willing to pay?

2. What information, or data-processing capacity, that we have can be used to start a new business?

3. Can we produce information that may help create new products (or services) that are related to our products (or services), or to other companies' products (or services)?

SISs FROM VERTICAL INFORMATION When you shop for a new car, dealers will offer you two services. First, they will offer to take a trade-in on your old car. Second, they will offer to help you finance the purchase of the new car. Why do they offer these services? Because they understand that these services solve the two main problems you are likely to have when buying a new car. The dealers stretch their business "backward" and "forward," known as **vertical extension**, to enhance their chances of getting your business.

Consider real estate agencies. Real estate agents expand their services vertically to offer financing information you need *before* your purchase, and relocation information that you need *after* your purchase. The agency can ask you for information that will help moving companies make you an offer as soon as you purchase your new home. Realtors who extend their services vertically will be more appealing to some clients.

ACUMAX: AN SIS SUCCESS

McKesson Drug Co., a wholesale distributor of pharmaceuticals, has implemented what is now considered one of the most successful strategic information systems. The company applied technology to automate its operations, and in the process it gained a competitive advantage by (1) enhancing existing services, (2) providing new services, (3) cutting costs, and (4) creating high switching costs for clients.

Used by permission from McKesson Corporation

AcuMax and its successor, AcuMax Plus, contributed to significant cost cutting and increased market share at McKesson Drugs Inc.

Understand the Notion of Strategic Information Systems?

Although it is mainly the responsibility of senior management to devise strategic moves, let us remember Napoleon's words: "Every French soldier carries a marshal's baton in his knapsack." To paraphrase: Every junior manager is a potential senior manager. Thus, it is incumbent on every manager to try to think strategically for his or her organization. In fact, some of the most brilliant strategic ideas have come from low-level managers. In today's highly competitive market, strategy may determine the rise or fall of organizations.

An increasing number of strategic moves are either possible only with the aid of ISs, or have ISs in the center of their strategy—that is, the technology provides the product, service, or method that gains the organization a strategic advantage. Thus, managers must understand how technology can be used in strategic moves. Understanding how strategic information systems are conceived and implemented may help you suggest good ideas for such systems in your organization, and facilitate your own promotion in the organizational ladder.

IMPROVING EXISTING SERVICES

In 1974, the wholesale drug industry had 180 distributors and over 50,000 customer stores. Many drugstores and drugstore chains purchased their supplies from several different distributors. McKesson and other drug suppliers were threatened because the large chains tended to order directly from manufacturers. McKesson's management decided to reduce the threat by devising a new information system that would automate order entry and order processing, eliminate duplicate activities, and improve overall performance.

Before the new system was implemented, receiving, processing, and filling customer orders at McKesson's 100 regional warehouses was labor-intensive, expensive, and slow. Erroneous delivery of ordered items was common. The new SIS, designed to automate the collection and fulfillment of orders using scanners to read and fulfill orders, changed all that. After using a hand-held scanner in the 1970s and 1980s, the company resolved to implement a new wearable computer and scanner called AcuMax throughout its shipping centers. The company has invested between $20 and $30 million in improvements to the system. It has paid off.

BUSINESS PROCESS REDESIGN

At any complex distribution center, the chore of tracking millions of individual items is extremely complicated and error-prone. The weakest point in the distribution function is mispicks that occur when orders get scrambled or miscounted. Managers at the company estimate that each mispick costs about $80 in lost time and shipping costs, seven times more than filling a customer's order correctly the first time. After two months of pilot-testing, McKesson estimated that AcuMax cut mispicks by more than 50%.

Typically, a druggist electronically places an order with McKesson by sending it via modem (a data communications device) to the company's computer center in Rancho Cordova, California. The order is then relayed to the McKesson distribution center nearest the store. Workers then complete the order by filling plastic tote boxes with the ordered products, which are shipped overnight to the customer.

The Butlers of the Digital Age

Electronic shopping is not new; after all, using your phone to place an order through an 800 number is a form of electronic shopping. And the World Wide Web has expanded electronic shopping even further. Companies that adopted these technologies when they were new gained a strategic advantage, until their competitors jumped on the bandwagon.

But in spite of the convenience of ordering anytime with 800 numbers and the Web, the drudgery of shopping still remains: You still need to spend time leafing through direct mail catalogs or visiting Web sites to find the best quality for the lowest price. The next big change in shopping will be to have an electronic agent do not only the purchasing, but the actual shopping as well.

INTELLIGENT AGENTS

Think of a proper English butler. Every morning long before his boss gets out of bed, the butler scurries through the house, anticipating his boss's every need. That's the basic concept behind "intelligent agents," software that travels through computer networks to fulfill users' requests. Agents can make travel reservations, collect interesting stories from news services, or sort through electronic mail—while their masters are miles from the keyboard.

Agents were not much more than a futurist's dream until recently. In 1993, General Magic, Inc. developed Telescript, software that includes features that may someday become the butlers of the digital age. Like the butler, Telescript relies on a small army of assistants to keep things running smoothly. Instead of housekeepers, footmen, and scullery maids, Telescript's success depends on a variety of programs running at the same time, carrying out different tasks. And, needless to say, these digital gofers can only do their jobs if there is a virtual world of electronic shopping, communication, and information services out there to navigate.

THE DIGITAL SHOPPER

Software developers who are working with General Magic believe that the day is near when everyone will have his or her own computerized butler. Matt Kursh, president of eShop Inc., says his company is designing the electronic stores that consumers—or their agents—will enter via personal computers or hand-held computing devices. These stores will exist only in cyberspace. But what Kursh's stores lack in real estate, they'll make up for in services.

(continued)

AcuMax relies on constant two-way radio communication between the human pickers on the warehouse floor and a database in the warehouse's minicomputer. The picker wears a scanner glove that is activated by pointing an index finger at the customer's bar-coded shipping label, generated by the system from the store's order. The minicomputer transmits the customer's shopping list to a small display screen mounted on the picker's forearm, which includes the exact location of the item to be picked. The picker goes to the case lot and confirms the order by using

In a recent demonstration, Kursh easily navigated through an electronic sporting-goods store with the aid of an incredibly courteous on-screen salesman who knew all of the customer's previous purchases and could explain the best features of everything from tennis racquets to golf clubs.

In Kursh's demonstration, the consumer guided the purchase personally. But once a network of electronic stores and information services is fully in place, Telescript's agents will theoretically be able to do the shopping on their own, following general instructions from the user. Say you want a new stereo system. You will list your specifications and send the agent out through the system to find the best price. The next time you turn on your computer, the agent will have drawn up a list of possibilities. If one seems right, you can instruct the agent to buy it and have the package delivered to your door.

BEYOND SHOPPING

The same agent can also monitor weather reports at favorite resorts or scan electronic forums run by online services to see if there's any cyberchat you might find interesting. An agent could remind you of your mother's birthday, suggest possible gifts it has found, and then arrange delivery. Electronic agents can arrange a date, including securing flowers and tickets; shop for the best price from mail-order firms; monitor stock prices; set up a meeting with a group of people at various companies; or find out what song is playing on the radio and let you order the CD instantly for delivery the next day. And the list goes on.

AGENTS AS RISKS

This high-tech version of a personal assistant worries some industry observers. They say that a badly designed agent might turn into a type of computer virus destroying every system it touches. Or these agents could be used to keep tabs on a consumer's personal life by tracking the agent's activities. They could open up a consumer to a greater onslaught of catalogs and other junk mail.

General Magic counters that the agents can be programmed to self-destruct when they have finished their task, reducing the risk of their being used for the wrong purposes. Security codes are also programmed in, to guard privacy. But the key question is, will the average American willingly give up crowded malls, surly clerks, and long lines at the check out counter?

Source: Kantrowitz, B., "The butlers of the digital age will be just a keystroke away," *Newsweek*, January 17, 1994, p. 58, and "Can They Pull Another Mac Out of Their Hats?", *Datamation*, April 15, 1994, p. 24

THINK CRITICALLY

Suppose electronic agents can be programmed to avoid the risks discussed above. What negative impact might the technology nonetheless have on society?

laser beams from the AcuMax to read data on bar codes up to 20 feet above the warehouse floor. The picker then selects the appropriate number of items for the tote, the next shelf location shows up on his forearm, and the cycle begins again.

Within a year of implementation, mispicks and shortages were reduced by 60%. In 1997, McKesson estimated an accuracy level of 99%. The new system tracks the exact location and status of over 20,000 different items stored in each warehouse. As a result, physical inventory counts can be less frequent, and will eventually be reduced to zero.

PROVIDING NEW SERVICES

About 93% of McKesson's over-the-counter items and 99% of prescribed drugs are delivered the next day. This service has created an almost just-in-time supply cycle. Customers no longer need to carry large quantities of drugs to ensure availability. They only need to carry what they display on the shelves. AcuMax also provides customers with valuable information, such as the number of units, dollars spent, and profit margin at different time intervals for different purchases. With the automation, McKesson now also offers additional services, including processing credit card purchases and third-party claims, and installing pharmacy terminal systems.

The system has benefited McKesson tremendously. The number of warehouses has been cut from 100 to 45. Telephone order clerks were reduced from 700 to 15. The national purchasing staff has been trimmed from 140 to 12. And the sales force has been reduced by 50% while the sales volume has increased sixfold. A senior vice president observed that getting customers connected to the company by computers was the key to all the company's advances.

The company succeeded in forming an alliance with drug stores, thereby also helping the drug stores save time. One druggist estimated that his store saved eight hours a week that were once spent on ordering. McKesson reported improvement in customer satisfaction. This helped the company create customer loyalty and increase the number of its clients.[1]

MORTGAGEPOWER PLUS: AN SIS FAILURE

For an SIS to succeed, it must of course be designed to achieve its specific organizational goal. But it must also follow a company's basic business principles, and it must integrate smoothly into day-to-day business operations. The company must ask: Are we willing to take on the risk inherent in this venture, and can the system deliver as promised? Citicorp's MortgagePower Plus is an example of an SIS that was consistent with the company's organizational goals and designed to create a competitive advantage by enhancing one of the company's services—but whose implementation failed.

IDENTIFYING THE COMPETITIVE ADVANTAGE

Suppose you are about to purchase a house. Would you rather borrow from a bank that takes a week to let you know if you have a mortgage, or from an institution that lets you know in 15 minutes? Imagine the huge business that the latter service could attract.

Citicorp is one of the most advanced users and developers of information technology (IT). It employs 4,000 programmers and spends an estimated $1.5 billion a year on ISs. It even designed its own ATMs. Apparently, Citicorp has all the ingredients necessary for successful implementation of new ideas using IT.

In 1987, Robert Horner, chairman of Citicorp's mortgage unit—the nation's biggest mortgage lender, originating nearly $15 billion in loans per year—conceived a great idea that required an SIS for implementation. The idea: a 15-minute mortgage approval process, equivalent to a ten-minute oil change or one-hour

[1]McKesson Publications Manager, March 1997; Daly, J., "McKesson Drug Curing Inaccuracy of Warehouse Labor with Wearable PCs," *Computerworld*, v19 n19, May 11, 1992, pp. 59, 61; LaPlante, A., "McKesson Cuts Costs with Wireless Scanner," *Infoworld* v14 n21, May 25, 1992, p. 50. Clemons, E. K., "A Strategic Information System: McKesson Drug Company's Economost," *Planning Review* v16 n5, Sept/Oct 1988, pp. 14–19.

Strategy and the Law

When is a company's strategic advantage a violation of free trade? When might the high switching costs or the installation of a system be so expensive that no other company can afford to compete, thereby not only deterring new entrants to the industry, but also preventing fair trade? These are questions that have arisen around the competitive use of information systems.

Fair trade laws were established in 1890 to protect the public against monopolies and ensure that the principles of laissez-faire capitalism would thrive in the U.S.: namely, that fair competition would create the greatest good. These laws were written long before information systems became a competitive tool, but they are relevant nonetheless.

Is an SIS a Barrier to Fair Trade? A case that raised some SISs issues with respect to fair trade evolved when American Airlines and United Airlines each created a new service in which they offered to give travel agencies computer terminals to book flights online, on any airline. AA and UA charged other airlines to be listed on their new services. However, there was a twist in the way the systems presented the options to travel agents that led to claims that the systems obstructed free trade.

Before the new systems, travel agents had to call each airline individually to get prices and schedules, and then advise their clients based on the information gathered. The process was slow and tedious, and the information was often unavailable. The new systems changed all that. In both systems, the terminals were connected to large databases containing schedule, seating, and reservation information for all airlines, and they were promoted as a tool that could save a lot of time for the agent—a one-stop shop for all flight information and for making reservations.

The key to the controversy that arose was that AA and UA designed their systems so that their own offerings appeared at the top of every list. So, if a travel agent had a terminal installed by American, whenever a customer asked for information on flights to a certain destination, American's flights appeared at the top of the list. Needless to say, this gave the airline a significant advantage. United's reservation system followed the same principle. The two systems serve approximately 80% of the travel agencies in the U.S.

The Complaint. Smaller companies complained that the practice was unfair and bordered on violation of antitrust laws. They alleged that the two airlines used means unavailable to others in the industry to gain a competitive advantage. One company, Braniff, claimed that this caused its bankruptcy in the early 1980s. United and American were sued. The initial ruling in favor of the other airlines was successfully overturned; the higher court concluded that both AA and UA were entitled to place their names first. The reason was that the opportunity to build a similar or better system was available to others who operate in the industry; therefore, using such a system was neither legally nor ethically a violation of fair trade practices.

American's reservations system, called Sabre, books 40% of U.S. airline tickets. Competitors complained that the airline charges them exorbitant prices for using the system and diverts some of their potential traffic to American. While denying the charges, American's president agreed, in June 1992, to divest Sabre if his rivals sold their shares in three smaller reservation systems.

Sometimes, there is a fine line between fair and unfair use of information in trade. The mere use of a novel information system is not considered unethical as long as a similar system is available to others.

photo processing. He wanted to connect real estate agents and brokers to a Citicorp electronic system through which an applicant could receive a quick approval or denial of a mortgage loan.

THE SIS PLAN

MortgagePower Plus was designed to work as follows. A real estate agent using Citicorp software types up an application at a personal computer and sends it over telephone lines to a mainframe computer in St. Louis. The system automatically accesses certain credit and other information, judges whether the applicant earns enough to afford the loan, and sends back a decision.

The launch of MortgagePower Plus was accompanied with much fanfare, but the program soon turned into a disaster, both strategically and operationally. Strategically, Citicorp misjudged the risk involved in lowering the loan standards in order to increase the number of their loans; operationally, the technological failure had to do with faulty modems and software modules.

Citicorp tried a procedure that is considered a "no-no" in mortgage lending. The bank removed the requirement that borrowers obtain private mortgage insurance, but did not compensate by increasing its reserve for resulting losses. Also, to facilitate the application process, the bank made low-document and no-document loans, in which it checked borrowers' credit reports and abridged employment histories, but not their assets or income. At worst, the executives believed, the bank could sell a foreclosed house at a profit and recoup the loan.

HOW THE SIS FAILED

In reality, the Citicorp system was often down, or the credit bureau's system was down, or there were connection problems. Static on the line caused computers in the real estate offices to disconnect from Citicorp's mainframe. This problem could have been fixed with available error detection and correction software, but it wasn't. The software's logic was wrong, too. Many credit-worthy applicants were denied loans. In addition, the bank experienced fraud from some brokers who lied to the system. The shortcuts the bank took were overly risky.

Mortgage companies often "sell" mortgages, that is they transfer loan contracts to other lenders for a fee. These lenders are referred to as the secondary market. Citicorp hoped to make huge profits by using its new system to originate loans that it would later sell. But the secondary market smelled trouble. It refused to buy mortgages from Citicorp and other banks that took such risks, unless the bank guaranteed to take them back when borrowers defaulted. The secondary market lenders' fears were probably realistic. In the first year that Citicorp used MortgagePower Plus, its overall mortgage portfolio showed a delinquency rate of 7%, five times the industry average.

LOSING GROUND

MortgagePower Plus rejected 70% of all applicants, well above the bank's normal 35% rate. The 15-minute objective was never met. Brokers waited hours for an electronic reply, and often did not get one at all. After several trials, they were embarrassed to use the system in front of clients.

In response to all these shortcomings, Citicorp's management reduced the size of the mortgage unit, and removed its responsibility for originating loans for later sale. The bank became a second-tier mortgage lender. In a way, the technological failure was fortunate; had the system succeeded, the bank would have made more loans, and the losses might have been higher.

Teleconferencing For Profit

At Flagstar Bank in Bloomfield Hills, Michigan, IT executives found a way to increase market share and profit. The company is the nation's fourth largest wholesale lender, boasting a loan portfolio of over $8 billion. It claims it got so big thanks to using Integrated Services Data Network (ISDN) and Intel's ProShare desktop video conferencing software. Flagstar does business with 4,500 brokers and other banks from which it buys mortgages. Of them, more than 500 are linked to the firm's ProShare network, and its goal is to connect all of the brokers and banks. These independent loan originators are the key to Flagstar's success. To gain an advantage over competitors, management decided to use technology to speed up mortgage approval.

"We can speed up the process with video-conferencing," says Michael Hillman, Flagstar's vice president of business development. "It brings the warm fuzzy of the face-to-face meeting [between Flagstar, the originators, and the mortgage customer].... The ability to share facial gestures, hand gestures, and even

the rolling of eyes is important." All this direct communication adds up to cutting down a loan approval cycle from several weeks or more to less than a week, he says.

But the application is designed to do more than let a loan officer see an applicant's nervous twitch. "We're able to electronically let [the originators and customers] see a copy of the loan documents to help us make our decision faster," Hillman says. Some loan originators on the ProShare network are equipped with PCs that include fax scanners in the keyboard so that applicants can not only go over the documents but mark them up and send them back to Flagstar. Video-conferencing is arranged between representatives at Flagstar's central video-conferencing center and mortgage originators and applicants at a remote site, typically a mortgage broker's office or a bank branch. The originator uses a ProShare PC, linked via ISDN lines to the local telephone company. The transmission goes through to Ameritech's (the regional telephone carrier) central office and then is switched out through a dedicated ISDN link to the video-conferencing center.

Source: McCarthy, V., "Bringing video on line," Datamation, February 1997, pp. 100–103.

Questions

1. How did Flagstar differentiate its service from the service of other firms in the industry?

2. What might motivate a mortgage broker to subscribe to the video-conferencing system?

3. As a mortgage applicant, would you be comfortable in a video-conference session as described in this case? Why, or why not?

Targeting The Customer

Specialty-produce wholesaler Frieda's Inc. claims it has changed the way America eats. That boast seems to have some truth to it: Los Angeles-based Frieda's began importing kiwis back in the 1960s when people still called the kiwi a Chinese gooseberry. Frieda's, whose distinctive purple heart logo has become a familiar sight in the produce section of supermarkets in all 50 states, starts with the basics of database marketing, which states that the better you know your customers, the easier it is to sell to them, and takes it one step further. Frieda's strives not only to get to know its customers, which are supermarkets, but also its customers' customers, the people who actually buy and eat the fruit. In many cases, Frieda's knows those supermarket shoppers better than the supermarkets do. All thanks to information systems.

"I don't think there are many other companies in our business that even know the names of their customers," says Karen Caplan, Frieda's 38-year-old president and daughter of company founder Frieda Caplan. "We do very little advertising. The database is our biggest marketing tool." Frieda's doesn't exactly measure its success one pomegranate buyer at a time. But by tracking buyers' purchasing habits and satisfaction level, the company has opened new distribution channels in the often hidebound retail grocery business.

Frieda's strategic weapon is the database that holds a total of some 100,000 customer names and addresses. Frieda's collects this information the old-fashioned way: by mail. Every piece of produce supplied to a supermarket by Frieda's bears a label that carries some information about the item to assist the average shopper who may be unfamiliar with the best way to prepare, say, daikon radish sprouts. The label also encourages consumers to write the company with their opinions about the produce they've just purchased, and, to make it easy, provides Frieda's address. Every year, some 18,000 of these consumers take the company up on the offer.

Back at Frieda's headquarters, every correspondent's name, address, and other relevant information is logged into a database running on the company's LAN. To ensure the accuracy of address listings, Frieda's checks the database once a year against post office change-of-address records. By knowing its customers, Frieda's has a leg up in competing for their attention and business, say marketing gurus. Consumers are starved for time and bombarded with telemarketing and advertising in every nook and cranny of the media. "Knowing who your best customers are is the key to any successful marketing program," says Robert McKim, a partner of M/S Database Marketing, a database-marketing consulting and implementation firm in Los Angeles.

The company customer database has also helped Frieda's reach new ethnic markets. Recently, a large Texas grocery chain balked at stocking Frieda's products, saying that its specialty items were too expensive. Undaunted, Frieda's information soldiers attacked. They combed the database, researched trade publications, and enlisted the help of a firm specializing in Hispanic marketing to analyze the supermarket chain's significantly Latin-American customer base.

Among other things, Frieda's convinced the chain that it could supply foods Guatemalan consumers were used to eating in their native country but couldn't find in the U.S. "We did a complete profile of their market to prove that our product line would be perfect for them," explains Caplan. "The idea was to profile their typical shopper and knock their socks off with information about their own customers."

Effective database marketing is, by definition, proactive database marketing. As a niche player in a business dominated by much larger companies and high volumes, Frieda's has always known it must work hard to be heard. By billing itself as the expert on the specialty-produce consumer, the firm convinces its retailers that stocking Frieda's produce is a no-lose proposition. In essence, Frieda's succeeds by flaunting its own database marketing excellence.

Source: Wilder, C., "Who'd eat a blue squash?", InformationWeek, *January 10, 1994, p. 31.*

Questions

1. Frieda's relies on little advertisement. What is its main marketing tool?

2. While the supermarkets are Frieda's customers, they are not the subject for data collection and analysis. Who is? Explain.

3. How does Frieda's ensure the accuracy of its data?

4. Could the company generate revenue from selling something other than produce? Explain.

Pioneering Supply Chain Information Systems

The term "supply chain" refers to the sequence of processes from ordering raw materials, through production of goods, to the supplying of goods to customers. Reducing the cost of overstocked inventory and maximizing the load on distribution trucks are the main benefits a manufacturer can gain from an IS that supports supply chain operations. Procter & Gamble Worldwide, Inc. (P&G), the giant supplier of consumer goods, realized the potential of such systems much earlier than other players in the industry.

Profit margins of grocery retailers average 2% of sales. The profit margin of the producer of these items is not much greater. Therefore, every penny the producer can "shave" from the price plays a critical role in the decision of supermarket chains and regional distributors to buy from this or another producer. The low profit margin also means that the turnover of inventory must be great to produce sustaining profit, which in turn means that greater efficiency in inventory management and shipping is crucial.

P&G had to address three major issues. It needed to reduce its own inventory of finished goods; it wanted to reduce the retailers' overstocks, while preventing stockouts; and it wished to make a more efficient use of its trucks, that is, to reduce the number of less than truckload (LTL) shipments. Achieving any of these goals alone could improve the company's strategic position in this highly competitive market.

In 1988, executives from P&G and from a large distributor met to discuss opportunities to use a new approach. The distributor had severe space constraints in its warehouses. Its executives suggested that P&G ship merchandise on a just-in-time (JIT) basis, that is, the distributor would not have to use its warehouses, but would distribute the merchandise immediately to the retailers. Thus was born CRP: Continuous Replenishment Program. Implementation of the new IS took less than two months.

The principle was simple. The distributor connected its ISs to P&G via telecommunications lines so that demand data could be channeled directly to P&G's ISs. CRP took this data and processed it through models that calculated the quantities that the different divisions needed to produce so that delivery dates could be met. This gave managers ample information to plan optimal production, and saved both P&G and the distributor warehousing costs. With improved information, P&G could also plan better shipping schedules so that fewer trucks left the docks not fully loaded.

By 1991, almost all of P&G's large distributors and three large retail chains had adopted the CRP. All participants enjoyed reduction of inventory and stockout levels. By 1994, another 47 grocery chains were connected to the system. More than 26% of the company's sales were processed through the system. In 1993 alone, P&G's market share increased by 4%. Executives agreed that even if only 1% of this increase was thanks to the system, CRP played a major strategic role in increasing market share in this crowded and competitive industry.

In 1993, P&G sold the CRP system to IBM, which now offered the system for sale to anyone. Executives explained that the sale was not for the purpose of generating revenue, but for strategic purposes. The company decided to sell this strategic asset so it could attain an important strategic goal: connecting as many retailers and distributors to its system as possible, even at the cost of seeing other producers enjoy the benefits of it. Furthermore, P&G decided to hire IBM to operate and maintain the system rather than use its own, more costly, staff.

Source: Harvard Business School Case Study 9-195-126: *"Procter & Gamble: Improving Consumer Value through Process Redesign,"* March 31, 1995.

Questions

1. Enumerate all the benefits that a system like CRP can give a consumer goods supplier, and explain how each benefit is attained.

2. If you were P&G's president at the time, would you have sold the system to IBM? Why, or why not?

3. Companies that develop strategic systems sometimes sell them, or give them away free of charge, to other businesses, including competitors. What is the rationale for such a move? (Hint: consider the word "standards.")

SUMMARY

•••• Information systems are no longer regarded as tools for mere automation of previously manual processes. Corporations now value ISs as competitive weapons. Rather than waiting complacently until a problem occurs, businesses are actively looking for opportunities to improve their position with information systems. An IS that wins an organization a **strategic advantage** is called a **strategic information system (SIS)**. To assure optimal utilization of the technology for **competitive advantage,** top managers must engage in idea-generating activities and champion new, innovative usages of information systems.

There are several ways to achieve a competitive advantage. Significant cost reduction enables a business to sell more units of its products or services while maintaining or increasing its profit margin. **Raising barriers** to potential entrants to the industry allows the organization to maintain market share rather than share it with others. By establishing high **switching costs,** a business makes it unattractive for clients to buy from competitors. Developing totally new products and services creates an entire market for an organization. And if the organization cannot create new products or services, it can still enjoy competitive advantage by **differentiating its products** so that customers view them as better than those of an competition. Organizations also attain advantage by enhancing existing products or services. Many of the new services we enjoy are the fruit of **alliances** between companies: each contributes its own expertise to provide a "package" of services that entices customers with an overall value greater than that offered by the separate services individually. Another approach to gaining strategic advantage is by **locking in** clients or suppliers, that is, by creating conditions that make it unattractive to deal with competitors.

Many of these initiatives to gain a strategic advantage can be obtained by the use of an innovative SIS. While many SISs were not originally planned with strategy in mind, organizations do try to devise SISs and develop them. Among the questions they need to ask are "Would better information help establish an advantage?" and "Can an information system be developed that would provide this information?" We proposed several steps for evaluating the potential for an SIS and for running meetings to generate ideas about an SIS. Sometimes, such sessions suggest ways to totally change a business process, which may be the start of a **re-engineering** effort.

SISs can evolve from different initiatives. They may create an advantage through massive automation of a manual process, thus significantly cutting costs. They may provide a new service that was not feasible without IT. An advantage may be gained thanks to a new technology, such as imaging. Some organizations obtain a strategic advantage by selling excess information obtained through daily operations (such as customer information collected by retail chains) to companies that can use that information—direct mail operations, for example. And some organizations use ISs to augment their services vertically by offering related services; this strategy is used by realtors when they offer financing and relocation information in addition to information about houses for sale.

Some ideas for SISs, such as Econoscan, have been implemented successfully. Others, such as MortgagePower Plus, failed because of attempted shortcuts and poor technical implementation. Good ideas must be carefully executed if a company is to seize opportunities.

Strategic advantages from information systems are usually short-lived because competitors quickly emulate the systems for their own benefit. Therefore, the process of looking for new opportunities must be ongoing. The owners must develop new features to maintain the system on the cutting edge.

SISs give their owners, at least for a while, a tool that competitors do not have. This has raised ethical questions about fair trade practices. However, it is generally believed that since every business is free to implement any IS it wishes, organizations should not be held back in their competitive initiatives.

REVIEW, DISCUSS, AND EXPLORE

REVIEW AND DISCUSSION QUESTIONS

1. How did the role of information systems change in the late 1970s and early 1980s?

2. What should an information system achieve for an organization, in order to be considered a strategic information system?

3. Sometimes it is difficult to convince top management to commit funds for the development and implementation of an SIS. Why?

4. Can an off-the-shelf program be used as an SIS? Why, or why not?

5. The advantages an SIS affords a corporation are often short-lived. Why?

6. *Ethics and Society:* It may be argued that an SIS gives a company an unfair advantage, and that it may even cause the demise of smaller and weaker companies that cannot afford to build similar systems. What is your opinion?

7. Refer to the *A Look Into the Future* section and consider the following: Intelligent agents have been described as great future helpers to individuals. Suggest some ways in which they will be able to enhance business processes

CONCEPT ACTIVITY

Use a literature search program to find a news story on a strategic information system. Write a short report that will explain: (1) the industry in which the business competes, (2) the function(s) of the system, and (3) how the system gives the company a strategic advantage. For (3), identify the type of strategic move that the organization made, from the list provided in Figure 2.1. Suggest how the company may improve the system to maintain its advantage in the future, when competitors mimic the system.

HANDS-ON ACTIVITY

Use PowerPoint or another presentation software program to present the ideas you generated in the Concept Activity above. Use the best features of the program to make your presentation convincing and visually pleasing.

TEAM ACTIVITY

Your team has opened a musical compact disc store. Assume that you have the resources to adopt new information systems. Conduct a brainstorming session with your team members: What can you do to achieve a strategic advantage in this market? How can you use information technology to attain and sustain the advantage? Write a short report describing the competition and your ideas.

EXPLORE THE WEB

Several IS trade journals provide extensive Web sites, some of which contain online articles (for example, *Information Week* and *Datamation*). Search the Web for an article on strategic information systems in general or a particular case of a strategic information system. Summarize the story and mention in your report the name of the Web site at which you found the article.

PART 2

Information
Technology

Chapter **3**

Information Technology in
Business: Hardware

R_x For Hospital ISs

Hospitals are prime candidates for computerizing data collection and storage: The same patient medical records are used repeatedly by different doctors in the hospital, first during initial examination and throughout a patient's treatment. If all data related to a patient were collected and recorded in one system, a patient profile could be available whenever it was needed, by anyone involved in treatment.

Unfortunately, computerizing hospital procedures is a challenge for many reasons. Computer selection alone is a problem. Desktop computers take up a lot of space, but smaller laptop and hand-held computers don't have the capacity needed to store medical records and necessary medical programs.

When the Long Beach Memorial Medical Center in Long Beach, California, wanted to equip its staff with computers, they initially tested desktop, pen-based, and portable models. In all three cases, physicians and nurses alike felt these devices came up short. If space wasn't the problem, weight was, said Virginia Moulton, the hospital's director for clinical informatics: "The devices are impossible to carry with all the other equipment nurses have to

carry. The lighter units can't hold enough information, and pen-based technology wasn't usable at all."

The Center's Information Technology department looked for, and found, a non-traditional solution. Physicians and nurses at the 850-bed hospital are now using 16 flat-panel PCs outfitted with 10.4-inch touch-sensitive displays and virtual keyboards. A unique feature: The PCs can fit flush on the wall. "I actually got approval from engineering to put them in our emergency department, in the hallways, because they won't violate the fire codes," says Moulton. "That's the first time I've had a computing device approved for hallway use."

Eventually, the hospital plans to install 68 of these devices in the hospital's hallways and rooms, wherever doctors and nurses need them. The units, tied into the hospital's data communication networks, can also be moved around on rolling pedestals, like other portable clinical equipment. "The doctors love it," says Moulton. "It's the first time I've seen them enthusiastic about a business computing device. They can sign on quickly, access their information, and it automatically logs them off."

Source: Levin, R., "The PC Challenge," InformationWeek, September 23, 1996, pp. 48–58.

Computers have changed the face of our business and personal lives as few other modern devices have done. As they increase in capability and decrease in price, they pervade every corner of our lives. Many people use computers but have no interest in how they work. If you expect to make a positive contribution in business, however, you must understand the basics of computer technology so you can bring educated judgment to both the promise and limitations of computing in business.

When you finish this chapter you will:

◆ Know the major components of an electronic computer

◆ Know how the different components work

◆ Know what the major function of each component is

◆ Understand hardware terminology and the functions of peripheral equipment

◆ Know what the different types of computers are, along with their strengths and weaknesses

◆ Know what criteria to consider when purchasing computers and related devices

◆ Understand some of the controversy regarding the health hazards of computers

◆ Know how to evaluate hardware so that you can harness it to improve managerial processes

The 1995/1996 *Computer Industry Almanac* confirms that the U.S. has more computers than any other country: six times as many as Japan, seven times as many as Germany, and nearly twice as many as all of Europe.

THE CENTRAL TOOL OF MODERN INFORMATION SYSTEMS

In the center of any modern information system stands a computer. It is this machine that has revolutionized the way we gather and process data and produce information. There have been few machines that have changed human life as radically as the electronic computer. And there have been few machines that became so affordable to so many businesses and individuals in such a short time. Imagine this: If the auto industry had advanced as fast as the computer industry, you would be able to buy a family car for less than $5 now. Because computers are central to information systems, to be successful in business, you will need to understand them. The purpose of this chapter is to provide you with the knowledge necessary to make intelligent decisions about computer hardware for the purpose of doing your job.

WHAT IS A COMPUTER?

Regardless of size, age, function, or capability, all computers have the same basic components and operate according to the same principles (see Figure 3.1). A computer has to handle four basic operations; it has to accept data, store data and instructions, process data, and output data. Computers conduct these operations with the same basic equipment. Most of the remainder of this chapter will describe the various components of different types of computer systems in some detail. But, in general, every computer is composed of the following:

◆ **Input Devices: Input devices** receive signals from outside the computer and transfer them into the computer; the most common input device is the computer keyboard, but some input devices accept voice or other signals.

◆ **Central Processing Unit:** The most important part of any computer is the **central processing unit**, or **CPU**. The CPU accepts instructions and data, decodes and executes the instructions, and stores the results (the output) in memory for later display. In technical terms, a CPU is a microprocessor chip made of silicon and numerous tiny wires that form complex circuitry. The circuitry is built and programmed so that it can interpret electrical signals to run computers.

◆ **Memory:** Computers store information internally and externally.

  ◆ **Internal Memory:** How much data and information can be stored in **internal memory**—the computer's internal storage capacity—and the speed with which stored information can be retrieved, are two of the properties that determine the power of a computer. Internal memory stores programs that are currently running on a machine, intermediate results of an arithmetic operation, intermediate versions of documents being word-processed, and data that represent the pictures and sounds displayed on a computer screen.

  ◆ **External Memory: External memory** stores the same types of data and information as internal memory; however, the storage is usually for longer periods of time. Thus, many external storage media are portable and can be moved from one computer to another.

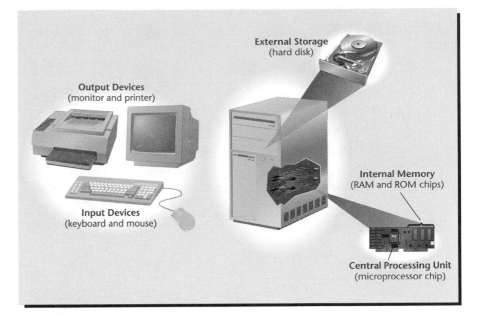

Figure 3.1 *All computers have the same basic system components.*

◆ **Output Devices: Output devices**—most commonly printers and computer monitors—deliver information from the computer to a person or another computer. There are also audio output devices and specialized output devices such as Braille writers.

BUSINESS EVOLVES WITH COMPUTING

There have been a lot of changes in computing technology over the years, and they have dictated to a great extent how business practices have changed. Today, computers come in a wide variety of sizes, from hand-held personal aides to supercomputers. However, for a long time, businesses depended upon mainframe computers, which are large computers generally used to retain all the data needed to run a business. Mainframes are housed in one central location, often at a corporate headquarters. Employees access data and programs from a mainframe computer by connecting from remote locations through "dumb" terminals: keyboards and video displays (with no local CPU) that use the mainframe's CPU and storage. While in some organizations this is still the situation, the great majority of businesses have moved to another arrangement: networked personal computers.

FROM MAINFRAME TO PC: NETWORKING BUSINESSES The first personal computer (PC) was introduced into businesses in 1981. While the impact on businesses was great, early PCs were treated as replacements for typewriters and calculators, while mainframe computers still dominated the information processing functions of business.

As the power of the PC increased and the price decreased, changes in business practices followed. On a PC, the CPU, the memory, the input, and the output could all be controlled locally by the user of the PC. With increasing power at their fingertips, managers started to devise their own local information systems to serve their own purposes. With information systems becoming

●● *POINT OF INTEREST*

Almost Checkless

Visionaries who predicted a checkless society were wrong. People still like to carry checks around in their wallets and mail them to pay their bills. Some do so because the canceled checks serve as legal documents for tax purposes. Banks, on the other hand, are not as crazy about checks. Soon, all of America's banks will use imaging to scan the 55 billion checks Americans write every year. Imaging systems scan up to 2,400 checks per minute. The systems are intelligent enough to convert the handwritten amount into computer-processable data. The clearing is done through computers connected in a network, rather than by shipping tons of checks on airplanes.

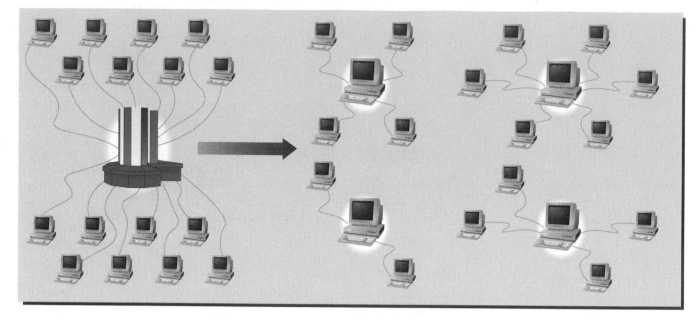

Figure 3.2 *Organizations have moved from using large mainframes to using networked PCs.*

localized, rather than centralized, companies found themselves struggling to balance the increasing ability of the PC to support local data pools and processing on one hand, and the need for centralized data, available and accessible company-wide, on the other hand.

Now, many companies have shifted away from mainframe computing, and have connected their PCs so that computing is more distributed, as shown in Figure 3.2. The most common computer arrangement is known as **client/server**.

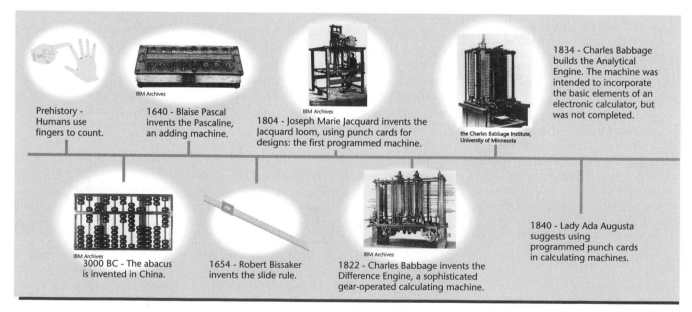

Prehistory - Humans use fingers to count.

1640 - Blaise Pascal invents the Pascaline, an adding machine.

IBM Archives

1804 - Joseph Marie Jacquard invents the Jacquard loom, using punch cards for designs: the first programmed machine.

IBM Archives

1834 - Charles Babbage builds the Analytical Engine. The machine was intended to incorporate the basic elements of an electronic calculator, but was not completed.

the Charles Babbage Institute, University of Minnesota

3000 BC - The abacus is invented in China.

IBM Archives

1654 - Robert Bissaker invents the slide rule.

1822 - Charles Babbage invents the Difference Engine, a sophisticated gear-operated calculating machine.

IBM Archives

1840 - Lady Ada Augusta suggests using programmed punch cards in calculating machines.

Figure 3.3 *A timeline of computing*

In this arrangement, individual departments create their own networks, dedicating one PC to be the "server," which maintains data, and other PCs to be connected as "clients," or users, of that server.

TRENDS IN COMPUTING The trends established since the birth of computing continue today: increasing power, decreasing cost, and shifting responsibilities from specialists to general users. Figure 3.3 shows the highlights of the computing journey, from prehistoric finger-counting to today's hand-held personal digital assistants (PDAs), which have the power of a mainframe computer of a few decades ago.

The road to electronic computing has included many mechanical counting machines. Charles Babbage's machine is probably the most famous. It laid the groundwork for the modern computer, but was not put to practical use. As machines evolved, electrical power was used to drive their mechanisms. This was the case with the electromechanical cash registers and calculators of the early twentieth century. The most significant leaps in the evolution of computing came in the 1930s and 1940s, when two teams started using electrical signals, not just electrical power, to create the first electronic computers.

Professor John Atanasoff and his assistant, Clifford Berry, built the first electronic computer in 1942 at Iowa State University. The purpose of the machine was to help physicists perform complex calculations. Several years later, two professors from the University of Pennsylvania, John Mauchly and J. Presper Eckert, built another electronic computer. This machine ushered in the age of true electronic computing.

The first organization to use computers was the only one that could afford the expensive machines: the U.S. government. But as IBM and other companies developed less expensive computers in the 1950s and 1960s, private businesses started to use them. Computers were no longer used for mere calculation, but

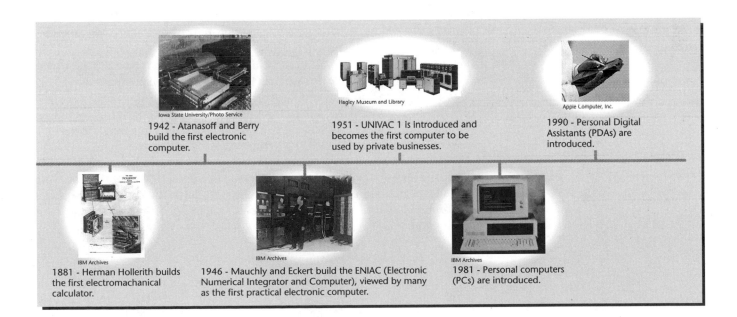

Iowa State University/Photo Service
1942 - Atanasoff and Berry build the first electronic computer.

Hagley Museum and Library
1951 - UNIVAC 1 is introduced and becomes the first computer to be used by private businesses.

Apple Computer, Inc.
1990 - Personal Digital Assistants (PDAs) are introduced.

IBM Archives
1881 - Herman Hollerith builds the first electromachanical calculator.

IBM Archives
1946 - Mauchly and Eckert build the ENIAC (Electronic Numerical Integrator and Computer), viewed by many as the first practical electronic computer.

IBM Archives
1981 - Personal computers (PCs) are introduced.

for many business purposes: record keeping, payroll, order entry, accounting, and finally to support sophisticated decision making.

COMPUTERS COMMUNICATING: BITS AND BYTES

To make the best use of the computer as an information system (IS) tool, you must understand how a computer processes data; therefore, you must first know how data and instructions are communicated to, in, and from the machine. Computers do not use human language either to run their operations or to communicate among their components; they use electricity (although some external storage devices also use magnetism and light).

Every communication made inside a computer is translated into a string of electrical signals that are in one of two states: low voltage or high voltage, which the computer translates into an "off" or "on" state respectively, in its circuitry. This applies to any signal, whether it is used to perform calculations, to display a scanned photograph on a screen, to run a video, or to run a computer game. The idea of translating communications into strings of signals that are in only one of two states may remind you of Morse code, which provides a good analogy for explaining computer communications. Morse code uses dots and dashes to transmit and receive words and numbers, whereas computers use on and off electrical signals.

Each on-or-off signal represents a *binary digit*, also called a **bit**. A binary digit is either a 0 (zero) or a 1. A standard-length string of bits is called a **byte**, as explained below, which is a unit of information used to represent characters, such as letters, numerals, and the like.

ENCODING SCHEMES

An **encoding scheme** is the agreed-upon representation of symbols (letters, numerals, and the like) by unique strings of bits. As a simple example, suppose our encoding scheme consisted of three bits per byte (which it does not). There would only be eight different binary codes available (000, 111, 001, 100, 010, 101, 110, 011) which would mean that we could represent only eight different characters or symbols. Obviously, we need more combinations, because each of the 26 lowercase letters, 26 capital letters, ten digits, the punctuation signs, and special signs such as @, #, $, %, and so on must be uniquely represented by a different byte. Larger bytes, seven or eight bits long, would allow us more combinations.

Indeed, the binary encoding schemes used by computers consist of eight bits per byte. Originally, **ASCII** (American Standard Code for Information Interchange, pronounced: AS-key) consisted of seven bits in a byte. However, a newer version of ASCII (ASCII-8) consists of eight bits per byte. **EBCDIC** (Extended Binary Coded Decimal Information Interchange, pronounced: EB-si-dik), developed by IBM, also has eight bits in a byte. However, the encoding schemes of the two methods are different. Virtually all of today's computers can process ASCII files. Figure 3.4 displays alphanumeric characters and their ASCII and EBCDIC representations.

UNDERSTANDING COMPUTER PROCESSING

In order to understand binary encoding schemes, it is essential to understand counting bases. Have you ever wondered why we use the decimal—or base 10—system for counting? The answer is, probably because we have ten fingers. Let us consider the numeral five thousand three hundred twenty-seven (5,327).

When someone communicates this to you, your mind does the following calculation, perhaps subconsciously:

$$5 \times 1000 = 5000 +$$
$$3 \times 100 = 300 +$$
$$2 \times 10 = 20 +$$
$$7 \times 1 = \underline{7}$$
$$5327$$

CHARACTER	ASCII-8	EBCDIC
0	10110000	11110000
1	10110001	11110001
2	10110010	11110010
3	10110011	11110011
4	10110100	11110100
5	10110101	11110101
6	10110110	11110110
7	10110111	11110111
8	10111000	11111000
9	10111001	11111001
A	10100001	11000001
B	10100010	11000010
C	10100011	11000011
D	10100100	11000100
E	10100101	11000101
F	10100110	11000110
G	10100111	11000111
H	10101000	11001000
I	10101001	11001001
J	10101010	11010001
K	10101011	11010010
L	10101100	11010011
M	10101101	11010100
N	10101110	11010101
O	10110110	10101111
P	10110000	11010111
Q	10110001	11011000
R	10110010	11011001
S	10110011	11100010
T	10110100	11100011
U	10110101	11100100
V	10110110	11100101
W	10110111	11100110
X	10111000	11100111
Y	10111001	11101000
Z	10111010	11101001
+	10101011	01001110
$	10100100	01011011
<	10111000	01001100

Figure 3.4 *Binary encoding schemes*

We could write this somewhat more elaborately as:

$$5 \times 10^3 = \quad 5000 +$$
$$3 \times 10^2 = \quad 300 +$$
$$2 \times 10^1 = \quad 20 +$$
$$7 \times 10^0 = \quad \underline{\quad 7}$$
$$5327$$

This second form illustrates that the decimal counting system is a base 10 system, that is, the base of the exponent by which each digit in the numeral is multiplied is 10. In base 10, the power of 10 by which we multiply the digits of a numeral depends on the position of that digit. If it is in the rightmost place, we multiply the digit by 10^0 (or 1); if it is in the second place, we multiply it by 10^1 (or 10); if it's in the third place, we multiply by 10^2 (or 100) and so forth. The base always remains 10, but the power increases by 1 as we move left.

The decimal system is simply an agreed-upon convention. We could just as well use another base as a convention. The binary, or base two, system used by computers is also a convention. Whereas in base 10, there are ten available digits that can be placed in each position (0–9), in the binary system (or base 2) only two digits are available for each position (0 and 1). Whereas in base 10, each digit is multiplied by the number 10 raised to a power, in base 2 each digit is multiplied by the number 2 raised to a power. Consider the value of the binary numeral 110101 in the same fashion as you considered 5327 above:

$$1 \times 2^5 = \quad 32+$$
$$1 \times 2^4 = \quad 16+$$
$$0 \times 2^3 = \quad 0+$$
$$1 \times 2^2 = \quad 4+$$
$$0 \times 2^1 = \quad 0+$$
$$1 \times 2^0 = \quad \underline{\quad 1}$$
$$53$$

Hence we could write that $110101_2 = 53_{10}$, or, in plain language, 110101 base 2 is equal to 53 base 10.

To perform addition, subtraction, multiplication, and division, computers use the same methods as human beings, except that they store all quantities and carry out all calculations in binary form.

A PEEK INSIDE THE COMPUTER

Two of the electronic computer's main functions are processing data into information and maintaining data and instructions in memory. In addition, computers are connected to other equipment, such as printers and keyboards, usually referred to as **peripheral equipment**. Remember, all communication within and among computer components and peripherals uses the binary mode of communication; therefore all components must have a mechanism for representing two modes, either "on" or "off." The following discussion introduces the most common parts of the computer and its peripheral equipment, and the way these devices fulfill their functions (see Figure 3.5).

THE CENTRAL PROCESSING UNIT

Remember that the CPU is the brain of the computer, where all processing takes place. The modern form of CPU, a silicon chip with multiple circuits,

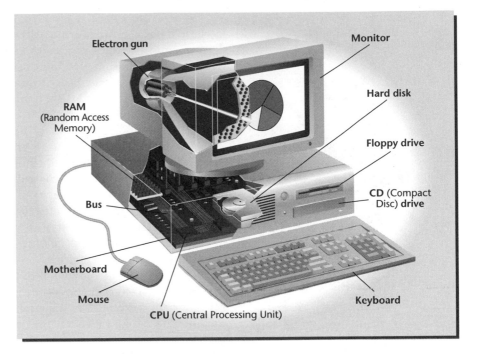

Figure 3.5 *A look inside a computer*

carries signals that execute all the processing that takes place within a computer. Because it is so small, it is referred to as a **microprocessor**. The CPU consists of two units: the **control unit** and the **arithmetic logic unit** (ALU). They conduct functions of storing and processing data.

WHAT IS A MICROPROCESSOR? Microprocessors are made of silicon embedded with transistors. A transistor is a semiconductor, a component that can serve both as a conductor and insulator, depending on the voltage of electricity that tries to flow through it. A semiconductor conducts electric current of a certain minimum voltage along special paths, but blocks current that is lower than that minimum voltage. This is an excellent property for computer communications, because it provides a means to represent binary code's two states: "voltage conducted" and "voltage not conducted." Thus, these transistors can sense binary signals that are encoded instructions to the computer to conduct different operations. In the computer, the 0 is represented by an open circuit, one in which no electric current flows, and the 1 is represented by a closed circuit, one in which there is a current (see Figure 3.6).

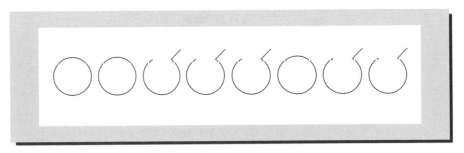

Figure 3.6 *Schematic of how circuits on a chip would be open and closed to represent the letter D in EBCDIC (11000100)*

Used by permission from Intel Corporation

Engineers continue to miniaturize microchips to help make computers smaller and more powerful.

INCREASING CPU CAPACITY Today's electronic semiconductors are called **integrated circuits** because a large number of circuits are integrated on each silicon chip. Early microprocessors contained only hundreds of circuits, but **large scale integration** (LSI) and **very large scale integration** (VLSI) techniques have enabled engineers to install millions of circuits on one microprocessor. This has allowed them to put more and more computing power into smaller and smaller machines.

THE MACHINE CYCLE Once a program starts running in a computer, the CPU performs a very routine sequence, as illustrated in Figure 3.7 for a simple arithmetic function. First, the **control unit**, one of the two parts of the CPU, **fetches** an instruction from a program in internal memory, and **decodes** it into binary code. This code is transmitted to the other part of the CPU, the **arithmetic logic unit (ALU)**, which **executes** the instruction. Usually, the result of the operation is needed for further operations. Therefore, the control unit takes the result and **stores** it in the internal memory. The control unit then fetches the *next* instruction, decodes it, and puts it in the ALU, which executes the instruction. The control unit stores the result in the internal memory, and so on, until the entire program is executed, or something happens that stops this cycle. Anything that stops the cycle is called an "interrupt." It may be an instruction in the program itself, a power failure, or any other reason for the CPU to stop.

As you can see, the CPU performs four functions in every cycle: fetch, decode, execute, and store. Each such cycle is called a **machine cycle**. Computers can perform at rates of millions of machine cycles per second. This rate of repetitive cycles is called **frequency**. One cycle per second is one **hertz**. The frequency of computers is measured in **mega hertz**, or millions of hertz, denoted **MHz**. Powerful computers reach frequencies in the **gigahertz**, or billions of cycles per second, denoted **GHz**.

During the time it takes to blink your eye (about .2 second), millions of instructions can be executed by a computer. Timing of computer operations is measured in infinitesimal fractions of a second (see Figure 3.8).

THE WORD The **data word** (or word for short) is the maximum number of bits that the control unit can fetch from internal memory in one machine cycle. The size of the word is determined by the size of the circuitry in the CPU which holds information for processing. Obviously, the larger the word, the more instructions or data can be retrieved per second. Therefore, all other things being equal, the larger the word, the faster the computer. Older computers had words that could contain just four bits, so each machine cycle could move only four bits at a time. Current microcomputers have words of 32 and 64 bits.

THE CLOCK The sequence of CPU operations must be paced so that the different tasks do not collide. To this end the control unit uses a **system clock**, which synchronizes all tasks. Often, computer frequency is referred to as clock rate.

THE ARITHMETIC LOGIC UNIT OPERATIONS As described in the section on the machine cycle above, the ALU is the part of the CPU in which all the arithmetic and logic operations take place. Arithmetic operations include addition, subtraction, multiplication, division, exponentiation, logarithmic calculations, trigonometric computations, and other complex mathematical tasks. Logic operations are

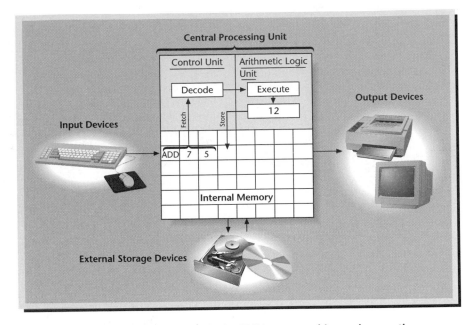

Figure 3.7 *What happens inside the CPU in one machine cycle executing the operation "7+5"*

those in which numbers and strings of characters are compared. For example, comparisons such as "greater than," "less than," and "equal to" are logic operations. The ALU also compares character strings that are not quantitative. For example, when you try to find a word in text processed by a word-processing program, the ALU compares all the words in the text to that specific word until it reaches an identical word.

MEMORY At various points in the machine cycle, program instructions and data must be stored, at least temporarily. The function of storing them is fulfilled by memory circuitry. Memory circuitry can be classified by its speed, that is, the amount of time it takes to store instructions and data in the memory location, or the amount of time it takes to retrieve them from the memory. The fastest memory in the computer is made up of registers (discussed on the next page), which are a part of the CPU. Less fast are internal memory chips, housed outside the CPU.

1 millisecond	= 1/1,000 (.002) second	
1 microsecond	= 1/1,000,000 (.000001) second	
1 nanosecond	= 1/1,000,000,000 (.000000001) second	
1 picosecond	= 1/1,000,000,000,000 (.000000000001) second	

Figure 3.8 *Computer time*

Bother with Technical Details?

Business majors often ask: "Why do I have to study computer hardware?" Ostensibly, the question makes sense. After all, you are not trained to be an engineer. The answer is that you must be at least familiar with the major terms and concepts of computer hardware because, as a manager, you will have to make decisions that depend on the capabilities of the machines. If you become a manager, chances are good that you will be involved in the purchase of computer equipment. You must know what makes one computer more or less powerful than another computer, and you should know the basic characteristics of computers so that you can follow their development.

In addition, knowledge of new technologies may give you ideas of how to develop new products and services to improve your organization's competitive position. Although throughout history, need has been the mother of invention, this is not so with information technology. Time and again, it has been shown that many inventions come to fruition long before they are put to use by businesses. Managers who realize that a certain development will give their companies an advantage will be rewarded for their vision.

REGISTERS The CPU chip itself has specific areas designated for the temporary storage of information that can be stored and retrieved very rapidly. These storage areas are called **registers**. A register is circuitry in the CPU which allows for the fast storage and retrieval of instructions and data during the various stages of the machine cycle. The different parts of the CPU—the control unit, ALU, and memory—all have registers.

For instance, the location in which the ALU accumulates the results of its operations during a machine cycle is a register called the **accumulator**. The control unit has an **instruction register** and an **address register**. The former holds the code that communicates the type of arithmetic or logic operation to be executed. The latter holds information on the location of the next instruction to be executed.

INTERNAL MEMORY None of the steps in the machine cycle can take place without a place for the CPU to store the instructions and data needed for a particular process. Every computer has both internal and external memory. **Internal memory**, also called **main memory** and **primary memory**, is used for storage of data and instructions just before they are processed by the CPU, and immediately after they are processed. Because the internal memory must exist in a computer for the CPU to do its job, many sources consider it to be another part of the CPU.

The internal memory of a computer comprises two types of storage spaces. The larger part is **random access memory (RAM)**, which is made up of microchips and is the first stop for instructions and data before the CPU can process them. The smaller part is **read-only memory (ROM)**, which is used for permanent storage.

External memory consists of **storage media** that allow for programs and data to be permanently stored. Such media include magnetic disks, magnetic tapes, and optical discs. It is imperative to distinguish between internal memory and external memory. Internal memory must be used in processing data inside the computer. On the other hand, external memory is not involved in the actual processing. Thus, even if the hard disk of your computer is of high capacity, the RAM may be too small to process some of the programs that you can store on the hard disk.

Random Access Memory. RAM is the first place all instructions and data are stored on their way to being processed by the CPU. The CPU does not directly deal with external storage devices, only with RAM. So, for a program to start running, all instructions and data must first be entered into RAM, either from a keyboard or other input device, or from an external storage device, such as a magnetic disk or CD.

Every RAM location has a unique address, which is how the CPU knows where to find instructions and data. As soon as an instruction is copied (or "read") into RAM, it is placed in a location with its unique address where it will stay until replaced by other instructions or data. Replacement will occur if the program sends another instruction, or if the computer finishes executing an entire program and another program is loaded.

You must pay attention to the RAM specifications indicated on software packages. For instance, if a program requires at least 50 MB of memory, that's an absolute minimum. It cannot run with less.

In most microcomputers, RAM is Dynamic RAM, or DRAM for short. DRAM chips must have periodic electrical pulses to retain the instructions and data stored in them. Static RAM, known as SRAM, does not require the periodic pulses, and is therefore faster than DRAM. Its main disadvantage is high cost; SRAM chips are significantly more expensive than DRAM.

Cache. A growing number of microcomputer models offer cache memory as an expansion to their RAM. **Cache** (pronounced *cash*) memory is made up of fast memory semiconductor chips. They are faster than DRAM and SRAM memory, but slower than registers. Cache memory stores the most frequently used instructions of the programs the computer runs, which allows the retrieval and execution of these instructions to be carried out faster.

Read-Only Memory. A small part of internal memory consists of chips called read-only memory, or ROM. These chips hold instructions that allow you to communicate with the computer until an operating system program, such as DOS or Windows in the IBM environment, or MacOS in the Macintosh environment, takes control. ROM also holds the ASCII codes for a character set: the 26 capital letters, another 26 lowercase letters, the digits 0 through 9, punctuation marks, and other symbols, such as &, $, #, and @, so that the computer can interpret character input even before any programs are installed.

ROM maintains instructions and data that the user need not, and should not, change. If the instructions and data were stored in RAM, the user might inadvertently delete them. On ROM chips, the instructions and data can never be changed.

ROM chips are installed in the computer by the manufacturer. To replace the data or programs etched in the chip, the user must remove it from the board and plug in a chip with the desired data and programs. There are also electronically erasable ROM chips, which do not require the removal of the chips before reprogramming.

Volatile vs. Nonvolatile Memory. One of the main distinctions among the different types of memory in a computer is whether the memory is **volatile**, meaning temporary, or **nonvolatile**, meaning permanent. Volatile memory is

According to an increasing number of studies, computerization of the office presents workers with a variety of hazards, including repetitive stress injuries (RSIs) due to long periods of typing, stress and strain injuries caused by computers and computer-related furniture that does not accommodate the human body, emotional stress, and eyestrain. Some people also believe that the electromagnetic radiation emitted by computer monitors poses a health hazard. The argument has been made that it is an employer's moral obligation to educate employees about risks, and to provide an environment that minimizes them.

Physical and Emotional Stress. Among the most common computer-related hazards are general physical and emotional stress; numerous muscular-skeletal problems (including RSIs); and vision problems (including eyestrain). One Japanese study found that while sitting in front of a computer monitor, a person blinks only one-sixth of the normal number of times. Extended periods of uninterrupted computer use may also cause emotional illness, by depriving workers of the office chatter and physical movement that are crucial buffers against emotional stress.

As recently as 1980, only 20% of reported occupational injuries were RSIs. (RSIs refer to a wide range of physical consequences caused by repeating the same motion, such as typing, over and over without interruption.) In 1992, the U.S. Department of Labor records showed that the percentage of all occupational injuries reported to be RSIs had risen to more than 50%. This has been explained by the increasing use of computers in the workplace, in many cases replacing typewriters. Typists had to stop typing periodically, changing hand positons to pull the carriage lever or insert a new sheet of paper. But word processing and other computer work requiring intensive repetitive keystrokes or mouse motion require no such breaks. In addition, in today's workplace, many people do not feel free to take a break and move around their workplace because the frequency and continuity of their keystrokes are being monitored.

Electromagnetic Radiation. Years ago, some scientists claimed that electromagnetic radiation from computer monitors might be a health hazard. There was heightened concern about pregnant women who spent long hours in front of monitors, which could possibly harm their fetuses. However, studies found that a person has to spend approximately 300 years in front of a

(continued)

stored in circuits that depend on electrical current to maintain the information. Information stored in volatile memory is not meant to be permanent. Because volatile memory depends upon electrical power to be maintained, it may be erased by power failure, or by machine shut-down. You may have experienced losing a file during a power outage or when someone unintentionally cut power to your computer. A file is lost because it was in volatile memory; if you had saved it, however, it would have been copied onto a nonvolatile storage device, such as a disk or a tape. RAM and registers are both volatile forms of memory.

Read-only memory is nonvolatile. Programs and data stored in ROM will stay in the chips when the power is turned off and can be accessed again when the computer is turned back on.

COMPUTER POWER What makes one computer more powerful than another? There are two major factors to consider: speed and memory capacity. The speed of a computer is determined mainly by (1) the rate at which the CPU

computer monitor (or a television set, for that matter) to absorb a dose of radiation considered to be a health risk. Obviously, this was not a problem, but there are other, very real, risks.

Lawsuits. One profession where RSIs are common is journalism. In 1990, four *Newsday* journalists filed a $40 million suit against Atex, Inc., a manufacturer of computer terminals. A few days later, eight reporters and editors from the Associated Press news agency and other publications in New York filed a $270 million dollar suit for personal injury against Atex. The plaintiffs claimed that they suffered chronic injuries because they used Atex computer terminals. Atex was charged with product liability for causing them economic loss and emotional damage due to repetitive stress injuries. They contended that the company should have known that the continuous use of the keyboards could result in cumulative trauma disorder.

In July 1991, a judge in New York consolidated 44 lawsuits against IBM, AT&T, Apple Computer, and Northern Telecom. The companies were charged with liability for RSIs, injuries inflicted on data entry clerks, supermarket cashiers, and journalists. Legal observers predict increasing litigation of this type.

New Laws. While employers are asked to voluntarily adopt policies to minimize such hazards, San Francisco adopted a law in 1991 that controls work with video display terminal (VDT) workstations. It requires employers with 15 or more workers to provide workstations that have user-adjustable chairs, keyboards, and VDT screens; appropriate lighting; nonglare screens and terminals, and arm, wrist, and foot rests if requested. Printers must be covered to attenuate noise. Employers are also required to provide either 15-minute breaks or alternative work for every two hours of continuous keyboard motion. Worker advocates are trying to spur legislatures throughout the U.S. to enact similar laws.

A distributor of computer components appealed the ordinance, and in February 1992 it was struck down by a judge. The judge said that only the state of California, not individual cities, could regulate worker safety. Not surprisingly the appeal was financially supported by large computer manufacturers.

operates (the computer's frequency, or clock rate, measured in cycles per second), and (2) the amount of information the CPU can process per cycle (determined by the size of the data word).

All other things being equal, the greater the frequency, the faster the machine, because it can fetch, decode, execute, and store more instructions per second. Also, the larger the data word, the faster the computer. And because a larger word means that in each trip to the internal memory, the control unit can retrieve more bits to process. Therefore, the CPU can execute a program faster.

You may have seen advertisements in which the vendor tries to sell a "64-bit computer." This means the data word's capacity is 64 bits. You have to be cautious with regard to word size. A larger word does not always mean a faster computer, because the bits may not be able to move within the computer at such a high rate. The **bus**, which is the wires used for communication inside the computer, may have a capacity of only 32 bits, while the word may

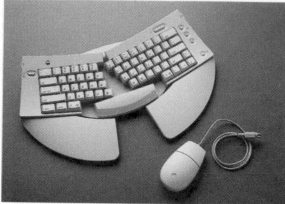

Used by permission from Apple Computer, Inc.

An increasing number of people prefer to use ergonomic keyboards.

contain 64 bits. In this case, the processing speed is limited to 32 bits in each machine cycle. This is analogous to a large water container connected to a narrow hose.

Neither of the above factors alone determines the computer's speed. Only the consideration of both factors will allow you to compare the speed of different computers.

The speed of large computers is measured in the billions of cycles per second, or GHz. Personal and notebook computers have speeds of millions of cycles per second, or MHz. Computer speed is also measured in MIPS, millions of instructions per second, which is not an accurate measure, because instructions may be of various levels of complexity.

INPUT DEVICES

Computers must receive input from which to produce desired output. Input devices include all machines and other apparatuses used to enter instructions and data into the computer's main memory. Input devices, the most common of which is the keyboard, come in many different forms.

KEYBOARD

The most pervasive input device is the **keyboard**. The keyboard allows data and instructions to be entered into primary memory and can be used to instruct programs to run. All keyboards have several **function keys** numbered F1, F2, and so on, that can be activated to execute preprogrammed functions, such as copying a highlighted sentence in a text file of a word processor. Many programs allow function keys to be programmed with **macros**, which are customized tasks that can then be activated by depressing the appropriate function key.

The Optimal Keyboard. The standard keyboard layout is called QWERTY, based on the top row of letter keys. Interestingly, the QWERTY keyboard was originally designed to slow down typing, because early mechanical typewriters jammed when users typed too fast. With today's electrical devices, this layout is counterproductive. Other keyboards, such as the Dvorak keyboard, are designed to facilitate the fastest typing possible. The Dvorak has the most frequently used keys in the home, or central, row. Using this keyboard can increase typing speed by 95%. However, most computer users are reluctant to retrain themselves or to purchase a new keyboard.

Ergonomic Keyboards. One of the most prevalent work-related injuries today is known as carpal tunnel syndrome, the pain caused by holding the forearms in an unnatural position when typing for long periods. In response to this problem, new ergonomic keyboards are gaining popularity. These keyboards are split in the middle, and the two parts are twisted outwards to better fit the natural angular position of the forearms when typing.

MOUSE, TRACKBALL, AND TRACK PAD

A **mouse** is an input device that controls a cursor on the screen to facilitate the point-and-click approach to executing different operations. It is most commonly used along with a keyboard, although some programs use it exclusively. Mice have two to four buttons. They allow the user to place the cursor anywhere on the screen, highlight portions of the screen, and select items from a menu.

Do computers cause cancer in the workplace? A mysterious cluster of cancers among journalists who use video display terminals (VDTs) on a regular basis raised some disturbing questions. There were apparent "epidemics" of cancer at such newspapers as the *St. Louis Post-Dispatch*, with nine cases of brain tumors among editorial employees (three of whom have died), and *The San Jose Mercury News*, with 18 assorted cancer cases. But when the National Institute of Occupational Safety and Health (NIOSH) investigated the *Post-Dispatch* at the request of the employees' union, the cancers' relationship to VDTs and the electromagnetic fields (EMFs) they generate could not be established. A NIOSH spokesman said tumors take 15 to 20 years to develop, meaning there's no way to pin down what might have caused them. A test of EMF levels at the newspaper showed a normal level of emission, not higher than in other offices where VDTs were used.

Source: "Are Computers Deadly?", *Datamation*, April 15, 1994, p. 23. Reprinted with permission of *Datamation* magazine. Copyright © 1994 by Cahners Publishing, Reed Elsevier Inc.

When the mouse is moved on the surface of a desk or a pad, the computer detects the movements, translates them into digital coordinates on the screen, and moves the cursor in a pattern that imitates the movement of the mouse. The buttons are used for clicking, locking, and dragging displayed information. A **trackball** is similar to a mouse, but the ball moves within the device, rather than over a surface. With a **track pad**, a user controls the cursor by moving his or her finger along a touch-sensitive pad.

TOUCH SCREEN

Sometimes a single device, such as a **touch screen**, may serve both as an input and output device. A touch screen allows the computer user to choose operations by touching the options displayed on the computer screen.

There are several types of touch screens. One technique uses the hit of a finger to sense the choice. In another technique ultrasonic waves are passed over the screen, and when the screen is touched, the computer senses the exact location where the waves are deflected. Touch screens are used in some common public applications, such as providing advice to tourists; selecting lottery numbers; and ringing in grocery items in self-serve supermarket check-out points.

SOURCE DATA INPUT DEVICES

Businesses in which speed of data entry is a top priority use machine reading devices, such as bar code scanners. These are known as **source data input devices** because they copy data directly from the source, such as the bar code, without the need for human intervention. Data can also be recorded directly from other sources, including checks and credit cards. Let's consider some settings where source data input devices have made an enormous difference in the efficiency of the operation.

With the huge number of corporate and personal checks processed daily by banks, entering check data manually was extremely slow and expensive. To facilitate source data entry, the bank identification number, account number, and check number are encoded into the bars printed in special magnetic ink at the bottom of each check, as shown in Figure 3.9. These are detectable by a special

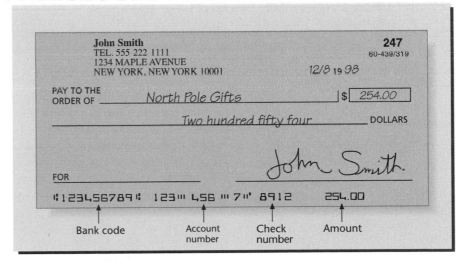

Figure 3.9 *Banks use magnetic-ink character recognition (MICR) to automate their input procedures.*

device called a magnetic-ink reader, using **magnetic-ink character recognition** (MICR, pronounced MIKE-er). A person at the bank enters the amount of the check, also in magnetic ink. Then banks record their check deposits by placing a large number of checks into a MICR device, which records the check amounts and the accounts from which the money is drawn.

Credit cards, too, facilitate source data entry. Card numbers and other data are coded onto the magnetic strip on the card's back. When you charge a purchase on your credit card, the person at the point of sale (POS) passes the card through the reader to record the account number and your name and address. The total amount charged is either manually keyed in or recorded automatically from the cash register.

Mark recognition devices are essential equipment to successful source data entry. **Optical mark recognition** is used by special devices to detect the positions of marks on source documents, such as standardized test response forms. **Optical bar recognition** is designed to sense data encoded in the ubiquitous series of thick and thin black bars that make up bar codes.

Another far less accurate technology used for source data entry is **optical character recognition (OCR)**. Unlike optical mark recognition, OCR technology is often used to try to interpret handwritten and printed texts not originally designed for data source entry. A device called a **scanner** scans the page and translates each character into a digitized representation of it. A special program then tries to correlate the images with characters and stores the interpreted text for further processing.

IMAGING

A growing number of organizations are **imaging** or **image processing** their documents, which allows not only the storage of enormous amounts of data in less space than paper, but also much more efficient retrieval and filing. Imaging, which is the process of scanning and storing, has already reduced millions of paper documents to digitized pictures, in many companies. The technology is used to store shipping documents, insurance policies and claims, personnel files, checks, and many other types of documents. The images are stored in large databases from which they can be retrieved and displayed on computer monitors. This technology is particularly useful when dealing with documents that include signatures and graphics. Once scanned, the original document can be destroyed. There is simply no need for the original piece of paper because an exact copy of it can be generated on demand.

Because storing pictures requires large amounts of storage capacity, imaging was often not feasible before the advent of laser compact discs. Writeable compact discs are now used as the main medium for maintaining images of business documents. This is expected to be the one technology that will actually reduce the amount of paper in organizations. Therefore, the prime candidates for adoption of imaging are companies in paper-intensive fields: law, retail, insurance, banking, health care, and shipping.

VOICE RECOGNITION

Engineers have developed machines called **voice recognition systems** that can translate human speech into computer-readable data and instructions. All voice recognition systems, which vary in their sophistication, receive input from

●● *POINT OF INTEREST*
▶ Mega Bytes

…IBM, the same company that introduced the first hard disk in 1956, has set a new record for magnetic storage capacity: 3 billion bits *per square inch.* At this density, a small hard drive could hold more than 3,400 megabytes of data—equivalent to information contained in a 565-foot-tall stack of typewritten pages. The new disk uses two improved technologies: more sensitive recording heads that can read smaller and smaller bits, and a finer alloy coating that prevents the magnetic signal from degrading into "noise." Expect to see these high-capacity disks move from the lab to the stores in three to five years, according to IBM. You may never need to copy to floppy again.

Source: *Newsweek,* May 1, 1995. Copyright © 1995, Newsweek, Inc. All rights reserved. Reprinted with permission.

a microphone and process the input with conversion software. The simplest voice recognition systems have to "learn" a person's speech. The prospective user feeds a large sample of spoken sentences into the computer along with the machine language equivalent so the computer can *learn* the speech patterns. The computer is programmed to recognize the person's accent, intonation, pauses, and other speech patterns. Only then will the machine be able to effectively recognize that person's voice—but not necessarily others'.

The more sophisticated and complex systems are programmed to allow any person to speak to a computer. The vocabulary of these systems tends to be more limited. Also, some of them force users to settle for short commands with unnatural pauses between transmissions. Certain more complex systems may recognize continuous streams of speech and up to 5,000 words.

Voice recognition is helpful in environments where both hands are occupied while commands must be given to a computer. In manufacturing, the technology is used to record the findings of product inspection and control. In medicine, operating surgeons may request patient data from a computer equipped with voice recognition.

Voice recognition technology is still limited. Research is being conducted in an effort to develop hardware and software that will enable computers to recognize a much greater vocabulary and many speech patterns. While the devices are being improved, some observers think voice-operated computers may increase already high noise levels and add to distraction. Imagine an office with many people in cubicles talking to computers. Also, voice recognition may be the source of pranks; people could walk by and shout commands to other workers' computers.

OUTPUT DEVICES

Output devices include all electronic and electromechanical apparatuses that deliver results of computer processing. We capture the output with any one or a combination of our senses. The sense that we use most frequently is sight. Indeed, most information is rendered in the form of visual reports, either on screen or on paper. When the output is intangible, such as a picture on a computer monitor, or information stored on disk, it is called **soft copy**. When it is tangible, such as a printout on a piece of paper, the output is called **hard copy**.

SOFT-COPY OUTPUT DEVICES

Soft-copy devices produce either an image or sound. Images include text and pictures. Sound includes speech, music, and other audio signals.

MONITORS The most pervasive output device is the computer monitor. Computer monitors look like television screens and use very similar technology. There are two major types of monitors: cathode-ray tube and flat-panel display.

Cathode-Ray Tube. In a **cathode-ray tube** (CRT) monitor, the inner side of the screen has a layer of tiny phosphoric dots called **pixels** (*pic*ture *el*ements), which respond to electronic beams by displaying different colored light. A ray of electrons is sprayed by an electron gun that sweeps the rows of pixels. When electrons hit a pixel, the pixel emits light for a limited amount of time. The electron gun receives its instructions from the computer. It bombards some pixels and skips others, whereby a picture develops on the screen.

There are several sites on the Web that provide interesting information on ergonomics in general and on ergonomics of computer equipment in particular. The most detailed one is *http://ergo.human.cornell.edu/* provided by Cornell University. Another two are: *http://www.virginia.edu/~enhealth/ERGONOMICS/toc.html* and *http://vered.rose.toronto.edu*. The latter site provides many links to other resources, and if your computer has video-playing software, you can download short movies that demonstrate ergonomic equipment.

Do a search on the keyword *ergonomics* to find more information.

The human eye perceives as a continuous picture any stream of frames that appear at a rate of 24 frames or more per second. Therefore, the electron gun has to sweep the screen at least that frequently. The frequency at which the screen is swept is called the **refresh rate**. The higher the rate the less the chance that the screen will flicker. The better, and more expensive, monitors have a refresh rate of 72 Hz (frames per second) or above.

The greater the number of pixels per unit area on the screen, the sharper the picture. The sharpness of the picture is called **resolution**. It is expressed in the number of pixels that fit in the width and height of a complete screen image. CRTs come in several resolutions. The resolution required for text to be clear is 640 x 350. If you multiply these numbers you will get the total number of pixels on the screen. For graphics to be clear, higher resolution is required, such as 640 x 480, 720 x 480, or higher.

Some monitors, called **monochrome monitors**, display pictures in just one color over a background of another color, such as amber over black. The bombardment of the pixels with different amounts of electrons may create different hues of the single color, which are called **gray scales**. These monitors are suitable for tasks that do not require different colors, such as word-processing. However, with the proliferation of so many colorful applications, few people would find it appealing to use even a word-processing program on a monochrome monitor.

Both organizations and individuals now purchase only **color monitors**. The inner side of a color monitor has an array of triads of pixels, rather than an array of single pixels. Because each triad consists of one **red**, one **green**, and one **blue** phosphor dot, such a device is called an **RGB monitor**. The entire triad is referred to as a pixel. When these colors are mixed electronically, they can produce many different colors. Three electron guns bombard the triads simultaneously with different amounts of power to create different colors and hues in each triad. The better color monitors can display over one million colors and hues (see Figure 3.10).

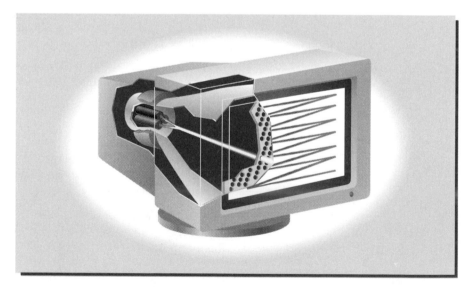

Figure 3.10 *In an RGB monitor, the electron gun creates many different colors and hues from the three primary colors: red, green and blue.*

Flat-Panel Monitors. Flat-panel monitors, used on laptop and notebook computers, use a different technology to display output. The main advantage of flat-panel monitors is their slim profile. One common type of flat-panel monitor is the **liquid crystal display (LCD)**, used in hand-held calculators and digital watches, as well as on some laptops.

In LCD, a conductive-film-covered screen is filled with a liquid crystal, in which molecules have the property of aligning in different planes when charged with electricity of a certain voltage. When the proper voltage is applied to segments of the screen, it disrupts the regular structure of the crystal in those areas, causing it to block light. Light continues to pass through the rest of the liquid. This combination of light and dark areas produces images of characters and pictures.

Early LCD displays were of poor quality. The user could see the picture only within a limited angle, and the resolution was low. Engineers managed to increase the difference in orientation between the crystals to create a greater contrast and improve visibility from greater angles. Current LCDs also have built-in fluorescent light to improve visibility in poor light conditions.

Another technology used for flat-screen display is **gas-plasma display**. The screen is made up of two glass plates with an ionized gas (plasma) between them. One plate contains an array of tiny horizontal wires, and the other plate contains vertical wires. The intersections of the wires serve as "pixels." When the wires are charged with electricity, the plasma at the intersections emits light. Arrays of lit intersections create the image of characters and pictures.

VOICE OUTPUT Although much of the output we receive from computers is visual, another of our senses, hearing, is used too. The speakers of many computers are now used not just to beep when you try an illegitimate operation, but to provide auditory information.

There are two main approaches to voice output. In one, a large number of human-produced phrases are recorded. A program selects the appropriate phrase and vocalizes it in response to certain signals from the user. You may have experienced this in the supermarket, when using a self-checkout system. Many providers of banking and insurance services also use this method. For example, a human voice can report your account balance over the phone in response to a series of signals you transmit by depressing the telephone keys. The advantage of this method is the authentic human voice. The disadvantage is the huge number of phrases that need to be recorded, which slows the system's response time. Also, the sentences may sound awkward especially when pronouncing numbers.

Voice synthesizing tries to use machine sounds to emulate a human voice, using special devices called synthesizers, which produce the voice electronically. This technology does not require engineers to maintain large banks of prerecorded human words and sentences, but the output does tend to sound artificial. There are still great difficulties in building devices that not only pronounce the words correctly, but also use the appropriate intonations and accents in specific contexts.

Voice output is used for visually impaired computer users and for users whose situation does not allow a constant view of a monitor. Some car manufacturers install voice output devices that warn the driver when fuel is low, or when a mechanical problem occurs.

Notebook computers would be impossible without flat-display technology.

Used by permission from IBM Corporation

A Decade Ahead

Here are some technological developments we should expect in the next decade.

ARE LIGHT-SPEED COMPUTERS AROUND THE CORNER?

A long-time goal of computer scientists is to create a machine that uses beams of light instead of electrons to process information. Such "optoelectronic" computers would offer a leap in speed and performance, and use a lot less power. But so far, the optical processors have only been able to do simple calculations.

OptiComp Corp. in Lake Tahoe, Nevada, has taken a big step forward. Backed by the Pentagon's Star Wars program, the company built a machine that can execute up to 12 million instructions per second, which rivals the speed of conventional high-performance computers. The leap in speed comes from using arrays of lasers with scores of light beams instead of a handful, as earlier machines did. OptiComp is already working on a machine that will run at least 100 times faster than current computers. Among other chores, optoelectronic computers are especially suited for high-speed searches of databases or number-crunching in low-power satellites.

Source: Reprinted from December 13, 1993, issue of *Business Week* by special permission, copyright © 1993 by the McGraw-Hill Companies, Inc.

THINK CRITICALLY

What will the impact of optoelectric computers be on daily management? Do you think the role of the desktop computer will remain the same in the future? Why?

SUPER TAG

British Technology Group (BTG) developed a technology that will significantly shorten shoppers' time at the cash register. Intended to replace bar codes, a Supertag is a simple electronic circuit containing a unique number encoded on a silicon chip. It acts as a sort of electronic label that can be scanned, identified, and counted at a distance of up to 13 feet. The supertag is powered by radio beams in the scanner and does not require an internal battery. The technology could be used to identify individual bags on a baggage cart, parcels shipped through delivery services, and books checked out of public libraries.

One of the first commercial applications of Supertag will probably be in supermarkets. The chip will permit shoppers to pile their goods into a cart, pass through a scanner built into an archway, and receive an itemized bill for all of their items a few seconds later.

Source: "Supertag Is It," *Datamation*, August 15, 1994, p. 24. Reprinted with permission of *Datamation* magazine. Copyright © 1994 by Cahners Publishing, Reed Elsevier Inc.

(continued)

Current check-out devices in supermarkets have met with a lukewarm reaction from customers. Will the above technology meet favorable response? Why?

ROLL YOUR COMPUTER UP

French scientists have produced a flexible all-plastic transistor from layers of polymers and insulating film, using graphite ink as electrodes. The paper-thin transistors could one day be used in car windshields that display information or in flat television or computer screens that could be rolled up like a scroll or window shade when not in use.

Source: "Roll Your Computer Up" from *St. Petersburg Times*, September 18, 1994, pA4. Reprinted by permission of the *St. Petersburg Times*.

What other uses do you foresee for the above technology?

WEARABLE COMPUTERS

Used by permission from Xybernaut Corporation Fairfax, VA

NEC Corp., the big Japanese computer maker, says wearable PCs, including those slung from the shoulder, will be in vogue by the end of the decade for users in various professions.

Noted fashion critic Mr. Blackwell would probably be horrified, but NEC continues its efforts to create wearable PCs. The company announced its effort late in 1991, saying that the PC will become such an essential part of daily life that we will add it to our wardrobes. At the time, researchers at the Advanced PC Design Center in Tokyo predicted that by the late 1990s, people would be wearing their PCs. NEC said that potential PC fashion plates might include paramedics, who would wear computers across their shoulders and use specialized trackballs to scan for injuries and check vital signs. They would dictate their findings into microphones and could also access CD-ROM-based medical encyclopedias.

For those who need a keyboard at all times, a notebook PC with shoulder straps is under development. Folding keyboards and display setups would allow this to become a reality. An NEC spokeswoman said that the company has not accelerated its timetable for these devices. While wearable computers have already been displayed in exhibitions, the future will tell whether we are going to adopt them as a business tool.

Source: Fitzgerald, M., "You look 'mahvelous'," *Computerworld*, April 12, 1993, p. 28. Reprinted with permission of Computerworld Magazine.

Hand-held calculators could be significantly reduced in size, but would then be unusable. Wearable computers may pose the same problem. What is the problem? How would wearable computers help workers in different business functions?

HARDCOPY OUTPUT DEVICES

A hard copy is any tangible, permanent copy of computer output. When people ask for a hard copy they almost always mean paper copy. Most computers are connected to an essential peripheral piece of equipment: the **printer**. Printers can be classified into two basic types: impact and nonimpact.

NONIMPACT PRINTERS The most common printer in use today is the laser printer, which is a **nonimpact printer** because images are created on a page without pressing any mechanism against the paper. Nonimpact printers include laser, ink-jet, electrostatic, and electrothermal printers. Laser printers are also **page printers** because they print one whole page at a time. Laser and ink-jet printers produce very high-quality output, including color. Laser printing technology can create typeset quality, that is the quality of typesetting you see in magazines and textbooks. Electrostatic and electrothermal printers produce low-quality output because they use dot-matrix images. All nonimpact printers use fewer moving parts than impact printers, and are therefore significantly quieter. They are also much faster.

The excellent quality of their output has made laser printers the choice of many individual and corporate users for desktop publishing. The prices of laser printers have gone down so rapidly that many individuals now purchase their personal computer along with a laser printer, although color laser printers are still too expensive for many private users.

The two qualities to check when purchasing a laser or ink-jet printer are the speed, measured in pages per minute (PPM), and the type density, measured in dots per inch (DPI). The higher the density, the greater the sharpness of the output. Desktop printers produce output at 300 or 600 DPI. The speed of desktop laser printers is 4–10 PPM. Larger, commercial laser printers reach speeds of over 400 PPM. It is also important to inquire about the number of resident fonts. The greater the number of fonts stored in the printer's ROM, the more flexibility you have with the type faces.

IMPACT PRINTERS Printers are considered **impact printers** if the reproduction of an image on a page requires a mechanical impact. **Character printers** create one character at a time, in a manner similar to typewriters. **Dot-matrix printers** have a print head consisting of a matrix of little pins. When certain pins strike the ribbon against the paper, the shape of a character, or another form, is marked on the paper. Thus, each character is made up of tiny dots. Dot-matrix printers produce low-quality output. **Thimble** and **daisy-wheel** printers have a rotating head with all the characters needed for word processing. The impact on the paper is created by a character hammer hitting the ribbon. These printers create letter-quality output because the character shapes are solid, not made of little dots. However, they are not suitable for graphical output. Whereas dot-matrix printers can create more than one font (typeface), the thimble and daisy wheel must be replaced for different fonts.

EXTERNAL STORAGE MEDIA

As discussed briefly above, to maintain programs, data, and information for later use, data must be stored on a nonvolatile storage medium. Often, we also want to move the stored data to a computer that is not part of a network, and we need to back up important programs and data as well. To this end we use **external storage media**.

External storage devices come in different forms and different materials, each with their strengths and weaknesses. The important properties to consider are capacity, access speed, and mode of access. Capacity is the amount of data the medium can hold per area of its surface; access speed is the amount of data that can be stored or retrieved per time unit; and mode of access refers to the organization of data on the medium, either random or sequential.

PUNCHED CARDS AND PUNCHED TAPES

Punched cards and punched tapes store information in the form of holes arranged in patterns that are code for characters, numerals, and other symbols. Punched cards and tapes were the earliest external storage media, but are rarely used today. Cards were used in collating and tabulating machines as early as 1890. Punched tapes are used mainly in rough manufacturing environments—for control of heavy machinery such as lathes, machining robots, and the like—because they are less prone than other media to damage from dust and grease. Special devices called card readers and tape readers, respectively, are used to copy the information from the media into the computer.

MAGNETIC TAPES

Magnetic tapes similar to the ones used in tape recorders and VCRs are also used to store computer data. They are made of polyester coated with an easily magnetized substance, such as ferrous oxide or chrome oxide. The information is coded in the form of patterns of tiny magnetized areas. Each column of magnetized and nonmagnetized spots across the tape represents a character. As you know from reusing video tapes, the information can be easily erased by demagnetizing the tape, which can then be loaded again with information.

Magnetic tapes are inexpensive. Therefore, they are frequently used as a backup storage medium. Special devices called tape drives are used to record computer output and read input.

MAGNETIC DISKS

The most widely used storage medium is the magnetic disk. In a similar manner to the magnetic tape, information on magnetic disks is coded in the form of magnetized spots on the disk's surface. There are many types of magnetic disks. The simplest are the common 3.5-inch "floppy" disks. They are made of mylar coated with an easily magnetized substance. The ubiquitous 1.4 MB floppy disks are likely to be replaced by the increasingly popular 100 MB disks. The disks currently must be used with special external drives, but as their prices drop, the drives will become a standard feature of personal computers.

Today's PCs always come with what are known as **hard disks** built in. A hard disk is a stack of rigid disks made of several aluminum platters and built into the same box that holds the CPU and other computer components. Hard disks can also be portable (known as portable disk cartridges).

Although very popular, magnetic disks are sensitive to environmental mishaps. Because data are encoded in the form of weak magnetic fields, the read/write head—the sensor that reads the disk by sensing the pattern of magnetized spots—must operate very close to the disk surface. Only this way can the head detect the magnetic fields. This means that if a small particle of dust, for

Used by permission from Toshiba America Information Systems, Inc.

Used by permission from Iomega Corporation

The 100 MB super-floppy disk (left) is a popular external storage medium. The removable hard disk drive (right) allows storage of up to 1 GB on its removable disk.

example, gets between the head and the disk, the head may crash, and data may be lost. Magnetic disks are also vulnerable to being inadvertently erased in electromagnetic environments.

OPTICAL DISCS

There are three types of optical discs, also called compact discs (CDs): CD-ROM (Compact Disc, Read Only Memory), WORM (Write Once Read Many), and erasable CD. CDs, which come in diameters of 4.72 to 14 inches, can store text and deliver graphics and sound of superb quality. Data are recorded on CDs by treating the disc surface to reflect light in two different ways. In the case of CD-ROMs and WORMs, parts of the surface are pitted with microscopic indentations and parts are left flat. As a laser beam illuminates the surface, the light is either reflected back to a sensor or scattered because of the pits on the disc. The two different reactions of light to the surface in response to the presence or absence of the pits creates the two states that allow binary coding of zeroes and ones.

CD-ROMs are read-only devices. In other words, data on them cannot be erased or changed. The capacity of CD-ROMs is 500 MB or more, with one CD-ROM storing as much data as more than 400 floppy discs. Libraries find CD-ROMs extremely useful for storing vast amounts of information from magazines and books as well as encyclopedias, dictionaries, and other large volumes. In fact, the *Academic American Encyclopedia* is stored on one disk with some space left unused. Software is now distributed on CD-ROMs as well.

Before they have data recorded on them, CD-ROMs are referred to as WORM discs. They are bought blank from the manufacturer so the user can record information on them. Once the information is stored on a WORM, it becomes a CD-ROM and the information cannot be erased or changed. In business, WORMs are used to store technical and operational manuals and for archival purposes. For example, Boeing uses WORM discs to store aircraft maintenance manuals. WORM discs are more expensive than CD-ROMs. They usually come in diameters of 5.25 inches and 14 inches with capacities of 12 and 30 GB respectively.

Erasable CDs, also called **writeable CDs** and **CD-R** (compact disc-recordable), use both light and magnetism to store and retrieve data. Instead of creating pits in the surface, a special head at the end of the access arm magnetizes the surface. Hence, they are also called **magneto-optic discs**. Spots that are magnetized on these magneto-optic discs reflect light at a different angle than spots that are left unmagnetized. This allows the user to erase data and rewrite the disc. Erasable CDs look like the usual 3.5-inch floppy disks. Therefore, they are popularly known as **flopticals**. A 5.25-inch floptical can hold up to 12 GB of data. They are more expensive than CD-ROMs and WORMs. The 3.5-inch floptical drives look like ordinary magnetic drives and can read from, and write to, ordinary 1.4 MB floppy disks as well as 128 MB optical discs.

OPTICAL TAPE

Optical tape uses the same technology as optical discs to store and retrieve data. The only difference is that the magnetic fields representing the bits are organized serially, which is the same way they are organized on a magnetic tape. Like magnetic tapes, optical tapes are made as reels or cassettes. Their storage capacity is enormous. A reel 14 inches in diameter stores one terabyte (1 terabyte = a thousand billion bytes). A cassette stores about nine gigabytes (1 gigabyte = 1 billion bytes).

While the storage capacity of optical media, both tapes and discs, is significantly greater than the capacity of magnetic media, they have a slower retrieval speed. It takes significantly more time to retrieve data from an optical disc than from a magnetic hard disk. Hence, many IS managers feel that optical media are still too slow for online storage, that is, storage for immediate processing.

BUSINESS CONSIDERATIONS OF STORAGE MEDIA

In evaluating what type of storage media is best for a particular business, managers must be clear about purpose and budget. If retrieval speed is of utmost importance, magnetic disks are the best choice. If large volumes of data must be stored, with little need for fast retrieval speed, then optical discs are the better choice. Retrieval speed is usually referred to as **transfer time**, or the time it takes one megabyte of data to be copied from the external storage medium into RAM.

When volume of storage is the important factor, than the managers must consider price per megabyte, that is, the ratio of dollars spent to storage capacity. If the medium will be used merely for backup, the low cost of magnetic tape makes it the ideal choice.

TRADE OFFS Often, both the transfer time and capacity of external storage are major factors, and must both be weighed against cost. Figure 3.11 summarizes the characteristics of the most popular storage media. One must also consider the reliability and life expectancy of the device. For instance, optical discs are more

Medium	Storage Capacity	Transfer Time	Cost (per 1 MB)
Magnetic hard disk	High	High	Moderate
Magnetic tape	Moderate	Low	Very low
Magneto-optical disc	Very high	Low	Very high
Optical tape	Very high	Very low	Very high
CD-ROM	Very high (but not rewritable)	Very low	Low

Figure 3.11 *Characteristics of storage media for business consideration*

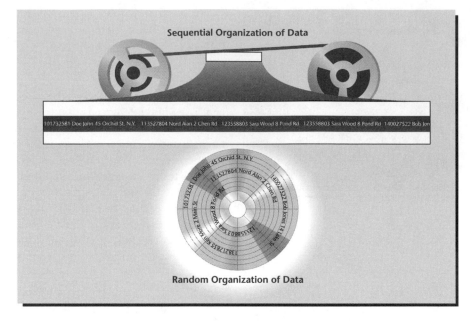

Figure 3.12 *Sequential and random organization of data*

reliable and durable than magnetic disks. Although the data transfer rate of current optical discs is low, discs with rates of up to 16.4 MB/sec will soon be available.

MODES OF ACCESS There are two basic types of data storage: sequential and direct (random) storage (see Figure 3.12). Sequential storage, such as on tapes, requires much data to be reviewed in order to access only a small part of the data. Direct storage, used on disks, allows data to be accessed by address, or location on the disk, and is therefore much faster for finding specific data.

Seqential data are stored in the form of whole bytes across a tape. In other words, the eight bits that make up a byte are stored across the width of the tape, one byte after another, like ties on a railroad track. When the data are coded on the tape, the tape drive moves in one direction only, laying down one byte after another in sequential order.

The records in a **sequential file** are organized by **key**, a field in the record that gives the record an ID number, such as the social security number in a human resource file, or part number in an inventory file. To retrieve a desired record, the computer must retrieve each record, one at a time, and compare its key with that of the desired record, then reject or further process the data. To do this on tape requires that the tape be processed from its beginning until the tape drive reaches the record with the specified information. If the record happens to be at the end of the tape, then the entire tape must be processed. Therefore, tapes and other sequential storage media are suitable only when processing a large percentage of the stored data, and for backup purposes, but they are much less desirable when only small amounts of data will be retrieved at a time.

When quick access to a single record, or to a small number of records at a time, is desired, direct access (also called **random access**) storage media are used. With such media, usually called **direct access storage devices**, or **DASD** (DAZ-dee), a single record can be reached without processing any other record. The key is translated into an address, a physical location on the medium. The access arm moves to the address on the device, and the record is copied into the computer's RAM.

DASDs also enable a third file organization, the **indexed sequential access method**. In a way, this is a hybrid of the sequential and direct organizations. The records are stored sequentially with a key. An index is stored on the storage device which provides the physical address of every record by the record key. When the user indicates a certain key value (such as a part number of an inventory item), the program first goes to the index to look up that value. It takes the physical address corresponding to the value and directs the access arm to that address. The record can then be retrieved. When sequential processing is required, the index may be used to process the records sequentially.

DASDs include magnetic disks, optical discs, and other media such as RAM disk and bubble memory. RAM disk is not really a disk but a board of RAM chips added to the original RAM in a desktop computer. Bubble memory is still an experimental technology.

CLASSIFICATION OF COMPUTERS

Computers are classified by their power, which is determined mainly by two characteristics: the computer's speed of processing, and the size of its memory. However, there are no clear lines between the classes. In fact, the same computer may be classified differently by two different vendors. In general, the more powerful the computer, the higher its price.

SUPERCOMPUTERS AND MAINFRAMES

Supercomputers are the largest, most powerful, and most expensive computers. They are used by universities, research institutions, and large corporations that engage in research and development. Manufacturers of these machines include Cray Research, Fujitsu, Hitachi, and NEC. The main memories of supercomputers consist of billions of bytes, and their processing speed is in the billions of instructions per second. Their prices are in the $10–30 million range.

New supercomputers contain multiple processors which allow them to perform parallel processing and run at great speeds. In parallel processing, several CPUs process different data at the same time. Uses of supercomputers include calculation of satellite orbits, weather forecasting, genetic decoding, optimization of oil exploration, and simulation testing of products that cannot otherwise be tested because of price or physical difficulty, as in the case of building the proposed space station or the future transatmospheric plane.

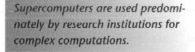
Supercomputers are used predominately by research institutions for complex computations.

Used by permission from Cray Research, A Silicon Graphics Company

MAINFRAME COMPUTERS

In terms of power, one class below supercomputers are **mainframe computers**. They are less powerful and significantly less expensive than supercomputers. Mainframes are used by businesses that must store large amounts of data in a central computer so that many users in multiple departments can access them. Typical purchasers include banks, insurance companies, large retail chains, and universities. Among manufacturers of the machines are IBM, DEC, Amdahl, and Unisys. IBM has produced a family of mainframes named 3090, which contain memory chips that store up to one million bits and can retrieve a record in a mere 80 billionths of a second.

Used by permission from IBM Corporation

Minicomputers satisfy many business needs for a fraction of a mainframe's price.

MINICOMPUTERS

Minicomputers are much smaller than mainframes and less powerful. For many years the DEC VAX family was a very popular choice for organizations that could not afford mainframes. In recent years IBM's AS/400 has been the computer of choice for such organizations. Hewlett-Packard is also a major player in this market. The price of minicomputers is in the tens of thousands to a few hundred thousand dollars. The machines are often used as the host computer in a network of smaller computers.

The term "minicomputers" is mentioned less and less in trade journals. Many vendors prefer to call these machines "midrange" computers. Some experts predict the disappearance of both terms as the performance of smaller machines steadily increases.

THE MICROCOMPUTER REVOLUTION

As of the late 1980s, companies have been moving from larger computers to smaller computers. Typically, companies replace their mainframes with a network of powerful microcomputers. **Microcomputers** is the collective name for all desktop computers, also known as personal computers (PCs), because a single machine serves a single user. The more powerful micros are sometimes called **workstations**. Among manufacturers of workstations, Sun Microsystems is a leader. What makes one machine a workstation and another just a PC? It depends on whom you ask!

The speed of a computer is largely determined by the microprocessor chip around which it is built. IBM and IBM-compatible machines have traditionally used microprocessors made by Intel Corp. The current series of Intel microprocessors is called Pentium. Macintosh computers are built around Motorola-made chips or around PowerPC chips. The latter are the result of a joint venture among Apple, IBM, and Motorola.

As the power of microcomputers rapidly increases, it is sometimes difficult to draw the line between the most powerful micros and the low-end minis. The term **low-end** means the cheaper, least powerful computer in its category; **high-end** refers to the most expensive, most powerful computers in a category.

	1992	1993	1994	1995
US PC Makers				
Units sold (million)	11.8	14.8	16.1	19.8
Increase from previous year		25.5%	8.8%	23%
Worldwide				
Units sold (million)	30.4	36.1	40.6	
Increase from previous year		18.8%	12.5%	

Source: International Data Corp., 1995 and U.S. Census Bureau, 1997.

Figure 3.13 *PC sales have increased tremendously in recent years.*

Compaq		Packard Bell
IBM		AST Research
Apple		NCR
Dell		Digital
Gateway		Hewlett-Packard

Figure 3.14 *The top ten PC makers*

The trend in the corporate world is clearly to equip offices with desktop computers. The power of microcomputers doubles every 18 months. The sharp drop in prices has made this class of machines very attractive to even the smallest of businesses.

Figure 3.13 shows how the microcomputer market grew 23% between 1994 and 1995, which considerably outpaces the growth of other computer markets. Figure 3.14 presents the biggest makers of microcomputers. For several years, these companies have been at the top of the industry in terms of units sold and revenues. Figure 3.15 shows the expected distribution of new PCs in the world. Note the great increase expected in Asia.

COMPUTERS ON THE GO: LAPTOP AND NOTEBOOK COMPUTERS

How can you use a computer outside the office? You use a laptop or notebook computer. The **laptop computer** is a compact, light, personal computer operated by a rechargeable battery. The monitor is flat. When folded, the computer looks like a small flat box and can be carried by hand or in a briefcase. Most laptops are about 12 x 8 inches in size, and weigh three–eight pounds. The battery allows them to operate for up to four hours without recharging. Thinner models of laptops are known as **notebooks**.

Many laptops have accessories through which the user can communicate with other computers, and even send and receive faxes. Prices of the machines are close to those of microcomputers, but with the spread of their use, prices are expected to drop.

	1995 (MILLIONS OF UNITS)	*2000* (MILLIONS OF UNITS)
North America	24.7	44.4
Western Europe	15.2	24.4
Asia	12.1	33.7
Rest of the world	6.1	13.9
Source: International Data Corporation 1996		

Figure 3.15 *Shipments of PCs, past and future (in millions of units)*

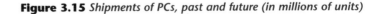

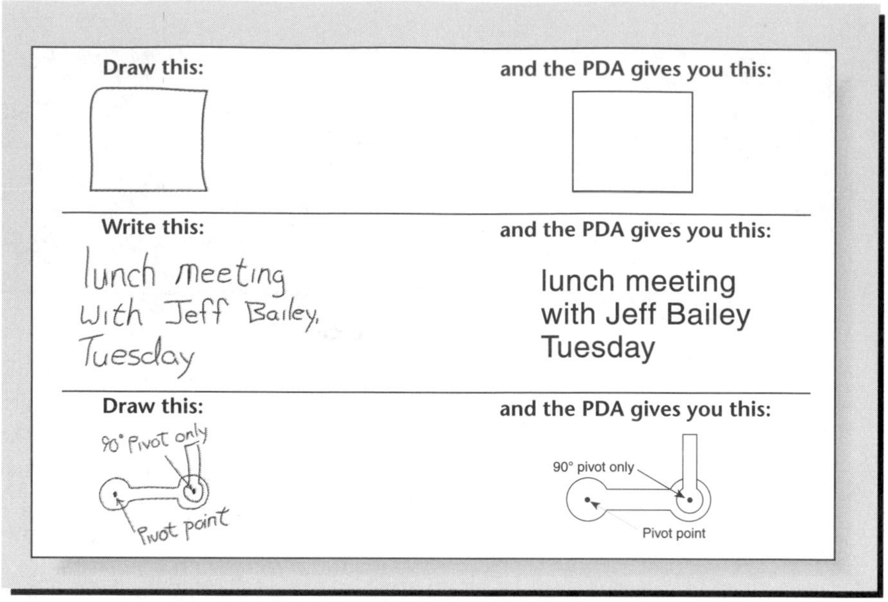

Figure 3.16 *A PDA's operating system is intelligent enough to turn rough drawings into neat ones or handwriting into text.*

The latest class of computing machinery is comprised of **hand-held computers** or **personal digital assistants** (PDAs). These are small enough to fit in the palm of a person's hand and typically use an electronic pen to enter data. Their most useful characteristic is their ability—still somewhat imperfect—to recognize handwritten text, numbers, and drawings, and turn them into word-processable documents and neat shapes, as shown in Figure 3.16.

While PDA's handwriting interpretation is imperfect, the small machines are very useful for storing notes and drawings when away from the office. These can then be either transferred to a larger computer or printed out. Many PDAs come with optional equipment that allows the user to transmit files to another computer or fax them via telephone lines.

REDUCED INSTRUCTION SET COMPUTING

Because the business market is so large, it is worthwhile for computer manufacturers to produce computers with CPUs designed especially for business. These CPUs lack the ability to execute instructions that are nonessential to most business applications, making them both less expensive and faster in a business setting. Computers with such CPUs are called **reduced instruction set computing**, or RISC, computers. The majority of high-end microcomputers, especially those called "workstations", are RISC computers. These computers trade off some computing functions for speed, but the user does not miss anything if those functions are not necessary for his or her work.

When software and peripheral devices from one computer can be used with another computer, the machines are said to be **compatible**. If the circuitry of one computer is different from the circuitry of the other computer, they are incompatible. Because there are no imposed standards in the computer industry, machines made by one vendor often are incompatible with those of another vendor. For example, an IBM microcomputer is incompatible with a Macintosh.

Before purchasing new computers, managers must consider the compatibility of the machines. If computers in different departments of an organization are not expected to "talk to each other," compatibility is not that important. But an increasing number of companies connect their computers in a network so that databases and other computing resources can be shared. Thus, in addition to power and cost, compatibility is an extremely important factor in purchasing decisions.

CONSIDERATIONS IN THE PURCHASE OF HARDWARE

Decisions about the purchase of computers are usually made by IS professionals in an organization or with the help of a consulting firm. But surveys show a new trend: an increasing number of end users are involved in the computer-purchase decision-making process. More and more companies realize that more effective usage will result if their employees are satisfied with the computers and other equipment installed in their workplace. The move from large computers to microcomputers is a contributor to this trend.

What should you ask when buying hardware? Managers must consider many things. First comes the equipment's power: the speed, the size of the memory, and the capacity of storage devices, such as the hard disk that is installed in the computer case. Some computers allow the expansion of RAM through the addition of RAM chips onto the motherboard. In other models, sockets are left unused for adding whole boards in the future.

It is important to check whether or not the computer has several sockets called **ports** to connect it to external devices: printers, hard disks, and communications devices. A greater number of ports gives more flexibility. If new needs arise in the future, you can simply buy the required device and attach it to the computer.

Most microcomputers come with a monitor and a keyboard. It is important to check the monitor's resolution. Higher resolution is more pleasing and less straining to the eyes. See how flexible the adjustment of the colors and hues is. Examine how ergonomic the hardware is. **Ergonomics** is the study of the comfort and safety of human beings in their working environment. An ergonomic computer does not strain the eyes and arms. For example, the keyboard must be comfortable to work with. Traditional keyboards cause muscle pain when used for long sessions. Consider purchasing a split ergonomic keyboard.

If space is scarce, you may want to consider the size of the computer and its peripheral equipment. The **footprint** is the area that a computer occupies. A smaller footprint will leave more desk space for other devices.

Inquire about the reliability of the vendor, the warranty policy, and the support you may receive after the warranty expires. Try to assess how soon the equipment will be obsolete. This is not an easy task in a reality of fast developments.

All of the above must be weighed against one important factor: cost. Careful study may yield hardware with excellent performance for an affordable price.

PDAs are becoming popular devices for people who spend a lot of time outside the office.

Used by permission from Apple Computer, Inc.

Factor	What to look for	Score
Power		
Speed	Greater frequency and word size	_____
RAM capacity	Larger	_____
Expandability	Greater number of board slots for additional RAM	_____
Ports	Greater number of ports for printer, external hard disk, communication devices and other peripherals	_____
Ergonomics	Greater comfort and safety	_____
Compatiblity		
with hardware	Compatibility with many other computers and peripheral devices from the same and other manufacturers	_____
with software	Compatibility with many software packages currently used and potentially to be used	_____
Footprint	Smaller area	_____
Support	Availability of telephone support for troubleshooting	_____
	Supply of information on new upgrades	_____
Warranty	Longer warranty period	_____
Cost	Lower cost	_____

Figure 3.17 *Example of a hardware evaluation form*

Perusing trade journals is extremely helpful. Many periodicals provide evaluation tables of comparable hardware. The hardware is tested in laboratories by impartial technicians. You do not have to be an IS professional to understand the evaluation.

The above-mentioned factors, and others that you should consider when purchasing hardware, are summarized in Figure 3.17. It is useful to attach a quantitative score to each category on a 10-point scale. The internal needs of your organization, or even of your department, may require you to add some factors. The equipment receiving the highest score is the best in the evaluator's opinion.

As you can see, the terms in Figure 3.17 are relative. It is often difficult to evaluate hardware in absolute terms. Therefore, it may be helpful to rank each

category while comparing each component with the hardware that is the best in that category.

Small but Powerful

During his residency at the University of Texas at Houston Medical School, Dr. Thomas Giannulli, an internist, first realized that the way doctors and other health-care workers handle information regarding patients' histories, diagnoses, and treatment could stand some improving. "I was required to capture so much data and report on so much information that was so critical, and I had no tools to help me," Giannulli said. "I used to write things down three times: once for a chart, once for me, and once for my colleagues."

Giannulli experimented with several devices, including laptops, and several computer programs to make his work more efficient, all to no avail. Each device had a critical disadvantage, from too short a battery life to a lack of portability. "Given the fact that there was always a power-supply or keyboard requirement, I could never get the speed and efficiency I was really looking for," Giannulli said. But

he didn't stop looking for the appropriate technology.

In 1994, he found the right device: Apple Computer's Newton MessagePad. It was ideal for the doctor's record keeping. It provided a relatively long battery life and used pen input requiring simple gestures, enabling users to communicate very quickly. Using his engineering background, he wrote special software that enabled users to simply point to items on their personal digital assistant (PDA) to quickly and easily create and track data files. He then founded a software development company to further develop the software. With the tap of a stylus, health-care providers can complete an entire patient record, send prescriptions to the pharmacy, collect billing information, and access other medical data.

He named the new software pocketCHART. As soon as the patient walks into a clinic or hospital, the staff using pocketCHART can begin inputting information including the patient's personal data and medical history. They can then create and store notes based on their conversation with the patient. Using information collected during the examination, the

doctor can select a course of treatment by pulling up menus within the software that list all of the various options for every possible recommendation, from lab tests to medications.

In 1997, more than 2,500 physicians used the device. Giannulli said: "The device gives you the dosage for the drugs prescribed and how to administer them, and it allows you to set up your care plans and maintain consistency in your treatment. It improves care in that you're less prone to error because you have past medical records and correct information at the point of decision ... and you have immediate access to all the information right in your pocket."

Source: Jacobson, V.B., "The Prescription: Palmtops," Mobile Computing & Communications, March 1997, pp. 52–54.

Questions

1. What features make the pocketCHART device so successful in clinics and hospitals? Enumerate the features and explain their benefits.

2. Doctors are notorious for being slow to adopt IT in their work. In what way does the device support the traditional manner doctors recorded information during their rounds?

Taking Off With Imaging

Northwest Airlines, the nation's fourth largest airline, has deployed a massive 45-user imaging system to capture and process the ticket stubs printed by Northwest gate agents and independent travel agents and carried by Northwest passengers. "We can now do everything on a timely basis, with a slightly smaller staff and a larger airline," said Scott Grengs, project analyst of distributed services, and one of the people closest to the passenger revenue accounting system.

Mainframe-based DB2 databases will continue to handle the marketing department's needs for the foreseeable future. The 442 users of the system, working on diskless workstations, are connected over a local area network, which is attached to an image server and image library. The library contains as many as 408 optical discs for a total online capacity of 40 million documents.

One notable benefit has been to bring the processing load up to date. "When I started here four years ago," says Grengs, "we were, at times, as much as six months behind in processing the ticket stubs." Today, the system produces revenue or audit reports "accurately and on time," Grengs said.

Under the 20-year-old manual system, the revenue and marketing departments could only extrapolate their numbers, manually conducting a 5% audit of all the tickets. The problem was the volume of these ticket coupons: in peak months, Northwest processes 270,000 daily. The 5% audit, while adequate for billing and revenue projections, fell far short of the needs of Northwest's marketing department, which wanted more timely and detailed information to monitor the effectiveness of its marketing campaigns.

"Marketing needs to know a lot more about what's happening, where and when people fly, and which products they're using," said Mike Shields, project manager of the marketing analysis system at Northwest's Information Services Group. "Now we capture 100%," said Shields, adding that several benefits have flowed from this change. For example, Northwest can now accurately monitor the fares and commissions charged by independent travel agents. An even greater value, he said, will be a subsystem to track incentive and promotional programs.

For example, this will let Northwest monitor, for the first time, the effectiveness of short-term flight discounts or promotional tie-ins with hotel chains. Shields emphasized that the data coming from the system are being integrated with other sources, such as Northwest's flight schedules. "We're working now on bringing these data sources together so that they can be accessed by marketing and applications development," Shields said.

Source: Booker, E., "Northwest productivity takes off with imaging," Computerworld, Vol 25 No 10, March 11, 1994, p. 31. Reprinted with the permission of Computerworld Magazine.

Questions

1. What were the problems that prompted Northwest to adopt imaging?

2. How does the imaging system solve these problems?

Saving With Optical Discs

A shift to optical storage has brought savings in time and payroll for a minicomputer support unit at Nynex Corp. subsidiaries New England Telephone and New York Telephone. The Telesector Resource Group is responsible for the operation and backup of the two companies' DEC VMS systems. Within the past 18 months, the department moved from using magnetic tape to collecting data from many systems to using an automated optical disc library from Eastman Kodak Co.

The Kodak library holds five 5.25-inch optical drives and stores up to 60 GB. At the same time, Telesector centralized its recovery storage. "We decided to centralize our methodology and get the labor out of it," said Jack Sullivan, senior systems specialist at Telesector. "We didn't want a different backup scheme on every single system," he said.

The Kodak system saved the company $25,000 in the first year because it obviated the need to hire additional operators to monitor the backup process. Another savings is time, according to Sullivan, who reported that the optical backup takes four hours, less than half the time operators needed to copy data onto magnetic tape.

With the new backup approach, three sets of optical discs are used, stored and reused in rotation. Data are copied onto optical discs once a week, and the discs are sent off-site for two weeks. Discs are returned for reuse after two weeks, once the data they contain have become obsolete.

"This is a different backup schedule than we had for the magnetic tape, since we can hold much more data on each disc," said Ed Macgillivray, technical support person at Telesector. One optical disc per system is required

today, compared with ten magnetic tapes before, he said.

Source: Booker, E., "Nynex unit opts for optical disc storage," Computerworld, January 10, 1994, p. 62. Reprinted with permission of Computerworld Magazine.

Questions

1. Why doesn't Nynex use CD-ROMs? What type of compact discs does it use, and why?

2. Many companies have moved from using magnetic tape as a backup medium to using magnetic disks. Nynex leaped to compact discs. What is the main advantage of this medium over magnetic disks?

3. Optical discs have a disadvantage, compared with magnetic disks. What is this disadvantage, and why is it a negligible factor in the company's decision to use optical discs?

SUMMARY

In a 1993 survey, 41% of IS executives said that they saw an increase in end-user influence over hardware buying decisions in the workplace. As a manager, you can no longer afford to say "Understanding hardware is not my job; it's the IS manager's responsibility." Eventually, it is you who will use the computer. If you are comfortable with it, your productivity may increase and you will draw more satisfaction from your performance. So, take advantage of any opportunity you have to participate in choosing new hardware and implementing new systems.

Regardless of size and power, all computers must have several components to function. The "brain" of every computer is its **central processing unit**, which consists of complex circuitry on a piece of silicon wafer, and controls four basic operations: it retrieves instructions from **internal memory**, decodes them, executes them, and stores the results in internal memory. The rate at which the CPU can do all of that is the computer's frequency. Frequency and the size of the **data word** (the number of bits that can be moved through the CPU in one machine cycle) are the primary determinants of computer speed, which is a major factor in measuring computer power. The other factor is the size of the internal memory.

Computer memory can be classified in two ways: by volatility and data organization. The larger part of the internal memory is **RAM** (random access memory)

and is **volatile**, but **ROM** (read-only memory) is **nonvolatile**. Unlike data in RAM, data stored in ROM are not erased when the computer is turned off. Similarly, all **external storage media**, such as **magnetic disks** and **optical discs**, are nonvolatile.

While internal memory is used directly by the CPU, data is also saved on external storage media. When evaluating external storage, the factors to consider are the capacity of the medium, its **transfer time**, and the form of data organization that it allows. Data on some storage media, such as magnetic tapes, can be organized and retrieved only sequentially; **direct access storage devices**, such as RAM, magnetic disks, and optical discs, allow both sequential and random organization and retrieval. The latter provides faster storage and retrieval of records that must be accessed individually and quickly, as in airline reservation systems.

To enter data and instructions into computers we use **input devices** such as **keyboards** and mice. **Imaging** devices help in processing large amounts of text and graphic data, and have made work in banks and other industries more productive. **Output devices**, such as monitors and **printers**, display the results of the processing.

When considering the purchase of external storage media, managers must be aware not only of cost, but also of the trade-offs among media capabilities. They should take into account the speed of storage and retrieval, and the purpose of storage. While the storage capacity of optical discs is several hundred times greater than that of magnetic disks, magnetic disks provide faster access. Thus, **compact discs** would be appropriate for storage of library material, but magnetic disks are the appropriate medium for transaction processing. If the purpose of the storage is backup, then magnetic tapes still provide a feasible low-cost alternative.

For ease of reference, computers are classified into several categories according to their power. The most powerful are **supercomputers**, which are used mainly by research institutions for massive calculations. Somewhat less powerful are **mainframe computers**, still used by many organizations to process large databases and perform other fast tasks. **Minicomputers**, also referred to as "midrange" computers are less powerful and often are not much larger, physically, than PCs. PCs are used by individuals, but many organizations connect them as clients to more powerful computers that are servers in a **client/server** arrangement.

When purchasing computers, managers should consider computer power and other factors in addition to cost. Managers should consider expandability of RAM, the availability of sockets for connection of **peripheral equipment**, and compatibility with existing hardware.

Like many new technologies, information technology threatens the health of users. For computer users, the most common problems are repetitive stress musculo-skeletal ailments, such as carpal tunnel syndrome, which are caused by the uninterrupted repetitive use of the keyboard over long periods of time. Today, manufacturers of computer equipment pay more attention to health hazards, and try to design the devices **ergonomically**.

As you will see throughout this book, hardware components are combined in many different configurations to help businesses streamline operations and attain strategic goals. But hardware is rarely the first consideration in the acquisition of a new IS. When planning a new IS, managers should first determine the business needs, and then consider which software can support those needs. Only then should they select the hardware that supports the software. Software is the focus of our next chapter.

REVIEW, DISCUSS, AND EXPLORE

REVIEW AND DISCUSSION QUESTIONS

1. Give two examples of tasks performed by the ALU.

2. Because information technology advances so rapidly, it is difficult for managers to make informed decisions regarding the purchase of computers and peripheral equipment. What are the factors that cause these difficulties?

3. Which industries *cannot* use imaging to improve their operations, and why?

4. Comment on the following statement: Large computers, such as mainframes and supercomputers, have no future.

5. What are the technological achievements that enabled the building of laptop and PDA computers?

6. What are the advantages and disadvantages of optical storage media (such as CDs and optical tape) and of magnetic media?

7. The role of end users in making hardware purchasing decisions is growing. Analyze the technological development and operational reasons for this trend.

8. *Ethics and Sociey*: What are the health hazards associated with the use of computers? What can be done to alleviate each type of health risk?

Recommend one of the three computer configurations in the table below for each of the scenarios listed below. Assume that the prices of all of the computer configurations are equal. Explain your choice.

The scenarios are:

1. Employees do a lot of graphic design work. Graphics require large programs. The printouts must be of high quality.

2. This firm will use the computer mainly for word processing. The biggest application occupies 24 MB.

3. The employees save their work on floppy disks. They use scientific programs that are small but run for many hours.

4. It is imperative that all the employees' work be stored on one disk, and that the material be available as soon as anyone logs on to the computer.

Features	Computer Configuration		
	A	B	C
RAM	32 MB	64 MB	32 MB
Secondary Storage			
Hard Disk	500 MB	250 MB	120 MB
Floppy Drive	1.44 MB	1.44 MB	1.44 MB
Speed	120 MHz	150 MHz	180 MHz
Printer			
	Laser	Ink Jet	Laser
	600	300 DPI	300 DPI
	4 PPM	2 PPM	8 PPM

HANDS-ON ACTIVITY

Choose a personal computer, preferably a computer at your school's PC lab. Research the hardware components. Use a word-processing program to prepare a full report on the computer: the computer model, the microprocessor it uses, the types of ports (outlets) it has, the amount of RAM, how much the RAM can be expanded by, and other specifications you find of interest. Similarly, describe the specifications of the peripheral equipment: the keyboard (is it ergonomic?), the monitor, and the printer to which the computer is connected.

TEAM ACTIVITY

You and your team members should type up the evaluation form found in Figure 3.17. Visit a computer hardware store and write down the specifications of three sets of equipment: a computer, a keyboard, a compatible 17-inch color monitor, and a laser printer. Each configuration should be for a student who needs it for his or her studies at your school. Obtain printed or verbal information on each configuration. For each configuration, the team should evaluate the features on a scale of 1–10 (1=worst; 10=best) and total the points. Which configuration would you recommend to your fellow students? Be ready to explain your recommendation.

EXPLORE THE WEB

"Shop" the Web for hardware. Access three vendors who sell via the Web. Summarize your impression of the sites, addressing these points: (1) Which site was the most informative? (2) Which site was the most attractive in appearance? (3) Which site provided the most convenient manner of "electronic" payment?

Chapter **4**

Information Technology in Business: Software

Off-the-Shelf or Homemade Software?

Like those of many companies, for years Chrysler Corp.'s computer programs, whether used by accountants to generate paychecks or by engineers to design cars, were developed in-house from scratch. Scores of programmers spent thousands of hours writing code. Over the years, however, a slew of vendor-developed and off-the-shelf programs became available to do the same jobs. The new programs could be purchased for a lot less money than the cost of development. The big auto maker started to ponder whether it needed to develop all the necessary programs by itself. The issue was not a simple one. Because not all available programs fit the company's needs exactly, Chrysler had to contemplate the trade-offs between cutting costs and adjusting operations. A policy was needed to decide which software to develop in-house, and which to purchase. What should the criteria be?

Chrysler Corp. decided to adopt a best-of-a-kind policy in its acquisition of software. "I am a big believer that we do not have to create everything ourselves," said Sue Unger, Chrysler's Chief Information Officer and executive director of information services. Chrysler installed PeopleSoft's human resources management software package and Dun & Bradstreet Software's SmartStream financial application.

But the $53 billion automaker's IS group, with worldwide staff of 1,300, built its own factory information system to monitor problems on the factory floor. "If something is out of our specifications, the system lets us know," Unger says. "We are trying to automate processes so that we get things right on the factory floor from the beginning, to eliminate errors and improve quality." Unger concluded that only Chrysler personnel could develop appropriate software to achieve this goal.

Chrysler also has a massive object-oriented development effort, using Smalltalk to replace 12 mainframe payroll systems with a single system. The company could have gone with an off-the-shelf package, but as Unger explains, none fits its needs: "We cannot find anything out there that can match what we are doing."

Source: Wilder, C., "Start with the Best, then Build on it," *InformationWeek*, September 9, 1996, pp. 158-166.

Hardware, the "nuts and bolts" of the computer and its peripheral equipment, can do nothing without proper instructions. Computer instructions are called programs, or software. Many IS professionals refer to computer programs as "systems" because they are comprised of components working to achieve a common goal. As a manager, you must be able to make educated decisions regarding the selection of software. To do so, you must understand the factors involved in developing, selecting, and running software.

When you finish this chapter you will:

◆ Understand why managers must keep abreast of developments in software

◆ Understand how different generations of programming languages differ

◆ Understand the difference between application software and system software

◆ Understand the strengths and weaknesses of tailored software vs. off-the-shelf software

◆ Be familiar with the latest developments in application and system software

◆ Have the basic tools for evaluating packaged software applications for business use

SOFTWARE: INSTRUCTIONS TO THE COMPUTER

As mentioned in the previous chapter, a computer program is a series of instructions to a computer to execute any and all processes, whether displaying text, mathematically manipulating numbers, or copying or deleting documents. As you may remember, the only type of instruction computers understand is made up of series of electrical signals alternating between two states, either on/off or high/low voltage: different signals sent through different wires in the computer represent different instructions. In the early days of computers, programming a computer meant actually changing the computer wiring, which was done by opening and closing switches or moving plugs from one circuit to another. Turning the computer on with the new arrangement triggered a series of electrical pulses that resulted in different computations.

The instructions that make up programs today, because they do not require the reconfiguring of hardware, have come to be known as **software**. The process of writing programs is **programming**. To write programs, programmers use programming languages.

PROGRAMMING LANGUAGES

Remember, the *only* "language" that computer hardware can understand is a series of on/off electrical signals that represent bits and bytes, which together provide the computer hardware with instructions to carry out certain operations. But to write programs in that "language"—which is called **machine language**—would require a programmer to literally create long lists of *ons* and *offs* to represent different characters and symbols. While it can be done, this process is painstaking and time-consuming. For computing to progress, the programming process had to become more efficient, and it did.

Computer experts started creating **programming languages**, which are abbreviated forms of instructions that are automatically translated into machine language so the computer can understand them. Regardless of the programming language used, every program must ultimately be translated into machine language in order for each computer to carry out the instructions. With new programming languages, the programming process became more efficient and easier to understand for people who were not necessarily hardware experts. Today, programmers have at their disposal literally thousands of different programming languages.

RUNNING PROGRAMS

Programs are needed for absolutely every operation a computer conducts. That operation can be as simple as adding 1+2, typing a word, or emitting a "beep," or as complicated as producing a color picture and calculating the trajectory of a spacecraft to Mars. Learning about software, programs, and programming languages can be confusing partly because programs are used to write programs, and the "translations" of programs to machine code are also conducted by programs—that also have to be written using programs! However, *writing* a program, which is developing a series of instructions, is not the same as *running* a program, which is translating the program into machine language and sending the series of instructions to the CPU.

In the previous chapter, we learned that in order for a computer to execute program instructions, the program must first reside in the computer's primary memory. Certain operations that are routine and must be performed every time the computer is turned on will most probably reside in **read-only memory** (**ROM**). These include, for example, the message "Non-System disk or disk error; Replace and strike any key when ready" on a PC, or a sad face on a Macintosh when the computer cannot find a proper program with which to run software.

Other instructions must first be "loaded," that is, read into **random access memory** (**RAM**). These instructions will be run only as long as they reside in the primary memory. Once the run is complete, another set of instructions may be run. Of course, some computers, if their RAM is large enough, can load and run more than one program at the same time.

LEVELS OF PROGRAMMING LANGUAGES

Programming languages have evolved dramatically over the years. Their different stages of development are known as **generations.** First- and second-generation languages were quite inefficient in terms of code writing. They required lengthy written code for even the simplest instructions. Third- and fourth-generation languages, developed over the past four decades, replaced lengthy code with shorter commands. Ultimately, it would be nice to be able to program using your native language—English, French, Hebrew, or any other. But even then, there would have to be a translation of the so-called "natural language" into machine language (see Figure 4.1).

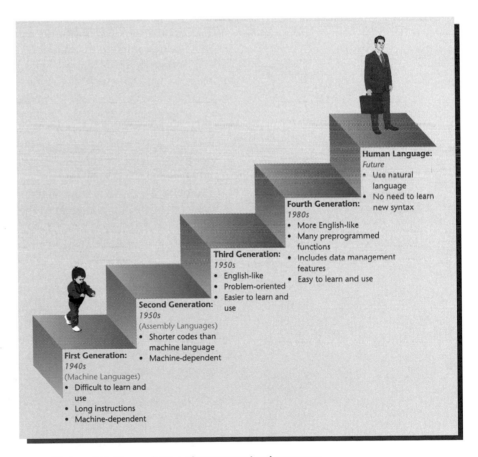

Figure 4.1 *The evolution of programming languages*

MACHINE LANGUAGES

Machine languages are the oldest programming languages and the only ones that computers can directly interpret to carry out instructions. They consist of groups of binary code, or bytes, that represent everything, from alphabet characters and arithmetic and logic operations to storage locations in RAM and the CPU. Remember that all this is written in zeroes and ones only.

Machine language programmers used coding sheets to write their programs. With each byte of seven or eight bits representing a single character, imagine how much code they had to write for each instruction. Not only was coding in machine language very time-consuming, but it offered myriad chances to make errors. Programmers had to concern themselves with details of the hardware that was to be used when the program ran, because the programs had to be written to manipulate a particular machine.

The term "machine language" does not refer to a single language. Every computer, or family of computers sharing the same features, has its own machine language that uses instructions that fit the hardware, including memory addresses, register numbers, and the like. Therefore, machine languages are said to be machine-dependent, or machine-specific.

ASSEMBLY LANGUAGES

In the early 1950s, programmers realized that many of the machine operations were used over and over again. There was no point in reprogramming routine instructions like *read*, which tells the computer to load something into RAM, *write*, which tells the computer to print, or *put*, which tells the computer to store. To save programming time, the long strings of zeroes and ones that represent such commands were represented by, or assembled into, a single three- or four-letter instruction. The newly created languages were called **assembly languages**. Like machine languages, assembly languages are machine-dependent, because the programmer must understand machine-specific details such as addressable CPU **registers**, in order to write programs. The main advantage of using assembly languages is that their code is more English-like and significantly shorter than code in machine language (see Figure 4.2).

Obviously, computers are unable to understand any languages whose level is higher than machine language. Therefore, a special program was needed to *translate* the assembly language into machine language. This translation program is called an **assembler**.

The main disadvantages of both machine and assembly languages are the long time it takes to learn them, and the high probability of errors. But these low-level languages have two major advantages. First, the programmer is in full control of how the hardware is used. Second, because the programmer has so much control over the hardware, programs written in low-level languages run, on the average, more efficiently than those written in higher-level languages. That is, the programs use minimum CPU time and memory space. Machine and assembly languages are referred to as first- and second-generation languages, respectively.

PROCEDURAL LANGUAGES

The growth of computer use in higher education and business in the 1950s prompted the creation of higher-level programming languages. **Third-generation** languages are significantly more English-like than assembly languages. Commands

PROGRAMMING LANGUAGE	CODE
IBM System 370 machine language:	00000101 00001000 00000010 00000000 00001100 00010000 00010000 00000000 00000101 00001010 00000010 00000000 00001100 00010000 00010000 00000100 00000101 00000000 00000010 00000000 00001100 00000001 00000000 00000000
IBM System 370 assembler language:	L R2, = F'2' A R2, = F'5' ST R2,Y
Third-generation languages	
FORTRAN:	y = 2+5
COBOL:	add 2,5 giving y
BASIC:	let y = 2+5;
C, C++:	y = 2+5;
Fourth-generation languages:	y = 2+5

Figure 4.2 *The instruction "ADD 2 and 5 and assign the result to variable y" is displayed in different programming languages.*

like *read, write, add a to b, let x=0*, and so on, became abundant. Third-generation languages are referred to as **problem-oriented** because they allow the programmer to focus on the problem at hand without having to be concerned with how the hardware will execute the program. Third-generation languages are also considered to be **procedural** because the programmer has to detail a logical procedure that will solve the problem at hand.

Procedural languages include **FORTRAN** (**FOR**mula **TRAN**slation), **COBOL** (**CO**mmon **B**usiness **O**riented **L**anguage), and **BASIC** (**B**eginners **A**ll-purpose **S**ymbolic **I**nstruction **C**ode). A third-generation program is a set of procedures or steps for the computer to carry out. Other software, called systems software discussed below, decides which registers to use, where in RAM to store the program and data, and other utilizations of the computer hardware, software, and data resources. In earlier languages, programmers had to make all those choices with the execution of each step.

Just as assembly languages need their assemblers, procedural languages need special programs to translate **source code**, which is the program as originally written, into **object code**, which is the same program in machine language.

Compared with assembly languages, third-generation languages offer programmers great advantages. They are relatively easy to learn; writing is easier thanks to the English-like commands; and debugging, which is the process of finding and correcting errors, is reasonably easy, especially for an experienced programmer. The main disadvantages are the lack of control over how the hardware is used, and, as a result, the fact that procedural programs usually run less efficiently.

However, as speed and memory space of computers are growing, the effectiveness of programs in helping organizations reach their goals is more important than the efficient use of computer resources.

Some languages, such as FORTRAN 77, COBOL, and some versions of BASIC, are said to be **standardized** or **portable**. A language is portable if its source code can run on different computers using different operating systems. Languages are considered portable even if they require some minute changes, such as replacing double quotation marks with single quotation marks, or dots with semicolons, in order to be executable on another type of machine. When applied to another machine, a portable source program may have to be modified for the new hardware, but this is usually an inconsequential task compared to rewriting the entire source program.

FOURTH-GENERATION LANGUAGES

Fourth-generation languages (4GLs) make application development even easier. They are often connected to database management systems that allow the programmer to create database structures, populate them with data, and manipulate the data. Many routine procedures are preprogrammed and can be incorporated into a program with simple insert procedures, such as making a selection from a menu or pressing a function key.

For example, if one of the columns in a database is AGE, the programmer can simply use the preprogrammed command LIST AVERAGE(AGE) to display on the screen the average age in all of the records. Similarly, there are preprogrammed functions for total, standard deviation, count, median, and so forth. Simple commands like LIST and LOCATE are used to list certain columns or records from the database, and to locate records that meet certain conditions.

4GL commands are more English-like than procedural languages' commands. In fact, 4GLs are significantly less procedural than 3GLs. This is because often the programmer only has to say what is to be done, but doesn't have to specify the procedure that will accomplish the task. For example, the programmer only needs to use the word AVERAGE, but does not need to specify how the average should be calculated. The 4GL already contains the procedure.

Popular 4GLs include PowerBuilder, FOCUS, NOMAD, and RAMIS. Because these languages are easy to learn and can be used to produce code quickly, some vendors prefer to call their 4GLs **application generators**. Indeed, more and more software houses use 4GLs to develop new application software.

Using some advanced 4GLs, programs can be written using input and output forms and menus and icons only, without ever writing code. The software creates the source code in the background, so that it can later be modified as needed. This type of language is often referred to as a **code generator**.

The advantages of 4GLs are obvious: the ease of learning and use shortens the time needed to develop new application software. The disadvantage is the fact that most programs written in 4GL use the computer's resources inefficiently and require an exorbitant amount of computer memory, due to the large size of the languages themselves. But, as mentioned above, these are usually not considered serious shortcomings.

OBJECT-ORIENTED PROGRAMMING

In recent years, another type of language has gained popularity—object-oriented programming (OOP) language The two great advantages of the modular

- OOP requires less code than other languages
- Programming in OOP requires less time than in other languages
- OOP enhances program modularity and reusability
- OOP makes code maintenance easier
- OOP enhances ability to create user-friendly interface
- OOP is appropiate for graphic- and sound-enhanced applicatons

Figure 4.3 *Advantages of object-oriented programming (OOP) over third- and fourth-generation languages*

approach used in this language are its ease of maintenance and its efficiency in applications development (see Figure 4.3). In traditional programming, programmers receive specifications of how a program should process data, and how it should interact with users, and then they write code. If the business changes and the program must be modified accordingly, the programmer then must return to the code and change it. In traditional programming, data and the operations to manipulate the data are kept separate. In **object-oriented programming (OOP)** the operations are linked to the data. For example, if the operation is to calculate an employee's gross pay, taxes, and net pay, selecting the record and clicking on it will trigger the calculation. Routine, frequent operations are kept with the data to be processed. Thus, the primary emphasis in OOP is not on the procedure for performing a task, but on the objects involved in the task.

WHAT IS AN OBJECT? An **object** encapsulates a set of data with the code that is used to operate on it. The data elements in the object are called "data members." The code elements of the object are called "member functions" or "methods." In object-oriented software there is no direct access to data members of an object; they can be accessed only through the methods of the interface, which is part of the object. The data are organized by attributes. For example, data in an hourly employee object may consist of social security number, last name, first name, address, date of birth, and hourly rate. As part of the object, three methods may be included: weekly pay, overtime pay, and age calculation. Figure 4.4 on the next page illustrates this object.

EASE OF MAINTENANCE Traditional programming is equivalent to making a new part every time a part in a car ceases to function. But mechanics do not make a new part; they take one off the shelf and replace the old with the new. One of the greatest advantages of object-oriented programming is that it allows for the equivalent of this in software development.

In object-oriented programming, software developers treat objects as parts or modules that are standardized and work together and can be used and reused. Instead of creating large, complex, tightly intertwined programs, programmers create objects. Objects are developed in standard ways, and have standard behaviors and interfaces. These modules enable software to be assembled rapidly rather than written laboriously.

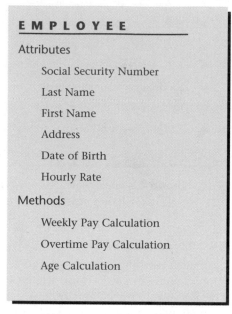

EMPLOYEE

Attributes

    Social Security Number

    Last Name

    First Name

    Address

    Date of Birth

    Hourly Rate

Methods

    Weekly Pay Calculation

    Overtime Pay Calculation

    Age Calculation

Figure 4.4 *The object EMPLOYEE*

In businesses, 60–85% of programmers' time is spent on maintenance of software. **Maintenance** includes ironing out bugs that were not detected in the final testing of a program, and modifying the program to meet new business needs. Imagine how much time could be saved if instead of writing new code the programmer could simply identify the old module and replace it with the new module. OOP allows reusability of code. Reusability saves much time and money.

OOP also makes it easier for nonprogrammers to create their programs. The inexperienced developer does not have to know how an object does what it does, only *what* it does. Thus, the developer can select and combine the appropriate objects from an **object library** to build a desired application.

Object-Oriented Programming Languages Object-oriented programming languages have been around for many years, but recently interest in them has become significant. The most popular OOP languages are SmallTalk and C++, an offshoot of the older C. While another popular language, Visual BASIC, does provide the programmer with the ability to use graphical objects, the language does not fulfill all the requirements of true OOP. For example, moving an icon to another application will not move the code with which it is associated. Some OOP languages are designed specifically for use in developing **graphical user interfaces (GUIs)**. These include windows, icons, and other graphical images that help the user interact with the program with minimum effort. For instance, the language Actor was used to develop Microsoft Windows applications.

Interestingly, object-oriented programming may be a concept more easily grasped by a beginning programmer than by an old-timer. Over the years, older programmers have become accustomed to the separation of data and procedures. The rigid distinction between data and instructions was dictated by procedural languages. A new learner naturally accepts the concept of data bundled with procedures when both the data and the procedures are used for a well-defined

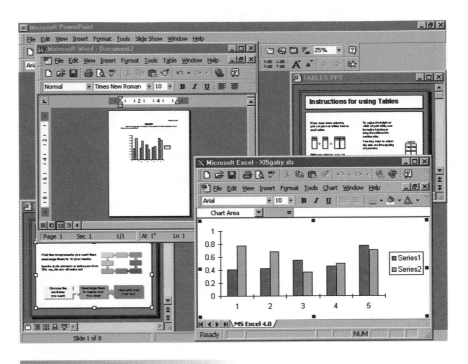

Object linking and embedding enables flexible and productive development of business reports and presentations.

purpose. Programmers who are comfortable with the concept immediately see the advantages of OOP: efficiency in application development and ease of maintenance.

OBJECT LINKING AND EMBEDDING Users often need to include data, graphics, and procedures in more than one document. Many operating systems and general application programs allow users to easily copy elements from one document to another. When the same element is to be used in different types of documents, an important feature is the ability to keep the connection, or "link," between these elements. Software that allows this type of operation provides a feature called **object linking and embedding (OLE)**.

Suppose you create a table in a spreadsheet that includes calculations of some of the cells. To prepare a report, you wish to include the table in your word-processed document. You copy the table from the spreadsheet to the document. If you change anything in the table, the changes are reflected in the report as well, because the software suite that you use keeps the link between the two documents. You can do similar things with charts that you import from a spreadsheet to a document created with presentation software.

Microsoft Office is a good example of an application set that supports OLE. You can create a chart using the spreadsheet program Excel, copy it into a text document created with the word processor Word, and then also copy it into a frame you create with the presentation program PowerPoint.

Like the links kept within a spreadsheet, OLE allows users to keep links among documents in different formats. This saves much time when preparing business reports and presentations: The user does not have to recreate an element that has already been prepared somewhere else.

Advantages of Higher Level Programming

◆ Ease of learning the language

◆ Ease of programming

◆ Code is significantly shorter

◆ Ease of debugging

◆ Ease of maintenance (for example, modification of a procedure)

Disadvantages of Higher Level Programming

◆ Less control over hardware

◆ Less efficient use of memory

◆ Program runs more slowly

Figure 4.5 *Advantages and disadvantages of higher-level programming languages*

While there are pros and cons to using higher-level languages, the pluses significantly outweigh the minuses (see Figure 4.5). Efficient use of memory and concerns about speed are becoming less important as computers come with increasing amounts of RAM and faster microprocessors. With the cost of computer power plummeting while the cost of personnel continues to increase, shorter training and less programming effort provide advantages that far outweigh the speed at which a computer runs a program.

APPLICATION SOFTWARE VS. SYSTEM SOFTWARE

Programming languages are used to develop many different types of software, which may be classified into two major categories: application software and system software. An **application** is a program that is developed to address a specific business need, or software that allows us to develop such programs. **System software** includes programs that are designed to carry out general routine operations, such as loading a file, copying a file, or deleting a file.

APPLICATION SOFTWARE

Application programs are designed either to address specific needs or to allow a user to develop programs that satisfy specific needs. Most of the programs used by managers, such as word-processing programs, spreadsheet programs, payroll programs, investment analysis programs, and work-scheduling and project management programs, are application programs. Some of these programs can be used to develop tailored programs.

Programs that are designed to perform specific jobs, such as calculating and executing a company's payroll, are called **application-specific software**. Programs that can be used for different purposes, such as developing decision-making tools or creating documents, are called **general-purpose application software**. Spreadsheets and word processors are general purpose applications.

Custom-Designed Applications

Often, an organization has a need that cannot be satisfied by any existing software. For example, if the cost-accounting procedures of a particular company are too specific to be met by any commercially available software, the company must develop its own **custom-designed** or **tailored** software. If the company has an information system department that can do the job, the application is developed in-house. If it does not, the company can hire a consulting firm that will develop the application for a fee.

Most of the software in organizations is tailored in some way to the company, often because of historical reasons. Many applications that are running today were developed in the 1960s and 1970s, when there were very few off-the-shelf applications available on the market. Another reason is that custom-designed programs are sometimes the only way to meet the specific needs of an organization. While custom-designed applications are more expensive than purchased ones, they afford several advantages: (1) the organization enjoys an application that meets its needs exactly, rather than having to settle for the "near" fit of an off-the-shelf program, (2) in-house developers are sensitive to the organizational culture, (3) special security measures can be integrated into the application, and (4) because the programmers are either employed by or easily accessible to the company, they are very familiar with the programs and can provide customized software maintenance.

The greatest disadvantage of tailored applications is the high cost. That is because in-house software development requires that all development costs be absorbed by the organization, whereas the costs of developing off-the-shelf applications are distributed over a large number of users. Another disadvantage of custom-designed development is that the production schedule is subject to long delays because IS personnel, either in-house or from a service provider, may not be available. The last but not least important downside of custom-designed software is that it is less likely to be compatible with other organizations' systems. ISs are more likely to be able to exchange data when they use the same application. If organizations with different tailor-made systems decide to link their systems, significant cost may be involved in the modification of one of the systems, or both (see Figure 4.6).

POINT OF INTEREST

Software Waste

Do PC users really need all their PC software? Egghead Software says no. The software reseller says that more than $2,000 worth of unnecessary or improperly licensed software is sitting on the average PC. Egghead has joined with Big Six accounting firm Deloitte & Touche to sell management tools for individuals to manage their financial assets, together with a database of licensing information on the 100 best-selling software products, to help track down and control that waste.

Source: "Stop Wasting Software," *Datamation*, January 15, 1994, p. 23. Reprinted with permission of Datamation Magazine. Copyright © 1994 by Cahners Publishing, Reed Elsevier Inc.

Advantages

- Good fit of features to business needs
- Good fit of features to organizational culture
- Available personnel for maintenance
- Smooth interfaces with other information systems

Disadvantages

- High cost
- Long wait for development if IS personnel are busy with other projects
- The application may be too organization-specific to be interfaced with other organizations' systems

Figure 4.6 *Advantages and disadvantages of tailored applications*

Advantages

- Low cost
- High quality
- Good vendor support
- Vendor upgrade for low cost
- Immediate availability
- Good documentation
- Conducive to sharing of applications and data

Disadvantages

- Features cater to the lowest common denominator of users' needs
- Often, the software addresses only a narrow spectrum of business needs
- Purchasers may be paying for features they don't need
- Impossible to alter to meet specific needs
- The vendor may go out of business, leaving the users without support

Figure 4.7 *Advantages and disadvantages of packaged software*

Net Notes

The University of Michigan Virtual Reality Lab maintains an interesting Web site on virtual reality and some demonstration software that you can load. Surf to *http://www-vrl.umich.edu*. Use the keywords *virtual reality* for other sites. Some sites offer free downloadable software that allows you to run demonstration applications. To see how VR is used in architecture, log on to the site of MRA (*http://www.mrabsi.com*), a firm which is a leader in VR use in this field.

Off-the-Shelf Software Packages Numerous software vendors now offer a large variety of off-the-shelf business software. Software ready to use is also called **packaged software** or **canned software**, because the users cannot revise the program. Many medium and small companies use packaged software for functions that are somewhat standardized across industries, such as operations in accounting, payroll, human resource management, project management, and the like. There are many similar programs for personal use as well: writing a will, preparing taxes, or managing personal finances, for example.

As described in Figure 4.7, there are several advantages to packaged software, including:

1. *Cost*: Since there are so many buyers, costs are distributed and prices are low. Many applications that would cost users thousands or hundreds of thousands of dollars to develop are sold for a few hundred dollars.
2. *Quality*: Because of the large market tapped by developers, off-the-shelf programs are tested and retested before being released for sale. When you buy a packaged program, chances are the program has been purged of all the bugs. However, it is advisable to wait a while and see what other businesses think about new software.
3. *Support*: Many software vendors offer a telephone support program for registered users. Usually, support is offered for a few months for free, and after that for a fee.
4. *Immediate availability*: Off-the-shelf software is available immediately. Developing customized business applications can take years.

Accent Multilingual Publisher

If you need more help, contact us at support@accentsoft.com

اما إذا كنت تحتاج إلى تعليمات أخرى فاتصل بنا على موقع support@accentsoft.com

Для получения дополнительной помощи обратитесь к нам по адресу support@accentsoft.com

לסיוע נוסף, התקשר עמנו לפי הכתובת support@accentsoft.com

Used by permission from Accent Software International Ltd.

New software packages allow users to work in many different languages.

To ensure the quality of the final release of a program into the mass market, many software companies finalize their programming according to feedback from companies that receive early test versions of their programs. The earliest testing is within the software development company, which is the alpha site; then, the developer releases the software to what are called beta sites, businesses that use the application for several months and report all problems found in the newly developed application. In return, these companies receive the final version either free of charge or for a reduced price.

The most common packaged software is general-use office software, such as word-processing programs, electronic spreadsheets, file managers, and database programs.

WORD PROCESSORS Word-processing software, programs used to prepare text documents, is the most widely used type of software, almost completely replacing the typewriter in the workplace. Writing is done by typing, and it is easy to perform copying, cutting, and pasting. With a little skill, a user can format any document, changing type fonts (or typefaces), type size, and even the color of the text. Searching to find a certain word or string of words takes seconds. When a letter must be sent to many addresses, it can be typed once and merged with a list of addresses stored in a separate file to produce personalized letters.

Advanced word processors come with large dictionaries and effective spell-checkers that help detect and correct misspelled words. Many programs come with a thesaurus to help users employ richer language and avoid duplication of words. Some programs allow the embedding of graphics within documents. Along with high-quality printers, advanced word-processing programs enable users to perform desktop publishing, preparing books and pamphlets for publication.

Among the popular word processors are WordPerfect and Microsoft Word, which are available for both IBM-compatible and Macintosh computers. Some programs, such as Accent, allow word processing in many different languages in the same document. The larger programs, such as Word, provide advanced features such as table-of-contents organization and indexing.

ELECTRONIC SPREADSHEETS Next to word processors, electronic spreadsheets have become the most popular type of software in business. Spreadsheet programs combine several tools that accountants have used for a long time into one computer-based application: a "sheet" divided into rows and columns that create "cells" for data, a calculator, and a way to enter information into the cells. The user enters data by typing, and conducts a calculation by entering an arithmetic formula into a cell that manipulates data from other cells; the program displays the results of the calculation in the cell that contains the formula. Whenever the value of any cell is changed, the values of all cells with formulas that reference the changed cell are recalculated automatically.

Managers Empowered by Spreadsheets. Spreadsheet programs run on desktop computers have put a powerful tool in the hands of managers. Although a user can see only that part of the spreadsheet that fits on the screen, the spreadsheet may be huge—several thousands of cells, allowing for the manipulation of enormous amounts of data. Early on, the most significant enhancement offered by spreadsheets was the elimination of human error in the manipulation of data; as long as the data entered in the appropriate cells are correct, the calculation of all the dependent values is correct. There is no need to check and recheck each calculation. This saved much time and greatly reduced the number of errors.

Many different fields and disciplines can benefit from spreadsheet technology. Businesspeople can use electronic spreadsheets to tabulate the number of units sold of each product at different time intervals, and quickly find out how much revenue and profit each product generated; human resource officers can tabulate and calculate corporate salaries of different positions; scientists can tabulate quantitative outcomes of scientific experiments; and social researchers can tabulate results of surveys and calculate different statistics.

Spreadsheets as Modeling Tools. The automatic recalculation of values in cells with underlying formulas provides a powerful modeling tool, allowing the user to view the effects of even slight changes in data. Spreadsheets can be set up with formulas representing relationships among data that mirror or "model" the relationships in an organization's operation. Then, the values of a cell or several cells can be changed to see the results of the change in other cells. This allows an easy way to conduct sensitivity analysis. For instance, if the mathematical relationships among several types of expenses and revenues are known, the value of a type of expense can be changed to see the impact on revenue.

Another example: a commodities trader may notice that there is a certain pattern in the price of flour over a 12-month period. She creates a spreadsheet with price data along with the apparent relationship predicting the price of flour in six months, expressed as a formula in one of the cells. The result appears in the cell with the underlying formula. When the trader changes the data to determine the effect on the six-month price, the new predicted price appears in the formula cell.

Spreadsheet programs provide graphical software that allows the user to create two-dimensional and three-dimensional diagrams from data contained in the spreadsheet: bars, lines, pie charts, turtle-wire graphs, and others. The data and diagrams can be placed in a text report in colors that make the presentation pleasing to the eye and easy to follow.

The programs also provide an increasing number of functions. Users can calculate net present values for investment analysis, statistics such as standard deviation and percentiles, frequency distribution, and other values.

The most popular spreadsheet programs are Lotus 1-2-3 and Excel. Both are available in versions for the most popular PC operating systems running on IBM-compatible and Macintosh computers. Figure 4.8 provides a simple example of spreadsheet use. The second table shows the values and formulas entered by the user. The top table shows the entered values and the results of formula calculations. The user chose a graph from a gallery of offered designs, and the program displayed it in the spreadsheet.

DATA MANAGEMENT PROGRAMS To manage data, managers use database management systems (DBMSs). These programs facilitate the construction of files, the ability to populate them with data, and the ability to find and manipulate the data flexibly to create a variety of reports. DBMSs can handle databases consisting of several files. We will devote Chapter 7, "Data Management," entirely to a discussion of data management.

Until the early 1980s, DBMSs were available only on mainframe computers. An application called dBASE pioneered their move to PCs. Now, managers can use their PCs to store records of thousands of employees, inventory parts,

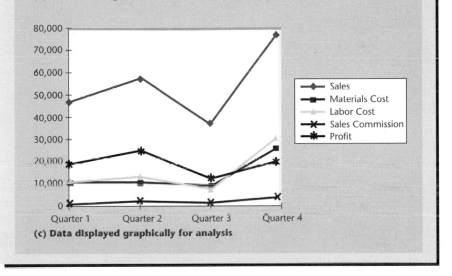

Oz Enterprises, Inc. — Revenue & Sales: 1999

	Quarter 1	Quarter 2	Quarter 3	Quarter 4	Total
Sales	45,766	56,990	34,320	76,562	213,638
Materials Cost	12,212	13,454	10,123	25,444	61,233
Labor Cost	13,099	15,666	9,005	31,702	69,472
Sales Commission	2,288	2,850	1,716	3,828	10,682
Profit	18,167	25,021	13,476	15,588	72,251

(a) Table displaying values only

Oz Enterprises, Inc. — Revenue & Sales: 1999

	Quarter 1	Quarter 2	Quarter 3	Quarter 4	Total
Sales	45766	56990	34320	76562	=SUM(B3:E3)
Materials Cost	12212	13454	10123	25444	=SUM(B4:E4)
Labor Cost	13099	15666	9005	31702	=SUM(B5:E5)
Sales Commission	=B3*0.05	=C3*0.05	=D3*0.05	=E3*0.05	=SUM(B6:E6)
Profit	=B3-SUM(B4,B5,B6)	=C-SUM(C4,C5,C6)	=D3-SUM(D4,D5,D6)	=E3-SUM(E4,E5,E6)	=SUM(B7:E7)

(b) Table showing both data and underlying formulas

(c) Data displayed graphically for analysis

Figure 4.8 *Electronic spreadsheets are powerful tools for (a) tabulation, (b) manipulation, and (c) analysis of data.*

or other data on which they need to perform powerful operations. Using a PC, a sales manager can instantly determine if a certain item is in stock; a human resource manager can view the entire employment record of an employee; and a financial manager can record and keep track of the firm's investments.

Some of the most powerful data management programs have been designed for microcomputers; dBASE V, FoxBase, Oracle, Paradox, and Microsoft Access are just five examples. Today's DBMSs are bundled with other capabilities of fourth-generation programming languages. In addition to building, populating, and manipulating data, the user can develop powerful applications with customized menus and security measures, to ease the access to data and to facilitate queries and report generation.

Speak to Your Spreadsheet

"**O**pen a new spreadsheet," Joe commands. He is facing a microcomputer set on his desk. "Name it ECON 301." On the computer monitor, a new window is filled with a spreadsheet. "Name the first column 'Student Name.' Name the second column 'Student ID.' Name the third column 'Assignment One.' Name the fourth column 'Assignment Two.'" Joe, an economics professor who has not mastered any programming language, continues to dictate to the computer. As he utters his commands, the screen is filled with new columns. "Name the next column 'Raw Grade.' Name the next column 'Scaled Grade.' Name the next column 'Letter Grade.'"

The little microphone attached to the computer top receives Joe's commands as he prepares the spreadsheet for recording the grades he will give his students over the upcoming term. A **voice recognition** program translates his commands into code. A special parsing program translates the code into instructions that the spreadsheet application can understand and execute. Through a speaker, the computer repeats every command before execution. "Please repeat," the pleasant female voice asks. Joe repeats the last command, this time slowly and with careful pronunciation. "Name the next column 'Letter Grade.'"

Now it's time to enter the formulas for calculating the future grades. Joe likes to prepare his grade spreadsheet at the beginning of the term. This way, as he records assignment and exam grades, the spreadsheet automatically calculates partial grades which Joe can report to inquiring students. "Enter formula in first row under 'Raw Grade.' The formula is: Average of left parenthesis Assignment One through Assignment Four right parenthesis times zero point four plus Midterm Exam times zero point twenty five plus Final Exam times zero point thirty five." As he pronounces the formula it is displayed in the formula box. Now Joe examines the formula. When satisfied that there are no mistakes, he commands "Enter." The formula is entered in the first cell under the heading Raw Grade.

Joe now tests the formula by entering perfect scores in the first row. "Go to cell three B." Cell 3B is highlighted. "Enter one hundred." The number 100 now shows up in the cell. Joe continues to fill the row up to the cell under "Final Exam." "Good," he whispers as the raw grade is calculated. The first cell under Raw Grade displays a perfect 100. "Please repeat," the voice says. "Ignore," Joe responds. "Delete row two." The numbers disappear. "Go to cell I2," he commands. "Fill down to I31." The spreadsheet is now ready to accept student grades. At the end of the term, Joe may enter a scaling formula. He will also enter the formula for calculating the letter grade for each student.

Joe's "programming" of the spreadsheet is only the tip of the iceberg of what we may expect to see in future programming. Professional programmers will be able to develop new programs using a human language, such as English, rather than computer language. This will also allow nonprogrammers to develop some simple programs because they will not have to master the rules and syntax of any programming language.

THINK CRITICALLY

Consider the career you have chosen to pursue. How would the combination of voice recognition and natural language processing affect your daily professional activities?

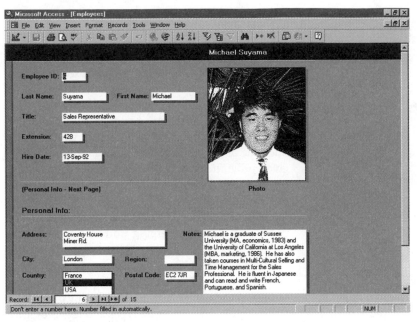

Data management applications provide powerful tools for data manipulation.

We have addressed DBMSs as applications software. However, the systems are so general in their purpose that an increasing number of professionals refer to them as system software. In fact, some operating systems (such as OS/400) come with DBMS capability.

SUITES Several vendors offer **integrated software**, which is a bundle of several applications. Usually, the bundle, or **suite**, includes the most widely used types of general applications: a word processor, an electronic spreadsheet, a database management system, a data communications program, and a drawing and painting application. The important advantage in these suites is the ability to move information from one application to another, while maintaining format. The use of OLE in today's suites makes linking documents across applications smoother.

For example, the user can create a spreadsheet, then create a chart from it and copy both into a document that was created using the suite's word processor. To embellish the document, or presentation, the user can create the company's logo and other drawings and paintings and integrate them into the document. The result is one document created with the aid of several different applications. Among the best-selling suites are Microsoft's Office and Office Professional, Lotus' SmartSuite, and Claris' Works.

HYPERTEXT

Hypertext is a feature that enables a user to access additional information by clicking on selected text or graphics displayed on the screen. When first conceived, hypertext was considered a huge step forward in the use of digital media. It is an excellent feature for creating documents that provide related information. Now, hypertext is fairly common, used widely on software stored on CDs and essential to Web based documents. For example, if you were reading a document about American history and came across the highlighted words "George Washington," you could click the mouse on the name, and a new window would open with information about George Washington. Within the newly opened document, you could click on a word, or a picture, to invoke another document. Often, hypertext is combined with multimedia to create easy-to-use, graphic-rich programs.

Vendors offer excellent software packages that allow users to build their own hypertext applications. Among the first ones was Hypercard, which is still popular. The application is used to create stacks of what the program calls cards, the basic unit of information used by the program. Each card contains a record, which can include text, graphics, animation, and "hot" buttons, which are the location the user clicks to access further information. Buttons may be pictures or parts of text. Hypercard and similar programs help teachers develop self-training applications. Private users can create trivia quizzes and other games, but the software is used for many business purposes as well.

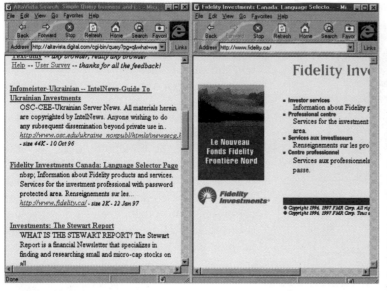

Hypertext in action: clicking the highlighted word on the left displays the page on the right.

MULTIMEDIA

Different programs handle different types of data. Some, such as spreadsheets, can handle and manipulate quantitative information; some, such as word-processing systems, handle mostly text; others, such as voice-mail and dictation systems, handle voice data; and still others handle image data. There used to be a division among programs, whereby only one type of data could be read and manipulated by a given program. But that has changed. Programs that can handle many different types of data are called **multimedia** software. A recent survey indicates that multimedia is viewed by top IS managers as the most promising among emerging information technologies. Multimedia is a powerful means of communicating because it does not limit the method of communication. It is a natural extension of the capabilities of the computer and provides flexibility that allows people to work the way they think, integrating all types and forms of information. Here are just a few examples of the use of multimedia.

Multimedia in Education. One of the most common uses of multimedia is in education. A student taking a lesson using multimedia can view a scenario in one window while listening to a recording of his or her professor and viewing text in another window. The student may then be asked to answer questions interactively, responding in another window on the screen. And the same program may be designed to provide that student with feedback on her performance. With more advanced voice-recognition software, multimedia programs used in language training will even be able to ask a student to pronounce certain new words and evaluate a student's performance.

Multimedia in Training. Another common use of multimedia is to simulate real-world situations for training exercises in many industries. For example, multimedia products that use video and voice and allow users to respond to questions about various situations have been used by the workers of an electric utility company to learn how to solve high-voltage wire problems. If they were to attempt the same cases in the field, their lives would be jeopardized.

Multimedia in Research. Another common use of multimedia is in compiling and integrating data from research. For instance, a researcher may use multimedia programs to view written articles and television news footage, and to listen to radio clips.

Multimedia in Business. Multimedia can be very useful in business situations as well. Consider this example: One manager writes a document, including digitized photographs or video clips and possibly a "live" spreadsheet, which allows the user to actually enter numbers and execute calculations. The document is sent to a colleague for review, who tacks on a video and voice clip requesting clarification of a certain point. The compound document can be filed electronically, retrieved, altered, and communicated as appropriate without ever being transformed into a paper document. In fact, multimedia by its very nature cannot be transferred to a paper document.

Multimedia technology allows users to enjoy text, audio, still pictures, and animation.

VIRTUAL REALITY

Virtual reality (VR) applications mimic sensory reality using software. There are several ways a user can sense a virtual reality. The most sophisticated VR devices are interactive; they include goggles, gloves, earphones, and sometimes a moving base on which the user stands, all of which sense movement, respond to signals, and provide feedback to the user. The user receives a three-dimensional visual sensation and stereophonic sound. With interactive gloves, the user's hand motions change the direction in which the user "moves" within the virtual environment. For instance, a VR system may be designed so the user can experience being a race car driver. In this case, when the user's hand makes a grabbing motion, sensors in the VR glove cause the hand in the VR image to "grab" the stick shift. The distinction between multimedia and VR can be hazy. Experts usually assert that only systems that include sensing helmets, gloves, and the like, which truly surround the user with a sense of a real experience, are VR. However, many people refer to sophisticated multimedia applications run on PCs as VR as well.

Virtual reality applications are used not only for game playing but as serious business tools.

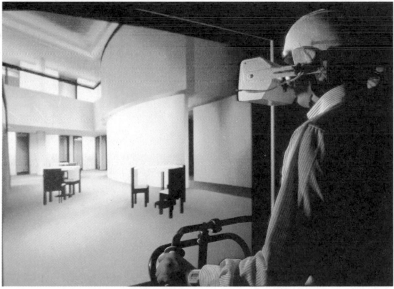

The business use of VR is expected to grow dramatically. VR business applications can decrease the cost of planned buildings, machines, and vehicles. They already help marketing efforts to lure buyers to try new products. For instance, architects can use VR to let a potential buyer "tour" a house. The buyer can then request changes in the floor plan and other features before the construction begins. Volvo, the Swedish car and truck maker, invites prospective buyers to test-drive its latest models in VR. Companies such as Raytheon and Fluor Daniel use VR to help design new plants.

Reliance on information technology often causes undesirable results. Consider: you receive an erroneous bill from your telephone company. There is a warning on the bill that service will be stopped if you do not pay within 30 days. You try to dispute the charge, but at the end of the 30-day period, your line is disconnected. Eventually the company apologizes, but blames the mistake on the computer. Can a computer be blamed for mistakes? Cases like this raise two questions. One: Is it appropriate to blame undesirable results on software? The other: What is a software developer's liability for malfunction, when a program does not perform as its developers expect? As you will read below, the message from the courts is clear: Computers do not make mistakes; people do. And whoever relies on a computer to run a business or to develop, produce, or sell goods or services, is responsible for the output of the computer. Computer professionals have an acronym to remind them how computers work: GIGO—garbage in, garbage out. In other words, bad programming will yield bad results.

Blaming the Computer. The courts have generally maintained that legal principles requiring a person or business to exercise reasonable care in conducting business do not change simply because a computer is involved. Thus, if a business could not hold a calculator legally responsible ten years ago, then that same business cannot hold a computer responsible for erroneous processing. Businesses providing products made, or services rendered, by computers cannot resort to blaming computers if the products or services do not meet expected standards. In one case in which electrical service was mistakenly terminated due to billing errors, the court stated: "While the computer is a useful instrument, it cannot serve as a shield to relieve Consolidated Edison of its obligation to exercise reasonable care when terminating service." A decision of a Federal Court of Appeals in a case of an erroneous insurance policy echoed this principle:

> Holding a company responsible for the actions of its computer does not exhibit a distaste for modern business practices as [the defendant] asserts. A computer operates only in accordance with the information and directions supplied by its human programmer. If the computer does not think like a man, it is man's fault.... The fact that the actual processing of the policy was carried out by an unimaginative mechanical device can have no effect on the company's responsibilities for... errors and oversights.

In another case, Ford Motor Credit Co. repossessed a car, claiming that the debtor defaulted on two payments. The debtor proved with canceled checks that he had never defaulted. The finance company admitted that its decision was wrong, but blamed it on a computer error. Rejecting the defense, the court stated:

> Ford explains that this whole incident occurred because of a mistake by a computer. Men feed data to a computer and men interpret the answer the computer spews forth. In this computerized age, the law must require that men in the use of computerized data regard those with whom they are dealing as more important than a perforation on a card. Trust in the infallibility of a computer is hardly a defense, when the opportunity to avoid the error is as apparent and repeated as was here presented.

(continued)

The jury awarded the plaintiff $600 for actual damages and $25,000 as punitive damages.

Financial service companies often suffer from consequences of software malfunction because of their high dependency on computers. In one case a computer error indirectly caused the arrest of a man. A client deposited $608 on January 4. He did not notice that the ATM stamped his deposit slip with the date of March 4. Within this period, he withdrew drew money from his account. In early April he received an overdraft notice from the bank, and discovered that his deposit did not appear on the bank statement. He notified the bank about the discrepancy, and postponed a vacation to ensure that the confusion was resolved. The president of the bank credited his account, but notified him that the investigation would continue. Without finding the source of the error, the bank's vice-president filed a complaint for theft. The man was arrested at his vacation site and spent two days in jail. He later sued the bank. The bank compensated him with $50,000.

Computer Malpractice? Suppose a business admits the error of its computer, and compensates the customer. Can the business look to the provider of the computer program for restitution? In other words, can the seller of the software be held liable for malfunction? The answer depends on how we regard software. Is software a good or a service? Goods are held to a stricter level of liability than services.

What are the options of a purchaser of flawed software? In the absence of adequate legal avenues to seek remedy, a few customers have tried to sue for malpractice. However, the courts have generally reacted unfavorably to claims of computer malpractice. In one case the court stated:

> The novel concept of a new tort called 'computer malpractice' is premised upon a theory of elevated responsibility on the part of those who render computer sales and service. Plaintiff equates the sale and servicing of computer systems with established theories of professional malpractice. Simply because an activity is technically complex and important to the business community does not mean that greater potential liability must attach. In the absence of sound precedential authority, the Court declines the invitation to create a new tort.

Plaintiffs have claimed that the services of computer specialists are similar to those of physicians, architects, and other professionals because of the expertise involved. A profession is recognized when its members possess a skill that is well above the mere competence of lay people, a skill acquired through learning and experience. Although the general public perceives computer specialists as professionals, the courts seem to be lagging behind. Yet, most businesses that purchase computer services (especially software) are totally dependent on computer specialists. A company that pays millions of dollars to a system developer counts on the expert as a patient counts on a doctor. But it may take years for the legal community to define a clear framework of culpability in cases of faulty software.

Source: Oz, E., *Ethics for the Information Age*, Wm. C. Brown, Dubuque, IA, 1994.

SYSTEM SOFTWARE

The purpose of system software is to manage computer resources and perform routine tasks—such as copying and pasting sections and files, printing documents, and allocating memory—that are not specific to any application. The presence of system software means that applications do not have to include these instructions. On the one hand, system software is developed with the goal of working in partnership with as many applications as possible; on the other hand, applications will work with system software only if the application is developed to be compatible with that software. The following discussion covers the major types of system programs.

OPERATING SYSTEMS

The **operating system (O/S)** is the most important system software. Without it, no application can be run on the computer. An operating system is developed for a certain **microprocessor**, or multiple microprocessors. Programmers know which operations each microprocessor can perform and how it performs them. The O/S must address technical details such as registers and RAM addresses. Therefore, O/Ss are usually developed with the aid of low-level programming languages, such as assembly languages or C.

The O/S is sometimes referred to as the "traffic cop" or the "boss" of computer resources. Indeed, it is charged with control functions such as optimally allocating RAM locations for an application program, copying the application from an external storage medium into RAM, passing control to the CPU for execution of program instructions, and sending processing results to output devices.

FROM USER TO O/S TO CPU Figure 4.9 describes where the O/S is positioned in the logical operation of a computer. The user interacts with the user interface using menus, icons, and commands provided by the application. The user's input is converted by the application into commands understandable to the O/S, and the O/S commands the CPU to carry out the operation.

For example, assume that you are using a word processor. You select a paragraph you wish to copy and paste. You select "copy" from the menu. The word processor converts your menu item into an appropriate command for the

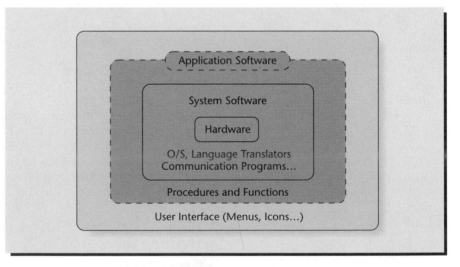

Figure 4.9 *Computers operate at a number of layers, starting from the user interface and moving inward to the hardware.*

O/S, which then instructs the CPU to copy. A similar action takes place when you select "paste" from the menu. Now assume that you are using an electronic spreadsheet on your computer. You select a portion of a column of numbers that you want to copy and paste. The menu here may not look the same as the word processor's menu. However, when you select "copy," the operating system receives a command from the application that is identical to the one it received when you used the word processor. And when you paste, the paste command that the O/S receives from the spreadsheet is the same one it received from the word processor. Thus, the developers of these two applications did not have to program the copy and paste operations; they only had to know how their programs must invoke these operations from the O/S.

In addition to performing input and output services and controlling the CPU, many O/Ss perform accounting and statistical jobs, including the recording of logon and logoff times, the number of seconds the CPU was used by the operator in every session, and the number of pages printed by a user. Some O/Ss also perform utilities such as hardware diagnostics, disk check, file comparison, file sorting, and the like. However, not all O/Ss provide all the utilities that might be necessary, in which case special utilities programs must be used.

TYPES OF O/Ss As mentioned above, operating systems are designed to work with a particular microprocessor; consequently, there is a different O/S for every computer that has a specific type of microprocessor. Popular operating systems for microcomputers include MS-DOS (Microsoft Disk Operating System) and MS-Windows for IBM-compatible computers (which use Intel microprocessors), and MacOS for the Macintosh (which uses PowerPC microprocessors). Popular mainframe O/Ss include MVS for IBM machines and VMS for DEC machines (see Figure 4.10).

NAME	O/S AUTHOR	RUNS ON
MVS	IBM	IBM mainframes
VMS	DEC	DEC minicomputers
AS/400	IBM	IBM AS/100 computers
MS-DOS	Microsoft	IBM and compatible PCs
Windows 3.x	Microsoft	IBM and compatible PCs
Windows NT	Microsoft	IBM and compatible PCs
Windows 95	Microsoft	IBM and compatible PCs
MacOS 7.5 (and other versions)	Apple Computer	Macintosh computers
Solaris	SunSoft, Inc.	Sun workstations
UNIX	Bellcore (originally) and other software companies	There are different versions for IBM, Macintosh, Sun, and other manufacturers' mainframes and PCs

Figure 4.10 *Popular operating systems*

OPERATING SYSTEM FUNCTIONS Operating systems provide several services, the most important of which is system management. **System management** refers to efficient allocation of the hardware resources to applications and includes tasks such as prompting the user for certain actions, allocating RAM locations for software and data, instructing the CPU to run or stop, allocating CPU time to different programs running at the same time, and instructing coprocessors and peripheral equipment.

User Interface. An important part of the O/S is the user interface, which can include prompts to enter commands, or icons and menus from which options can be chosen with a mouse click. The better O/Ss provide a graphical user interface (GUI), which makes the use of the computer intuitive and easy to learn.

Memory Allocation. One of the most important functions of an operating system is the management of memory, especially RAM. RAM, you may remember, is the memory locations where data and programming code must reside before being executed. Ideally, an entire application and all the data it processes would reside in RAM until the end of the processing. However, large applications and data pools require memory capacity that may be greater than the computer's RAM. So, RAM is used as an interim storage point for segments of code and pieces of data as programs run. The management of that space, which moves pieces of different programs and data in and out of this "holding" station, is a challenge addressed by the operating system.

One way the O/S deals with insufficient RAM is the use of what is called **virtual memory**, which allows the user to proceed as if significantly more RAM were available than really exists. This is achieved by using the hard disk as an extension of RAM. A special module of the O/S continually detects which parts of the application program are used frequently. The O/S keeps these parts in RAM while leaving on the disk the least frequently used parts. In professional language, this activity is called "page swapping," where the "pages" are program parts of equal size that the O/S swaps between RAM and the disk.

Multitasking, Multiprogramming, and Multiprocessing. **Multitasking** is the running of several applications at the same time. Usually each application that is running has its own window on the screen. Again, it is the O/S's responsibility to keep track of programs that run simultaneously and make sure that one application code does not overwrite another application code in RAM.

Many computers provide **multiprogramming**, which allows several people to use the same computer simultaneously. It is important to understand that a CPU works on only one program at a time. However, because the O/S can instruct the CPU to alternate among programs at intervals as short as a billionth of a second, it appears to users that each program is running uninterrupted.

Multitasking and multiprogramming should not be confused with multiprocessing, also called parallel processing. **Multiprocessing** can take place only in a computer with several CPUs rather than a single one. Processing is divided and assigned to different CPUs that work in parallel, completing a job more quickly than a single CPU can.

Times and Statistics. Another important task undertaken by operating systems in many businesses and academic institutions is helping to keep track of the services their computers provide to employees, clients, or students. The O/S contains modules that keep **times and statistics** by user: logon (start) and logoff (end) time, amount of CPU time used, number of input and output

There are several reasons why managers must be familiar with different types of software.

1. Software can automate many processes that managers and their subordinates are responsible for. These start with word-processing programs and electronic spreadsheets, and progress to sophisticated manufacturing control programs. Time and money can be saved by using software to do what could previously be done only manually.

2. New functions available in easy-to-use high-level software allow managers to develop their own tools for daily monitoring and control of their operations. Even simple software such as electronic spreadsheets can be used to build decision-support programs.

3. Software vendors offer a huge variety of programs. While it is doubtful that any individual can become knowledgeable about all available software, a working knowledge of the *types* of software will allow you to make informed comparisons and suggestions for improving your organization's software portfolio.

4. There is a strong relationship between hardware and software. Not every program can run on the hardware that is available to you. Understanding compatibility and incompatibility is important for making decisions on purchasing hardware or software.

5. Similarly, some programs may not be compatible with other programs. As organizations are moving toward integrated systems, it is extremely important to understand software-to-software compatibility.

6. As hardware prices decrease, companies spend significantly more money on software than on hardware. As more and more tasks are supported by software, the decision-making process of which software to adopt includes a growing circle of people. You need a working knowledge of software to be a contributing member of the decision-making team.

---

operations, number of pages printed, and so on. This information is used to keep track of organizational and individual budgets.

Increasing Services from O/Ss. The trend in O/S development is to include services that used to be provided by special systems or application programs. These services include database management, networking, and security.

For instance, **security** measures, such as tracking account numbers and passwords and controlling access to files and programs, are now an important function expected from an O/S. Windows NT provides networking functions, previously handled by separate programs.

Many **utilities**, which are programs that provide help in routine user operations outside applications, are also built directly into the O/S. These services include automatic backup of files, duplication of files on demand, location of files in a file-directory, retrieval of files flagged for erasure, prearranged shut-off when the computer is not in use for a certain amount of time, and many other services.

Quality. In addition to the sophistication of an operating system's operations, the quality of an O/S is judged by how easy it is to learn and use, how intuitive the user-interface is, and how transparent the operations are. **Transparency** means that the user is not made aware of operations that are not directly related to what he or she wishes to do. For example, the user should not be bothered with memory allocation.

A good operating system should also facilitate fairly simple changes to hardware configuration. When a new device, such as an external magnetic or optical disc drive, an external communication device, or a joystick, is attached to a computer, it is the job of the operating system to recognize the new attachment and its function. If the O/S can do so immediately after you attach the device (without your intervention), it is said to be a **plug-and-play** O/S. While MacOS and Windows 95 do not require significant involvement of the user in configuring newly attached devices, they are not completely plug-and-play because the user must follow specific instructions as part of the installation.

COMPILERS AND INTERPRETERS

In our discussion of programming languages we emphasized that computers understand only machine language. To run programs requires another specialized program whose only job is to translate the source code into object code, which is the equivalent code in machine language. There are two types of language translators, compilers and interpreters. The main difference between them is that compilers allow a user to save an entire program in object code, while an interpreter does not.

A **compiler** (as shown in Figure 4.11) scans the entire source code and looks for syntactic errors and execution errors. If it finds an error, it does not compile the program, it generates an error message, or a list of error messages. An error in a statement may render subsequent statements erroneous even if they are legitimate. Imagine that the fifth statement requires the computer to divide a number by zero. The compiler generates an error message. If subsequent statements depend on the result of the division, they also become erroneous statements, and the compiler will generate error messages for them. Therefore, the programmer must locate the first error and figure out that one error caused all these messages. This is not an easy task.

If the compiler finds no syntactic or execution errors, it translates the source code into object code, and the computer can execute the program. At this point, the programmer may save the object code. From now on the user can run the object code only. This saves the translation time.

An **interpreter** checks one statement at a time. If the first statement is free of syntactic and execution errors, it interprets the statement into machine language, and the computer executes it. If the statement is erroneous, the interpreter issues an error message. In some environments, the programmer can immediately correct the statement. It will then be executed, and the interpreter will move on to check the next statement. Error free statements are executed immediately.

Although using an interpreter makes debugging easier, interpreters have a major flaw: they do not produce object code that can be saved for future runs.

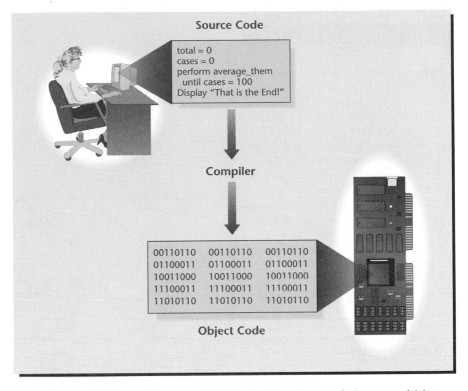

Figure 4.11 *A compiler converts higher-level-language code (source code) into machine language (object code), which the computer can process.*

Most BASIC translators are interpreters. Translators of FORTRAN, COBOL, and most other third-generation languages are compilers. Assemblers are actually compilers.

DATA COMMUNICATIONS PROGRAMS

Data communications software controls and supports data communications activities in a network. It includes programs to set up rules that govern transmission and reception, connect and disconnect communications links (such as phone lines for modems), assign priorities among terminals in a network, and detect and correct transmission errors. Note that communications programs must be compatible not only with the computer and the O/S, but also with the communications devices in use, such as modems. Later in this book we will explain how these devices work.

PROPRIETARY VS. OPEN OPERATING SYSTEMS

When an organization uses a certain O/S, it commits itself to that O/S. That is, because applications depend on a machine's O/S, the organization will not be able to use applications that are incompatible with its system software. Hence, there is talk about moving to **open systems**. While a proprietary O/S is limited to using applications compatible with it, an open O/S would be compatible with virtually all applications.

Sometimes, a little unnoticed error in a line of code can cause nightmarish situations. A bug in a single line in an updated computer program installed by Chemical Bank (now merged into Chase Manhattan Bank) in its New Jersey computer center caused the bank to process every withdrawal and transfer at its automated teller machines twice, meaning that customers' accounts were charged $2 for every $1 withdrawn. The bug hit 150,000 transactions before it was discovered a day later, having set back 100,000 customers some $15 million. Chemical Bank's response? "Executives were very apologetic."

Source: "Only in NY: $15M Debug Tab," *Datamation*, April 1, 1994, p. 21. Reprinted with permission of Datamation Magazine. Copyright © 1994 by Cahners Publishing, Reed Elsevier Inc.

FACTOR	WHAT TO LOOK FOR	SCORE
Fitness for purpose	◆ Try to maximize the number of needs satisfied.	_____
Ease of learning to use	◆ The shorter the training time needed, the better.	_____
Ease of use	◆ The easier a program is to use, the better. ◆ Try to minimize the number of commands that need to be memorized.	_____
Compatibility with other sofware	◆ Try to maximize compatibility with related software and with other operating systems. ◆ Try to maximize portability of data and output to other programs.	_____
Reputation of vendor	◆ Use professional contacts and references to gather background information on vendor. ◆ Be sure vendor can deliver what it promises. ◆ Be sure vendor stands by his pricing.	_____
Availability and quality of telephone support	◆ Ask references about their experience. ◆ Look for knowledgeable staff on phone support.	_____
Networking	◆ Try to maximize ability of many computers to share the software.	_____
Cost	◆ Seek detailed pricing information. ◆ Seek the best price, while maintaining quality and performance.	_____

Figure 4.12 *A sample software evaluation form*

The problem with the term "open O/S" is that such an O/S does not exist and may not exist at any time in the near future. While some O/Ss, such as UNIX, are said to be nonproprietary, it is still impossible to run many applications on different versions of such O/Ss because corporate users have modified the original version into multiple versions.

Do not confuse applications that have the same name but run on different O/Ss. Although these applications have the same functions, they are actually different programs. For example, there is a version of Lotus 1-2-3 for Windows, and another for the MacO/S.

In 1995, a partnership between IBM and Apple Computer produced a single computer that runs what were then the three most popular operating systems: the MacOS, Microsoft Windows NT, and IBM OS/2. IBM introduced a computer that runs Windows NT, OS/2, Solaris, NetWare, and AIX, a version of UNIX. Both computers are built around the PowerPC microprocessor. These developments are a major advancement toward a truly open system. However, in this case, it is the hardware that can run several O/Ss, not a single O/S that can run all applications. A truly open system environment will be a reality only when users can run every application on the single O/S that they use in their machine.

CONSIDERATIONS IN THE PURCHASE OF SOFTWARE

When an application is developed specifically for an organization, the specific program goals and custom requirements are considered during the development process. Such requirements include business needs, organization culture needs, the need for interface with other systems, and performance issues, such as response time. However, as discussed above, organizations find ways to satisfy many of their needs with off-the-shelf software as well. Figure 4.12 summarizes the important factors to consider when purchasing software. For each factor, the table details what you should look for.

Business requirements can be very complex. To avoid decisions that may prove to be costly mistakes, organizations often trust the choice of software to consulting companies. A consulting company brings to the selection process experience that an individual enterprise may not have. This includes information about successful and unsuccessful installations and experience with a wide range of software at similar businesses.

While Figure 4.12 provides a general framework for evaluating off-the-shelf software, each item may be augmented with further inquiry depending on the main function of the program. For example, a word-processing program is often tested by potential buyers for features like availability of different fonts, the size of its dictionary, the response time to search operations, the availability of table-of-contents and indexing functions, and other features. Electronic spreadsheet programs are tested for speed of recalculation of formulas, charting, and other features typical of this type of software, in addition to the above criteria. Some trade journals provide results of tests performed by their own experts, rating different software features on a numerical scale. See a sample rating report in Figure 4.13.

Note that the evaluation is helpful but very general. When you evaluate software for your organization, you should also take into account the specific needs and constraints of the organization, the users, and the typical operations in which the software will be used.

Reliability	4.0	Tools & utilities	4.1
Technical support	4.2	Spreadsheet editing	4.4
Ease of use	4.2	Programming	4.2
Performance	3.5	Formulas & analysis	4.4
Installation	3.5	Charting & graphics	4.2
Networking	3.0	Compatibility	4.1
		Overall rating	4.5

Figure 4.13 *Sample results of software evaluation (5 is the highest score)*

The following story exemplifies the year 2000 problem. In 1997, Visa and MasterCard asked banks to stop issuing new credit cards with expiration dates of 2000 and beyond. The credit companies wanted the banks to prepare their computer systems first. Unfortunately, some banks had already issued named cards with "00" expiration dates embossed on them. One such card was issued to a programmer named Robert Nicholson in Virginia. When Nicholson tried to use the card at a Citibank branch in New York, he was told that the card had expired on January 1, 1900. Although the bank eventually approved the transaction, Nicholson asked for another card, this time with an expiration date of 1999.

THE YEAR 2000 PROBLEM

Unless they take precautions, many organizations will find their ISs fail to operate properly one year before we enter the next century. The problem they are facing is called the **year 2000 problem**.

Numerous business applications process dates: payroll, billing, and accounting programs; cash management systems and investment tracking systems; and programs that process long-term project planning data. For several decades, programmers have designated years using their last two digits. Thus, December 8, 1997, would be 12/08/97. Dates are updated according to the internal clocks of the computers on which the programs run, and calculations are executed accordingly. For example, if you bought an interest-bearing security in 1995 that matures in 1998, the application will subtract 95 from 98 and calculate interest for three years.

But what happens if you bought a similar security in 1995 that matures in the year 2001? The application will subtract 95 from 01. The "01" will be internally interpreted as "1" and the result will be interest calculated for -94 years. Similar problems exist in many other business applications. If the owners of date-sensitive ISs do not fix the appropriate code, they will experience chaos once we enter the last year of the millennium (01/01/00).

To avoid the problem, businesses need to change every date from a six-digit format (07/01/01) to an eight-digit format (07/10/2001). There are different estimates of how many lines of code must be changed to fix the problem, but experts agree that millions of lines must be modified. The problem is actually greater than that, because organizations must first scour all their business applications for modules that have the problem. Once these are identified, the recoding itself may start.

How many business applications are date-sensitive? Approximately 30 million in the U.S. alone, about 40% of which are still written in COBOL, a programming language that has been out of use for almost two decades. Until the year 2000 problem, COBOL programmers were considered an "extinct" breed, but now they will be needed to help fix the problem.

What is it going to cost to solve this problem? Each affected application may have many date fields that must be modified. Depending on whose estimate you accept, the total cost to the corporate world and to governments will reach either a few or hundreds of billions of dollars. One research firm estimates that the overall cost of fixing a single date field so that a computer will recognize the year 2000 was $0.90–1.50 in 1996, but would rise by 20–40% for each subsequent year because fewer and fewer programmers would be available for the work. According to one estimate, fixing the year 2000 problem will cost the U.S. federal government $30 billion.

Quaker's Sliced And Diced Information

The trend in software is to present information in three dimensions. The Chicago-based Quaker Oats Co. now uses such software to glean essential facts and ratios. How many boxes are stacked on that shelf, who buys them and why, and how much profit was made on each are all information pieces tracked by the company's new data manipulation program.

Express, designed by IRI Software, is a multidimensional database and tool set, to analyze sales, marketing, and financial data. Quaker can now analyze data on all of its food products worldwide: Gatorade drinks, Life cereal, Cap'n Crunch, and Rice-a-Roni.

Says the company's manager of finance and planning systems David Breig: "We now have an overall worldwide competitive picture that we never had before. We now know where we stand relative to our competitors, and we understand our total profitability picture. We used to know how much we sold in total in Germany or France, but we really couldn't break that down for each product in those countries or anywhere

else. We just didn't have the tools to do that."

Using the new analysis, Quaker can now decide almost instantly which products it should market in what part of the world and at what price, to beat its competitors. Quaker began using Express five years ago, and it is gradually replacing an aging mainframe-based executive information system that relied on hard-coded analyses and only serviced a few of the top brass.

Now Quaker has rolled out Express to about 60 users in marketing, sales, and financial decisions. Whereas the previous system showed general trends in Quaker's overall business, Express lets users drill down to product details by brand and even by product bar code.

End-of-period financial closings and consolidations are still done on a general ledger system and on Excel spreadsheets, but "that's really one of the bottlenecks in the entire process, right now," says Breig. "We'll soon handle all of that with Express. When you analyze data, everything fits nicely in a two-dimensional world. But if you want to sort by region, by channel, by customer, etc., and keep slicing the data, such systems don't fit that model."

Breig says that eventually all Quaker's financial data will be contained in a single multidimensional database. End users can then tap into the database using multidimensional analytical tools. Despite the success Breig's group and other similar groups at Quaker have had, Breig says his own IS department isn't sold on multidimensional technology. "Our IS department has been immersed in transactional systems. So there is still a bit of a bias toward relational systems. One of the things a typical IS organization overlooks is that data by itself doesn't always mean a lot to end users," he says. "Dumping data onto somebody's PC is okay, but you need a system that can do some baseline analytics for you."

Source: Ricciuti, M., *"Oatmeal, Sliced and Diced,"* Datamation, February 15, 1994, p. 26. Reprinted *with permission of Datamation Magazine. Copyright* © 1994 by Cahners Publishing, Reed Elsevier Inc.

Questions

1. What is a "three-dimensional database"?

2. What can Quaker's managers now do that they could not do before?

Multimedia for Better Training

Multimedia has decreased costs and increased the effectiveness of training programs. Consider the following:

- Bell South uses an extensive sales training system to train its customer representatives, account executives, and marketing representatives. The system is expected to save the company an estimated $5 million and 20,000 training days over a five-year period. Before the new system was implemented, some courses required an employee to be in training five days. The time has been reduced to seven hours. The company reported that the calendar training period was reduced by 80% for marketing representatives, while the retention level of the learned skills has increased by 40%.

- Michigan-based Consumer Power Company converted its employee training to incorporate multimedia. Proper training is of the utmost importance because the lives of both employees and customers are at risk if the employee makes a mistake. Previously, employees were required to undergo extensive training sessions, including a 12-hour stand-up class. Since the company switched to multimedia-based training, it has been able to provide consistent, self-paced instruction to its employees, presenting real work-related scenarios. The company reported that the average training session had been reduced from 12 hours to 7 hours, while trainee retention had increased.

- Steelcase, Inc., a large manufacturer of office furniture, has attributed savings in training costs to multimedia. It has reduced cost from $200 per employee per year to only $20 per employee, for training its 4,000 employees, using 300 multimedia training programs. The programs vary in content, and cover topics such as project management, leadership skills, and product information.

Questions

1. The use of multimedia in training Bell South and Consumer Power personnel solved a serious problem. What was the problem?

2. In what other business areas can companies use multimedia applications to solve problems or seize opportunities?

Gutenberg Would Be Proud Of Them

You may have heard the name of Standard & Poor (S&P) more than once. The company earns its income from rating the credit status of businesses and selling the reports. Businesses like to get good grades from S&P, but when the New York firm reviewed its own publishing process in 1996, the grade it gave itself was not so good. Analysts, editors, and production staff all were frustrated by a paper-intensive editing and production system that was riddled with inefficiencies.

S&P's Rating Information Services division produces 400 different publications intended to help readers evaluate credit risks. The division's output has grown in the last few years, but until 1995, its publication process was tedious and error-prone. S&P laid out documents using publication software, then faxed or hand-delivered pages to analysts for corrections and comments. After the analysts had written their revisions on the galley pages by hand, they faxed pages back to the editor or had them hand-delivered to the editor's office.

S&P didn't have an automated system for managing the progress of copy through the publishing process. Another problem was the difficulty of tracking down previously published information to reformat and reuse it in new publications. This was time consuming and difficult. "The problem got put in our faces when a production person came to us and said, 'We lay out the same page eight times because we have multiple product,'" said Laurel Bernstein, director of design production and manufacturing for Rating Information Services at S&P. "The system was manually intensive and time-consuming. We used every form of paper."

Rating Information Services produces an increasing number of weekly and monthly magazines, newsletters, books, and special reports aimed at institutional investors and fund managers. The division's output has grown tremendously; from 1990 to 1995, the number of pages S&P published per year more than tripled, from 28,000 to 90,000. Faced with customer demand for more publications and a rising tide of dissatisfaction among its staff, S&P had to upgrade its technology to smooth out the publishing process and handle future growth.

Managers examined document management and electronic publishing applications from several vendors. After a nine-month evaluation process, they selected software that included document managing and distribution applications. The document managing application includes a document repository; a workflow component for routing articles and reports among writers, editors, and designers; full-text search and retrieval; and configuration management for tracking objects that are used in multiple documents. The software uses the Windows operating system and a widely used database management system.

An important factor in deciding on the software was that it allowed S&P to keep its existing hardware and software investment. This also meant that editors and analysts could continue using Microsoft Word (the popular word processor) on their PCs to create and edit documents, and the production staff could continue using the publishing application to design pages.

Because the technology had to support Rating Information Services' business processes, a committee with representatives from the S&P IS department and its production and editorial teams, as well as external consultants, was involved in designing and implementing the new system. Linx, as S&P named the system, was rolled out early in 1996. Some 150 employees now use it, and the publishing company planned to roll it out worldwide on 1,200 computers by the end of the year.

The use of Linx immediately changed the publishing process. For instance, S&P programmers have developed filters to retrieve data from the repository and format it for specific publications. Using the software's workflow and distribution capabilities, the system automatically tracks documents as they are passed between the different members of the publishing group, creating an electronic audit trail. This has simplified the trafficking of pages, reducing anxiety for deadline-driven analysts and editors.

"You no longer have to worry about where a document is," said Ronald Barone, director in the corporate finance utilities group and an analyst who writes reports and articles. "The system reminds you. It beeps every few minutes if the document is in your queue." Analysts no longer write out their corrections longhand on printed documents; instead, they submit them on the electronic document as a digital note. As a result, the process of faxing and hand-delivering pages between offices has been eliminated. In addition, analysts now have the most current credit data available at the tips of their fingers because Linx is integrated with S&P's corporate database. This lets analysts point and click on information in the database, such as an up-to-the-minute credit rating, and drop it into an article.

Source: Gambon, J, "S&P Raises its Own Productivity Rating," InformationWeek, *November 25, 1996, pp. 81–84.*

Questions

1. What development in S&P's business pushed toward adoption of the new software?

2. The new software allows sharing of information that was impossible before. Explain. How does the sharing of information help S&P in its publishing operations?

3. The firm did not want to incur more hardware costs. Did it succeed?

SUMMARY

Software is the collective term for programs, sets of instruction to the computer. Managers must understand the different types of software and how to evaluate programs, because much of their work is highly dependent on software.

To develop software, programmers use **programming languages**. Languages of the first generation were **machine languages**, which address the hardware directly and were difficult to learn and use. Over time, more powerful languages were developed that are easier to learn and use because they use syntax that is more like English. **Fourth-generation languages (4GLs)** are more English-like and provide many preprogrammed functions. **Object-oriented programming languages** facilitate the creation of re-usable objects, which are data encapsulated along with the procedures that manipulate them.

Software is classified into two general categories. **System software** manages the computer resources, such as CPU time and memory allocation, and carries out routine operations, such as **utilities**. This category includes **operating systems**, communications software, and translators. **Applications** are programs developed to specifically satisfy some business need, such as payroll or market analysis. Application software includes **general applications**, such as spreadsheets and word processors.

Among application programs, some are **custom-designed**, but many are purchased off the shelf. While the former are expensive to develop, they are often the only way a business can obtain a system that will cater to its special needs. The advantages of off-the-shelf applications are high quality and low cost.

Popular off-the-shelf general applications include word processors, electronic spreadsheet programs, and data management programs. Word processors help create text documents and prepare text for publication. Spreadsheet applications provide a powerful tool for tabulation, manipulation, and analysis of business data. Data management applications ease the tasks of constructing databases, manipulating data, and creating useful reports. **Hypertext**, **multimedia**, and **virtual reality** applications provide highly useful tools for education, training, and business.

It is important to learn about new off-the-shelf applications from trade journals, but managers should also consider the specific business environment of their organizations before purchasing applications. Businesses can follow a systematic evaluation to determine the suitability of off-the-shelf software to their needs. Applications should be tested with real transactions to find out whether they satisfy minimum requirements, such as response time.

Many business applications store only the last two digits of year dates. If corrective measures are not taken, many businesses will find their ISs interpreting 00 as 1900 instead of 2000. This is referred to as the **year 2000 problem**. Software is a relatively new type of product. Thus, the legal responsibility for problems caused by faulty software has not been determined in a consistent manner in the courts. Several years may pass before legal doctrines are established.

REVIEW, DISCUSS, AND EXPLORE

REVIEW AND DISCUSSION QUESTIONS

1. What are the advantages of machine and assembly languages over higher-level languages?

2. What are the advantages of third-generation languages over lower-level languages?

3. What are the benefits of 4GLs?

4. What is hypertext? How can it be used in searching literature, in training, in learning a foreign language?

5. What is multimedia? Give five examples of how the technology can be used in training, customer service, and education.

6. Give examples of GUI in operating systems. What else can developers of operating systems do to simplify the use of software?

7. *Ethics and Society*: You are a programmer on a team that develops software for a nuclear reactor. The software you and your team members develop is to

monitor radioactive leaks and trigger an alarm. The consulting company for which you work promised bonuses for early completion of the project. Three months into the effort you realize that there is a one in a million chance that the software will fail to activate the alarm system. You communicate your findings to your project leader. She dismisses your "overreaction" and instructs you not to mention your concerns to the client. Discussions with your team members reveal that they, too, would like you to keep silent. It is clear that you will lose your lucrative job if you blow the whistle. What do you do?

CONCEPT ACTIVITY

ZZZ Inc. is a new personnel recruiting and "head-hunting" company. It was recently started by a well-established and cash-rich management consulting company intent on providing adequate financial resources for the new firm to acquire information systems. ZZZ has opened offices in eight major cities in the U.S. and two in Europe.

The recruiting specialists exchange written correspondence with prospective clients, both managers looking for new positions and companies that may hire them. Records of both recruits and client companies must be kept and updated. All the ten branches should be able to exchange information in real time so as to maximize the potential markets on both continents. ZZZ professionals will travel often to make presentations before human resource managers and other executives.

The majority of ZZZ's own personnel are college graduates who lack programming skills. ZZZ management would like to adopt software that is easy to learn and use.

1. List the *types* of software the firm needs, both system software and applications.

2. Research trade journals. Suggest specific software packages for the firm.

HANDS-ON ACTIVITY

Use a spreadsheet program for the following activity:

Honest Abe and Cars R Us are two car dealerships. Their competition is fierce. Recently, both started to sell Sniper, a new model from Eternal Motors. Dealers' cost of the car is $9,600. A dealership is paid $200 for each car sold plus whatever mark-up it adds to the cost. Honest Abe decided to offer the car for $10,500, while Cars R Us's initial price was set at $10,600.

Immediately after the two dealerships started to offer the car, they each decided to lower the price until the other dealership stopped selling the car. However, they have different price reduction policies. Honest Abe's policy is as follows: at the end of each day, their price is set for the next day at the competitor's price minus $50. Cars R Us's policy: at the end of each day, their price is set for the next day at the competitor's price minus 2%.

Amazingly, each dealership manages to sell all the cars it orders: ten per day. This wild competition goes on for 20 days. The dealership whose total profit after the 20 days is smaller (or whose loss is greater) gives up and stops selling the car.

Enter the initial numbers. Build a model that will help you decide:

a. How much profit will each dealership make on the Sniper sales over the 20-day period?

b. Who will go out of the Sniper business?

1. Print out your spreadsheet.

2. Print out the spreadsheet with *formulas* where applicable (instead of the numbers calculated).

3. Print your name and ID# in the heading of each printout.

4. Label your disk. Staple your printouts.

5. Turn in your disk and printouts.

TEAM ACTIVITY

Your team should choose two operating systems that run on PCs. Research their features. If both operating systems are available at your school, try them. Write up a comparison of their features. Conclude with recommendations: which would you prefer to adopt for a small business, and why?

EXPLORE THE WEB

Access ten sites that offer software for sale through the Web. Prepare a list of the applications each offers. Next to the application name, write the name of the operating systems on which the application runs. For which operating system are the majority of applications offered? Which comes second, third, fourth, etc.? How do your findings relate to the discussion on operating systems in this chapter?

Chapter 5

Information Technology in Business: Telecommunications and Networks

A Quicker Route to Success

Until recently, Domino's Pizza knew almost nothing about its customers. The company did not know who was buying its products. It did not know which segments of its customer population preferred what type of pizza, nor did it know its customers' preferences by region. This meant that the company was probably maintaining far-from-optimal amounts of ingredients in its warehouses. It also meant that its delivery operations could be improved: with an integrated IS, orders for delivery could be routed to the nearest store. Since deliveries account for most of Domino's business, the company felt that better communication with its 700 outlets would provide the information it needed for faster and more streamlined service. The right data were out there at the individual stores, but how could headquarters receive it in a timely fashion to make the right decisions?

Domino's Pizza embarked on a new project to streamline its inventory, customer service, and delivery costs. The company installed a PC and a network of terminals in each of the 700 company-owned outlets in the United States. Every night, each store sends detailed sales data and other information to a large database stored on an IBM RS/6000 computer at Domino's headquarters in Ann Arbor, Michigan.

Outlets enter customer data into the system: names, addresses, and phone numbers, along with what and when they ordered and how much they paid. "That lets us really target our marketing and increases sales and profits," said Kenneth Herr, Domino's national director of IS. "We are now getting a wealth of knowledge that helps us track performance in different areas of the country and different market segments, such as our college stores versus military installations, and we can keep track of what is selling best."

Customers receive faster service. Domino's now uses a telephone-caller-ID system linked to the database, which allows order takers to view the identity, address, and preferences of customers as soon as they call in. The caller-ID system also offers the shortest delivery route, by making it easier for customers to contact the nearest store in a metropolitan area where there may be as many as 40 stores. The customer enjoys the pizza sooner, and the company saves delivery costs.

Source: Needle, D., "Betting the Store on Technology," *InformationWeek*, September 9, 1996, pp. 192–197.

Modern telecommunications technology allows businesses to send and receive messages in seconds. Unless a physical transfer of goods is involved, geographic distances are becoming meaningless in business transactions. When using computers, people can now work together as if they were sitting next to each other, even when they are thousands of miles apart. Understanding the technology underlying telecommunications—its strengths and weaknesses, and the available options—is essential to making informed decisions regarding business operations that depend on telecommunications.

When you finish this chapter, you will:

◆ Understand why successful managers must be familiar with telecommunications concepts and terminology

◆ Understand the principles of communication within a computer system and among computers

◆ Be able to identify the major media that are used in telecommunications

◆ Be familiar with different network layouts and the concept of protocols

◆ Understand how telecommunications can improve operations in organizations

TELECOMMUNICATIONS IN BUSINESS

Telecommunications, which is essential to today's smooth business operations, is the transmittal of data from one computer to another over a distance. Telephoning, faxing, e-mail, the World Wide Web, none of these essential business services would be available without fast reliable telecommunications. Much of this chapter will help you understand the technical foundations of telecommunications, an essential ingredient to managing its role in business. We will discuss the hardware and software needed for telecommunications, the cost/benefit trade-offs of different systems, and the technical trade-offs a successful manager needs to understand, to participate in business decisions essential to effective managing. It is equally, if not more, important to understand how telecommunications affects the way business is run and how managers can use technology to do a better job. Telecommunications has improved business processes in three main ways:

◆ *Improved communication.* When no physical objects need to be transferred from one place to another, telecommunications technology can reduce geographical distance to an unimportant factor in business communications. E-mail, voice mail, faxing, file transfer, cellular telephony, and teleconferencing (all of which are discussed below) allow for full communication, whether among managers, between managers and their staffs, or among different organizations. Telecommunications can also be used by one person to monitor another person's performance in real time. Telecommunications is used to communicate directions and receive feedback without requiring that people coordinate their schedules to hold a meeting. And the use of e-mail has brought some secondary benefits to business communications, by establishing a permanent written record of and accountability for ideas. The result is more accurate business communications.

◆ *Increased efficiency.* Telecommunications has allowed a number of business processes to become more efficient. Many business processes are serial in nature: One department must have the input of another department to act, and must then produce its own information, which in turn serves as input for a third department, and so on. For example, when the sales department receives a purchase order from a customer it must communicate the order to the warehouse, which needs the information for the preparation of the package. The warehouse workers must then forward shipping documents to the accounts receivable department for billing, and so forth. With telecommunications, all documents can be accessed electronically by many different departments at the same time. Processes that used to take place one after another can take place in parallel (at the same time) or at greatly shortened time intervals.

◆ *More effective distribution of data.* Organizations with the means to transmit vital data fast from one computer to another no longer need to have databases centralized in one location. Business units that need certain data most frequently may store it locally, while others can access it by telecommunication. Only fast, reliable transfer of data makes this efficient arrangement possible.

Telecommunications applications, such as e-mail, improve communication among employees and expedites business processes.

File Edit View Insert Format Tools Table Compose Help

To... allan_becket@alrco.com

Cc... Elain Watters; Edward Kay; Brian Ried; Alison Stone; Dennis Williams

Subject: Mission Statement

Dear Allan:

Thanks for your input on the mission statement draft. We've incorporated many of your changes.

I've attached the file for your review. Please let me know if you have further changes.

Mission Statement.doc

Jane

● ● ● *POINT OF INTEREST*

We Have Gathered (?) Here...

Two "high-tech fanatics" used video-conferencing technology to get married. While attending the PC Expo in New York City, Cassandra Lehman and Chris Thorne were married by a judge in California. Family and friends attended on both coasts. Using ISDN (Integrated Services Digital Network) links provided by Pacific Bell and videoconferencing systems at both locations, the bride, groom, judge, and family could all see and hear each other in real time. Because the hookup satisfied the legal requirement that the bride and groom were "in his presence," the high-tech vows are legal and binding.

Source: Pacific Bell, 7/1/94, quoted in *PC link*, No 2, Fall 1994, p. 7.

As a manager, you will have the responsibility of ensuring that your organization maximizes its benefits from fast and reliable telecommunications. In order to do so, you may be involved in selecting a telecommunications system or in exploring the demands you may put on your organization's system. In order to be a creative and productive contributor to these key decisions, it is essential that you grasp the basic technology behind telecommunications.

DATA COMMUNICATIONS AND TELECOMMUNICATIONS

Data communications is any transfer of data within a computer, between a computer and another device, or between two computers. As you remember from previous chapters, in order for a computer to function, binary data in the form of electrical impulses must flow from one component to another, such as from the CPU to the primary memory, from the CPU to the monitor, or from the primary memory to the hard disk. This type of communication is done through the computer's **bus**. The bus is a system of wires, or strings of conductive material soldered on the surface of a computer board. It is a communications channel that allows the transmission of a whole byte or more in one pass.

The Greek word *tele*, which means "distance," is part of words like "telegraph," "telephone," "teleprinter," and other words referring to technologies that allow communications over large distances. Thus, **telecommunications** is data communication between two computers over a distance. The data may represent any number of media, including voice, video, animation, or text. Once communications are transmitted between computer systems rather than within a single system, the rules of the communications game become more complex. A number of questions arise, such as:

◆ What physical channels should be used to transmit and receive signals?

◆ At what speed should the data be transmitted?

◆ Depending upon our business, what is the best layout of the nodes in a network?

There are other issues that must be taken into account as well when considering a telecommunications system. For instance, communications devices must be capable of working compatibly. As always, the benefits of the devices and software acquired to implement a telecommunications system have to be weighed against their costs.

WHAT IS DATA COMMUNICATIONS?

Data communications is the transmission and reception of digitized data, represented in binary code. There are two basic modes in which data can be transmitted: a whole byte at a time, which is feasible only over very short distances, or a single bit at a time, which is currently the only feasible mode for long distances.

Within the computer, and between the computer and its peripheral equipment (such as the printer, external hard disk, and the like), the transmission can easily take the form of **parallel transmission** (see Figure 5.1 on the next page). In parallel transmission, each byte is transmitted in its entirety. The electrical impulses representing all the bits of a byte are transmitted through a bundle of lines, one bit through each line. The line is actually several lines, often called a bus. In **serial transmission**, on the other hand, data are transmitted one bit at a time through a single line.

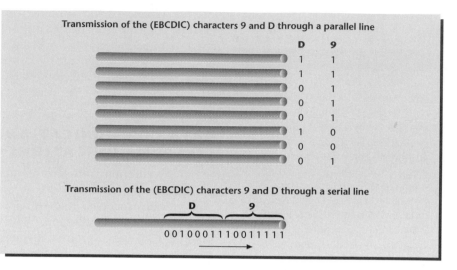

Figure 5.1 *Parallel and serial transmission*

Parallel and serial data transmission require different types of wiring. In the back of a computer there are several outlets for connecting different cables. An outlet that can accept multiwire cord to transmit in parallel is called a **parallel port**. An outlet that accepts a cord for serial transmission is a **serial port**.

In serial transmission, rules must be set so that both the transmitting device and the receiving device can "understand" each other. For instance, rules must be set to determine if each byte is transmitted with bits indicating the start and stop of the byte, the rate at which the bits are transmitted, and other features without which the transmission may result in a long stream of meaningless bits. Sets of such rules are called **protocols**. We discuss protocols later in this chapter.

Why not transmit only in parallel? Because currently there is limited public infrastructure to accommodate such transmission. The communications network available to most people is the telephone network, and it can accommodate only serial transmission of data.

COMMUNICATION DIRECTION

There are three modes of communication between devices—simplex, half-duplex, and full-duplex—distinguished by whether communication is one-way in one direction, one-way at a time in two directions, or two-way (see Figure 5.2).

SIMPLEX

In simplex communication, device A can transmit to device B, but device B cannot transmit to device A. An example of simplex communication is commercial radio transmission. Your car radio can receive signals from a radio station but cannot transmit back to it.

HALF-DUPLEX

In half-duplex mode, device A can transmit to device B while device B receives the signal. Device B can transmit to device A while device A receives the signal. However, the two devices cannot transmit to each other at once,

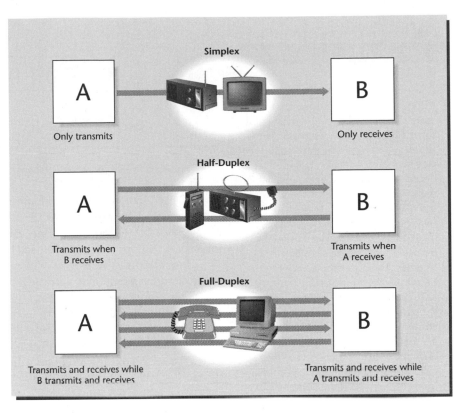

Figure 5.2 *Simplex, half-duplex, and full duplex communication*

and one device can transmit to the other only when the other device is in reception mode. One example of half-duplex is CB (Citizens Band) communication. Half-duplex may also take place when you use a computer terminal to communicate with a mainframe computer.

FULL-DUPLEX

In full-duplex communication, either device can transmit to the other device while simultaneously receiving signals from the other device. That is, device A can transmit to B and receive from B at the same time, and vice versa. Telephony is an example of full-duplex: both parties can talk and listen at once (although this is neither a practical nor a polite way to use the telephone). Full-duplex data communication is often used between computers.

SYNCHRONIZATION

Telecommunications can work only if the transmitting and receiving devices are synchronized, or "time-coordinated." Otherwise, the receiving device will not be able to correctly interpret the message encoded in the stream of bits it receives. There are two ways to synchronize communication: one is called synchronous and, despite the seeming contradiction in terminology, the other is called asynchronous.

ASYNCHRONOUS COMMUNICATION

In **asynchronous transmission**, the devices are not synchronized by timing aides as they are in synchronous communication. Rather, each character

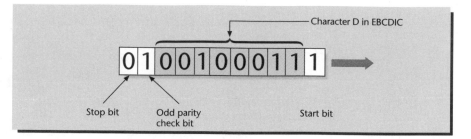

Figure 5.3 *The character D transmitted in asynchronous mode*

(that is, each byte) is transmitted along with additional special bits that tell the receiving device how to interpret the transmission. A start bit indicates the beginning of the byte, a stop bit indicates its end, and an additional bit may be added for error detection, which is discussed below (see Figure 5.3).

Regardless of the type of transmission, synchronous or asynchronous, to ensure accurate reception of a stream of bytes, the receiving end has to "sample the line" at the same rate at which the transmitting end is sending. **Sampling** means detecting the signal at preset time intervals. For example, if the transmitter transmits at a rate of 28,800 bits per second, the receiver must sample the transmission once every 1/28,800 of a second. If the receiver samples at a different rate, after several thousand bits the reception will be out of sequence with the transmission; the receiver will be misinterpreting the location and meaning of bits.

The timing of communications devices—that is, the sampling rate—can vary slightly from one machine to another, throwing off the coordination between the transmitting and receiving devices. To overcome any timing differences that may arise, a start bit (a "1") is added to the beginning of the transmittal of each byte, and a stop bit (a "0") is added at the end of each byte. The start-bit signal tells the receiver to realign with the transmitter. At worst, there will be very small sampling rate differences between the parties, too small to disrupt smooth communication. The realigning at the beginning of each byte ensures that the sampling gap never reaches a point where an entire bit is missed by the receiving device. Still, we call this type of data communication asynchronous, because the transmission and reception are synchronized only at the byte level, not for every single bit.

Sometimes, brownouts or other mishaps may disrupt a connection during transmission, resulting in unintended addition or loss of bits. **Parity check** is an error detection method used to assure that no bits are added or deleted during transmission. In parity check, a bit is added to ensure that the total number of 1s (ones) received is either odd or even. In odd parity check, each byte and its accompanying bits must have an odd number of 1s. So the transmission device will add a 1 bit if the total number of 1s is even (thereby making the total number odd), or a 0 bit if the total number of 1s is odd (thereby keeping it odd). The receiving device counts the number of 1s in every byte. If the receiving device counts an even number of 1s, it will stop the reception and demand retransmission of the byte. Even parity check works in exactly the same fashion, except that every byte must have an even number of 1s. While parity check methods eliminate a lot of errors in communication, they do not eliminate errors completely.

The advantage of asynchronous transmission is that it does not necessitate the employment of sophisticated and expensive timing hardware. The disadvantage is the high **overhead**, or time spent transmitting bits that are not a part of the primary data, but are rather the "start," "stop," and "parity" bits. Consider the

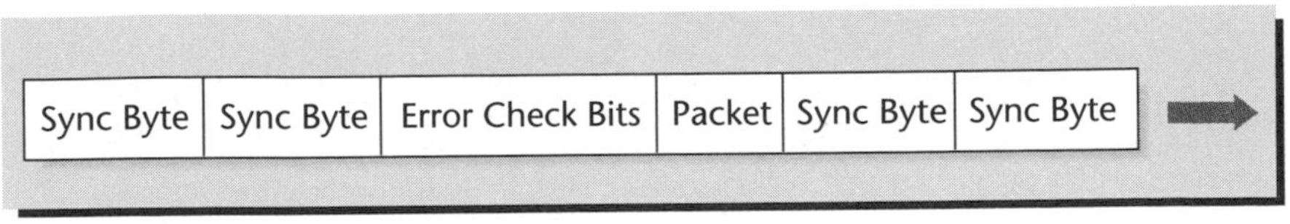

| Sync Byte | Sync Byte | Error Check Bits | Packet | Sync Byte | Sync Byte | →

Figure 5.4 *Synchronous transmission*

example of Figure 5.3. To transmit eight bits of data requires the transmission of another three nondata bits. This means that over 27% of the transmission time is spent on bits that do not convey business data; these are referred to as overhead bits. Asynchronous transmission is suitable for low-speed communications, either between two personal computers or between a PC and a larger computer.

SYNCHRONOUS COMMUNICATION

The use of timing devices in **synchronous transmission** allows several bytes to be transmitted without the great overhead of start, stop, and parity check bits for each byte. The basic unit transmitted is called a packet, rather than a single byte (see Figure 5.4). A **packet** is a group of bytes transmitted together with no overhead bits added between them, although there are some before and after the packet. Messages are divided into packets. Each of the message's packets is passed from the source computer to the destination computer through intermediate nodes. (A **node** is a computer or a communications device, in a communications network.) At each node, the entire message is received, stored, and then passed on to the next node, until the message reaches the destination. Since overhead bits only precede and trail each packet, the overall overhead in synchronous communication is significantly smaller than in asynchronous communication.

As indicated in the figure, a single message consists of several streams of bits that make up synchronization bytes ("sync bytes," to announce the beginning and end of an entire packet), a packet, and error check bits.

CHANNELS AND MEDIA

A **communications channel** is the physical medium through which data can be communicated. In our context, the term is synonymous with **communications links** and **communications paths**. The capacity of the channel is the speed at which the data are communicated, which is also called the transmission rate. Capacity is measured in **bits per second**, (bps); the greater the capacity, the faster the transmission.

CHANNEL CAPACITY

When the channel is of small capacity, it is said to be **narrow band**. (Media with the lowest capacity—such as copper telephone wires—are considered to have **baseband** capacity.) When a channel is of great capacity and can carry several streams of data simultaneously, it is said to be **broadband**. For example, copper wire telephone lines are a baseband, media that cannot transmit effectively at speeds of more than 28,800 bps. Other, specially treated or "conditioned" telephone lines can reach greater capacities. Of course, you may

bps	= bits per second
Kbps	= Thousand bps
Mbps	= Million bps (mega bps)
Gbps	= Billion bps (giga bps)

Figure 5.5 *Transmission speed measurement units*

force your computer to deliver signals into the line at a higher rate, but the destination end will receive a garbled message.

To understand why one type of channel has a greater capacity than another, consider this analogy. Think of transmitting bits through a channel to a friend as if you were sending bursts of water through a hose: for each bit, you either leave the spigot open (for a 1) or closed (for a 0). At the receiving end, your friend samples the hose at equal time intervals. When you transmit at a low rate, she can receive a clear message. You can't double the speed, because it will be difficult for her to distinguish between bits. Now consider you and your friend stand at a great distance from each other on a dark beach, and you transmit bursts of light from a flashlight. Your friend can perceive many more light signals per given time than she can perceive water bursts. Thus, dark air is a faster channel than a garden hose because it allows the transmission of a greater number of signals in the same period of time.

Improving technology is allowing data to be transmitted at greater and greater speeds, to millions of bits per second, and more (see Figure 5.5).

Net Notes

An increasing number of people carry out e-mailing via Web browsers. Virtually all browsers provide e-mail capability. But even if you still wish to do your e-mailing outside a browser, you may obtain good telecommunications software for your PC via the Web. Several sites offer such software free or for a nominal price ($10–25). Use the keywords *Communications Software*, *PPP*, *Winsock*, and *TCP*.

For a Macintosh, you may need to use either PPP (point-to-point protocol) or Open Transport software. Both are available from Web sites. TCP (TeleCommunications Protocol) is popular in the Windows environment, but you may obtain an emulation program for the Macintosh. TCP is easy to set up and easy to use. Downloadable telecommunications applications usually come with good downloadable documentation. Several sites also offer excellent information about the features of popular PC communications applications and the differences among them.

MEDIA

A channel is also called a medium, but not every medium requires a physical line. A **medium** is anything through which data are transmitted. In the example above, the first transmission was carried out through a guided medium, the hose. The second transmission was sent through an unguided medium, air, which has no physical channel. Another example of unguided media is outer space.

TRANSMISSION SPEEDS

A medium's capacity is determined by the range of bits per second at which it can operate (see Figure 5.6). You should remember, though, that the number of signals per second is not always equal to the number of bits per second. Sometimes one signal can represent two or more bits. The number of signals per second is called **baud**. If the baud rate is 28,800 and each signal represents two bits, then the bps rate is 57,600.

The bit rate of any communication should be chosen on the basis of the distance over which it is to be carried, because the greater the distance the less clear the signal. Therefore, the farther a signal must travel, the more slowly it must be transmitted, in order to be received correctly. To illustrate this, consider again the flashlight example. If your friend is standing nearby, she can easily detect the flashes of light. But if she is standing at a great distance, the bursts of light will not be detectable; the signals will get blurred. Even sending the bursts more slowly (at greater intervals) will not help. The signals will be too weak to be perceived, unless you use a repeater—such as a reflector—to capture the signal

Transmission Medium	Typical Speed
Twisted pair, voice telephone	300–28,800 bps
Twisted pair, conditioned	64 Kbps–1 Mbps
Twisted pair in LAN	4 Mbps–16 Mbps
Coaxial cable, baseband	10 Mbps–264 Mbps
Coaxial cable, broadband	10 Mbps–550 Mbps
Optical fibers in LAN	500 Kbps–30 Gbps
Microwave (terrestrial)	12 Mbps–50 Mbps
Microwave (satellite)	56 Mbps–274 Gbps

Figure 5.6 *Telecommunications transmission speeds of different media*

and retransmit it at its original strength. A **repeater** receives and strengthens the message and then sends it on to the next leg of its journey.

There are many different media—including twisted pair and coaxial cable, microwaves, and optical fibers—that vary in a number of ways: the amount of information they can carry, their vulnerability to interference that corrupts the data being transmitted, their cost, whether they guide the data or not, and their availability (see Figure 5.7).

TWISTED PAIR

The most pervasive and commonly available communications network is the telephone network. Telephones are connected either directly to a local telephone company office, or to a local **private branch exchange** (**PBX**), which is connected to a telephone company office. A traditional telephone line is made of a pair of twisted copper wires that act as a single communications link. The wires are twisted to reduce electromagnetic interference (EMI), which can alter voice and data and make them unclear.

Medium	Capacity	Vulnerability to Electromagnetic Interference	Cost	Guided/ Unguided	Availability
Twisted Pair	Lower	High	Lower	Guided	Everywhere
Coaxial Cable		Low		Guided	Low
Microwave		Low		Unguided	High
Optical Fiber	Higher	Nonexistent	Higher	Guided	Most of U.S. and parts of other countries

Figure 5.7 *Characteristics of channel media*

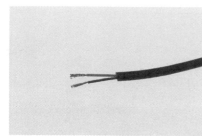

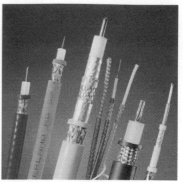

Twisted pairs (left), previously the most common telecommunications medium, are being replaced by optical fibers (center). Coaxial cables (right) are used primarily for television transmission, but are also used for data communications.

Typically, a number of twisted wire lines are bundled together into a cable by wrapping them in a protective sheath. Regular telephone lines allow transmission at speeds of up to 28.8 Kbps. Twisted pair lines can be conditioned to reach much higher capacities by shielding the wire with metallic braid or other material to reduce EMI.

The rate at which digital data completes its transmittal depends on the distance it travels. When twisted pair is used for local area networks (LANs) supporting personal computers, they may reach 100 Mbps.

COAXIAL CABLE

Coaxial cable is sometimes called TV cable because of its common use for cable television transmission. Like telephone lines, it is made of two conductors, but it is constructed differently to permit operation over a wider range of frequencies. It consists of a hollow outer conductor and an inner wire conductor, with an insulator between them, usually of wax or plastic. The outer conductor is covered with PVC, a special plastic.

Coaxial cable is a significantly more expensive medium than twisted pair, but its transmission rate is greater. Thanks to its shielded concentric construction, coaxial cable is much less susceptible to EMI. In voice communication, it is less prone to crosstalk (the intrusion of a third party's conversation on your line) than twisted pair.

MICROWAVES

Microwaves are high-frequency, short radio-frequency (RF) waves. Short radio waves have the quality of carrying signals over long distances with high accuracy. RF is used to transmit different waves to represent bits. You have probably noticed the ubiquitous parabolic antennas on the roofs of many buildings. Because microwave communication can be effective only if there is an unobstructed line of sight between the transmitter and receiver, the

Microwave transceivers are used by many businesses to communicate data.

Large companies lease frequencies of telecommunications satellites to transmit data coast-to-coast and across national borders.

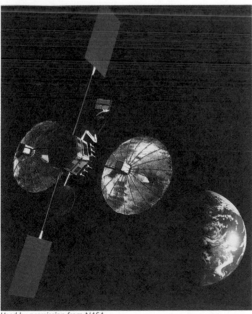

antennas are placed on the roofs of high buildings and the tops of mountains.

TERRESTRIAL MICROWAVE Microwave communication requires far fewer repeaters and amplifiers than coaxial cable and optical fibers, for the same distance. Terrestrial microwave communication—so-called because signals are sent and received from stations on the ground—is good for long-distance telecommunications, but can also be used in local area networks (LANs) in and among buildings. It is commonly used for voice and television communications.

SATELLITE MICROWAVE Signals can also be transmitted using microwaves via satellite technology. Communications satellites that serve as microwave relay stations are placed in orbit 35,784 kilometers (about 22,600 miles) above earth. At this distance the satellite is geosynchronized (synchronized with the earth); that is, once it starts its orbit, the satellite will stay above the same point on earth at all times, without being propelled. Microwave transceivers are aimed at the satellite, which has antennas, amplifiers, and transmitters. The satellite receives a signal, amplifies it, and retransmits it to the destination.

Communications satellites are launched by governments and private enterprises. They are used for television broadcasts, long-distance telephone transmissions, and private business networks. A satellite owner can divide the frequency (that is the band) into several channels and lease different channels to different users. Large companies, such as Kmart and Wal-mart, have bought satellite channels. They use the links for fast transmission of business data among stores and distribution centers.

OPTICAL FIBER

Fiber-optic technology uses light instead of electricity to represent bits. Fiber-optic lines are made of thin fiberglass filaments. A transmitter sends bursts of light using a laser or a light-emitting diode device. The receiver detects the light and samples the line to determine the data bits. Optical-fiber systems operate in the infrared and visible light frequencies (10^{14}–10^{15} Hz). Because light is not susceptible to EMI and RFI (radio frequency interference), fiber-optic communication is much less error prone than twisted pair and radio transmission.

Optical fibers, which compare favorably with coaxial cable networks in providing a fast, reliable medium for telecommunications, are rapidly replacing both twisted-pair and coaxial cable telephone lines. Sprint Communications, a major telephone carrier, implemented its entire network using trunk lines of optical fiber, and other carriers have followed suit. In 1991 optical fiber surpassed satellites as the dominant medium for global digital network communications.

The expanding fiber-optic networks and their declining prices offer great opportunities for businesses. Teleconferencing, electronic mail, and Integrated Services Digital Network (ISDN) (which provides a much greater bandwidth) are available to more and more enterprises. Some experts expect fiber-optic networks to displace all other communications media within several years.

MODULATION

Until several years ago, the most available communications network was a huge web of twisted-pair telephone lines designed to carry signals for voice communication. More recently, however, business demands and technological progress have required that the same lines be used to transmit data. Unfortunately, the type of signal used to transmit voice messages—called **analog**, or continuous signals—is not well suited to the communication of **digital** signals, such as data communications.

ANALOG VS. DIGITAL

As illustrated in Figure 5.8, an analog signal can be graphically represented as a continuous series of waves, while a digital signal can be represented as a stream of short lines of two different heights. Voice communication is transmitted well by analog signals because they are not limited to one high pitch and one low pitch, but can reproduce all the variations of voice, with an infinite number of pitches and sound levels over a wide continuous range. Computer data, on the other hand, is digital because it consists of a series of discrete bits that can be represented by only two different states and nothing in between. For data communications we need a line that can carry a digital signal. If the line can carry only analog signals, we must

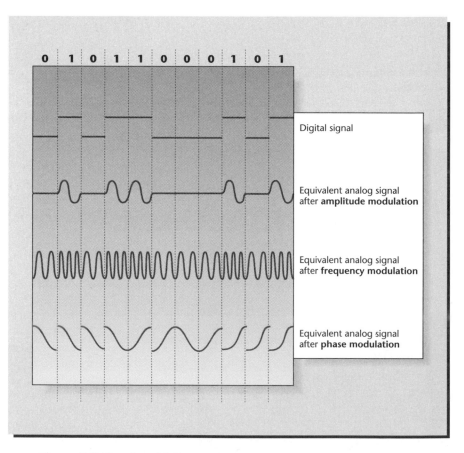

Figure 5.8 *Signal modulation*

Now that managers have realized that information has no geographical boundaries, businesses are quickly moving into remote operations. New applications are taking advantage of telecommunications technology, helping to bring a wide range of benefits to remote business operations:

- Telecommunications allows managers to receive information as it is being developed, in real time, a powerful factor in good decision making.

- Telecommunications makes it possible for people working even thousands of miles apart to share information easily. The increased use of "groupware" software allows several users to compute and design on the same screen remotely, enhances team work, and shortens response time to customers' requirements.

- Telecommunications enhances the efficiency of resource use. Databases and software applications are at the disposal of everyone connected to them, regardless of distance. Distributed processing and the client/server approach empower workers to share the same data but with applications that they can tailor to their specific needs.

To enjoy the benefits of telecommunications, managers must understand the basic concepts of the technology. If you know what is technologically available, you will know what to ask for. You will be able to contribute to the decision making involved in the implementation of different telecommunications features for your own use and for the use of your peers and subordinates.

employ devices that translate the digital signals to equivalent analog signals in their passage from the computer to the line, and then translate them back to the original digital signals just before they are transferred to the receiving computer. This modification of a digital signal (from the computer) into an analog signal (for the phone line to transmit) is called **modulation**. The transformation of an analog signal (from the phone line) into a digital signal (so the computer can understand it) is called **demodulation**. There are three different types of modulation: amplitude modulation, frequency modulation, and phase modulation.

AMPLITUDE MODULATION

As explained above, an analog signal can be graphically represented as a continuous series of waves of different heights. The height of the wave is its amplitude. In amplitude modulation (AM), the 0 bits are transformed into an analog signal whose amplitude is either zero (flat), or very low. The 1 bits are transformed into a higher wave of a fixed amplitude. The two amplitudes represent the 0s and 1s of digital transmission.

FREQUENCY MODULATION

In frequency modulation (FM), the amplitude of the wave remains constant, but the frequency varies. The frequency is the number of waves per second. Whenever a 0 bit is transmitted, the frequency is low. Whenever a 1 bit is transmitted, the frequency is greater. The two frequencies represent the 0s and 1s.

PHASE MODULATION

In phase modulation, the transmission always starts with a certain bit, 0 or 1. When the wave abruptly stops and immediately continues at another phase, it indicates a shift from the previously transmitted bit to the next bit, such as from 0 to 1, or from 1 to 0.

MODEMS

Although much of the telephone networking in the U.S., Western Europe, and Japan is technically ready for direct digital transmission, modulation/demodulation devices are still needed because the networks predominantly serve voice communication.

A device whose purpose is to modulate and demodulate communications signals is called a **modem**, a contraction of modulator-demodulator. A modem can be internal (plugged into the computer's motherboard) or external (outside the computer, plugged into a serial port). To use a modem, the user needs to attach it to a computer and install communications software, which determines the protocol of different communications and generally manages data communications. Modems are rated by their transmission speed; models are available that can transmit up to 56 Kbps and cost between $50 and $200.

SETUP To set up a modem for transmission and reception, a user must select the communication protocol, that is, the number of data bits in each byte, the number of start and stop bits, whether there is a parity check bit, and if so, whether it is odd or even. The setup of some other features may be done automatically by the communications software.

FAX/VOICE Most modems are also fax-capable, that is, they allow the computer to be used as a fax machine. Any page that needs to be faxed is first "digitized" by the modem. Digitization is a way of "taking a picture" of a page and relaying it as an array of dots. Special software divides the page into many tiny areas. Each area is assigned a binary code that represents its location on the page and its color, or hue. This digital code is then transmitted as a stream of bits. The receiving device transforms the digitized stream and reconstructs the picture.

To receive a fax through a fax-modem, the receiving computer must be on. The received digitized page is saved in a file. Note that the fax is an *image* of the page. If a letter or other text is faxed, the digital file is *not* the ASCII code representing the characters, it is just a picture of the characters. As such, the file cannot be manipulated and edited with a word processor. (Character recognition programs, discussed in Chapter 3, "Information Technology in Business: Hardware," can translate the image into text code.) Many modems also allow callers to leave voice messages, which are digitized and stored for later retrieval.

Most modems are connected to telephone lines. More recently, cable modems have started to take advantage of the high transmission rates of coaxial cable. Cable modems are likely to become increasingly popular as the use of coaxial cable becomes more widespread.

MULTIPLEXERS

Multiplexers are communications devices that allow several telephones or computers to transmit voice or digital data through a single line. If data are transmitted through telephone lines, the multiplexers may also incorporate modems.

The multiplexer (right) will connect standalone computers, such as the one shown here, to each other using radio waves rather than hard wiring.

Used by permission from Dayna Communications, Inc.

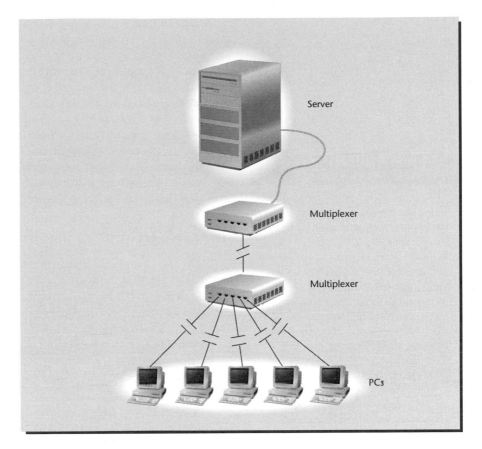

Figure 5.9 *Multiplexing*

The great advantage of multiplexers is cost savings. Instead of installing a line between a central computer and each of the terminals with which it communicates, terminals can be connected to one channel through a multiplexer (see Figure 5.9). Another multiplexer serves the host computer. There are two types of multiplexing: **frequency division** and **time division**.

Frequency Division Multiplexing. If the bandwidth of a carrier channel—that is, the range of frequencies it can carry—is large enough, it can be divided into several narrower bandwidths. This allows for frequency division multiplexing, where several computers transmit data, each at its own assigned frequency, to the host computer. As illustrated in Figure 5.10, the multiplexer can literally transmit data from several computers at the same time. The multiplexer attached to the host computer identifies the source of the data according to its unique frequency.

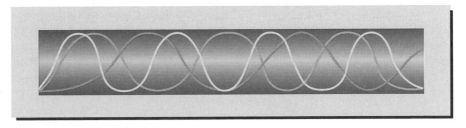

Figure 5.10 *Frequency division*

Time-Division Multiplexing. Some multiplexers allocate prespecified equal amounts of time to each connected terminal, receiving a part of each terminal's signal at a time, in a round-robin fashion, and piecing the signals together again. This is called **time-division multiplexing** and is most commonly used by terminals interacting with a host computer.

In time-division multiplexing, each terminal is allotted its time slots whether it uses the time to communicate or not. Often, some of the terminals use their time slots less than others, which causes inefficient use of the communication resources. A **statistical multiplexer** dynamically allocates time slots to those devices that need to transmit more frequently. This way, time that would otherwise be automatically allocated and not used can be used by terminals that need the line more frequently.

NETWORKS

The key to fast and efficient telecommunications is networks. In the context of data communications, a **network** is created by connecting a combination of devices (at least two computers) through one of the communication channels just discussed. Networks in which a single host computer serves only dumb terminals (computers with no processing capability of their own) are becoming obsolete as prices of microcomputers (also called "smart terminals" when they are connected to a larger computer) are plummeting.

LANs

A computer network within a building, or within a group of adjacent buildings, is called a **local area network**, or **LAN**. There is no specific distance that classifies a network as local, but as long as it is confined to a radius of 3–4 miles it is referred to as a LAN. LANs, which can be hardwired or wireless, are the most common way to let users share software and hardware resources, and to enhance communication among workers.

In LANs there is usually one computer used as a central repository of programs and files that can be used by all connected computers; this computer is called a **file server**. Connected computers can store documents on their own disks or on the file server, can share hardware such as printers, and can exchange e-mail.

LANs with a server usually have centralized control of communications among the connected computers and between the computers and the server itself. This control can be excercised by a computer or special communications device. A peer-to-peer LAN is one in which there is no central device controlling communications.

Although wireless LANs are still expensive, they offer significant benefits: companies don't have to drill holes to install wires, and they are free to move equipment around. Despite costs as high as $1,000 per node, wireless networks offer significant savings in some environments. Wireless LANs are less costly to maintain when the network spans two or more buildings. Figure 5.11 presents suggested environments in which the investment in wireless units may be justified despite their high cost, and Figure 5.12 indicates that the use of wireless hardware is expected to grow significantly over the next few years.

WANs

A network that crosses organizational boundaries, or, in the case of a multisite organization, reaches outside the immediate environment of local offices and

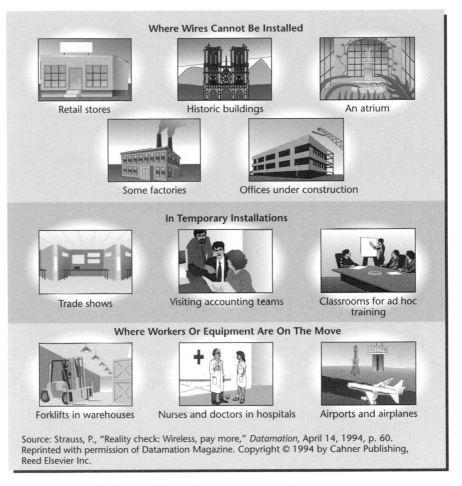

Where Wires Cannot Be Installed

Retail stores

Historic buildings

An atrium

Some factories

Offices under construction

In Temporary Installations

Trade shows

Visiting accounting teams

Classrooms for ad hoc training

Where Workers Or Equipment Are On The Move

Forklifts in warehouses

Nurses and doctors in hospitals

Airports and airplanes

Source: Strauss, P., "Reality check: Wireless, pay more," *Datamation*, April 14, 1994, p. 60. Reprinted with permission of Datamation Magazine. Copyright © 1994 by Cahner Publishing, Reed Elsevier Inc.

Figure 5.11 *Where wireless LANs may be worth the cost*

factory facilities is called a **wide area network (WAN)**. WANs can be public or private. A private WAN may use either dedicated lines or very-small-aperture-terminal satellites (VSATs), which provide narrow bandwidths and are less expensive.

YEAR	SALES ($ MILLION)	YEAR	SALES ($ MILLION)
1990	7.3	1996	565.3
1991	19.4	1997	836.9
1992	44.2	1998	1,155.9
1993	100.7	1999	1,522.1
1994	206.1	2000	1,923.1
1995	359.7		

Source: Frost & Sullivan, quoted in *MacWEEK*, Vol. 8, No. 44, November 7, 1994, p. 32.

Figure 5.12 *Past and estimated growth of wireless hardware sales*

Many organizations cannot afford to maintain a private WAN. They pay for the use of already existing networks, which are provided in two basic formats: common carriers or value-added networks.

A **common carrier** is any communications company that provides general access public telephone lines, which anyone can use by dialing, and leased lines, such as AT&T, MCI, and Sprint. The user pays for public lines based on the time used and the distance called. Leased lines are dedicated to the leasing organization. They do not serve anyone else. Leased lines have a lower error rate than dial-up lines.

Value-added networks (VANs) such as Tymnet and Sprintnet provide enhanced network services such as protocol conversion and error detection and correction. VANs fulfill organizational needs for reliable data communications while relieving the organization of the necessity for network management and maintenance.

As with LANs, **wireless communication** is winning turf in WANs (see Figure 5.13). Outfitted with a radio modem, which is a regular modem with an antenna for communicating radio signals, a user can send data on a radio frequency to a selected recipient. There are no wires to connect, no telephone jack to look for, and no unreliable cellular phone service. However, the service is still expensive. For example, subscribers to RadioMail's service must buy a radio modem, purchase an e-mail software package, pay RadioMail a start-up fee, and assume a monthly service charge. The monthly charge alone is about four times what users currently pay for e-mail services. Also, current commercial services do not provide many messaging gateways; a wireless communication from New York to Dallas may have to go through a gateway in San Mateo, California.

However, the advantages are attractive, especially to professionals who work outside their offices, such as consultants. Normally, when at a client site, a consultant must locate a suitable telephone data jack and determine the local telephone access number in order to dial into his or her e-mail service—a procedure that may take a number of tries if the access number is busy or temporarily unavailable.

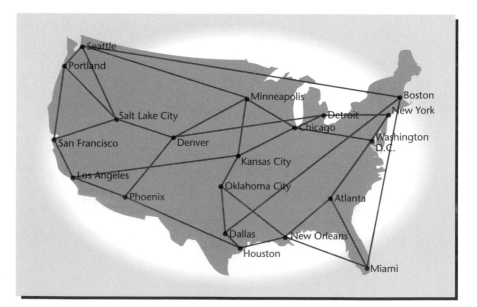

Figure 5.13 *Wireless e-mail often travels a circuitous route.*

With wireless communication, the consultant can give the client access to vast resources from a notebook computer that doesn't even appear to be connected, from anywhere in or outside an office.

NETWORK TOPOLOGY

Network topology is the physical layout of the nodes in a network, which often dictates the type of communications protocol used by the network. (For the sake of simplicity, we use the term **node** to denote any computer or communications device.) In reality, only small LANs follow a single topology. Larger networks are actually a combination of two or more different topologies. The following are descriptions of the main network topologies, and their strengths and weaknessess (see Figure 5.14).

STAR As illustrated in Figure 5.14, in a star topology all the nodes are connected to one central device. That device may be a file sever, a private branch exchange (PBX), or a network "hub." When the user of a node wants to transmit to another node, the communication is managed by, and transmitted through, the central device, which contains the communication software.

Star topology is the most popular network topology at the present time. The advantage of star topology is that it is easy to identify the source of a network problem such as a cable failure. The main disadvantage of star topology is that if

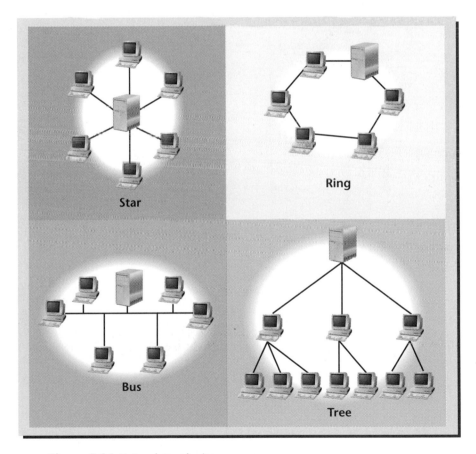

Figure 5.14 *Network topologies*

the central device is not working, the entire network is not working. Another disadvantage is that it can be costly to add computers, which necessitates the installation of a cable from the central device to each additional device.

Ring In ring topology, every node is connected to another two nodes through a single line: a twisted pair, coaxial cable, or optical fiber. There is no central computer that manages the communication. One of the computers, with a large storage capacity, is usually used as a file server.

The main disadvantage of ring topology is that signals from one computer to another nonadjacent computer must flow through the computers between them, so communication between two computers can affect any number of other computers, and can also be quite slow. The major advantage is the network's simplicity. It is easy to add a new computer to the existing network.

Bus Bus topology is an open-ended ring. All the devices are connected to a line whose ends are disconnected. The great advantage of the bus topology is the ease of adding devices to the network. Like a ring, a bus supports peer-to-peer protocols. The great disadvantage is that communication between two devices on either side of a failed device is impossible, whereas in ring topology communication can be rerouted.

spend on commuting. In 1991 a study by technology consultants Arthur D. Little estimated that if 10–20% of the activities currently involving transportation were performed by telecommunications, the U.S. economy could save $24 billion annually. Telecommuting would eliminate at least 1.8 million tons of pollutants, save 3.5 billion gallons of gasoline, and free up 3.1 billion personal hours for increasing productivity or leisure time. Some studies show that working from the home increases output by 15–50%. However, not everyone is so enthusiastic about telecommuting.

Sociologists have mixed opinions about the phenomenon. On one hand, telecommuting allows people to work who would otherwise be outside the workforce, such as older professionals and many disabled people. On the other hand, it was found that employers tend to pressure telecommuters to work harder than workers who perform their jobs in the office. In the office an employee works a preset number of hours, but the home worker has no defined workday; his or her workday is, the employer assumes, 24 hours per day. Inevitably, telecommuters are more estranged from their fellow workers. For telecommuters, there is no office in which to foster new social ties and camaraderie. Also, midlevel managers do not support the trend. They experience a lack of control when they cannot see their subordinates at work, or communicate their instructions face to face.

Many workers who were given the option to work at home have decided to return to the office. They claim that they missed the social interaction with their peers, the hallway chat, lunch with their friends, and the direct communication with fellow workers and supervisors. But telecommuting will probably continue to grow among knowledge workers. It is estimated that by the year 2000, one fourth of the American workforce will telecommute; in the not-so-remote future, as much as half of the workforce may work at home. The offices occupied by organizations will be significantly smaller than they are now, and will serve as the logical, more than the physical, center of an organization's activities.

TREE Tree topology—or hierarchical topology—consists of several stars connected to form a tree-like structure. This configuration is typical of large computer networks. It lends itself to broadcasting messages in organizations because once the "root" computer launches a message, the message can be transmitted further in parallel by the next layer of computers, each sending the message to several other computers. This is its main advantage. The main disadvantage is that if a link is disabled, all the computers of that branch of the tree are disconnected from the rest of the network.

PROTOCOLS

As discussed above, a **communications protocol** is a set of rules that governs the communication between computers or between computers and other computer-related devices that exchange data. When these rules govern a network of devices, the rule set is often referred to as **network protocol**. If a device does not know what the agreed-upon protocol of a network is, or cannot comply with it, that device cannot communicate on that network.

In a way, a protocol is like human language and basic understanding. Human beings make certain gestures when they start a conversation. Certain words signal the end of a conversation. And each element of the language, be it

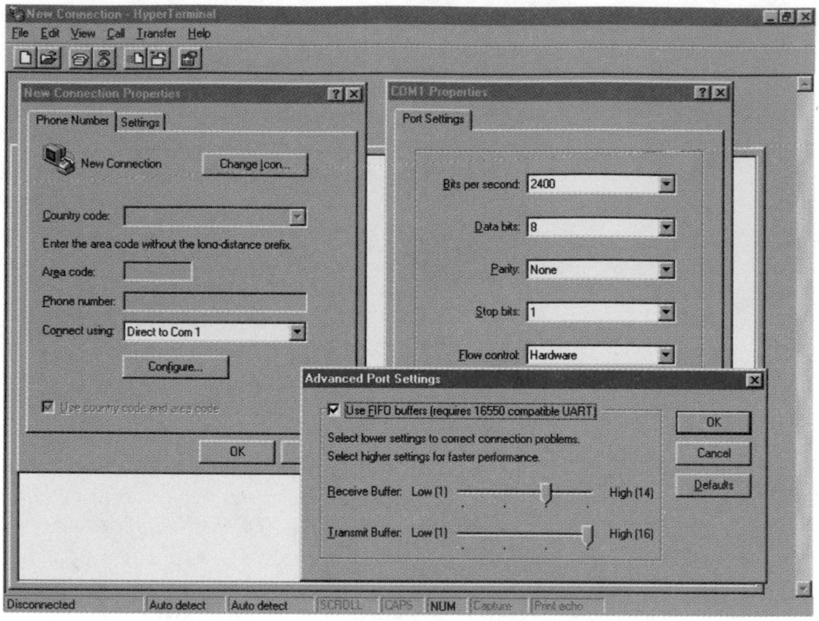

Figure 5.15 *Some communications software allows a user to establish protocols: bit rate, parity, number of data bits, stop bits, and a handshake procedure.*

English, French, or German, means the same thing to all parties. Computers, too, need an agreed-upon set of rules.

The protocol determines whether the transmission is synchronous or asynchronous; if asynchronous, the protocol determines how many data bits and how many control bits (start bit, stop bit, and parity check bit) are transmitted at a time. Both transmitter and receiver must "understand" which stream of bits signals the beginning of the transmission, and which one signals the end. And, of course, both parties must transmit and receive at an agreed-upon speed. If the transmission is synchronous, a specified protocol will determine for all parties such features as the number of bytes per packet and the specific header and trailer bytes.

As illustrated in Figure 5.15, before you log on to a network, such as your campus network, from your PC, you must ascertain that your communication software is set to conform with the corresponding elements of the network's protocol. If your computer is not instructed to follow the protocol, you cannot communicate on the network.

LAN Protocols

Before sending a message, a node must announce its intention and determine that the receiving node is ready. There are several methods for establishing this understanding before the actual transmittal of data. The most popular methods are polling, contention, and token passing.

In **polling**, a communications processor—a special device or a host computer—conducts a continuous roll call of the nodes. It sends an electrical pulse to each node in the network in a sequence. A node that has a message to send responds to the call. The communications processor then instructs the node to send the message. When this communication is over, the polling resumes.

In **contention**, each node has to contend for the line. When a node has a message to send, it checks the line. If the line is not in use, the message will be sent. Obviously, two or more nodes may start sending messages at the same time, and the messages may be garbled. To prevent this, a protocol called CSMA/CD (carrier sense multiple access with collision detection) is used. When a collision occurs, the communications processor stops both transmissions and forces the colliding nodes to wait for varying lengths of time. Then, the first node to seize the line transmits first.

The contention approach was first introduced by Xerox and subsequently adopted by Digital Equipment Corporation and Novell. The design is usually referred to as **Ethernet**, the name given it by Xerox. It is typically used in bus networks.

Another popular access method is token passing. In **token passing**, a special signal is transmitted on the line by the communications processor. Usually, the signal—or token—is a byte that is not used for any other purpose. The token is sent to each node in a sequence. A node that has a message to send seizes the token, sends the message, and retransmits the token to the processor. Then, the processor sends the token to the next node. A node without a message to send will simply not take the token.

Token passing is used both in bus and ring LAN. IBM developed the token passing standard called Token Ring, for use in ring LANs. The token moves in one direction. When a node needs to send a message, it waits until the token reaches it, stops it, sends the message, and releases the token back to the ring.

Typically, all the above protocols are implemented in networks that use either twisted pair or coaxial cables.

WAN Protocols

Wide area network protocols are significantly more complex than LAN networks. WANs are often made up of incompatible lines, communications processors, and nodes. Also, because of the long distances between nodes, signals may deteriorate and be garbled. There are several WAN protocols. After many years of international negotiations, **Open Systems Interconnection (OSI)**, developed by the International Standards Organization (ISO), has emerged as the dominant standard. Note that although OSI is often referred to as a protocol, it is actually a general model for protocols.

To understand how the model works, imagine a telephone conversation between two diplomats speaking different languages, let's say Chinese and Arabic. Since neither can speak or understand the other's language, they wish to conduct the conversation in their native languages. To do so, they must employ another "layer" of aides, interpreters. The interpreter at the Chinese end has a good command of Chinese and English; the interpreter at the Egyptian end has a good command of Arabic and English. When the diplomats wish to speak, they give their respective interpreters a signal. The interpreters give a signal to another "layer," the respective telephone operators. The telephone operators establish a connection. The interpreters then establish the rules of communication between them: they will use English. They then give the diplomats their respective signals to begin the conversation. The diplomats can then converse through these "layers" using their native languages. In other words, what makes the communication possible is a set of "layers" and the rules to which the two sides adhere. The only difference between this kind of communication and data communications in a WAN is that the latter involves more machines than human beings, and thus requires more layers and rules that can be "understood" by computers.

As illustrated in Figure 5.16, OSI consists of seven layers. Conceptually, they operate in the following way: the devices need only concern themselves with the message and identifying the receiver. The OSI views the telecommunication process as a layered activity, where each layer deals with another aspect of the process, which must have a protocol in order for any communication to take place. OSI establishes a protocol for each layer.

The *physical layer* protocols are concerned with the physical medium, or the channel, such as wires, radio waves, and optical fibers. This layer deals with the transmission of an unstructured stream of bits over the physical channel and the properties of the transmission. Included at this level is information about (1) what voltages are used to represent a 1 and a 0 respectively, (2) the duration of bit transmission, and (3) what procedures are used to maintain the channel.

The next OSI layer, the **data link layer**, takes a raw stream of bits and organizes it into **frames** by adding special header and trailer bits to indicate the boundaries of each frame. The data link layer transmits the message frames to the physical layer for actual transmittal over the line and provides error detection and control.

In the third layer, the **network layer**, the computer interacts with the network to specify the destination address and to request network facilities and priorities. The network layer is the one in which the switching and routing take place.

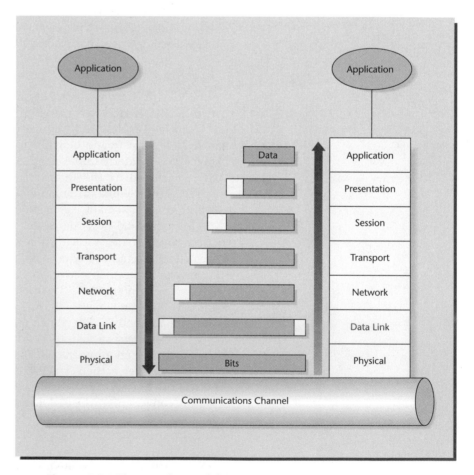

Figure 5.16 *The seven layers of the OSI model*

The **transport layer** provides a transparent transport of data from one computer to another free of error or duplication. "Transparent" means that neither the user nor other layers need to be aware of error detection. This layer may also be concerned with optimizing the use of network services. At this layer, security measures are taken.

The **session layer** provides the mechanism for controlling the dialogue between the communicating systems. For example, it is this layer in which the dialogue type is coordinated: half-duplex or full-duplex.

The **presentation layer** defines the format of the communicated data. For example, data encryption and data compression would take place at this layer. Data **encryption** is the scrambling of data at the transmitting end to minimize the risk that an unauthorized party will understand it, if it is intercepted. The receiving end has the appropriate de-scrambling device or software. **Data compression** procedures allow the transmission of significantly fewer bits to convey a message. For example, instead of using five bytes for five spaces, the transmitter can send one byte for the number "five" and one byte for a "space."

The **application layer** contains management functions and useful mechanisms to support distributed applications such as file transfer, electronic mail, and node access to remote computers.

Figure 5.16 illustrates the seven layers of OSI. The sending and receiving ends transmit and receive data only. Like the two diplomats in the above example, senders do not have to concern themselves with anything except the message itself and the address to which they wish to send it. At each layer, special software adds a header to the message frame in the form of several special bytes. The next level adds its own header while regarding the previous headers as part of the stream of bits. At the data link layer, in addition to a header, a trailer is added as a rear boundary of the frame. The physical layer regards the data bits and the headers and trailers as one long stream of bits. At the receiving end, each layer strips the frame off the corresponding header and trailer, until the user receives a data-only message at the application layer. The other layers are said to be transparent to the users.

SWITCHING TECHNIQUES AND TRANSFER MODES

For reliable transmission of a message, the sending and receiving nodes have to conform to a certain switching technique. That is, they have to agree on how the connection between communicating devices will be managed, to accommodate the transmission of data. Will the transmitter send its messages all at once, broken up into a few pieces, or broken up into many pieces? Will the entire message travel the same path, or will different parts travel different paths?

There are two major switching types: circuit switching and packet switching.

CIRCUIT SWITCHING

In **circuit switching**, the sending node signals the receiving node that it is going to send a message. The receiver must acknowledge. It then receives the entire message. The advantages of circuit switching are that data and voice can use the same line, and that no special training or protocols are needed to handle data traffic. The disadvantages are the need for compatibility of the communications devices at both ends and the need for a separate line for each node that is connected to a host computer.

Customer-Managed Inventory

Here is a look into the near future. For years, stores were responsible for managing their own shelf stock and inventory. They tracked their own supplies and placed orders with vendors as needed. The current trend in managing inventory in retail establishments is moving toward what is referred to as vendor-managed inventory. Vendors install systems in stores that allow store employees to easily and automatically transmit information regarding shelf stock and store inventory to vendor warehouses; the vendor then determines what the store needs. Most of these systems depend upon Electronic Data Interchange (EDI) and vertical data communications systems, both of which facilitate the use of data and information by many different systems.

But vendor-managed inventory systems may be just a transition phase to a more sophisticated form of *customer*-managed inventory, where data will be transmitted from the point of sale directly to the manufacturer, according to André Martin, chief executive officer of LogicNet, a division of Information Resources, Inc.

LogicNet provides software for inventory replenishment programs, as well as for managing point-of-sale data from Information Resources' databases. Martin says LogicNet can handle inventory replenishment tasks regardless of whether the retailer or the vendor is doing the managing, but he believes that, fundamentally, the individual store is the "central nervous system" of the whole supply chain—and that is where the control should be.

"Who knows best what the consumer really wants? It is the one who is closest to the firing line, the people in the stores. The further you get from the store operations, the less chance you have of forecasting what the consumer really wants," Martin says. For some time, there will be a hodge-podge of both vendor- and customer-managed replenishment systems across the nation, he predicts. So, in the near future, we may see an interorganizational chain of manufacturing resource planning systems, EDI, and other ISs, all triggered by several key-strokes at the POS in the retail store. Inventories will be reduced to virtually zero, first on retailers' premises, then on the vendors' as well.

Source: Betts, M., "Customer-managed inventory," *Computerworld*, January 31, 1994, p. 94. Reprinted with the permission of Computerworld Magazine.

THINK CRITICALLY

1. Telecommunications technology has already shifted many activities from employees of an organization to the customers of the organization. Name some of these activities in several industries.

2. With the trend toward automation of inventory replenishment and purchasing, will there still be a need for customer service and purchase officers in commercial organizations? Why, or why not?

PACKET SWITCHING

In **packet switching** the message is divided into packets, each of which is a fixed number of bytes or a frame of a variable number of bytes. The packets are transmitted separately to intermediate nodes on their way to their final destination. Different packets of the same message may be routed through different paths to minimize delay. There are some advantages to this type of switching. The sending and receiving devices do not have to be data-rate compatible because buffers in the network may receive the data at one rate and retransmit it at another rate. The lines are used on demand rather than having their capacity dedicated to a particular call. Packet switching lends the lines to multiplexing: a host computer can have simultaneous exchanges with several nodes over a single line. The main disadvantage of packet switching is the requirement for complex routing and control software. When there is a high load, there are delays. When the network is used for voice communication, a conversation with long delays may sound unnatural, so voice communication uses circuit switching only.

THE CHANGING BUSINESS ENVIRONMENT

As was discussed at the opening of this chapter, it is just as important to understand the technical foundations of telecommunications as it is to understand its continuing impact on business operations. We discussed how telecommunications makes sharing and exchanging information and ideas fast, easy, and convenient. But what are the main business areas where telecommunications is having the most impact? And how do commonly used technologies such as cellular phoning, teleconferencing, voice mail, and facsimile work?

CELLULAR PHONES

Cellular phones are so called because of the territories—known as cells—into which an area serviced by a particular provider is divided. Each cell has at its center a computer called a **transceiver** (transmitter-receiver) because it both transmits and receives: it transmits to another receiver and receives from another transmitter. When a call is placed on a cellular phone, the signal is first transmitted to the closest transceiver, which sends a signal that dials the desired phone number. If the receiving telephone is not in the same cell with the sending phone, a series of transceivers receive and retransmit the message until it reaches the destination phone. Communication takes place between the cellular phone and the receiving party through the transceivers. As the user moves from one area, or cell, to another, other transceivers pick up the transmission and receiving tasks.

By 1996, millions of people were sharing the advantages of cellular phoning: As long as a cellular service is available, people can transmit and receive calls anywhere, allowing them independence from a fixed office location. Cellular phones can also be used for e-mail and faxing. Since modems work through telephone lines, many managers use their cellular car phones to connect to their computers and use them as if they were in the office. "My car is my office" has become a reality for many managers who spend much of their time traveling.

TELECONFERENCING

Until recently, when managers from two remote sites had to confer in person, they had to travel to a meeting place. Now, people sitting in conference rooms thousands of miles apart are brought together by transmitting their images and speech to each other in what is called **teleconferencing**.

Teleconferencing saves the travel costs and time of highly salaried employees, whether they work in different organizations or in different offices of the same organization.

VOICE MAIL

Virtually every personal computer can be equipped with hardware and software that will allow its user to transmit and receive **voice mail**. With voice mail, a person who calls the number to which the modem of the PC is connected can leave a voice message. The message is digitized into bytes and stored for the user in a queue. The user can open the mail file, retrieve the message, and play it through the PC's speakers. Voice mail has largely replaced answering machines in the business environment.

FACSIMILE

As discussed above, **facsimile** (from Latin: duplicate), or **fax**, is the transmission and reception of images over telephone lines. The fax machine at the transmitting end digitizes the image and transmits the bits representing it to the receiving fax machine. The receiving machine transforms the digitized codes back into an image. The great advantage of using fax machines is the ability to transmit original documents, both text and images, without the need to convert them into a computer file for transmission. It also provides an easy means of communicating pictorial images.

Virtually every modem offered on the market now is a fax/modem, a device that allows the transmission of a file to, and receiving of a file from, a fax machine, as well as operating as a modem.

WHAT'S AHEAD?

Probably the most profound effect of telecommunications has been the internationalization of business. Even the smallest "mom and pop" businesses can now communicate with countries thousands of miles away just by making a local call on a computer, or by publishing a home page on the World Wide Web.

But this global business village is only possible if all participants agree to the technological protocols needed to communicate. In recent years there have been international agreements on two concepts that will have a significant effect on both business organizations and households: ISDN and ATM. We'll devote a short discussion to each topic here.

INTEGRATED SERVICES DIGITAL NETWORKS

Integrated Services Digital Network (ISDN) is a set of protocols and services now being implemented that allows the integrated transmission of voice, data, and video communications. Whereas we now receive television through radio-wave transmission or cable, and usually receive telephone and computer transmission through twisted-pair telephone wires, ISDN allows all signals to be transmitted over the same conduit.

The idea of ISDN is to make all of the signals that we receive, including telephony and digital, and communicate them through the same communications link. Thus, ISDN enhances the already existing concept of multimedia, allowing the reception of many different types of input, from text to graphics to animation and sound. Eventually, ISDN will be a world-wide public telecommunications network that will replace the current analog public networks and deliver a wide variety of services.

The integration of these services requires fast communications lines. Indeed, ISDN lines accommodate faster bit-rate than regular telephone lines: they allow transmission at a rate of up to 128 Kbps. Many regions in the U.S. offer such lines for use by organizations and private citizens.

Imagine what will happen when this concept is widely implemented. Offices and homes will have a single device, a combination of today's computer and television set, which will be used to compute, store and retrieve data, receive television programs, and place telephone calls. The technology will enable interactive TV. You will be able to respond to questions presented by program hosts; you will be able to select video tapes from vast collections and view them when you want to.

In business, managers will be able to view actual operations as they occur, on one part of the monitor, receive text and numeric data on another part, and receive a "voice" briefing, all through the same device.

ISDN lines are already offered by telephone companies in many regions of the U.S. However, their maximum speed of 128 Kbps is quickly becoming too slow for the graphic-heavy information communicated through the Internet, discussed at length in Chapter 6, "The Internet and Intranets."

ASYNCHRONOUS TRANSFER MODE

For many years the term ATM meant only Automatic Teller Machine, but since the early 1990s, the acronym has also meant something in telecommunications: **Asynchronous Transfer Mode (ATM)**. ATM is a digital multiplexing and high-speed switching protocol developed to support the architecture for Broadband ISDN (B-ISDN). It can offer bandwidth on demand and support a union of local and wide area networks.

The adjective "asynchronous" may be confusing here, because ATM actually sends data synchronously. It is called asynchronous because it does not require synchronization devices. It is defined to operate over electrical or optical transmission links. The key concept underlying ATM is **cell switching**. **Cells**, in this context, are fixed-length blocks of data carrying user information as well as basic routing and control information.

In the international standard of ATM, cells are short. Each cell comprises 53 bytes: a five-byte header containing the address, and 48 bytes of information. Each group of information bytes, regardless of length, must be transmitted with header bytes, so small cells have more overhead than large cells. However, large cells have disadvantages as well. The longer the cell for voice transmission, the longer the time the telephone network must wait before it has enough voice to fill a cell and transmit it. If the cells are large, significant delays will occur and the quality of speech will deteriorate.

In long-distance voice communication, some bytes must be included in each message to cancel echo, the reflection of the transmitted signal from the received signal in the telephone network. Over small distances there is no risk of echo.

In Europe, distances between senders and receivers are shorter than in the U.S. Hence, in the international negotiations, the Europeans preferred 32-byte cells, and U.S. representatives preferred 64-byte cells. The longer cell accommodates both echo cancellation and higher efficiency in data communications. The compromise was 48-byte cells. With this convention, the Europeans still need to use some of the cells for echo cancellation in voice communication, and the data transmission efficiency is lower than with 64-byte cells.

It is expected that ATM will be the dominant standard of the future. Some experts predict that the protocol will eventually replace current protocols not only in WANs but also in LANs.

IMPACT OF TELECOMMUNICATIONS ON THE INFORMATION SYSTEMS ARCHITECTURE

Unfortunately, the word "architecture" is used to convey many different things. In this chapter, **architecture** refers to an organization's hardware and software system configuration. Advances in telecommunications have been a major contributor to drastic changes in IS architectures. Many companies are **downsizing** their systems, that is, moving from one architecture (using a few large computers to which many smaller computers and terminals are connected) to another architecture (using small powerful machines connected to each other). Although most commonly used to describe dramatic decreases in staffing, the term downsizing was first used in the context of systems architecture.

With fast and reliable telecommunications, organizations can move from an architecture of shared resources to a client/server architecture. With shared resources, computing power is centrally located and accessed from terminals; in a client/server arrangement, computing power and many applications are located in each computer, and large data files that need to be shared are housed in a server. The issues surrounding client/server architecture are closely related to databases. Both topics are discussed further in Chapter 7, "Data Management."

SECURITY

On a final note, we must recognize the great risks that come with the great opportunities of telecommunications technology. Once an organization connects its IS to a public network, security issues become extremely important. Unauthorized access and data destruction are constant threats. Thus, organizations must establish proper security measures as preventive measures. We discuss the risks and preventive measures in Chapter 17, "Controls and Security Measures."

Reconcile Checks Remotely

Telecommunications allows businesses to do some of their accounting remotely. For instance, American Express Co. is trying to help its business customers use electronic expense reports instead of paper expense reports. In June 1996, the company's Corporate Services unit released Expense Manager, an application that lets employees download their charges from American Express computers, drag them into customized software expense forms, and submit the report to their employers via e-mail. Users have to type in only the information American Express doesn't know, such as the names of clients they took to dinner.

The application includes four modules. One allows employees to create and file expense reports. The second lets managers approve reports, using a personal identification number for security, and send them to their corporate accounting department. The third module helps companies to audit expenses. The fourth module creates a database of expense information that managers can examine. Users can request updates of transactions by

sending e-mail to American Express, or businesses can have statements sent to them at regular intervals.

Similar expense-reporting software is available from other issuers of corporate credit cards as well as from independent software vendors. But American Express's 6.4 million corporate-card holders constitute a big advantage for the new software. "They are playing from a position of strength here," said Karen Epper, an analyst for Forrester Research Inc. in Cambridge, Massachussetts. "They are the predominant player in this business, by a long shot."

According to American Express, the average company spends $22 processing each paper expense form, not including the cost of the employee's time to fill out the form. American Express is aiming Expense Manager primarily at large customers such as Philips Electronics NV, which in 1997 was testing the software for possible rollout to all 25 of its U.S. divisions. Since Philips has standardized on American Express corporate cards, it would prefer to use expense reporting software from American Express, said Cindy Scanlon, travel manager at Philips Medical Systems in Shelton, Connecticut. American Express charges fees for the service, with a

maximum charge of $50,000 for large customers. A $2,500 fee is added for helping organizations set up and incorporate company policies into the software.

Source: Swenson, J., "Filing expenses via American Express," InformationWeek, July 1, 1996, p. 103.

Questions

1. Assume that you are the chief financial officer for a large corporation. For your organization, what are the advantages and disadvantages of using the above service?

2. Assess Expense Manager from a strategic point of view. Can the new application give American Express a strategic advantage? Why, or why not?

Forget the Wires

When Younkers, the department store chain based in Des Moines, Iowa, was shopping for a state-of-the-art platform to replace its aging point-of-sale (POS) system, it faced two problems. One was its recent acquisition of the former H.C. Prange department stores, based in Green Bay, Wisconsin. Prange's POS system was not compatible with the existing Younkers system, and the need to integrate the two rendered the need for a fast installation of the new system critical. The second problem was the need to rewire every store in the Younkers chain, 29 original Younkers stores and 25 former Prange stores, to accommodate the high-bandwidth LAN that Younkers wanted to implement in connection with its POS upgrade. This, of course, threatened to be an extremely costly and time-consuming process that could prevent the quick installation needed to keep business running smoothly. The only way Younkers believed that it could accomplish a "rollout" (the term used to describe the start-up of a new system) within a reasonably short time frame was to "go wireless" with all terminals in all stores.

NCR and its software partner, Post Software International, helped Younkers come up with an innovative solution using several leading-edge components:

◆ NCR's WaveLAN for wireless communications between the back-room processor and all sales floor terminals

◆ An in-store processor in each store running a relational database

◆ A menu-driven full-screen POS transaction set

Dan Smith, chief information officer and senior vice president of Younkers, says the LAN provided several benefits. Since no wiring was necessary, the rollout schedule, which began after a two-month pilot, was shortened by at least 60 days relative to a schedule requiring hard wiring. Also, normal work at the store went on without disturbance.

The preset and preloaded terminals were installed in each store without affecting the existing wired network. Training on the new equipment took place without delay. Most importantly, from a customer service perspective, Younkers gained the capability to easily move its POS terminals to where they could be most effective, from low-volume areas of the store to heavy traffic areas, depending on the season or on sales in particular departments.

This also had the effect of reducing the number of terminals required per store by 10%, Smith says. With 15 to 100 terminals in each store, that translated into "roughly 250 fewer terminals chain-wide than we would have needed otherwise." Add to that the cost of peripherals and maintenance, and "we figure we saved about a million dollars right off the bat," he says.

Smith acknowledges that he initially considered the wireless LAN to be somewhat of a risk for Younkers, in that it's "hardly a mainstream product," and involves "very leading-edge technology." His fears were allayed, he says, by the fact that J.C. Penny had tested the product in seven stores and was pleased with it. "Penny spent a long time studying WaveLAN, and they were remarkably helpful and cooperative in giving us access to their findings, and letting us observe their operations," Smith says.

Source: "Younkers goes wireless," Chain Store Age Executive with Shopping Center Age, © Information Access Company; © Lebhar-Friedman Inc, 1993, Vol. 69 No 11, p. 18A ISSN 0193–1199.

Questions

1. What were the problems Younkers faced?

2. What are the benefits of the new system?

3. Can you think of another business environment in which this technology could benefit the organization? Explain.

Go on LAN

As United Science Industries grew to reach sales of $4 million per year, CEO Jay Koch watched labor overhead eat up his profits. The Woodlawn, Illinois, environmental-service provider hadn't yet set up a computer network; employees were duplicating work and the collection and use of data were extremely time-consuming. Just as an example, accounting had to gather and enter data from the field managers' handwritten sheets to generate invoices, a process that usually took at least two months. Koch realized that if the system were networked and automated, field managers could enter data in field computers, which could be accessed and used by accounting and other departments in the store. United needed networking power.

In late 1994 Koch decided to replace his ten Macintoshes with PCs. A consultant determined that United needed a local area network. The total cost was about $76,000. Wiring 15 networked computers cost $8,000, while the Novell NetWare software for 50 users and the server cost $11,400. The computers and software came to $47,500, and in-house training cost another $9,000.

With the proper software installed, everyone has access to project files. "With the network, people spend less time hunting for information and more time working on tasks crucial to operations," Koch says. There's less paperwork floating around the office, since all workers can gain access to the same information from their computers.

Now accounting has access to field managers' files, so invoicing takes only ten to twelve days, and Koch thinks that, in time, it will take only three to four days. He estimates that he has speeded up accounts receivable by five to ten days and lowered labor costs by $20,000 per month.

Source: "The Need for Speed," Inc., *March 1996, p. 103. Reprinted with permission,* Inc. *Magazine. Copyright ©1996 by Goldhirsch Group, 38 Commercial Wharf, Boston MA 02110.*

Questions

1. Identify the cost items involved in the new LAN.

2. What are the different types of benefits of the new LAN?

Riding the Data Highway

On a stormy Wisconsin evening, a beep breaks Brian Bertram's concentration. The bearded 34-year-old reaches for his laptop, punches a key, and watches text scroll onto the screen: "Icy road conditions exist in much of Wisconsin and Illinois. Please slow down." It's a reminder Bertram appreciates as he steers his truck through drifting snow on I-94. "I couldn't work for a company that's pushing me," he says. But that message reveals more than benevolence. It also tells his employer, Schneider National, where he is, which way he's headed and when he's likely to deliver 24 rolls of paper to a printing plant in Covington, Tenn.

If trucking makes you think of CB radios and cowboys in CAT caps hightailing through the night, better update that image: the lonely road is quickly becoming an information highway. No one is traveling it faster that Schneider National, which has emerged from the obscurity of Green Bay, Wis., to become the nation's largest hauler of full-truckload freight. Although it owns 9,000 bright-orange trucks, Schneider is really an information system masquerading as a trucking line. Last week its ability to gather and mine vast amounts of data won it a contract worth hundreds of millions of dollars to manage logistics for General Motors' auto parts operation. No wonder Wall Street is watching. Says CEO Don Schneider: "People get the mistaken impression that our business is running trucks."

Schneider's sophistication is extraordinary. When Procter & Gamble advises that a trailer of detergent needed in Denver will be ready in Cincinnati at 3 p.m., the computer lists drivers headed for Cincinnati and their arrival times, updated every two hours via a satellite link on each truck. Should driver 11839, who will be free at 1 p.m., take the load? The system says no; it knows that 11839 has been driving since 3 a.m. and, by law, must take a break. What about driver 27536, who'll be empty at 2:30? On a Tuesday he might handle it, but on a Thursday this load would mean a weekend away from his Georgia home. The system gives 27536 an Atlanta load, while the Denver freight goes to driver 83620. The time and place of pickup are beamed to the computer in his cab,

sparing him the need to phone in. Later, the computer will register his speed—and if he exceeds Schneider's 55-mile-an-hour limit, he may lose his monthly bonus.

Keeping its equipment busy, its drivers moving and its customers happy enabled the closely held company to post $1.25 billion in revenue in 1993, nearly double its revenue for 1989. That growth, in turn, allows Schneider to buy trucks by the thousands and run a network of company-owned centers that lets it save on fuel and maintenance. When Brian Bertram puts a card into the pump at a Schneider center, his fuel consumption is automatically recorded in a computer back in Green Bay, letting the company spot mechanical problems early.

Investment bankers are beating a path to Don Schneider's spartan office, but the 58-year-old Schneider sees no need to sell the firm his father began with one truck in 1935. The company refuses to file profit data with the Interstate Commerce Commission, but Don Schneider says its earnings provide enough capital to grow as much as 20% a year. If competitors think trucks are their business, they have plenty to fear.

Source: "Riding the Data Highway," Newsweek, *March 21, 1994, Newsweek Inc. All rights reserved. Reprinted by permission.*

Questions

1. What does efficiency mean in the trucking industry? How has telecommunications made Schneider's operations more efficient?

2. Some benefits of a new IS cannot be quantified. What impact has the telecommunications system had on drivers?

•••• In recent years, the major developments in the way we disseminate and use information have been driven by telecommunications technology. Organizations are increasingly dependent on fast, reliable means of communicating business data both internally and with other organizations. Thus, to succeed as a manager, you must understand the underlying technological developments and the ways in which the technology is used to facilitate business processes.

Telecommunications is communication over distance. Nowadays, it refers primarily to communication of digital data over distance. There are three modes in which telecommunications is performed: **simplex**, whereby only one party transmits and the other receives; **half-duplex**, whereby a party can only transmit or only receive during communications; and **full-duplex**, in which both parties, that is, computers, can both transmit and receive at the same time.

Bits are used to represent data in data communications. Inside the computer and between a computer and its peripheral devices, data can be communicated using **parallel transmission**, in which all bits of a byte are transmitted at the same time through a bundle of wires, with one bit traveling through each wire. Over a long distance, however, the bits must be transmitted one following another, which is called **serial transmission**.

Different media are said to have different capacities, meaning that they are capable of carrying different numbers of bits per second (bps) without garbling messages. To ensure correct reception of data, communications devices must be **synchronous**. When special synchronization devices are employed, the transmission is said to be **synchronized**. When communication is **synchronized** without synchronization devices, the transmission is said to be **asynchronous**. Asynchronous transmission adds extra bits to each byte to indicate the beginning and end of the byte and for error detection.

Between computers, data is transmitted digitally as bits, in the form of zeroes and ones, represented in some form of two states, either using electrical impulses or bursts of light. However, most telephone lines are still capable of transmitting only **analog** (continuous) **signals**, not **digital** (discrete) **signals**. To transmit digital data using an analog line requires that the amplitude, frequency, or phase of the analog signal be **modulated** to represent equivalent digital signals.

This modulation is executed by a **modem**, which is an abbreviation of modulator/demodulator. When the computer is sending data, the modem modulates the digital signal into an analog signal. When the computer is receiving data, the modem accepts the modulated signal and demodulates it into the original digital signal.

While often incorporating modems, **multiplexers** are more sophisticated devices that allow several computers to communicate with another computer via the same channel, thereby making the use of the channel more efficient.

Data is transmitted through different media. Telecommunications media include the old telephone lines made of **twisted pairs** of copper wires, **coaxial cables**, **microwave devices**, and **fiber-optic devices**. The devices use different types of channels, or paths, through which the streams of bits flow. Twisted pair, coaxial cable, and optical fiber are **guided channels**. Microwave devices transmit data through air and outer space, which are **unguided channels**.

When computers are connected locally within an office, we refer to the arrangement as a **local area network (LAN)**. When computers communicate over long distances, the network is referred to as a **wide area network (WAN)**. Both LANs and WANs can be organized in several physical layouts: star, ring, bus, tree, or a combination thereof—all of which have strengths and weaknesses. Both LANs and WANs increasingly employ wireless technology, which significantly reduces the need for expensive wiring.

To ensure that a receiving computer receives accurate messages, some rules must be established to which all computers on a network must adhere. A set of rules that governs telecommunications is called a **protocol**. One of the rules is the form of switching, or the manner in which a message is communicated: in its entirety from the transmitting computer to the receiving computer (**circuit switching**), or divided into packets of bytes and transmitted via several nodes on the network (**packet switching**).

Telecommunications technology has changed the business environment. Businesspeople are now more mobile; they can use cellular phones not only for voice communication but also for data communications. Teleconferencing brings managers together across thousands of miles. **Voice mail** allows business people to record voice messages on computers so that the person receiving the message does not have to pick up the phone to receive it. **Fax** capability is now incorporated into modems and allows the communication of graphic information in addition to text.

Until recently, the major obstacle in turning the world into a global village was standardization, but there have been great strides toward international agreements. The **Asynchronous Transmission Mode (ATM)** protocol for the **Integrated Services Digital Network (ISDN)** is an example of such cooperation. Soon, these international standards will usher in the ultimate means of communication: a single device providing the capabilities of the current television set, computer, and telephone.

These great advances in technology also have some negative impacts. We are witnessing the emergence of the "virtual organization," an organization that is independent of a physical location, and whose members don't commute but telecommute. Telecommuting has its advantages, but it can also erode some of the basic human needs, like socializing, the short hallway chat during lunch break, and a clear separation between work and family obligations.

When an organization connects its information systems to public networks, it must protect them against risks of unauthorized access. Preventive measures must be taken to provide adequate security. These measures are discussed in Chapter 17, "Controls and Security Measures."

REVIEW, DISCUSS, AND EXPLORE

REVIEW AND DISCUSSION QUESTIONS

1. What are the benefits of LANs?

2. What are the advantages and disadvantages of the following telecommunications topologies: star, ring, and bus?

3. ISDN integrates computing with telecommunications in businesses. What are the advantages of this integration?

4. What are the implications of telecommunications for group work?

5. How is telecommunications changing the nature of organizations and work style?

6. What are the risks to organizations that are involved in the growing use of networks for business?

7. What can a company that does not have access to computer networks do to utilize the technology?

8. *Ethics and Society:* Consider your own life and preferences. Would you prefer to work in an office or to telecommute? Why?

CONCEPT ACTIVITY

Consider an industry with which you are familiar. Prepare a short paper in which you suggest how telecommunications could help the industry.

HANDS-ON ACTIVITY

1. Joan Smith completed her book *I Graduated from Wisdom University, Now What?* She used a word processor to type up the manuscript. The book took exactly one 3.5-inch disk with a capacity of 1.4 MB (ASCII-8). Since she lives in Detroit, the publisher asked that she transmit the book to the publisher's office in New York. Both Joan and the publisher have 28,800 bps modems that are set to transmit each ASCII-8 byte with 1 start bit, no stop bit, and 1 even parity check bit.

   How long (in minutes) does it take to transmit the book? Ignore the distance between the cities. Remember how many bytes make up 1 K. Show your calculations clearly. Use measurement units throughout your calculation.

2. Alex Pushkin uses a 28.8 Kbps modem to transmit a report from his office to headquarters. The data communications protocol is identical to the one in Question 1. The report is transmitted in ASCII-8. On the average, a page contains 4,000 characters including spaces. Alex is allotted only ten minutes for the transmission. *How many pages can he transmit?*

TEAM ACTIVITY

Select a bank branch that is close to your school. Interview the branch personnel about the telecommunications equipment used between the branch and (1) other branches, (2) headquarters, and (3) other institutions (such as credit information companies), if any. Use the discussion in this chapter to identify the different communications devices that are used by the branch. List the devices and state their roles in the bank.

EXPLORE THE WEB

Use your browser to look for five companies that develop and manufacture telecommunications hardware (such as modems, cable modems, multiplexers, and the like). Prepare a list of the manufacturers and their main products. Explain the functions of each product. If the site does not give enough information, send an inquiry to the e-mail address mentioned at the site.

Chapter **6**

The Internet and Intranets

A Virtual Home Office

When Xerox Corp.'s U.S. Customer Operations branch introduced a virtual office strategy for its field representatives in 1995, it hoped the move would cut costs and let sales representatives spend more time with customers. The idea of the virtual office was to provide all the communications and computation technology necessary—phone, FAX, e-mail, and the like—so that sales and service people would no longer need to be *at* the office to be *in* the office. What the Xerox division did not anticipate was the extent to which this strategy would change the way field representatives keep in touch with the office.

There were some unexpected challenges in keeping people up to date on office operations when they weren't in the office, explained Jim Roth, systems consultant for the company. One of the biggest challenges was that the representatives did not have easy access to the latest marketing data and other presales support. Even though fax capability was available through portable computers, that didn't help much because it was inconvenient to use and not very interactive. The division looked for a better solution.

The Xerox Customer Operations division found the solution to its virtual office woes in the new Internet and intranet concept. Now field representatives use their Web browsers to point and click their way through HTML documents with current marketing data and other important information. Like other organizations that have launched corporate intranets, Xerox saw the potential for implementing easy-to-use, Web-based technologies to let employees share information more efficiently. Xerox Wide Web, the company's internal version of the World Wide Web, is hosted on more than 800 Web servers and accessed by more than 25,000 employees.

But it does not stop there. Xerox found that intranets also affect the way people and departments interact, redefine job responsibilities, and give employees a role in developing applications that make their work more efficient.

Source: Maddox, K., "The Work Connection," *InformationWeek*, September 16, 1996, pp. 98–102.

LEARNING OBJECTIVES

The Internet has been the most exciting development in the field of information systems and telecommunications in recent years. The combination of advanced telecommunications technology and innovative software is changing the way we communicate, shop, make payments and contracts, educate, and learn. With the introduction of a graphical user interface (GUI) on the Internet's World Wide Web, numerous companies throughout the world have established a "Net" presence.

When you finish this chapter you will:

- Know what the Internet is
- Understand how the World Wide Web has developed and what its visual, audio, and animation capabilities are
- Have a good idea of how Web sites are built
- Know the business potential of the Web
- Realize the risks and limitations of using the Web for business activities

WHAT IS THE INTERNET?

Imagine you need a bookkeeping program for your home-based business selling advertising space for your local newspaper. You've heard that the World Wide Web is a good place to research any purchase. You go to your computer and connect to your school's main computer, which is a node on the vast network known as the Internet. You use your Web browser to search for information about bookkeeping software and soon find an online mall that lists all bookkeeping programs, their features, and their prices. From your computer, you select the programs that seem to most closely match your needs. You click on their descriptions, and download the demonstration files that show you the user interface and basic functionality of the programs. You make your choice based on your budget and need, enter your credit card number into the online purchase form presented on the Web, and proceed to download your copy of the software and its supporting documentation, which you install on your computer and begin using with the next day's sales.

Just a few years ago, most businesses had absolutely no use for the Internet. Back then, the **Internet** was a communications network connected to government and researchers that could transmit text only. All that has changed. Technology only a few years old has brought multimedia to the Internet—full-color graphics, animation, video, and sound, as well as graphically-based interactivity. The part of the Internet that carries all these new features has come to be known as the **World Wide Web** (**WWW**). With new visual tools and interactivity to grab people's attention and make online business transactions (such as purchases and payments) a reality, companies quickly saw a new opportunity to advertise their wares and ultimately to conduct their business.

As of this writing, few businesses have managed to actually make money on the Web. But experts agree that in any area of business, an understanding of the Internet will be essential to your career. To know how to best apply the Internet in business, it is important that you understand the basic technology that drives it, where the most important advances are being made, and the limitations and risks of this new tool as well.

THE DEVELOPMENT OF THE INTERNET

Today, the Internet is a network of networks with hundreds of thousands of servers. Tens of millions of people take for granted that with a simple phone call via their modems, they can access a huge number of files of all types from all Internet servers, do research, purchase items, and participate in electronic discussions. It has not always been so.

In 1969, the U.S. Department of Defense's Advanced Research Projects Agency (ARPA) wanted to establish a communications network that would operate in case of a nuclear strike, as an alternative to telephone, radio, and television, all of which might quickly become nonfunctional in a military crisis. One of the most important features ARPA sought was that the network have no central point for controlling communications. A system was developed in which messages could travel from one point to another through any number of routes. Thus, if one line was destroyed, there would be other lines through which to route messages to a node. The result was the Internet's predecessor, ARPANET, a network that was launched with a mere four computers. ARPANET's computers exchanged information in the form of digitized data, operating according to standards agreed upon by all participants, with no one person, institution, or organization "in charge." And with distributed control, the system had no one centralized vulnerable point through which anyone could either control or disable the entire system.

In today's terms, ARPANET was a modest network. Participants placed files on their computers so that others could find and access them. The government soon found that ARPANET provided an effective way for researchers to communicate easily with each other. ARPANET was an open system designed for the free flow of information, but available only to members of academic institutions and some of the defense community.

The number of computers on the Internet has grown steadily since that time. At a certain point, the U.S. Government decided to split the network into a civilian one and a military one. The civilian network came to be known as the Internet. Soon, other networks connected to the Internet, and the Internet is now known as a network of networks.

GROWTH OF THE INTERNET

Physically, the Internet is a network of communications media to which hundreds of thousands of computers are connected (see Figure 6.1). This major line of communication is called the **backbone**, and the computers that are linked directly to the backbone and carry the files accessed over the Internet are called Internet **servers**. A typical Internet user connects to the backbone through a local area network at work or by dialing up and connecting directly to a server via a modem and phone lines. When people speak of 100 million Internet users, they refer to people who have dial-up or network access to an Internet server.

When speaking of Internet growth, some people are referring to the addition of *servers* to the network (that is the linking of additional computers directly to the backbone), and others are referring to the increase in the number of *users* of the network (that is the number of people with accounts to *access* the Internet). Indeed, the growth on both counts is impressive: in May 1993 there were 100 servers on the

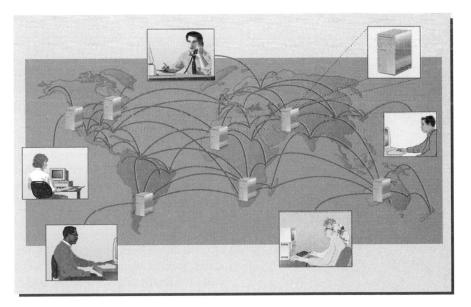

Figure 6.1 *The Internet has over 100,000 networks and almost 100 million users.*

Internet; two years later there were 22,000, and by 1997 there were about 100,000. By the time you read this book, these numbers will have grown significantly. It has been estimated that there are another 30 million or so Internet computers at the disposal of some 100 million users who could access those servers. In fact, some of the fastest growing businesses in the United States are Internet Service Providers (ISPs), the companies that set up servers on the Internet and provide access to organizations and individuals who do not have their own servers on the backbone.

As mentioned above, the Internet is not owned or controlled by anybody. Nobody decides who may connect another server to the backbone, nor who may log on, nor how the resource should be used. As explained below, the only element that is determined by an organized body is the assignment of a unique address to a newly connected server. This freedom from authority and rules may be one reason for the tremendous growth of what is often referred to as *the Net*.

COMMERCIAL ONLINE SERVICES

Several companies offer "online" services to the public; such as the widely-known America Online (AOL), Prodigy, and CompuServe. What are these online services, and how do they relate to the Internet? Before the World Wide Web made the Internet attractive as well as useful, a number of independent companies created commercial online networks, such as the American ones listed above and others abroad. These services are networks that are private; the information on their servers is controlled completely by these companies and is accessible, by dial-in to their servers, only to paying subscribers who are assigned special user IDs and passwords. The private networks compete with each other by providing a wide variety of different information services, including news, sporting events, online games, e-mail, and subscriber-only chat rooms where people can exchange information and the like. Originally, subscribers to a private network could communicate electronically only with other subscribers to the same network. Furthermore, the early services of the private networks did not include connecting their subscribers to the Internet.

The popularity of the Web pushed online service companies to offer their subscribers Internet access. The private services connected their computers to the Internet backbone and installed software that allows subscribers to connect, seamlessly, to the Internet. This gateway to the Internet allows subscribers to exchange e-mail messages with anyone who has access to the Internet, not only with other subscribers to a particular online service.

INTERNET DOMAINS

If you have ever been on the Internet, you are familiar with .com, .org, .gov, and the like. But, what do these names mean and where do they come from? Every machine on the Internet backbone is uniquely identified with a numerical label known as an **Internet Protocol** or **IP number**, which has four parts separated by periods, such as 146.186.87.220. Some years after the Internet was established, the Internet Community (IC) agreed that it would be helpful for servers to have a unique name that was easy to remember. So while every Internet server had a unique IP number, those who wanted one could apply to have a unique *name* assigned to that IP number. Internet computers are named using a domain naming system, which breaks down all Internet servers into different groups—called **domains**—and makes each domain responsible for the names of computers in its group. Usually, server names include between two and four parts, designating their domains (see Figure 6.2).

Internet Computer Suffix	Organization Type	Example	
		Web Domain Name	Web Server Name
	United States		
.com	Commercial Organization	www.ibm.com	IBM Corp.
.edu	Academic Institution	www.psu.edu	The Pennsylvania State University
.gov	Government Agency	www.irs.ustreas.gov	Internal Revenue Service
.org	Not-for-Profit Organization	www.acm.org	Association for Computing Machiner
.mil	Military Unit	www.usma.army.mil	U.S. Military Academy, West Point
.net	Internet Service Provider	www.gi.net	Global Internet Com., Inc.
	All Other Countries		
.jp	Japan	www.netlaputa.or.jp	The NetLaputa Organization
.uk	United Kingdom	www.fco.gov.uk	Foreign & Commonwealth Office
.au	Australia	www.ida.com.au	Blue Tongue Online
.il	Israel	www.tau.ac.il	Tel-Aviv University

Figure 6.2 *Internet address suffixes*

•• POINT OF INTEREST

Vying for Domain Names

Securing an Internet domain name no longer depends on how quickly an organization chooses a name, but also on how careful the organization is to pay InterNIC the $100 annual fee charged by the registry. If the owner misses a payment, another applicant can ask for, and be granted, the right to the name. When IBM discovered that *www.ibm.com* was legally owned by Iqmar's Baltic Mints, it entered negotiations with the small company and paid the company to ensure that IBM could continue using the name. Many companies are insuring their domain names with Lloyds, the famous insurance organization in London. Many others have litigated their cases in federal courts. Undoubtedly, Internet domain names have become an important commodity.

Source: Niksanek, C., "Are you the master of your domain?" *Datamation*, February 1997, p. 137.

The coordinator of domain names is known as the Internet Network Information Center, or InterNIC. The last part, or suffix, for each Internet server domain name designates the top-level domain where that server operates. The top-level domain for Internet servers in all countries except the U.S. is a two-letter country code, such as "ca" for Canada, "au" for Australia, "uk" for the United Kingdom, and the like. The U.S., however, has several top-level domains that identify the type of business being conducted on the server. As shown in Figure 6.2, the most common are .com, .edu, .gov, .mil, .org, and .net. If an organization outside the U.S. is a research or educational institution, the country code is usually preceded by an "ac" (academic) rather than the American "edu."

Here is an example of how the domain naming system works. Let's say you addressed e-mail to a friend at *ux.cso.uiuc.edu*. This name has four domain levels, each separated by a period. The highest is *.edu*, which is responsible for all names within it, of which *uiuc* is only one. The next domain is *uiuc* (University

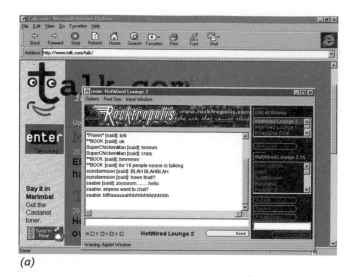

(a)

(b)

There are many different types of information on the Internet, from text-only shown in (a) a real-time chat window, (b) usenet news, and (c) e-mail, to full multimedia shown in (d) the World Wide Web.

of Illinois at Urbana Champaign), which is responsible for all names at that campus, of which *cso* is one, and so on. The model is similar to addressing mail sent through the postal service, where the country is the top-level domain, and the state or province is the second level domain.

Note that every computer that is connected to the Net—even a computer only connected from time to time to collect e-mail or surf the Web—is assigned an IP number. The computer of a user who connects to the Internet infrequently is assigned an IP number for the duration of its connection. The IP number is associated with the server to which it is connected (it is created by adding a numeral to the server's permanent IP number). This allows sites on computers that are not directly on the backbone, but connected via a server on the backbone, to have their own assigned names.

What Else Is on the Internet?

The Internet is a lot more than the multimedia world of the World Wide Web. One way to consider the massive amount of information available via the Internet is to segment it by the manner in which it is organized, searched, and transmitted. These different so-called *segments* are not separate networks, they are simply a particular use of the Internet network, defined by the types of files that are included, the way they are stored on their servers, and the software that is used to access them. One of those segments is the World Wide Web, which is discussed at length below. The other most heavily used segments of the Internet are Usenet and Internet Relay Chat. There are also some older file access applications, such as Archie and Veronica.

Text-only Internet Content As described above, before the Web, only text files were stored on Internet servers, with files formatted and structured so that they could be searched by programs known as Archie, Veronica, WAIS, and Gopher. These programs were specifically designed to navigate specific file formats and directories. Some of these programs are still in use, but since they allow only the use of text, their popularity is dwindling, and, therefore, we will not discuss them here. Currently, the most heavily trafficked text-only segments on the Internet are Usenet and Internet relay chat (IRC). The Usenet is a global system of free discussion forums, known as *newsgroups*; anyone can join a newsgroup to

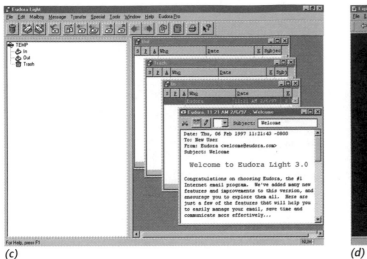

(c)

(d)

post ideas, ask questions, and respond to others in the same group. IRC is a global system of online real-time discussion groups.

Usenet allows users to search and retrieve news on many different subjects, but users do not interact simultaneously with each other online. Online real-time interactivity is the world of IRC, another Internet feature or free forums on different topics, which allows a number of users to share their thoughts simultaneously, an activity that has come to be known as "chatting online."

Groups of people can view the Web together, using stand-alone Web devices. Shown here is the Philips Magnavox WebTV™ Internet Product.

Used by permission from Philips Magnavox

POINT-TO-POINT TRANSFER In addition to being used as a platform on which to "publish" content that then becomes accessible to millions, the Internet is also used as a conduit for transferring information from one computer to another. The two most common point-to-point transfer modes are e-mail and file transfer protocol. **E-mail** is used to send text messages from one computer to another, and also allows for attaching files of any type. **File transfer protocol (FTP)** is used to transmit whole files from one computer to another

All these different types of information—Usenet, IRC, e-mail, and FTP—are accessible from the World Wide Web, which has become the main point of entry into the online world for millions of people. Therefore, the remainder of this chapter will focus on the Web, the starting point for engaging in business on the Internet.

STANDALONE WEB DEVICES

As the number of people connected to the Internet has grown, so has the number of different ways to connect. Early (ARPANET) connections were by mainframe only, and now most are by desktop or laptop through a modem and phone line. With the World Wide Web becoming the most common way for people to enter the online world, there are now standalone devices designed just to provide Web access. Popularly termed **PC-TV**, **Network Computer (NC)**, or **telecomputer**, these devices consist of a small CPU box, a keyboard, and a mouse. The box is hooked up to a television set and to a telephone line. With some devices, the keyboard and mouse are cordless, allowing the user remote operation.

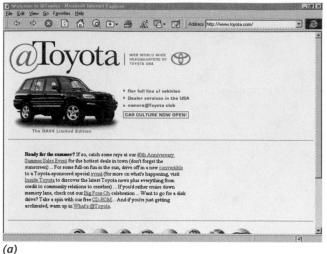

(a)　　　　*(b)*

This trend in standalone Internet access devices seems to support what some experts have observed, that "the network is the computer." This summarizes the idea that an increasing number of people will use their computers to retrieve information from the Net rather than to create it on their own computers. The phrase also expresses the idea that standalone computers (computers without Net access) have no future in our society. In fact, some observers claim that many individual users would rather just have access to the Internet than buy a PC whose local services they do not need. For these people electronics companies have developed what is known as a **telecomputer**.

A telecomputer lets a user log onto the Internet and provides a browser for "surfing the Net." The television set is used instead of a computer monitor. It has no other computer capabilities, no word processing, spreadsheet software, or the like that can run on a PC. The price of such devices is about one fourth of the price of a personal computer. In addition to offering low cost and ease of use, a telecomputer allows the user to view a television broadcast and to receive information from the Internet at the same time. For instance, someone might watch a sporting event on one side of the screen while receiving game statistics on the other.

THE WORLD WIDE WEB

The text-only world of the Internet changed in 1993, when a software protocol invented by Tim Berners-Lee, a British scientist in Geneva, expanded the world of Internet communication, allowing full-color graphics, tables, forms, video, and animation to be shared over the Internet. Berners-Lee's **hypertext transfer protocol (HTTP)** dictates how data in files—whether they represent text, images, or animation—should be coded, stored, transferred, and viewed on the Internet so that they will be displayed as desired.

The code that is used to tag files for display on the Web is called HTML, or hypertext markup language, which is discussed at some length below. The seminal feature of HTML is that it uses hypertext, which is the ability to provide easy access to additional files by clicking on marked text or images displayed on the monitor. The software programs used to access Web files, known as browsers, are programmed to use HTTP to transmit, receive, and interpret HTML files, and to display the various images on the user's computer screen. In fact, all Web addresses—

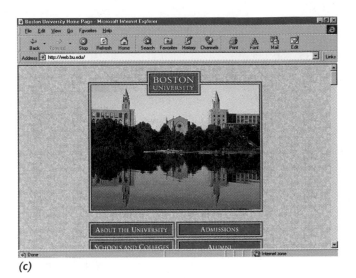

(c)

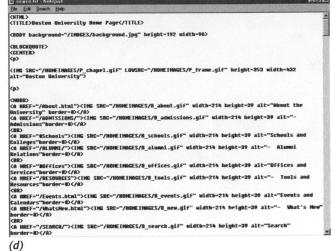

(d)

known as **Uniform Resource Locators** (URLs)—start with "http://" to indicate that their content follows hypertext transfer protocol. The Internet servers with HTML files using this new display technology are known as the World Wide Web, the section of the Internet currently most heavily trafficked. Since the greatest use of the Internet now is through utilization of the Web, there are many people who refer to "the Web" when they mean the Internet, and vice versa.

CREATING WEB FILES

You can establish your own presence on the Web by mounting HTML files on a Web server, which is referred to as "publishing on the Web." A series of HTML files is usually structured into **pages**, so-called because they fill approximately one screen when viewed with a browser. Some pages do extend beyond the screen and require the user to scroll to see the entire page. A series of pages stored on a server and accessible on the Web is called a **Web site**, the opening page of which is called the site's **home page**. A single site is usually identified with a particular organization or individual. A single server, which is the physical computer that is directly linked to the Internet backbone may hold any number of Web sites, although some large organizations run their own server for their Web site alone.

HTML editors expedite the construction of Web pages through user-friendly menus and intuitive graphical interfaces.

HTML Every file displayed on the Web is coded with HTML. Simply put, HTML is a system of standardized "tags" that format elements of an HTML document: strings of text, graphics, animation, or the like. Elements are formatted by providing an opening tag and a closing tag for the particular instruction. **Tags** are combinations of letters surrounded by "< >". For instance, if you wanted to italicize the text, you would put <IT> and </IT> at the beginning and end of the text, respectively. These tags are interpreted by Web publishing software to display the elements in a particular fashion. There are also tags to turn designated text into a "hot link" that a user will be able to click on to access additional material. Other tags link marked text to e-mail addresses or other Web sites.

HTML Editors HTML is a relatively easy-to-learn programming language, but the design of advanced features such as tables and frames is quite time-consuming. The process has become easier with **HTML editors**, programs that automate the design work by translating well-known or intuitive commands into HTML code, much as word processing programs have automated the formatting of text in written documents.

With an HTML editor, if you wish to center certain text you simply highlight it, then select a Center option from a pull-down menu. To create more advanced features, such as tables, editors provide templates that users can fill in.

Some HTML editors let the designers simply type as if they were using a popular word-processing application, such as MS Word, and then turn the text into HTML code. This way, the users need only know how to use the word processor. Some browsers, such as Netscape Navigator Gold and Communicator, have an HTML editor as an added feature.

Java The single most significant recent advance in Web technology was the 1995 introduction of Sun Microsystems, Inc.'s **Java**, a programming language that significantly expanded on HTML's display abilities. If a browser clicks on a Java feature on a Web site, a small program—called an **applet**—is automatically downloaded from the site to the browser's machine and then runs, displaying images that enliven pages with animation and highly interactive features. Many of the elaborate animation and sound elements of today's Web sites would be impossible without Java.

The power of Java is that, like HTML (but unlike most of the programming languages we discussed in Chapter 4, "Information Technology in Business: Software") programs written in Java are independent of the type of operating system running on a machine, so they can be developed on any type of computer, downloaded from another type of computer, and run on still another type of computer. Software developers writing programs in other programming languages have to write a different version for every operating system; Java programming does not require multiple versions of the same program.

Common Gateway Interfaces and Forms The availability of hypertext and graphics was essential for business to be conducted successfully on the Web, but other features, not originally available on the text-only Internet, have allowed those business applications to grow. Among the most important of these features is interactivity, made possible on the Web by **common gateway interface (CGI)** software. CGI software allows a computer that is accessing a particular Web site to have some similar functions, such as a client might have with a server. The user can fill out a form online and can submit the data into a database that resides on a server; then the CGI program can separate the data and field names from the form, run a program on the server that utilizes the new data, and provide feedback to the user by creating and transmitting a revised HTML page that is often in the form of a table (see Figure 6.3).

Interactive Web forms make it easy for users to subscribe to Web-based services, participate in Web-based surveys, or use the Web to update data on a site. Forms are also used for access codes and payment.

Tables are useful for the display of data retrieved from corporate databases, and forms allow interactivity between a user and the site's business owner.

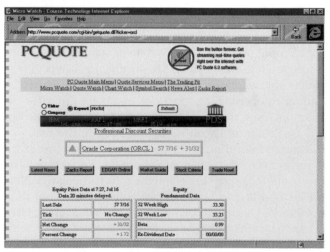

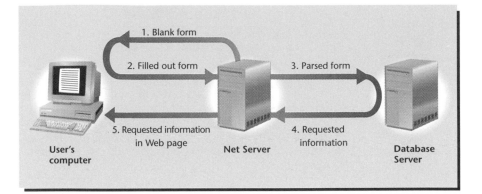

Figure 6.3 *How a CGI works*

FRAMES HTML also allows displayed pages to be split into **frames**, sections of a Web page that let a browser explore a site in different ways on the same page, scrolling and linking by hypertext to different places in the different frames. Since few people use monitors larger than 17 inches (measured on the diagonal), frames often simply cut off images and can be quite irritating to view.

VRML In Chapter 4 we discussed virtual reality applications and how they help in different business activities. As the Web evolved, the need arose to use it for communication of three-dimensional graphics. The **Virtual Reality Modeling Language** (VRML) is a developing standard for describing interactive three-dimensional scenes delivered across the Internet. You can browse virtual environments that include links to other VRML spaces or WWW pages.

CREATING YOUR OWN WEB PAGES Designing Web pages is not as complicated as it may sound, although building feature-rich graphical pages is obviously more complicated than basic tagging. One of the best ways to learn how to design pages is to log onto the Web and search for HTML tutorials. It is recommended that you first search for a free downloadable HTML editor and copy it onto your hard disk.

One helpful feature provided by Web browsers is the ability to copy a Web page's **document source**, which is the page's file showing all the HTML tagging (usually available from the view menu). Selecting Document Source while a Web page is displayed retrieves and displays the HTML source code of the page. Examining this document can teach you tags and commands used to build the features you see in the output. Invoke the document source, then look at the resulting page and try to figure out which HTML tags and instructions create which features.

> *Frames split Web page displays into two or more independent parts.*

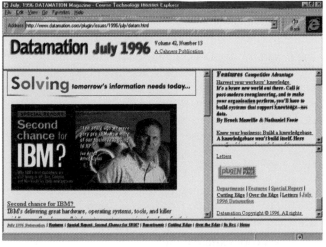

BROWSERS

To use the Web one needs special **browsing** software that was originally designed to (1) search the Web for specific sites, and (2) retrieve information from the site in the form of text, pictures, sound, and animation; more recent versions of this software have included the ability to (3) send and receive e-mail, and (4) engage other applications that allow the user to conduct telephone conversations and play video movies via the

Learn About the Internet?

As a product manager, you have been asked to compile a set of recent articles representing press coverage of the type of product your company designs and manufactures. You need the information for a meeting this afternoon, and do not have the time to research the project the way you usually would. When you mention this to a colleague from another firm, she tells you how to use the Internet to get the job done. What you will find is that compiling information is only a very small part of how the Internet can serve management.

The Internet is one of the most exciting technological developments humankind has experienced since the advent of the printing press. It is a huge source of information and also a tool that can facilitate many business activities. We have already seen how managers need external as well as internal information for their decision making. The Internet is a great source of external information, and much of the useful information it provides is free of charge.

The Net also allows organizations to save labor by (1) giving suppliers and customers access to information, (2) enhancing marketing efforts through online advertisement and letting customers sample goods, such as software applications and music, (3) providing online means of order placing, and (4) allowing customers to pay for goods and services electronically. Because the Net has no international barriers, it can become a great contributor to international trade.

One important outgrowth of the Internet is intranets. Managers and their subordinates can relatively easily use intranets to communicate ideas and facilitate business operations within a site and among multiple sites of an organization. While managers may not need to develop software for their Internet or intranet nodes, they can benefit from staying abreast of Internet developments and knowing how to utilize the technology to their advantage.

Web. Netscape's Navigator and Communicator, and Microsoft's Internet Explorer are the most popular browsers, but there are others, as Figure 6.4 shows.

Most browsers offer nearly identical capabilities because there is a tendency for browser designers to voluntarily adhere to certain standards. However, there are some differences among browsers in the types of features and the graphical and menu interface.

Software vendors have developed add-on applications that enhance browser capabilities. These add-on applications—usually automatically integrated into the basic program through a point-and-click instruction—are called **plug-ins**. Plug-ins allow the user to conduct certain background processes that make navigating easier, such as decompressing compressed software copied from servers, automatically running video software, and performing other advanced operations while accessing Web sites.

BEYOND BROWSING: OTHER ACTIVITIES ON THE WEB

There is a wide variety of activities (some of which were discussed above) that can be undertaken on the Web in addition to browsing. Some of the activities were available on the Internet before the advent of the Web, but they are now integrated into Web capability. The following are the most popular activities.

Vendor	Browser
Netscape	Navigator, Communicator
Microsoft	Internet Explorer
NCSA	Mosaic
ABSI	Skyway
Alis	Alis Multilingual Browser
InterVista	WorldView
NetManage	WebSurfer
PathLink Technologies	NetRunner
Oracle	Oracle Power Browser
Pipeline USA	Pipeline
InterCon	NetShark
TradeWave	WinWeb, MacWeb
Quarterdeck	QMosaic
Spry	SPRYNET Mosaic
Spyglass	Spyglass Mosaic
Stac	InterAP
Virtus	Virtus Voyager

Figure 6.4 *Popular Web browsers*

E-MAIL The first use of the Internet was **electronic mail**, or **e-mail**, as it is popularly called. It is still the most useful feature of the network. There are numerous applications that allow users to type and launch messages to designated addresses. E-mail has improved communications not only because it is fast, but because it is convenient: like regular mail, e-mail messages are stored to be read whenever the recipient becomes available. The latest trend is to integrate e-mail capability into Web browsers. You may have noticed the little envelope icon in the frames of some browsers. Clicking the icon opens a window for e-mail. You can then check to see if you have received messages and send your own.

As explained above, an e-mail address can be composed of three, four, or more parts separated by periods and the @ sign. The part of the e-mail address to the left of the @ sign uniquely identifies the user. The part of the e-mail address to the right of the @ sign indicates the **domain** name of the server where that user's e-mail may be found. Domains are groups of computers and computer networks organized into a structured hierarchy on the Internet backbone. Note that Web sites are treated somewhat differently, because the address identifies a *site*, not an individual. Also, keep in mind that, although you need a browser to access a Web site, you can use e-mail with a number of different types of software, not necessarily embedded in browsers.

INTERNET RELAY CHAT Internet relay chat (IRC) is an Internet feature that allows two or more people to communicate text at the same time, sometimes known as "real-time e-mail." A user must run an IRC applications program—available free of charge from a number of Web sites—in order to participate in an IRC conversation. The user can browse for a "chat" site and check if anyone is online. IRC allows people with shared interests to exchange ideas on any subject, such as products and their features, research results, or just plain gossip.

TELEPHONING ON THE WEB While regular long-distance telephone companies charge according to the number of minutes a call lasts, **internet service providers** (**ISPs**), almost always charge customers a flat monthly fee. With the proper software and microphones attached to their computers, Internet users can conduct long-distance and international conversations via their Internet connection, and pay for only the *local* call to their ISP. VocalTec, Voxware, and other companies provide software that digitizes and compresses voice signals, and with slight delays, transmits the bits via the Internet link. Some Internet-phone (I-phone) applications are bundled within browsers.

In the early days of Internet telephoning, each vocalization (any utterance separated by pauses) was recorded, digitized, and transmitted. This caused a noticeable delay. Also, pieces of data were often lost before arrival at the destination, leaving the recipient with a garbled communication. Current applications use buffers, that is, memory space, to first record a "chunk" of the digitized sound and then transmit it. The buffer is refilled with a chunk while the previous chunk is decoded and listened to at the receiving end. In addition, vendors have continuously improved data compression techniques to allow transmission of greater amounts of digitized sound per second. These developments have significantly improved the quality and speed of telephoning on the Net. Eventually, the quality is expected to reach that of high-quality telephone lines. Experts expect long-distance carriers to reduce their tariffs significantly when this happens.

An increasing number of callers prefer to use Internet telephoning to cut their long-distance costs.

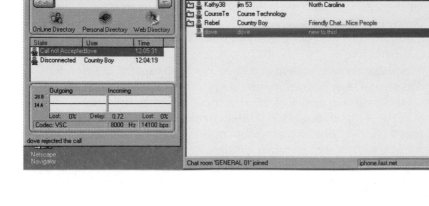

FILE TRANSFER In addition to displaying information, many organizations and individuals install software on the Net that users can download. **Downloading** is the transferring of software from one computer to another via communications lines. The user designates a storage device onto which the downloaded file is to be copied. Usually, the user chooses the computer's hard disk, especially if the copied file is large.

File transfer is expected to change the way in which software applications are sold. Instead of purchasing a box that contains disks with the program, buyers will simply download the software directly from vendor-designated Web sites, and pay for it by transmitting a credit card number to the seller.

INTRANETS

Soon after the Web caught the interest of the corporate world, IS managers conceived a simple idea: if HTML can be used to communicate information effectively on the Internet, why not use the same technology for communications *within* an organization?

So a new concept was created: the intranet. An **intranet** is a within-organization computer network that uses Web pages to communicate. The designers use the same tools to build sites and pages, and the users can use the same browsers they use to access external sites. In fact, many of today's intranets did not require any additional hardware; the existing LANs and other intra-organizational networks are used for telecommunications, but the Web applications, such as server programs and browsers, add to these networks all the advanced features that are available on the Web (see Figure 6.5).

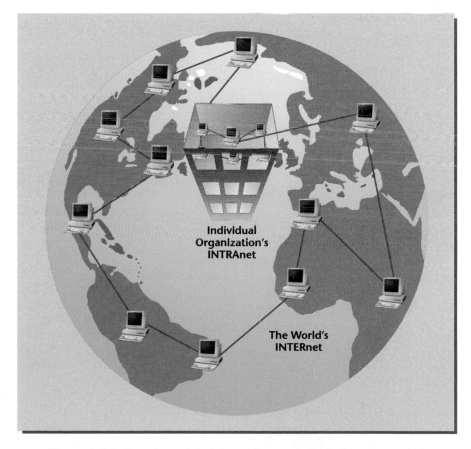

Figure 6.5 An intranet and the Internet from an individual user's perspective

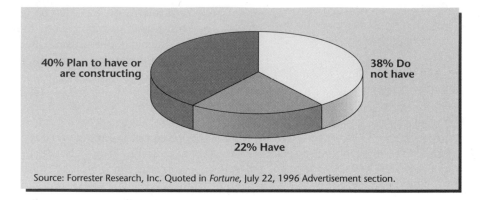

Source: Forrester Research, Inc. Quoted in *Fortune*, July 22, 1996 Advertisement section.

Figure 6.6 *The percentage of U.S. companies using Web servers for internal applications in 1996*

Figure 6.6 indicates that, in 1996, when the idea of intranets was about one year old, approximately one quarter of American corporations had intranets, and another 40% were planning to adopt the concept. Figure 6.7 clearly shows that the rush to establish intranet servers has outpaced the installation of Internet servers. Figure 6.8 displays the potential of both the Internet and intranets to enhance productivity for a business.

ESTABLISHING A WEB SITE

An organization that wishes to establish a presence on the Web must first establish a connection to the Internet's backbone, by either installing an Internet server or connecting to the server of an ISP. A number of business decisions regarding naming the site, choosing the capacity of the site, and establishing the capacity of the lines entering the site must be made.

SITE NAME Choosing a Web site name can make the difference between having browsers find your site easily, or not find it at all. An organization can obtain a Web site name through its service provider or, if it establishes its own server, directly through InterNIC, the organization responsible for naming Web sites. When someone applies for a new site name, InterNIC, through a licensed

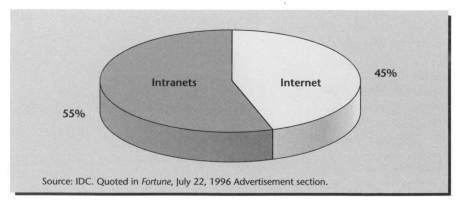

Source: IDC. Quoted in *Fortune*, July 22, 1996 Advertisement section.

Figure 6.7 *Distribution of Internet and intranet servers worldwide*

While an Internet Web site can enhance productivity through...

◆ Providing Product Information

◆ External E-mail

◆ Placing Orders

◆ Processing Orders and Payment

◆ Conducting Research

An Intranet can enhance productivity through...

◆ Internal E-mail

◆ Collaborative Processing

◆ Access to "Organizational Memory" Residing in Databases

◆ Order Processing

◆ Personal Web Pages

◆ Departmental Web Pages

◆ Group Communications

◆ Organization-wide Communications

◆ Product and Company Information

Figure 6.8 *Internet and intranet productivity enhancement potential*

private firm, checks its database to ensure that the name has not been given to an existing site. Site names combine a company's choice of name with the domain in which it operates (.com, .org., etc.). A new Web-based business has emerged, based on site-name acquisition. Companies buy what they believe will become desirable site names and then auction them off to the highest bidder, or create online "trading floors" where the names are bought and sold by site-name investors, until a company finally uses the name.

POINTS OF PRESENCE Some organizations run secure Internet servers, so that employees from around the world can have access to exactly the same information. For multisite companies paying for phone time this can be an expensive proposition. To cut the communications expenses, an organization can establish more than one connection point for the Internet; that is, it can have a number of **points of presence** (**POP**) that can be positioned across the globe to be as close as possible to as many employees as possible. Most access calls will thus be less expensive than with one POP.

LINE CAPACITY Management must consider the transfer rate, or speed, it needs for its site. If the site is expected to be accessed by many users, or to be heavily loaded with graphical information, it may be wise to purchase a link with high capacity. Slow links force users to wait a long time for pages to be retrieved. (Thus, some users sarcastically interpret WWW as World Wide Wait.) Obviously, communication speed depends both on the bit rate of the accessing devices, and

MEDIUM	TRANSFER TIME
28.8-Kbps telephone modem	2.3 hours
56-Kbps telephone modem	1.5 hours
128-Kbps ISDN modem	10 minutes
1.54-Mbps T1 link	52 seconds
10-Mbps cable modem	8 seconds

Source: Digital Nation, quoted in *InformationWeek*, June 3, 1996, p. 40.

Figure 6.9 *Transfer times for a 10 MB file by different media*

the bit rate of the communications lines. Faster communications devices let users enjoy the superior bit rate of communications lines. Although we discussed the subject of data communications speed in Chapter 5, "Information Technology in Business: Telecommunications," Figure 6.9 gives you an indication of how long it takes to transmit data with different communications media.

SITE MAINTENANCE Once the link to the Internet has been established, a professional called a "Webmaster" installs server applications on the computer designated as a server, and stores the Web pages on a storage medium connected to that computer directly, or on other computers connected to the server. Servers are usually connected to a high-capacity magnetic disk, or to a series of magnetic disks, to allow the storage of many Web pages. The Web master is the person in charge of updating the content of the pages according to corporate guidelines and decisions.

BUSINESS ON THE INTERNET

The Internet offers not only a means for conducting day-to-day business, but opportunities for companies to generate revenue as well. Web pages can provide different types of interactivity. The simplest is static publication through a home page of information that does not change unless the owner changes it. This is similar to a billboard. The more advanced form is dynamic publishing facilitated by CGI, described earlier: The user enters data or selects data from a database, and a computer program reconstructs the page accordingly with new information.

An example of dynamic publishing is the service Federal Express offers: You can type in a package number, and the page will tell you what point the package has reached on its route to the destination. Another form of dynamic publishing is to connect a business' own IS to the Net so that it can dynamically communicate with, and take orders from, remote users. A similar form, which is somewhat more advanced, uses special software to allow continual two-way dealing via the Net. For example, a brokerage house can connect its computers with such software to buy and sell stocks.

Hooked on the Internet

Alec T. Ronic is a senior manager for an electronics manufacturer. His typical day starts at 6 a.m. While having his breakfast he examines information displayed on the extended screen of his laptop computer. He logs onto the Web and examines the weather forecast for the day. It is going to rain again. This will probably slow down traffic. Alec selects a new bookmark from the browser's menu. A traffic analysis Web site shows up. Alec selects the name of the region where he lives. A street map appears on the monitor. He asks for the fastest route from his home to the office. From experience he knows that traffic conditions in the area change frequently, so he inserts a floppy disk into the laptop and records key leads. Later, he will insert the disk in his car computer which will combine the information with the data provided by the car's Global Positioning System (GPS) to direct him.

Alec calls up the Internet phone application and selects a number from a pull-down menu. There is a momentary blip on the screen. A holographic image of Lynda, his assistant, appears. "Good morning, Lynda. I had a feeling I'd find you in the office at this early hour. Just wanted to let you know I might be a little late for the 9 a.m. meeting." "I'll represent you well there," Lynda answers.

Alec does much of his business with the aid of the Internet and the company's intranet. He often tells his associates, "I don't know how I could live without the Net."

The basic operation described above may seem a large leap from the virtual office of today, but it may not be. Scientists are already working on the development of computer-generated holographic images, although years may pass before we see the widespread application of their efforts. On the other hand, systems that take advantage of GPS have already been installed in cars. The greatest challenge in utilizing these and other technologies via the Internet is communication speed. The transmission of ever-growing amounts of text, pictures, and sound is slowed down by the limits on the bit-rate communication that technology can support. It is expected that this gap will be closed in the next few years.

THINK CRITICALLY

Do you foresee a greater dependence on Internet resources in our daily lives, or do you think the current enthusiasm is a fad that will soon plateau?

Cambridge Physics Outlet is a Woburn, Massachusetts, start-up that makes up experiments used in teaching science and math. CFO Peter Hamilton figures it costs his company roughly $2 to generate a sales lead from the company's Web site, compared with $8 to $12 to generate a lead by direct mail or cold calling. The company spends roughly $500 per year for Web service and an undetermined amount for internal development. In return, the Web site generates leads at the rate of 1,000 per year. "Even if the cost per lead doubled, [the Web] is much cheaper than other methods of generating leads," Hamilton says.

Source: Excerpted from Radosevich, L., "Can you measure Web ROI?", *Datamation*, July 1996, p. 94.

CONDUCTING BUSINESS ON THE WEB

Organizations as well as individuals can use several types of services to do business on the Internet:

◆ *E-mail*. Businesses can send and receive messages to and from anyone who has access to the Net. E-mail provides the convenience of "store and forward" communications.

◆ *Bulletin Boards*. Electronic bulletin boards allow businesses and individuals to post questions, answers, and information on specific subjects. The majority of bulletin boards on the Net still provide access free of charge, but many organizations have started to provide information for a fee. For example, some entrepreneurial bulletin boards offer companies space for "help wanted" advertisements. Individual subscribers can then look for a job by searching the bulletin board's help-wanteds, using their own specific parameters. Both pay the owner of the service a fee.

◆ *Index and Retrieval Services*. These services facilitate retrieval of specialized information from a multitude of sources. They may help businesses to establish contacts with potential institutional clients, suppliers, or allies. They help businesses narrow the search of vast amounts of data for specific information in different specialties, such as engineering, pharmaceuticals, law, and government regulations.

◆ *File Transfer Protocol (ftp)*. Organizations can send and receive large batches of data using file transfer protocol. The data can then be conveniently routed into the organization's own databases and applications for further processing and manipulation.

◆ *Data Push*. Until 1997, organizations in need of news and new articles on specialized topics had to spend their employee time on long searches. Designated employees scoured the print and electronic media. As of 1997, however, several firms have offered a service called *data push* or *Webcast*; for a monthly fee, the vendor uses special software to electronically search for the new literature and news on the topics desired by the client. Special applications then dynamically transmit the found information to the computers of the client's employees. This Web-based tool is being used by many people to combat information overload.

GENERATING REVENUE ON THE WEB

There are several commercial uses of the Internet, as listed in Figure 6.10 and described below. Sometimes businesses use the Internet to provide traditional services, such as customer support, in place of or in addition to providing them in traditional ways. Some use the Internet in innovative ways not previously possible, either to provide a new service or product, or to package information for online distribution. Most businesses require a full- or part-time Webmaster, who can have varying degrees of responsibility (see Figure 6.11).

ONLINE ADVERTISING One way publishing companies generate revenue is by selling space in their magazines and newspapers to advertisers at a price based on the number of published copies circulated. The online equivalent to that is companies that generate revenue by selling space on their Web sites. Anyone who visits the site sees the advertisement. Web ads may be anything from colorful pictures illustrating products and price listings to flight schedules or online discount coupons.

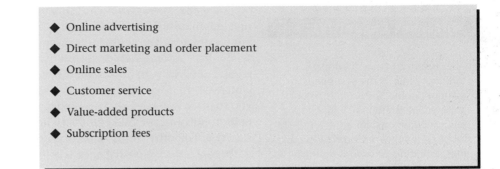

- ◆ Online advertising
- ◆ Direct marketing and order placement
- ◆ Online sales
- ◆ Customer service
- ◆ Value-added products
- ◆ Subscription fees

Figure 6.10 *Revenue sources on the Web*

Advertising rates are established slightly differently online than in print. The magazine equivalent of circulation on a Web site is the number of different people who visit that site, a number that was difficult to establish until the development of **counter** software. Counter software is connected to the server and counts the number of visits to a site by adding one every time someone visits the site. In professional jargon these visits are known as **hits**. One must bear in mind, though, that the same user may visit a site multiple times. Thus, hits alone do not provide a good rating of the site. In fact, a prankster can simply click the "reload" button of the browser time after time to run a counter up. For now, however, it's the most common tool for determining potential customers at a site.

Online advertising is most popular on Web sites that provide services for free. For instance, many search engine sites, such as Yahoo! and Infoseek, do not charge for their service, but charge advertisers to place banner announcements on the Yahoo! pages. Other types of sites include those providing sports statistics or free downloadable software. Some sites provide news collected from the home country of immigrants.

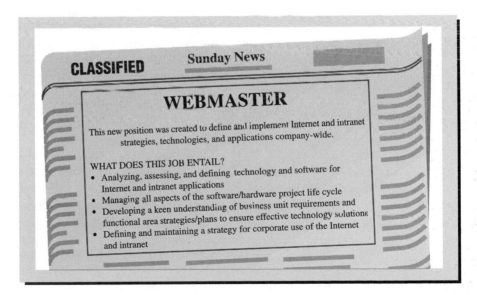

Figure 6.11 *Part of an actual help-wanted advertisement listing the typical skills required of a Webmaster, especially the need to understand business unit operations (see the third bullet).*

After nearly 20 years of bringing together some of the best minds in computing, the Boston Computer Society closed shop in 1996. The society gained renown for attracting a long list of computer luminaries to its meetings, including, at various times, Bill Gates, Mitch Kapor, and Steve Jobs. David Drucker, a former board member, blamed the society's demise on the Internet, technical support groups, and computer publications. "They've taken the place of what many users were drawn to, a place to share ideas, information, and camaraderie," he said. Steve Longo, a former president of the Philadelphia Association of Computer Users, fears the Boston society was outpaced by Internet time. "Computer neophytes were drawn to these groups as a way to get information quickly," Longo said. "But today's neophytes can't get that by attending a meeting once a month, they're turning elsewhere." The BCS's Web site (*http://www.bcs.org*) will stay active for members wishing to keep in touch.

Source: "Boston Computer Society, R.I.P.," *InformationWeek*, September 23, 1996, p. 12.

DIRECT MARKETING AND ORDER PLACEMENT Just as direct mail companies purchase lists of names and use them to fill mailboxes with junk mail around the country, companies can now purchase lists of e-mail addresses and send e-mail information about products and services. Rather than filling your regular mailbox with junk mail, they send messages to your electronic mailbox, which for many consumers is much more convenient. The Net can then allow you to place orders for desired products and services. If what you order is information, software, or video products, delivery can also be accomplished over the Internet. The other form of text-based advertising is to send messages to subscribers of list-servs. A **list-serv** is a list of e-mail addresses of people who are interested in a particular subject.

ONLINE SALES Companies are selling all kinds of products online, from makeup to used cars, and they are providing a wide variety of services as part of their sales efforts. Some simply provide information about their products, with instructions on how to purchase them off-line. Others have automated customer support for their products. And still others offer customers the ability to pay over the Internet and, in the case of software, to actually receive what they have purchased over the Internet. Companies that allow purchasers to use credit cards to pay for products and services over the Internet save the costs of printing and mailing invoices, and processing check or money order payments. They also often receive payment sooner than with more traditional methods.

Online stores offer a wide variety of goods on the Web, including the biggest sellers, which are books and music CDs. With graphics and sound, companies can now charge for entertainment provided over the Internet, such as movies or live rock concerts, much as is done over cable television services. Some services are actually more convenient to use on the Internet than when provided by traditional means, via telephone or mail. Securities trading is just such an example. In the past, customers who wanted to buy and sell stock had three alternatives: to look up quotes in the newspaper, to call their broker during business hours, or to wait for their statements from the brokerage house. Now, they also have the opportunity to log on to a Web site that lets them view quotes of any stocks they wish to consider, and then place buy or sell instructions. By clicking the "reload" button of the browser, the user receives an up-to-the-minute (or a few minutes delayed) quote.

Such services allow brokerage houses to offer trades for fees that are a fraction of the fees charged for trades executed the old way by placing a transaction via the phone. Many brokerage houses add other useful services, such as valuations of customer portfolios, reports on portfolio daily gains and losses, and stock analyses by experts.

Web brokerage houses may soon offer combined services that are considered by some experts the ultimate financial service: brokerage, banking, and checking as one package. Customers will be able to easily move funds from one account to another to maximize their financial opportunities.

CUSTOMER SERVICE Companies can now provide free customer support for products already purchased as well as service for a fee via the Internet. This may include online or downloadable instructions for maintenance, upgrades for software packages, and the ability to ask questions via e-mail. There are even some companies that sell hardware and software servicing online. These companies can access a customer's local hardware to diagnose and treat computer malfunctions.

VALUE-ADDED SERVICES Many businesses are providing customers with online tools to find information or execute transactions that in the past required the intervention of employees. Because these services lead to increased sales and/or significant cost savings by adding value to the company's product, they are called **value-added services**. For example, instead of using a phone operator to provide information, a shipping company may allow clients to track their packages online, an airline may let passengers see which seats are available on an airplane, and a bank may provide account balances and transaction histories online.

Some businesses have found original ways to sell value-added services by offering products that complement those already offered in more traditional manners. For example, a publisher may offer an online extension to its popular Web-related books. The publisher charges a little more for these extensions than it would charge for the same material had it been marketed as part of the printed books.

SUBSCRIPTION FEES Another method for generating revenues is to collect a periodic fee for a service rendered via the Web. Several companies tried this method but failed to convince prospective clients to subscribe. The approach has been more successful with organizations than with individuals, however. Businesses that benefit from timely specialized information are willing to subscribe to online services for a fee.

WHO USES THE WEB?

The demographics of Web users are changing all the time. Therefore, it is difficult to glean a clear picture of the characteristics of organizations and individuals who use this fast-developing resource. At press time, the following patterns were apparent.

ORGANIZATIONS While the Internet offers great business opportunities, small and medium size companies are joining the user circle at a slower pace than large organizations. It seems that the larger, richer organizations have rushed to establish a presence on the Web first.

INDIVIDUALS Several surveys have been conducted to find out the demographic characteristics of typical Web users. Although the user group was dominated for years by people in their late teens and early twenties, older people are now joining the user population. And while the Web still attracts more men than women, an increasing proportion of the Net surfers does come from the female population.

Surveys have also indicated a changing picture in terms of income. Early users came from affluent households, but the average income of users is declining as the number of users with lower incomes increases. And while the early users came exclusively from the U.S. (which is the country that established the Net), members of other nations are joining the crowd in large numbers. In fact, you may stumble over numerous sites that offer information in languages other than English. All these developments suggest an encouraging picture: the Web is fast becoming a universal resource for individuals from different socioeconomic backgrounds.

WEB COSTS

The costs involved in building and maintaining a corporate Web site depend on what management wants to achieve. The least costly sites are those constructed simply to showcase the company's products or services, without providing

Net Notes

If we all want to maintain a pleasant and courteous Internet, we must adhere to some rules of proper behavior. How one "behaves" on the Net is often referred to as *netiquette*. Use the term as a keyword to find sites discussing the topic.

Do's

◆ Clearly and briefly communicate who you are and what you offer.

◆ Clearly show all the options available on the home page.

◆ Keep the site dynamic. Offer something new every day to lure the user to make more visits.

◆ Make your site useful rather than just attractive.

◆ Link your site to search engines and "what's new" and "what's cool" lists.

◆ Create links to sites of related businesses, in return for their linking to yours.

Don'ts

◆ Do not overload pages with graphics, because this may slow down reception.

◆ Do not build too many "layers"; it is easier to browse within a page than between pages.

◆ Do not use unclear icons; text always communicates ideas more clearly.

◆ Never activate an "under construction" site. Surfers are unlikely to return to unfinished sites.

◆ Do not use in-house company jargon.

Figure 6.12 *Do's and Don'ts in Web site construction for commercial purposes*

customer service, CGI, or the ability to purchase, pay for, or receive products on the Internet. Such sites usually cost only a few thousand dollars. An example of this kind of site is Hershey Foods, the famous chocolate maker. There, as in other companies that have chosen not to have a highly sophisticated interactive site, the employees themselves learned enough HTML to design the company's Web page. The annual maintenance cost is only several thousand dollars.

Regardless of the level of site provided, there are some basic Do's and Don'ts to Web site design, which are summarized in Figure 6.12.

The most expensive sites are those designed to enable electronic commerce. The cost of such sites can reach several million dollars. The annual maintenance cost can be tens or hundreds of thousands of dollars. In addition to the cost of interfacing the Web site to other ISs, the cost may reach six figures, depending on the complexity of graphic design, animation, forms, and frames, the frequency of updating information, and the level of interactivity provided.

Before managers opt to establish a corporate Web site, they must decide what they want to achieve. At Hershey, management realized that no one would buy sweets via the Web. It is also unlikely to conceive a value-added product in this industry. Therefore, despite its huge resources, the company decided to build a simple site, so as to have a presence on the Web. Other companies may determine that they can benefit from a complex site that supports electronic commerce. They should expect to spend millions of dollars, as Figure 6.13 shows.

Hardware	$ 151,000
Off-the-shelf Software	$ 30,000
Professional Services	$ 488,000
Labor/Dedicated Personnel	$ 350,000
Facilities Management; Data Conversion; Telecommunications Costs	$ 280,000
Total	$1,299,000

Source: IDC, quoted in Radosevich, L., "Can you measure Web ROI?," *Datamation*, July 1996, p. 94.

Figure 6.13 *The average cost to a company offering a Web site for electronic commerce*

RISKS

The Internet is a great resource for research, education, entertainment, and business. However, using it for business purposes does involve some risks.

RISKS TO ORGANIZATIONS

Before an organization decides to do business via the Net, it should consider the risks. Management must realize that once its information systems are linked to a public network, they are no longer disconnected from the outside world. This means that without proper precautions, the business may suffer one or more of the following mishaps: (1) contracting of computer viruses, (2) interception of passwords and codes by an unauthorized hacker, and (3) interception of charge account numbers.

A company must realize that if it does business via the Internet, its organizational IS is constantly (or for the duration of business hours) up and running, while connected to the Net via some communications line. This potentially exposes the IS to unauthorized access by hackers who figure out a way to circumvent protection measures. Many companies have suffered serious losses from this criminal activity, in the form of ruined or altered data files or theft of proprietary information.

Unauthorized parties may also intercept passwords and access codes, and then use them to access the organization's resources. At best, they use services without paying for them; at worst, access is only the prelude to destroying data and applications. In several cases, hackers who intercepted access codes to commercial services later posted them on electronic bulletin boards for everyone to use.

Since the Net is so vulnerable to hacking, the use of electronic payment through the network is still limited. Many companies and individuals are

"mb121@abc.com, nice to meet you"
"twilliams@xyz.com, pleased to meet you"

Road Bumps on the Electronic Superhighway

The Internet, and especially its most exciting section, the World Wide Web, has produced an excellent medium of communication. Adults and children alike can easily access huge amounts of information in the form of text, pictures, sound, and movies. But as with other means of communications, moral issues have emerged as well.

Who Controls the Internet? A quick search of the Web will reveal that many servers contain adult-oriented material. Many also contain information of defamatory and violent nature. When transmitted through other communications channels such as the mail, telephone, radio, television, and motion pictures, this type of information is subject to regulation in many countries. In some countries, including the United States, the texts of these other laws do not apply the regulation to general communications; instead, the texts refer to the specific communications channels to which the law applies, thereby excluding the Internet from the same regulation. Some examples of existing controls on other communications include the following. Movies are rated to allow parents to decide what their children should or should not view. Noncable television networks avoid broadcasting sexually explicit programs. Even cable television stations precede movies with an appropriate warning, and will usually not broadcast explicit adult and violent movies. It is against the law in many countries to use the postal service to mail adult-oriented material without prior consent of the recipient.

But who controls the Internet? The answer is no one. More appropriately, the question should probably be who *can* control the Internet? Unlike postal services that can be fully controlled by governments, or radio and television stations whose broadcasting is limited to certain territories, the Internet is a world-wide network under the control of no government, organization, or individual. Even if control could be established, is censorship the appropriate solution to smut and verbal venom?

Consider the case of America Online (AOL), the world's most popular online information system. Like other online services, AOL provides gateways to the Internet. After some subscribers complained, the Bavarian government threatened to terminate AOL services unless the company blocked access to sites communicating pornographic content. The company agreed. Since it could not block specific material to only one territory all AOL subscribers were denied access to material that was unacceptable to one government.

1996 Telecommunications Act: The U.S. Government Weighs In. Civil rights advocates argue that the purpose of the Internet from its origination has

(continued)

reluctant to transmit their credit card account numbers while hackers are lurking to capture and use them. Thus, many companies warn users that any personal data they provide, especially credit card information, may be captured by unauthorized parties.

There are several protective measures that can alleviate these dangers, but business activity on the Net cannot be totally risk free. The reason is simple: the more stringent the protective measure, the more limited the communication. The two major protective measures are "firewalls" and authentication.

Firewalls are special computer programs that protect the organization's IS, which is connected to the Net, from certain access activity directed at it from users of the network. This may involve the total denial of access to certain parts of the IS, or the practical disconnection from certain parts of the Internet.

been to allow everyone free exchange of information. In democratic countries, the claim of many Internet users is that any regulation of the Internet poses a threat to free speech. Nevertheless, the U.S. Congress passed the Telecommunications Act of 1996 including a clause known as the Telecommunications Decency Act. This clause made a criminal of anyone who makes, creates, or solicits and initiates the transmission of any comment, request, suggestion, proposal, image, or other communication which is obscene or indecent, knowing that the recipient of the communication is under 18 years of age, regardless of whether the transmitter of such communication placed the call or initiated the communication. The Act's enforcement was suspended pending its review by the U.S. Supreme Court.

Many respected organizations joined a call to denounce the measure. The main argument was that the operator of a server cannot know the age of every recipient of the information offered. The operator may also be responsible for the content of Web pages prepared by and maintained by a subscriber to the service. In addition, critics said it was simply impractical to try to control who attains access to what material on the Web. To comply with the new law many operators posted warnings, such as "You must be 18 years or older to access…" but there could not be a guarantee that the recipient was not younger. In June 1997, the law was struck down by the U.S. Supreme Court, partly because it recognized that censoring parts of the Internet is impractical.

The Internet is unlike radio, television, and motion pictures. Free speech advocates say it is the responsibility of the receiving end to screen the content of what is accessed on the Net, and to use proper measures to prevent young children or sensitive people from retrieving inappropriate material. Indeed, several software companies have developed applications that block access to certain servers. Usually, these programs screen sites by keywords found in the titles and several lines registered with search engines. However, no such software can cull out all sites intended to be blocked.

Visionaries regard the Internet as an important tool to making the world freer, better educated, and more prosperous. Opponents of Web supervision claim that free exchange of information is the rule that facilitates democratization and education. Proponents of control advocate a free exchange of information only if it maintains a measure of respect for people of all creeds, races, religions, and other demographic backgrounds. They would like to remove the "Internet graffiti," and establish a Web free of defamation and material that may offend some users and prevent younger audiences from enjoying this resource. We are faced with the old problem of finding the right balance, but this time it is not one community or nation that has to find a solution—it's the entire world.

Authentication measures ensure that the person who accesses an organization's IS is indeed the person he or she claims to be. Among other methods is the use of a series of access codes and specific information known only to authorized users.

In addition to these risks there is the potential for misrepresentation. One of the greatest advantages of the Net is the ability of the users to remain anonymous. This ability has been termed "the great equalizer": it protects the users from any prejudice because they cannot be seen or heard; only the information they communicate can be judged by the receiving parties. But this also makes it easy to misrepresent oneself. For example, a high-school student can easily introduce herself as a representative of a large foreign company and place a multimillion dollar order with a business that offers its products on the Net. Therefore, organizations doing business on the Internet must take precautions to minimize misrepresentation.

Chastity on the I-way

The information superhighway has many sites parents may not want their children to visit. Help is on the way from several companies offering software that screens the sites and blocks access to those whose names or short introductions contain certain keywords. One journalist who tried such a program said that each time he tried to access one of the adult-oriented discussion groups, the program blocked his efforts. His only complaint? "The program denied me access to my local newspaper, the *Middlesex News*."

Source: Bowman, W., "Chastity Beltway," *Inc. Technology*, No. 3 1995, p. 82.

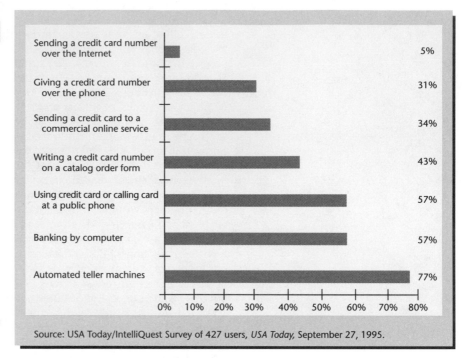

Source: USA Today/IntelliQuest Survey of 427 users, *USA Today,* September 27, 1995.

Figure 6.14 *How much do people trust various online charging methods?*

Business parties on the Internet should also keep in mind the legal loopholes regarding electronic contracts and payments. The legal aspect of doing business over computer networks will be discussed in the EDI (electronic data interchange) section of Chapter 11, "Inter-organizational and International Information Systems."

RISKS TO CONSUMERS

The Internet will probably never be fully secure against eavesdropping and interception. This poses the major obstacle to our advancement toward a cashless society and "virtual shopping." A great majority of Internet users are wary of volunteering credit information (see Figure 6.14). When you purchase goods or services via the Internet, you are required to furnish the number and expiration date of a credit card. Usually, before you enter the data a message pops up on the screen warning you that the information you are about to enter is not secure. Other "Net surfers" may intercept the information and misuse it. Figure 6.14 indicates how reluctant people are to send a credit card number through the Internet.

THE NATIONS: WHO IS ON THE NET?

While the U.S. is leading in developing new technologies for the Net, other nations are not far behind. Governments recognize the great economic potential of being part of the network, and try to relax regulations so that more businesses and individuals can gain access to this great resource. As can be seen from Figure 6.15, Finland has the highest ratio of Internet servers to users. Israeli companies are heavily involved in developing high-quality Internet phone software, and Singapore's government has invested over $2 billion in a state-of-the-art technology infrastructure that is intended to make this tiny island-nation an "intelligent island." Its citizens are offered the most advanced information-related services in the world.

POINT OF INTEREST

A Company By Any Other Name

Your e-mail address conveys something about you: If you work for an academic institution, your address ends with .edu (such as john_doe@psu.edu); if you work for a commercial organization, your address probably ends with .com. Say you own a small company but you want to project a big company image out there in cyberspace. What you need is a .com name. Now American Information Services, a company that specializes in connecting companies to the Internet, will set you up with a tailor-made address even though you may actually be connected to a standard ISP. For example, AIS will allow you to have your customer contact you at prez@intergalactic.com, while your e-mail will be routed to your real address, which is Mike1234@delphi.com or some similar site. The e-mail address remains the same, even if you switch Internet service providers.

Source: Parts excerpted from "What's in a Name?" *Datamation,* May 15, 1995, p. 22.

Finland	25
U.S.	50
Australia	60
Canada	70
Netherlands	90
Singapore	125
United Kingdom	130
Germany	180
Israel	185
Hong Kong	310
Japan	470
Taiwan	850
South Africa	930
South Korea	1,550
Brazil	8,000
Thailand	15,000
Indonesia	87,000
China	561,000
India	1,200,000

Source: Network Wizards; Killen & Associates, 1997.

Figure 6.15 ***The number of citizens per Internet server around the world***

Pay Us a Virtual Visit

Marshall Industries of El Monte, California, is one of the largest distributors of electronic components to the major computer manufacturers of the world (refered to as OEMs, or original equipment manufacturers). Marshall's clients require timely information about part specifications and availability, but printed catalogs—the traditional means of letting customers know what is available—are often outdated before they are even shipped. World Wide Web technology has created an alternative.

Directed by its CEO Rob Rodin, Marshall in July 1993 joined the World Wide Web Internet marketplace. Marshall on the Internet (Address: *http://www.marshall.com*) serves a number of purposes: it is a Web server with a comprehensive and up-to-date product catalog readable and searchable through standard browsing technology; it is a customer service rep that can receive orders online; it is an online sales rep, providing demonstration software and other promotional information to any person who requests it online, and it is a type of in-house bulletin board, posting requests for proposals to potential vendors.

Marshall software engineer Steve Knipping says the creation and maintenance of the Web site is a joint effort of the marketing and MIS departments. Knipping says Marshall has a staff of Web programmers and experts in page editing, who update the materials, which amount to some 10,000 pages of parts inventory, technical specifications, demonstration versions of software, and schedules of Marshall's technical seminars.

Vice president Bob Edelman says that Marshall receives some 100,000 Web visits per month from all over the world and that it has become a hit with electronic component designers. Rather than flipping through technical references, designers can keep the Web page with the spec sheets open in a window on their monitor; coincidentally displaying Marshall's corporate logo right on their computer desktop.

Marshall's clients can search through the Web page material by keywords. When they find the part they want, a menu of links at the bottom delivers them to pages that hold directions for ordering the parts or samples through the phone or by mail. Marshall is developing a secure system to take payment directly through the Internet using corporate credit cards that companies assign to engineers for purchases of small lots of components. Marshall is also developing a system for RFPs (requests for proposals) for its potential vendors.

While Marshall explores the interactive edge of the digital frontier, its trading partner AVEX Electronics, headquartered in Huntsville, Alabama, is investigating another exciting opportunity in business-to-business Web commerce: Internet-mediated Electronic Data Interchange (EDI). EDI allows organizations to exchange price lists, invoices, and other business documents electronically rather than as paper documents. Until recently, the concept was implemented using dedicated communications lines rather than the Internet. AVEX, a contract-manufacturing and engineering services company, has made a considerable investment in EDI, creating a database of all technical specifications and drawings that are EDI-compatible. Internet-mediated EDI—the transfer of EDI data or the display of EDI data on the Internet—would be the best of both worlds for AVEX, fusing the Internet's robust information transport technology and low costs with the data-formatting standards of EDI.

AVEX selected a secure Internet EDI authentication software package called Templar that reviews a database to be sure it conforms to EDI specifications. The software was mounted on an AVEX host computer in Huntsville and linked through a high-capacity line to the corporate Web server at AVEX's parent company J. M. Huber in Edison, N.J.

Mike Gordon, manager of AVEX's Electronic Commerce Group, says that AVEX now receives all of its EDI invoices from client National Semiconductor through Templar, which operates between the mail protocol and the EDI translator at the corporate server. AVEX receives the orders, no matter what kind of service they may have originated from, with no data loss.

AVEX had used EDI via the Internet as of 1995. By 1997, the EDI operation had saved AVEX $750,000. "VANs [Value Added Network firms] charge by character [transmitted], whereas once you have paid for the initial connection, the Internet is basically free," explained Gordon. But the benefits went beyond pure costs savings. "As a contract manufacturer for the electronics industry, we exchange a lot of design drawings and files between the original equipment manufacturers and ourselves and with our suppliers," Gordon said. "When we looked at that process, there was a significant amount of time taken to exchange that information. So we saw the Internet as a means to reduce that time."

Source: Cassidy, P., "Wholesale Success on the Web," Datamation, June 15, 1995, pp. 48–51; Trommer, D. "AVEX Tightens up Supply Cahin with Net-based EDI," Electronic Buyer's News, Issue 1039, January 6, 1997.

Questions

1. What cost does Marshall save with its Web site?

2. What type of cost will AVEX be able to curb when it fully implements its EDI via the Web?

Online Riches

In the fall of 1994 Windham Hill Records set up its Web site, and marketing director Roy Gattinella made sure he could track its popularity. As Gattinella explained, the company had always tracked the number of viewers its magazine and newspaper ads received, and they had to do the same on the Internet. Unfortunately, most Web-service providers offer "hit rate" information that reports only the number of inquires at a site rather than the number of people who visit: For example, three quick visits by five people in an evening register as 15 "hits." So Gattinella made sure that his Web-page service provider, Intersé, in Sunnyvale, California, could provide daily "user feedback" reports that track the site's visitors, about 1,000 people.

To his satisfaction, Gattinella has found that he can learn much more about the promotional effectiveness of his Web site than he can about the effectiveness of a print campaign.

With Interse's tracking system, Gattinella can find out what ads people look at, for how long, and how involved they get. The data can be broken down by artist's page, which also provides information on which artists are currently the most popular. And, Web customers can sample products by downloading a song, or even place orders. Compared to trying to track a response to a print ad, the Web comes out ahead. A print ad is only a call to action, that is, providing an 800 number or a list of local retailers, but Web promotion actually follows through to sales.

Windham Hill pays for a number of Web listings, or hypertext links, that let users click directly to the company's Web page. So Gattinella particularly values the section of Intersés report that details the directories his visitors use to find Windham Hill's site. The company spends less than 5% of its marketing budget on the Web site. That's roughly the cost of a limited national print campaign, but Gattinella views the Web as an investment in the future. With the accuracy and detail of online feedback, Gattinella has said he can make daily changes on the Web, as well as in written or telephone promotions. The geographic feedback has led the company to schedule a number of successful concerts around the country.

The Web site reports have also uncovered some unanticipated marketing errors. User printouts indicated that artists whose names started with A's or B's were significantly more popular than others. Gattinella plans to rearrange the list, from alphabetical order to an order that emphasizes whom the company wants to market.

Source: Hise, P., "Hits that Rate Attention," Inc., September 1995, p. 115.

Questions

1. What is the main element of communication with buyers that the business has which it could not have via other modes of advertisement?

2. Windham Hill managers receive a great deal of information about people who explore their Web site? How?

Fruit of the Web

For many businesses, electronic commerce provides the opportunity to eliminate middlemen and bypass distributors, in order to conduct business directly with consumers. Contrary to this approach, Fruit of the Loom (FTL) sees electronic commerce as a way to strengthen ties with its distributors. The company's Activewear division in Bowling Green, Kentucky, is empowering its distributors by building Web sites for them at no charge. The logic is simple: If distributors reach more customers via the Web, they will generate more demand for apparel manufactured by FTL.

"We're intermediating, not disintermediating," said Charles Kirk, senior vice president and chief information officer for FTL Activewear. "If we help our distributors get lots of small orders, that makes large orders for us.

Anything that moves more shirts helps our bottom line." More than half of FTL's 50 distributors across the U.S. have signed up for the Web initiative, called Activewear Online.

FTL hired three companies to set up the sites for the distributors: an online commerce software provider, a Web site designer, and a systems integrator. The distributors don't pay anything for these sites, although they are dedicated to serving *their* clientele. However, FTL took the approach that American Airlines took with its SABRE reservation system in the 1970s (discussed in Chapter 2, "Strategic Uses of Information Systems"). Each distributor is required to list FTL products first in the online catalog. The FTL logo must appear at the top of each page, across from the distributor's logo. The sites are open to the public, but when users move from catalog browsing to order placement, they enter a protected part of the site requiring registration and passwords.

The sites are physically maintained by Connect, one of the companies FTL hired. Each site also provides the distributor a means to order FTL T-shirts, sweatshirts, and gym shorts with logos of sports teams, colleges, rock bands, restaurants, bars, and the like. The server that connects users includes order processing software and a database that holds FTL's catalog. "The database is key," said James Strohecker, director of interactive communications at Connect. "Distributors, who typically have a huge warehouse with a tiny office at one

end, can put their entire catalog on the Web."

FTL has spent $3 million on Activewear Online, and Kirk expects the project to pay for itself in incremental business for the $800 million division. "We're saving the distributor $10 to $20 in order entry costs for every order," said Kirk. "We see a big public relations and goodwill lift from this project. All the rest is gravy, and I think the gravy is huge."

Source: Wilder, C., "Web Sites a Gift to Distributors," InformationWeek, August 26, 1996, pp. 36–38.

Questions

1. List and explain the benefits to FTL of this collaboration. List and explain the benefits to the distributors.

2. In what other industries can a win-win situation like this take place if a manufacturer establishes and funds Web sites for its clients? Explain.

Let the Clients Serve Themselves

The Environmental Protection Agency (EPA) maintains databases to support individual environmental programs, such as the Clean Air Program, launched in accordance with Congressional statutes such as the Clean Air Act. The programs are run by a program office, but the EPA must examine information on pollution on a geographical basis. For example, EPA personnel now assess the impact of all environmental hazards across a county, town, or state.

To this end, the EPA developed five program databases:

1. Aeronautic Information Retrieval System Facility Subsystem: data covering air pollution by some 150,000 facilities regulated by the EPA and state and local air regulatory agencies.

2. Permit Compliance System: data on more than 75,000 water-discharge permits, including permit issuance and permit limits.

3. Comprehensive Environmental Response, Compensation, and Liability Information System: data from the Superfund Authorization Bill on hazardous waste site assessment and remediation.

4. Toxic Release Inventory System: data about the release and transfer of more than 300 toxic chemicals and compounds according to medium of release (air, water, underground injection, land disposal, and off-site) reported by more than 33,000 submitters.

5. Resource Conservation and Recovery Information System: data used to track handler permits of 450,000 facilities and transporters of hazardous waste, cleanup activities, and closure status of hazardous waste sites.

In addition to the program databases, the agency provides these auxiliary databases:

1. Facility Index System: a central inventory of more than 675,000 facilities regulated or monitored by EPA program offices.

2. Envirofacts Master Chemical Integrator: an index of chemical data in the program databases.

How does one give thousands of users easy access to five mainframe databases? The EPA chose to make them accessible through the Internet. Its Envirofacts database lets EPA staff and the public access the databases. Since Envirofacts' launch in March 1995, the public has gained access over the Internet via Web browsers.

In 1986, Congress passed the Community Right to Know Act, requiring the EPA to share the information in its databases with the public. The agency has 24,000 PCs of its own, many of which now access the databases. Before Envirofacts, IS personnel were deluged by information requests from EPA employees and the public. "We used to be a bunch of gofers getting data for people," said Patrick Garvey, Envirofacts Director of the EPA's IS department. "Now we can spend more time thinking about [information technology] tools."

In addition to being a boon to the EPA's IS department, Envirofacts has helped local branches tremendously. "It used to be, 'I don't know if there are any Superfund sites in my neighborhood; how can I access information from them?'" said Karen Schneider, director of the EPA's regional library in New York. "But now when we describe our services, people say, 'We already researched that from home over the Internet.'"

The EPA's Web site has 80,000 pages and receives about 100,000 hits per month from the public and 2,000 per month from EPA staff. The EPA's staff now has more time for more creative work.

Source: Adhikari, R. "Saved by the Web: Internet access to the EPA's databases cuts IS staff burden," InformationWeek, March 17, 1997, pp. 95–96.

Questions

1. Enumerate all the benefits that the EPA derived from the new Web site.

2. Which technology does EPA use to "fill out" user requests in the forms displayed on their computers?

The **Internet** is a huge network connecting millions of computers throughout the world. It allows organizations and individuals to send and receive electronic mail, transfer data files, and communicate a wide variety of text, pictures, sounds, and animation. Its most exciting section is the **World Wide Web**, which has elevated the network from a text-based medium to one that facilitates the communication of graphical and sound content as well.

The Web is defined by a common programming language, **HTML (Hypertext Markup Language)**. **Java**, another Web programming language, supplements HTML with advanced features such as animation. Web users can use special applications called **browsers** to access different **servers**, which are computers connected to the Internet. A **Web site** is a collection of **Web pages** stored on a server. Many servers allow users to **download**, that is, to copy software.

Web pages may contain text, graphics, tables, forms, and frames. **Forms** let servers capture information remotely. **CGI** applications process data captured in forms and either store them for later use or respond to the user with requested information. Other Web applications allow real-time interactive correspondence and telephoning. **Telephoning** via the Web is expected to improve and reach the quality available with conventional telephone lines.

Some companies have developed network computers that are devices solely for use with the Web. The device comes with a keyboard and mouse, and uses a home television set as its monitor. Some observers say that these devices will soon be more popular than home PCs because of the fast growth of the Web and the increasing population of individual users. Recent studies show greater numbers of older people, women, and lower income earners among Web surfers.

Intranets are the local version of the Internet. Many organizations have adopted HTML and Java for use in building Web sites for internal use by their employees. Usually, the development of new internal Web sites does not require a significant investment in additional hardware and telecommunications devices, because they have already been installed for local area networks and corporate intersite communications.

Studies show a greater rate of growth in the number of intranets than of Internet sites.

To establish a Web site, an organization purchases a link to the Internet and pays a periodic fee for its maintenance. It obtains a unique **Internet Protocol Number** and reserves an address that can identify it and the nature of its business. Addresses outside the U.S. also include a country identifier. Either the organization or a **service provider** prepares and maintains the **home page** and other pages of the Web site.

Business opportunities on the Internet include **e-mail**, use of **bulletin boards**, indexing and retrieval services, **file transfer**, advertising, direct marketing and order placing, customer support, payment, and entertainment. Generation of revenue on the Web has taken four forms: online sales, online advertisement, **value-added services**, and subscription fees for services rendered through the Web. Organizations planning to establish Web sites should expect to spend several thousand to several million dollars. The least expensive sites are those that establish a mere presence on the Web, to simply introduce the organization and its goods or services. The most expensive sites are those that enable electronic commerce. Cost items include hardware, software, professional services, dedicated personnel for maintaining the site, and telecommunications costs.

Along with the business opportunities come risks to both organizations and consumers. They include computer viruses, unauthorized access, and interception of access codes and credit card numbers.

The Internet is a world-wide network that nobody controls. From the advent of its exciting section, the Web, "inappropriate" material has been posted and disseminated throughout the world. There have been calls to censor what is transmitted, especially pornography, violence, and racial slurs. The U.S. Congress included special provisions in the Telecommunications Decency Act of 1996 that criminalized transmission of such content to people under 18 years of age. In June 1997, the law was struck down by the U.S. Supreme Court. Critics of such attempts to control the Internet said the law contradicted principles of free speech; they argued that only a totally free Internet can enhance education, freedom, democracy, and the welfare of humankind.

REVIEW, DISCUSS, AND EXPLORE

REVIEW AND DISCUSSION QUESTIONS

1. The Internet has existed for decades, but only the emergence of the World Wide Web created excitement in the business world. Why?

2. What is HTML and why is it needed to use the Web?

3. Major manufacturers of computers claim that network computers have a bleak future. What is your opinion, and why?

4. What are the main opportunities for doing business on the Web?

5. What are the main risks in doing business on the Web? How can these risks be mitigated?

6. What are the two main ways to generate revenues with a Web site? Can you think of other ways?

7. How does Internet telephoning work? How do you expect that telephone companies will react to long-distance Internet telephoning?

8. It is expected that software developers will sell their products via the Internet. How?

9. Refer to the Do's and Don'ts in Figure 6.12. From your experience with the Web, what other Do's and Don'ts would you add to the list?

10. Many people are comfortable with the feeling of being anonymous when using the Web. Are they really anonymous? How can software capture information about people who visit a Web site?

11. *Ethics and Society*: The Telecommunications Act of 1996 included a "decency" provision (which was struck down by the U.S. Supreme Court) that limited the presentation of some information on the Web. Should it be the responsibility of information providers or of parents to limit children's access to inappropriate material?

CONCEPT ACTIVITY

Use your browser to shop for an item of your choice (such as sports shoes, clothes, or CDs). Use Figure 6.12 as an outline for your critical report of the sites. Evaluate each site according to the Do's and Don'ts, and say which of the sites you found most effective, overall.

HANDS-ON ACTIVITY

1. Choose a topic in which you are interested. Select three different search engines to look for information about the subject. Prepare a short report in which you (1) describe the manner in which the search was performed, including the list of categories you used, or list of sites that have the keywords in their title, and (2) rank the search engines based on your results. Explain your ranking.

2. Ask a professor in one of your other classes to allow you to prepare an assigned term paper in the form of an HTML file. Instead of outlining topics and subtopics, use marked text. Submit the file on a disk.

3. Prepare your resume as an HTML document. If you wish, include your scanned photograph. Submit your work on a disk.

TEAM ACTIVITY

Your team has been hired by a pizza delivery service to design a Web site. The site should be attractive to families and young professionals, and should allow them to order home delivery. Use an HTML editor to build the home page of the business. Submit your page on disk.

EXPLORE THE WEB

1. To establish a Web site, a business must either use someone else's server or establish a direct link to the Internet. Use your browser to find information from three different Internet Service Providers (ISPs). Prepare a comparative table of the charges. Below the table explain what each charge item means and how the charge is determined.

2. You own a music store that specializes in a variety of music styles and sells compact discs. Of the three ISPs, whose service would you purchase? Explain your decision.

Chapter **7**
Data Management

Banking on Data

Like other banks in the course of normal business operations, KeyCorp gathered large amounts of data about their customers that could be useful for marketing purposes, if only it could be accessed and pulled together in certain ways. The company knew how old their customers were, how much money they made, what communities they lived in, and where they spent their money. But KeyCorp was unable to use the data for marketing purposes. Executives of the Cleveland, Ohio-based bank rarely regarded the data as more than a by-product of conducting business. That's because the data sat in scores of separate files, in different departments, in different types of computers and information systems, and in different types of programs.

Information that customers provided when they applied for automobile loans was channeled into one group of files, mortgages into another, and checking and savings transactions into others, each remaining unconnected to the rest. How could the bank use this huge wealth of data to increase its clientele? How could managers identify something as fundamental as which customers were profitable to the bank and which were not? How could the bank figure out which customers of one service might be good candidates for another service?

Like many other banks, KeyCorp turned to structuring their files into a database that would provide transparent links among all the bank's data, using an easy-to-use client/server application. The "transparency" allows users to retrieve data from other computers without even knowing which computers actually provide the data, or where they are located. Client/server applications let bank personnel quickly capture a view of a customer, which allows the employees to provide better service. By "mining" its data, KeyCorp can now cross-sell other bank services, increasing the profitability of each employee contact with each customer.

For example, with all the data collected in one system, the bank could determine that a person is most likely to buy a new car within six months of making the last payment on a car loan. That information could provide the sales department with a series of leads to promote attractive loan rates. Also, the integration of data allows the company to segment its customer base however it pleases, to figure out which characteristics describe the most profitable clients.

Source: Johnston, S.J., "How to Get a Better Return on Data," *InformationWeek*, September 9, 1996, p. 82.

Data are usually not collected in a way that make them immediately useful. Imagine a pile of building blocks dumped on your desk. You have a good idea of what you want to build, but you first have to organize the blocks in a way that will make it easy for you to select only the blocks you need, and then combine them into substructures that eventually will be integrated into your desired model palace. Similarly, data collected by organizations must be organized and stored so that useful information can be extracted from them flexibly.

When you finish this chapter you will:

◆ Know the difference between traditional file organization methods and the database approach

◆ Know how database management systems are used to construct databases, populate them with data, manipulate the data to produce information, and maintain databases to keep them current, accurate, and relevant

◆ Be familiar with the different database models and the advantages and disadvantages of each model

◆ Know the most important operations of a relational database, the most popular database model

◆ Understand how databases are changing business operations across industries and what impact they might have on our personal lives

FILE MANAGEMENT

As we discussed in Chapter 4, "Information Technology in Business: Software," digital data can be stored in a variety of ways on different types of media. They can be stored in what is called the **traditional file** format, where the different pieces of information are not labeled and categorized, but are stored as continuous strings of bytes. While the chief advantage of this format is the efficient use of space, the data are nonetheless difficult to locate and manipulate, and are therefore of limited use. By contrast, the **database** format, in which each piece of data is labeled or categorized, provides a much more powerful information management tool. Data in this format can be easily accessed and manipulated in almost any way desired, to create useful information and optimize productivity.

The impact of **database technology** on business cannot be overstated. Not only has it changed the way almost every industry conducts business, it has also created an information industry with far-reaching effects on both our business and personal lives. Databases are behind the successful use of automated teller machines, increased efficiency in retail stores, almost every marketing effort, and the numerous storehouses of information on the World Wide Web as well. Their impact on business has allowed fewer people to do more work, and their power has allowed organizations to learn more about us than we may realize.

If you are entering business today, you must understand the power of databases. This chapter will review the different approaches to organizing data.

THE TRADITIONAL FILE APPROACH

We can roughly distinguish between two different approaches to maintaining data: the traditional file organization—which has no mechanism for tagging, retrieving, and manipulating data—and the **database approach**. To appreciate the benefits of the database approach, one must keep in mind the inconvenience involved in accessing and manipulating data in the **traditional file approach**: data/program dependency, high data redundancy, and low data integrity.

PROGRAM/DATA DEPENDENCE In Chapter 3, "Information Technology in Business: Hardware," we discussed different ways that data is stored in files. Remember that in *sequential file storage*, the bits and bytes are laid down on the storage medium one after another; in *direct file storage*, the bits and bytes may be organized in no particular sequence, but are accessed via a physical address; and in *indexed sequential file storage*, the bits and bytes are organized sequentially but can also be accessed directly, as in direct organization. These are considered traditional or flat file format types of organization.

Consider Figure 7.1, which is an example of a human resource file in traditional file format. Suppose a programmer wanted to retrieve and print out only the last name and department number of each employee from this file. The programmer must clearly instruct the computer to first retrieve the data between position 10 and position 20. Then he must instruct the computer to skip the positions up to position 35 and retrieve the data between positions 36 and 39. He cannot instruct the computer to retrieve a piece of data by its column or category name, because column and category names do not exist. To create the reports,

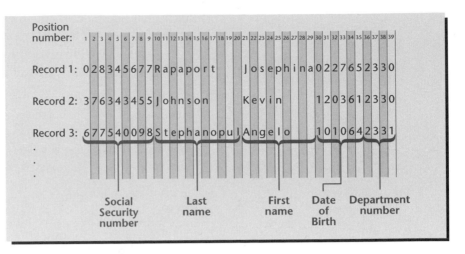

Figure 7.1 *The layout of a personnel file in traditional file organization*

the programmer must insert the appropriate headings, "Last Name" and "Department," so that the reviewer of the output can understand what the data are. If the programmer miscounts the positions, the printout may include output like "677Rapap" as a last name instead of "Rapaport." This illustrates one major problem with traditional file storage: the dependency between programs and data. The programmer *must* know how data is stored in order to use it. Perhaps most importantly, the very fact that manipulation of the data *requires* a programmer is probably the greatest disadvantage of the file approach.

DATA REDUNDANCY AND DATA INTEGRITY Other problems with traditional file storage are high data redundancy and low data integrity. Imagine three departments of your university keeping completely separate records about you in traditional format. As Figure 7.2 shows, the registrar's office, the financial aid office, and the housing office maintain a total of nine different pieces of data about you, four

STUDENT RECORD INFORMATION		
REGISTRAR'S OFFICE	FINANCIAL AID OFFICE	HOUSING OFFICE
last name	last name	last name
first name	first name	first name
SSN	SSN	SSN
home address	home address	home address
major	loan amount	campus address
grades		monthly rent

Figure 7.2 *Different information making up a student record retained in three different sites*

of which are identical. But because these three offices use the information separately, these four data appear *three different* times in *three separate* places. This situation is called **data redundancy**, which causes a waste of storage space (and consequently money), and is extremely inefficient. When it comes to implementing any corrections or modifications, every change has to be made three separate times, which takes time and may introduce errors. If someone in the financial aid office has misspelled your last name or misentered your SSN, then it may be impossible to match the records from the different departments. Inaccurate data in a database are referred to as violations of **data integrity**. Usually, the traditional file approach to storing data leads to low data integrity.

MOVING TO DATABASES

Continuing our analysis of the university records: Would it be easier if the four pieces of data used by all three departments were stored only once, and accessed and manipulated by the different departments into whatever reports they needed? In fact, would it be easier if *all the data* were stored only once, and accessible to everyone in the university system to do with as they please? The answer is yes, and that is the basic idea behind the database approach.

To understand how data are organized in a database, you must first understand the "data hierarchy," described in Figure 7.3, which shows a compilation of information about students: their first names, last names, years of birth, SSNs, majors, and campus phone numbers. The smallest piece of data is a **character** (the letter in a first or last name or address and so on). Several characters make up data in a **field**, such as last name, first name, and the like. A field is one piece of information about an entity, such as a student. Several fields related to the same entity make up a **record**. A collection of related records is called a **file**. Often, there is a need to keep several related files together. A collection of such files is referred to as a **database**. However, the features of a database can be enjoyed by builders and users of databases even when a database consists of a single file.

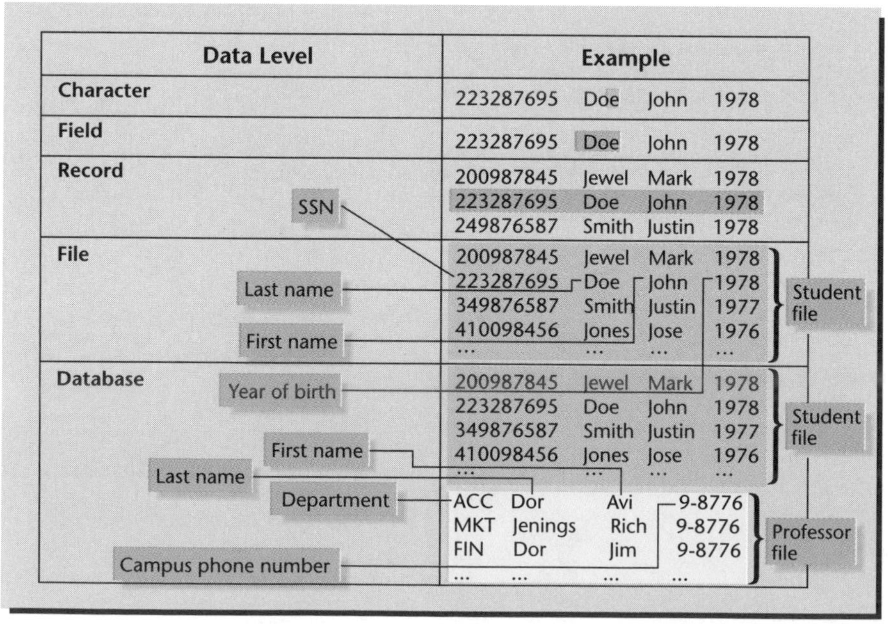

Figure 7.3 *Data hierarchy*

To continue with the above example, lets' assume the university is now storing all nine pieces of student data once, in a database, which is a **union** of the necessary data. Once the fields are assigned names, including Last Name, First Name, SSN, and the like, the data in each field carry a tag in the form of a field name and can be easily accessed by that name, no matter where the data are physically stored. One of the greatest strengths of databases is their promotion of **application/data independence**. In other words, if an application is written to process data in a database, the application designer need only know the names of the fields, not their physical organization, nor their length.

DBMSs A computer program that supports the database approach is called a **database management system (DBMS)**. While a database is a collection of several related *files*, the program used to build databases, populate them with data, and manipulate the data is the database management system. While the files themselves *are* the database, DBMSs do all the work—structuring files, storing data, and linking records. As you saw above, in the traditional file approach you would have to organize the records, establishing exactly how many characters were designated for each type of data, but the DBMS does much of this work for you. Because of the need to move rapidly from one record to another and produce different types of sorting, databases are stored on direct access storage devices (DASDs), such as CDs or magnetic drives, but cannot be stored on sequential storage devices such as magnetic or optical tapes.

QUERIES Data are accessed in a database by sending messages called **queries**, which request data from specific fields and direct the computer to display the results on the monitor. Usually, the same software that is used to construct and populate the database, that is, the DBMS, is also used to present queries. Modern DBMS programs provide fairly intuitive means of querying a program. Queries can be entered either via the keyboard, or as part of more complex applications that are designed beforehand for routine and more complex reports.

SECURITY The use of databases raises issues regarding security and **privacy**. The fact that data are stored only once in a database does not mean that everyone with access to that database should have access to all the data in it. This is easily dealt with by menus and access codes that block access by certain users to certain fields or records. That is, users have different **views** of the database, as illustrated in Figure 7.4. This gives the database administrator (the person who

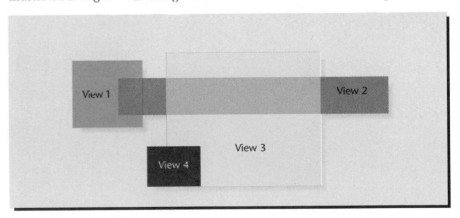

Figure 7.4 *Different database views reveal different combinations of data.*

plans the database and ensures that the database is up and running) another advantage: ease of implementation of security measures. The measures are implemented once for the database, rather than multiple times for different files. For instance, in the database in Figure 7.5, while a human resource manager has access to all fields of the employee file (the EMPLOYEE table), and the payroll personnel have access to the four fields of the employee file (the PAYROLL table), a project manager has access only to the Name and Hours Worked fields. Views may be limited to certain fields in a database, or certain records, or a combination thereof.

TRADITIONAL FILES VS. DATABASES: PROS AND CONS

The advantages of storing data in database files far outweigh the advantages of storing them in flat files. While there are some trade-offs, in general, databases allow for much greater flexibility, easier access by different applications, easier maintenance of data currency and integrity, and savings in both cost and time, all of which make them far superior to flat files. The database advantages include:

1. *Reduced data redundancy*. Although there may still be some data redundancy in a database, it is significantly less than in the traditional file approach. This saves storage space.

2. *Application/data independence*. Writing an application to use data from a database is much simpler than writing one to use data from flat files. To access data in a database, a program can use field names and the names of data sets in which the data exist. This saves programming time and allows users with limited knowledge of programming to enter queries or even develop simple applications.

3. *Better control*. Since all data are concentrated in one place in a database, it is easier to control access and data maintenance, and it is easier to get an overall view of an entity. It is also easier to access procedures and keep data updated.

4. *Flexibility*. Modifying a database by adding additional data related to each entity is much simpler than adding data to flat files.

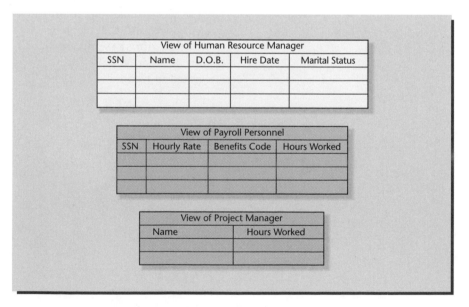

Figure 7.5 *Different views of one employee database*

In general, the reverse characteristics of these advantages are the disadvantages of using traditional files to store data. The traditional file approach creates data redundancy and application/data dependence. It does not support as tight control over data currency, accuracy, and integrity as the database approach, and it provides less flexibility in data maintenance. However, the traditional file approach does have some advantages, including:

1. *Efficiency*. Applications written for flat files run more efficiently than those written for databases because they do not use the additional CPU time and memory space required by the preprogrammed functions that are a part of the DBMS.

2. *Simplicity*. Constructing a database can be very complex and time-consuming. Sometimes, it may be simpler to create simple files and to develop applications for them, especially when an application accesses just one flat file.

3. *Customization*. Using a third generation language to build files and to access them allows a tight tailoring of the applications to business needs—more so than using a DBMS, because the preprogrammed features of the DBMS may restrict some relationships among data. However, this advantage of flat files does not hold for the few DBMSs that are now packaged with fourth-generation languages (4GLs) that include procedural languages.

The advantages of databases raise the question: Why use flat files at all? However, the historical accumulation of data means that businesses will be dealing with flat files for many years to come. Because vast amounts of data in businesses are still stored in flat files and accessed through applications that were written with third-generation languages such as COBOL (which by their nature are designed to access flat files), it may be too costly to switch to databases. However, almost all new data banks are developed and maintained with the aid of DBMSs.

Databases now include more than just text: For instance, an airline personnel database may include digitized images of employees and the equipment they run.

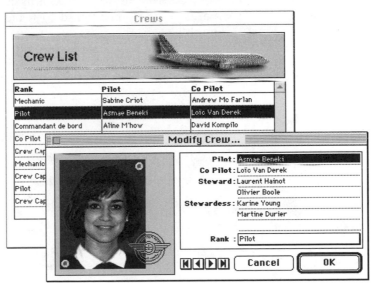

Used by permission from 4th Dimension ©1985–1997ACI US, Inc.

DATABASE MODELS

A database model is the general logical structure in which records are stored within a database. There are three different methods—called **database models**—used to store data in databases. The difference lies in the manner in which records are linked to each other. This, in turn, dictates the manner in which a user can navigate the database and retrieve desired records. As summarized in Figure 7.6 and discussed below, each model has advantages and disadvantages when compared with the other two.

To understand the different models, consider a database for storing university data: there are records about colleges, departments, professors, and students.

THE HIERARCHICAL MODEL

Logically, these four types of university records are hierarchical, meaning that each category is a subcategory of the next level up. The highest level is college; each college has several departments; each department consists of several professors; and each professor has several students. The **hierarchical model** follows the pattern of an upside-down tree, and is sometimes referred to as the **tree model**. Therefore, if the university chose to follow a hierarchical model, the records would be stored as indicated in Figure 7.7, where Figure 7.7a indicates schematically the relationship among the various levels, and Figure 7.7b shows the details within the first few levels. Note that Figure 7.7b does not show the files of all the departments, all the professors, or all the students.

There are as many College records as there are colleges in the university. Each record contains the appropriate values of the following data items: College Name, Dean's Last Name, College Address, and College Telephone Number. To each College record are linked the records of its departments. For example: The College of Business is linked to the records of the Accounting, Marketing, Finance, and other Business departments. The record of each department is linked to the record of each of its professors. And the record of each professor is linked to the record of every student he or she has.

A record to which several records of a lower level are linked is called a **parent**. The records linked to it are its **children**. In our example, College records have no parents, because they are the highest level in the hierarchy, called the **roots**. Student records, on the other hand, have no children, because

	DATABASE MODEL		
	HIERARCHICAL	NETWORK	RELATIONAL
CONCEPTUALIZATION	Moderately easy	Difficult	Easy
EASE OF DESIGN	Very difficult	Moderately difficult	Difficult
EASE OF MAINTENANCE	Difficult	Very difficult	Easy
DATA REDUNDANCY	High	Low	High
EASE OF USE	Moderate	Low	High

Figure 7.6 *Advantages and disadvantages of database models*

they are the lowest level of the hierarchy, called **leaves**, like the leaves of a tree. As you can see in the figure, a College record's children are the departments, and a Department record's children are the professors, and so on. A glance at the diagram reveals that while a parent may have several children, every child has only one parent. This is described mathematically by saying that hierarchical databases have one-to-many (1:M) relationships.

How is a child record linked to a parent record? This is done by adding **pointer** fields to the records. Pointers maintain the links among parent and children records. One pointer field contains the address of the first child record; another pointer field contains the address of the record's parent.

The advantage of hierarchical databases is their suitability for maintaining data on hierarchical environments. But hierarchical databases also have several disadvantages. To retrieve a certain record, a user must start the search at the root and then navigate the hierarchy. If, for some reason, a link is broken, the entire branch is lost. And, because child records can have only one parent, hierarchical databases require considerable data redundancy. For example, the records of students who take several classes with several professors must be stored multiple times, each time as a child of another professor. Thus, in our example, the entire records of students Khori and Williams must appear in both the classes of Professor Munro and Professor AlNajjar.

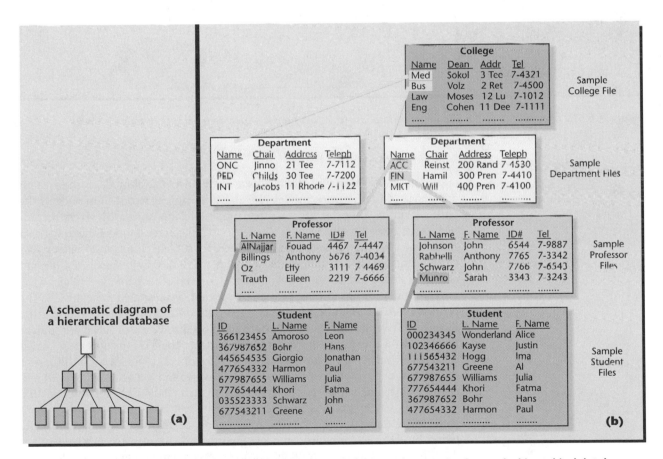

A schematic diagram of a hierarchical database

Figure 7.7 *The schematic diagram of a hierarchical database (a) and a sample of part of a hierarchical database showing relationships among different records (b).*

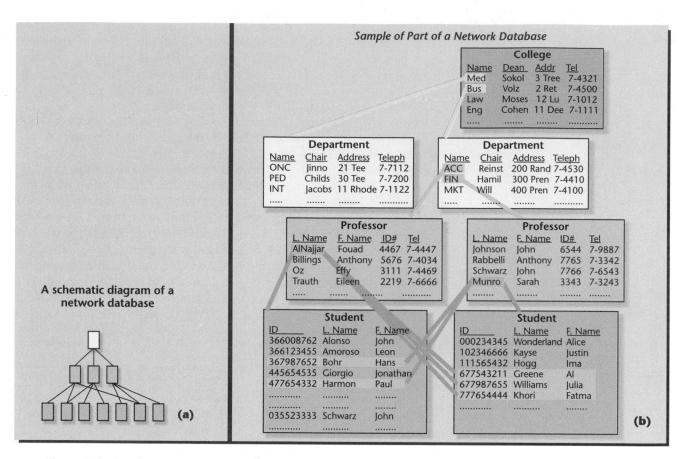

Figure 7.8 *The schematic diagram of a network database (a) and a sample of part of a network database showing relationships among different records (b).*

THE NETWORK MODEL

The reverse of the last disadvantage of the hierarchical model is the greatest advantage of the **network model**: the ability to store a record only once in the entire database, while creating links that establish relationships with several records of another type of entity. Remember that in the hierarchical model there was data redundancy because separate repetitive records for students Khori and Williams had to be maintained in two different student files, one linked to Professor AlNajjar and one to Professor Munro. The network model, on the other hand, would allow the same record to be linked to more than one parent, as illustrated in Figure 7.8. The records of Williams and Greene are stored only once, in the file containing the records of Professor Munro, but they are also linked to Professor AlNajjar's student file. When the user lists Professor AlNajjar's students, these two records are included in the list. Similarly, the records of students Hans Bohr and Paul Harmon will appear in only one of the professors' student files, AlNajjar's, and will be linked to both parents: AlNajjar and Munro. Now imagine many such relationships. If you draw the relationships as lines connecting the records, you will create a network of relationships, as illustrated in Figure 7.8. This is the reason for this model's name. Unlike the hierarchical model, the network model supports many-to-many (N:M) relationships.

Network databases create significantly less data redundancy than hierarchical databases, but are complicated to build and difficult to maintain. While the user does not have to start a search at the root, it is difficult to navigate in the database. The complex network of relationships creates "spaghetti" that is hard to follow. For these reasons, the network structure is the least popular model.

THE RELATIONAL MODEL

A **relational model** database has all the advantages of a network database without the complications. The relational model consists of tables. Its roots are in relational algebra, although you do not have to know relational algebra to build and use relational databases. However, database experts still use relational algebra terminology: in a relational database, a record is called a *tuple*; a field is called an *attribute*; and a relation is simply a table. We will use the simpler terms, as do the popular software packages: fields, records, and tables.

Relational databases are easier to conceptualize and maintain than hierarchical and network ones. To build a relational database, one only needs to have a clear idea of the different **objects**. In our example, the objects are: college, department, professor, and student. A single table is built for each object.

Retrieving a desired record is easy. To find a record of a certain professor, one needs to access the Professor table and make an inquiry. Maintenance is easy, because the user does not have to keep in mind any relationships. Each table stands alone. To add a student record, the user accesses the Student table. Similar actions take place to change or delete a record. Figure 7.9 presents our example as a relational database. The advantages of this model make relational database management systems the most popular in the software market. Virtually all DBMSs that are offered for microcomputers accommodate the relational model.

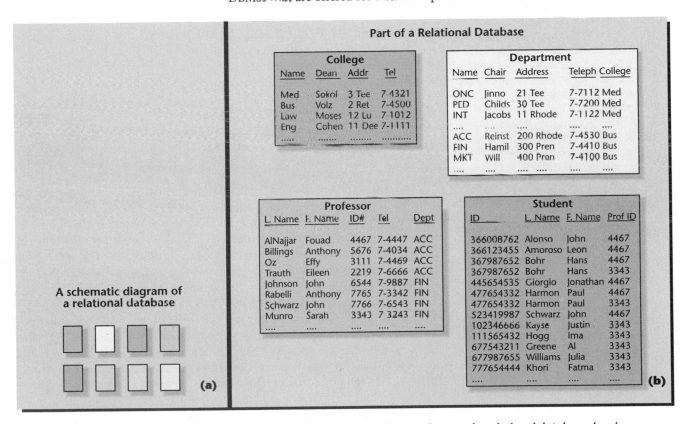

Part of a Relational Database

College

Name	Dean	Addr	Tel
Med	Sokol	3 Tee	7-4321
Bus	Volz	2 Ret	7-4500
Law	Moses	12 Lu	7-1012
Eng	Cohen	11 Dee	7-1111
.....			

Department

Name	Chair	Address	Teleph	College
ONC	Jinno	21 Tee	7-7112	Med
PED	Childs	30 Tee	7-7200	Med
INT	Jacobs	11 Rhode	7-1122	Med
....	....	....	....	....
ACC	Reinst	200 Rhode	7-4530	Bus
FIN	Hamil	300 Pren	7-4410	Bus
MKT	Will	400 Pren	7-4100	Bus
....	....	....	....	....

Professor

L. Name	F. Name	ID#	Tel	Dept
AlNajjar	Fouad	4467	7-4447	ACC
Billings	Anthony	5676	7-4034	ACC
Oz	Effy	3111	7-4469	ACC
Trauth	Eileen	2219	7-6666	ACC
Johnson	John	6544	7-9887	FIN
Rabelli	Anthony	7765	7-3342	FIN
Schwarz	John	7766	7-6543	FIN
Munro	Sarah	3343	7-3243	FIN
....	....	....	....	....

Student

ID	L. Name	F. Name	Prof ID
366008762	Alonso	John	4467
366123455	Amoroso	Leon	4467
367987652	Bohr	Hans	4467
367987652	Bohr	Hans	3343
445654535	Giorgio	Jonathan	4467
477654332	Harmon	Paul	4467
477654332	Harmon	Paul	3343
523419987	Schwarz	John	4467
102346666	Kayse	Justin	3343
111565432	Hogg	Ima	3343
677543211	Greene	Al	3343
677987655	Williams	Julia	3343
777654444	Khori	Fatma	3343
....	....	....	....

A schematic diagram of a relational database

(a)

(b)

Figure 7.9 *The schematic diagram of a relational database (a) and a sample part of a relational database showing different tables (b).*

KEYS

To retrieve records from a relational database, you must use a key. A **key** is a field that identifies a record. For example, you could ask the database for the record of Professor Munro from the Professor table by using the L. Name field as a key. That is, you enter a query, a condition that instructs the DBMS to retrieve a record in which the value of its L. Name is "Munro."

PRIMARY KEY If there is more than one record with "Munro" in the L. Name field, you may not retrieve the record you desired. Depending on the software you use, the record you retrieve is probably the first one that meets the condition. The only way to be sure you are retrieving the desired record is to use a value in the record that you know to be unique in the table (such as a social security number). This type of key is called a **primary key**. If your query specified that you wanted the record whose ID# value is "3343," the system will retrieve the record of Sarah Munro.

Every record in a relational database must have a unique value that can be used as the primary key in each table. Once the primary key is determined, when constructing the records' format, the DBMS will not allow a user to enter two records with the same value in that column. Note that there may be situations where more than one field may be used as a primary key. Such is the case with motor vehicles, because both the vehicle identification number (VIN) and the license plate number uniquely identify a car. Thus, a database designer may establish either field as a primary key to retrieve records.

Note that many DBMSs will force you to designate a primary key in each table you construct. Usually, the software will require that the primary key be the leftmost field in the schema. By default, many DBMSs automatically sort the records the user enters in ascending order of the primary key, which is not the case in our College, Department, and Professor tables in Figure 7.9.

Some relational databases use **composite keys**, a combination of two or more fields that together serve as a primary key. An example: the last name, first name, and department in a table that holds professors' records. Unless we expect two people with the same name to lecture for the same department, the combination will be a valid primary key.

LINKING To link records from one table with records of another table, both tables must have a column (that is, a field) containing the same type of data, and that field must be a primary key field for one of the tables. This repeated field is a primary key in one table, and a **foreign key** field in the other table. In our example, to create a table showing the last name of every professor and, next to each name, a listing of all the students of that professor, both the Professor and Student tables must contain the unique ID number of the professors. In the Professor table, the ID number is the primary key. In the Student table, the Professor ID number is a foreign key field. To generate a list of the students of the professor whose ID number is 4467, the DBMS calls for the last name of the professor whose ID number is 4467 (AlNajjar), and a list of names of all student records for which the Professor ID number field contains 4467. This is called a **join table**. As long as each student's record contains a field with his or her professor's ID number, it is possible to create the join file. We will elaborate upon the join operation later in this chapter.

As you can see, all database design requires a lot of forethought. The designer must include fields for foreign keys from other tables so that join

A national car rental company knows the precise number of automobiles to hold for late-booking, high-paying travelers. A restaurant chain detects consumer buying patterns that the company uses to boost its sales of specialty meals. A department store chain discovers that people who buy diapers on Thursdays purchase, on average, another 19 items; therefore, the company puts diapers on sale every Thursday to lure more customers. How do businesses find this information?

Data and information are the lifeblood of organizations. Transactions are recorded at the boundaries of a company in its contacts with external entities, such as customers and suppliers. Internal data captured this way make up the greater part of most organizational databases. They provide the raw material for essential information which helps answer questions like: What is the total amount of money we owe debtors? What is the backlog of a certain product that we manufacture? What was the average sales volume per employee last quarter?

If we can manipulate the data, we can produce accurate and current answers to these and other important questions. Data manipulation includes all those arithmetic and logical operations that help produce information: totals, averages, standard deviations, selection of records that meet certain conditions, creation of a joint file from two or more different files, ranges of values, and many other operations as well.

Imagine a sales clerk who cannot immediately respond to a customer about the availability of an item. The customer is not likely to patronize the business again. Imagine a treasurer who cannot figure out in real time how much cash the company has in the bank. The company may miss an important deal. Available and reliable information is the most important resource of any business, in any industry. Thus, managers must understand at least the fundamentals of data organization and manipulation.

tables can be created in the future. The inclusion of foreign keys may cause considerable data redundancy. This has not diminished the popularity of relational databases however. Since the links between tables are created as part of manipulating the table, the relational model supports both one-to-many (1:M) and many-to-many (N:M) relationships between records of different tables.

THE OBJECT-ORIENTED STRUCTURE

While the move from traditional file systems to databases was a leap forward in data management efficiency, recent years have seen a new development that may afford even greater benefits: **object-oriented** databases. We introduced the concept of *objects* in our discussion of object-oriented programming in Chapter 4, "Information Technology in Business: Software." An object consists of both data and the procedures that manipulate the data. In addition to the attributes of an entity it also contains the relationships with other entities. The combined storage of both data and the procedures that manipulate them is referred to as **encapsulation**. Thus, an object can be "planted" in different data sets. The ability in object-oriented structures to automatically create a new object by replicating all or some of the characteristics of a previously developed object (called the **parent object**) is called **inheritance**.

Modern Databases:
A Threat to Privacy

The widespread use of database management systems allows organizations and individuals to easily and cheaply collect, maintain, and sell vast amounts of private personal data. Millions of credit card transactions take place in America and other countries, each carrying private information. Millions of personal data items are routed, daily, to corporate databases, through sales calls and credit checks. This opens the door to the abuse of a fundamental human right: privacy. This is the downside to database technology, but there is also an upside. Consider the following.

Out of Hand—Out of Control. You have just recieved a letter from John Doe Investment Co. In the letter, the president tells you that at your age, with a nice income like yours, the company could provide you with innovative investment services. How did the company know about your existence? About your annual income? Well, remember the free sample questionnaire about your shopping habits you filled out the previous month, in exchange for product samples? The company that received your completed questionnaire entered your record into its database. It later sold the entire database, or selected portions of it, to John Doe Investment Co. You enjoyed your product samples, but you paid a price you didn't know about.

Where is the Information Going? In the above example, you were at least aware that you gave somebody information. But many consumers daily provide information without really being aware of it. For example, a car dealership installed a computer terminal to help potential customers make purchase decisions. The interactive program invited them to answer questions about their personalities and attitudes so that the computer could recommend the best car for them. When customers answered the questions, they indeed received a printed "recommended car profile," but the information was also channeled into a permanent record for the car company. The dealer kept the data to later target customers for sales promotions. Do you know where the information you provide ends up? If not, simply ask.

Personal Data Matched, Sliced, and Diced. Database technology allows organizations to easily match and mix data from different sources. As a consumer, you may give away just a few details at every purchase. But the little pieces may be matched and put together like a jigsaw puzzle to produce a bigger, intimate picture that exposes much of your private life in a way you never expected. Here is one example:

Let's say you fill out a survey questionnaire that asks you to supply percentages of your expenditure on different products and services. You are

(continued)

All these capabilities make object-oriented DBMSs (OODBMS) handy in computer-aided design (CAD) because they can handle a wide range of data—such as graphics, voice, and text—more easily than the other models. OODBMSs are also more effective than other database models in complex information systems, such as geographic information systems and systems that use a lot of multimedia components. In manufacturing and engineering, OODBMSs have been used in CAD and computer-aided manufacturing (CAM) systems. These are systems that use complex data relations as well as multiple data types. OODBMSs provide graphical user interface (GUI) to manage the DBMS. The user can choose objects from classes, which are groups of objects that share similar characteristics.

not asked to divulge your income, or to mention dollar amounts. A few days later a market-research firm has a pretty good estimate of the actual amounts you spend on these products and services. How could that happen? Simple. A few weeks ago you applied for a new credit card. You had to provide an exact amount of your income, the number of your dependents, and your monthly mortgage payments. The credit company sold the data to the market research company. It was quite easy to calculate your net income. The firm used a well-tested statistical model to estimate the distribution of that income by the products and services.

Error Propagation. Many individuals have complained that some data maintained by organizations about them are erroneous. There are especially sad cases of individuals who could not receive credit to buy a house or pay tuition because of erroneous credit histories. Even if an individual learns about such errors, it is often too late to completely eliminate the damage. Perhaps you were fortunate to find out that your record in the database of Company A was erroneous. The company took your complaint seriously and straightened the data out. Now, who can guarantee that the same correction will be made in the databases of Companies B, C, and D, all of whom bought parts of Company A's data? It may be practically impossible to trace your data to all of the organizations that now own it.

The Upside. Against all these examples, there is also a positive side to giving up some of our privacy. Database technology enables companies to provide us with better and faster services. It also makes the market more competitive. Small firms cannot afford the great expense of data collection. For much less money they can purchase sorted data. Now the same data are available to both the big, strong industry leader and the small, still weak, new enterprise. The wide availability of data contributes to a more egalitarian and democratic business environment. The winners are not only vendors, but also the consumers, who can purchase new and cheaper products.

And while many of us complain that these huge databases contribute to the glut of junk mail, better information in the hands of marketers may actually save consumers from junk mail and junk telephone calls. After all, junk mail and junk telephone calls are the ones that tout products and services we don't need. With more specific information, marketers can target only those households that may be interested in their offerings.

ENTITY-RELATIONSHIP DIAGRAMS

It is quite easy, even for a lay user, to plan flat file databases (databases that contain only one type of record). However, many business databases consist of multiple files with some relationships among them. For example, a hospital may use a database that has a file holding the records of all its physicians, another one with all its nurses, another one with all the current patients, and so on. The administrative staff must be able to create reports that link data from multiple files. Thus, the database must be carefully planned to allow useful data manipulation and report generation. The planning task often involves the creation of a conceptual blueprint of the database. This blueprint is called an **entity-relationship (ER) diagram**. An ER diagram is a graphical representation of all entity relationships, an example of which is shown in Figure 7.10, and they are often consulted to determine a problem with a query or to implement changes. Boxes are used to identify entities, also referred to as objects. Lines are used to indicate a relationship between entities. When crow's feet are pointing to an object, there may be many instances of that object. When a link with a crow's foot also includes a crossbar, then all instances of the object on the side of the crow's feet are linked with a single instance of the object on the side of the crossbar. Let's refer to the example for clarification.

In the figure, the crow's foot on the Department end of the Department/School relationship indicates that there are several departments in one school, indicating a one-to-many relationship between school and department. However, a department belongs to only one school, thus the crossbar at the School end of the School/Department link. A department has many professors, but a professor may belong to more than one department, thus the relationship between Professor and Department is many-to-many, represented by the crow's foot at both ends of the link. Similarly, a course is offered by a single department, indicated by the crossbar at the Department end of the Department Course link. A professor may teach more than one student, and a student may have more than one professor, thus the crow's foot at both the Professor and Student ends of the many-to-many relationship between professor and student. However, the ring at the Student end indicates that a professor does not have to have students at all. The ring means "optional," and is there for cases in which professors do not teach.

You should be aware that database designers may use different notations. Therefore, before you review an ER diagram, be sure you first understand what each symbol means.

COMPONENTS OF DATABASE MANAGEMENT SYSTEMS

When designers have a good idea of how a database should be **structured** to accommodate the different data sets and the relationships among them, they select a DBMS to construct the new database. While DBMSs have different interfaces, almost all of them share the same components. These components allow the user to create a set of objects, define a set of fields within those objects, organize the record types within the objects, create a set of files, and manipulate the data in the different files, records, and fields. Be aware that lay users often design simple databases, but higher degrees of complexity usually require the involvement of an experienced database designer. The components of a DBMS are the data definition language, which enables the building of schemas and data dictionaries, and the data manipulation language, which allows the user to manipulate data.

Note the difference between a record type and a record: A "record type" is the general structure of a record, defining the types of fields that make it up; a "record" is the actual data that pertain to a specific instance. Therefore, for a file that holds the records of professors, we need to design a record type that describes which fields will appear in *every* actual data record of the professors' (for instance, ID number, last name, first name, department name, and telephone number). A record will be the row of data describing a specific professor in the professors' file (such as, 120-33-7685, Weinrib, Janet, English, 209-8256). That is, a record contains the actual data values.

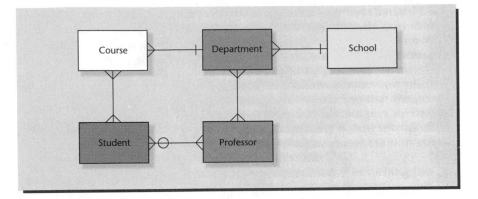

Figure 7.10 *An entity-relationship diagram*

THE SCHEMA

When building a new database, users must first build a **schema** (from Greek: plan). The schema describes the structure of the database being designed: the names and types of fields in each record type, and the general relationships among different sets of records, or files. It includes a description of the database's structure, the names and sizes of fields, and details such as which field is a primary key. The number of records is never specified, because it may change, and the maximum number of records is determined by the capacity of the storage medium.

TYPES OF DATA Fields can hold different types of data: numeric, alphanumeric, graphic, or date. Numeric fields hold numbers that can be manipulated as quantities to add, multiply, average, and so on. Alphanumeric fields hold textual values: words, numerals, and special symbols, which make up names, addresses, and identification numbers. Numerals entered in alphanumeric fields, such as social security numbers or zip codes, cannot be manipulated as numbers. In addition to numeric and alphanumeric fields, DBMSs offer date fields and graphic fields. While date fields are displayed in the standard fashions of mm/dd/yy, mmm dd, yyyy, or some other format, the dates are actually stored in the form of so many days elapsed from a certain base date, such as January 1, 1901. An increasing number of microcomputer-based DBMSs offer graphical fields in which pictures can be maintained. For example, employee pictures can be scanned and entered into the Photo field in a human resource database.

In a hierarchical DBMS, the schema includes the relationships between parent and child record types. Similarly, relationships must be detailed in the schema of a network database. The schema of a relational database is simpler. It describes only the record type of each table. The builder of a new database must also indicate which fields will be used as keys. Many DBMSs also allow the builder to indicate that the field is not unique, meaning that the database should accept the same value in more than one record when the database is populated or updated.

BUILDING THE DATABASE Once the schema is complete, the users may start entering values in the tables. Figure 7.11 on the next page presents the schema of a database created with the DBMS Paradox and the equivalent schema in the DBMS Access. The user is prompted to enter the names and types of fields. As you can see, in the Paradox schema the length of numeric fields in this DBMS is not specified. The user enters the letter N for "Numeric" to indicate that the field is numeric. The letter D indicates that the field will maintain dates. The "*" indicates that the field will be used as a primary key. Access lets the user name the fields and determine the data types. The Description part allows the designer to spell out the nature and function of the respective fields for people who maintain the database. However, in the lower part of the window the user is offered many options for each field, such as field size, format, and so on. Rather than an asterisk, in Access a primary key field is indicated by a little key icon to its left.

THE DATA DICTIONARY

All the information supplied by the database developer when constructing the schema is maintained in the **data dictionary**, which includes the file names, record names and types, field names and types, and, if applicable, the relationships among record types. In addition, the data dictionary contains the notation of who is responsible for updating each part of the database and a characterization, or actual list, of the people who are authorized to access the different parts of the database. Figure 7.12 shows a typical data dictionary entry.

Data dictionaries are often referred to as **metadata** meaning "data about the data." They are useful when trying to understand a database designed by someone else. Many PC DBMSs do not allow the users direct access to the data dictionary. The user can view, and to a certain extent change, only the schema. But some mainframe DBMSs provide users with a facility to add to the data dictionary information such as the name of the database designer, the date the database was built, the purpose of each field and minimum and maximum values of a data field, who may make changes in the schema, who is authorized to access which data in the database, and other valuable information.

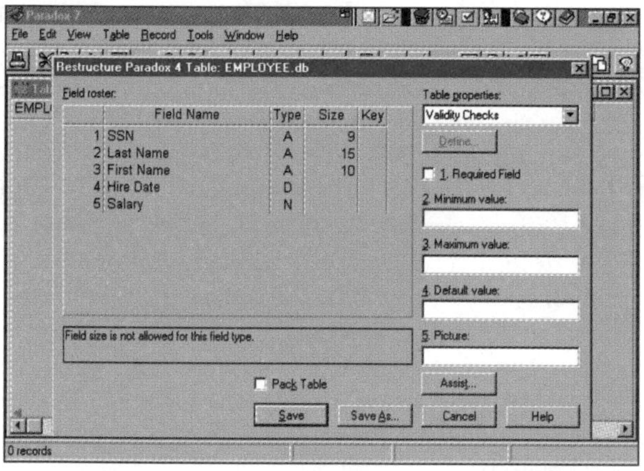

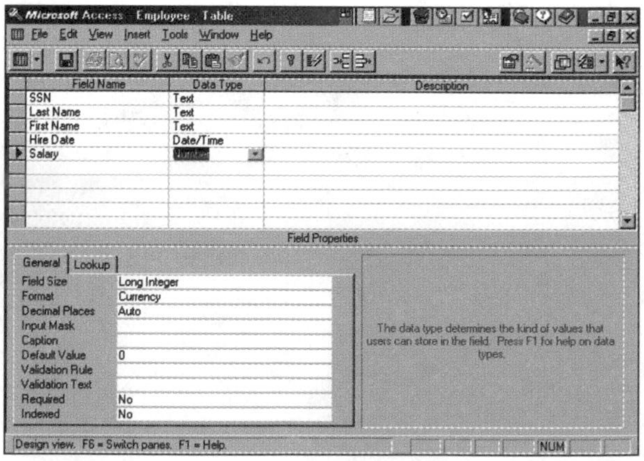

Figure 7.11 *Schemas of the Employee table of a database in Paradox (left) and in Access (right)*

```
File:  STAFF
PREPARED BY:        J. HORN
DATE:              APR 5, 1997
APPROVED BY:       M. WILLIAMS
DATE:              JUN 7, 1997
OWNED BY:          HUMAN RESOURCES
MASTER:            PHYSICIAN
ACCESS:            PAYROLL DATA ENTRY CLERK, BENEFITS
                   CLERK, ACCOUNTS PAYABLE MANAGER
DATA ELEMENT:      ID
DESCRIPTION:       PHYSICIAN IDENTIFICATION NUMBER
OTHER NAMES:       NONE
VALUE RANGE:       1000-9999
DATA TYPE:         ALPHANUMERIC
```

Figure 7.12 *A typical data dictionary entry for a staff file*

THE DATA DEFINITION LANGUAGE

Every DBMS must include a subprogram (in this case a language) called a **data definition language** (DDL) that is used to construct the schema. This language has various commands and protocols the database designer uses to define and name the files, records, and fields in a database before beginning to populate them. In most PC DBMSs, the user interface of the DDL presents screens and prompts the designer to enter the appropriate parameters from a menu. These interfaces are intuitive and allow a database to be created by someone who may have relatively little experience. In other DBMSs, the user must know the commands used in the DDL to construct the schema.

It is unlikely that you will have to deal with DDLs directly, unless you choose a career in MIS. If you use a modern relational DBMS, you will use a GUI to create a schema, and the DDL will be transparent to you. However, Figure 7.13 is an example

```
!This is a hospital schema. Created 4/1/98 by Rich Little!
MASTER doctor KEYED(last_name);
    ITEM last_name AS A15;
    ITEM first_name AS A10;
    ITEM dept AS A12 LIMITS ('internal', 'oncology', 'ob/gyn',
'urology') HEADING
       'Department';
MASTER patient KEYED(ssn,A);
    ITEM ssn as A11 MASK '999-99-9999' HEADING
'Social:Security:Number';
    ITEM lname AS A15 HEADING 'Last Name';
    ITEM fname AS A10 HEADING 'First Name';
    ITEM age AS 999 LIMIT (0:120);
    ITEM doctor AS A15;
    ITEM adm_date AS DATE'mm/dd/yy' HEADING 'Admission:Date';
END;
```

Figure 7.13 *Data definition language to create a schema in NOMAD*

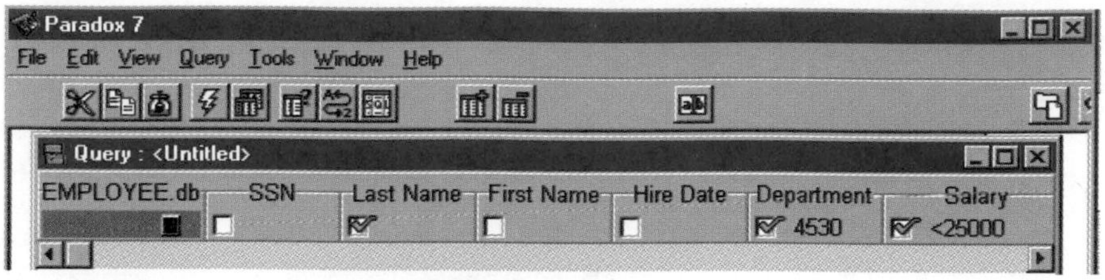

Figure 7.14 *A Paradox query by example*

of a schema described by statements used by the DDL of the DBMS called NOMAD. The word MASTER indicates a record type. ITEM indicates a data item type, that is a field type. The letter A indicates that the field is alphanumeric, and the number next to it specifies its length. When a field is defined with 9s, it is numeric. The number of 9s determines the maximal number of digits that the field will display.

> **Net Notes**
>
> The Web is getting crowded. Organizations find it harder and harder to reserve a desired Web name. Access *http://www.primehost.com/domain/index.htm* to explore Primehosts database, or use the keywords *check web address* to access other locations that let you check which names are still available.

The Data Manipulation Language

Data manipulation language (DML) is the software that serves the user in querying the database. Some DBMSs require that the user type in commands. For example, consider a database holding personnel data: ID, Last_Name, First_Name, Department, and Salary. Suppose you want a list showing the last names, department number, and salaries of employees whose department number is 4530 and whose salary is less than $25,000. It is the DML that allows such a query to be placed and executed.

In NOMAD, for instance, the user asks for the EMPLOYEE master, the record set that holds employee records, and specifies the required output, as follows:

```
FROM EMPLOYEE LIST LAST_NAME DEPARTMENT SALARY WHERE
DEPARTMENT="4530" AND SALARY<25000
```

Some DBMSs hide the DML from the user. Instead of statements, the user expresses a **query by example (QBE)**. The user invokes the query module of the program, which displays the fields available, and then places check marks in the fields to be listed and conditions in the proper fields. The above query would be made in Paradox as illustrated in Figure 7.14. Virtually all the popular PC relational DBMSs provide QBE dialog interfaces.

Many DBMSs are now part of 4GLs. 4GLs are flexible enough to allow programmers to use the language both to develop applications that retrieve and manipulate data from a database, and also to perform tasks that have nothing to do with the database, all in the same application.

RELATIONAL OPERATIONS

As mentioned before, by far the most popular DBMSs are those that support the relational model. Therefore, it would be beneficial for you to familiarize yourself with a widely used relational database, such as Microsoft Access, dBASE V, Oracle, Paradox, or FoxBase. To use the database you must know how to use relational operations. A **relational operation** creates a temporary table that is a subset of the original table or tables. If so desired, the user can save the newly created table. Often, the temporary table is needed only for ad hoc reporting and is immediately discarded.

DATA MANIPULATION

There are several types of data manipulation in relational databases. We will discuss the three most important relational operations. **Select** is the selection of records that meet certain conditions. For example, a human resource manager may need a report showing the entire record of every employee whose salary exceeds $30,000.

Project is the selection of certain columns from a table, such as the salaries of all the employees. A query may specify a combination of selection and projection. In the above example, the manager may require only the ID number, last name (project), and salary of the employees whose salary is greater than $30,000 (select).

One of the most useful manipulations of a relational database is the creation of a new table from two or more other tables. As you may recall from our discussion of the relational model, the joining of data from multiple tables is called a join. For example, a relational business database may have four tables: salespeople, catalog, order log, and customer. The sales manager may wish to create a report showing, for each salesperson, a list of all of the customers who purchased anything last month, the items each customer purchased, and the total amount spent by each customer. The new table is created from data that come from the different tables.

In our university example, a report showing the name of every professor with his or her students' names is a join table, as shown in Figure 7.15. Note that some DBMSs will not allow the same field name to be used more than once in a table, so the second "L. Name" may automatically be changed to "L. Name-1." Also, in this example the user indicated that for display purposes she does not desire the professor name and ID number repeated for each student.

The join operation is a powerful and useful manipulation that can create very useful reports for decision making. A join table is created "on the fly" as a result of a query and only for the duration the user wishes to view it or create a paper report from it. Design features allow the user to change the field headings

Professor		Student	
L. Name	Prof ID	L. Name	F. Name
AlNajjar	4467	Alonso	John
		Amoroso	Leon
		Bohr	Hans
		Georgio	Jonathan
		Harmon	Paul
		Schwarz	John
Munro	3343	Bohr	Hans
		Harmon	Paul
		Wonderland	Alice
		Kayse	Justin
		Hogg	Ima
		Koholik	Al
		Williams	Julia
		Khori	Fatma
...	...	...	...

Figure 7.15 *A join table of professors and their students*

(although the field names are kept the same in the internal table), and to add graphics and text to the report. However, the new table may be saved at any time. The DBMS then treats it like any other table.

STRUCTURED QUERY LANGUAGE

Structured query language (SQL) is quickly becoming the DDL and DML of choice for many developers of relational DBMS. SQL is now an international standard and is provided with most relational database management programs. Its strength is in its easy-to-remember intuitive commands. For instance, to perform the query mentioned above from the EMPLOYEE table, the command would be:

```
SELECT LAST_NAME DEPARTMENT SALARY FROM EMPLOYEE
WHERE DEPARTMENT="4530"
AND SALARY<25000
```

Statements like this can be used for ad hoc queries, or integrated in a program that is saved for repeated use. Commands for updating the database are also easy to remember: INSERT, DELETE, and UPDATE.

There are several advantages to integrating SQL in a DBMS:

1. With a standard language, users do not have to learn different DDLs and DMLs to create and manipulate databases in different DBMSs.

2. SQL statements can be embedded in widely used third-generation languages such as COBOL. The combination of highly tailored and efficient third-generation language statements with SQL statements increases the efficiency and effectiveness of applications accessing relational databases.

3. Because SQL statements are portable from one operating system to another, the programmer is not forced to rewrite statements.

As described above with respect to DDLs, some relational DBMSs provide GUIs for SQL queries that allow the use of SQL by users who are not familiar with the language. SQL queries can be placed by clicking icons and selecting menu items, which are internally converted into SQL queries and executed.

POPULAR DATABASE MANAGEMENT SYSTEMS

There are numerous database management packages for mainframes and PCs, all listed in Figure 7.16. One of the oldest mainframe DBMSs is IMS, a hierarchical DBMS developed by IBM. Also widely used is FOCUS by Information Builders International. In the network model arena, ADABAS and IDMS are leaders.

In the mainframe arena, DB2 (Data Base 2) and FOCUS reign. DB2 was developed by IBM in 1982 and is used on IBM large mainframes. Information Builders International has successfully marketed FOCUS, a 4GL and hierarchical DBMS. Some vendors developed a PC version from their mainframe packages, such as PC FOCUS and PC NOMAD. Other popular DBMSs include dBASE V, which started as a mere file manager in its early versions. The V version is a full-blown relational DBMS. Microsoft Access, Paradox, Oracle, and Ingres are also widely used by organizations and individuals. All include a 4GL for development of database applications. Some packages allow the presentation of data in more than one format. For example, in NOMAD, the user can arrange and access the data hierarchically, but also join data from tables in a relational manner.

Database Model	Product	Vendor	Hardware
Hierarchical	Focus	Information Builders International	Mainframe/PC
	IMS	IBM	Mainframe
	Ramis	On-line Software International	Mainframe
Network	ADABAS	Software AG of North America	Mainframe
	IDMS	Computer Associates	Mainframe
	Image	Hewlett-Packard	Mainframe
Relational	DB2	IBM	Mainframe
	dBASE V	Borland International	PC
	EDA/SQL	Information Builders International	PC
	FoxPro	Microsoft	PC
	Ingres	Ask Group	PC
	NOMAD	Must Software International	Mainframe/PC
	Oracle	Oracle	Mainframe/PC
	Paradox	Borland International	PC
	Rbase	Microrim	PC
	SQL/DS	IBM	Mainframe
	Sybase	Sybase	PC
Object-Relational	ObjectStore	Object Design	PC
	Universal Server	Informix	PC
	Illustra	Informix	PC

Figure 7.16 *Commercial DBMSs*

DATABASE ARCHITECTURE

Database architecture refers both to the physical and logical layouts of databases in an organization. In the past, most organizations' databases—data and programs alike—were centrally located on mainframes and accessed from remote locations throughout the company from dumb terminals. There have been significant changes in database architecture as both databases and the programs running them have moved from mainframes to PCs, from a centralized to a distributed model.

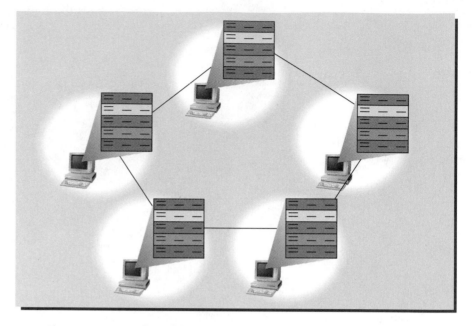

Figure 7.17 *A replicated database: Each computer holds a copy of the entire database.*

DISTRIBUTED DATABASES

Many organizations operate through geographically remote sites. Still, much of the data used by one site is often also used by other sites. Of course, the organization can use a centrally located database and let the other sites use it through communications lines. A less expensive solution, however, is to distribute the database at different sites for all to use. This arrangement is called a **distributed database**. There are two distributed database models:

The database administrator (DBA) can either replicate the database or fragment it. **Replication** of the database means that a full copy of the entire database is stored at all the sites that need access to it (see Figure 7.17). This approach is expensive and not conducive to data integrity, because all the updates must be performed at all the sites, and the chance of errors occurring due to delayed updates and copying errors is high.

Many organizations have opted for the other alternative: a **fragmented** database. Different parts of the database are stored in the locations where they are accessed most often, but they continue to be fully accessible to others through telecommunications (see Figure 7.18). The result is just one copy of the database, distributed among the various sites by way of communications lines. Applications make the use of remote fragments of the database transparent to the users. The users do not know, and need not bother to know, which part of the database resides locally at their site, and which is processed remotely. One advantage of a fragmented database is the lower communications costs. With only one copy of the database, another advantage is better data integrity. Many experts refer to fragmented databases as **distributed** databases.

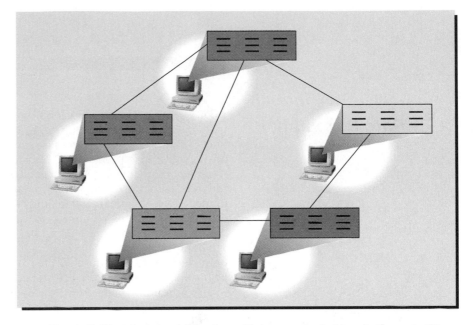

Figure 7.18 *A fragmented database: Each computer holds only the part of the database which is most frequently accessed by the local users.*

SHARED RESOURCE AND CLIENT/SERVER SYSTEMS

As described above, some organizations store their databases and the applications that run them on mainframe or minicomputers accessible remotely from dumb terminals. Others distribute their database, but leave the processing of the data centralized. Some experts refer to either arrangement as **shared resource** architecture. The central resource is used by remote terminals and PCs not only for the data in its databases, but also for the applications that process the data.

However, the increasing power of microcomputers and the great progress and declining cost of data communications are driving organizations to move to what is called **client/server** architecture, which is a loose term IS professionals use to describe any distribution of data and applications between a server and its clients. This includes allowing users to access data remotely, but process it locally (see Figure 7.19 on the next page). The server is a computer, usually a powerful PC or a minicomputer, that serves the clients —the users' PCs—by storing databases and managing remote access communications. Once the desired data are downloaded, that is, copied, from the server, the users can use the applications they developed locally on their PCs to process them.

In a client/server network, software may run not only on a host, but wherever it makes most sense. In fact, software can be processed "cooperatively" on various computers across the network. Seemingly, the computer becomes the network, and the network becomes the computer. Often, the physical location where the processing takes place is transparent to the user.

To use a human analogy, thoughts are processed throughout an office, not just in the mind of the boss. And thoughts are communicated as requirements of the collective process. In a client/server network, more computing power is transferred to the individual users, locally, where they can process data, produce information, and then decide what to save on the server, and what to save locally in their own computers. This is the reason that many experts say that the

A Spatial Data Presentation

Joan Reynolds sits down in her office with a freshly brewed cup of coffee in her hand. She turns to face the large flat screen attached to the wall and utters: "On, sesame." The screen is painted light blue, and a soft voice answers: "Ready, Ms. Reynolds." "Open the Customer database," she orders. A large window opens on the screen with the word "Customer" in its title bar. "Show sales for the month of May by age," she says, pronouncing her command to the computer in a loud and clear voice. Within a second, a table is displayed showing two columns: age groups with five-year ranges, and corresponding dollar amounts. "Clear," she says, and the columns disappear.

She sips her coffee. "Show sales for the month of May by region." A column showing regions in the United States and Canada appears, followed by a column containing the corresponding dollar amounts. She examines the information. "Breakdown Northeast," she commands, and the system zooms in on the Northeast region. A new window appears, partly covering the original window, showing a list of names and dollar amounts. These are the company's salespeople covering the Northeast region.

This is a scenario not far in the future. But it's not just the smooth vocal interactivity of the system that makes it somewhat futuristic; it's also the type of computing and data storage that could easily be used in this setting.

Joan is the vice president of marketing for an apparel company. A guest to her office-of-the-future would expect to see a large computer serving the staff, with a huge amount of data collected and analyzed daily in numerous ways. But the computer that could make this all possible would take up

(continued)

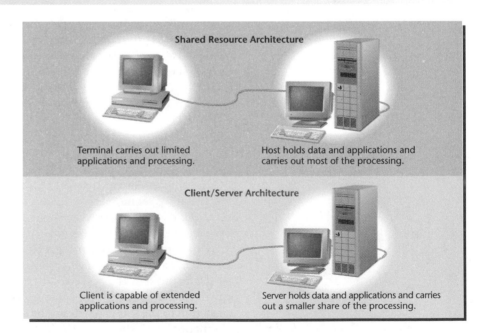

Figure 7.19 *Shared resource and client/server architectures*

very little space: The company could use a massively-parallel processing system that stores data holographically. Several thousand processors, each attached to its own main memory, would increase data processing and reduce the time needed to store, retrieve, and update data.

The system uses laser technology and crystals, rather than magnetic media, to store bytes in holograms. The technology reduces the physical storage space because it provides higher storage densities than magnetic or older optical disks.

Holograms can also be used for the visual presentation of data. Joan commands: "Three-dimensional. Show sales by region by age." A holographic picture appears in front of the screen. It looks as if the cube is hanging in the air. "Rotate up," she commands. She can now see the regions and dollar amounts. "Rotate, down." The age ranges and corresponding dollar amount sides of the cube show now.

When Joan says, "Show ages 26 to 30 by item," the age range side is replaced with a list of apparel items offered by the company. The column displays item numbers and short descriptions. The title above the dollar amounts column reads: "Age 26-30." She examines the information. "Two-dimensional. New note." The holographic report collapses back into a two-dimensional blank window on the screen. A small "sticky-note"-like window opens in the top left corner. "Remind Paul to discuss possible boost in advertising of Item 301 in Northeast for age 26-30," she says to the screen. As she utters the words, they appear on the virtual yellow note.

THINK CRITICALLY

Will holographic 3-D databases help businesses in more than simply better presentation? How?

client/server architecture empowers employees; it gives them more independence and the ability to make their own decisions regarding information.

Unfortunately, some people use the term client/server to describe what is, practically, the older shared resource approach. A client/server architecture can follow any of the following four basic models:

◆ Applications run at the server; the PC serves as a terminal, primarily formatting and validating data.
◆ Applications run on the local PC; the database resides at the server; no significant part of the application runs on the server.
◆ Applications are run on both the local PC and the server; the database resides at the server.
◆ Applications and key elements of the database are split between the local PCs and the server. Applications call data or other procedures at other locations.

Organizations seem to spend significant portions of their IS budgets moving to some kind of client/server architecture. Since the early 1990s, client/server budgets of U.S. corporations have increased significantly more than their total IS budgets. The trend of devoting an increasing proportion of the IS budget to client/server systems is expected to continue in the foreseeable future.

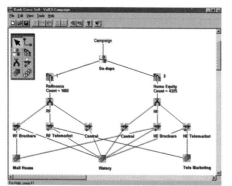

Used by permission from Exchange Applications, Inc. © 1997

DATA WAREHOUSING AND DATA MINING

Information technology allows even the smallest company to collect or purchase huge amounts of data, but the large size of some databases makes them difficult to maintain and manipulate. This created the need for new expertise: data warehousing. **Data warehousing** is the organization of very large amounts of data in databases, usually relational databases, for efficient use. Data warehousing experts must be well versed in the business activities that the data support. They also have to design databases in a way that leaves ample flexibility for modifications in years to come, when business activities change, or when different information is to be extracted.

Often, firms that specialize in data warehousing also specialize in **data mining**. Data mining software searches through large amounts of data for meaningful patterns of information (see Figure 7.20). Data mining is most often used by marketing managers who are constantly analyzing purchasing patterns, so that potential buyers can be targeted more efficiently through special sales, product displays, or direct mail campaigns.

To illustrate the difference between "traditional" queries and data mining queries, consider the following examples. A typical "traditional" query would be: "Is there a relationship between the amount of product X and the amount of product Y that we sold over the past quarter?" A typical data mining query would be: "Discover two products most likely to sell well together on a weekend." The latter query lets the software find patterns that may never be detected by observation. While we traditionally used data to see if this or that pattern existed, data mining allows us to ask *what* patterns exist. Thus, some experts say that in data mining we let the computer answer questions that we do not know to ask. The combination of data warehousing techniques and data mining software makes it easier to predict future outcomes based on patterns discovered within historical data.

DATA MINING APPLICATION	DESCRIPTION
Market segmentation	Identify the common characteristics of customers who buy the same products from your company
Customer churn	Predict which customers are likely to leave your company and go to a competitor
Fraud detection	Identify which transactions are most likely to be fraudulent
Direct marketing	Identify which prospective clients should be included in a mailing list to obtain the highest response rate
Interactive marketing	Predict what each individual accessing a Web site is most likely to be interested in seeing
Market basket analysis	Understand what products or services are commonly purchased together
Trend analysis	Reveal the difference between a typical customer this month and a typical customer last month

Source: Datamind Corp., quoted in McCarthy, V., "Strike it rich!", *Datamation*, February 1997, p. 47.

Figure 7.20 *Potential applications of data mining*

Customer Data as a Gold Mine

Information gleaned from customer service databases can help detect defects in products and save money by avoiding lawsuits. This was a lesson Whirlpool learned when it started using such information. The giant manufacturer of home appliances used to maintain a customer service database so that its service personnel could answer phone calls from customers and give them advice on how to solve mechanical problems with the appliances they had purchased. The service representative would bring the customer's record up to a computer monitor and use whatever information was there (such as appliance model, purchase date, etc.) to provide help.

But the company discovered that if it collected the information provided by complaining customers, it could extract even more important information. The complaints are entered into a large database. Engineers look for patterns in the complaints, diagnose the situation, and as soon as they find the reason for the malfunction, halt manufacturing of the model under investigation. The faulty part is examined and redesigned. So, when in 1994 several customers called in and complained about a bad leak from their washing machines, the engineers

traced the problem to a faulty hose clamp. They immediately stopped the manufacturing of that model and fixed the clamp. Service representatives used the customer service database to contact every customer who owned that machine so that mechanics could be sent out to replace the bad part.

Whirlpool collects the information to track problems with parts it purchases. If a certain part is repeatedly reported as faulty, the company uses the information either to stop purchasing from one vendor and start purchasing from another, or to renegotiate warranty terms with the supplier. Knowing which parts are more prone to fail has allowed the company to lower its spare-parts inventories and drive harder bargains with suppliers.

Source: Verity, J., "The gold mine of data in customer service," Business Week, March 21, 1994, p. 113.

Questions

1. What was the primary purpose of Whirlpool's new database system?

2. Collecting and analyzing data helped the company in more ways than originally thought. How?

Data Warehousing at TWA

...Trans World Airlines vice-president of revenue management

Marilyn Hoppe muses, "My life is data." Hoppe, in charge of revenue management, does nothing less than set ticket prices for about 800 daily TWA departures. Like her industry counterparts, she relies on databases...

For Hoppe at TWA, tapping legacy [older] data has been a source of incredible frustration. Hoppe took over TWA's revenue management last fall, after leaving a similar post at America West Airlines. Her job: to crank up revenue through savvy pricing and promotions, maximizing how much passengers spend on each individual flight. To do that, she needed to pull data from a variety of databases, including databases for scheduling, reservations, pricing, booking and frequent fliers, among others.

Hoppe expected the company's old, disparate systems to be disjointed, but things were worse than she had anticipated. "I can't move as fast as I had hoped to until I get the data I need," she says. Hoppe wants to repeat her success at America West, where she says she generated $84 million in her first 12 months. But, she notes, "I need data to get that revenue."...

Source: Halper, M. "Setting up is hard to do. Data warehouses do not grow on trees," Forbes, April 8, 1996, pp. 50–51. Reprinted by permission of Forbes ASAP Magazine. Copyright © 1996 by Forbes, Inc.

Questions

1. What is "data warehousing"?

2. Hoppe relies on different types of data for pricing. What data would you use to determine flight pricing?

Mining Data for Precious Information

Data warehousing, the massive storage of business data, does not yield much if the data are not mined for useful information. Capital One Financial Corp., one of America's largest credit card issuers, uses data mining techniques to finetune the marketing of its 3,000 different financial services. Its potential-clients base includes 150 million customers. To this end, the company maintains a database of two terabytes (two trillion bytes). Before Capital One starts a marketing blitz, analysts create a list of targeted customers.

The company uses demographic and behavioral data to track the success of past marketing efforts with the 8.6 million customers who have purchased its services. It also tracks the profitability of the marketing efforts. Knowing which customers maintain a credit balance with other card issuers helped Capital One develop a program that offers new customers a low interest rate for several months so they can more quickly pay up their balances if they sign up with Capital One. The "balance transfer" strategy has been copied by many other credit card issuers. Data mining helped the company increase sales from $1 billion to $12.8 billion over the period of 1988–1996. Data mining also helped the company maintain customers with a very low delinquency rate: most customers pay

the balance on their credit cards quite promptly.

Another benefit of data mining is fraud detection. Credit card fraud damages of Visa and Master Card were $702 million in 1995. By tracking payment behavior, the company managed to cut such fraud damages in half in 1996.

Source: Wreden, N., "The Mother Lode - Data Mining Digs Deep for Business Intelligence," Communications Week, *February 17, 1997, Issue 650.*

Questions

1. What demographic and behavioral data would a data mining application use for targeted marketing in the credit card industry?

2. What questions would you like a data mining application to "ask" to detect credit card fraud?

S U M M A R Y

In their daily operations, organizations can collect vast amounts of data. These data are raw material for highly valuable information, but they are useless without tools to organize them, store them in an easily accessible manner, and manipulate them flexibly to produce that information. These functions are the great strength of **databases**, collections of interrelated data that, within an organization and sometimes between organizations, are shared by many units and contribute to productivity and efficiency. The **database approach** has several advantages over the more **traditional file approach**: less **data redundancy**, data/program independence, greater **data integrity**, and a higher level of security. **Database technology**, which affords managers a powerful tool for daily operations and decision making, has had dramatic and far-reaching impacts on our business and personal lives.

To understand how databases are built, one first must know the "data hierarchy." The smallest piece of data is a **character**. Several characters make up a **field**. Several

fields make up a **record**. A collection of related records is a **file**. Databases usually comprise several files, but the database approach can be applied to a single file.

The manner in which the data are organized and linked in a database can follow one of three general models. In a **hierarchical database** each entity value may have several entity values linked to it in what is called a parent-child relationship. This model affords only one-to-many relationships. The **network model** allows a **child** to have more than one **parent**, thereby allowing many-to-many relationships. In the **relational model** the links among entities are maintained by the use of **foreign keys**. The latter model is the most popular nowadays. **Object-oriented** databases afford the maintenance of data along with the applications that process them. Some vendors offer DBMSs that accommodate a combination of relational and object-oriented models, called object-relational.

The software tool that enables us to apply the database approach to managing data is called a **database** management system (DBMS). DBMSs allow managers and other users to construct databases, populate them with data, and manipulate the data. Most DBMSs come as part of 4GLs that can be used to develop applications that facilitate queries and produce reports. Usually, a DBMS supports one specific type of the three database models. The relational model has gained popularity thanks to its ease of conceptualization and relatively easy maintenance. Virtually all recent PC-based DBMSs are relational.

To plan databases, designers need to lay out a diagram showing the relationships among the different entities. Then they can move on to constructing a **schema**, which is the structure of all record types of the entities, and the relationships among them. To construct a schema, one uses a **data definition language (DDL)**. The DDL is also used to build the **data dictionary**, which is a repository of information about the data and their organization. To **query** the database, one uses a **data manipulation language (DML)**. **SQL**, a language that serves as DDL and DML, has been adopted as an international standard language for relational databases. Modern PC DBMSs provide intuitive interfaces with menus and icons that make the DDL and DML transparent to the users for ease of operation.

Due to the drop in cost and increasing power of microcomputers, organizations are gradually moving from an architecture of a mainframe and terminals to a network consisting of a computer that is used as a server, with smart microcomputers as its clients. This is a move from the traditional shared resource architecture to the newer **client/server** architecture. The latter affords more flexible utilization of data and applications and empowers workers to develop simple applications for their specific tasks.

Data warehousing is the organization of very large amounts of data in databases. Usually, organizations that own such large databases also use **data mining** software, which helps them find useful, unexpected patterns such as clients' purchasing patterns. The new information helps them improve operations.

The low price of efficient and effective database software exacerbates a societal problem of the information age: invasion of **privacy**. Since every transaction of an individual can be easily recorded and later combined with other personal data, it is inexpensive to produce whole dossiers on individual consumers. Although individuals are giving away some of their privacy, commercial organizations insist that they need other information to improve their products and services, and to target their marketing only to interested consumers.

REVIEW, DISCUSS, AND EXPLORE

REVIEW AND DISCUSSION QUESTIONS

1. Why is it important to know how to use database management systems in organizations?

2. What can be done with database management systems that cannot be done with word-processing and spreadsheet applications?

3. What are the advantages of the database approach over the file approach to data management?

4. Compare the three database models. Which one would you favor, and why?

5. What are the principles of object-oriented databases?

6. Which industries are the most dependent on operation of large databases, and why?

7. Database management packages are usually bundled with 4GLs. Why?

8. What is SQL? What are the benefits of using SQL in different database management systems?

9. Explain the concept of client/server. Which two developments prompted the move from a shared resource system to client/server?

10. The client/server architecture is said to "empower employees." Why?

11. *Ethics and Society*: The proliferation of organizational databases poses a threat to privacy. After reading this section, what would you say to someone in response to these statements: "I'm a law-abiding citizen and pay my taxes promptly. I don't care if anyone reviews my college grades or my income statements, because I have nothing to hide. I have no reason to worry about violation of my privacy. All these complaints about violation of privacy are not valid. Only individuals who have something to hide need to worry."

12. *Ethics and Society*: Civil rights advocates demand that organizations ask individuals for permission to sell personal information about the individuals. Some also demand that the subjects of the information be paid for their consent. Organizations have argued that they cannot practically comply with these demands, and that the demands interfere with free flow of information. What is your opinion?

CONCEPT ACTIVITY

Research trade journals and use your word-processing program to write up a research paper titled "Object-Oriented Databases" in which you explain the differences and similarities between relational databases and object-oriented databases, and the advantages of the latter over the former.

HANDS-ON ACTIVITY

Mid-County Hospital holds data on doctors and patients in two tables in its database (see below): DOCTOR and PATIENT. Use your DBMS to build the appropriate schema, enter the records, and create the desired reports.

DOCTOR ID#	LIC#	LAST NAME	FIRST NAME	WARD	SALARY
102	8234	Hogg	Yura	INT	87,000
104	4666	Tyme	Justin	INT	91,300
221	2908	Jones	Jane	OBGYN	89,650
243	7876	Anderson	Ralph	ONC	101,800
256	5676	Jones	Ernest	ORT	123,400
376	1909	Washington	Jaleel	INT	87,000
410	4531	Carrera	Carlos	ORT	97,000

PATIENT SSN	LAST N	FIRST N	ADMISSION DATE	INSURANCE	DOC ID
055675432	Hopkins	Jonathan	4/1/95	BlueCross	221
101234566	Bernstein	Miriam	4/28/95	HAP	243
111654456	McCole	John	3/31/95	Kemper	221
200987898	Meanny	Marc	2/27/95	HAP	221
367887654	Mornay	Rebecca	4/3/95	HAP	410
378626254	Blanchard	George	3/30/95	BlueCross	243
366511122	Rubin	David	4/1/95	Brook	243

1. A report showing the following details for each doctor in this order: Last Name, First Name, and Ward. Arrange the report by ascending alphabetic order of the last names

2. A report showing the entire record with the original order of columns of all the doctors whose salary is greater than $90,000

3. A report showing the following data values for all of Dr. Anderson's patients. In each record, the join report should show: Doctor's ID, last name, and ward (from the DOCTOR table), and Patient's Last Name, First Name, and date of Admission (from the PATIENT table)

TEAM ACTIVITY

Your team should contact a large organization, such as a bank, an insurance company, or a hospital. Interview the database administrator about the database he or she maintains on customers. What are the measures that the DBA has taken to protect the privacy of the subjects whose records are kept in the databases? Consider accuracy, timeliness, and appropriate access to personal records. Write a report on your findings. If you found loopholes in the procedures, list them and explain why they are loopholes and how they can be remedied.

EXPLORE THE WEB

The U.S. government provides access to many of its databases via the Web. Explore the databases of at least three government agencies (such as agencies of the Department of Labor and the Department of Commerce). Prepare a list of general topics on which data are offered to the public. Print out a sample from each database.

PART 3

Information Technology in Management

Chapter **8**

Managers and **T**heir Information **N**eeds

Less Paper, More Customers

Just a few years ago, the Aetna Health Plan business unit relied on a manual system to process new insurance policies, and it had stacks upon stacks of paper to prove it. So when DeAnn Anderson arrived as director of insurance quality, she found the "case installation" process topping the list of candidates for re-engineering.

The first step was to understand the current installation process. Some concerns emerged immediately. First, the various Aetna regional offices handled the installation process differently, so the company did not have a consistent set of procedures in place. Second, new case managers were working with almost unmanageable amounts of paper. One case alone could take up three 4-inch binders. Third, managers were working with small differences in options and nuances with every potential business client, so each installation was like starting anew. What could be done to cut back on the paperwork and manage the case installation process more efficiently? A customer installation management system was the answer.

First step: analyze the existing process. After nine months, the re-engineering team determined that there were 800 potential tasks that any given case could require. The group decided the new system needed three key tools: a database management system to store customer profiles, a project management system to cut back on the paper volume and automate the work flow, and a front-end application to help automate the marketing and installation managers' jobs, as well as to interface to the back-end applications to process the new contracts.

Dianna Cowles, Aetna's director of national accounts, has explained that the company opted for an entirely PC-based system because it wanted the system to be flexible and easy to use. The group selected off-the-shelf DBMS and project management software. The staff participated in developing an icon-driven, user-friendly graphical user interface (GUI).

Now, the marketing staff uses the system's front-end to select options that potential clients want as part of their health plans. They complete the profile, and move it, via electronic mail, to Cowles, and then to an installation manager. This software is directly tied to the project management software.

Today, about 90 users from the marketing and case installation groups work with the system. In the first full year of use, the team was able to turn around 24% more cases than before the system was installed, and they have not missed any deadlines preparing health plans for new clients.

Source: Cafasso, R., "Manual no more: Aetna unit gets PCs, result," *Computerworld*, January 18, 1993, p. 37.

Information is needed for decision making and operations at all levels of management, but managers at different levels of the organization's hierarchy need different types of information. By making information available to virtually every level of an organization, ISs are changing the way organizations operate.

When you finish this chapter, you will:

◆ See the link between an organization's structure and information flow

◆ Understand the main functions and information needs at different managerial levels

◆ Be able to identify the characteristics of information and the data needed by different managerial levels

◆ Recognize the influence of politics on information systems

◆ Understand the connection between information systems and trends in employment levels

MANAGERS AND INFORMATION

Generally speaking, managers at different levels of an organizational hierarchy make different types of decisions, control different types of processes, and therefore have different information needs. While there are different types of organizational structures, in this chapter we will discuss the most common: a generic pyramid-shaped hierarchy with a few leaders at the top and an increasing number of workers at each subsequent managerial and operational level below (see Figure 8.1). There has long been a fairly close correlation between the level of work being done in an organization and the type of IS being used, but, with computers on every desk, that relationship is no longer so clear. The availability of increasingly flexible and powerful information systems as tools, throughout all organizational levels, has had a profound effect on organizational structure. For instance, placing the ability to generate information directly into managers' hands has led to a massive trend in the downsizing of middle management. Technology aside, the politics of information within an organization can undermine optimal business decision making if it is not taken into account when developing systems, and deciding how people will support these systems.

THE ORGANIZATIONAL PYRAMID

Every organization needs leadership. The leaders of an organization are a small group of people responsible for running the organization and reporting to one person in the group who usually bears the title Chief Executive Officer (CEO). Some small, knowledge-intensive companies have adopted a matrix pattern as their organizational structure, with no one leader, and leadership distributed among many more people, varying by project, product, or discipline. However, the management of most organizations still follows a pyramid model: the CEO at the top, a small group of senior managers who report to the CEO one level down, a larger number of middle managers who report to the top managers, many more lower-level managers who report to the middle managers, and so on down the line (see Figure 8.1).

In general, at the bottom of the **organizational pyramid** are general and clerical workers; in the next layer up are operational managers; next up is a much narrower layer of middle managers; and at the top are a few senior managers. Due to the nature of their decisions, the top two layers are often referred to as tactical (middle) and strategic (senior) management. There is variation among organizations; not every organization has exactly three layers, and there are often sublayers in the management levels. Also, the distinction between operational and middle managers is not always clear, nor is it necessarily important. Remember that this rough categorization is just for the purpose of discussing information needs. It is best to think of managerial levels as a continuum between two ends, the lowest level being operational managers and the highest level being top management. It is very likely that your first managerial position will be as an operational manager.

CLERICAL AND SHOP FLOOR WORKERS

In many organizations, **clerical and shop floor workers** make up the largest group of employees. These terms are carried over from manufacturing

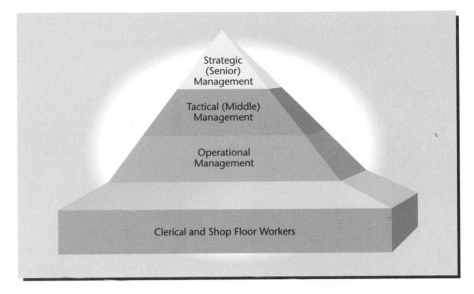

Figure 8.1 *The management pyramid*

enterprises, and we continue to use them for brevity. However, we now include in this group service workers, such as tellers in banks, receptionists in hospitals, and sales associates in retail stores. The main characteristic of this level of work is that it is not managerial. While clerical and floor workers may have high levels of expertise in a particular technology, equipment, or process, they are not required—and are not expected—to make management-level judgments. Many of these workers operate at their organizations' boundaries, where they interact with other organizations or individuals. Many take orders for products and services, record sales, make the billings, record raw material received and services performed, maintain machinery leased or purchased from the company, and perform any other nonmanagerial work

To illustrate who these workers are, here are some examples. In a manufacturing plant, they are the laborers who control machines. In a retail chain they are the salespeople who are in direct contact with the customers. In a hospital they are the reception clerks and maintenance people. At a bank, clerical workers are the tellers and other clerks.

OPERATIONAL MANAGEMENT

Operational managers are in charge of small groups of clerical and shop floor workers. Examples include the foreperson on a shop floor, a department manager in a department store, and a manager in a bank or insurance company who is in charge of a small unit and authorized to obligate the company for small amounts of money. The people in these positions comply with general policies handed down by their superiors. Within these policies, they make decisions that affect their small units in the short term, that is, within days. For instance, if a subordinate calls in sick, an operational manager is empowered to decide whether to call another employee in from home, in which case the person will probably report late, or to ask another worker to stay for another shift, in which case the company must pay time and a half.

Operational managers are in charge of small groups of workers and carry out daily tasks of planning and control. Clerical and shop floor workers carry out daily operations handed down from operational managers.

Used by permission from McDonnell Douglas

Used by permission from Steven Peters/Tony Stone Images

Senior managers make strategic decisions.

TACTICAL MANAGEMENT

Tactical managers, also called middle managers, are handed general directions from their superiors and, within those guidelines, they make wider-ranging decisions for their subordinates, affecting the near and somewhat more distant future. Usually, they are in charge of several operational managers. Tactical managers are so-called because they are responsible for finding the best *operational* measures to accomplish their superiors' strategic decisions. As you remember from Chapter 2, "Strategic Uses of Information Systems," a strategic decision focuses on *what* to do, while a tactical decision concentrates on *how* to do it.

For example, corporate management makes the strategic decision to provide more of a bank's services through electronic means: the telephone and personal computers. This leaves the tactical managers to determine *how* to provide those services. Should the bank develop the necessary computer software in-house? Should it hire a consulting firm? Which services should be offered first? How should the bank educate staff and customers about the new offerings? Tactical managers are expected to provide the best solutions to these problems, and refer issues to the strategic level only if their decisions may affect the general strategy outlined.

STRATEGIC MANAGEMENT

It is easier to determine which managers make up the strategic level than it is to discern who belongs to the other two levels. The reason is simple: these are the highest-ranking officers of the organization. In many companies, the president and vice-presidents make up the strategic management. When members of the board of directors play an active role in the company's business, they too contribute their share to strategic decision making. However, do not be misled by titles. Some corporations, such as banks, grant vice-presidential titles to thousands of their managers. This alone does not place those people in the strategic level of their organizations.

Strategic managers make decisions that affect the entire organization, or large parts of it, and leave an impact in the long run. For example, such decisions may include mergers with other companies and acquisitions of other companies, the opening of branches overseas, developing a completely new product or service, or recommending major restructuring of the organization.

CHARACTERISTICS OF INFORMATION AT DIFFERENT MANAGERIAL LEVELS

People in different management levels have different information needs. As shown in Figure 8.2, the information needed varies as to the time span covered, level of detail, source, and other characteristics over a broad spectrum, depending on whether it is needed for lower or higher management or operations. For instance, clerical workers need data that allow them to fulfill daily operations but not necessarily make decisions. To serve customers and other workers, they must have access to information such as: how many units of a certain item are available for sale, the cost of a certain customer service, and how much overtime a certain employee worked last week. Usually, these people make inquiries on demand to satisfy immediate information needs.

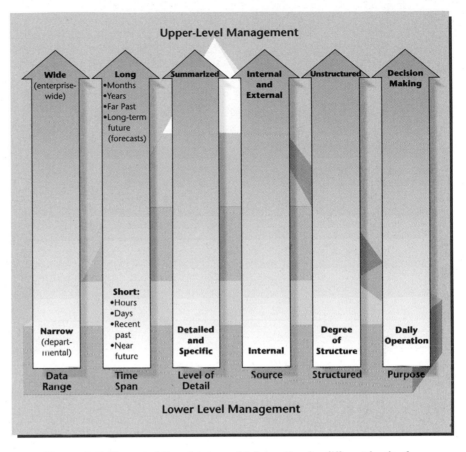

Figure 8.2 *Characteristics of data and information for different levels of management*

On the other hand, most of the information that managers require is used to make decisions. Operational managers need information based on data that are narrow in scope, gathered over a short period of time, and useful for decisions that have an impact in the short run, that is, hours, days, and weeks. The decisions made by middle managers, on the other hand, impact a greater number of organizational units for longer periods of time, and require information extracted from data that are broader in scope and time, and may come from outside their departments. The decision-making process of middle managers and above is less structured than that of operational managers; despite the broader scope of the data—and sometimes *because* of it—there are no proven methods for selecting a course of action that guarantees a predicted outcome.

The decisions that senior managers make affect whole divisions or the entire organization, and have a long-standing impact. Their decision making is very unstructured. **Senior managers** need information gleaned from vast amounts of raw data that have been collected over long periods of time from many or all of the organization's units. The original data for the information come from internal organizational sources as well as external sources, such as the mass media, national and international trade bulletins, and consulting firms.

Electronic Monitoring
of Employees

One of the most important tasks of managers, especially operational managers, is to monitor the performance of their subordinates. Traditionally, this has been done by direct observation ("walking the floor") and tracking productivity. But modern information technology now allows supervisors not only to tap phones and watch employees through video cameras, but also to log on to their computers, observing their work and reading their e-mail. An estimated 26 million American workers in more than 60,000 companies are subject to electronic surveillance. Of these people, several million are monitored by computers. And as the use of computers in all aspects of business is increasing, such monitoring is expected to grow. Among U.S. office workers, probably as many as 50% are monitored. Many managers maintain that "people won't do what they are expected to do, but what they're inspected to do." But is the practice of electronic monitoring ethical? If it is, what should and should not be monitored? Should employees be forewarned when they are monitored?

We've Come a Long Way. Technology allows a supervisor to essentially follow employees from the moment they show up at work until they leave for home, tapping their telephone lines, intercepting their e-mail messages, and even videotaping their activities. All of this may be done with or without the awareness of the employee.

A video camera tiny enough to fit in a computer chip is already used to tape ATM transactions, but it could be used to monitor employees, too. A person's every move can now be monitored by a standard-looking ID badge developed by Olivetti, the giant Italian computer maker. It uses infrared light to transmit location information to selected computers.

The Employers' Position. Employers feel that, because they pay for their employees' time, they are entitled to know how that time is being spent. Furthermore, employers insist that it is their right to monitor employees how they want to, when they want to, and with or without warning. Employers are especially adamant about the need for monitoring in the service sector. In a manufacturing setting, products can be inspected both in terms of quantity produced per time unit and in terms of quality, but when service is being provided, the work and the "product" are inseparable. Therefore, the reasoning goes, service must be monitored to ensure acceptable quality. And electronic monitoring provides an effective means.

Companies that monitor insist that there is no other way for managers to know how workers perform and interact with customers, and they believe that monitoring is an objective, nondiscriminatory method of gauging employee output.

The Employees' Position. Employees often claim that electronic monitoring deprives them of autonomy and dignity, and can increase stress and stress-related illness and injury. Civil rights groups say employers have gone too far with electronic monitoring, creating adverse working conditions with poor peer social support, reduced supervisory support, fear of job loss, regimented work activity, and lack of control over tasks.

In an environment where PCs are used, the situation may be especially unpleasant. Karen Nussbaum, in a national meeting of Computer Professionals for Social Responsibility, quoted an ad in *PC Week*:

> "Close-Up LAN brings you to a level of control never before possible. It connects PCs on your network giving you the versatility to

(continued)

instantly share screens and keyboards… You decide to look in on Sue's computer screen… Sue won't even know you are there! … All from the comfort of your chair."

And employers use the technology to do exactly that. A reporter complained that while she was typing a story, her computer flashed: "I don't like that lead." A supervisor was butting in on a first draft. Data processing workers have complained that occasionally their computer screens display the message: "You are not working as fast as the person next to you," which can appear as part of a program that automates the monitoring process.

Attempted Legislation. In 1991, Congressman Pat Williams introduced HR1218, The Privacy for Consumers and Workers Act, and Senator Paul Simon presented S516 in the Senate, both bills meant to deal with these issues. The Privacy for Consumers and Workers Act was not meant to eliminate monitoring altogether, but to curb and control it.

"Electronic monitoring" was defined in the proposed law as "the collection, storage, analysis, and reporting of information concerning an employee's activities by means of a computer, electronic observation and supervision, remote telephone surveillance, telephone call accounting, or other form of visual, auditory, or computer-based surveillance conducted by any transfer of signs, signals, writing, images, sounds, data, or intelligence of any nature transmitted in whole or in part by a wire, radio, electromagnetic, photoelectronic, or photo-optical system."

The bill:

◆ Required employers to give employees prior notification and warning whenever they are being monitored electronically

◆ Required employers to identify and to disclose to employees the various types of monitoring being used. If monitoring is not performed on a continuous basis, an audio or visual signal should be given to warn employees whenever they are under surveillance.

◆ Prohibited employers from collecting personal data not related to the employee's work performance

◆ Limited disclosure and use of the collected data

◆ Granted the employees access to the collected data

Representatives of large service and manufacturing companies testified before Congress against the proposed legislation, arguing that employee notification would cause employees to behave uncharacteristically during performance monitoring, which would result in inaccurate readings of performance levels. They also claimed that the bill would hamper efforts to uncover fraud or corporate spying, or even preclude general surveillance efforts. One interesting claim was that, since electronic monitoring is broadly defined in the bill as including all forms of "visual, auditory, or computer-based surveillance," it includes computer-based manufacturing and the equipment used to automatically monitor employee productivity within factories. A representative of a large organization of manufacturing industries said: "Corporate management should not be prohibited from using information obtained through computer-aided manufacturing unless managers are physically on the shop floor looking over the shoulders of employees." The bill "died" in Congress.

Video cameras have been used for years to monitor employee productivity, and for security purposes.

Used by permission from Surveillance Systems, Inc., Pottstown, PA

DATA RANGE

Data range refers to the amount of data from which information is extracted, in terms of number of organizational units supplying data, or the length of time that the data cover. For example, data gathered from just one department have a narrower range than data from every department of the organization. At the same time, one department's data from several months have a broader range than the same department's data from one week.

Data range is different from level of detail. To make a strategic decision, top management may need a single figure that comes from a wide range of data, such as the average monthly expenditure on television advertising of sports shoes in the U.S. over the past decade. Although the information required is a single figure, it is derived from vast amounts of data spanning a long time and many corporations. Therefore, the data range is wide. At the other extreme, the manager of a shop in a manufacturing plant may need only information that is extracted from data collected within that organizational unit. The data range is then narrow.

TIME SPAN

The **time span** of data refers to how long a period of time the data cover. Data that cover hours or days, the time span usually needed by lower-level managers, are said to have a short time span relative to data that cover months, years, or decades, which are said to have a long time span. Senior managers typically use data that reach far into the past. They also make **extrapolations** based on the patterns of performance in the past, to forecast what might be expected to happen in the future.

LEVEL OF DETAIL

The **level of detail** is the degree to which the information generated is specific. When a department manager looks at the total number of shoes that were sold every day of the week from every design the department carries, the information is, obviously, very detailed. Indeed, operational managers usually consider highly detailed information. Senior managers, in contrast, consider information that is the result of highly summarized data, such as totals and averages for categories of products (rather than individual products) over long periods of time.

Usually, the more detailed the information, the closer it is to the data from which it is derived, and thus the less processing is involved to generate it. Daily totals of sales in the shoe department are more detailed than an annual total for the entire chain of stores. The latter requires significantly more processing because it combines data from many sources.

SOURCE: INTERNAL VS. EXTERNAL

Internal data are collected within the organization, usually by transaction processing systems, but also through employee and customer surveys. **External data** are collected from a wide array of sources outside the organization, including mass communications media such as television, radio, and newspapers; specialized newsletters published by private organizations; government agencies; and the Internet. For instance, to plan the expansion or contraction of a national supermarket chain, top managers cannot rely only on their own organization's internal

Net Notes

Several Web sites provide information on the organization of information systems and the IS profession. Use the keywords *IS World* to explore what is probably the most comprehensive site on anything involving research and practice in the field. Try also national and international professional organizations: *Association for Computing Machinery, Data Processing Management Association, British Computer Society,* and *Canadian Society for Information Processing.*

data. They must keep track of national trends. Thus, they need information on annual demographic changes. Without it, they may spend resources on increasing the number of stores, only to find, a few years later, that their customer base has shrunk.

STRUCTURED AND UNSTRUCTURED DATA

Structured data are numbers and facts that can be conveniently stored and retrieved in an orderly manner for operations and decision making. The sources of such data are primarily internal files and databases that capture transactions. **Unstructured** data are drawn from meeting discussions, private conversations, textual documents, graphical representations, and other "nonuniform" sources.

Structured data are used for daily operations and decisions that are relatively easy to make with the help of previously proven models. The higher the managerial position, the less structured the decisions that a manager faces; therefore, unstructured data are extremely valuable in managerial decision making, especially at the higher levels of the organization. Many of us refer to "management science," but, as you may have surmised, many managerial processes are more an art than a science. Structured and unstructured environments and their managerial context are further discussed in Chapter 12, "Decision Support and Executive Information Systems."

THE NATURE OF MANAGERIAL WORK

Managers are paid to plan and control. They plan to minimize uncertainty and reduce risks; they control to assure adherence to plans. Both responsibilities involve decision making and leadership, and information systems are a great support throughout the management process.

PLANNING

Ideally, managers would know what the future will bring, so they could make their decisions to bring about desired outcomes. Unfortunately, managers do not have a crystal ball, but through both short- and long-term **planning**, they can have something better: a hand in shaping the future. As illustrated in Figure 8.3 on the next page, planning starts with a long-term mission and vision, and includes establishing goals and objectives, resource planning, and budgeting for both the short and long term. Most of all, good planning requires good information. The better the information, the clearer the picture managers have of the present; the clearer the present picture, the better prepared managers are to plan their moves. By extracting only the most useful facts from raw data, ISs can provide the most salient information.

As any entrepreneur will tell you, the first step in planning is to create a mission statement: How do you envision the organization in one year, five years, and ten years in the future? Within the framework of the mission statement, top management sets goals. Goals are a wish list without specific quantities or dates. Goals roughly correspond to strategy. Within the framework of each goal, top managers and middle managers set objectives. Unlike goals, objectives are specific in dollar terms, market share percentages, completion dates, and other results that can be measured. Whereas the mission statement is the basis for long-term planning, objectives are the basis for short-term planning.

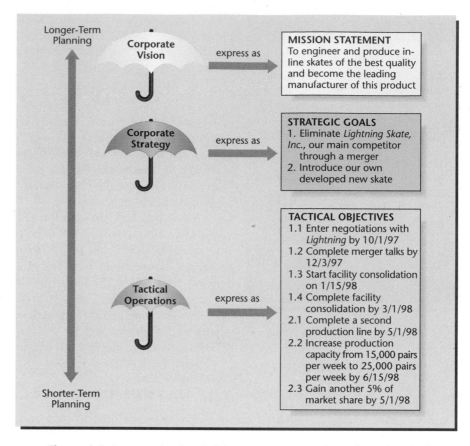

Figure 8.3 *An example of a mission statement, strategic goals, and tactical objectives for an in-line skate manufacturer*

After objectives are outlined, planning includes such things as the calculation of person-hours required to complete a project, and thus, the size of staff needed; detailing a master production schedule; and specifying quantities of raw materials and their supply lead-times. Probably the most important part of any business plan is the budget. The organization's budget is the aggregate of the budgets of all its units. Examples of the steps involved in planning are shown in Figure 8.4.

CONTROL

Once plans are in place, managers use them to **control** actual activities by comparing them to results, as shown in Figure 8.5. Thus plans are the control tools of an organization. When discrepancies between the planned and actual performance are found, managers determine the reason for the variance. If the actual performance is better than planned, then the plan may be modified. If the actual performance is worse than planned, then the cause of the discrepancy is corrected, if possible, or the remaining plan is revised to be more realistic. Different parts of plans are used by different levels of management to control different aspects of an operation. For instance, strategic and tactical managers are concerned with allocating resources to projects, while operational managers are usually concerned with further, more specific allocation of the resources to the different tasks of a project.

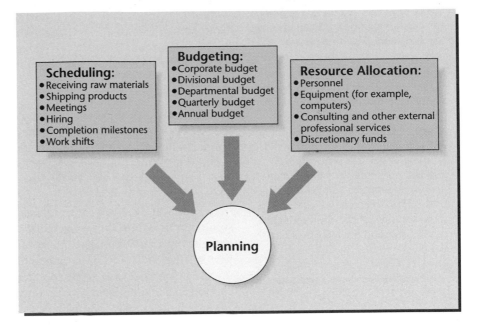

Figure 8.4 *Main ingredients of planning*

DECISION MAKING

Both planning and control activities call for decision making. While we will cover decision making at length in Chapter 12, you may remember from previous chapters that a **decision** is a commitment to act. A decision must be made when one selects a course of action out of several possible courses. For the time being, it will suffice to say that the higher the level of management, the less routine the manager's activities are, the more open the options are, and the more decision making is involved. For instance, operational managers make relatively simple decisions, such as resolving problems with individual customers, scheduling work shifts, and evaluating employee performance. Many of their other activities do not call for judgment but for fulfillment of the directives of

◆ Reviewing project resources and updating milestones

◆ Tracking receiving times of raw materials

◆ Tracking shipping dates

◆ Periodically comparing actual expenditures with budgetary figures

◆ Periodically examining exception reports

◆ Discussing project progress

◆ Periodically examining project progress reports

◆ Periodically examining performance ratios (for example, revenue-per-employee, inventory turnover)

Figure 8.5 *Examples of processes used to control projects*

tactical managers. At the very top of the organizational pyramid, on the other hand, virtually all of an executive's work day is devoted to meetings that result in some decisions. All along the managerial hierarchy, information systems are used to provide information to support decision-making activities.

MANAGEMENT BY EXCEPTION

Some people think that more information is always better than less information. However, there is a limit to the amount of information that managers can handle. A better statement would be that managers need information that communicates the most important facts. Too much information creates **information overload**, a situation where a person is confused and cannot make optimal decisions.

One way to ensure that managers use their time optimally when consuming information is **management by exception**. The manager reviews only those exceptions from preset plans that are of a certain size or type, assuming that smaller deviations are immaterial (see Figure 8.6). For example, a department manager may ask for a periodic report that compares actual expenditures to budgeted figures, and reports only those line items that are greater than 110% or less than 90% of the budgeted figures. Or a periodic report on a project schedule may include only activities that have not been completed within seven days past schedule. These exception reports require a manager to determine the cause and make a decision about how to deal with the situation.

LEADERSHIP

Reviewing exception reports is only a small part of a manager's job, focused specifically on adhering to an organization's agreed-upon plan. Managers are also expected to **lead**, which requires having a vision and creating confidence in others, encouraging them to follow the vision. This requires a manager to initiate activities that make work more efficient and effective, create new techniques to achieve corporate goals, inspire subordinates, present a role model for desired behavior, take responsibility for undesired consequences of decisions made under his or her direction, and delegate authority. A person may technically be a good manager and still not be regarded as a leader. Many experts hold that true leadership is an innate trait that may be honed but cannot be learned. Therefore, leadership "skills" are really techniques that hone already existing traits. Although some

10% Exception Report			
Plant: 3706 Cockpit Wiring			
Period: 1/1/97-3/31/97			
ITEM	BUDGET AMOUNT	ACTUAL AMOUNT	DEVIATION
Wages	$12,236,000	$10,236,876.34	(-16.4%)
Telephone	$4,700	$5,202.87	10.7%
Office Supply	$2,500	$3,002.00	12.8%

Figure 8.6 *Example of budgetary exception report*

expressions of leadership may depend on personal qualities—inspiring confidence and communicating well—information systems can help managers become better leaders. ISs can provide an overall picture of an organization's operation that supports brainstorming and generation of new ideas—another important element in leadership. They may inspire innovation and the pursuit of new goals as well.

ORGANIZATIONAL STRUCTURE

Information technology (IT) is the most powerful tool available for increasing efficiency, solving problems, and making decisions in businesses today. Its impact contributed to vast organizational restructuring in the 1980s and 1990s, with a trend toward downsizing and "flattening," which usually translates into eliminating levels of management.

IT FLATTENS THE ORGANIZATION

Before the introduction of computers in businesses, lower-level managers spent much of their time processing data to produce useful information for their supervisors. Over the past two decades, many companies have used ISs to automate these activities, eliminating the need for several layers of middle managers. This shift has led to flatter organizational structures (as shown in Figure 8.7) and has been a major force behind the enormous downsizing in both the manufacturing and service sectors. In 1993, in the U.S. alone, some 450,000 middle managers lost their jobs. In 1994, over a half million workers lost their jobs, almost all of them middle managers.

Strategic and operational managers have suffered much less from this trend. Strategic managers are still needed because of their traditional responsibilities. Operational managers run the daily operations of the organization. Easy-to-use graphical user interfaces and affordable data communication allow senior managers to produce their own information and communicate directly with lower-level managers who used to be at least two or three layers away. In some small organizations there are simply no middle managers at all between strategic managers and operational managers.

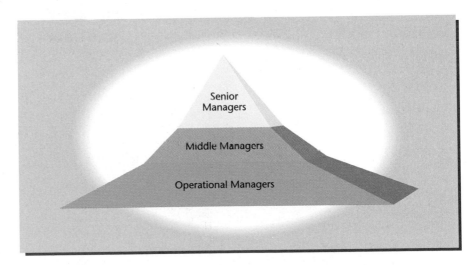

Figure 8.7 *Information systems flatten managerial layers.*

> **Net Notes**
>
> Nonprofit membership associations and organizations are an excellent resource for exploring career opportunities and other issues related to a particular field. A good place to start exploring opportunities in information studies is the University of Toronto's Web site (*http://www.fis.utoronto.ca/internet/assocs.htm*), which maintains a long list of hyperlinks to organizations related to information studies.

THE MATRIX STRUCTURE

The increasing power and integration of information systems in organizations led in the 1980s to an organizational experiment: **matrix management**. Matrix management replaced a strict hierarchy structure with a flexible reporting structure, where people reported to different supervisors, depending on the project, product, or location of the work. While this has been successful in some small entrepreneurial organizations that consist predominantly of knowledge workers (such as young high-tech companies), it was less successful in larger, non-high-tech organizations.

Figure 8.8 shows how a matrix organization might work, with the personnel of each unit reporting to both a divisional and a functional manager. The manager of the personnel in cell 1 reports to both the vice president of marketing and sales and the general manager of Division A. While the vice president of marketing is responsible for only the marketing of all the company's products and services, the general manager of Division A is responsible for all the activities taking place to produce the products and services that come out of the division: engineering, manufacturing, and marketing. Technologically, IT supports the matrix structure well, because both divisional and functional managers can have access to cross-sectional information.

The matrix structure came about because sometimes divisional organization (by geography or product, for instance) and functional supervision are equally important. If so, then top management has to be composed of both divisional executives (such as general managers of the divisions and corporate vice presidents) and functional executives (such as vice presidents of finance, marketing, engineering, and the like).

Unfortunately, human nature sometimes stands in the way of implementing this approach, leading most of the organizations that tried a matrix management to abandon it for the traditional pyramid, in which each manager reports to a single supervisor. There are a lot of problems when people report to more than one authority, especially when business is not going well or an individual's performance is in question. Also, power plays may interfere and undermine rational decision making.

Functions	Divisions		
	General Manager of Product A Division	General Manager of Product B Division	General Manager of Product C Division
V.P. of Marketing and Sales (M&S)	1 M&S manager personnel assigned to Div. A	2 Manager and M&S personnel assigned to Div. B	3 Manager and M&S personnel assigned to Div. C
V.P. of Manufacturing (Mfg.)	4 Mfg. personnel assigned to Div. A	5 Mfg. personnel assigned to Div. B	6 Mfg. personnel assigned to Div. C
V.P. of Engineering (Eng.)	7 Eng. personnel assigned to Div. A	8 Eng. personnel assigned to Div. B	9 Eng. personnel assigned to Div. C

Figure 8.8 *Example of a matrix organization*

A LOOK INTO THE FUTURE ▶

Far, and Yet So Close

Irma Gaines is a department head at Ogden Technologies, a leading aerospace company in Connecticut. Eleven months ago she was assigned to design a new executive jet. In addition to her regular duties as department head, she is also involved in the daily monitoring of this project. The team was given 18 months to complete the task, but Irma expects to complete this assignment within a month or, at the latest, a month and a half.

Although her staff comprises well-trained engineers and technicians, these are high expectations. Some members of Irma's project team have never met her in person. How will she manage them from three facilities thousands of miles apart, one in the Connecticut headquarters, another in Tulsa, Oklahoma, and a third in Brighton, England?

The answer is through teleconferencing. Not "simple" teleconferencing, in which people gather periodically to discuss burning issues, with mixed results. That has been used for almost ten years by Ogden, and managers and engineers have had mixed reactions. They found communicating with "pictures" rather than "people" frustrating, and they missed their desktop tools when trying to communicate, especially detailed information.

Irma's project team was the first to use three-dimensional desktop-teleconferencing. The engineers in Connecticut did not have to get off their chairs in order to exchange ideas with staff from Oklahoma and England. They used their own desktop computers, the very same machines they used to crunch numbers and draw detailed structural designs. When an engineer needed information from the Brighton designers, he or she simply connected to a desktop computer in that office. Each computer has a special set of cameras through which the parties can receive three-dimensional images of their peers' faces.

Sometimes, the engineers feel somewhat limited explaining drawings and formulas on the computer screen. When that happens, they get up and draw their ideas on a white board. Sophisticated software directs the cameras to follow their motion. When the remote peers wish to take a closer look at part of the information on the white board, they press a zoom button on their keyboard, much as they would when using a video camera.

The engineers can work together, seeing each other all of the time, and collaborate in the design. If the engineers wish to copy what another, remote, engineer is presenting either on the computer monitor or the white board, they use their mice to frame the information and copy it into a screen window.

The technology allows very flexible and timely management of large projects. Corporate management can use the best and least costly labor force for engineering, design, and prototyping, where that labor force actually resides. This is the next step toward realization of the virtual organization.

THINK CRITICALLY

The business advantages of the described groupware technology are obvious. Do you foresee any social impediments? Explain.

Be Information-Conscious?

Managers are rarely involved in the actual production of their organizations' products and services. Managerial work involves activities that facilitate the generation of products and services. The "material" managers use in their daily activities is information. They either extract information by themselves, or have someone else extract it for them; they exchange information with other managers and with subordinates; and they communicate instructions to their subordinates to attain objectives.

To do all that, managers must know the best sources of useful information, and the best ways to communicate information. The flow of information is closely linked to the organizational structure. In fact, we often inquire about an organization's structure by asking, "Whom do you report to?", a question connoting the direction of information flow.

As a manager, you must know which type of information, derived from which type of data, will serve your needs best. This does not mean that more information is necessarily better; too much information may be confusing and time-consuming to analyze. Understanding what data to rely on, and how to best extract information from it, helps managers optimize their efforts.

A matrix structure facilitates flow of information because workers have easier access to their managers. They do not need approval to pass information outside an organizational unit because the lines of reporting are more flexible than in a hierarchical structure. There is less tendency to block access to information, and there are more vertical and lateral lines of communication. This has an impact on information needs, and thus on the design of ISs. Disparate ISs must be integrated, and they must provide easy access to, and incorporation of, different databases and applications.

CHARACTERISTICS OF EFFECTIVE INFORMATION

ISs can be designed to accommodate the different ways in which human beings process data. Some managers like their information in graphic format, some like it in text, some like tables and some like to hear the information from their staff. Most people are most comfortable with some form of visual data, such as diagrams and pictures.

TABULAR AND GRAPHICAL REPRESENTATION

A large number of studies have been conducted to find relationships between personal characteristics and data-representation preferences. A recent study found that when solving problems, engineering students performed better when the data were presented as tables of numbers, while business students solved the problems more successfully when the data appeared as graphs.

There are certain types of information that most people grasp more quickly when presented graphically (see Figure 8.9). For instance, trends are immediately recognized when presented as lines; distributions (such as percentages of respondents' responses) are easily comprehended when displayed as pie charts; and a

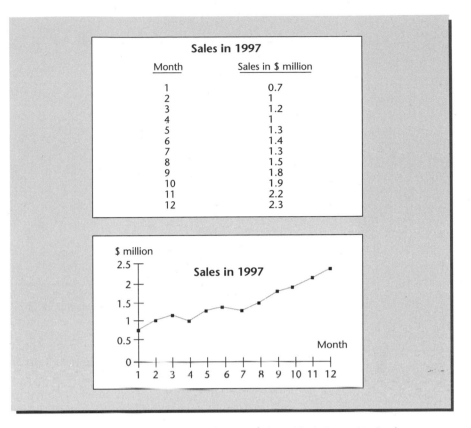

Figure 8.9 *Tabular and graphical presentations: The information in the two presentations is identical, but the trend is detected faster with the line graph.*

comparison of performance is best displayed with bars. However, when complex problem solving must be done, many people prefer tabular raw data so that they can extract the information *they* deem necessary to solve the problem. They feel that a graph renders only one interpretation of the data.

In the past, researchers asserted that information systems should be designed with the psychological type of the person who will use them in mind, but the widespread use of computers has made this suggestion highly impractical or prohibitively expensive. Now, however, many applications allow the user to select how the data will be presented. The raw data are selected from a database, or a spreadsheet, and the user may display and examine it in tables or graphs. Many applications allow the user to present the same information on the monitor in tables and in graphs at the same time, or to embed graphs in tables and vice versa.

Until recently, information presentation was only two-dimensional, but a growing number of new applications let the user display three-dimensional data (see Figure 8.10 on the next page). For example, instead of displaying a table showing the quarterly sales figures for each division for just one quarter, the user can do so for many quarters. The user enters a command that rotates the displayed picture on a desired axis, much as she would rotate the sides of a Rubik's Cube.

DYNAMIC REPRESENTATION

In many circumstances, knowledge workers and managers must make decisions based on real-time activity, not on data about something that has already taken place. This requires a new type of display, called **dynamic representation**

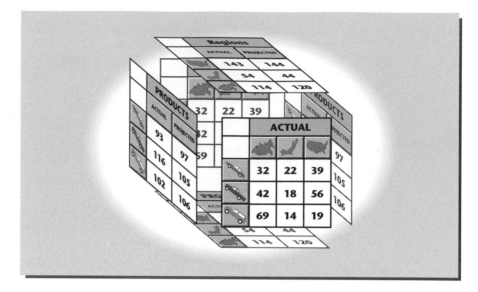

Figure 8.10 *Three-dimensional tables provide useful data matrices.*

because it usually includes moving images that represent either the speed or direction of what is happening in real time. For instance, in stock trading, brokers are interested not just in the stock's price but also in how fast its price changes, which indicates the level of activity of buying and selling. In new stock-trading software, columns with lists of selected stocks rotate to indicate buying and selling activity: the faster they rotate, the greater the activity. The direction in which the stock price has changed since the start of the trading day may be represented by a column above a surface for "up" and under the surface for "down," where the length of the column changes to represent how far the price rose or fell. Raw data for this representation are taken directly from the price board on the trading floor. Rates of change may also be represented by changing colors: blue for slowest, red for fastest, and other colors for intermediate rates. It is expected that the use of dynamic representation will grow in information systems.

Dynamic yield representation lets investment traders and analysts immediately sense market changes.

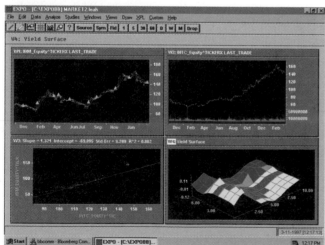

Used by permission form Leading Market Technologies, Cambridge, MA

MANAGERS AND THEIR INFORMATION SYSTEMS

Figure 8.11 shows the traditional view of what types of information systems are needed for the different levels of operations and management. These relationships may be generally true, but information needs vary widely in practice. With ISs making information available throughout organizational hierarchies, these traditional correlations can become inaccurate.

TRANSACTION PROCESSING SYSTEMS

As you may remember from Chapter 1, "Business Information Systems: An Introduction," workers at the bottom of the organizational hierarchy use Point-of-Sale (POS) terminals, order-entry systems, and other transaction-processing systems (TPSs) to enter data at its source at the time the transaction

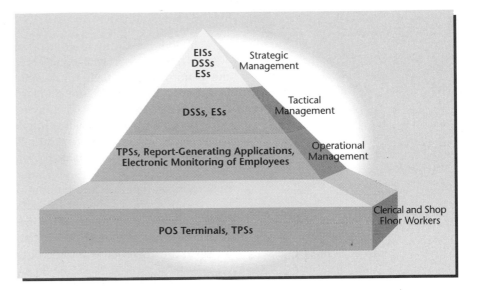

Figure 8.11 *Types of information systems typically used at different levels of an organization's hierarchy*

takes place. These are the raw materials for producing useful information. TPSs are interfaced with applications that provide clerical workers and operational managers with up-to-date information, such as the quantity-on-hand of a certain inventory item, the latest deposit in the bank account of a customer, the shipping date and contents of a shipment to a customer, or the latest prescription filled for a customer in a drugstore. Clerical workers use the systems to perform their routine responsibilities: serving customers, placing purchase orders with suppliers, and providing information to other employees.

TPSs are also used by operational managers, mainly to generate ad hoc reports, usually on-screen.

DECISION SUPPORT SYSTEMS AND EXPERT SYSTEMS

Middle managers must solve problems that are more complex and nonroutine than those faced by operational managers. Their decision making requires significantly more data. Therefore, they use computer-based decision aids, including decision support systems (DSSs) and expert systems (ESs), which play an important role in these managers' problem-solving and decision-making activities.

DSSs and ESs are also used by senior managers. Historically, senior managers have been more reluctant to be assisted by computers in their decision making. Until several years ago it was rare to find a PC on the desks of corporate presidents and vice presidents. One reason may be the reluctance to work in a mode that was perceived to be more appropriate for lower-level managers and clerical staff. The other reason may be the genuine paucity of computer-based decision aids that fit the way senior managers think and decide.

Senior managers realize they need to use computerized decision aids to keep their companies competitive.

Executive Information Systems

In addition to the more traditional DSSs and ESs, executive information systems (EISs) now provide managers with timely and concise information about the performance of their organization. DSSs, ESs and EISs are discussed in Chapters 12 and 13, "Decision Support and Executive Information Systems" and "Artificial Intelligence and Expert Systems."

In addition to reviewing internal information, many executives have their microcomputers connected to commercial services that provide business and general news from outside the organization, including economic indices, stock and commodity prices, and summaries of information sorted by industry, on a regional, national, and international basis.

While there is a general correlation between managerial level and type of IS, it is important to note that nothing prevents any member of the organization from using any type of IS. Of course, management may not choose to put an EIS at the discretion of a clerk, but clerks may use DSSs for their work.

Information Politics

The development and control of ISs are not free of politics. In the case of organizations, **politics** is the decision to act in the interest of the individual decision maker, rather than in the interest of the organization as a whole. Opposed to political decisions stand **rational decisions**, which are made to achieve organizational goals. Information systems become embroiled in politics when the desire for power motivates managers to control systems, or when managers refuse to use systems that are not designed especially for their organizational unit.

Power

Anyone who has worked for an organization recognizes that information often affords power. And power is something that people do not give away willingly. When management slates a new IS for development, managers of departments that will use it do usually concur on several issues. But questions arise:

◆ *Who owns the system?* Managers tend to build "empires." They are perceived as more powerful when they control more resources: people, machinery, and funds. A new system added to this pool of resources adds to their perceived (and often, real) power. Usually, the department that owns the system also controls it. That department has the final say in determining its features and in modifying it. When a system is to serve more than one department, the struggle among managers may result in a system that is not used properly, or that is not used at all by those who were denied ownership. Management is often forced to announce which unit owns the system and what "rights" other units have to it. If the system is to be used by more than one unit for similar amounts of time and volumes of data storage and retrieval, a good solution to the ownership problem may be the pronouncement that the system is owned by top management.

◆ *Who pays for the system?* When several units share a newly conceived system, managers often try to burden the other units with the cost of development and the current operational expenditures. Management must be fair in allocating the costs to the units that use the system. The costs must be commensurate with the benefits each business unit derives from it.

POINT OF INTEREST
Computer Comfort

The level of comfort with information technology is on the rise, from the business unit to the boardroom. A 1997 survey of 100 CEOs and other senior executives reveals the following: 85% felt comfortable dealing with technology issues, 69% claimed to have a working knowledge of technologies used in their companies and of the impact those technologies have on organizational performance, and 40% said they spent more than 10% of their time learning about relevant technologies. The survey also showed a relationship between technology literacy at the top of an organization and the number of IT projects initiated at that level. Top executives claiming to have a very good working knowledge of technology initiated 29% of all IT projects, while CEOs with fairly good or poor working knowledge initiated fewer than 15%.

Source: Caldwell, B. "Top Execs Take IT Reins," InformationWeek, March 17, 1997, p. 100.

◆ *Who accesses what information?* Since information is power, managers often try to gain access to as much information as they can, while at the same time trying to deny access to others—people who, in their view, do not, or should not, have a "need to know." If others have access to information pertaining to your unit, they may question your decisions. Also, managers feel more powerful when others who need information turn to them first.

◆ *Who has "write" privileges?* "Write" privilege is the authority to modify information in files and databases. Keep in mind that other managers make some of their decisions based on "your" data. If you control the data, you have influence on their decisions. Management should give "view access" on a "need to know" basis. "Write" access should be given only to users who must update data or applications as part of their jobs. Usually, these are the database administrator or another high-ranking MIS officer and some of their staff. These decisions must be made carefully in order not to alienate other managers. The decisions must be followed with satisfactory explanations to those who may challenge them.

Political struggles are especially harmful when systems are to be shared by several organizational units. Tactics include the insistence on adding features that will afford the manager more control, trying to derail the development effort by not cooperating with the developers, and promotion of alternatives to the system.

THE NOT-INVENTED-HERE PHENOMENON

Sometimes, managers do whatever they can *not* to use ISs. The reason is known as the Not-Invented-Here (NIH) phenomenon: Managers and their subordinates feel that if the new system is the fruit of an outsider's idea, it will not serve them well. Often, they know this is not true, but it is human nature to seek credit and not to give others credit for something you feel *you* should have "invented." Again, managers use different tactics to foil attempts to introduce the new system in their department. They may try to convince top management that the system is not needed, or that it does not satisfy their "unique" business needs.

Top management must be aware of these issues. This is particularly true since an increasing number of ISs are not only developed for individual departments, but also integrated to form **enterprise-wide systems** shared by many business units and managerial levels.

Useful Information from Bulletin Boards

Managers used to look for external information in the mass media, such as newspapers, magazines, newsletters, and even TV news. But over the last few years, managers have started reaching to a resource that technical people have been using for decades: the electronic bulletin board.

When Bill Vick needed ideas to drum up business for his Dallas-based executive-recruiting firm, he placed a request for some ideas on a business-related bulletin board used by thousands of other entrepreneurs. Many responded with suggestions. Acting on one of them, Mr. Vick mailed scores of postcards to prospective executives he suspected would be attending a conference a few days later, letting them know that he would be available to talk to them. When many of the executives showed up as expected, Vick was there, shaking hands. "That one idea must have gotten me $25,000 worth of business," says Mr. Vick, president of Vick & Associates.

Many small business owners still view computers as alien machines and use them only for bookkeeping and word processing.

But others are logging on to computer bulletin boards every day to swap advice, information, and marketing tips. Experts say that small businesses must use computers as tools for research and planning if they want to keep pace with the competition.

"You can only go so far on your [own] steam. With bulletin boards, I've gotten advice from Albany, NY, and Tokyo," says Mr. Vick, who has only three employees. "Some of it is junk, but some of it is good, solid stuff." It seems that bulletin boards have become an effective external source of information. This is especially so with new businesses. Entrepreneurs starting from scratch are attracted to the expert advice available informally on electronic bulletin boards. "They're a great leveler. Important people who have secretaries to answer their regular mail will answer their own electronic mail," says Jane Rettig, a New York computer consultant.

Source: Saddler, J., "Electronic Bulletin Boards Help Businesses Post Success," New York Times, October 28, 1994.

Questions

1. Within the framework described in Figure 8.2, enumerate the types of information entrepreneurs like Mr. Vick need.

2. Ms. Rettig said, "They are a great leveler." Indeed, many business people say that public information resources such as the Internet and electronic bulletin boards democratize the business world. Explain what they mean.

Uniting Engineers at United Technologies

It should not be surprising that United Technologies Corp. (UTC) has been a pioneer among desktop-video-conferencing users. The corporate parent of the companies that manufacture Otis elevators, Pratt & Whitney aircraft engines, Sikorsky helicopters, and Carrier heating and cooling systems depends on the ability of its engineers throughout the world to effectively collaborate in designing new products.

UTC has been steadily increasing its use of room-based video-conferencing systems for groups, convinced that video-based collaboration increases productivity and cuts travel costs. And just over three years ago, the company decided to explore desktop video-conferencing.

"We wanted to make collaboration between personnel in different locations more immediate and as easy as if they were in the same room," says Dr. Joseph Caspar, principal scientist at the company's Research Center in East Hartford, Connecticut. At the time, says Caspar, UTC thought putting the technology on the users' desktops could make video-conferencing more immediate in the same way that a PC makes applications more immediate and personal than mainframes. And integrating desktop computing and video-conferencing might enable users to more easily combine multiple collaborative forms such as electronic white-boards, shared applications and files with video.

UTC has found that desktop video-conferencing can indeed deliver all of those benefits. As part of a pilot project internally called TOP-DESK, engineers from UTC and collaborating companies in Dearborn, Michigan; East Hartford; Montreal; and Ulm, Germany, participated in a two-hour seminar in which machine parts were rapidly prototyped using drawings and models made of plastic and other materials. The process helped cut design verification and testing time to a fraction of what it normally takes, Caspar says.

Source: Moad, J., "Uniting engineers at United Technologies," Datamation, May 1, 1994, p. 31.

Questions

1. What are the advantages of video-conferencing compared with other types of remote collaboration?

2. Video-conferencing on the Internet is already used by some corporations. Would you be comfortable conducting business with managers from other companies via this medium? Which topics would you not discuss via this medium?

Where Is My Information Buried?

..."Any company that doesn't have a comprehensive plan to deliver data to its employees will miss the boat," warns Howard Dresner, program director for the Gartner Group, Stamford, CT.

Don Waddell knew he had excess petroleum idling in storage tanks throughout Chevron's nearly 100 U.S. refineries and marketing terminals. But until early 1993, the inventory manager had no way of quantifying how much cash was tied up—and, subsequently, no idea how to free it. The amount turned out to be a staggering $50 million. This didn't count the $5 million annually it cost Chevron to finance this excess inventory. "Mostly, we used Big Chief writing tablets to track inventory," Waddell recalls.

Pat Ellis shudders when he remembers those days. Formerly the superintendent of operations coordination for Chevron's El Segundo, Calif., refinery, he is now on special assignment to the company's inventory management task force. Recalls Ellis, "All I knew was how much I had in each tank at my own refinery at any given moment." Forget about looking at historical trends at his own facility, much less knowing what was happening at other Chevron sites. Poor Ellis. He was responsible for processing the right amount of crude oil and delivering to market terminals according to a monthly production plan. His ignorance led to some "seat of the pants" management decisions, he admits.

"We have to hold inventory until marketing is ready for it," Ellis explains. "Unless I know how much crude oil is already being held by marketing—and how much is on its way to me on supply ships—it is pure guesswork figuring out how much to produce on any given day." What was maddening was that the data Ellis needed *existed*. Somewhere within the bowels of Chevron's San Ramon, Calif.-based Information Technology Co. (which employs some 2,000 people to stoke the information furnaces), a wealth of valuable data was hidden. Massive transaction databases running on mainframe and minicomputers...tracked oil production and sales data in infinitesimal detail for accounting and billing purposes. Yet there was no way for line managers like Waddell and Ellis to get their hands on it.

Enter a new category of software tools designed to break down the technological vaults and distribute the wealth. Called BIS, Business Intelligence Systems, these desktop tools let line managers go "data dipping" into...suddenly accessible corporate knowledge. Now, by 2 p.m. each Friday, Ellis, Waddell and other interested Chevron workers can sit down at their PCs and use Cognos Corp.'s PowerPlay BIS to call up vivid graphics that show how oil moved through the company's supply chain during that production week. Managers can paste the numbers to a favorite spreadsheet or word processing program for further analysis or reporting. They can send via e-mail relevant charts and figures to colleagues at any Chevron site in the country.

Bottom line: They can do their jobs much more effectively. "I can ramp production up, slow it down, or hold steady—now that I know what's happening elsewhere," says Ellis, who confesses to having been technology illiterate until this year. "I used to joke that my computer was just a $4,000 clock until this was put on my desk," says Ellis of the Window-based inventory tracking program that cost Chevron $750,000. "Now I can't imagine life without it."...

Source: LaPlante, A., "Liberate your data," Forbes ASAP, February 28, 1994, p. 58.

Questions:

1. What were Ellis' problems?

2. Use Figure 8.11 to pinpoint the type of IS Ellis and his fellow managers now utilize.

SUMMARY

Organizations are run by managers. The majority of organizations are structured like **pyramids** with several layers of management. Managers can be roughly classified into these levels: **strategic**, at the top of the organizational hierarchy; **tactical**, below top managers; and **operational** managers, below tactical. Managers at the three levels have different information needs, and typically use different types of information systems to satisfy these needs.

Top managers make decisions that affect the entire organization, or large parts of it, in the long run. They use highly summarized information that is based on wide-range data, both in terms of the number of organizational units that the data cover, and in terms of time span: long historic periods, and periods well into the future. They use both internal and external sources. Strategic managers operate in highly **unstructured environments**. The typical information systems they use are **executive information systems (EISs)**, **decision support systems (DSSs)**, and, to a smaller extent, **expert systems (ESs)**.

Middle managers receive strategic decisions as general directives within which they develop tactics to achieve specific objectives. The information they use is processed from data that cover narrower organizational units and shorter time spans. Their typical information systems consist of DSSs and ESs. Like top managers, they must make unstructured decisions.

Operational managers are responsible for daily operations. They make relatively simple decisions that affect only their departments in the short run. The information they need reflects transactions of their own small units and very narrow time spans. However, the information is very detailed. Operational managers use transaction processing systems to generate reports. Much of their work involves **monitoring**. This sometimes includes **electronic monitoring** of employees, which may infringe on the employees' right to privacy.

At the bottom of the organizational chart, we find **clerical** and other workers who carry out their supervisors' orders. They use transaction processing systems to record transactions and satisfy queries from other employees, customers, and suppliers.

A major task of middle managers in the past was to screen information and pass it on to higher-level managers. Since information technology allows top managers to extract their information directly and conveniently, many organizations have reduced whole layers of middle management, resulting in a **flatter** organizational structure.

Effective information conveys a message with minimum necessity for interpretation. Many applications allow users to present information in the form that best suits their individual preferences: tabular or graphical. Innovative applications also provide three-dimensional information and **dynamic information**.

Information systems have not escaped the influence of **politics**. On the contrary—because information is power, managers often do not use **rational** approaches to the development and control of ISs. Often, managers try to obtain power by controlling ISs beyond their real business need. Sometimes, they reject new ISs because they were "not invented here." Politics harm the effort to deliver and share information for the benefit of the organization as a whole.

REVIEW, DISCUSS, AND EXPLORE

REVIEW AND DISCUSSION QUESTIONS

1. Why are the majority of organizations structured like pyramids?

2. What are the major tasks of managers in the three levels of management?

3. Often, it is difficult to distinguish between middle managers and operational managers. Why?

4. Explain the generally accepted adage that: "The higher you are in the organizational hierarchy, the more decisions you have to make."

5. Why don't operational managers usually use DSSs?

6. Why do senior managers rely on external information?

7. Give five examples of external information sources.

8. "A picture is worth a thousand words." Is this always true? Why, or why not? Give an example of a situation in which you would prefer information in tabular rather than graphical form.

9. What is dynamic information? Give three examples of industries in which applications of dynamic information could be used for effective decision making or operations.

10. In the past decade, many middle managers have lost their jobs. Why?

11. Senior managers and operational managers have not been hurt by information systems as much as middle managers. Why?

12. A major task of operational managers is to monitor the performance of their subordinates. This task can be effectively executed with the help of electronic devices. What issues does this practice raise?

13. *Ethics and Society:* Employers argue that it is their right to monitor employees for productivity and for security reasons. What guidelines would you require employers to follow, to ease employee resentment?

CONCEPT ACTIVITY

Interview a controller of a small or medium-sized company. List the tasks that he or she could not perform without a computer-based IS. List the tasks that are still performed manually. Which of these tasks could be automated, and how?

HANDS-ON ACTIVITY

You are the marketing manager of the irrigation products of Water, Inc. The following are your budgeted and actual figures.

WATER, INC. IRRIGATION PRODUCTS DEPARTMENT BUDGET, QUARTER 1

ITEM	FORECAST	ACTUAL	5% EXCEPTION
Income			
Model P12 Sales	1,250,000	1,452,375	
Model P15 Sales	13,500,000	12,788,992	
Drip Valve V2	450,000	452,344	
Expenditures			
Sales Reps' Commissions	750,000	763,000	
Advertising	500,000	425,000	
Packaging Materials	270,000	298,000	
Telephone	5,200	5,790	

Using a spreadsheet, create an exception report that will aid in making decisions as to which items to investigate. Add the "5% Exception." Have an asterisk (*) appear in every column for which the actual expense of an item deviated by at least 5% from the budget. Hint: Try the absolute value function.

Use the appropriate fonts and styles as used here. *Turn in:* (1) a printout showing the reports (2) a printout showing the formulas where applicable.

Many ISs, especially in large organizations, are used by more than one department. Contact a large organization where a system like this is used. Split your team into two groups, each assigned to interview a manager from a different department using the system. Each subteam should pose to the manager the questions appearing in the section *Information Politics*: ("Who owns the system?", "Who paid for the system?", and so on). When the interviews are over, compare the information you received from the two managers. Did they supply the same answers? What are the areas of disagreement? Write a report that summarizes your findings, including your suggestions. As a top manager championing the system, how would you have acted *before* the system was introduced for operation, so as to avoid the disagreements? If there are no disagreements, what did management do to achieve a harmonious work atmosphere regarding the IS?

EXPLORE THE WEB

The Web offers much external information that is not available in the more traditional external sources, such as newspapers, printed bulletins, trade journals, and newsletters. Assume that you are a human resource manager looking to hire qualified chemical engineers for your petrochemical company. Explore the Web for three sites offering candidates. Prepare a short report answering the following questions: What are the advantages or disadvantages of using the Web, compared with advertising in newspaper help-wanted ads? What are the advantages or disadvantages compared with using a "headhunting" firm?

Chapter **9**

Organization of Information Systems and Services

Divide And Conquer

For many years Corning had a centralized approach to IT operations. The $5.3 billion diversified maker of cookware, specialty glass, fiber optics, flat-panel displays, video tubes, and optical lenses ran its information systems operation like most other large corporations at the time: A large group of IS professionals reported to a single executive and served all organizational units. The decision-making process for development of new ISs became extremely long and frustrating. The individual organizational units often felt that they were not receiving the services they expected from the IS personnel. Top management, on the other hand, felt that it was spending too much money on IS services that might not be really needed.

In the early 1990s, the Corning, New York, company embarked on a series of **re-engineering** projects whose main purpose was to streamline purchasing, manufacturing, and delivery processes. Management felt that the individual business units had to be more accountable for their activities. As a key target of the re-engineering effort, Corning decided to reorganize the IS staff. The centralized IS approach was not compatible with re-engineering initiatives.

The company dispersed its formerly centralized IS group among business units, with only a small central corporate team in charge of overall technology direction and functions such as e-mail, groupware, and other systems common to the various business units. The different divisions are now fully accountable for the systems they develop and maintain. Corporate management feels that the decentralization is saving the company millions of dollars.

Source: Wilder, C., "Start with the Best, Then Build on It," *InformationWeek*, September 9, 1996, pp. 158–166.

Information systems and their management must be organized wisely to deliver services promptly and effectively. Their deployment must work smoothly with an organization's general approach to management and the dissemination of information. When you finish this chapter you will:

◆ Know the different ways in which ISs are deployed in organizations

◆ Understand the advantages and disadvantages of each IS architecture

◆ Realize the importance of collaboration between IS managers and line managers, and understand the relationships between the two groups

◆ Recognize the importance of chargeback methods for IS services

◆ Have a good idea of career paths and responsibilities in the IS field

INFORMATION SYSTEMS ARCHITECTURE AND MANAGEMENT

Organizations tend to have their own distinct managerial styles, most of which fall somewhere on the spectrum between two extremes. One extreme is **centralized management**, which designates staff positions and departments in a strict vertical hierarchy, and places control of the organization in a few hands. The other is **decentralized management**, which delegates more authority to lower-level managers. In most organizations, the management and structure of information systems follow the same pattern as the organization's overall management: centralized management tends to want centralized control over ISs; decentralized management is more likely to be comfortable with decentralized ISs.

Similarly, the structure of IS management tends to be mirrored in the general layout of **information systems architecture**, which in this context refers to the physical layout of computers and data communications networks, discussed at length in Chapter 5, "Information Technology in Business: Telecommunications and Networks." Companies with centralized IS management tend to have centralized IS architecture, and companies with decentralized IS management tend to have decentralized IS architecture although exceptions may be found. Remember that architecture does not strictly dictate how systems are managed (a decentralized architecture can be managed centrally, and a centralized architecture can be decentrally managed), but architecture always has an impact on the way access to data is controlled.

CENTRALIZED INFORMATION SYSTEMS ARCHITECTURE

For a long time, mainframes were the only computers available for business. By their nature, they dictated that IS architecture be centralized because typically all applications and data were stored on a company's single mainframe. As an example, Figure 9.1 shows a typical physical layout of a centralized IS of a single-site company whose general management philosophy advocates tight control of operations. A centralized IS is still favored in some organizations, but with the introduction of inexpensive desktop computers and reliable data communications technology, many organizations moved to a decentralized or distributed architecture.

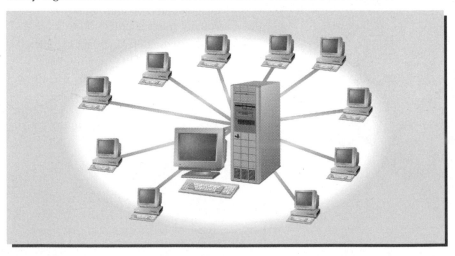

Figure 9.1 *In centralized IS architecture, information resources are maintained on one or several large computers that are centrally controlled.*

The great advantage of a centralized architecture is that it affords top management and the IS department a high degree of control, making it easy to maintain standards of hardware, software, procedures, and operations, and to control access to information. The main disadvantage of a centralized system is its inflexibility. A centralized system is run so that it can be used by everyone, but that does not mean that the system is optimal for everyone. Different departments and remote sites have different information needs; usually, with a centralized system, everyone is served, but few are completely satisfied. These disadvantages are especially problematic when an organization consists of multiple remote sites.

DECENTRALIZED INFORMATION SYSTEMS ARCHITECTURE

A decentralized architecture allows departments and remote sites a large degree of independence in organizing and utilizing their information systems (see Figure 9.2). In a decentralized model, each unit within an organization has its own local IS department to establish an infrastructure, and to select hardware and software to satisfy the specific information needs of that unit, without necessarily considering other units. Although rare nowadays, in fully decentralized architecture the systems of the independent units are linked neither to that of the organization's headquarters nor to each other.

The major disadvantage of decentralized ISs is that with a variety of independent systems, it can be difficult to share applications and data. It is also more expensive for the organization to establish maintenance and service contracts with many vendors than with just one or a few.

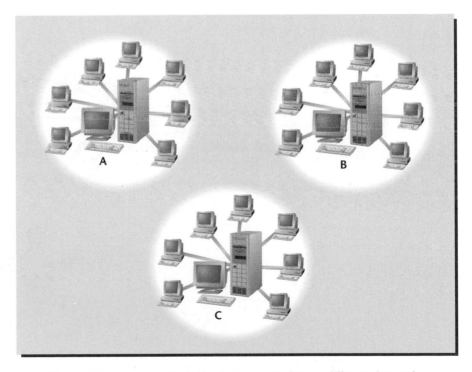

Figure 9.2 *In decentralized IS architecture, workers at different sites and departments (A, B, C) use information resources that are dedicated to their site or department.*

DISTRIBUTED INFORMATION SYSTEMS

Organizations that wish to afford independence to their employees without losing centralized control prefer to rely on what is called **distributed architecture**, with which an organization can enjoy the benefits of both decentralized and centralized architectures. Each unit enjoys sufficient independence in selecting and implementing its own system to optimize its operation, but it can also share resources, remotely, with other units through communications lines (see Figure 9.3).

The increasing reliability and affordability of data communications and PC technology have encouraged organizations to change from centralized and decentralized architectures to distributed architecture. Now, when IS professionals say "decentralized systems" they usually mean "distributed systems."

CENTRALIZED VS. DECENTRALIZED ISs: ADVANTAGES AND DISADVANTAGES

Thanks to telecommunications technology, organizations can choose to manage any type of architecture centrally or decentrally. However, the different architectures make some operational factors easier to manage, and others harder. As summarized in Figure 9.4, when choosing between more or less centralized or decentralized IS architectures, organizations trade off different advantages and disadvantages in IS efficiency, economies of scale, ease of training, level of control, and other factors, as discussed below.

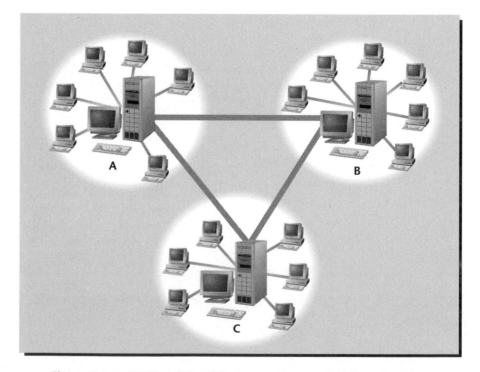

Figure 9.3 *In distributed IS architecture, workers use the information resources of their own site or department, but can also use the resources of other sites or departments through communications lines.*

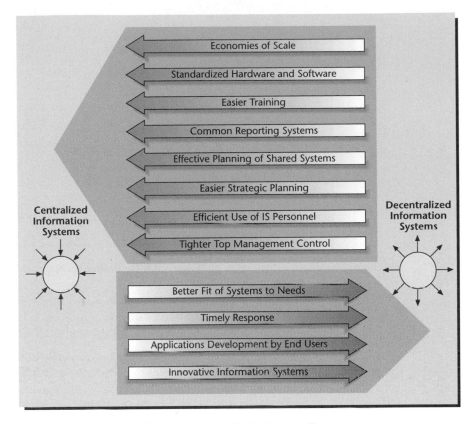

Figure 9.4 *Centralized vs. decentralized IS trade-offs*

ADVANTAGES OF CENTRALIZED IS MANAGEMENT Centralized IS management, as illustrated in Figure 9.5 on the next page, has several major advantages:

Economies of Scale. A centralized IS staff may save time and money in the development of systems because they apply their unique specialized experience with the corporate and business culture when developing information systems for their company. In addition, purchasing hardware and software is often less expensive for an entire organization, thanks to the large quantity ordered.

Standardized Hardware and Software. Centralized ISs can establish corporate software and hardware standards, which saves time and money in purchasing and installation, and simplifies interdepartmental sharing of data and information. Standardizing software is particularly important for facilitating data exchange and the sharing of applications.

Easier Training. Training, often a major expense in a company's budget, is much more efficient and less expensive when an organization uses standardized hardware and software.

Encouragement of Common Reporting Systems. Central IS management can easily standardize reporting systems and formats across departments, which many companies and some laws and regulations require for accounting or tax reporting.

Effective Planning of Shared Systems. Large and complex systems that are shared by several organizational units can best be developed by a central IS department that knows the "big picture."

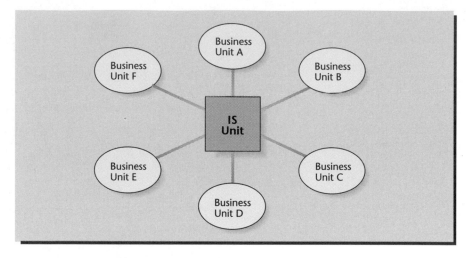

Figure 9.5 *Centralized management of an IS*

Easier Strategic Planning. Strategic IS planning takes into consideration an organization's entire IS resources. It is easier to link an IS strategic plan to an organization's overall strategic plan when IS management is centralized.

Efficient Use of IS Personnel. With a centralized IS department, an organization is more likely to employ highly specialized IS professionals who are better qualified to develop information systems, especially the larger and more complex ones, than are IS professionals who are dispersed in non-IS organizational units.

Accommodation of Tight Control by Top Management. A centralized IS management allows top management to maintain control over the often vast resources spent on ISs.

ADVANTAGES OF DECENTRALIZED IS MANAGEMENT Historically, most organizations have moved from a centralized IS architecture to a decentralized deployment, and then to a distributed architecture. Decentralized IS management, illustrated in Figure 9.6, has several advantages that are the opposite of the advantages of centralized management. In addition, consider the following advantages:

Better Fit of IS To Business Needs. The individual IS units can use their familiarity with their departments' information needs to develop systems that fit those needs more closely.

Timely Responsiveness of IS Units To Business Demands. Individual IS units can arrange IS priorities in development and maintenance to fit their business units' priorities. They can be more responsive because their responsibility is more focused.

Encouragement of End User Development of Applications. In a decentralized setting, end users are usually encouraged to develop their own small applications to increase their productivity.

More Innovative Use of ISs. Since a business IS unit knows its clients better than central management, it has a better chance at devising innovative ISs.

Accommodation to Decentralized Enterprise-Wide Management Style. Decentralized IS management works best if top management wishes to delegate more authority to lower-level managers.

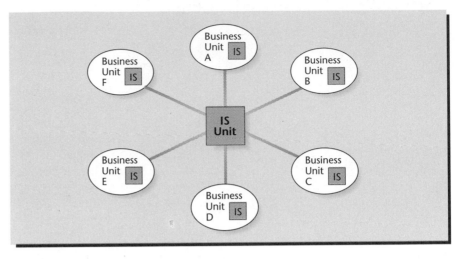

Figure 9.6 *Decentralized management of an IS (In fully decentralized management, the central IS unit would not exist.)*

While you will find many companies with centralized IS architecture, fully decentralized IS architecture is rare. It may be employed if an organization has divisions that produce completely different products and services, so that the advantage of sharing IS resources does not outweigh communications costs.

TRENDS IN INFORMATION SYSTEMS ORGANIZATION

There is a lot of talk about "trends" in the organization and management of information systems. Perhaps the two that have had the most profound effect on the way companies run their businesses are downsizing/rightsizing, and re-engineering.

DOWNSIZING/RIGHTSIZING In the business and popular press, **downsizing** refers to massive layoffs from companies, usually the result of re-evaluating business processes and reorganizing that includes removing layers of management. The goal is to recreate an organization that produces the same or better goods and services for less cost (that is, with fewer employees). However, the term originated in the IS world, and refered to the smaller-sized computers used when companies change from a centralized mainframe to decentralized networked systems. As shown in Figure 9.7 on the next page, the decentralized systems are usually in a client/server arrangement and are at least as powerful as their predecessors. Figure 9.8 on the next page indicates the trend in IS downsizing, showing how U.S. sales of "big iron" (as many professionals call mainframe computers) increased until 1990, and then decreased dramatically between 1991 and 1994, while server unit sales increased at the same time.

Because downsizing supports a distributed IS architecture, the benefits gained by downsizing are generally the same as those enjoyed with a distributed IS architecture. But ridding an organization of large computers has additional benefits. For instance, the maintenance of PCs is easier and less expensive than the maintenance of mainframes. Also, if an organization's mainframe is down,

Year	Mainframes	Servers
1985	11,000	N/A
1986	11,200	N/A
1987	11,630	253,000
1988	13,100	229,800
1989	14,690	309,000
1990	15,130	421,500
1991	13,565	573,900
1992	9,411	1,032,600
1993*	8,500	1,374,500
1994*	8,700	1,528,800

*Estimate

Source: "Downsizing the Machine: Northrop Latest to Ditch Mainframe Computing," *Los Angeles Times*, May 25, 1994. Reprinted with permission of Los Angeles Times Syndicate.

Figure 9.7 *Mainframe and server unit sales in the U.S.*

the entire company may be left without computing resources, whereas with a network of microcomputers, one computer can go down and have no effect on other computers.

The term "downsizing" sometimes takes on a negative meaning in IS systems. Downsizing for its own sake is not necessarily in the long-term best interests of an organization. Some IS professionals argue that downsizing often leaves organizations without sufficient computing power. The term **rightsizing** has come into favor, to reflect downsizing that continues to allow a company to

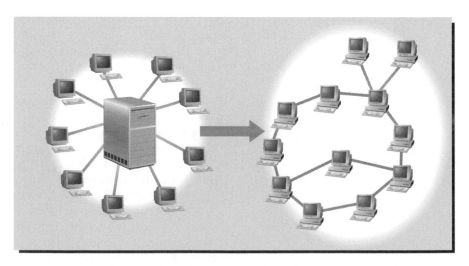

Figure 9.8 *Decentralizing ISs leads to downsizing from larger to smaller computers.*

deliver its goods and services in an uncompromised fashion. In IS terminology, rightsizing means finding the right combination of mainframe, or midrange, computers and PCs.

Many large companies that have millions of customers and perform millions of business transactions daily must hold on to their large computers. No combination of small computers can provide the processing power of a supercomputer, whose number-crunching power is still required by some government agencies, research institutions, and large corporations. In these environments, the traditional approach of centralized systems will continue for quite a while.

RE-ENGINEERING WITH INFORMATION TECHNOLOGY The past decade has brought with it many new ideas about how to improve business. As mentioned above, many of these ideas include evaluating and revising business processes to improve quality and/or reduce cost. When critical business processes and the systems that support them undergo radical changes that cause breakthrough gains in performance, the shift is referred to as re-engineering. Re-engineering does not *have* to involve information technology, but because information is involved in every step of a business process, re-engineering almost always leads to integrating IT in all processes.

As part of business re-evaluation, managers analyze how their organization could use information to improve processes; then IS managers contemplate how to translate the requirements into practical solutions that involve state-of-the-art IT. Successful re-engineering improves service and product quality, reduces costs, and enhances revenue.

Perhaps the best evidence that process re-engineering is tightly related to innovative use of IT is the finding of a recent survey, in which top IS managers rank the limitations of existing systems as the second most significant obstacle to re-engineering success. (The first is resistance to change.) Thus they perceive advanced ISs as critical to the success of re-engineering.

Several software companies offer special applications that aid in the business process analysis. For instance, FlowCharter from Micrografx provides several graphic tools for visualizing workflow and then modeling the business process. A statistical component lets the analyst chart data for evaluation of performance by different departments involved in the process.

Business process re-engineering (BPR) software tools help analyze processes and suggest radical improvements.

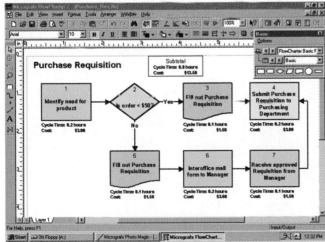

Used by permission from Micrografx

ORGANIZATION OF THE IS FUNCTION

As discussed above, there are several ways to organize IS professionals within an organization, regardless of IS architecture. These arrangements range from having a central IS team to whom all units turn with their IS needs to having a separate IS team for each business unit. The former approach is referred to as **central IS management**; the latter is referred to as **functional IS management**. Some arrangements combine elements of both. The management approach has a direct effect on how the IS professionals are positioned in the organizational structure of the business. In any case, the goal in choosing an IS management style is to place IS personnel in the organizational structure in a way that optimizes IS services, and in a manner that fits the organization's goals and culture.

CENTRAL IS MANAGEMENT

A centrally managed IS department has what we will call in this book an IS director, who may in fact be a member of top management or a high-level manager who reports to a vice president (usually of finance or operations). The highest-ranking IS officer in an organization is often given the title of chief information officer (CIO) and, in many organizations, is also a vice president.

CENTRAL IS UNITS As seen in Figure 9.9, the most common central IS unit organization has the IS director overseeing several departments within the IS unit. One department develops new systems and maintains current systems. Another department runs the information center, whose function is to provide ad hoc advice about hardware and software to business units. The communications department develops and manages local area and wide area networks. And the data administration department develops and maintains corporate databases. In large organizations there may also be a research and development department, which keeps the IS unit abreast of technological advances, and develops ideas for the strategic use of ISs.

A central IS unit is usually involved in virtually every aspect of IS in the organization. It determines which computers and peripheral equipment are approved for purchasing, and in some cases it is the only unit that is authorized to purchase hardware. It approves or rejects software purchases, is in charge of training new users, and (except for small and simple programs) is the only body that is authorized to develop ISs for business units.

TRADE-OFFS The advantages and disadvantages of a centrally managed IS unit are essentially the same as the advantages and disadvantages of using a centralized IS architecture, even though the architecture and management types do not have to coincide. When centrally managed, the IS unit assures compatibility of hardware and software and seamless interfaces between different systems that must work together, such as purchasing and cost accounting; payroll, accounts payable, and cost accounting; sales and accounts receivable,

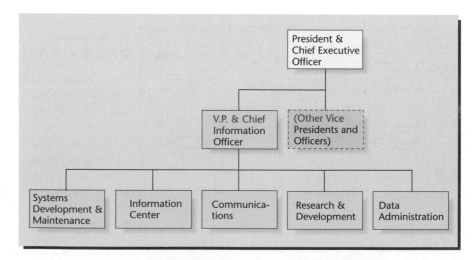

Figure 9.9 *An example of an IS unit's organization with centrally managed IS*

and so on. This approach helps all top managers share an organizational vision of how information technology will serve the corporation in the future.

Regardless of architecture, central IS management usually includes a **steering committee** with representatives from a variety of key business units. It establishes priorities for systems development and implementation of communications networks; it considers and prioritizes requests for new systems; and it commits funds to projects.

It is often easier to integrate an IS plan into an organization's overall strategic plan when there is centralized IS management, rather than decentralized. On the other hand, when only a central systems department is available, business units often find themselves overly dependent on—and at times resentful of—the central unit, over which they have no control, although they depend upon it for their success. Business units must receive approval for almost anything they do with computers and software. Centralized IS management tends to create an atmosphere that discourages the development of applications by end users, even if they are technologically knowledgeable enough to do so.

FUNCTIONAL IS MANAGEMENT

At the other end of the IS management spectrum is the approach whereby each unit fulfills its IS needs independently, deciding for itself which systems it needs and how to develop them (see Figure 9.10). There is usually still a central IS unit, which is relatively small and serves to coordinate IS needs for those departments that cannot handle their needs for themselves. Only large and complex systems, especially those that impact several departments, are developed under the auspices of the central IS unit.

Each functional unit has one or several IS professionals who report to the unit's manager. These workers know their colleagues' daily operations well and understand their information needs better than central IS personnel do.

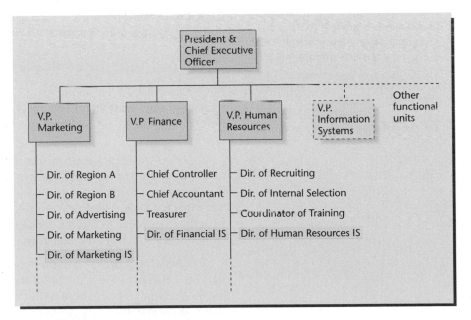

Figure 9.10 *An example of IS personnel locations in an organization with functionally managed IS*

In functional IS management, funds for development and maintenance of ISs always come from the unit's budget. This optimizes the use of resources. While the unit's IS professionals may seek input from their central IS colleagues, decisions are made fairly independently.

In this environment, IS professionals are often involved in many aspects of operations that do not necessarily involve IT, and may be promoted from an IT position into another type of position within the business. This enhances their chances of advancing up the organizational ladder to general managerial positions.

As Figure 9.10, indicates, an organization that chooses a functional IS management approach may still have a corporate IS director, possibly a vice president, who oversees a small central IS unit, consults with functional IS units, and concentrates on larger, more complex corporate-wide IS projects. However, the IS personnel of the various units do not report to the central IS unit.

THE BEST OF BOTH

Many companies use elements of both central and functional IS management. For instance, a large corporate IS unit may have liaisons in the functional units who report to the corporate IS unit. Gilette, the world's largest supplier of shaving blades and other toiletry products, has established such an arrangement and found it very beneficial. The corporate IS unit coordinates intraorganizational systems, while the different sites (including international divisions) develop and maintain their own local systems. This helped the company remain on the leading edge of IT while maintaining a strong sense of ownership at the local sites.

Regardless of how the ISs are managed, surveys show that IS implementation is handled differently according to the position of the highest IS officer in the organizational structure. If this person reports to the vice president of finance or another vice president, the IS personnel tend to provide mere technical solutions to business problems. However, if the highest ranking IS manager reports to the CEO, the IS professionals are significantly more involved in strategic planning, and they also search for opportunities rather than just solve problems.

CHALLENGES FOR IS MANAGERS AND LINE MANAGERS

To succeed in development and maintenance of ISs, IS managers and line managers must understand what each party expects from the other, and must find the best way to respond to those expectations. What are those expectations?

LINE MANAGER EXPECTATIONS OF AN IS UNIT The first thing that line managers must remember is that they should keep up a continuous dialog with the IS manager, to explore new ways to help their operations. Although they are not expected to be well-versed in the cutting edge of IT, they should collaborate with the IS manager to explore the capability of new technologies to support the work of their subordinates. Line managers need the following from the IS unit:

A Broad Understanding of the Business Activities. IS professionals must understand the nature of the activities of the business unit they support: Whom does the business unit serve? Where do its raw data come from? What information does it use? What systems do the business unit's systems interface with? Understanding the business helps systems analysts put themselves in the users' shoes and develop systems from the users' point of view.

Be Interested in Deployment of ISs?

As discussed in previous chapters, managers must obtain good information to make good decisions. Knowing how information technology is deployed in an organization helps managers know how to inquire about, and obtain, useful information. Thus, not only IS managers but line managers as well must be involved in the organization of IS resources in a business.

To ensure convenient access to data, managers must not rely on IS professionals to dictate deployment, responsibilities, and charges; they should be proactive and participate in the decisions leading to IS organization and policies.

In today's businesses, managers are expected to be knowledgeable consumers of information services. Thus, they should have a clear picture of the organization of the ISs and the responsibilities of different IS professionals, whose job it is to satisfy the information needs of line managers.

Prompt Response to the Information Needs of the Business Unit. Line managers are often disappointed with the long time it takes IS units to react to business needs. A business unit that cannot elicit a prompt response may resort to finding haphazard—and ultimately problematic—solutions to its information needs.

A Clear, Jargon-Free Explanation of What the Technology Can and Cannot Do for the Business Unit. To show off their expertise, IS professionals sometime use technological jargon to communicate ideas. While use of technical terminology facilitates communication among professionals, it may cause problems for lay users. If line managers and their employees are reluctant to admit that they do not understand certain terms, communication breaks down and costly misunderstandings can arise. If technical terms must be used, IS professionals should explain them.

Candid Explanation of What Information Systems Can and Cannot Do. Line managers and their employees count on IS professionals to tell them not only what marvels a planned information system will accomplish, but also what the system's limitations are. Outlining the limitations of a system will eliminate disappointment and assure proper useage of the system.

Honest Budgeting. Line managers depend on IS managers for an honest, detailed assessment of the resources needed to develop a new IS and maintain an existing one. Time and budget overruns occur often in systems development projects. IS managers must detail the work that will be done, how much it will cost in terms of person hours and other resources, and how much time each project phase will take.

Reference Personnel. To serve the business units after an IS is installed or modified, IS managers should assign one contact person to be responsible for responding to the business units' questions and problems.

In general, IS managers should treat line managers as clients, although they all work for the same organization. This approach has been adopted in an increasing number of companies. Some have taken the client/vendor model to such an extreme that line managers are allowed to use outside IS vendors if the internal IS unit cannot offer comparable service.

IS MANAGER EXPECTATIONS OF BUSINESS MANAGER IS managers are expected to keep themselves abreast of developments in the IT field, suggest adoption of new technologies, and make suggestions to improve business operations. To do this job well, IS managers also need clear communication from line managers, in three basic areas: basic business planning, general systems planning, and specific systems development.

A Projected List of Basic IS Needs. In order to plan ahead by a few years, IS managers need to know their own business, but they also need to know their clients' (the business units') plans. For instance, if a business department is planning to hire ten new people to introduce a new product, the IS manager must be informed in order to budget for purchasing and installing new equipment, installing new software, and training personnel to use it. Business plans for three years in the future may be a mere "wish list," but they will become a part of the organization's overall IS plan, which in turn is a part of the organization's overall strategic plan.

Once an IS Unit is Called Upon to Develop a New System, It Needs a Clear Explanation of Business Processes That Need Support. An IS manager can only develop an effective IS if line managers and their employees clearly communicate the exact processes they want automated.

Once the General Automation Process is Agreed Upon, the IS Manager Needs to Know What Features the Business Manager Wants in the New System. Although IS professionals are more familiar with IT than many users, they still need to know how a new system will be used in daily operations, in order to design it correctly. The business manager is responsible for communicating desired features, such as the sequence of input and output in a database. This information helps systems analysts and programmers design interface dialogues that are intuitive, easy to learn, and easy to use.

The dialogue between IS managers and general managers must be an ongoing process for an organization to take full advantage of IT to improve business operations.

THE INFORMATION CENTER

Even if management keeps tight control on information flow through centralized architecture and systems management, users who have PCs at their disposal will probably try to develop some applications independently. This is certainly so when the company maintains a decentralized IS organization and when management encourages the development of applications by non-IS employees. Local systems development may create problems: incompatibility of applications, inability to share data files and databases, development of isolated "private" databases, and inability to control sensitive information. Also, individual users, even in organizations with functional IS management, find they need advice on new software and the compatibility of applications created with different software packages.

COORDINATION AND CONTROL

One way to allow sufficient local independence in IS acquisition and use, while trying to control the problems it can create, is to have an **information center** that coordinates and controls hardware and software purchases of

end users. If a user needs a certain application, the center may inform that person that someone else has already developed a similar application. The information center also notifies departments of new hardware or software that may be of interest to them. The center may also determine which hardware or software to purchase for a department, to avoid incompatibility.

The same approach applies to collections of data. To avoid the duplication of databases, a user could check with the center to see if someone else in the business has already organized a database that would fit his or her needs. Information center personnel may also determine which data may or may not be gathered and kept by individual departments.

SUPPORT

Another important function of the information center is providing hardware and software support through both training and responding to ongoing requests for help. The latter is usually accomplished through a **help desk**.

The help desk usually consists of small units specializing in troubleshooting problems in different areas: hardware, software, communications, and so on. The success of the help desk depends largely on its ability to provide a single point of contact that can connect the user to the appropriate expert, on demand (see Figure 9.11).

CHARGEBACK METHODS

Some companies treat the IS function as a part of overhead, a general expense carried by all departments that is considered a part of running the company. In these companies, business units don't purchase services from the IS departments, they simply call on IS services at will and expect to receive them "free" (or at least for no additional charge over the department's general overhead). The service is provided to business units as a part of the normal equipment

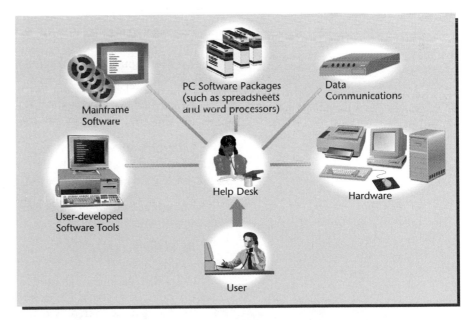

Figure 9.11 *The help desk is an essential resource for IS users.*

and services for doing business, like the lights above everyone's desk or the phones at everyone's disposal. In this arrangement, IS services can be easily, if not intentionally, abused, mostly because departments order services even when they are not essential, because no cost is directly associated with them.

To mitigate this problem, many organizations have established chargeback systems. A **chargeback** system is a method by which organizational units are charged for the services they receive, and the charges are referred to as **service charges**. Chargeback systems reduce tension between the providers and the receivers of IS services, because the receivers know what they are being charged for. It also makes the allocation of the services more efficient, because it encourages the individual departments to use only those services that they really need for their operations.

SERVICE CHARGES

Without a chargeback system, politics often prevails as the controlling factor in who receives IS services. Even if top management limits IS services, business units with strong political clout tend to receive more service than other units that may, objectively, need it more. This becomes less of a problem as units started paying for their service, but other problems appear.

For instance, although many users now know how to develop their own simple applications, they still must count on a central IS unit to satisfy most of their information needs. When a functional unit depends upon a central IS unit to provide a service, tensions may grow. The functional IS has only its department as a priority, while the central IS personnel prioritize requests from a corporate perspective. When a service is eventually delivered and charged, tension may build up if the users do not understand what their department is being charged for, and by what criteria.

WHAT IS CHARGEABLE? The items for which the serviced unit may be charged are:

Personnel Hours. Usually, this is the largest part of the charge for systems development or systems maintenance. The IS unit charges either a fixed hourly rate, or hourly rates that differ according to the level of expertise being provided.

Computer Time. This charge is normally billed to departments for the use of mainframe computers or computers on loan.

External Storage Space. IS departments charge for storing data based on the amount stored, charging by dollars per month using magnetic space (number of tracks) or tape (number of feet) per month.

Number of Input and Output Operations. Some IS departments charge business departments for each logon involving a shared computer.

Paper Output. Some IS departments charge business departments per page of paper printout.

Costs that cannot be definitely attributed to specific business units are generally not charged back. For example, the purchase price of any hardware or software that is to be shared by many departments cannot be charged directly to any one department.

DESIRABLE CHARGEBACK FEATURES

Chargeback methods are successful when they have the following features:

Accountability. Every element of the IS service—including personnel time, computer time, and paper—must be accounted for and attributed to the manager who has used it. The cost of some services, such as intraorganizational communication time, cannot be accurately allocated to individual units. Such costs are considered overhead and are absorbed by divisional or corporate headquarters.

Controllability. Managers who order services should be able to control what they purchase. The chargeback system should be designed so that business managers can determine the type and amount of service to purchase to best fit their specific information needs.

Timeliness. The IS unit must bill managers periodically, with reasonable intervals between billings, so that the managers can keep track of the IS costs they incur and change their request if they so wish.

Congruence with Organizational Goals. Chargeback rates should be established to encourage business units to use resources that are in the interests of the corporation, and to discourage business units from using services that are not in the corporation's overall interest. For example, a low hourly rate may be charged for IS personnel time spent on training employees to use their PC software to develop applications, if management wishes to encourage application development by users. A high per-page rate may be charged for the generation of paper reports if management wants to encourage online ad hoc reports.

CHARGEBACK CRITICISM The chargeback approach is not without its critics. The major argument against chargeback systems is that the expense may discourage managers from exploring IT opportunities for business activities. Because there is an element of long-term investment in adoption of IS technology, managers may opt to spend their budgets on other resources that they believe would generate immediate benefits.

OVERHEAD EXPENDITURES

IS units incur some costs that cannot be accurately attributed to individual activities performed for specific business units, such as research and development, and corporation-wide data communications installation and maintenance. These costs are often excluded from the chargeback scheme and treated as overhead expenses shared by the entire organization. If overhead charges were included in service charges, the company would end up either not doing any research and development or not providing any services.

CAREERS IN INFORMATION SYSTEMS

Like most professions, the IS trade is not fully cohesive. While systems analysis and software development occupy the majority of IS professionals, many specialize in narrowly defined areas. For example, some provide management consulting services, advising clients how to use technology to improve business processes without ever touching a client's computer. The following is a discussion of the responsibilities of IS professionals in typical areas of specialization.

IS personnel usually start their careers as **programmer/analysts** or **systems analysts**, a position that requires a broad range of skills (see Figure 9.12). A programmer/analyst is somewhat involved in the analysis of business needs and ISs, but the greater part of the job involves the programming of business applications. A systems analyst is involved in designing new ISs and in updating and maintaining existing ISs. This includes developing alternate system plans based on (1) analyzing system requirements provided by user input, (2) documenting development efforts and system features, and (3) providing adequate specifications for programmers to write code.

To succeed, systems analysts must possess excellent communication skills to translate users' descriptions of business processes into system concepts. They must be flexible enough to understand a wide range of business processes and ways in which IT can be applied to support them. Since analysts often deal with systems that serve more than one organizational unit, they must also understand organizational politics and be shrewd negotiators.

Most importantly, systems analysts must always keep in mind that they are **agents of change**, and that most people do not like change. Unlike many other occupations, theirs always involves the creation of a new system or the modification of existing ones. The new or modified system often changes human activities and organizational cultures. Since workers tend to resist change, systems analysts must be able to convince both line workers and managers that the change will benefit them. Thus, these professionals must possess good persuasion and presentation skills.

Senior systems analysts advance to become **project leaders**. In this capacity, they are put in charge of several analysts and programmers. They seek and allocate resources, such as personnel, hardware, and software, which are used in the development process. They use project management methods to plan activities and milestones, to control the utilization of resources, and to determine completion times.

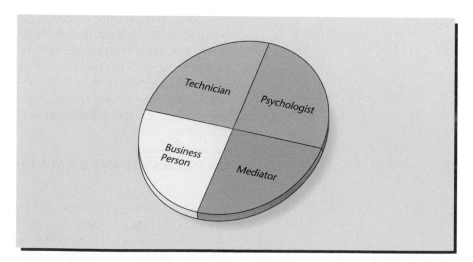

Figure 9.12 *The multiple skills of a systems analyst*

POINT OF INTEREST

3-D To The Rescue

Computer Associates, a large software development company, offers a three-dimensional set of network management tools. Imagine the system as applied to a corporation with offices in 60 different North American cities. The system administrator would hover over a map of North America with the company's office cities highlighted and connected by a web of lines. If there was a problem in San Francisco, a colored ball would appear over that city and the administrator could fly over and get a blow-up of the city block where the company's offices are located. The administrator could "fly" into the building, go to the appropriate floor, view the network layout, see an indicator showing which computer has a problem, go into the computer, and see whether it is a hardware or software problem. The administrator then can initiate the appropriate action, such as starting up a trouble ticker. "Looking at that visual interface is a lot better than looking at alarms or reports," said one expert.

Source: Adhikari, R., "VR: A Corporate Reality," InformationWeek, September 23, 1996, pp. 33–40.

Used by permission from Computer Associates International

THE DATABASE ADMINISTRATOR

The **database administrator** (DBA), the officer responsible for the databases of an organization, holds a very sensitive and powerful position. Since access to information often connotes power, this person must be not only technologically qualified, but also astute enough to reject requests for access to data from managers who do not have a real "need to know." (Recall our discussion of information politics in Chapter 8, "Managers and Their Information Needs.") The DBA must carefully consider how the data will be used, and is therefore also responsible for the development of database applications. In addition, the DBA must adhere to federal, state, and corporate regulations to ensure protection of the privacy of customers and employees. DBAs are responsible for the following areas:

◆ Overall planning and design of corporate databases

◆ Adoption of appropriate DBMSs and 4GLs for development of databases and database applications

◆ Planning and implementation of the physical organization and storage of databases

◆ Planning and implementation of the logical organization of databases

◆ Development of schemas

◆ Development and maintenance of data dictionaries

◆ Establishing security measures to assure authorized access and proper use

◆ Establishing failure-recovery and backup measures

◆ Establishing procedures to assure proper updates and data integrity

◆ Planning and implementing interfaces of internal databases with other organizations' ISs

◆ Managing database personnel

Soon, when object technology becomes ubiquitous, many of the database applications will be encapsulated in reusable objects. The DBA will also have to oversee the construction and maintenance of objects.

Usually, it takes 5–10 years of experience to qualify for this position, which commands salaries that may exceed $100,000, especially in large companies. In recent years, the position has become increasingly challenging because of rapid developments: new DBMSs, downsizing, and the move toward client/server architectures.

The latter development requires much attention from the DBA, because more and more employees access corporate databases. It is the responsibility of the DBA to provide appropriate software to employees so that they can create their own data-manipulation applications without compromising the integrity of the data.

THE TELECOMMUNICATIONS MANAGER

Among the IS areas, data communications is the one that has seen the most exciting developments in recent years. Not surprisingly, this area has also seen the greatest increase in corporate allocation of IS personnel since the early 1990s. The importance of telecommunications as an enabling technology is expected to sustain this trend for some years, allowing specialized professionals to be in great demand and to command high salaries.

ETHICS AND SOCIETY

Worker Displacements

Technological progress often leads to more efficient production processes, usually created by replacing labor with technology. When the first steam machines were installed in factories to mechanize the production of clothing and other products, thousands of manual workers lost their jobs. In a different industry, motorized agricultural machines replaced millions of human hands in the production of food. General Motors' layoff of some 23,000 employees in 1982, and thousands more in subsequent years, was directly or indirectly related to the deployment of modern computer-based robots. Information-intensive industries such as banking, insurance, and other service-oriented industries have gradually downsized their workforce because computers can do so many jobs more quickly, reliably, and efficiently than people. This phenomenon, known as "worker displacement," is widespread and will no doubt continue to grow. While some companies provide retraining, and others provide services to assist people in adjusting to loss of employment, economic realities dictate the need for this type of change. Worker displacement affects all industries where competition requires businesses to make decisions that optimize their performance. Trade unions have tried to stop the ongoing wave of worker displacement, but to no avail. Computer-based machinery and information systems are too appealing to commercial organizations to forego them.

Worker Displacement Reaches Out. Even the once most labor-intensive industries have replaced people with computers. For instance, consider Nucor, a steel mill in Crawfordsville, Indiana. As machines perform most of the dirty work, workers monitor computers to ensure that products meet quality standards. The workers have to be comfortable with statistical process control methods, not just with huge furnaces of molten lead.

While victims of worker displacement cannot be divided along age lines, there is some indication that older workers may find it more difficult to adapt to new technology, even though any new job they may find will probably require knowledge of computers as well. The economic reality is that within any given industry, workers who can use computers earn, on average, 15% more than those who cannot.

The Price of Progress. Worker displacement frequently involves cutting whole layers of middle managers. This is true because executives no longer need a "middleperson" to collect, process, and analyze data. Higher executives have direct access to information through the computers sitting on their desks.

Frustrated workers often blame their misfortune on the machines. In some cases, workers have tried to sabotage new computer systems that were perceived as threatening their job security. Employees of the U.S. Postal Service inserted paper clips into a computer that improved sorting productivity. But by and large, the days of destroying machines are gone. It is impossible to stop modernization in the workplace. And most people agree that, in the long run, a more efficient economy is good for all of us, even

(continued)

at the cost of many individuals' unhappiness. Even a U.S. Senator from New Jersey who lost her seat to the owner of Automated Data Processing (ADP) said: "In my campaign, I could argue that because of his computers many people had lost their jobs. It's a fact. But saying that would be unfair, because computers are good for society."

Consider what AT&T, the world's largest telephone service, figured in 1981: If the company were to serve its customers with the efficiency achieved by that year, but with the equipment of the 1930s, it would have to employ approximately 1 billion switchboard operators! Now, the switching is performed by computers. In 1992 the company announced that new computers with voice-recognition features would replace a third of its 18,000 long-distance operators within two years.

How much money is saved by using information technology instead of manual work? Figures are not available for every industry, but ATMs alone save American banks at least $1 billion per year in teller salaries.

Worker displacement also happens indirectly. Telecommunications reduce the need for travel and hotel services. The hotel and airline industries see a major portion of their business gone for good. As a result, workers are laid off. On the other hand, telecommunications specialists enjoy a growing demand for their expertise.

Worker Replacement. In the face of displacement claims, some studies show that computers do not always replace people. An extensive study for the British government showed that, on a national scale, the introduction of computers in business organizations did not cause a net reduction in personnel. In other studies, it was found that in many organizations the implementation of information systems actually created a need for additional workers. These organizations needed new skilled personnel to operate systems, which means that the same or a greater number of workers led to greater productivity.

For example, Japanese construction companies use robots to assemble buildings, as well as for support chores such as painting walls, pouring and smoothing concrete, and repotting plants. All of these jobs were once labor-intensive. Did the changes lead to worker displacement? Yes. But the Japanese companies retrained the manual construction workers to handle computerized controls, providing new jobs that are less dangerous.

In recent years, the term "retraining" has become almost synonymous with learning how to use a computer. However, ironically, progress in the computer field is gradually reducing the need for computer-training, as artificial intelligence and voice recognition remove the need for specialized training to run programs.

Regardless of the impact on society of worker displacement and worker replacement, it is the nature of business to make decisions based on business operations only. With increasing familiarity with computers, cross-training may make the redeployment of displaced workers increasingly likely.

The **telecommunications manager** is responsible for the acquisition, implementation, management, maintenance, and troubleshooting of computer networks throughout the organization. Since investment in telecommunications involves great amounts of money, data communications managers must carefully assess the future needs of the business, including finding the optimal answers to questions such as:

◆ What is the transmission capacity that will be needed over the next several years?

◆ What is the most cost-effective way to connect the various facilities?

◆ What are the most cost-beneficial measures for protecting our local networks from unauthorized intruders?

◆ Whom should we contract with for our Internet services?

The duties of the telecommunications manager include:

◆ Assessing current and future communications needs

◆ Planning local and wide area network topologies

◆ Recommending specific communications hardware and software

◆ Supervising technicians and support personnel, and hiring qualified consultants

◆ Providing ad hoc solutions to connectivity problems

◆ Providing advice in the purchase of hardware and software when shared networks are involved

THE WEBMASTER

The fast development of the World Wide Web and Web-like intraorganizational networks has created a new IS career: the Webmaster. The **Webmaster** is responsible for creating and maintaining the organization's Web site and its intranet's pages. (The WWW is discussed in detail in Chapter 6, "The Internet and Intranets.") Professional Webmasters must understand not only the technology of Web use, but the business and security schemes as well.

Increasingly, Webmasters are assigned also to help individual departments to create their own Web pages. As HTML editing programs become easier to use, increasing numbers of employees venture into developing personal and departmental Web pages, relying on Webmasters for support. As our discussion in Chapter 6 indicates, Web sites must be constantly changed and enhanced to draw visitors. Thus, Webmasters are increasingly involved in creative decision making that determines how to represent the organization on the Web. These decisions involve elements of marketing and graphic design. Depending on the size of a company and its Web and intranet activity, salaries range from $30,000 to $100,000. It is expected that the great demand for Webmasters will continue to grow as long as the growth in corporate utilization of the Web continues.

THE CHIEF INFORMATION OFFICER

The fact that a corporation has a **chief information officer (CIO)** reflects the importance that a company places in ISs as a strategic resource. Currently, more than half of the Fortune 500 companies have a CIO. About 8% of North American CIOs are women, and this rate is growing. As explained above, the CIO, who is responsible for all of the aspects of an organization's ISs, is often, but not always, a corporate vice president. In a centralized IS organization, the CIO supervises all the IS professionals. In a distributed organization, this person supervises the corporate IS unit directly, and the divisional IS personnel professionally.

1. **Be a leader**; do not only empower IS workers but lead by example.

2. **Be business-driven**, understand company strategy and know such things as why it's important to cut product development cycle times.

3. **Have a proven track record** as an experienced manager of IS projects.

4. **Be a pioneer** who can thrive on chaos.

5. **Be technologically adept.** You may not know how each technology works, but you must know how to ask the right questions.

6. **Be humble**, willing to admit when you don't understand something.

7. **Play on a team** and be comfortable working in a sometimes confusing matrix structure.

8. **Have intuition** and be able to make decisions quickly, without having every piece of information in hand first.

9. **Be entrepreneurial** and able to translate internal projects into externally marketed products when required.

Source: *Datamation*, April 15, 1994, p. 36.

Figure 9.13 *Nine commandments for successful, effective CIOs*

Unlike a lot of large companies, Roadway's CIO doesn't report to the vice president of finance. And technology isn't considered a mere subset of operations. Gerry Long, Roadway's chief technology executive, reports directly to the company president and sits in on top-level planning meetings at the transportation giant.

It hasn't always been that way. When Roadway's IS overhaul began in 1987, the firm's operations divisions were not well integrated with its technology functions. A complete reorganization of IS created a highly decentralized organization, with all systems projects "owned" by business groups. No technology is ever implemented without the full support and financial funding of a line manager.

"My people serve as technical tool builders, but they are guided by a model designed by the business users themselves," Long says. "Without this level of integration and cooperation, we wouldn't be nearly as successful."

Source: LaPlante, A., "Roadway CIO in the Executive Loop," *InfoWorld*, March 8, 1993. Reprinted by permission of InfoWorld.

A person who holds the position of CIO must have a wide variety of strengths, outlined in Figure 9.13, and must be prepared to play an important role in integrating the IS strategic plan into the organization's overall strategic plan. He or she must not only keep abreast of technical developments, but must also have a keen understanding of how different technologies can improve business processes or aid in the creation of new products and services.

The most important duties of a CIO are:

◆ Overseeing all IS research and development, including scouting new technologies that can be applied to emerging business needs and developing new products and services

◆ Overseeing the development of an IS infrastructure, including creating standard technologies and using organizational skills that will yield greater flexibility and shorter system development times

◆ Being the chief technologist, discovering how new technologies, such as data mining and virtual reality, can be applied to existing business needs

◆ Being the chief agent of change, using his or her company-wide perspective, knowledge of technology, and change-management skills to lead or guide the redesign of business processes

The CIO position may be very demanding. A survey of 400 U.S. and Canadian CIOs revealed an 18.8% annual turnover rate. The CIOs reported that "dismissed or demoted" was the reason for their predecessors' departures. Every year, about one fifth of North American CIOs leave their positions voluntarily, possibly for a more lucrative position with another company. About 10% are promoted to another top management position within the organization[1].

---

[1] "Leading Trends in Information Services," *Sixth Annual Survey of North American CIOs 1994*, Deloitte & Touche, 1994.

Soon to Come: A New Profession

Observers say that within a decade we should expect to see the rise of a new occupation: the **information engineer**. This person will be a well-rounded expert who can quickly solve problems that involve ISs in virtually any given area: databases, data communications, objects, systems prototyping, and perhaps also artificial intelligence.

The information engineer profession will arise in response to the need for IS operations to be cross-functional. This professional will not report to any business unit, but to the central IS organization. He or she will have to learn the needs of the entire enterprise, or of big parts of it, to be able to define requirements and design enterprise-wide ISs. The information engineer will be an expert at overcoming the two major challenges in planning and designing ISs: how to give the users access to the information they need, and only to the information they need; and how to enable business units to share information and communicate with each other in a timely fashion.

The information engineer will, most probably, head efforts of business-process re-engineering. This person will constantly look for opportunities to integrate IT into processes and create new business opportunities for the firm. Is there a school for training such professionals? Not yet. Perhaps the trend in some business schools to churn out the "techno-MBA" will produce the future information engineers.

THINK CRITICALLY

Is information engineer really a new occupation? If your answer is positive, what functions will this person fulfill that have not been fulfilled by other professionals? If your answer is negative, what (and whose) existing responsibilities will this occupation combine?

THE CHIEF KNOWLEDGE OFFICER

The **chief knowledge officer (CKO)** is a recently established top management position, most often found in large companies. While the CIO is responsible for the management of IT and the technical issues of ISs, the CKO is responsible for finding the appropriate resources of knowledge that are strategically important for the organization, including databases, Internet sites, and data resources offered commercially either through communications lines or on storage media such as compact discs. In service businesses, such as public accounting or management consulting firms, the CKO also devises methods to retain knowledge accumulated through interaction with clients. This reduces the need to "reinvent the wheel" with other clients who may need similar advice in the future.

In some organizations, the CKO is also responsible for making the business a **learning organization**. Therefore, some organizations call this person a **chief learning officer**. This officer looks for means to retain knowledge accumulated over time and ensure that managers and other professionals have access to information resources that help them learn how to perform their jobs better. When the CKO finds the resources, the CIO oversees the implementation of the knowledge dissemination through the firm's ISs. To succeed, the CKO must closely cooperate with the CIO.

THE INDEPENDENT CONSULTANT

Many IS professionals work for organizations for several years, accumulate experience, and then leave to become consultants. They offer their services as consultants to companies who lack qualified personnel for specific tasks. Usually, **IS consultants** are hired for a limited period of time, from several days to several months. In some cases, they are integrated into project teams composed of regular employees of the company.

While many consultants are simply programmers for hire, many others are experts in a specific area, such as telecommunications or database design. Some specialize in business process re-engineering. The latter provide advice to top management and are not involved in technical work.

With the rapid developments in telecommunications, we may see increasing numbers of IS professionals choosing this career path. Consultants can do much of their job from home via communications lines and collaborative software. This may promote a more flexible lifestyle, allowing a consultant to live in a desired, remote place, but do business with organizations located in large cities.

Restructuring the IS Organization at TransCanada

TransCanada Pipeline is Canada's largest transporter of natural gas and one of the largest on the American continent. Headquartered in Calgary, Alberta, its 1992 revenue was $3.8 billion, the company has a net income of $329 million, and it employs 1,800 people, 140 of whom are in the IS organization. The company grew to its current size over a very short period of time, with the number of customers increasing from 16 to 1,400 within five years amid major changes in the industry—including deregulation, which usually changes the way companies price their products and services.

Until 1986, TransCanada had a traditional highly centralized IS organization, but the huge growth in business led the company to hire a new chief information officer, who found the existing centralized system unable to cope with the new business. He encountered a conventional mainframe environment, home-grown applications down to the general ledger level, layers of old code, operational troubles, and lagging performance in information technology compared to other firms in the industry.

The new CIO decided to shake up the IS organization. He started with an overall evaluation conducted by an outside consulting firm. The consultants recommended the following measures: (1) reorganize the IS function into a combination of decentralized IS teams supporting the business units, and a centralized body of expertise, (2) provide personal productivity software tools, such as spreadsheets, to users to improve IS operations credibility, (3) freeze the current computing environment and stop purchases or application development in the old style, and (4) initiate pilot projects to "build small," using midrange computers.

This was followed by a preliminary development plan and a five-year conversion and development plan. The policy and direction were widely published. More than 200 projects were launched during 1987 and 1988, and every existing system was rewritten over three and a half years.

In 1990, TransCanada headquarters was moved from Toronto to Calgary. In the same year, the company moved from the old mainframe to a network of 65 VAX minicomputers, 1,400 Macintoshes, 70 other PCs, and 37 client/server applications.

The crucial point was the creation of IS teams to support the business of different functional units. The TransCanada IS organization now has a total of 21 business units and a central Shared Resource Group. The IS teams consist of between one and ten members in each business unit. The functional systems teams are responsible for requirements, application development, and systems support. The Shared Resource Group sets and enforces IT standards, controls the IT budget, and retains responsibility for IS training and human resource issues. The teams are physically located in the business units, but they report to the central IS group to ensure professional training and career development, flexibility to shift resources, and adherence to established standards.

IS personnel are actively transferred between business units and back to the Shared Resources Group to give them a variety of experience, as well as ongoing contact with other IS professionals. "We feel it's really important for IS people to be a part of a group of people from the same profession with whom they can share ideas," says Eric Baerg, manager of engineering field systems. He says this approach helps the IS staff build strong links with line business units, without sacrificing training and career-planning support or adherence to the company-wide IT architecture.

Each team acts as an IT advocate. It becomes intimately familiar with the business operations and competitive requirements. It links the worlds of business and technology. However, the support team does not develop applications on its own. It determines the application requirements, works out the justifications, timing, and migration to the new system, and creates development teams by calling on the central staff, other IS support teams, and temporary hires.

The central body of technological experts has several responsibilities, including: desktop productivity tools, data management, technical services and support, the communications network, the help desk, budgeting, and planning. The talent split and orientation of these two groups are clearly different, so policies are established to guarantee cross-functional awareness to ensure that the experts are kept in close contact with the users.

TransCanada's adoption of a hybrid IS organization reaped great benefits: (1) better responsiveness to the user, and allowing the user to call the shots, (2) cost control that puts the responsibility for justifying spending with the user (along with the elimination of an arbitrary spending limit for the IS department), (3) better productivity in systems development through distributed IS resources and new development styles based on standards that provide economies of scale, and (4) flexible human and equipment resources to meet changing requirements. One measure of how successful this program has been is that each of the 18 business units has significantly increased its demands for new ISs from year to year. The partnership concept is working.

Source: Rosser, W., "The new model IS organization: A case study," IS Research Note K-970–1045, 2/21/94, the Gartner Group, and "How one hybrid IS works," Datamation, July 15, 1994, p. 62.

Questions

1. What is the hardware equipment that indicates TransCanada's originally had a highly centralized IS architecture?

2. The consultants recommended redeploying the IS personnel. Which figure in this chapter reflects best the recommended deployment?

3. IS personnel are frequently transferred between their line units and the headquarters' Shared Resources Group. What is the purpose of this practice?

Infighting at Company X

This is the case of the IS organization of a large, diversified manufacturing company, and the solutions its IS groups developed to meet client demands. This company had a central IS group whose mission was to maintain an enterprise-wide IT architecture plan and to provide utility services, such as the data center and wide area communications to the entire organization. Because the central group was the sole support organization for corporate headquarters, it also offered help desk services, telecommunications support, education and training, and applications development. The company's five operating divisions could either secure services from the central IS group, or hire their own IS personnel. Although all the operating divisions used some services from the central IS group, each had chosen to establish its own IS organization.

Conflicts

There was no restriction on the type of services these divisional IS groups could provide, even if central IS could provide the same service more cost-effectively. Consequently, the central IS group and the divisional IS groups became competitors, and their working relationships became strained. The operational IS groups viewed the central group as a mainframe-oriented, power-seeking bureaucracy. While this negative perception might have been true in the past, the central IS group had taken several steps to change. A client representative was assigned to each operating division to facilitate communications between the central and divisional IS groups. Quarterly meetings were held with the senior staff of the divisional IS groups to cover service and planning issues. None of these actions seemed to have a positive impact.

From a practical viewpoint, the corporate IS group served two groups: the end users throughout the organization, and the divisional IS groups. The challenges of running divisional IS groups' customized applications together with services provided by the central IS group (such as the centralized data center) exacerbated the already strained relationships. Whereas end users used to call one help desk number to report any application problem, now it was sometimes difficult to determine whom to consult to resolve problems. Although the divisional IS groups believed that end user problems were resolved quickly, much time was lost "behind the scenes" in negotiating which technical-support group should absorb the responsibility and costs of problem resolution.

Gauging the Problem

In seeking a solution to this operational problem, the central IS group decided to conduct a client satisfaction survey. In doing so, it regarded divisional IS professionals and end users as two distinct client groups. To ensure that the survey results would be viewed as reliable by all IS organizations, the central IS group's survey team included its divisional peers in every step of the process. Two separate survey questionnaires were developed—one for divisional IS group members and one for end users. The questionnaire for the divisional IS professionals contained detailed information about the quality of specific central IS services. The questionnaire for end users focused on overall service quality and the responsiveness of IS professionals.

What were the survey findings? The divisional IS professionals did not view the central IS group as a leader or facilitator in helping the enterprise leverage IT. They thought chargeback costs were too high and technical support was inadequate. The feedback on specific services showed that the more familiar the users were with a system, the lower they rated its quality. In addition, divisional IS professionals did not feel that the central IS organization treated them as valued clients.

End users were enthusiastic about the potential of IT to resolve their business problems, but more than half of them did not know about the services available to them. Most found it difficult to find the right IS person to help them resolve a problem. In addition, users felt they had inadequate training, and that the training they were given was not customized enough to their own system use.

While the central and divisional IS groups had recognized that there were problems among the organizations, none had expected the impact on the end users to be so strong. All of the IS groups recognized that their clients felt disenfranchised from any IS organization. In fact, the survey confirmed that some divisional end user departments had avoided both the central and divisional IS groups by setting up small IS groups to manage local systems.

Fixing the Problem

The survey underscored the need to resolve territorial disputes and refocus the groups' energies on improving customer service. In addition, the divisional IS groups recognized that they were spending too much time trying to control how the central IS group managed its core business. The central IS group and the five divisional groups realized that organization and culture had to change across the board. Organizational changes implemented included:

Centralizing End User Technical Support. One person would "take ownership" of an end user until problem resolution. End users would work with only one IS person in reporting and resolving a request for technical support. To do this, the help desk function was centralized. Although it might be necessary for more than one person to contact the end user to resolve a problem, the primary client contact would keep the client informed of how and when a problem would be resolved.

Empowering the Client Representative. Although the central IS group had set up a client representative program, which had a representative from each division communicating requests to the central IS group, business managers had come to rely on their representative for matters relating to services provided both centrally and locally. Client representatives frequently found themselves caught in the middle of intradepartmental friction, with no power to resolve disputes. To rectify this situation, the client representative was given the authority to assign someone to fix the client's problem, with disputes resolved at a later time. In addition, the client representative's position was raised and opened to central and divisional IS professionals, as well as to (non-IS) business-unit members. In time, the client representative position was regarded as a career "stepping stone" within the IS community.

Rotating IS Staff. IS staff would rotate between central and divisional IS organizations. Rotation would accelerate career opportunities for IS professionals and facilitate knowledge-base transfer across business units. In addition, rotation would draw loyalty away from a particular IS organization and toward the client.

Training IS Managers in Product Marketing, and Establishing Interdepartmental Teams for Bundled Services. Each IS manager was responsible for developing a product development plan and was measured against that plan. The most important measurement criterion was client satisfaction with that service. Bundled services (composed of central and divisional IS service elements) were measured as a single product. Recognizing that some clients had already chosen other IT suppliers, IS managers realized that real competition was from external suppliers and clients themselves— not other internal IS shops.

Providing Rewards and Incentives at All Levels of IS for Achieving Client Service Goals. IS staff who did not personally interact with clients had difficulty understanding that their jobs ultimately affected the quality of client service. Therefore, IS managers created a client service recognition program that recognized staff members each quarter with small bonuses and gifts for achieving service goals.

Re-evaluating Roles of the Central and Divisional IS Organizations. In addition to continuing to provide utility services, the divisional IS groups asked the central IS group to take on a larger IT consulting role. The divisional groups also charged the central IS group with the responsibility of helping the divisions exchange information with one another, as well as with the central IS group.

Like children whose parents do not get along, end users ultimately are affected by infighting among IS groups. The solution is establishing common goals and improving communications among organizational units.

Source: Flynn, S., "Case study of a hybrid IS organization, Part 1," Research Note K-970–1043, and -1044 2/21/94, Gartner Group.

Questions

1. Relationships between the central IS group and the divisional IS groups became strained. Why?

2. There were several missed potentials in the company with respect to IS services and development of new applications. List them and explain why the opportunities were missed.

3. One of the changes that took place was that end user problems would be resolved by a single IS professional from beginning to end. Why is a "single-point of contact" so important in providing end user support?

The IT-Conscious CEO

When he took over Schlage Lock as CEO, Tom Fields didn't have any IS experience on his resume, nor was he much of an IT user himself. A large business-process re-engineering project, however, has forced Fields not only to take a hard look at IT but to actually take an active role in establishing IT strategy and to help implement projects. His new relationship to IT serves as at least one model of how a modern CEO should view IT.

Schlage is in a relatively slow-growing business, making door hardware for residential and commercial buildings. Fields decided that, in order to increase growth, Schlage had to improve customer service, and replace the order fulfillment process, which had become too complex. Fields initiated a major study of all of Schlage's key business processes and systems. That led to a two-pronged improvement approach: re-engineer critical business processes and, in parallel, rewrite major systems, moving them from their existing batch mainframe platforms to PCs.

But, unlike other CEOs, Fields didn't just delegate the implementation. He got involved, putting together cross-functional IS and user teams, sponsoring critical projects, and beefing up his own IT user skills. Fields even joined other Schlage business and IT managers in classes at The Center for Project

Management in San Ramon, California, where he learned about running IT and other types of projects. Fields says he decided to drive the IT changes himself in order to set an example for others at Schlage.

"We were coming into a period of radical change, and the rest of the organization needed to know clearly that this was coming from the top and that it was supported there," says Fields. "It kind of says, 'You don't have a choice anymore.'" Fields says he has learned plenty about IT. "It's a whole different world out there now with client/server," he says. "The hardware's less expensive, and application development is quicker. But it's still a very complex process."

Source: "This CEO Gets IT," Datamation, September 15, 1994, p. 60.

Questions

1. Some people would say that Fields is a bad delegator. Do you agree? Why, or why not?

2. Why did Fields take IT classes? Should all CEOs take such classes? Explain.

SUMMARY

Organizations deploy their IS resources in different ways. The manner in which the resources are organized is often referred to as **IS architecture**. In a **centralized architecture**, the organization is served by a mainframe computer or several smaller computers centrally located. Workers use PCs and terminals to access data and applications that reside on these central computers. The main advantage of this arrangement is the tight control that management retains over information resources.

In a **decentralized architecture**, business units, often geographically remote, have their own local area networks connecting PCs and terminals to a local larger computer. In extreme cases, the local resources are not connected to those of headquarters or other sites. Such an arrangement affords independent decision making regarding IS resources, so that the resources can best fit local needs.

In a **distributed IS architecture**, local resources are connected to headquarters and other sites of the organization. While maintaining a measure of independent decision making on IS resources, each site can enjoy the resources of other sites. Management still maintains main control. Many organizations are now moving in this direction.

There are many ways to organize an IS unit. At one extreme is a centralized organization where all of the IS professionals report to the **CIO** or another person who is the highest IS authority. The unit is responsible for systems development and maintenance, communications networks, research and development, data administration, and the **information center**. The information center coordinates and controls the purchasing of hardware and software and also provides training and support. The best information centers provide a single contact point from which calls for help are routed to the appropriate expert. At the other end of the organization spectrum is the **functionally managed IS** where business units have their own IS personnel to deal with their daily needs. However, responsibility for larger systems, especially those serving several departments, remains with the corporate IS unit, as do responsibilities for corporate communications networks, research and development, and other activities that impact the organization as a whole.

Centralized IS management has several advantages: standardized hardware, common software, easier training, common reporting systems, effective planning of shared systems, efficient use of personnel, and accommodation of tight control by management.

Factors influencing decentralization of IS management include: better fit of systems to particular needs of business units, timely response to requests by business units, encouragement of end user computing, reduced telecommunications costs, encouragement of innovation, and accommodation of decentralized management style.

In recent years, organizations have moved from mainframes to smaller, powerful computers. This is popularly called **downsizing**. Also, the notion of **re-engineering** is taking hold in many organizations. Re-engineering of business processes almost always involves the implementation of new ISs.

Successful use of IS technology depends on understanding and collaboration between managers of business units and IS managers. IS managers must have a broad understanding of business activities. They are expected to respond promptly to the information needs of business units, use jargon-free language when dealing with their non-IS clients, explain what is and what is not possible with ISs, detail the resources that would be needed to develop and maintain a new IS, and designate personnel who will be responsible for resolving problems reported by the users.

IS managers expect business managers to project their future information needs, clearly explain the business processes that IS should support, and thoroughly detail the features they desire in the new IS.

To encourage proper utilization of resources, organizations implement **chargeback** methods, by which departments are charged for their use of IS resources. Successful chargeback systems make managers accountable for their use of IS resources. They let managers control IS use, provide timely usage reports, link the charges to the benefits of usage, and are congruent with general IS goals.

In a chargeback system, IS departments often charge users for personnel hours, computer time, external storage space per period, the number of input and output operations on shared computers, and the amount of paper output.

IS professionals pursue different careers, including **systems analyst, database administrator, data communications manager, Webmaster, chief information officer**, and **chief knowledge officer**. Many IS professionals elect to be **independent consultants**.

The integration of ISs in almost every aspect of business creates an inevitable problem of worker displacement. Millions of people have lost their jobs, but businesses can retain some workers to perform their former jobs with the newly installed computers.

REVIEW, DISCUSS, AND EXPLORE

REVIEW AND DISCUSSION QUESTIONS

1. What are centralized and decentralized IS architectures?

2. Many organizations prefer distributed IS architecture. What is it, and what are its advantages over fully centralized and fully decentralized architectures?

3. What are the advantages of centralized and decentralized IS management?

4. What is "downsizing"? Why do we find only limited downsizing in research institutions and organizations that process large amounts of data?

5. What is business process re-engineering? Why is it so often carried out with new ways of using ISs?

6. Why should IS managers understand business processes, even though their expertise is IT?

7. What is professional jargon? When is it fine to use professional jargon, and when should it not be used?

8. What type of businesses are most likely to adopt a centrally managed IS organization?

9. What type of businesses are most likely to adopt a functionally managed IS organization?

10. What are the responsibilities of the information center?

11. Why is it important for the help desk to provide users with a single point of contact?

12. What is the purpose of chargebacks?

13. Can you think of chargeable items that are not mentioned in this chapter?

14. If you were to choose a career in IS, what would you choose (other than CIO), and why?

15. One of the desired qualities of a CIO is to "be entrepreneurial." Why?

16. *Ethics and Society*: Many workers have lost their jobs because of new computer systems. Can these people still be utilized? How? Can the solution you suggest be implemented in all situations?

CONCEPT ACTIVITY

Interview an experienced systems analyst. Ask for examples that show how the person handles different aspects of the profession: psychological, political, and so on. Write a report listing at least one example for each of these aspects of the person's career.

Elk-tronix, Inc. has a chargeback system for IS services. Each department is charged for direct services rendered by IS personnel. Prepare a spreadsheet for the charges of departments 3424, 3556, and 3644 according to the following elements:

a. Systems analyst: $45.30/hour

b. Help desk: $25.50/hour

c. CPU time of the company's mainframe computer: $10.75/second

d. Printed page: $0.02 each

e. Mainframe's disk space: $7/MB per month

f. 3.5-inch floppy disk: $0.50 each

g. Dedicated local equipment: at cost

Last month, Dept. 3556 consumed the following services:

Two systems analysts spent seven hours each with department workers to help the department develop a small application. The department personnel spent a total of 56 hours on the project. It used nine 3.5-inch disks.

The department continued to maintain its 45 MB database on the mainframe. At the beginning of the month, another MB of data were added. Sixteen seconds of CPU time were used.

The IS personnel purchased a $495.00 laser printer for the department.

Enter the appropriate amounts in a spreadsheet. What was the total charge of IS services to Dept. 3556 for last month?

Turn in: (1) a disk with your spreadsheet, (2) a paper report for Dept. 3556.

TEAM ACTIVITY

Approach the CIO of a local company and ask permission to interview that person and an end user in the same company who uses IS applications and services frequently. Ask both people to tell you the strengths and weaknesses of the services rendered by the company's IS personnel. Prepare a list of the points you collected from each party. Compare the two lists. What are the points of difference? Write your own analysis: Why do the parties have different perceptions of those points?

EXPLORE THE WEB

Many organizations use the Web to recruit professionals. Explore the Web and find three job offers for systems analysts. Write down the URL of each site (so that your professor can verify your work) and summarize the qualifications required. Compare the requirements with those mentioned in this chapter. What is missing in this chapter? What is not listed by the firms?

Chapter **10**

Information Systems in Business Functions

Streamlining With IT

3M in Minneapolis, Minnesota, is one of the world's largest mining and manufacturing corporations. In 1996, the company sold 50,000 different products for more than $15 billion. The company knew it was wasting millions of dollars maintaining too much inventory, and that it was compromising its competitive edge by taking too long to deliver its multitude of products through its intricate distribution systems. Management set out to meet the challenge of cutting delivery time and reducing inventory levels to the minimum necessary to keep delivery satisfactory.

The solution to 3M's ill-managed inventory and too-long delivery times came with Rhythm, a system that creates schedules based on operational limits or constraints set by the user, such as: the maximum amount of time allowed between receiving and shipping an order, the maximum amount of inventory allowed in the warehouse, the maximum number of workers available, or the maximum amount of time between ordering and receiving raw goods. Referred to as a constraint-based scheduling system, Rhythm computes the optimum way to schedule both production and distribution, within the set constraints.

Because the application works in real time, a plant manager or scheduler can take a rush order and, using a desktop computer, juggle production schedules right away. One of the results described by Dave Drew, 3M' vice-president of information technology, is that manufacturing applications are more closely integrated with the supply chain, and all the other facets of the business, than they were before using Rhythm. Informed, up-to-the-minute decision making for supply-chain issues is something manufacturers desperately need and want, according to Drew and other experts.

The supply chain is the sequence of activities in a manufacturing enterprise, from purchasing raw materials, through using them in the different phases of the manufacture and assembly stages, to the supply of the finished product. Rhythm reports bottlenecks in the supply chain, and helps managers to quickly open them. For instance, the system may designate another production line where managers can move resources, to minimize delays that would increase labor and warehousing costs. The new system saves many dollars.

Source: Kerr, D., "In Rhythm with Users," *InformationWeek*, September 16, 1996, pp. 61–62.

LEARNING OBJECTIVES

In an economy that produces and consumes so much information, managers must know how to use information systems in virtually every business activity. Managers must have an overall understanding of all elements of a system, so that they know what options are available to them to control costs, prices, and the uses of resources. None of these activities or the decision making that underlies management is possible without useful information. And the best tool to handle this important resource is information technology, which is used in a broad range of business functions across different industries.

When you finish this chapter, you will:

◆ Understand how processes in different business functions relate to each other

◆ Understand how ISs of different business functions can support each other

◆ Understand how information technology is used in the most common business functions to make business processes more effective and more efficient

◆ Be able to identify areas in business where information technology can facilitate the work of managers and knowledge workers (such as engineers, designers, and sales representatives)

EFFECTIVENESS AND EFFICIENCY

It is often stated that the use of information technology makes our work more effective, more efficient, or both. What do these terms mean? **Effectiveness** defines the degree to which a goal is achieved. Thus, a system is more or less effective depending upon (1) how much of its goal is achieved, and (2) the degree to which it brings about better outcomes than another system.

Efficiency is determined by the relationship between the resources expended and the benefits gained in achieving a goal. Expressed mathematically,

$$\text{Efficiency} = \frac{\text{Benefits}}{\text{Costs}}$$

Thus, one system is more efficient than another if the costs to operate it are lower for the same or greater quality of the product, or if the quality of the product is greater for the same or lower costs. The term **productivity** is commonly used as a synonym for efficiency. However, productivity is specifically the efficiency of *human* resources. Productivity is improved when fewer workers are required to produce the same amount of output, or, alternately, when the same number of workers produce a larger output. The closer the result of an effort is to the ultimate goal, the more effective the effort is. The fewer the resources spent on achieving a goal, the more efficient the effort.

Suppose you designed a new car to reach a speed of 60 miles per hour in 10 seconds. If you managed to build it, then you produced the product effectively. If the car does not meet the requirement, your effort has been ineffective. If a competitor made a car with the same features and performance, but used fewer people and fewer resources, then he was as effective but more efficient than you.

ISs have proven to contribute both to the effectiveness and efficiency of businesses, especially when strategically positioned in specific business functions, such as accounting, finance, and engineering, and especially when used to help companies achieve their goals more quickly by facilitating collaborative work (see Figure 10.1). ISs can be used in a wide variety of applications, from

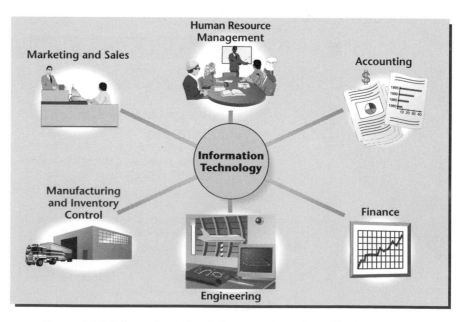

Figure 10.1 *Information technology supports a variety of business functions.*

automating manual processes to creating innovative products and services; from shortening routine processes, to placing an organization in a strategic position. The following is a discussion of how ISs have changed some of the most common functions in business.

You will notice below that the role of information systems in business is addressed one business function at a time. While organizing the information this way is less than ideal, most businesses do operate many ISs separately: one for engineering, one for marketing, one for finance, and so on. This is usually done because systems developed at different times for different business functions are often incompatible in hardware, software, data sharing, and the like. However, as you may remember from Chapter 1, "Business Information Systems: An Introduction," business functions do in fact have substantial information interdependencies. Systems thinking tells us that ideally, ISs supporting different functions would be connected so that information from one system could flow into another accurately and without delay. For example, information resulting from market research could serve the formulation of product requirements on one hand, and the sales force on the other. Figure 10.2 illustrates information systems that are commonly used in business functions, and the interdependencies among them. Organizations lucky enough to create systems from the ground up try to implement this model.

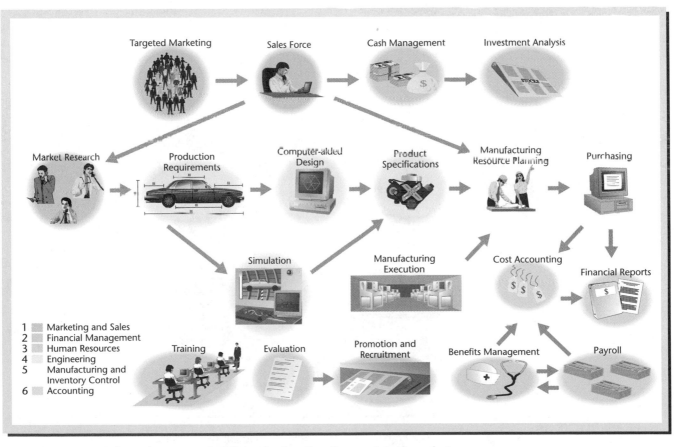

Figure 10.2 *Information systems in different business functions are interdependent.*

The End of A Tradition

ACCOUNTING

Several years ago, the board of directors of the Chicago futures exchange tried to computerize bidding. The attempt failed because traders preferred the traditional "scribble and shout" method. With the advent of PDAs (personal digital assistants), the board tried again and failed for the same reason. But a new custom handheld machine has made the grade, now that its cordless stylus has been redesigned to withstand being dropped and stomped in a trading-pit frenzy. Other features required in the pits: an interface anyone can figure out, weight under a pound, eight-hour battery life, a vibrating hand grip to signal when a trade doesn't go through (a buzzer wouldn't be heard over the din), handwriting recognition that actually works (thanks to the limited range of codes the device is required to translate), and a strap to keep the device from flying off when traders frantically wave their arms to bid and offer.

Source: "An audit trail for pork belly futures," *Datamation*, May 1, 1994, p. 24.

Accounting was among the earliest business functions to embrace IS technology because of the routine manner in which transactions are posted and processed. Virtually all of the businesses in the western world use IT for accounting. General ledger, accounts receivable, accounts payable, and cash flow books conveniently lend themselves to computerization, and balance sheets and profit and loss statements can easily be generated from the records. There are also systems to manage capital investments (see Figure 10.3).

Typically, accounting ISs receive records of routine business transactions—such as the purchase of raw materials or services, or the sale of manufactured goods—from transaction processing systems (TPSs). Every purchase of raw materials or services is automatically routed to the accounts payable system. The information is later used to produce checks, and a check reconciliation program reconciles the checks against the company's bank account. Whenever a sale is recorded, the transaction is routed to the accounts receivable system, among other destinations. The firm's comptroller can pull a list of outstanding customer debts to keep track of cash receipts. The totals of the accounts receivable and accounts payable are automatically transferred to the balance sheet whenever one is requested. Balance sheets, profit and loss statements, and cash flow information with accounting ISs can be prepared for perusal at any given time, not only at the end of the year.

Cost accounting systems, which are used to accumulate data about the costs involved in producing specific products—including the costs of labor, raw materials, and purchased services—make excellent use of ISs to compile data to establish pricing. ISs are also used to help allocate costs to specific work orders. When interfaced with payroll and purchasing ISs, a cost accounting system automatically captures records of every penny spent (originally recorded in the payroll and purchasing system) and routes the expenses to the appropriate work order.

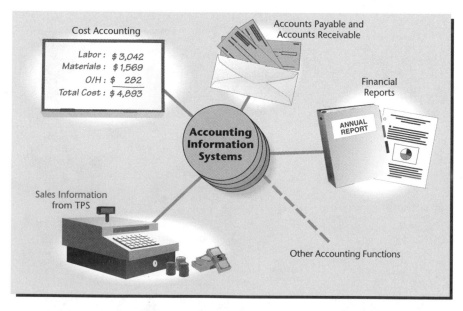

Figure 10.3 *Accounting information systems include features that reflect up-to-date performance of the organization in financial terms.*

Accounting ISs are also used extensively for managerial purposes, assisting in organizing quarterly and annual divisional and corporate budgets, and helping managers control budgets by tracking income and expense in real time. Effective **budget systems** can be interfaced with cash management ISs, requiring that payments be allocated to appropriate budgetary line items, and that cash receipts be credited to appropriate income budgetary items.

The widespread use of accounting ISs has placed new demands on auditors, creating a new specialty called **electronic data processing audit** or **EDP audit**, which ensures that electronic systems comply with standard regulations and acceptable rules, and ensures that the systems cannot be manipulated to circumvent these principles.

FINANCE

The health of a firm is often measured by its finances, and financial management can be significantly improved by using ISs (see Figure 10.4). The job of financial managers, including the firm's comptroller and treasurer, is (1) to collect payables as soon as possible, (2) to make payments by the latest time allowable by contract or law, (3) to ensure that sufficient funds are available for day-to-day operations, and (4) to take advantage of opportunities to accrue the highest yield on funds not used for current activities.

CASH MANAGEMENT

Financial information systems help managers keep track of a company's finances. Every payment and cash receipt is recorded to reflect cash movement, plans for company finances are tracked using budgeting software, and investments are managed using capital investment systems, which balance a company's need to accrue interest on idle money versus the need to access cash for business operations. Systems that deal specifically with cash are often called **cash management systems**. They are used to execute cash transactions, with financial institutions transferring huge amounts of money using electronic funds transfer (EFT). EFT is used in more than $200 billion of transactions daily in New York City alone, and twice that amount throughout the U.S.

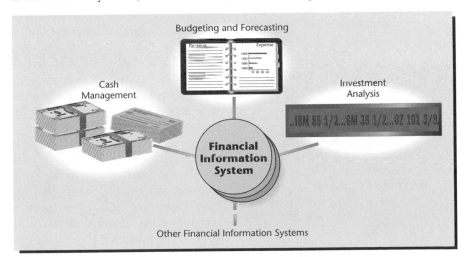

Figure 10.4 *Financial information systems help manage cash and investment portfolios.*

INVESTMENT ANALYSIS AND SERVICE

The ability of financial ISs to record thousands and millions of security prices and their daily changes over long periods of time, coupled with flexible DBMS operations, puts powerful analysis tools in the hands of investment managers. Within seconds, using a financial IS, an investment analyst can chart the prices of a specific stock or bond over a given period and build extrapolation models to help delineate trends.

The same systems can be used to transmit buy and sell orders through communications lines in a matter of seconds. Even the smallest investment firm can inexpensively provide clients with a detailed statement listing their portfolio, periodic yield, and the current price of the portfolio, with all calculations performed by the system.

Some financial services would simply not be possible without IS technology. Consider the cash management accounts used by millions of businesses to manage investments. Extra cash can be invested in securities only because all records are connected through an IS, so that any amount of investment can be liquidated by simply writing a check. And the system also automatically generates a combined statement of deposits, investments, and liquidations. In the same way, mutual fund investors can track their investments and even buy securities, sell securities, and transfer funds, by accessing the IS of the managing company and receiving a daily update of their investment—through the telephone or via the Internet—directly from the system. Before the late 1970s, this type of transaction took days or more, and was done totally by hand.

ISs now combine with other special services to provide subscriber brokers with news, in addition to stock prices, commodity prices, and currency exchanges from multiple locations across the world, within seconds. Consider what happens when the exchange rate of a foreign currency fluctuates by a fraction of a percent. A brokerage house can make a profit of several thousand dollars within three minutes of buying and selling several million dollars' worth of the foreign currency. Information technology has enabled many smaller companies

Used by permission from Fidelity Investments

to enter the arena, thereby making the international financial market a more stable one.

Financial ISs provide new tools for visualizing decision-making factors in three-dimensional graphics, which managers at financial institutions such as insurance companies find useful in managing their portfolios of stocks, bonds, and other commercial papers. Some of the most important factors these financiers must consider are (1) risk, measured as the variability of the paper's yield in the past, (2) expected return, and (3) liquidity (a measure of how fast an investment can be turned into cash). Special programs help calculate these factors and present the results either in tables or as graphs.

ENGINEERING

The time between the adoption of an idea for a product and the completion of a prototype that can be mass-manufactured is devoted to engineering, and is known as **engineering lead time** or **time-to-market**. Minimizing this time is one of the keys to maintaining a competitive edge, because it doesn't give competitors time to introduce their products first. The automotive industry shows how ISs can contribute significantly to this effort. Over the past decade, these companies have used ISs to reduce the time from product concept to market from seven to three years, mostly by using ISs in engineering.

The greatest contribution of IT to engineering is in the area of **computer-aided design (CAD)** and rapid **prototyping** (creation of one-of-a-kind products to test design in three dimensions). Instead of using the traditional paper and pencil, engineers and technicians can use computers to quickly modify and store drawings electronically. With groupware software, much of this process can be performed in collaboration: Engineers can conduct remote conferences while viewing and developing plans and drawings together. Sophisticated systems then allow manufacturing departments to feed the data of the electronic drawings into **computerized numeric control (CNC)** machines that take the

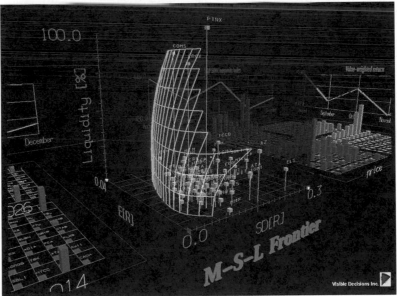

Used by permission from Andrew W. Lo, Director MIT Laboratory for Financial Engineering and Visible Decisions, Inc.

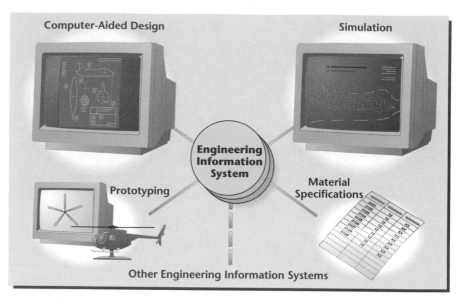

Figure 10.5 *Engineering information systems aid engineers in designing new products and simulating operations.*

data and create instructions for robots on how to manufacture and assemble prototypes. Ultimately, engineers can design the manufacturing process directly from the original drawings, a process that in the past was enormously time-consuming (see Figure 10.5).

One example of applying IT to make engineering more precise and the engineering process more efficient is the design and manufacture of the Boeing 777 aircraft, unveiled in 1994. Executives from various airline companies (who are the potential buyers of the aircraft) assisted Boeing engineers with valuable information for its design. Every component and system—from toilet seats to the fold-up wings—was designed using computer-aided systems. This eliminated the extremely time-consuming and expensive step of building a wooden model of the full-sized plane to check that all systems work together and that the aircraft can in fact be constructed. With the new computerized system, Boeing enjoyed 20% fewer errors in manufacturing.

Computer-aided design systems significantly shorten the time needed to produce drawings and complete the design of new products.

Used by permission from Ashlar, Inc.

MANUFACTURING AND INVENTORY CONTROL

Manufacturing is the processing of raw materials into physical products. Manufacturing is more complex to manage than most services, because, in addition to customers and personnel, it involves elements that the service sector does not deal with: purchasing of raw materials, warehousing of raw materials, and running of production and assembly lines. ISs have been instrumental in reducing manufacturing costs, including the costs of managing resources and controlling inventory (see Figure 10.6).

Qiagen, a biotech company, has a 40-person sales force spread over the United States and Canada. Headquarters used to share information with sales reps via phone and overnight delivery. With no formal structure in place, reps were often in the dark about new sales leads in their area. To rectify the problem, Qiagen invested $1,500 per user in a sales force automation program, and gave each of its reps laptops. Now reps dial in via modem to the company for weekly updates. Hot leads no longer fall through the cracks, and Qiagen no longer pays a fortune to Federal Express.

Source: "Tapping in Remote Reps," *Inc.*, July 1996. Reprinted with permission, *Inc.* magazine. Copyright ©1996 by Goldhirsh Group, 38 Commercial Wharf, Boston MA 02110.

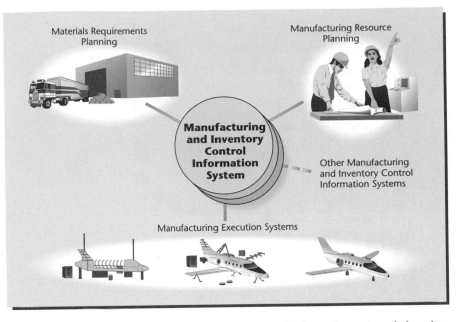

Figure 10.6 *Manufacturing and inventory control information systems help reduce cycle times and the cost of maintaining inventory.*

Information technology helps in the following manufacturing activities:

◆ It helps schedule activities in the plant, taking into account the capacity and availability of all resources: machines, personnel, tooling, and raw and interim materials.

◆ It helps plan material requirements based on current and forecast demand.

◆ It helps reallocate material rapidly from one order to another, to fulfill required due dates.

◆ It allows users to manage inventories dynamically, taking into consideration demand and the responsiveness of all work centers.

◆ It helps to group work orders by "characteristics" of the items ordered, such as color and width of products, and to balance setup minimization versus on-time deliveries.

◆ It considers the qualifications of each resource (such as qualified labor, setup crews, and specialized tools) to accomplish its task.

Probably the most important achievement of IT in manufacturing is that it improves agility: the ability of a company to adjust its manufacturing process in real time to meet both market and manufacturing demands. For instance, people and raw materials can be moved from one plant to another to accommodate machine breakdown or customer emergency, and design changes can be implemented quickly to respond to changes in customer wishes.

Surveys show that manufacturing companies realize the great potential of ISs. A 1994 survey by Deloitte & Touche found that both in 1992 and in 1993 manufacturing companies led other sectors in the number of re-engineering projects (the massive changes that lead to huge improvements in performance), with an average of 4.8 projects per respondent company[1]. These efforts all involved information technology.

---

[1] "Leading Trends in Information Services," *Sixth Annual Survey of North American CIOs 1994*, Deloitte & Touche, 1994.

Used by permission from Stewart Cohen/Tony Stone Images

MRP systems help reduce inventory cost while ensuring availability.

MATERIALS REQUIREMENT PLANNING

One of the areas of manufacturing that has experienced the greatest improvement from IS is inventory control, or **materials requirement planning (MRP)** (see Figure 10.7). Traditional inventory control techniques operated according to the basic principle that future inventory needs are based on past use: once used up, inventory was replaced. By contrast, replenishment in MRP is based on *future* need, calculated by MRP software from a master schedule of materials information and projected inventory availability. MRP programs take customer demand as their initial input. They use long-range forecasts to put long-lead material on order, with actual receipt schedules adjusted to match actual demand. The main input to MRP programs is the number of product units needed and the time at which they are needed; the programs then work back to calculate the amounts of resources required to produce subparts and assemblies.

Other important input to MRP applications includes: a list of all the raw materials and subcomponent demands, called the **bill of materials (BOM)**, and the economic order quantity of the different raw materials. The **economic order quantity (EOQ)** of a specific raw material is the optimal quantity that allows the business to minimize overstocking and save cost, without risking understocking and missing production deadlines. It is calculated by a special program that takes into consideration several factors: the cost of the item, the discount schedule for large quantities ordered, the cost of storing the ordered parts in the warehouse, the cost of alternate use of the money (such as the interest rate the money could yield had it not been spent on inventory), and other factors affecting the cost of ordering the item.

Some MRP applications are tied to a purchasing IS, to automatically produce purchase orders when the quantity on hand reaches a reorder level. The purchase order includes the economic order quantity.

MANUFACTURING RESOURCE PLANNING

Manufacturing resource planning (MRP II) combines MRP with other manufacturing-related activities to plan the entire manufacturing process. It

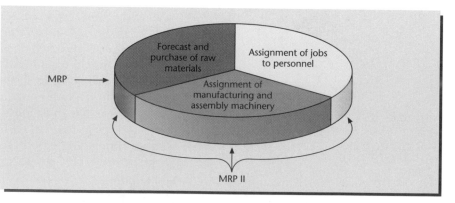

Figure 10.7 *Materials requirement planning (MRP) and manufacturing resource planning (MRP II)*

Used by permission from Andy Sacks/Tony Stone Images

MPR II systems help manage production and assembly lines, and reduce manufacturing cost.

joins material planning to the functions that execute the plan: shop activity control and purchasing; the source of demand; customer order entry and forecasting; and support functions such as financial management, sales analysis, and data collection.

MRP II systems can quickly modify schedules to accommodate orders, track production in real time, and fix quality slippage. The most important input of MRP II systems is the **master production schedule (MPS)**, which specifies how production capacity will be used to meet customer demands and maintain inventories. Virtually every report generated by an MRP II package starts with, or is based upon, the MPS. Purchases of materials and internal control of manufacturing work flow, for example, actually start with the MPS, thereby giving it direct impact on the cost of operations and the use of assets.

MRP II systems help balance production economies, customer demands, manufacturing capacity, and inventory levels over a planning horizon of several months. Successful MRP II systems have made a significant contribution to **just-in-time (JIT)** manufacturing, where parts are shipped by suppliers directly to assembly lines, and products are shipped to consumers or retailers, saving the cost of warehousing parts or products.

JIT is an idea more than a technique. It refers to a change in management thinking, rather than a set of computer programs or calculation techniques. With JIT, managers identify and eliminate any cost that does not add value. They reduce inventories, rearrange plant layouts to minimize handling, introduce automation to reduce setup and changeover times, bring quality out of the testing lab onto the shop floor, and focus on performing in the most efficient manner. The information obtained from MRP II systems helps in identifying opportunities, and in measuring the results of the changes that have been made.

MANUFACTURING EXECUTION SYSTEMS

MRP and MRP II systems are designed to plan for manufacturing, not control it. That is, they are fed with information on the current conditions: expected demand, EOQs, the production capacity of each machine in the production line, and projected demands. But some of these very conditions can still be improved. The production manager should ask: Is the maximum capacity of Machine A really just X units per month? What are the bottlenecks in the line? **Manufacturing execution systems (MESs)** are developed to help answer these questions. Their purpose is to track, schedule, and control manufacturing processes. The systems collect data such as: the number of hours the machine is operated every day of the month; how many hours the machine was idle, and why. Analysis of the data can pinpoint reasons for idle time that can, sometimes, easily be resolved.

MARKETING AND SALES

No commercial organization can survive without selling its products or services. Thus, businesses seek ways to entice consumers to buy what they produce. Marketing efforts are exerted to pinpoint the demographic groups that are most likely to buy, the product features that are most desirable to consumers,

Marketing is one business function that depends very heavily on personal customer data. As you may remember from the discussion in the "Ethics and Society" section of Chapter 7, "Data Management," consumer privacy is becoming an increasingly hot issue as IT, and especially DBMS technology, evolves. Here we review how corporations obtain the personal data they use, and introduce the principles they should heed to minimize invasion of privacy.

How Did You Get My Data? Here are some scenarios of how personal data is collected about you:

Scenario #1: A manufacturer of personal health care products asks customers to fill out a long questionnaire. In addition to questions about the electric toothbrush the person purchased (price paid, who recommended the purchase, and so on), the company also asks about marital status, annual income, education, and interests, "to help us understand our customers' lifestyles," according to the company. At the end of the questionnaire, the fine print reads something like: "Your answers will be used for market research studies and reports, and will help us better serve you in the future. They will also allow you to receive important mailings and special offers from a number of fine companies. Through this selective program, you will be able to obtain more information about activities in which you are involved and less about those in which you are not."

"Fine companies" are those to which the corporation sells your information. "Important mailings" are promotional material from other companies trying to sell you their products. And before you send the form out, be sure you really want individuals unknown to you to know that among your personal interests are "Wines," "Dieting/Weight Control," or "Casino Gambling." The manufacturer is kind enough to add: "Please check here if, for some reason, you would prefer *not* to participate in this opportunity." Well, if you don't want to participate, why don't you just throw the questionnaire away?

Scenario #2: When you buy a computer from a local retailer, you provide your home address and phone number to the inquiring salesperson, who keys them into the terminal supposedly "for the receipt." You have just been entered into the chain's database. From now on, you will receive its periodic sales flyers as well as telemarketing calls to sell you more products.

Scenario #3: Grocery chains, drugstores, and mass merchandisers such as Wal-Mart stores, Inc., and Kmart Corp. sell their point of sale (POS) (cash register) scanner data to suppliers and information brokers, which sell the data to food, drug, clothing, and appliance manufacturers. Some of the better-known brokers include Chicago-based Information Resources Inc. (IRI) and Northbrook, Ill.-based A.C. Nielsen Co. (the television viewing rating firm). According to IIA (Information Industry Association), sales of marketing information in America has reached several billion dollars per year.

(continued)

The Seven Commandments of Personal Data Collection and Maintenance. In a free, market-oriented society, it is inconceivable not to allow organizations to collect personal data. However, as you remember from the Chapter 7 ethics discussion, there are ways this data is misused, such as combining data from different sources in a way that would disclose more information about you than you intended, and selling your data to a third party without your permission. What can businesses do to minimize invasion of privacy? They can try to adhere to the following rules to assure the public that data banks are not misused:

◆ *Purpose.* Companies should inform people who provide information about themselves of the specific, exclusive purpose for which the company maintains their data, and only use the data for another purpose with the subjects' consent. For example, this practice could protect psychiatric patients from having their insurance companies sell information about their psychiatric treatments.

◆ *Relevance.* Companies should record and use only those data necessary to fulfill their own purposes. For example, an applicant's credit record should not contain the applicant's political views, because that information is irrelevant in credit considerations and would only be useful if sold.

◆ *Accuracy.* Companies should ensure that their data are accurate. For example, many loan applicants have had terrible experiences due to erroneous data held by credit history companies. Accuracy can be enhanced through careful data entry and periodic verification.

◆ *Currency.* Companies should make sure that all data about an individual are current. If currency cannot be guaranteed, then the data should be discarded altogether within a certain period of time. Outdated information can have horribly negative repercussions. For example, a person who may have been unemployable due to illness in the past may not be able to get a job, even though she may be healthy now.

◆ *Security.* Companies should limit access to data to only those who need to know. In addition to passwords, audit trails (which identify every employee who has accessed a personal record, and for what purpose) are also very effective tools for implementing security.

◆ *Time Limitation.* Companies should retain data only for the period of time necessary.

◆ *Scrutiny.* Companies should establish procedures to allow individuals to review their records and correct inaccuracies.

Of course, many consumers will still feel that their privacy is invaded even if every business adopts all of the above "commandments" as policy.

and the most efficient and effective ways to execute a sale once a consumer has shown interest in the product or service. Since these efforts focus mainly on the analysis of huge amounts of data, ISs have become key tools to conceiving of and executing marketing strategies (see Figure 10.8).

MARKET RESEARCH

Few organizations can sell their products and services without promotion, and fewer can promote successfully without market research. **Market research systems** help to find the populations and regions that are most likely to purchase a new product or service. They also help in analyzing how a new product fared in the first several months.

Through interviews with consumers and retailers, market researchers collect information indicating what consumers like and do not like about products. When sufficient data have been collected, statistical models are used by the marketing department to predict the sales volumes of different products, and of different designs of the same product. This critical information aids in the planning of manufacturing capacities and production lines. It is also extremely important for budgeting purposes.

TARGETED MARKETING

To save resources, businesses use IT to promote to those who are most likely to purchase their products (called **targeted marketing**), and they use the same system to actually execute the sale. The great advances in database technology enable even the smallest and poorest business to use targeted marketing. The principle of targeted marketing is for a company to define the prospective customer as accurately as possible, so that promotional dollars can be concentrated only on those people most likely to purchase the product. Perhaps the best evidence of how much companies use ISs for targeted marketing is the huge

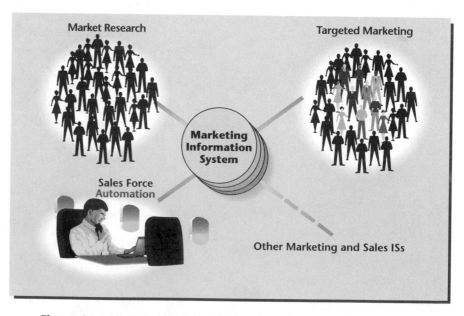

Figure 10.8 *Marketing and sales information systems help target potential buyers and serve clients.*

In the 1980s, Continental Can managers thought they had devised a simple method to improve the company's financial condition, but they may not have anticipated the ultimate price they had to pay. Management dubbed the plan BELL, the reversed acronym of Lowest Level Employee Benefits. Employees who had worked almost 20 years for the company were laid off for no apparent reason, some fired just a few days short of completing 20 years, when they would become eligible for a pension. As was determined years after the layoffs started, Continental Can used a computer program to identify veteran employees shortly before they qualified for pension payments. The computer was also programmed to alert executives to any check paid to an employee who had been fired, because this might indicate that the person was rehired, in which case he or she would be eligible for the accumulated benefits. As soon as the computer indicated such an occurrence, the program manager had to find out within 30 minutes if the payment has been made to a rehired person. If he could not resolve the case, or if it was a payment to a rehired employee, the manager was to call the president of the company immediately. The program "saved" the company hundreds of millions of dollars, except that the dismissed employees sued the company, and the judge decided the employees were fired for no legitimate reason. They won a total compensation of $415 million.

amount of promotional mail—usually called "junk mail"—we receive daily. While many people hate to receive junk mail, commercial organizations know that it is one of the least costly and most effective means to market their products and services.

In order to define their target, businesses collect data everywhere they can: from sales transactions and warranty cards, or by purchasing databases about organizations and individuals. Using DBMSs, a company can sort and categorize the names by age group, gender, income, previous purchase of a related product, or any combination of these facts and other demographic information. The company then selects those whose characteristics match the company's customer profile, and spends its promotional dollars to try to sell to those select customers.

Telemarketing (marketing over the telephone) reduces the need for sales personnel. Telemarketing no longer requires a person. A computer can be programmed to retrieve designated records one at a time from a database, call the person, and launch the marketing pitch, either through a recorded or synthesized voice.

Although not considered targeted marketing, marketing via television also involves information technology. When you call to order an item that has just been displayed on your TV set, it is most likely a computer that takes your order. All you have to do is press keys on your phone according to the instructions that the computer gives you.

Some mail-order firms have recently started to use caller-ID to better serve their customers. Caller-ID was originally intended to identify the telephone number from which one calls, but mail-order businesses quickly found a new use for the gadget. They connect it to their customer database. When you call to order, a simple program runs a search of your number, retrieves your record, and displays it on a PC monitor. You may be surprised when the receiver of your call greets you by name, and later asks if you would like to use the same credit card number you used in your last purchase.

THE PERSONAL COMPUTER AS A MARKETING MEDIUM

For several decades, radio and television were the only nonprint media for marketing. Now, the household computer is becoming a means of promoting products. In the mid-1980s, several companies, especially in the auto industry, started to develop disk programs with information on their products, usually referred to as **promotional disks**. The disks were then sent to previous buyers and other prospective customers for examination on their personal computers.

While a television commercial can keep the attention of a viewer for an average of 30 seconds, computer programs can do so for up to 30 minutes. Also, a 30-second television commercial is many times more expensive than the production and distribution of promotional disks. These are two great advantages of this marketing avenue. While there is no research that shows how effective it is, there is a clear indication that companies like the new idea. SoftAd is one of a few companies that develop promotional disks for industrial giants like General Motors, Ford, AT&T, and others. It was established with two employees in the mid-1980s and has doubled its revenue annually ever since.

Commercial announcements are also pervasive on public bulletin board systems. Prodigy, America Online, and other online services integrate commercials into their regular news and entertainment programs. Interactive software allows subscribers to receive several levels of information on products and services, and, if they wish, to purchase them immediately. For several years, sales of PCs

Your Wallet in the Year 2000

If you have been in the work force for more than a year, you probably have a problem fitting all your "stuff" into your wallet: a phone card, three credit cards and a bunch of receipts, an ATM card, frequent-flier cards, insurance card, prescription care card, company ID, and, of course, cash. With the ability to store more and more data on a simple magnetic strip, and with microprocessors so small that they fit neatly into a credit-type card, someday you will literally be carrying a computer in your wallet. Here are some ways that computer may be used.

COMPANY ID

Even today, your company ID lets you into your office, but soon it will carry a microchip and a three-year battery, and will become the key to your company's computer network from any computer anywhere. Say you are on the road and need to check a file. You turn on your laptop, dial up the Internet, and connect to your office's network. To get in, type your password and enter your dynamic access code, a number that appears in the window of your ID card. It is generated by the card's microprocessor; it changes each minute, and is coordinated with the same number on the network. The constantly changing access code creates a double lock: if someone steals your card, he still can't get in without the password; if somebody guesses the password, he can't get in without your card.

CREDIT CARDS

Now let's look at the future of your credit cards. You are likely to need only one major card because every merchant will take all the major credit cards. Your card will likely give you mileage on any airline. Associated with your card will be your digital signature to protect against fraud when making purchases online. A digital signature will probably be created using "public-key cryptography," invented in the 1970s in California by Whitefield Diffie and Martin Hellman. Every person will have two keys: an encryption key, which is private, and a decoding key, which is public. The private encryption can only be unscrambled with your public key. Here is how the keys work. You send an order over the Internet to L.L. Bean. It consists of your name and, encrypted with your private key, the list of items you want and your credit

(continued)

have exceeded sales of television sets. Marketing executives cannot ignore this great potential.

The growth of the Internet as a medium open to the public has enhanced the PC as a marketing and sales medium. Many Web sites display promotional material and applications to support interaction between sellers and buyers. The Web provides excellent marketing and sales opportunities, as discussed in Chapter 6, "The Internet and Intranets."

card number. When Bean receives it, they look up your public key. If it unlocks the message, only you could have sent it. The process takes no longer than giving your card number over the phone, and it's safer.

It is more than likely that your future driver's license and medical card will also both incorporate microchips. The former would hold your car registration and insurance data, as well as a record of the speeding ticket you received last week. The health card would hold your medical history. At each medical visit, your doctor would update the card, and use it to receive an immediate reimbursement from your managed care network, as well.

Another big change in the wallet of the future is that instead of carrying money, you will likely have a cash card, which holds the equivalent of digital cash that can be withdrawn by you or deducted by a store or vendor you purchase from. Cash cards evolved from the "smart" cards used by European phone and transportation systems. The user passes a card with prepaid calls or trips recorded on its magnetic strip across a reader, to make calls or enter the transportation system. Back in 1993, GemPlus, a French outfit, and VeriFone, a U.S. maker of credit card scanning systems, introduced a cash card in a small Northeastern state, but it worked only with certain supermarkets, fast food stores, convenience stores, gas stations, and at least one big bank. In the future, you will be able to use your card to retrieve cash and to make purchases at any store. To get coffee at the 7-Eleven, put the card in the cash register slot, and it deducts 75 cents.

What will be nice about the new cash card is that it will be anonymous. You can buy sweets on the fly, pay your housekeeper, and pick up a copy of *Fortune* without getting a subscription come-on in the next day's e-mail. You can even use digital cash online. (The gambling action on Super Bowl XXXIV was amazing.) Via "remailers," computers that hide the origin of a message, you can make transactions hard to trace.

This is all technology that existed in 1993. Amazing how long it takes to catch on.

Source: Stewart, T., *Fortune*, Autumn 1993 (Special Issue on Information Technology), pp. 153–162.

Apparently, the technology described above may be very helpful. Do you see any "downside" to it? What do you foresee that you do not like?

SALES FORCE AUTOMATION

Sales force automation is the equipping of traveling salespeople with information technology to facilitate their productivity. Typically, salespeople are equipped with notebook computers with promotional information for prospective customers, software for manipulation of this information, and computerized forms. Sales force automation can increase sales productivity significantly, making sales presentations more efficient and allowing field representatives to close deals on the spot, using preformatted contracts and forms.

Information technology allows salespeople to present different options for products and services on the computer, rather than having to ask prospective customers to wait until the information can be faxed or mailed from the main office. At the end of the day or the week, the sales information can be downloaded to a computer at the main office, where it is raw input to the order processing department, the manufacturing unit, or to the shipping and invoicing departments.

Used by permission from Gerard Yunker/Sight Photographers, Inc.

Sales force automation increases marketing and sales productivity.

Text and pictures can be combined to store and retrieve employee records.

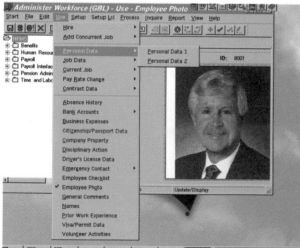

Used by permission from PeopleSoft, Inc.

HUMAN RESOURCES

Human resource management has become more complex than in previous years due to the fast growth in specialized occupations, the need to train and promote highly-skilled employees, and the growing variety of benefits programs. Human resource management can be roughly classified into five main activities: employee record management, promotion and recruitment, training, evaluation, and compensation and benefits management (see Figure 10.9).

EMPLOYEE RECORD MANAGEMENT

Employee record management can be easily facilitated with ISs. Human resource departments have to keep personnel records to satisfy both external regulations (such as federal and state laws) and internal regulations, as well as for payroll and tax calculation and deposit, promotion consideration, and periodic reporting. Many HR ISs are now completely digitized (even including a picture of the employee), which dramatically reduces the space needed to store records, the time needed to retrieve them, and the attendant costs of both.

PROMOTION AND RECRUITMENT

To select the best qualified person for a position, a human resource manager can search a database of applicants and existing employees' records for set criteria, such as a specific type and length of education, particular experience, specific talents, and required licenses. Automating the selection process significantly minimizes the time and money spent on recruitment, but does require that a current database be maintained.

TRAINING

One important function of human resource departments is the improvement of employee skills. Training programs involving classrooms and teachers are increasingly being replaced with **multimedia software training** in both the manufacturing and service sectors. Although the initial investment in multimedia training systems may be high, human resource managers find that the systems are very effective.

Training software emulates situations in which the employee must act, and includes tests and modules to evaluate the trainee's performance. In addition to savings in trainers' time,

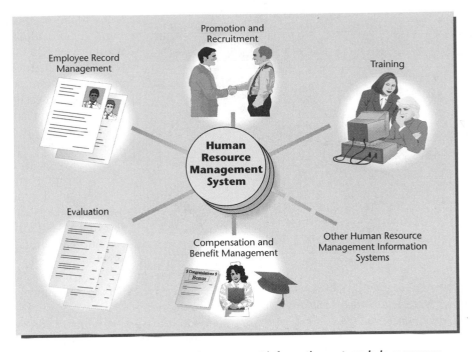

Figure 10.9 *Human resource management information systems help managers optimize the assignment of employees and provide payroll, benefits, and other employee-related services.*

there are other benefits. The trainee is more comfortable because he or she controls the speed at which the sessions run. The software allows the trainee to go back to a certain point in the training session if a point is missed. Also, the software can emulate dangerous situations, thereby testing employee performance in a safe environment.

EVALUATION

Multimedia has become the training method of choice for many organizations.

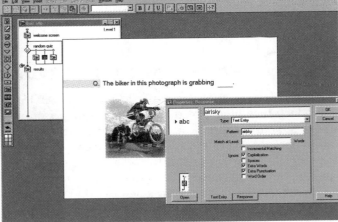

Used by permission from Macromedia

One of the difficult, and often unpleasant, tasks of supervisors is the periodic evaluation of the technical ability, communications skills, professional conduct, and general behavior of employees on the job. While there are objective factors involved in evaluation—such as attendance rates and punctuality—employee evaluation is often a very subjective undertaking. Assessing levels of performance and effort, and their relative weights of importance, can vary significantly depending upon who is doing the evaluating. In some cases a supervisor may forget to include some factors altogether, or may place inappropriate weight on a particular aspect of performance. Subjectivity is particularly problematic when more than one employee is being considered for a promotion, and their evaluations are compared to determine the strongest candidate. Evaluation software helps standardize the evaluation process across employees and departments, and adds a certain measure of objectivity and consistency.

In an evaluation, a supervisor provides feedback to an employee, records the evaluation for official records and future comparison, and accepts input from the employee.

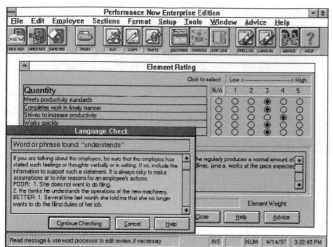

Used by permission from KnowledgePoint

ISs help supervisors create accurate and thorough employee performance evaluations.

An employee using an interactive benefits plans system to optimize the combination of benefits.

Used by permission from USX

Software helps managers standardize their employee evaluations, by providing: step-by-step guides to writing performance reviews, a checklist of performance areas that should be included in the evaluation (with the option to add or remove topics), scales for indicating how strong the employee is in each area, and the ability to select the relative importance each factor should hold in the overall evaluation, as well. Areas of performance include written and oral communication, job knowledge, and management, with each topic broken down into its basic elements to assist the supervisor in creating an accurate evaluation.

A typical application guides the user through all the necessary factors and includes a help guide. When the evaluator finishes entering the data, the application automatically computes a subtotal for each category and a weighted grade, which can then be electronically stored as part of the employee's record.

Recently, expert systems have been introduced to track and analyze aberrant conduct. The systems can be programmed to track patterns or can be queried for existing patterns of absenteeism, low productivity, or performance inconsistency that may indicate that an employee is having substance abuse or other problems.

COMPENSATION AND BENEFITS MANAGEMENT

ISs help HR officers manage compensation (salaries, hourly pay, and commissions) efficiently and effectively. Programs can easily calculate weekly, monthly, and hourly pay according to annual salaries, and can include federal, state, and local tax tables to assist in complying with compensation regulations. This same system can also automatically generate paychecks or **direct deposits**, which are the electronic transfer of compensation funds from the firm's bank account to the employee's.

There is also special software to help the HR department manage benefits, such as health insurance, life insurance, retirement plans, and sick and leave days, which are determined by seniority, amounts individuals pay into programs, and other factors. To optimize benefits, some companies use special software, incorporating expert systems that determine the optimal health and retirement plans for each employee based on factors such as marital status, age, occupation, and other data.

GROUPWARE AND COLLABORATIVE WORK

When people work together, either to provide a service or create a product, they often do so in sequence: one person provides his or her input to the project, then passes it along to another person, who does the same, and so on along a chain. This is not necessarily the most efficient or effective way to undertake a particular project, but it is dictated by the *tools* being used to do the job. For instance, engineers developing a new car must wait for the body design from the designers so that they can figure out how to fit the engine and other mechanical items. Or, lawyers representing a buyer and a seller must wait for each other's modifications to a draft contract until a final version is agreed upon. Almost without exception, IT provides opportunities to shorten work flow time and deliver products and services significantly sooner, across both industries and business functions, by allowing people to work together in real time rather than in sequence.

Software that lets users work together is called **groupware**, a term that refers to a broad and somewhat diverse collection of technologies, including electronic mail, group calendaring and scheduling, collaborative document handling, group application development tools, audio/video/desktop conferencing, group decision-support systems, conferencing products, electronic-meeting systems, and work flow and group project management. There are three major types of collaborative work that ISs can help with: document control, collaborative projects, and brainstorming.

DOCUMENT CONTROL

Thousands of documents are produced in business processes, many of which are repeatedly accessed from world-wide locations and continually revised through collaborative efforts. This often creates the problem of people inadvertently working with outdated information, because they are not aware of revisions that have been made. For instance, engineering design sheets and blueprints are updated so frequently that engineers often find themselves working with outdated plans. Programs such as LinkWorks and TeamLinks from DEC, and Notes from Lotus let users distribute and track electronic documents containing text, graphics, and video or audio data, to help prevent these types of problems.

In these programs, annotations tracked by time and source immediately become a part of the electronic document, so that the document is current whenever accessed. This can be extremely important to accurate, efficient work, especially when it involves engineering.

COLLABORATIVE PROJECTS

Several groupware programs, such as MarkUp from Mainstay and Instant Update from ON Technology, allow multiple users to coordinate their work on a single document from many different terminals. Keeping the original document intact, MarkUp lets workers use on-screen tools to change parts of drawings, add notes, and delete other material. Instant Update, on the other hand, maintains an unchanged original text document while allowing each user to edit the document on his or her local PC. Authorized participants may permanently replace the master copy with the desired changes, and other users can then retrieve the updated document. Such applications are extremely helpful in law offices, publishing houses, and other text-intensive environments.

Some applications allow individuals to participate remotely in a collaborative writing effort. For example, Face-to-Face from Crosswise Inc. allows any combination of Windows and Macintosh users to simultaneously view and annotate entire documents. Document layering distinguishes each user's input, and a chat box at the bottom of the screen allows workers to communicate. Another example is ScreenLink from Datawatch Corp., which also lets remote users view each other's screen images. This is an excellent feature for user- or customer-support desks. Users seeking help can simply link their screen with that of the support person, eliminating the need to describe what's on the screen.

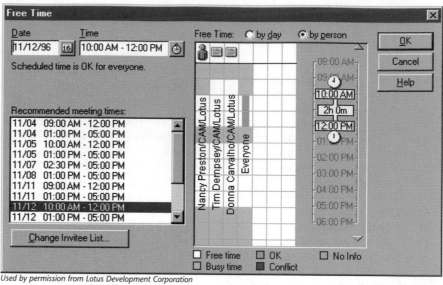

Used by permission from Lotus Development Corporation

A project-management tool lets all connected users make changes to the same document simultaneously.

There are also project planning groupware programs that allow users to see modifications in project schedules and activities as soon as they are made.

BRAINSTORMING

In business, "brainstorming" refers to the process of a group of colleagues generating creative solutions and new ideas by meeting together and working collaboratively. Groupware software can facilitate this process without the expensive practice of bringing everyone to the same location. Groupware allows users to type up ideas on a "whiteboard" that is one window on everyone's monitor. The same technology can be used when people are physically together, as well: the "whiteboard" can be a large monitor, while all participants may use their own computers for ideas and information they do not wish to share.

Ideas can be organized and reorganized, discussed, and then voted on. One of the major advantages of this type of decision-making process is that it allows individual users to bring up revolutionary ideas anonymously, motivating discussion without exposing themselves to criticism.

NO GUARANTEED SUCCESS

Success with information systems is never guaranteed. Despite the spending of billions of dollars on information technology in the past decade, many companies are finding that their systems come nowhere near generating the anticipated benefits. At the national level, some call this phenomenon "the productivity paradox." Some researchers claim that part of the blame should be attributed to the inadequate ways in which we measure the contribution of IT. Many systems do not simply cut the number of employees or increase the output of existing products; they create whole new products and services. This makes the measurement of productivity difficult, if not impossible.

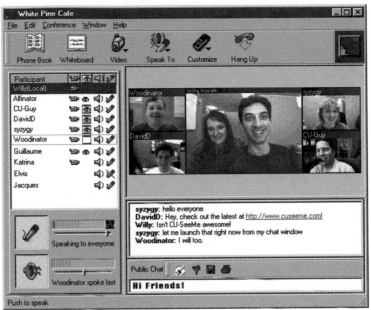

Used by permission from White Pine Software

A team workstation allows the parties to see facial expressions. One monitor is used for shared information, the other for individual view. One of the cameras lets the other party view hand-drawn sketches.

But in many cases, the problem lies elsewhere. A 1993 survey indicates that the shortfall is most often the result of a poorly developed system or detective technology. Problems arise for the following reasons:

◆ ISs are infrequently or improperly used.

◆ ISs are not appropriate or were never implemented.

◆ ISs are not developed with a total system approach, and overlook cross-functional issues. This happens when developers focus on the system in terms of only one function, disregarding the need for smooth interfaces with systems that serve other functions.

◆ Expectations are imprecise.

Instead of dealing with the true nature and source of these problems at their root by redesigning or replacing systems, many companies respond to the situation by initiating diagnostic projects that focus on such activities as:

◆ Leveraging information already being generated to make better decisions

◆ Identifying new information requirements that can be satisfied with minimal investment

◆ Redesigning processes to make them more efficient and to position them better to harness the system's power

The best way to assure success with information systems is to follow careful planning and development procedures, which are discussed in Chapter 14, "Planning of Information Systems" and in Chapter 15, "Systems Development."

Alcan Improves Manufacturing

Alcan is a world-wide manufacturer of aluminum components. Its building products factory in Point-Claire, Canada, manufactures aluminum siding for the residential and commercial marketplace. From the heyday of the '70s and '80s, when growth was the norm, the market has suddenly become extremely competitive where cost, quality, and ability to deliver rapidly have become basic ingredients to survival. Facing high demand from customers that wanted made-to-order products with new colors and styles, the company decided in 1991 that only a huge shift in its manufacturing process would allow the company to remain responsive to customer demands and competitive in the market. A consulting firm was recruited to re-engineer its business and manufacturing process. Scheduling was immediately identified as a critical component.

Today's manufacturing process at Alcan Building Products exhibits all the complexity that would have made it impossible to schedule only five years ago. Aluminum rolls must be painted, slit, and roll-formed to shape. The efficiency of the paint process depends upon the color chosen and the width of the product. Because each change in setup requires time and costs money, grouping jobs by colors and grading them from wide to narrow is essential to the efficiency of the process. Alcan can custom manufacture items that are not grouped by type to respond to customer demand, but it can only afford to do so provided the repercussion of such a decision on all the other orders in the plant is clearly understood. Unlike other phases of the manufacturing process, the paint shop was previously not very responsive to irregular requests; now it can be.

To optimize the manufacturing process, the capacity of all the shops—such as cutting and painting—had to be coordinated. (The capacity of a shop is the number of items it can process per time unit.) Scheduling and optimizing the entire plant was extremely difficult without raising the levels of work-in-process (WIP), that is, the number of unfinished goods in the pipeline, whose storage costs money and which, unfinished, could not create revenue. If one phase is slower than others, unfinished goods accumulate; in this case, unpainted aluminum products.

After a six-month search, Alcan selected MOOPI, a capacity scheduling system developed by Berclain. The system considers the capacity of each shop and determines the quantities of different materials it needs, and when, for optimal operation. Besides being able to rapidly release a detailed schedule to the shop floor, the system was selected due to its ability to balance all manufacturing parameters (machine efficiency, inventory levels, and on-time delivery). The manager could, for example, determine the effect of increasing WIP levels, at the output of the paint process, on the factory's manufacturing cycle time and with respect to delivery dates. He could then decide whether or not the cost of additional inventory is worth the reduction in cycle time. In other words, the system could quantify these decisions, eliminating the guesswork, and hence reducing the risk factor.

Christian Gachignard, project leader and material manager at Alcan, states that lead time reduction was identified as the main goal of the overall project. Lead time is the time it takes a series of activities (including planning, acquisition of materials, and production) to conclude. Several benefits were derived from that single objective (lower inventory, customer satisfaction). Lead time reduction in this case required more than installing a scheduling system. Streamlining the product line, real-time dispatching and shop floor feedback were among the additional steps necessary to create an agile manufacturing environment.

Armed with this weapon, Alcan was able to reduce its manufacturing cycle time from 40 days to eight within one year. Going from eight to five days necessitated the installation of a real-time dispatch and feedback system and took another 12 months. By properly managing the WIP buffer at the output of the paint process, and operating all subsequent work centers in a made-to-order mode, Alcan was able to eliminate all other inventories within its plant and reduce the overall inventories within its plant by 60 percent within the same time frame. Gachignard considers MOOPI to be an essential tool to his process of continuing improvement. Besides its day-to-day scheduling ability, the system is a powerful simulation tool to analyze and improve the efficiency of the whole plant.

Source: "A Case Study," in APICS - The Performance Advantage, March 1994, p. 23. Reprinted by permission of Lionheart Publishing Inc.

Questions

1. Enumerate and explain Alcan's main problems before the re-engineering process.

2. Explain the three main types of information that Alcan's managers can now receive from MOOPI. Why are these types of information so important in the management of a manufacturing company?

3. Besides its day-to-day support, the system is a powerful simulation tool. What would you simulate with it, and for what purpose?

3-D Computing For Securities Trading

Imagine being able to see in a single display what is happening to stocks and other securities in a half-dozen markets around the world. Metaphor Mixer, a PC program by Maxus Systems International of New York City, does just that. Using up-to-the-minute data from financial wire services, the program represents the various markets as a kind of checkerboard on which individual stocks appear as graphic symbols. If a stock is outperforming the market's moving average, its symbol appears to rise above the board; if it is lagging behind, the symbol seems to sink below the surface. The symbol blinks when a stock is trading actively and spins when it becomes volatile

Metaphor Mixer is a virtual reality system that allows the client to "fly" over the entire financial world, represented as a huge grid with each square corresponding to a country and industry group. Real-time data reports are fed into the system; stocks are represented by color-coded shapes. Spinning and blinking shapes

symbolize various performance patterns—spinners, for example, represent optimal price to earnings ratios—and "profit missiles" home in on attractive securities.

George M. Gabriel of ABD Securities Corp., the Wall Street trading arm of Germany's Dresdener Bank, uses Metaphor Mixer to help watch German stocks. His system is programmed so that if a stock lags behind the market, but the company it represents is financially strong, its symbol glows red as it sinks below the board. "The color red is a tip-off to a potential buy," says Gabriel. Using a mouse, he zooms in on a symbol that is blushing brightly on his screen. He clicks on it, and up come the latest analysts' reports on the stock. In seconds, Gabriel explains, a portfolio manager can spot "a sunken treasure," investigate the opportunity, and act on it.

Source: Bylinsky, G., Fortune, Autumn 1993 (Special Issue on Information Technology), pp. 32–40, and http://www.hotwired.com/wired/1.6/departments/electric.word.html, April 1, 1997.

Questions

1. Metaphor Mixer provides different information than other stock ISs linked to the stock exchange. What is its main advantage?

2. Identify all the visual elements in the system that are meant to help stock traders.

Paperless Service

AT&T, the world's biggest communications company, is also the world's biggest IT spender. In 1995, it spent about $5 billion on technology. A knowledge management system that runs over an intranet gives 15,000 AT&T customer-service agents easy point-and-click access to data on products, services, and procedures. Previously, these agents had to rely on paper-based sources that took too long to decipher. "The task of getting all that paper out, considering the breadth of services we offer, was a Herculean task," said Rod Mack, vice president and general manager for business services. The intranet system "allows us to get information out instantly" by updating the database five times a day. AT&T also has developed software that consolidates 25 different systems needed by the agents.

The company established a Web-based offering called ATT.ALL featuring a billing service that bundles long-distance, local, and wireless services. The company is also testing a system that will significantly reduce the time it takes to activate services.

On the consumer side, AT&T developed "intelligent call processing" software, which routes customers to the right agent, depending on customer preferences. "If the customer prefers to speak Spanish, he'll automatically be routed to a center where he'll be greeted in Spanish," said Alan Jones, a vice president and general manager of consumer operations and technology. Another intranet gives customer service agents access to information about all AT&T consumer products and services. AT&T also uses mainframe processing, optical records storage, customized software, and the

Internet to provide faster and more diversified billing services.

AT&T is spending big on multiple-terabyte databases and data mining tools, Jones said, to learn more about the buying trends of its 80 million customers. "This will be a strategic differentiator for us," he said. "We routinely process billions of call detail records."

Source: Viloino, R., "AT&T Sees End to Paper Trail," InformationWeek, November 25, 1996, p. 36.

Questions

1. How does the Web site help AT&T agents provide better customer service?

2. The company has implemented data mining software. Give some examples of the "buying trends" mentioned by Jones that AT&T could find when analyzing the data.

3. What did Jones mean by "differentiator?" How can the data mining software be a differentiator?

Summary

Effectiveness is the degree to which a task is accomplished. The better one performs a job, the more effective one is. **Efficiency** is measured as the ratio of output to input. The more output with the same input, or the less input for the same output used in a process, the more efficient the process. ISs can help companies attain more effective and efficient business processes. **Productivity** is the measure of efficiency of people.

ISs have been integrated into almost every functional area in business. The earliest business ISs were implemented in **accounting** and payroll because of the routine and structured nature of accounting tasks. The systems automatically post transactions in the books and automate the generation of reports for management and for legal requirements.

Financial ISs help manage cash. Managers can keep track of available cash for transactions, while ensuring that the money is invested in short- or long-term programs to yield the highest interest possible. **Investment analysis ISs** help build portfolios based on historical performance and other characteristics of securities.

ISs are an important tool in modern engineering processes. **Computer-aided design** systems help engineers design new products and save and modify drawings electronically. **Manufacturing ISs**, especially **materials requirement planning (MRP)** and **manufacturing resource planning (MRP II)** systems, facilitate production scheduling and material requirement planning, and shorten lead times. **Manufacturing execution systems** help pinpoint production bottlenecks.

Many of today's marketing and sales techniques would be impossible without ISs. For instance, database technology is instrumental in **targeted marketing**, in which potential customers are defined as narrowly as possible. And computers can fully automate **telemarketing**, eliminating the need for a person to speak directly to a customer. Statistical models help market researchers find the best populations for new and existing products.

Selection of staff and efficient record keeping have been improved mainly thanks to **human resource ISs**. Some innovative systems are also being used to detect aberrant performance that may be caused by substance abuse or other problems that can then be addressed.

Groupware helps workers communicate ideas, brainstorm, and work together remotely as if they were sitting in the same room, resulting in better ideas and shorter processes.

There are many potential obstacles to acquiring successful ISs. To ensure success, managers and developers must express requirements clearly and consider related systems for compatibility and possible interface. Often, redesign of an entire business process, before developing an IS, contributes to its success.

Ethical issues are abundant in the use of business ISs, especially for marketing. The chief problem is how to utilize the technology for efficient and effective marketing without violating individual privacy.

REVIEW AND DISCUSSION QUESTIONS

1. What business functions were the first to adopt ISs? Why?

2. About 80% of the investment in IT has been made in service companies. Why?

3. Some experts say that ISs have great potential in manufacturing. Explain why. (Hint: business process re-engineering)

4. What is groupware? How does it help in the publishing industry? In engineering?

5. What is JIT? How do MRP and MRP II systems help achieve it?

6. What are manufacturing execution systems, and what is their contribution?

7. Over the past decade, banks and investment firms have offered many services that would be impossible without ISs. Describe three such services and explain why IT makes them possible.

8. What are the information technologies that play a crucial role in marketing today?

9. Sales force automation is not a new concept, but for many years it did not succeed in many organizations. What is meant by "sales force automation," and what has been the major obstacle in implementing it?

10. *Ethics and Society*: Some consumer advocates argue that organizations should pay every individual whenever they sell his or her records to another organization. (They suggest 5 or 10 cents per occurrence.) Do you agree? Why?

11. *Ethics and Society:* Examine the list of precautions suggested in "Ethics and Society" for ensuring minimum invasion of privacy when businesses use personal data. Which of the steps can be taken without, or with small, added cost? Which steps would entail financial burden on businesses? Why?

CONCEPT ACTIVITY

1. Select a business function that is not mentioned in this chapter. Write an essay explaining how IS technology could be used to make processes (1) more efficient and (2) more effective. Can ISs achieve a strategic advantage? How?

2. Choose two distinct business functions. Write a short paper describing how the information systems of these two functions can be interfaced to improve their performance.

HANDS-ON ACTIVITY

Winter Springs Inc., a manufacturer of industrial springs, uses an old Hymana machine whose capacity has deteriorated over the years due to an increasing rate of stoppages. The company now has three alternatives.

Alternative 1: Upgrade the machine.
Background:
- The upgrade will cost $9,600.
- The upgrade would extend the machine life another seven years.
- The maintenance costs for the upgraded machine would be about $1,400 per year. (Maintenance is performed by Winter Springs personnel.)

- The salvage value (the price the company can get for the machine at the end of the seventh year) is $1,000.
- The capacity of the upgraded machine would be 30,000 units per year.
- The current machine could sell for $5,000 now.

Alternative 2: Buy an advanced machine, Super Hymana.

Background:
- The new machine costs $32,000.
- Manufacturer-supplied maintenance cost would be $900 per year including parts and labor.
- The productive life of a new machine is estimated to be 20 years.
- A Super Hymana's economic worth after seven years is $25,000.
- The new machine's capacity is 40,000 units per year.

Alternative 3: Rent a Super Hymana.

Background:
- The machine can be returned whenever the company wishes.
- Rental is $1,700 per year including service.

Other information:

Winter borrows money from the bank for 11.5% per year. The company's comptroller considers this as the firm's interest rate in her calculations. Assume that the firm can sell all the springs it manufactures.

Question:

Which alternative would serve Winter Spring, Inc. best? Using a spreadsheet, print a discounted cash-flow analysis of this problem, and provide an explanation of which approach should be selected, and why.

TEAM ACTIVITY

Form a team and design an IS for a small mail-order business that will have to handle customer order processing, sales, salesperson commissions, billing, and accounts receivable. Prepare a report describing the different components and their points of interface. What files are necessary? How will the data in each file be used?

EXPLORE THE WEB

Assume that you are about to start a mail-order business for sporting goods. You wish to mail information to potential customers. Determine the demographic characteristics of your target audience. Search the Web for companies that sell consumer data that can serve you. Prepare a report listing the names of the companies, their services, and (if available) the prices.

Chapter **11**

Interorganizational and International Information Systems

Higher Standards for Hamilton Standard

Hamilton Standard, a division of United Technologies in Windsor Locks, Connecticut, used to send weekly or monthly production schedules on paper to its suppliers, who would provide delivery dates about three weeks later. The process was so slow that Hamilton could not adopt a just-in-time (JIT) inventory program, which was essential to saving money and staying competitive. Instead, Hamilton Standard held significantly more inventory than was needed, incurring excessive warehousing costs, much paperwork, and uncertain supply schedules. Management felt that these problems could be solved with IT, and, specifically, EDI.

With the implementation of EDI, production schedules are now sent electronically to the suppliers the day after they are created by Hamilton's application, and the suppliers electronically respond with promised ship dates three days after receipt of the schedules, cutting the processing time to a fraction of its original. The suppliers also send advance shipment notices, informing the company of what is coming.

With the new system in place, Hamilton was able to cut the cost of carrying raw material inventory by adopting a JIT inventory program, with automatic replenishment when possible. Hamilton now enjoys reduced raw-material-ordering cycle time, streamlined purchasing and receipt processing, more manageable cash flow, reduced personnel, and a reduction in the cost of carrying inventory. The benefits to the suppliers are the ability to improve their production planning as a result of earlier knowledge of what is needed, reduced inventories, and earlier payment.

Source: Reilly, B., "Making EDI Work at Hamilton Standard," *Note Number 617–625,* The Gartner Group, 1993.

LEARNING OBJECTIVES

As organizations realize that many of their operations are intertwined, they find that sharing information by linking their information systems results in increased efficiency. When multiple organizations link their ISs, they all enjoy great benefits. Organizations are meeting the challenge of operating international information systems to accommodate the free flow of information among a single company's divisions, as well as between multinational corporations.

When you finish this chapter, you will:

- ◆ Understand the importance of interorganizational and international ISs

- ◆ Understand the role EDI plays in saving costs on business operations

- ◆ Understand both vertical and horizontal information integration among companies

- ◆ Understand the legal, cultural, and practical challenges to implementing information exchange systems

SHARING INFORMATION SYSTEMS

A careful look at the evolution of information systems in organizations reveals an interesting, but not unexpected, phenomenon. Until the 1970s, organizations obtained **departmental ISs**, that is systems that typically served one department. There was an accounting system that supported the comptroller's department, an order entry system that served the sales department, and other systems that were devoted to serving specific functions and business units. In the early 1980s, in keeping with systems thinking, managers realized that they could achieve higher efficiency and effectiveness if information were integrated to serve several business units, because the nature of the work required interaction. Organizations moved to integrating their various business systems into one enterprise-wide IS designed to serve all or part of the organization's business, from marketing, through the production of a product or service, to delivery.

The 1990s have seen the emergence of even larger-scope ISs. Most organizations have learned that seamless exchange of information *within* an organization increases efficiency and effectiveness. In recent years, many organizations have concluded that operations could be further optimized if information were exchanged in a similarly seamless fashion between the ISs of *different* organizations, for instance between suppliers and buyers. Such a system is called an **interorganizational IS** because it serves more than one organization. Interorganizational information systems are systems shared by two or more organizations to transfer data electronically. Note, however, that an interorganizational IS usually is built and owned by only one organization. Now, there are many systems that serve more than one organization, to the benefit of all participants. Multinational organizations have implemented similar systems that serve multiple sites across national borders.

The future of many organizations depends on their ability to adopt an IS perspective that takes into consideration the organizations with which they interact. Large organizations have discovered the benefits of sharing their ISs with other organizations. Small organizations are slowly realizing that they must collaborate with their more powerful clients when flow of information is involved. And in the global arena, the future of the world economy depends, to a large extent, on the flow of information across borders. Many organizations now acknowledge that they are just links in a series of activities performed by a chain of players, as in a relay race. They do not just exchange goods and services for money; they also interchange information to facilitate their interactions.

VERTICAL INFORMATION INTERCHANGE

When the output of one organization is used in the processes of another organization, the two organizations are said to be **vertically related**. This relationship exists when one organization produces another organization's raw materials, and also when this second organization's products are sold to retailers for resale to consumers, in which case three organizations are trading vertically (see Figure 11.1). Integrating ISs to facilitate this relationship has brought great benefits to all participating companies.

Thinking along these lines, Kmart, Wal-mart, Toys Я Us, and other companies allowed their suppliers to connect to their inventory systems. The retailers save time and money because now the suppliers do all the control work: tracking customers' stocks, shipping supplies and adjusting customers' inventory records as needed, and billing customers accordingly. Of course, retailers need to track the activity as well, to assure that there is no deliberate overstocking by a supplier.

With the information systems connected, the entire transaction described above can be conducted without a shred of paper. Obviously, an organization that opens its systems to outside organizations takes a great risk. Therefore, there must be a true sense of trust between the parties for this relationship to succeed. When an organization allows the access described to all of its suppliers, it actually renders full control of its inventory to its suppliers. This has been the trend in many large companies for several years now.

Another purpose of interorganizational ISs is to better serve the consumer. The manufacturer of a product realizes that *its* customers will do better if *their* customers are happy. For instance, as you may remember from our discussion in Chapter 2, "Strategic Uses of Information Systems," Saturn Automobile Corp.

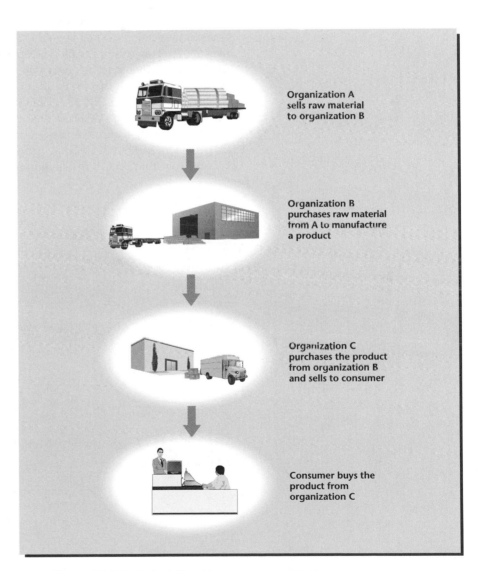

Figure 11.1 *Vertical relationships among organizations*

connected its dealers to its manufacturing information system through a satellite communications system, creating a link between the customer demand
(individuals purchasing from the dealer) and the manufacturer. When a customer wishes to purchase a Saturn car with certain specifications, a dealer can
query the manufacturing IS and tell the customer when his car will be available.

ELECTRONIC DATA INTERCHANGE

A significant portion of the cost of products and services can be attributed
to the creation, handling, and storage of paper documents: requests for proposals, purchase orders, shipping documents, invoices, payment approvals, checks,
equipment such as file cabinets and shelves to store the documents, and time
required for document preparation and shipment. (In the auto industry, these
costs were estimated at $200 per vehicle in 1996.) An increasing number of orga-
nizations that share information for their mutual benefits are replacing paper-
based transactions with interorganizational information systems that use
telecommunications to exchange electronic data, much as described in the examples above. This concept, called **electronic data interchange (EDI)**, has been
used in some industries for over two decades, but the popularity of EDI grew
tremendously in the late 1980s and in the 1990s. According to the technology
research firm Input, some $130 billion worth of transactions were conducted
throughout the world via EDI in 1996. As enumerated in Figure 11.2, tremendous
benefits are being realized in the estimated more than 100,000 companies using
EDI, of which 40,000 are U.S. firms. An increasing number of businesses
acknowledge that belated installation of EDI would put them at a disadvantage.

Cost Savings	◆ Reduction of employee hours involved in creation and handling of paper documents ◆ Reduction in the cost of funds transfer ◆ EDI reduces cost of storage space
Speed	◆ Forwarding of documents through computer network is faster than mail
Accuracy	◆ EDI minimizes the need for rekeying information ◆ Communication is direct and easily verifiable ◆ No mail is lost
Security	◆ Information is less susceptible to interception and false modification
System Integration	◆ EDI software can be interfaced with internal systems so that incoming data trigger applications and further automation of data processing
Just-In-Time Support	◆ Speeding up communication enhances intercompany just-in-time operations, which significantly reduce inventory costs. Only the necessary items are shipped by the vendor and arrive directly at the manufacturing or assembly line.

Figure 11.2 *Benefits of EDI*

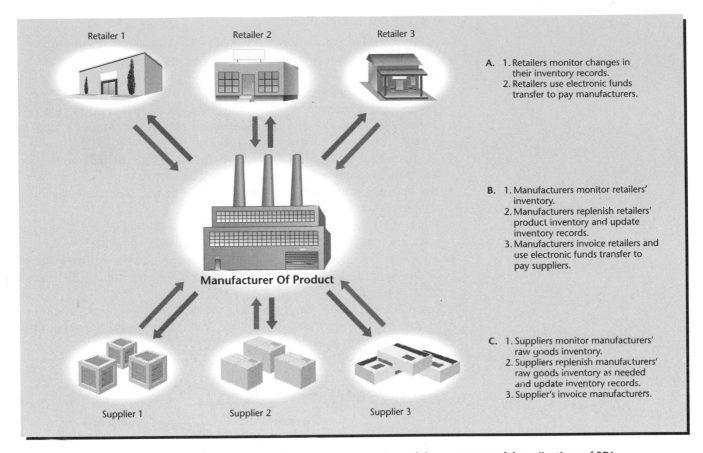

A. 1. Retailers monitor changes in their inventory records.
2. Retailers use electronic funds transfer to pay manufacturers.

B. 1. Manufacturers monitor retailers' inventory.
2. Manufacturers replenish retailers' product inventory and update inventory records.
3. Manufacturers invoice retailers and use electronic funds transfer to pay suppliers.

C. 1. Suppliers monitor manufacturers' raw goods inventory.
2. Suppliers replenish manufacturers' raw goods inventory as needed and update inventory records.
3. Supplier's invoice manufacturers.

Figure 11.3 *Suppliers, manufacturers, and retailers cooperate in some of the most successful applications of EDI.*

WHAT IS EDI?

In addition to being a concept, EDI is also a set of hardware, software, and standards that accommodates interorganizational exchange of data. The most common types of interorganizational information systems use EDI, which, when used along with bar coding and imaging, can increase the efficiency of an organization tremendously. For instance, the creation and handling of a paper document such as a purchase order might cost an organization $25–$50, but the cost of an equivalent electronic document would be as low as $12. In addition, because electronic recording is more accurate than manual recording, EDI contributes to a higher level of information accuracy and integrity, which saves additional costs.

EDI can also shape the long-term direction of a manufacturing firm. By linking a firm to its vendors, customers, and subcontractors, EDI enables manufacturers to quickly query vendors, who in turn can provide on-time delivery of the exact amount of resources needed. The technology also allows changes in production schedules to be communicated quickly and acted upon with minimal disruption in the plans of either the buying or supplying firm (see Figure 11.3).

How Does EDI Work?

Figure 11.4 illustrates how EDI would work between two organizations.

◆ First, the supplier's proposal is sent electronically to the purchasing organization.

◆ Next, an electronic contract is approved over the network, with both organizations maintaining a digital copy.

◆ The supplier manufactures and packages the goods, attaching to each box shipping data recorded on a bar code, which are scanned into the system as the shipments are loaded onto the truck.

◆ The items shipped, their quantities, and their prices are entered into the system and flow automatically to an invoicing program.

◆ The documents and invoices are transmitted to the purchasing organization, so they know what parts they will receive.

◆ When the packages are received at the purchasing organization, the bar codes are scanned, and the data are compared to the actual items received.

◆ If there are no discrepancies, an approval for payment is transferred electronically to the Accounts Payable department, which instructs the bank to pay the supplier.

◆ Using EFT (electronic funds transfer), the bank reduces the organization's balance by the proper amount, and electronically transfers the sum to the supplier's account at his bank.

None of the documents involved in the process is on paper.

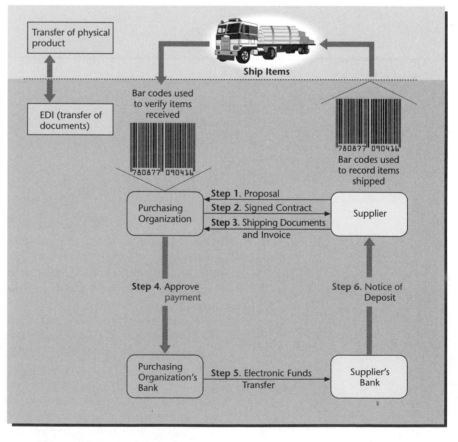

Figure 11.4 *How EDI works*

Using the Internet for EDI purposes was unheard of until 1996, when Heineken decided to implement the idea. Forecasting inventory needs over the Net helps smooth interorganizational communications, eliminating a major bottleneck in the companies' **supply chain** (the series of operations from purchasing of raw materials, through production phases, to delivery of the finished product). Special software lets manufacturers and retailers conduct real-time collaborative planning and reduce excess inventory. Heineken USA, Inc., a large beer distributor, incorporates such special software into its Heineken Operational Planning System (HOPS), and supplies more than 100 independent U.S. distributors with a client version of the software. Using a standard Web browser, distributors log on to Heineken's intranet to view forecast information and adjust beer supplies based on customer demand. Supply information is automatically entered into the HOPS database. The system cut lead times by almost half. That means a supplier is able to receive beer shipments in four to six weeks, instead of the previous 10 to 12 weeks.

Source: Stein, T., "Inventory Control Online," *InformationWeek*, December 9, 1996, p. 28.

EDI Standards

EDI is not a new concept. In fact, electronic funds transfer, which is EDI in the banking industry, has been around for at least three decades. The main obstacle to EDI becoming a common practice is standardization. For two organizations to transmit documents to each other, they must have compatible hardware and software, and must agree on the formats of the electronic forms they will use. Participating organizations must agree on details down to the length of each field and its location in the document, how many lines should be left for "comments," and so on and so on.

The auto industry has made the greatest strides in this regard. General Motors, Ford, and Chrysler have collaborated for years. Along with another 300 auto parts manufacturers, they established the Automotive Industry Action Group (AIAG) to set standards for transmitting forms among companies. All three organizations now pressure their suppliers to adopt their EDI standards. They do not sign contracts with a new supplier unless the supplier agrees to use EDI for transactions.

Different industries have different needs. National and international committees have adopted standards for customs organizations, hospitals, shipping, and other industries. In the U.S., a standard called X.12 was developed by the **American National Standards Institute** (ANSI) and has become the the de facto umbrella standard for EDI in the U.S. and Canada. In Europe, the **EDI For Administration, Commerce, and Trade** (EDIFACT), first issued in 1987 and developed under the auspices of the United Nations, is becoming the prevailing umbrella of standards. It is expected that EDIFACT will eventually govern EDI globally.

How to Subscribe to EDI

Large companies usually install their own EDI hardware and software, with the latter representing the bulk of the investment. Medium and small companies prefer to purchase the services of third parties that specialize in providing managed network services, sometimes called **value added networking** (VAN). VAN companies, such as General Electric, Sprint, and MCI, connect the subscriber's computer to their managed network. For a fee, they allow the subscriber to use the network for EDI. Some VANs provide only the communications links. Others provide both communications and the translation of the business documents into acceptable EDI formats.

Legal Problems of EDI

The legal issues that arise with the use of EDI include the increased risk of unauthorized external interception (which necessitates sophisticated measures of security), the challenge of resolving contractual responsibility for incomplete or corrupted telecommunications, the questionable validity of digital contracts in general, and protection against the ease of collaborative pricing and other activities that may violate antitrust laws (see Figure 11.5 on the next page).

One challenge to a smooth EDI operation is finding a way to deal with bilateral problems, which arise when one party does not receive a promised document on time, or receives a document corrupted by a bad communications line. Currently, it is unclear whether the sender or receiver would be responsible if, for example, a power blackout, or brownout, destroyed a transmitted message such as a request for a proposal, order, invoice, or payment

Figure 11.5 *Legal issues that arise in the use of EDI*

instructions to a bank. In the absence of clear legal contractual standards for EDI transactions, cooperating parties have to establish a relationship of trust, and agree to some rules governing their EDI activities. In fact, currently, EDI typically involves only close trading partners. The long-term relationship is an effective incentive to avoid misunderstandings, or to quickly resolve them when they occur. But in the future, more casual trading partners will use the technology, which may create fertile ground for lawsuits.

Another challenge in EDI is dealing with contract law and its requirements for a legally binding agreement. Section 2-201(1) of the Uniform Commercial Code (UCC), which governs commercial transactions in the U.S., provides that any contract for goods valued at $500 or more is not legally enforceable unless a writing "sufficient to indicate a contract for sale" has been made between the parties. No one has yet tried to test in court the validity of electronic contracts.

Kmart has opened its information system to help suppliers better serve customers. The interface has a heavily graphical user interface and allows 50 to 100 vendors to look at Kmart's merchandising database. For instance, the system gives Black and Decker access to any data (except information about their competitors) that Kmart believes helps B&D better serve Kmart. Kmart implemented the program in exchange for more frequent and smaller deliveries, but also because it was in the best interests of the company, its customers, and its suppliers. It is in Kmart's interests for B&D to spot a sales trend as early as possible, because it helps them better fulfill Kmart's needs. B&D wins because it has a channel to customers who want to buy its products. Customers win because there will be stock of products they want to purchase.

However, legally, a digitized signature is not valid; only an original signature on paper is legally binding. What happens if a party to a business transaction challenges the authenticity of a person's signature? As long as this legal issue is not resolved, most EDI trading partners sign a contract (with ink, on paper) in which they agree that electronically transmitted contracts bind them legally. These written contracts also outline how events such as lost, or criminally intercepted, electronic messages will be handled.

Lawyers specializing in legal issues of EDI suggest that the trading parties at the very least agree on what they consider "written" and "signed," to meet the definition of a contract under U.S. law. The attorneys recommend that a "Trading Partner Agreement," which is an agreement between organizations that plan to use EDI, establish the following points:

1. The precise EDI standard to be used (such as X.12 or EDIFACT)

2. The point in the transaction at which the contract becomes valid

3. Auditing and error detection procedures

4. Security measures

5. An "act of God" clause to address the results of natural events beyond human control, such as fires, floods, and earthquakes

Another important legal aspect of all interorganizational data interchange, including EDI, falls into the antitrust regulation arena. There is often a fine line between cooperation for mutual improvement of operations and illegal collaboration that results in what the government may perceive as price fixing, directly or indirectly. CEOs of large organizations in the auto industry and other industries complain that they must think twice every time they want to exchange information.

Despite the legal risks, EDI is rapidly becoming a fact of life in many organizations. Large corporations realize the great efficiency that the technology affords. Many of them simply refuse to trade with suppliers who do not adopt EDI. As the pressure from buyers on suppliers continues, we should expect the entire business community to use EDI in the foreseeable future.

THE IMPORTANCE OF EDI

The increasing demand, in a wide range of industries, for flexibility and the improved reliability of telecommunications technology is compelling more and more organizations to adopt EDI. Some of the factors contributing to this development are:

1. *The need for timely, reliable data exchange in response to rapidly changing markets.* Organizations cannot afford to rely solely on internal data to respond to market demands. Continuous exchange of data with cooperating organizations is vital for both suppliers and buyers.

2. *The emergence of standards and guidelines.* Great progress has been made in developing standards and guidelines for EDI in different industries, thereby eliminating the need for lengthy negotiations about the formats of forms, which often slowed the move to EDI.

3. *The spread of information into many organizational units.* A growing number of organizational units already generate and store data in computers, paving the way for the exchange of data with sources outside the organization. It is easier to exchange the data electronically than to enter it again, or print and send it in paper form.

Toys Я Us became the world's largest children's specialty chain, in part through using electronic data interchange (EDI) to make information transactions with suppliers digital rather than paper-based. Annually, the company processes over half a million invoices electronically, dramatically reducing costs and improving the integrity and management of related information. Some of its most important suppliers even have direct access to point-of-sale information, to determine sales trends and generate purchase orders on behalf of Toys Я Us. Everybody wins: the company and its suppliers.

4. *The greater reliability of information technology.* The more robust telecommunications technology makes electronic business transactions more reliable.

5. *The globalization of organizations.* A common method of communication simplifies processes among units of the same organization located in different countries.

Frost & Sullivan, a market research firm, estimates that the world-wide EDI market will more than quadruple from $700 million in 1994 to $3.2 billion in 2001. These figures include hardware, software, and services. The largest number of EDI end users are in health care, insurance, and retailing. Other major end-user industries include finance and banking, automotive, petroleum and chemical, and transportation companies.

For small businesses, the question of adopting EDI is becoming a question of life or death. Many of them cannot join the circle of a large organization's suppliers if they do not join the EDI network.

HORIZONTAL INFORMATION INTERCHANGE

Horizontal information interchange occurs when organizations performing similar activities share information. Usually, this is done by connecting to a central IS that collects data from all the participants, rather than by one organization connecting into the system of another organization, as is done in vertical interchange (see Figure 11.6).

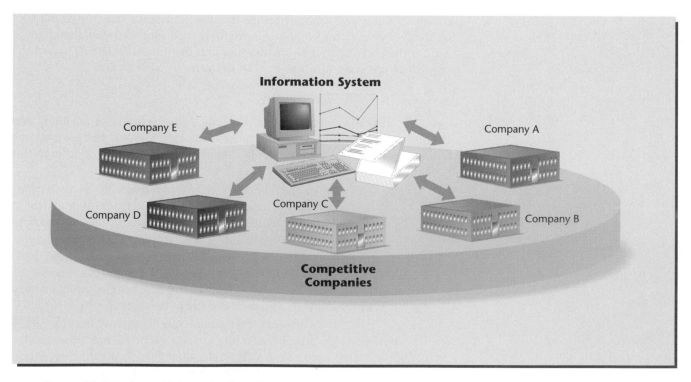

Figure 11.6 *Horizontal information interchange*

Used by permission from the SABRE Groupdisk

The SABRE information system, used by many airlines and travel agencies to make reservations and other travel services, is shown here being accessed through the user-friendly Planet SABRE interface.

Net Notes

Fast evolving electronic commerce has raised many legal issues. The Cyberspace Law Institute, an organization which, not surprisingly, has neither centralized offices nor personnel, is a virtual legal think tank with a Website at *http://www.cli.org*. If you are interested in legal issues on the Net, log on, and use the keywords *web legal issues* and *electronic commerce law* to find other sites.

For example, real estate agencies have shared information for years. They maintain a multiple listing system (MLS) containing the details and digitized picture of the houses listed for sale or rent. Whenever a participating agency lists a house, it automatically enters the MLS database. By using the MLS, every agency greatly increases its access to potential customers.

Similarly, insurance companies and auto repair shops can subscribe to services that allow them to browse databases containing information on junk yards and their used spare parts.

In the airline industry, reservation systems are an example of information interchange and sharing. The SABRE and APOLLO systems connect about 80% of U.S. travel agencies to huge databases that provide real-time seating information from different airlines.

In a recent move, the 17 largest U.S. hotel chains have joined together to create THISCO (The Hotel Industry Switch Company), which provides the participating hotels with a reservation switching capability and network. Fierce competitors benefit through a technology-enabled collaboration.

The oldest type of horizontal information interchange takes place among financial institutions, especially banks and credit card companies. Credit card companies access thousands of bank accounts daily to determine the credit-worthiness of credit applicants. Mortgage companies do the same thing for decisions on mortgage loan approvals.

Law enforcement agencies have taken great strides in opening their systems to their counterparts in other localities and states. The detectives of one city's police force can now receive information from federal, state, or local agencies within minutes. Such information includes digitized pictures and fingerprints. To a lesser extent, transfer of criminal information takes place internationally, for example, between the FBI and the international police organization Interpol.

The legal implications and risks in the use of horizontal electronic information exchange are similar to those faced by EDI, which are detailed above. These include risks involving loss of data due to power disturbances, and late shipments due to interrupted electronic communication, as well as the overall question of the validity of agreements executed electronically.

INTERNATIONAL AND MULTINATIONAL ORGANIZATIONS

An increasing number of the world's corporations are **multinational**. While they may have headquarters in a single country, they operate through divisions and subsidiaries located in different countries, where they take advantage of the local benefits offered. For instance, a company might establish engineering facilities in countries that offer large pools of qualified engineers, build production lines in countries that can supply inexpensive labor, and open sales offices in countries that are strategically situated for effective marketing.

Because of this spread of operations, a company's nationality is not always clear. For example, consider IBM and Philips. While IBM is known as an "American" corporation because its headquarters and most of its research

Learn About Inter-organizational and International ISs?

Two developments have contributed to the proliferation of international and interorganizational corporate alliances: the democratization of many countries, and the fast progress in telecommunications technology. To function successfully in this environment, managers must understand how both interorganizational and international information systems can serve their companies by identifying what information is needed, how it can be harnessed to improve business performance, and how their own information might benefit others.

Interorganizational ISs—both within one country and between countries—promote increased efficiency and paperless transactions as well. In order to contribute to this effort, a standard expectation of corporations today, managers must understand how the systems work.

These skills have become increasingly important as companies break up into smaller units, or closely collaborate with other companies in the same or similar industries, a trend supported in part by deregulation in the U.S. and Europe. In these situations, sharing of information by two or more organizations becomes extremely important. Managers now working for multinational corporations need an understanding of the problems and challenges involved in international data flow, to support efficient and effective decision making.

Net Notes

Use the keywords *chat* or *IRC* (Internet Relay Chat) and try to participate in a chat group. You will find many participants from other countries. What is the language used by those from non-English speaking countries?

activities are in the U.S., the company has numerous subsidiaries in other countries. These subsidiaries are registered and operate under the laws of the respective countries, and they employ local workers. Likewise, not many Americans realize that Philips's headquarters is in the Netherlands and that it owns one of the largest U.S. sellers of electric razors: Norelco.

One hundred of the largest 500 Canadian companies have majority U.S. ownership, and 90% of U.S. multinational companies have Canadian offices. Japanese companies own whole U.S. subsidiaries in every imaginable industry. British companies have the largest foreign investment in the U.S. Soon, thanks to the North American Free Trade Agreement (NAFTA) and agreements between the U.S. and the European Community, we may witness the internationalization of many more American, Canadian, Mexican, and European corporations.

For the management of an international corporation, the flow of information among divisions across national borders is often as essential as the flow of information among departments within a single-location company.

A number of surveys reflect the fact that IS managers are giving increasing attention to international integration of their ISs. A Deloitte & Touche survey shows that a great majority of CIOs working for companies with foreign operations consider international integration of ISs important or very important (see Figure 11.7). Eighty-two percent of the respondents said they planned further international integration of their IS operations.

Some larger multinational corporations build their own international ISs. EDS built EDSNET for General Motors. The network integrates data, voice, and video communications and is spread over five continents.

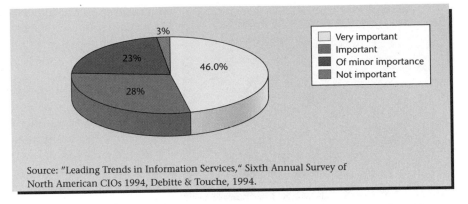

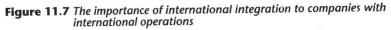

Source: "Leading Trends in Information Services," Sixth Annual Survey of North American CIOs 1994, Debitte & Touche, 1994.

Figure 11.7 *The importance of international integration to companies with international operations*

THE GLOBAL VILLAGE

Telecommunications technology has turned the world into what many people call a **global village**. The term connotes that with almost the entire world networked, individuals and organizations are location-independent for their information needs.

Consider today's vast network resources:

◆ BITNET, the Internet-based academic network started in the 1980s, connects thousands of universities and research institutions around the world.

◆ CSNET consists of some 200 host computers providing services to government and private research institutions in the U.S., Canada, Australia, France, Germany, Israel, Japan, Korea, Sweden, and England.

◆ SWIFT (Society for Worldwide Interbank Financial Telecommunications) and CHIPS (Clearing House for Interbank Payments System) are operated by banks and credit institutions.

◆ Airline reservation systems service airlines world-wide.

◆ EURONET serves European countries and is connected through gateways to U.S. and Canadian networks.

◆ TRANSAC (France), ACSNET (Australia), IPSS/PSS (England), NORDIC (Scandinavia), Junet (Japan), and VNIIPAS (the former Soviet Union) are connected through gateways to form one huge meganetwork. Soon, the meganetwork will expand to millions of users in the People's Republic of China.

◆ And, finally, the Internet, "the mother of all networks," has grown from an American network to a global network with millions of people logging on to it daily.

As you remember from Chapter 6, "The Internet and Intranets," the Internet is the infrastructure for the **electronic superhighway**, which supports not only text but also video, audio, and animated information, as well as interactive communication for shopping and entertainment. Once they expanded from America to the rest of the world, such networks opened excellent opportunities for direct business activities within and across national borders.

Communications networks promote the phenomena of **telecommuting** and the **virtual office**. Workers can receive tasks at home and transmit their

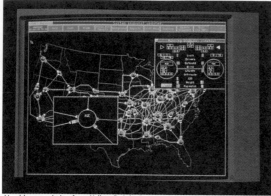

Used by permission from Yellow Freight System

Networks link businesses and individuals across the country and worldwide.

products back to the "office," which may be nothing more than a very few managers and secretaries in a small suite, while the "organization" comprises hundreds or thousands of employees who telecommute. This geographically loose form of organization is often referred to as a **virtual organization**.

Now, the phenomenon is spreading to include international telecommuting. Companies whose business is information or software employ workers from other countries. If one can telecommute from Albany to New York City, there is no reason, technically, why one could not do the same from New Delhi. Indeed, some U.S. software companies employ non-American programmers. Such practices may soon create a challenge: **electronic immigration**. Electronic immigrants may have an immense impact on the world economy and an adverse effect on national interests (see this chapter's *Ethics and Society*).

CHALLENGES TO GLOBAL INFORMATION SYSTEMS

Establishing global ISs is not without its problems. Although most of the purely technical problems have been resolved, there are still several obstacles that multinational companies must overcome.

LANGUAGE DIFFERENCES

Naturally, text and voice information is language-dependent. To communicate internationally, parties must agree on one acceptable language, and that can create problems. For instance, data processing may not be transmittable internationally in real time because the information must first be translated. Another hurdle is that national laws usually forbid businesses to run accounting and other systems in a foreign language, leading to the use by multinational companies of an awkward and expensive solution: running these systems in two languages, the local one and English, which is the defacto international language.

CULTURAL DIFFERENCES

Lingual differences must be overcome to integrate international information systems.

Cultural differences refer in general to the many ways countries differ from each other, such as in their laws, in their attitudes about work, and in their opinions about different ethical issues. For example, some European countries, such as Germany, Sweden, and Denmark, severely restrict businesses from collecting and maintaining personal data because they view these practices as infringing on their citizens' rights to privacy. U.S. and Canadian laws do not impose any restrictions of this sort. One result is that German and Swedish divisions of an American company are forbidden to transfer any personal data from their databases to the U.S. for marketing or other purposes.

Information systems play an important role in determining what information other nations receive. ISs may challenge cultural traditions by imposing the culture of one nation upon another. Conservative groups in some countries have complained about the "Americanization" of their young generation. Governments may be inclined to forbid the reception of some information for reasons of undesirable cultural influence.

The Electronic Immigrant

Telecommuting, working from home through computers and communications lines, is becoming increasingly popular in America and Europe. It has many advantages, including a reduction in energy costs, fewer congested highways, less air pollution, and a more flexible workday. But on the national level, it also poses a great threat. Currently, if a foreign national wishes to work in the U.S., he or she needs permission from the federal government, which controls the flow of foreign workers into the country in order to secure jobs for its own citizens. Other countries have similar policies. In fact, the laws of some countries practically close their borders to foreign workers. The control is enforced by physically blocking entry at borders, seaports, and airports.

Telecommuting, which does not require physically crossing national boundaries, significantly reduces the ability of governments to control immigration effectively. As communications costs go down, we will see an increasing number of **electronic immigrants** and no one can stop an electronic immigrant at a port of entry. He or she competes with local workers in foreign countries. Sometimes this means that professionals in countries with low standards of living and low wages are competing directly with workers in affluent countries with relatively high wages.

As long as national governments prefer to employ their own citizens for job openings, they have to carefully consider methods that can block electronic immigration, while not hampering the free flow of information. If new methods of blocking electronic immigration are not found, the world will take a huge step toward a job market that lacks political boundaries, at least in the service sector. In the long run, this shift may lead to a more efficient allocation of resources, and the world economy as a whole may in fact win. But in the short run, which may last several years, electronic immigrants may cause pockets of unemployment in host countries, and in extreme cases, the phenomenon may eliminate entire occupations in some other countries.

An example of such fear is the French directive against usage of foreign words in government-supported mass media and official communications.

ECONOMIC, SCIENTIFIC, AND SECURITY INTERESTS

The goal of corporate management is to seize a large market share and maximize profits for its organization. The goal of a national government is to protect the economic, scientific, and security interests of its people. Scientific information is both an important national resource for a country and a great source of income for corporations; occasionally, those interests conflict.

For instance, companies that design and manufacture military weapons have technical drawings and specifications that are of financial value to the company, but also of security value to their country. Hence, many governments, including the U.S. federal government, do not allow the exchange of information regarding such designs. Transfer of such information to another country, even if the receiving party is a part of an American business, is prohibited. Often, products whose intended purpose has nothing to do with military use are included in the list of prohibited trade, because of the fear that those items could be used against the country of origin. In recent years, the list has included many software packages. The result is that, while American divisions of a company may use such software, their sister divisions in other countries cannot.

A LOOK INTO THE FUTURE ▶

Virtual Yet Real

We have mentioned the terms "virtual organization" and "virtual office" several times. How will the virtual organization function in the future? Consider the following scenario.

Tony Tang is the marketing manager of a small but thriving software company. The firm specializes in applications for graphic designers. Its products are popular on three continents: America, Europe, and Asia. Business is booming.

You would expect the offices to be full of programmers working hard on new applications. But the "offices" are actually one modest office. In addition to Tony, who has a cubicle in an open-space office 20 by 15 feet, only three other people have office space: the firm's president and two senior programmers. Where is everybody?

"Everybody" is not here. These four people are the only ones who occupy the office. They are the only employees of the company who live in this city. In fact, they are the only employees who live in this country and on this continent. In addition to the programmers, the firm has a part-time employee who duplicates floppy disks, and packages them for shipment. The other 23 employees, all experienced programmers, live and work in other countries.

The president, Mr. Probish, checks daily with his international staff. Because of the time differences, he does that at strange hours, like 6 p.m. or later. Yesterday, he had a long discussion with Jayant Trewn from Bombay, India. In one window on his computer monitor he saw Jayant's real-time image. In another, Jayant displayed some program code with which he had a problem. Mr. Probish fixed the code in two of the lines, and was satisfied with it.

Tony uses his PC to check the status of two new program modules that Hans Sterner and Clive Horn are working on. He has placed several ads in trade journals, for the upcoming version 4.3 of the successful QuickPaint application, and he is determined to make it available in time as promised. Hans works from his home in Hamburg, Germany. Clive works from his home in Greenwich, England. Each is working on a different module. Tony checks with them frequently.

When he joined the firm, Tony found that, in a way, he was also a shipping officer. He uses his computer to log on to the systems of eight large software retailers, four in the U.S., two in England, and two in Japan. When the numbers indicate that supply is down to a minimum level, he issues an electronic shipping order and an electronic invoice, which he transmits to the retailer.

At month's end, Tony consolidates sales figures from all retailers. Of course, the figures come in different currencies, but he has programmed his spreadsheet to convert the amounts according to the current rates of exchange. And he doesn't need to plug the rates into the spreadsheet. Since the firm subscribes to the services of an international financial reporting firm, he has programmed his spreadsheet application to capture the rates automatically whenever he consolidates the sales.

THINK CRITICALLY

What managerial problems do you foresee in "virtual organizations" like the one described here? What will the impact of such cross-border activity be on national economies?

Used by permission from Jane Evelyn Atwood/Contact; The Stock Market

Some nations are afraid that cross-border information flow promotes "cultural imperialism".

Governments prohibit the sharing of sensitive information with other countries, especially if the information can compromise national security.

Used by permission from Lockheed Martin Corporation

Another problem that arises with international information interchange is that different countries treat trade secrets, patents, and copyrights differently. Sometimes, business partners from different countries are reluctant to transfer documents when one partner is in a country with strict intellectual property rights, while another is in a country that lacks laws protecting such rights. On the other hand, the employees of a division of a multinational corporation may divulge information locally with impunity.

As intellectual property is tightly protected in the U.S., trade negotiators and diplomats have pressured some countries to pass and enforce similar laws. Reportedly, the legislatures of several Asian nations have passed such laws or revised existing laws, under American pressure.

POLITICAL CHALLENGES

As we have mentioned several times in this book, information is power. And some countries fear that a policy of free access to all information may threaten their sovereignty. For instance, a nation's government may feel that access to certain data, such as the location and quantity of natural resources, may give other nations an opportunity to control an indigenous resource, thereby gaining a business advantage that would adversely affect the resource-rich country's political interests.

Governments are also increasingly recognizing software as an important economic resource, leading some countries to dictate that companies operating within their borders must purchase software from within their borders. For example, until 1997 Brazil's authorities allow local business to purchase software from outside its boundaries only after demonstrating that the software was not available locally. The rule was enforced even if the business was owned by a foreign company. Similar laws regulate the purchase and installation of telecommunications hardware and software. These policies can hinder standardization and compatibility of international ISs by preventing the use of the same software throughout a multinational corporation.

STANDARDS

Because nations use different standards and rules in their daily business functions, sometimes records within one company are incompatible. For instance, the bookkeeping records of one division of a multinational company may be incompatible with the records of other divisions and headquarters. As another example, the U.S. still uses the "English" system of weights and measures (inches, feet, miles, quarts, pounds, and so on), while the rest of the world (including England) officially uses the metric system (centimeters, meters, liters, kilograms, and the like). Simple differences such as the way dates and addresses are displayed can create problems, especially in ISs. These differences must be taken into consideration when integrating ISs internationally.

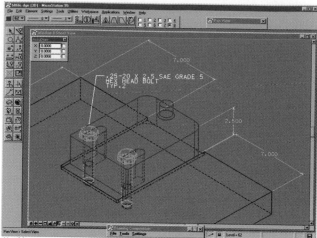

Used by permission from Bentley Systems

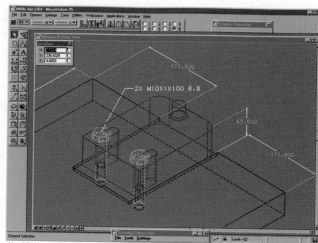

Used by permission from Bentley Systems

LEGAL BARRIERS TO INTERNATIONAL DATA TRANSFER

While many of the challenges involved in cross-border data transfer have been resolved through international agreements, one remains unresolved: respecting differing national views on privacy while conducting international business with very little restriction. Interestingly, despite the importance we attach to privacy, that value is not even mentioned in the constitutions of the U.S. and many other countries. Nonetheless, a majority of the democratic nations try to protect privacy.

Different nations have different approaches to the issue, as is reflected in their laws. Some are willing to forego some privacy for the sake of a freer flow of information and better marketing. Others restrict any collection of private data without the consent of the individual.

To a large extent, laws governing cross-border data transfer stem from a nation's approach to the privacy of its citizens and organizations. Over 30 nations have data privacy laws, and many more are considering either regulations or national legislation. Austria, Denmark, France, Germany, Norway, and Sweden enacted their laws in the 1970s. Luxembourg, England, and Holland followed suit in the 1980s. On other continents, Canada and New Zealand enacted privacy statutes. Almost all of the Western European countries have laws that protect private data.

Data protection laws from various countries can be generally described by three different criteria:

1. Whether the law applies to the collection and treatment of data by the private sector (companies), the public sector (governments), or by both
2. Whether the laws apply to manual data, to automated data, or to both
3. Whether data protected under the law are only those about human beings, or those about both human and "legal" persons (that is, organizations)

Except for the American and Canadian privacy acts, privacy laws apply to both the public and private sectors; that is, government and private organizations are subject to the same regulation of collection, maintenance, and disclosure of personal data. Over half the laws (including U.S. federal statutes) encompass manual as well as computerized record-keeping systems. A minority of the laws apply to legal persons. Denmark, Austria, and Luxembourg are among the countries that protect the privacy of legal persons' data.

Countries that favor protection of data about legal persons argue that it is difficult to separate data about individuals from data on business activities involving or performed by individuals. This is especially true with respect to small businesses.

For example, the financial information of a small business also reveals information about the people involved with and/or running the business. Furthermore, a large corporation may unfairly compete against a smaller firm if it has access to the smaller firm's data.

The conditions of these differing laws hinder development of international trade, and especially hurt multinational corporations. Therefore, international organizations try to harmonize the laws. The EC has considered a uniform law that will prohibit the transfer of personal data without the individual's knowledge and agreement. There are two problematic points in the draft. One is how to treat countries that are not signatories to the Council of Europe agreement on data protection, especially with respect to international use of credit cards. The other stems from an article in the draft that states: "An individual shall not be subject to an administrative or private decision involving an assessment of conduct which has, as its sole basis, the automatic processing of personal data defining his profile or personality." This provision, which is stipulated in the French law, limits the use of a computer as a decision aid in certain circumstances. For instance, no automatic decisions as to credit, admittance to a college, or the like would be permitted.

THE ADVANTAGE OF WAITING

Those of us who live and work in countries where IT and telecommunications have developed rapidly often "pity" less developed countries that are not at the forefront of these technologies. Before rushing to make judgment, however, one should recall the old story about the roasted pig that economists like to tell when discussing developing countries and economic growth.

As the story goes, many years ago, a shed caught fire in a small village. The shed's owner had a pig locked in it. The villagers helped put the fire out, but the shed was almost fully consumed. Then they smelled something delicious they had never smelled before. As the owner looked somberly at the smoldering remains of the shed, some of his friends tore pieces from the roasted pig, and they liked what they tasted. As of that day people started to eat roasted pigs. And eventually they learned that they didn't need to burn down a shed to roast a pig...

What is the lesson, and what does this have to do with our topic? Countries and companies that are on the so-called *bleeding edge* of technology take a much longer and more expensive road to more advanced technologies; latecomers have the privilege of learning from their predecessors' mistakes, and often take the shortcut to the more advanced solutions. For instance, many nations that couldn't afford the expense of wiring an infrastructure for physical telecommunications networks have skipped those technologies and adopted the relatively inexpensive cellular phone option. It is the more technologically advanced nations who had to go through the research and development and heavy expenses of creating the networks. Other nations do not have to pay dearly by "burning the shed." They can quickly deploy the same technology that the more developed nations now have. This will, to some extent, close the gap in networking and the use of global information resources.

---

[1] Oz, E., *Ethics for the Information Age*, Wm.C. Brown, Dubuque, IA, 1994.

Invoicing in 13 Currencies

Six foreign languages and 13 currencies made overseas invoicing a headache for Cannondale, a bicycle manufacturer in Georgetown, Connecticut, that conducts 37% of its sales in Europe. So the company adapted an off-the-shelf software program to produce invoices in each customer's currency and language.

Why go to such lengths? The translation software simplifies the billing of Cannondale's European distributors and retailers, and makes it easier for the U.S. company to blend in. "We're 'transparent' to the local customer because we can invoice in the local language and currency," says Cannondale Europe president Dan Alloway. Cannondale's programmer Peg Beasley spent about three weeks rewriting the invoicing and billing functions of the company's business planning software, which comes from a Chicago-based company named SSA.

At first, Beasley organized files by country, until she realized that a Swiss customer could speak German or French, at which point she switched to organizing the

files by language. It took another week to work out the technical snags. Here's how the ordering process works today: A sales representative enters an order into the computer; the order is then downloaded to Cannondale Europe's central office in Holland, where invoices are created according to the customer's "language code."

The system ensures accurate billing by accounting for fluctuating currencies. Once a month, staffers key in current exchange rates for 13 countries, based on exchange rates given by Cannondale's bank. The system recalculates any outstanding accounts receivable. That's a helpful feature, whether you're booking $1 million or $40 million, as Cannondale does.

Source: "Invoicing in 13 Currencies," Inc., November 1995, p. 101.

Questions

1. "We are 'transparent' to the local customer." What does the term 'transparent' mean in this context? Why is it important that the language and currency conversions are transparent to the local customer?

2. Enumerate the advantages of a system like the one described here.

3. What could Cannondale do to automate the updating of the currency exchange rates?

FedEx Opens the Doors to the World

FedEx is the world's leader in physical logistics, but not without competitors. UPS, DHL, and Airborne Express, fiercely compete with the company. Thus, FedEx works hard to keep its strategic edge. In 1997, FedEx ran a fleet of 570 aircraft and 37,000 trucks and vans. The company had already established a Web site that allows institutional and individual clients to track their parcels remotely. However, to accommodate large corporations that ship great volumes of items through FedEx, the company had to take an extra step. It had to establish electronic commerce with its corporate clients. The company decided to establish EDI through the Internet. This practice is often called "extranet" by some observers because the network reaches *outside* the organization.

"The focus for the Internet over the last few years has been business-to-customer," said Laurie Tucker, senior vice president of FedEx Logistics, Electronic Commerce and Catalog Division. "But in everything I've read in the last six months, I see the focus shifting toward business-to-business." The company established links to large distributors such as Blobelle Corp. and Intelligent Electronics, Inc., helping those companies cut costs and become more efficient. In 1997, FedEx handled an average of 54.7 million electronic transmissions daily.

FedEx uses a mainframe computer connected to multiple servers. It arms partners such as merchandise distributors and resellers with hardware and software that allow them to tap into FedEx's own shipping information system, to gain information about shipments the moment an order is placed, arrange for courier pickups, track packages, and create paperless transaction records. The systems have become quite sophisticated, allowing FedEx to coordinate their pickups for the same shipment from different warehouses, to ensure that all the pieces arrive at the customer site at the same time.

In 1996, FedEx gave customers the ability to send packages without having to fill out any paperwork, by using its InterNetShip software. This program allows the user to process the transaction data, and dials FedEx over a modem through the Internet to request a courier pickup, as well as to log in the outgoing shipment. The only paper involved is a package label that any laser printer can produce.

The freight carrier has gained a considerable competitive edge by integrating its information sys-

tems with those of its partners. The level of access stems from FedEx's philosophy that information is crucial to cutting the cost of doing business. "The information on the shipment has become more important than the physical shipment itself," said the chief operating officer of one client, which has closely integrated its warehouse management and information system with FedEx's. The client ships about 50% of its freight with FedEx, which amounts to eight million pounds per quarter. "The customer who doesn't want to keep inventory needs to know where the product is," said an executive for another client. The distributors use the hardware and software provided by FedEx to let their own customers track the items they ordered. "By the time customers wake up the next morning and sign on to our Web site, they can go into it and look up their tracking number," said the executive.

One of the systems FedEx provided resellers is BusinessLink, an online ordering system. The resellers' customers can use it to place orders from the distributors. FedEx uses the information to pick up the ordered item from the original supplier (the seller to the distributor), and ship it directly to the consumer. The distributor never sees or touches the item. "A lot of times we never touch the product; we just collect the money," said the executive of one reseller.

Source: Pereira, P., "Instant Delivery: FedEx Opens Doors to World," Computer Reseller News, Issue 723, February 17, 1997.

Questions

1. Why is FedEx so eager to provide distributors with hardware and software for electronic commerce?

2. The supply chain of many products passes through several "hands" before the products reach the final buyer: manufacturer, national distributor, regional distributor, and so on. Consider BusinessLink. What may be the impact of such a system for distributors?

A Global Web of Procurement Agents

Manufacturers' Services Ltd. (MSL), headquartered in Concord, Massachusetts, provides manufacturing services to large computer and telecommunications manufacturers, such as AT&T, IBM, LM Ericsson, Thomson Multimedia, and 46 others. For the subcontracts it carries out, the company procures items from many suppliers, including Cypress Semiconductor Corp., Mitsubishi, National Semiconductor Corp., and Toshiba.

When Steve Darendinger was called to oversee MSL's purchasing in 1996, he was faced with a daunting task: implement a seamless procurement process at a company that had become one of the world's biggest contract manufacturers. Instead of centralizing the purchasing system, he decentralized it. The different manufacturing plants, scattered all over the U.S. and the world, perform with considerable independence, but still work in tandem.

The plan was to decentralize purchasing and disperse it globally.

He placed procurement organizations at each site (Minnesota, California, Singapore, Malaysia, Spain, and Ireland) to execute purchases for customers in their respective regions. He also established international procurement offices (IPOs) in California, Singapore, and Tokyo. Until that move, the company had no IPOs in place. While each IPO is responsible for the suppliers in its own region, it can also provide help to the others.

For instance, if U.S. supplies of a particular component are low, an MSL procurement manager can use an information system to tap another warehouse or manufacturer for the order. The IS will replenish any site with material or components for assembling products within the subsequent two weeks. For that reason, the U.S. sites and warehouses carry little inventory. "We can rapidly shift product from Singapore to the U.S. if it's required," Darendinger said. For instance, MSL was able to fulfill an order for memory chips within the 24 hours a major networking customer required.

Linking the site procurement offices with the IPOs are seven global commodity managers, each in charge of a different commodity, such as memory chips, microprocessors, PC boards, plastics, and sheet metal. The global commodity managers e-mail monthly commodity reports not only to Darendinger, but to each of the other sites as well, to ensure a homogeneity of standards for the company as a whole.

To help reduce materials costs, MSL uses enterprise-resource-planning software to connect its supply sites and procurement and corporate offices in the U.S. and other countries to each other and, in turn, to suppliers and customers. The software tracks component requirements and inventory world-wide, and saves money in the process. By using the software to link MSL clients, the original equipment manufacturers (OEMs), the company is able to consolidate requests for identical items, and bargain with vendors to get the lowest price possible.

Darendinger has succeeded in reducing the number of MSL's suppliers from about 600 to 350, while reducing the cost of materials by 5.8%. He has also managed to achieve a 24-hour response to clients' item orders. Since purchasing constitutes 70–75% of MSL's operating costs, this is a significant contribution both to the company's profits and to its reputation.

Source: Jonas, G., "Decentralizing Pays Dividends for Contractor: Manufacturer's Services Trims Suppliers, Reduces Its Cost of Materials by 5.8%," Electronic Buyers' News, Issue 1045, February 17, 1997.

Questions

1. Why did Darendinger decide to decentralize the procurement system? To what extent is the system still centralized?

2. Consider the vertical supply chain discussed in the *Vertical Information Interchange* section of this chapter. What are the organizations involved in the chain of which MSL is a part?

3. While the system has saved MSL money, it is not fully automated. What would you implement to improve it?

Organizations find that sharing ISs benefits all participants in business activities. In **vertical information interchange**, companies such as Toys Я Us and Kmart save costs by opening their ISs to suppliers, who then take over the cost of inventory control, while also making their own operations more efficient and effective. **Horizontal information interchange** occurs among companies in the same line of business. This is common in the banking industry, which shares databases of credit histories, and the airline industry, which shares reservation information, and among realtors, who share data about available real estate.

Electronic data interchange (EDI) networks have been established by many businesses to support vertical interaction with their suppliers. EDI not only speeds up communication between organizations, but also saves money by reducing the number of paper documents and the costs involved in handling them. However, the use of EDI has raised some legal issues. For one, since the law regards only signed commercial agreements, on paper, as binding, EDI can be successfully used only if the parties trust each other. Companies have to be careful not to share so much information that their increasingly efficient processes may be interpreted as violating antitrust laws, through price fixing and the like.

Thanks to advancements in communications technology, the world is turning into a **global village**, where geographic distance is unimportant in business as far as information interchange is concerned. The number of **multinational corporations** is growing, and so is the need for **international ISs.** However, implementation of international ISs faces some challenges. Linguistic, cultural, economic, and political interests may interfere in the flow of information across national borders, as can different standards, and the privacy laws of the individual nations.

Telecommuting takes place not only within countries, but also between countries. This may cause unforeseen problems. The phenomenon has created the **electronic immigrant**, a person employed by a business in a country other than the one in which he or she lives. Such practices reduce governments' ability to enforce employment regulations.

The Internet, the world's largest computer network, is fast becoming the target of many commercial organizations, for business purposes. While the opportunities are exciting, there are also risks: unauthorized access, interception of access codes and credit information, and misrepresentation. Participating businesses adopt protective measures, but the activity is never fully risk-free.

REVIEW, DISCUSS, AND EXPLORE

REVIEW AND DISCUSSION QUESTIONS

1. What is meant by the term "interorganizational information systems"?

2. What is vertical information interchange? Give examples.

3. What is horizontal information interchange? Give examples.

4. What are international information systems?

5. EDI experts argue that staffs should be educated on the concept of EDI. What do they mean by "the concept of EDI," and why is it important to educate employees?

6. What technology plays a major role in interorganizational and international information systems? Why?

7. Partners in interorganizational information systems say the key to success is mutual trust. Why?

8. What are the challenges faced by companies that wish to implement an international IS?

9. What does the term "virtual organization" mean? What are the implications of the term to international organizations?

10. In your opinion, what is the most difficult legal issue that nations must resolve before full cross-border flow of information takes place?

11. *Ethics and Society*: What is the "electronic immigrant"? What are the advantages and disadvantages of this phenomenon? Who benefits, and who loses?

CONCEPT ACTIVITY

Interview the highest ranking IS officer of a multinational corporation. Use the challenges mentioned in this chapter as a framework: What are the challenges this organization is facing in data flows with overseas sites? Prepare a short report.

HANDS-ON ACTIVITY

You are the international sales manager for a multinational company headquartered in the U.S. At the end of every month you receive reports from the national sales managers of your company's operations in England, France, and Germany. The products are sold by area. The managers report the units sold and income from sales in their national standards: Pounds Sterling (£), French Francs (FF), and Deutsche Marks (DM). Use your spreadsheet program to consolidate the sales reports you received, as follows.

Aladdin Yarns, Inc.

UK		FRANCE		GERMANY		US		TOTAL	
m²	£	m²	FF	m²	DM	yd²	US $	m²	US $

1. Under "total," enter formulas to convert square yards to square meters and enter another formula to total the area in square meters for all four countries.

2. Enter a formula that will convert all foreign currencies to U.S. $ according to the rate of exchange for the day this activity was assigned. (Extra challenge: program a macro to do the calculations.)

3. Test all formulas with actual numbers.

TEAM ACTIVITY

Your team should conduct research with four companies in four different industries, one of which is in software development. The title of your research is "The Electronic Immigrant: Economic and Political Implications." Contact the CEOs of the four companies, present the issue, and ask for the CEO's opinion: Can the company use "electronic immigrants?" Can it be hurt if competitors use them? Do the CEOs think the national economy can gain or lose from the phenomenon? Do they foresee any political ramifications? Your team should use a word processor to prepare a neat report starting with half a page of background on each company.

EXPLORE THE WEB

Non-U.S. Web sites have addresses with suffixes denoting the country where they are located, such as .ca for Canada, .nl for the Netherlands, .fr for France, .uk for the United Kingdom, and .il for Israel. Assume that you are shopping for sporting goods. Use the keywords *sporting goods*. Write down the URLs (addresses) of four sites, one American and three each of another country. Click to retrieve the home pages of these sites, and time the retrieval from the click to the moment the retrieval is complete. Repeat the retrieval at least three times. Compare the average times for each site. Write a short report detailing the names and countries of the sites.

Many IS professionals say it is too early to conduct regular business through the Web because of the low speed of retrieval. Write your own opinion, bearing in mind what you experienced. Is it practical to use the Web for international business with the speed of your modem (or other communications devices)?

PART 4

IBM S/370 machine language

```
00001000 00000010 00000000 0000
00001010 00000010 00000000 0000
00000000 0        010 0000000 00001100 00000001 00000
```

BM System 370 Assembler

```
L R2, = F '2'
A R2, = F '5'
ST R2, Y
```

Third generation lang

```
AN:     y = 2+5
        add 2, 5
        let y =
        y := 2
        y =  2+5
```

urth generation

```
y = 2+
```

Information Systems in Decision Making

Chapter 12

Decision Support and Executive Information Systems

Predicting Defectors

"Northwest Cellular" sells cellular phones and resells long distance service for a national telephone carrier. The company faced a serious problem: many customers left it to subscribe to services of competitors, but Northwest didn't know why. On average, the company lost 23% of its customers per year. The cost of subscribing a new customer is $350. Management figured out that the company could sustain a defection rate of no more that 20% per year. To remain competitive, the company had to find a way to reduce defections. In order to reduce the defection rate, the sales manager wanted to target the department's marketing efforts to those customers most likely to defect. But how do you find who the likely defectors were?

Northwest acquired a decision support system to help it. The system is connected with the company's database. For the purpose of analysis, the system considers as defectors not only those customers who have actually left, but also those whose monthly calling has dropped drastically. The system takes the characteristics of individuals from these two groups to identify who is likely to defect. For each customer, Northwest's database includes credit information, contract terms, phone type, and aggregate calling activity. The system uses these data to create a model reflecting the overall profile of the previous year's defectors. The system then applies this model to predict which of the current year's customers are likely to defect. Customers are assigned to segments based on how closely their information matches the previous year's defectors' profile. The company then targets the likely defectors with its marketing efforts. In 1997, likely defectors constituted 40% of the company's customers.

In addition to this help, the DSS provides a profit model that helps the sales manager estimate the return on investment from conducting marketing campaigns with each of the customer groups. Targeted marketing helped Northwest Cellular reduce defection in 1997 from 23% to 19.7%.

Source: "Predicting Defections among Customers," Pilot Software, Inc., April 25, 1997. ©1997 Pilot Software, Inc. Reprinted courtesy of Pilot® Software, Inc.

Much of managerial work is decision making. Managers must often consider great amounts of data, synthesize from it only the relevant information, and make decisions that will benefit the organization. As the amount of available data grows, so does the need for computer-based decision aids to assist managers in their decision-making process.

When you finish this chapter, you will:

◆ Understand the steps followed in decision making

◆ Understand the difference between structured and unstructured decision making

◆ Know the typical software components that decision support systems comprise

◆ Be familiar with the main types of decision support systems

Net Notes

Decision Science Institute is the premier nonprofit organization whose main interest is to research and disseminate information on decision making. Log on to the organization's Web site (*http://www.gsu.edu/~dsiadm/index.html*) to explore the organization's activities.

DECISION MAKING IN BUSINESS

The success of an organization largely depends on the quality of the decisions that its managers make. When decision making involves large amounts of information and a lot of processing, computer-based systems can make the process effective and efficient. There are several types of information systems that support decision making: decision support systems, executive information systems, and expert systems. The former two are discussed in this chapter, and the latter in Chapter 13, "Artificial Intelligence and Expert Systems."

THE DECISION-MAKING PROCESS

When does one have to make a decision? As we reviewed in Chapter 1, "Business Information Systems: An Introduction," when you drive your car to a certain destination and there is only one road, you do not have to make a decision. The road will take you there. But if you come to a fork without a sign, you have to decide which way to go. In fact, whenever there is more than one alternative action available, a **decision** must be made.

A decision is easy to make when one option will clearly bring about a better outcome than any other. Decisions become more difficult when more than one alternative seems reasonable and when the number of alternatives grows. In business, there can be dozens, hundreds, or even millions of different courses of action available to achieve a desired result. The problem is deciding on the best course of action. (You can see why problem solving and decision making are so closely related.)

Herbert Simon, a long-time researcher of management and decision making, described decision making as a three-phase process (see Figure 12.1).

- ◆ ***Intelligence***: In the intelligence phase we collect facts, beliefs, and ideas. In business, the facts may be millions of pieces of data.
- ◆ ***Design:*** In the design phase, we design the method by which we will consider the data. The methods are sequences of steps, formulas, models, and other tools that enable us to systematically reduce the alternatives to a manageable number.
- ◆ ***Choice:*** When we are left with a reduced number of alternatives, we make a choice; that is, we select the one alternative we find most promising.

As you may remember from Chapter 8, "Managers and Their Information Needs," businesses collect data internally (from within the organization) and externally (from outside sources). They either use universal models, such as

Intelligence	◆ Collect data inside the organization. ◆ Collect data outside the organization. ◆ Collect information on possible ways to solve the problem.
Design	◆ Organize the data; select a model to process the data. ◆ Produce reasonable, potential courses of action.
Choice	◆ Select a course of action.

Figure 12.1 *The three phases of decision making*

some statistical models, or design their own models to analyze their data. Then they select what they perceive as the best course of action. Sometimes an individual manager makes a decision. At other times, the decision process is carried out by a group of managers. There are computer-based aids that can support almost any style of decision making.

STRUCTURED AND UNSTRUCTURED PROBLEMS

Consider the following scenario: You have a sum of money you want to invest for a period of two years at a yield of 20%. You consult an investment specialist who considers the total amount, the length of time you are willing to separate yourself from the money, and the desired yield. You invest your savings in the stocks she recommends. At the end of the two-year period, you are left with less money than you put in.

You complain to the specialist, but she says: "There are no guarantees. We are dealing with an unstructured area." "Look," you say, "I am a mathematician. Give me a problem, give me the parameters, and I will give you the number you are looking for. Guaranteed. Why can't you guarantee that your decision will yield what you expect?"

The answer is that the confidence that can be placed in the solution to a problem depends on the nature of the data and data analysis that are used to solve the problem. Depending on the amount of data and the availability of data analysis methods, the problems with which we are faced daily can be classified as structured, semistructured, or unstructured (see Figure 12.2).

STRUCTURED PROBLEMS

A fully **structured problem** is one whose optimal solution can be reached through a single set of steps. Since the one set of steps is known, and since the steps must be followed in a known sequence, solving a structured problem with

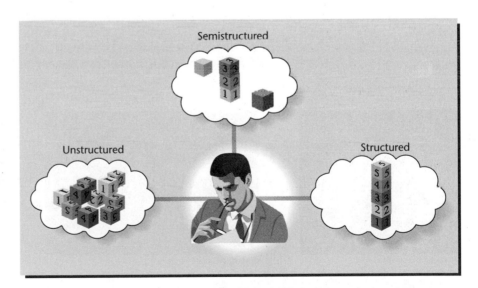

Figure 12.2 *Business problems vary from structured to unstructured. Many fall between the two extremes and are considered semistructured.*

the same data will always yield the same solution. Mathematicians call a sequence of steps an **algorithm**, and the categories of data that are considered when following those steps **parameters**. For instance, when we consider the problem of the shortest route for picking up and delivering shipments, the parameters are the time when shipments are ready for pickup, the time when shipments are needed at their destinations, the distance of existing vehicles from the various destinations, the work schedules of the drivers, the capacities of the trucks, and so on. Most mathematical and physical problems are structured. Finding the roots of a quadratic equation is a structured problem: There is a formula (an algorithm) one can use to solve the problem. For the same equation the roots will always be the same. Predicting how hot a liquid will get in a particular setting is a structured problem: If you know the properties of the liquid, the size of its container, the properties of the energy source heating the liquid, and the exact length of time the energy will be applied, you can figure out what temperature the liquid will reach.

Unstructured Problems

An **unstructured problem** is one for which there is no algorithm to follow to reach an optimal solution—either because there is not enough information about the factors that may affect the solution, or because there are so many potential factors that no algorithm can be formulated to guarantee a unique optimal solution. Unstructuredness is closely related to uncertainty. We cannot be sure what the weather will be tomorrow; nobody can guarantee what an investment in a certain portfolio of stocks will yield by year's end; and two physicians may diagnose the same symptoms differently. These are all areas where unstructured problems predominate.

Semistructured Problems

A **semistructured problem** is one that is neither fully structured nor totally unstructured. The examples cited above would be considered semistructured by experts in their fields because they have enough knowledge to narrow down the number of different possible solutions.

The problem "How much will I earn after two years if I invest $100,000 in municipal bonds that pay 3% per annum tax free?" is structured. To find the

Used by permission from NYSE

Used by permission from Corel Corporation

Used by permission from Corel Corporation

Stock investment, weather forecasting, and medicine are domains of semistructured decision making.

solution you have to follow a simple algorithm that takes as parameters your $100,000, the two years, and the 3% interest rate. Unless the city that issued the bonds goes bankrupt, your calculated income is guaranteed. However, the problem "If I invest $100,000 in the stock of XYZ, Inc. and sell the stock after two years, how much money will I make?" is semistructured. It cannot be considered structured because too many factors must be taken into consideration: the demand for the company's products, entrance of competitors into its market, the market of its products in this country and overseas, and so on. So many factors that affect the price of the stocks may change over the next two years that the problem is semistructured at best, and totally unstructured at worst.

PROGRAMMABLE PROBLEMS

Structured problems are often referred to as **programmable problems** because it is feasible to write a program to solve them. Similarly, unstructured problems are considered unprogrammable, because there is no specific program that can solve them. Nevertheless, computer programs (decision aids) have been written to solve unstructured problems. Although the programs may not yield perfect results, and two different programs addressing the problem may even yield slightly different results, they do significantly minimize the time that would otherwise be necessary to solve these problems.

MANAGERS AND SEMISTRUCTURED PROBLEMS

Managers are faced with semistructured problems almost daily, in many different industries and in many different business functions (see Figure 12.3).

STRUCTURED PROBLEMS	SEMISTRUCTURED PROBLEMS
How many workers are needed to fully staff production line A?	What are the benefits of merging with XYZ Inc.?
What is our optimal order quantity for raw material Z based on our production?	Where should we deploy the next five stores of our retail chain?
How many turbines are needed to supply power to Hickstown?	How will the consumer react if we lower the price of our product by 10%?
Which of our regions yields the highest revenue per salesperson?	What is the best advertisement campaign to launch our new financial service?
Which money market fund currently yields the highest return?	What are the benefits of opening an office in Paris, France?
How much would the implementation of pollution-preventing devices cost us?	Which stock will yield the highest return by the end of the year?

Figure 12.3 *Examples of structured and semistructured problems*

A manager solving a typical semistructured problem faces multiple possible courses of action. The task becomes choosing the one alternative that will bring about the best outcome. For example:

◆ In manufacturing, managers must provide solutions to semistructured problems such as: (1) Which supplier should we use, so as to receive the best price for purchased raw materials? (2) There is a stoppage in assembly line B; should we transfer workers to another assembly line, or wait for B to be fixed? (3) Demand for product X has decreased; should we dismantle one of the production lines, or should we continue to manufacture at the current rate, stock the finished products, and wait for an upswing in demand?

◆ Managers of investment portfolios must face semistructured decision making when they decide which securities to sell and which to buy, so as to maximize the overall return on investment.

◆ Human resource managers are faced with semistructured problems, when they have to decide whom to recommend for a new position, taking into consideration a person's qualifications and his or her ability to learn and assume new responsibilities.

◆ Marketing professionals face semistructured problems constantly: Should they spend the money on print, television, or direct mail advertisements? Which sector of the population should they target?

DSS COMPONENTS

Decision support systems (DSSs) are computer-based information systems designed to help managers select one of many alternate solutions to a problem, and to help corporations increase market share, reduce costs, increase profitability, and enhance product quality. By automating some of the decision-making process, the systems actually give managers access to some analyses that were previously completely unavailable. Certain analyses could be performed by managers, but would be prohibitively time-consuming and would render late, and therefore bad, decisions. DSSs provide sophisticated and fast analysis. Although the use of DSSs increases with the level of management, the systems are used at all levels of management.

The majority of DSSs have three major components: a data management module, a model management module, and a dialog management module (see Figure 12.4). Together, these modules (1) help the user enter a request in a convenient manner, (2) search vast amounts of data to focus on the relevant facts, (3) use the data in desired models, and (4) present the results in one or several manners for easy grasp by the user.

THE DATA MANAGEMENT MODULE

A DSS's **data management module** is a database that allows the decision maker to conduct the intelligence phase of decision making. For example, an investment consultant always needs access to stock prices for the past several years; a data management module would maintain that data and provide a means for the DSS to select data according to certain criteria: type of stock, range of years, and so on.

A DSS may use a database created only for that system, but DSSs are usually linked to external databases used for other purposes as well, such as purchasing,

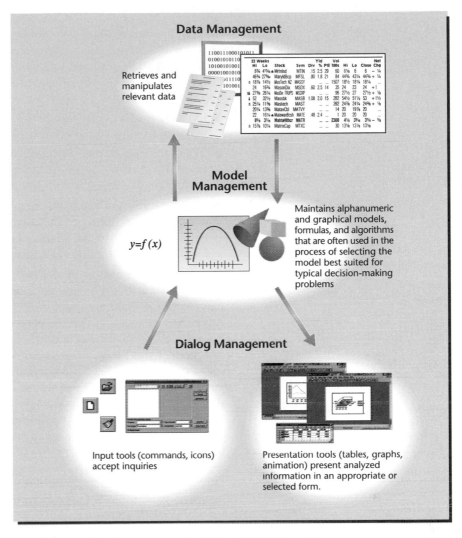

Data Management

Retrieves and manipulates relevant data

Model Management

$y = f(x)$

Maintains alphanumeric and graphical models, formulas, and algorithms that are often used in the process of selecting the model best suited for typical decision-making problems

Dialog Management

Input tools (commands, icons) accept inquiries

Presentation tools (tables, graphs, animation) present analyzed information in an appropriate or selected form.

Figure 12.4 *Components of a DSS and their interaction*

shipping, billing, and other daily transactions. Often, databases that have been in use for other purposes before a DSS is built can be linked to become part of the data management module.

THE MODEL MANAGEMENT MODULE

To turn data into useful information, the user selects a model from the **model management module**, which is a collection of models the DSS draws upon to assist in decision making. A sequence of events or pattern of behavior becomes a **model** when the relationships among its inputs, outputs, and conditions are described well enough that they can be used to analyze the responses to different inputs, outputs, and conditions. Models are used to predict the output based on different input or different conditions, or to estimate what combination of conditions and input might lead to a desired output. Models are often based on mathematical research or on experience. A model may be a widely used method to predict performance, such as "best-fit" linear analysis, or it may be built by the organization, using the experience that knowledge workers in the firm have accumulated over time. Many companies will not divulge details of the models they have programmed because they view them as important trade secrets and as valuable assets that may give them competitive advantages. Patterns or models may be unique to a certain industry or even to an individual business. For example:

◆ In trying to serve customers better in a bank, operations research experts try to create a model that predicts the best positioning and scheduling of tellers.

◆ In the trucking business, models are developed to reduce the total mileage trucks must travel, while maintaining a satisfactory delivery time. Similar models are developed in the airline industry to maximize revenue.

◆ A model for revenue maximization in the airline industry will automatically price tickets according to the parameters the user enters: date of the flight, day of the week of the flight, departure and destination points, and the length of stay if the ticket is for a round-trip flight.

A **linear regression model** is the best-fit linear relationship between two types of data, such as sales and the money spent on marketing. A private business may develop a linear regression model to estimate future sales based on its past experience. For example, the marketing department of a shoe store chain may apply linear regression to the relationship between the dollar amount spent on television commercials and change in sales volume. This linear relationship can be translated into a program in a DSS. Then the user can enter the total amount to be spent on television commercials for the next year into the DSS, and the program will enter that figure into the model and find the estimated change in the sales volume. The relationship between the two variables can be plotted as shown in Figure 12.5.

Usually, models are not so simple. In this example, for instance, many more factors may play a role: the number of salespeople, the location of the stores, the types of shoes offered for sale, the television programs in which the commercials are presented, and many more parameters. Therefore, before models are programmed to become a part of a DSS, the environment in which the decision will be executed must be carefully considered.

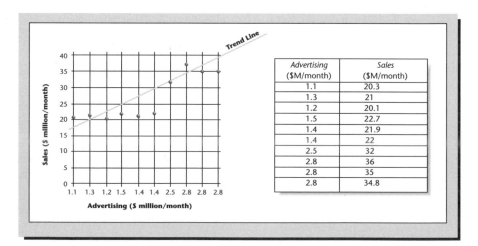

Figure 12.5 *A linear regression model for predicting sales volume as a function of dollars spent on advertising*

Privacy in the EC

Banks, credit bureaus, marketers, and government agencies maintain mountains of personal information. Privacy advocates claim that there is too much personal information in these data banks and that control over its use, and possible abuse, is too loose. In general, Europeans are more sensitive to the collection, maintenance, and use of such data than Americans. Privacy seems to be a value more highly regarded in Europe than in the U.S., at least from a legal point of view.

In their effort to harmonize their laws governing personal data, members of the European Community (EC) have formulated strict rules. For example, the rules require both government and private organizations to notify a Data Commissioner of the establishment of every automated database in which personal data are held, and to ask each individual for permission when transferring his or her data to another organization.

But the members could not agree on one rule. Several members demanded that personal data not be used for decision making. The fear is that individuals may be denied admission or service because of harsh criteria. On the face of it, the rule seems to be fair. The EC governments wish to protect their citizens against discrimination of any kind. But this would have a severe impact on business practices.

Businesses *want* to discriminate among their potential clients and consumers. Financial institutions want to be able to deny credit to one person, and grant credit to another. Universities and other educational institutions want to be able to admit students with high academic potential, and reject students with poor performance. And employers want to be able to make hiring decisions based on personal data.

Personal data are not used just for targeting populations for marketing. Much of the information maintained in organizational databases is used exactly for the purpose that the EC wishes to forbid: decision making. What is the purpose of DSSs if not to automate time-consuming processes like determination of credit worthiness or academic potential?

Not surprisingly, the issue of automated decision making has been the most difficult to resolve in the effort to harmonize the laws and reach a single unified privacy law for the EC. It is expected that the privacy extremists will ease their resistance in return for a commitment to high standards of control: accuracy, periodic currency checks, and perhaps government scrutiny of decision criteria.

Not all DSSs are business-oriented. In some areas, especially engineering, models in DSSs may simulate physical environments rather than business environments. For example, aeronautical engineers build computer models of wind tunnels to view how an aircraft with a new wing design might behave. It is significantly less expensive to construct a software model than to build a physical model. The simulation provides valuable information on vibrations, metal fatigue, and other factors, in relation to various speeds and weather conditions. The output, in the form of both animated pictures and numerical tables, enables engineers to make important decisions before spending huge amounts of money to actually build aircraft.

Used by permission from Lockheed Martin Corporation

Using a model for simulation saves costs.

THE DIALOG MANAGEMENT MODULE

In order for the user to interact with the DSS, the system must provide an easy way to interact with the program. The part of the DSS that allows the user to interact with it is called the **dialog management module**. It prompts the user to select a model. It allows the user to access the database and select data for the decision process, or set criteria for selecting such data. It lets the user enter parameters and change them to see how the change affects the result of the analysis. The dialog may be in the form of commands, pull-down menus, icons, dialog boxes, or any other approach.

The dialog component is also responsible for displaying the results of the analysis. DSSs use various textual, tabular, and graphical displays from which the decision maker can choose. In disciplines that require decisions regarding the physical construction of objects, such as aircraft or buildings, the output is often animated. For example, an architect may want to test the strength of a new structure by creating a computer model and subjecting the model to increasing pressures until the construction collapses. Decisions can then be based on the sequence of events that appears on the monitor, along with the display of textual and tabular data. Different colors and patterns may also play an important role in DSS output, by quickly drawing attention to exceptional results that do not comply with certain rules of analysis.

Take the previous advertising effort scenario, for example, where the marketing manager of the company is trying to decide how to spend promotional dollars (see Figure 12.6). The dialog management component of the DSS presents a menu allowing the marketing executive to select "TV advertising" from a variety

Decision support systems help process collected data and produce a suggested solution to a problem.

Many DSSs can display the results of an analysis as a graph.

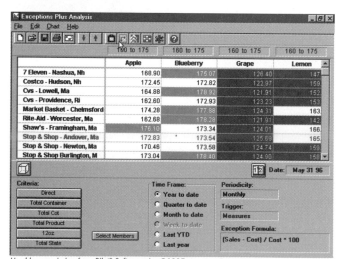

Used by permission from Pilot® Software, Inc.©1997

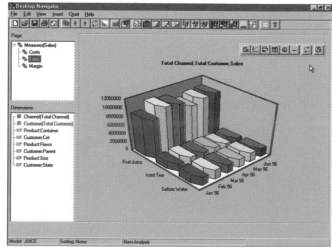

Used by permission from Pilot® Software, Inc.©1997

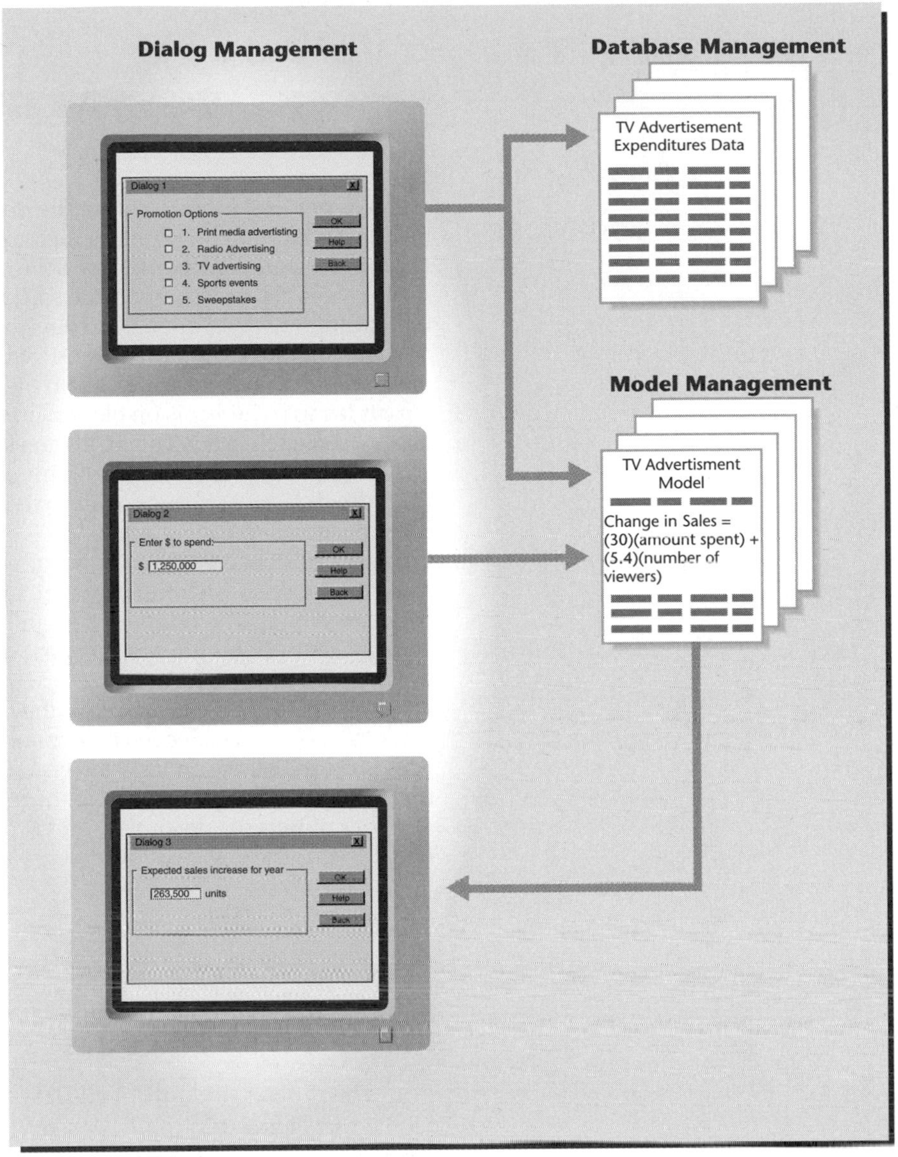

Dialog Management

Database Management

TV Advertisement
Expenditures Data

Model Management

TV Advertisment
Model

Change in Sales =
(30)(amount spent) +
(5.4)(number of
viewers)

Dialog 1

Promotion Options
☐ 1. Print media advertising
☐ 2. Radio Advertising
☐ 3. TV advertising
☐ 4. Sports events
☐ 5. Sweepstakes

OK
Help
Back

Dialog 2

Enter $ to spend:
$ 1,250,000

OK
Help
Back

Dialog 3

Expected sales increase for year
263,500 units

OK
Help
Back

Figure 12.6 *A DSS helps marketers make decisions.*

of promotional choices, and to choose the amount to be spent in that channel. Now the dialog management module invokes the part of the database that holds current data on advertising expenditures and sales volumes for the corresponding months. At this point, the system may either present a list of models for analyzing the data, from which the user can choose, or, if it is sophisticated enough, it may select a model automatically, based on the problem at hand. The model projects sales figures based on the data from the database, and the dialog management component presents the results of the analysis. The output helps the executive make a decision by answering the question: Will the proposed amount to be spent on television commercials yield a large enough boost in sales?

Every Move You Make

The richer and more accurate the data used by DSSs, the better decisions businesses can make. With the increasing power of smaller and smaller microprocessors, companies are devising means for collecting actual data rather than depending upon the sampling of data via surveys. Consider the consumer wristwatch as used in the following scenario.

Mel C. Smith just returned home from the office. He pours himself a big glass of cold orange juice, walks into his den, and turns on the television set. On his left wrist he wears an old watch. On his right wrist is a device that looks like a wristwatch, but isn't one. It's an electronic device that collects data.

Mel holds the remote control unit and switches channels until he sees the title of a movie he was waiting to watch. Several seconds later, commercials flash on the monitor. Mel is not aware of what happens in the little device attached to his right wrist, but it's hard at work. It collects signals from the TV set, which indicate which channel is on and what commercials are shown. The data are kept in a small but powerful chip.

Mel likes to do his grocery shopping at night, around 11 p.m., or even closer to midnight, when there are no lines. Later that night, he goes to his favorite supermarket and buys groceries for the next two weeks. As he passes the products over the bar code reader, it's not only the register that records the data; so does the small device on his right wrist. It captures the item numbers and stores them in the little chip, which is, for all practical purposes, a database.

Like millions of consumers, Mel is paid $100 per month for his willingness to wear the device at all times. To ensure that he does not remove it,

(continued)

TYPES OF DECISION SUPPORT SYSTEMS

The general structure of all DSSs is similar and comprises the components detailed in Figure 12.4, but DSSs may differ in their degree of sophistication and the manner in which they are used.

PERSONAL DECISION SUPPORT SYSTEMS

Personal DSSs are built for the use of the individual knowledge worker in his or her daily work. They can be run on desktop or mainframe computers, and often contain a single model for data processing. Personal DSSs are developed with the participation of all prospective users or of those who are most experienced.

With personal DSSs, raw data may be entered directly into a program by the user, or it may be drawn from the firm's database, from an external source, or from a combination of sources. Some companies have policies to accept whatever output personal DSSs produce, in which case the worker acts upon the system's decision. For example, Mrs. Fields Cookies provides store managers with DSSs that decide for the managers which types of cookies to make, what quantities of each type, and which ingredients to use. The decisions are based

an operator for the company with which he signed the contract attached it in much the same way that electronic bracelets are attached to inmates on furlough. Like many other people, Mel balked at first, at the thought that he was under surveillance, but the company assured him that his geographic whereabouts were not among the data collected. But what does the company do with the data collected?

At the end of the month, Mel connects the device to his personal computer through a special wire and plug kit. He brings up the program with which the company provided him. The data are transmitted to the company's supercomputer in Dallas, Texas. The small device is now ready for collection of another month's data.

The company maintains the data in huge databases. This is the raw material for valuable information. Statisticians use it to build and modify models of buying trends. They observe the relationships between the length of time viewers watch various commercials and the resulting impact on buying habits. These models are a major component of marketing decision support systems. The results of the analyses are sold to marketers and retail chains. With the new device, television viewing is accounted for significantly more accurately than Nielsen could calculate, with its limited sample of households. Businesses can have better information on which to base their advertising decisions. Television networks can have more accurate information on which to base their pricing of advertising time slots.

Does all this sound somewhat far-fetched? Maybe. But some firms are already hard at work on these wrist devices. The "consumer wristwatch" will be a conspicuous phenomenon on many forearms in the future.

THINK CRITICALLY

If offered a modest fee, would you volunteer to wear a device like the one described above? Why, or why not?

---

on sales volumes and corporate-dictated baking instructions. However, if the user works in a highly unstructured environment, he or she must carefully examine output before acting upon it, or rejecting it.

INTELLIGENT DECISION SUPPORT SYSTEMS

Some personal DSSs provide several models from which the user chooses the most appropriate. A personal DSS that includes a special selection module to help the user select the right model, based on the type of problem being analyzed, is called an **intelligent DSS (IDSS)**. Because IDSSs use an element of artificial intelligence, they are similar to expert systems.

GROUP DECISION SUPPORT SYSTEMS

Often, business decisions are made by a group of managers rather than a single person. **Group decision support systems (GDSSs)** are usually installed in conference-room settings or through a group of networked computers. They are designed specifically to take input from multiple users interacting with the program at the same time and converging on a decision as a group. Although personal DSSs can help groups make decisions, the nature of group decision making is different from that of a single individual. In individual decision making, the

Net Notes

ISWorld, a nonprofit organization of IS professionals, offers Web pages on DSSs and GDSSs. Use *http://midir .ucd.ie/~mbsft-4b/global/frame.html* to read more about GDSSs, or use the keywords *DSS* and *GDSS* for more information on the Web. You will be surprised how many sites have information on these topics. A search for "decision support systems" will yield several million (!) sites.

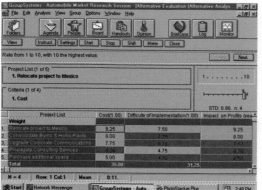
Used by permission from Ventana East

GDSSs allow users to rank and weight factors considered in group decision making.

The GDSS shown here provides privacy for each participant, and a central monitor for sharing ideas.

Used by permission from Cathy Span/College of Business and Public Administration, The University of Arizona

individual may share ideas with others, but he or she does not have to agree with any other person about the data collected, the ideas raised, or the decision made. A decision made by a group, on the other hand, can be the result of a consensus or majority vote. GDSSs are designed to provide methods such as weighing votes to overcome impasses.

Unlike personal DSSs, the physical arrangement of a facility designed to support GDSSs is important. A typical GDSS is installed in a special conference room where PCs are networked to each other and to a shared display screen at the front of the room. Each participant can use his or her local computer, and can display text and spreadsheet material on the central screen as well.

One of the most important activities in group decision making is **brainstorming**, a word used to describe a group process aimed at generating ideas in a creative setting, so as to ultimately lead a group to the best decision possible. In face-to-face meetings, people are often too shy to raise ideas that their peers may judge as being "crazy," even though these are often the best ideas. The GDSS protects the participant's anonymity, if he or she so desires. In some installations, the monitors are recessed in the desks for further privacy and for ergonomic reasons.

The University of Arizona, a pioneer in research of the subject, developed a GDSS named GroupSystemV, used by Coca Cola, BellSouth, Ford Motor Co., Chevron, Texaco, and other corporations. The program has saved time and money, and, by using a meeting facilitator and giving all participants an anonymous voice in decisions, it has eliminated the typical phenomenon of a few people dominating decision-making meetings. The system displays the anonymous comments on the central monitor, tallies votes, and outlines options available. Verbal interaction is allowed, but kept to a minimum by the moderator. The GroupSystemV developers emphasize the advantages of using their GDSS conference room: shorter meetings, less stressful conferences, a focus on shared values and concerns, and increased meeting efficiency.

Similarly, the University of Minnesota developed a GDSS called SAMM (Software Aided Meeting Management). The menu options of this system are presented in Figure 12.7. There are three ways in which a participant can generate ideas in a meeting: by using the public scratch pad, by using his or her private scratch pad, or by sending a message to another participant.

SENSITIVITY ANALYSIS

An outcome is almost always affected by more than one parameter; for instance, the sales volume of a product is affected by the number of salespeople, the number of regional sales representatives, the amount spent on national television advertisement, the price per unit of product sold, and so on. However, outcome is rarely equally sensitive to variation in all parameters. A small change in price per unit may have a hugely positive effect on sales, an effect known as **high sensitivity**; however, the same sales may increase only slightly in spite of a huge investment in advertising dollars, which would mean that sales have a **low senstivity** to the advertising factor. Sometimes the parameters to which outcome is most sensitive also affect other parameters. It is important to pinpoint the parameters to which the outcome is highly sensitive, so that efforts can be focused where they will be most effective.

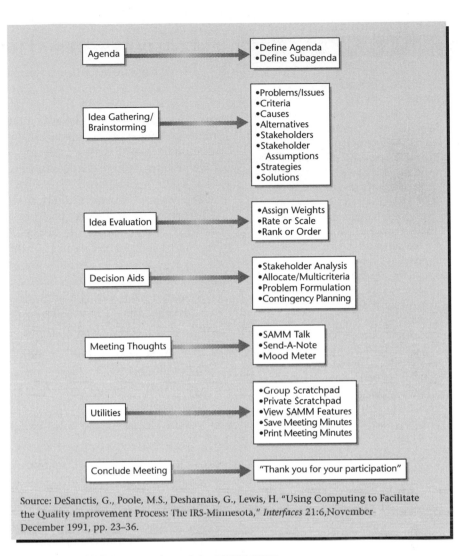

Agenda → •Define Agenda / •Define Subagenda

Idea Gathering/ Brainstorming → •Problems/Issues / •Criteria / •Causes / •Alternatives / •Stakeholders / •Stakeholder Assumptions / •Strategies / •Solutions

Idea Evaluation → •Assign Weights / •Rate or Scale / •Rank or Order

Decision Aids → •Stakeholder Analysis / •Allocate/Multicriteria / •Problem Formulation / •Contingency Planning

Meeting Thoughts → •SAMM Talk / •Send-A-Note / •Mood Meter

Utilities → •Group Scratchpad / •Private Scratchpad / •View SAMM Features / •Save Meeting Minutes / •Print Meeting Minutes

Conclude Meeting → "Thank you for your participation"

Source: DeSanctis, G., Poole, M.S., Desharnais, G., Lewis, H. "Using Computing to Facilitate the Quality Improvement Process: The IRS-Minnesota," *Interfaces* 21:6, November-December 1991, pp. 23–36.

Figure 12.7 *Menu options of the SAMM GDSS*

If the purpose of a company is to maximize profit, managers must find the optimal combination of many factors. To equip a DSS to help achieve this goal, a model is built into the DSS that takes into consideration the approximate arithmetic formula that expresses the relationship between each factor and the total profit. A **sensitivity analysis** is conducted to test the degree to which the total profit grows or decreases if one or more of the factors is increased or decreased, and the results indicate the relative sensitivity of the profit to the changes. If the outcome is affected significantly even when the parameter is changed only a little, then the sensitivity of the outcome to the parameter is said to be high. The opposite is also true: If the outcome is affected a little even when the parameter is varied widely, the outcome is said to be insensitive to the parameter.

For instance, a manager may ask: What is the impact on total quarterly profits if television advertising is decreased by 10% and the number of commissioned sales representatives is increased by 5%? Thus, sensitivity analysis is often referred to as **what if analysis.**

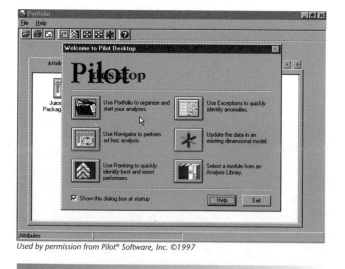

POINT OF INTEREST
Executives, Too, Use Computers

A survey by *Computerworld* and Andersen Consulting of top executives in 200 large U.S. corporations showed that executive use of desktop technology is rising. The percentage of chief executives and operating and financial officers who said they use a PC or terminal in their daily work rose to about 56% by 1993. Many expressed interest in knowledge-based and executive information systems (EISs).

Executive fervor can help spread technology in the ranks across an entire company. That's what happened at Bay State Gas in Westboro, Massachusetts, where high-level enthusiasm helped expand a PC-based EIS into general use, said John Doucette, Vice President of Administration at the 270,000-customer utility. "It's the first thing top executives turn on in the morning," he said. Company officers use their point-and-click EIS to access group calendars, shipping and financial information, and more.

Source: Maglitta, J., "More users! This time, it's your CEO," *Computerworld*, December 28, 1992/ January 4, 1993, p. 38.

EXECUTIVE INFORMATION SYSTEMS

Executive information systems (EISs) are a type of decision support system especially designed for high-ranking managers, to provide them with the most essential information for running their organizations. EISs are useful to executives, who almost always suffer from **information overload**, the phenomenon of having so much information that the very volume creates the additional work of having to decide what is important, rather than helping to solve problems and make decisions.

You may recall from our discussion in Chapter 8 that high-level managers make decisions based on highly summarized information. They review ratios like sales per employee per quarter or year, regional sales, return on investment, and inventory turnover for different items, and EISs can display these data graphically so exceptions can be easily spotted. Unlike regular DSSs, many EISs do not require that a user enter any parameters. The system is interfaced with the organization's databases, and uses predetermined or selected models to respond to queries, displaying the results in the fashion requested.

An effective EIS has the following features:

◆ An easy-to-use and easy-to-learn graphical user interface

◆ On-request "drill down" capability that allows the executive to reach information in further detail

◆ On-demand financial and other indicators, to reflect organizational strengths and weaknesses

◆ Easy-to-use but sophisticated tools to allow navigation in databases

◆ Statistical analysis tools

◆ Functionality for ad hoc queries and sensitivity analysis

◆ Access to external data pools

◆ Ability to solve diverse business problems

◆ Constant access and analysis of information that reflects the results of activities that impact the entire organization or large parts of it

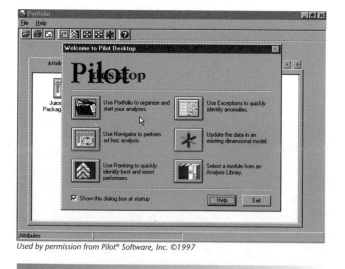

Used by permission from Pilot® Software, Inc. ©1997

EISs are becoming popular among high-ranking executives.

DEVELOPING DECISION SUPPORT SYSTEMS

Managers who consider the acquisition of a new DSS must understand what circumstances justify such an effort and the time that potential users may have to devote to the development process.

WHEN SHOULD A DSS BE BUILT?

Like the investment in developing any information system, the investment in developing a DSS may be hundreds of thousands or even millions of dollars. Therefore, management must consider several factors before making a commitment to a new DSS.

◆ *What type of problem are we trying to address, and how structured is it?* Not every decision needs a DSS or EIS. In general, the less structured the problem, the more analysis it requires, and the more likely it is that managers will benefit from a decision aid. But many decisions can be made with a quick look at the appropriate data. In fact, some analyses are so simple that they can be performed within seconds. Even some unstructured problems can be solved easily with common sense. But for solving highly unstructured problems, with many different models as possible analysis tools, and many factors and parameters to be considered, even the most experienced managers can benefit from using a DSS.

These problems are usually qualitative rather than quantitative. For instance, consider a purchasing manager deciding which supplier to use for a certain item. He or she must consider several factors, including the quality of the item, delivery time, price, payment terms, and warranty. If there are only two manufacturers of the item, and the factors listed have similar values for both, then the manager does not need a DSS to make a decision; he or she may simply negotiate a better price.

However, if the company has many potential suppliers, the manager must consider many combinations of values of the above factors, in which case a DSS could aid in the evaluation and selection of the best supplier.

◆ *Are the data that are required for the analysis available in automated databases?* The accessibility of relevant data from existing internal and external databases, or from the creation of a combined new database, is an important consideration in the development of a DSS. A DSS designer may determine that an entire database needs to be maintained just for the operation of the system, or that adequate interfaces with existing databases can be developed. In general, the higher the level of the managers who use decision aids, the greater the amount of external data required. Hence, developers have the added challenge of effectively combining internal and external sources.

◆ *How often do managers encounter the problem?* The more frequently the problem occurs, the more justified is the development of a DSS to solve it. If the problem is encountered rarely, the development cost will outweigh the benefits.

◆ *Who will use the system?* In general, the greater the number of prospective users and the higher the level of user, the greater the positive impact a DSS will have. Depending on the level of management, if only one person, or a handful of people, would use the system, it may be more economical to have them develop their own individual systems using a 4GL or spreadsheet. However, if the sole prospective user is the company's president, and this person would use it frequently, then the investment may be justified because of the great benefit the DSS might have for the entire organization.

◆ *Can the prospective users spare adequate time for the development process?* The development of automated decision aids requires the time and effort of the users, so management has to be willing to let people from their staffs take time from their regular duties.

PARTICIPANTS IN THE DEVELOPMENT EFFORT

As mentioned above, the success of a DSS depends heavily on active involvement of prospective users in its development. The systems analysts and programmers must understand the decision process thoroughly. The users have to explain which data sources they would like to draw from, which models are relevant for analysis, and what form of output they prefer.

In the past, users complained that DSSs were inflexible. They felt that the systems did not follow their human decision-making process. Hence, developers now try to provide systems that are versatile and flexible, and offer several modes of dialog to fit the individual user's preference. The development process is a continuous series of input from the users and design modifications from the analysts and programmers. This method of developing a DSS through an iterative process that passes the system back and forth from user for feedback to designer for revision is called **prototyping** and is discussed in Chapter 15, "Systems Development."

BUILDING YOUR OWN DECISION SUPPORT SYSTEM

If data must be drawn from external databases, and decisions require complex, special calculations, a DSS may have to be programmed from scratch. But

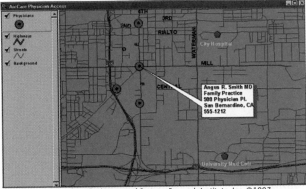

Used by permission from Environmental Systems Research Institute, Inc. ©1997

Here, a GIS maps the number of physicians located in a particular neighborhood to determine the ease of access to health care.

many DSSs can now be developed using inexpensive off-the-shelf software referred to as **DSS tools**. The most widely used tools are electronic spreadsheets.

Spreadsheets provide two facilities for building DSSs: (1) preprogrammed functions, such as totals, averages, net present values, and the like, and (2) the ability to use IF-THEN statements. Coupling the preprogrammed functions with IF-THEN statements can create quite complex decision models. A lot of spreadsheet programs allow the user to fully automate a model (that is, create the dialog management component of the DSS) using macros, which can also be used to display information in the form of charts. Many users who are not professional programmers have developed excellent DSSs and EISs for their organizations using DSS tools such as spreadsheets.

Spreadsheet DSSs usually require that data used in the analysis be present in the spreadsheet that contains the model itself, or in a linked spreadsheet. This is because spreadsheets serve to contain both models and the data that the models process.

GEOGRAPHIC INFORMATION SYSTEMS

Many business decisions are made with relation to maps, such as choosing the best locations for new stores, and determining how to optimally deploy police forces. For map-related decisions, **geographic information systems (GISs)** are often the best decision aids to use. GISs are systems for which location is a major factor in both processing data and providing output. For instance, a GIS could be used to help a housing developer determine where to invest, by tracking and displaying population changes on a map. Increases in population greater than 10% over the past three years could be displayed in red, while all other changes could be displayed in various shades of gray, from light for small changes to black for large changes. With this information, a developer could easily decide where to invest on the basis of population growth trends. Other examples include:

◆ Delivery managers looking for the shortest distance a truck can travel to deliver ordered goods at the lowest cost

◆ School district officials looking for the most efficient routes for busing school children to and from their homes

◆ City planners looking to deploy services to better serve residents, which might include police officers deciding how to deploy their forces based on precinct maps indicating criminal activity

◆ Oil companies looking to determine drilling locations

A typical GIS consists of a database from which information is extracted for display, a database of maps, and a program that translates information and displays it in the form of easily understood symbols and colors, which are displayed on the maps. For instance, an oil exploration map may show different concentrations of expected oil in the form of different hues of red. Or, population density may be similarly displayed on a map. A more sophisticated GIS may display, in colors or icons, concentrations of specific consumer groups by age, income, and other characteristics.

Deep-Dish DSS

Pizzeria Uno, the Chicago-style pizza and full-service restaurant chain, consisted of 150 eateries in 1997, located throughout the U.S., Puerto Rico, and Canada, with sales of $175 million. Before 1995, executives as well as individual restaurant managers reviewed restaurant performance data without the use of computers. "The reports were labor intensive to produce and the information was not very timely," said Alan LaBatte, vice president of information systems. In addition, some critical information was not available at all. Other data was so outdated by the time it became available, management decided to deploy a system to give executives and restaurant managers access to timely sales and labor costs information.

The company installed a system called Pilot Analysis Server™ from Pilot Software, Inc., a leading global supplier of customer and market analysis software. The software runs on a server that allows executives and restaurant managers to interactively access and analyze information about store performance and staffing at both individual and regional levels. To this end,

the software includes a library of analytical models.

Each evening, daily sales and labor information is downloaded from each restaurant point-of-sale onto the server located at the company's Boston headquarters. Marketing, operations, and finance executives at Uno headquarters access the server each day to download up-to-date data onto their own computers.

The software allows executives and managers to quickly produce graphical information that compares performance of restaurants and whole regions. In a way that doesn't require much experience with computers, managers can receive information such as which type of pizza has been the most popular over the past week, or month, or any other period. They can use models that forecast costs for any restaurant based on its previous performance.

"For example," said one executive, "if on a Sunday I see that our costs for some restaurants in a particular region will be too high for the upcoming week, I can discuss the problem with the divisional vice president, and we can determine an appropriate course of action. The more quickly we can respond to increasing costs, the greater our profits." Before the implementation

of the DSS, regional managers could manage only six restaurants each. Now, each manager can run nine restaurants.

Marketing executives have also found the system to be a valuable tool. For example, they use it to measure the results of test marketing of a new menu or the success of a special lunch promotion and how it relates to labor and other costs.

Source: Pilot Software, Inc., "Customer Profiles: Pizzeria Uno," April 25, 1997. ©1997 Pilot Software, Inc. Reprinted courtesy of Pilot® Software, Inc.

Questions

1. Enumerate some typical business questions to which you would like to find answers using a DSS in a restaurant chain.

2. How could the new DSS allow regional managers to manage more restaurants?

DSS for Survival

In 1995, the management of National Car Rental was given a clear choice: significantly increase profitability, or the company will be liquidated. The General Motors subsidiary headquarters in Edina, Minnesota, hired Aeronomics to provide consulting and try to resolve its problems.

Kevin Geraghty, senior consultant at Aeronomics and business manager of the National Car Rental project, used a software suite of analytic models that handle capacity management [the managing of an inventory of products that can be used in different places, for different periods of time, at different costs], pricing, and reservation controls. The DSS was to pinpoint National's weaknesses and help make decisions in correcting the situation.

Geraghty discovered that National did not have effective pricing strategies, [partly because] there was no central responsibility for pricing within the company. Thus, the lack of a pricing strategy was the first obstacle to be overcome. The consultants developed a rate recommendation, albeit a simple one, but one that produced rates that were dependent on demand.

National's information systems were fragmented. Geraghty said: "Picture a system that handles the daily activity on the rental lot, another one that handles reservations, another that handles the actual prices, and then the airline centralized reservation systems into which we communicated information. Into this we had to drop our revenue management system. It had to be able to tie these different systems together so that a user could look at his monitor and see how many cars were on the lot, see what prices the company had to work with, and see how bookings were coming in."

Keeping track of the location of the cars in the fleet was a major problem. When you are planning on what rate to charge based on demand and availability, you need a forecast of where the cars will be. "So we had to figure out where the fleet was and where the fleet was going to be at a certain date. And we had to develop a system that would allow the user to override the system with updated information as necessary," Geraghty said. "We paid attention to user expertise and to what was going to be required of the guys who would actually use the system."

The final program was a very comprehensive solution. Looking at the system as a whole, the capacity management function optimizes fleet utilization; the pricing function capitalizes on consumers' price sensitivity (which varies in response to competitive pressures in the marketplace); rate levels are linked with availability and booking activity; the reservation and control function maximizes revenues by accepting or rejecting booking requests; and length-of-rent controls are determined through mathematical programming to optimize management of National's rental car inventory.

For Geraghty, the pivotal point of the system developed for National involves the integration of two approaches: automated decision making and decision support for user decision making. Automated decision making, the method typically used for revenue management, helped the team implement numerous new ideas. "We wanted to build the users closely into the models to give a decision support feel as well," Geraghty said. "So, we had to take the users and insert them into the models so they could look at the system as it's halfway through generating its recommendations, make little changes, and then run the program again to see what-if scenarios. For example, if the user didn't agree with the forecast, he could go in, change the forecast, rerun the system and get new recommendations. It's the same with pricing; the user can change those recommendations and re-optimize the inventory controls. There was a lot of trade-off between automated decision making and decision support."

Using the methods employed by National also allows the company to expand its market downward. "Basically, if you're not managing your pricing and capacity very well, all you can do is pick a price, and it's got to be somewhere in a range where you get enough people booking, but not so much that you dilute your revenues too much," Geraghty said. "Now, if you can manage multiple pricing, it allows for people who are not willing to pay as much to make use of capacity that would otherwise just sit there." The new DSS provides easy means to simulate situations, so it can make better decisions. Interestingly, the new system changed other things as well.

"We had to change the culture of the organization to implement the system," said Ernest Johnson, National's vice president of revenue management, "and this change enabled us to alter our control of leisure pricing, which had formerly been under the control of two people who handled pricing for the whole country without sophisticated systems to forecast demand,

and no easy tool to change pricing or inventory. It was mostly done via a manual process. So it was very difficult, if not impossible, for us to get ahead of the demand curve.

"We also changed the way we handled inventory, which is done by means of reservation inventory through a computerized reservation system. Through this change, we found that field management did not have the tools to make decisions on inventory that would maximize our return. So we took control of these inventories from our field locations all over the country and brought them into a centralized team here at headquarters."

Source: Greenfield, D., "OR Overhaul," ORMS Today, April 1996, pp. 12–14.

Questions

1. What was the problem in the way National ran its inventory?

2. How was pricing done before the implementation of the new system? How is it done now?

3. What is the difference between "automated decision making" and "decision support"? Which approach was implemented?

4. Why was it important to centralize the system?

5. Of the three components of a DSS (data management, model management, and dialog management), what are the data, and what are the models in this system?

Efficient Decision Making in the Paint Industry

Sherwin-Williams Co.'s $1.8 billion Paint Stores Group in Cleveland spent two years giving some 110 district managers access to a new executive information system (EIS). Before they had access to the system, managers had the unenviable task every Monday morning of telephoning the 20 to 25 stores in their districts to get sales figures for the previous week. Each manager would then draft a sales report for the district and send it up the chain of command to one of the 14 area vice presidents.

"The goal was not to get rid of the phone procedure but to give the district managers more information to work with," said Bill Thompson, Director of MIS at the Paint Stores Group. "It's kind of intuitive that you'll do better when you know more," he said.

Sherwin-Williams selected the Arthur Performance Tracking System from Comshare Retail, a division of Comshare, Inc., in Ann Arbor, Michigan. The Arthur Databases, fed by NCR Corp. point-of-sale (POS) systems in the retail outlets, reside on Sherwin-Williams' mainframe computer.

While many EIS applications start at the top of a company and only later trickle down the organization chart, Sherwin-Williams started the EIS application with its numerous mid-level managers and moved it up to senior executives. According to Thompson, all the area vice presidents use the system, as does at least one of the four division heads. Senior executives have the same graphical user interface as the managers, although the executives are able to compare a larger set of stores.

Thompson's information systems staff analyzed district managers' needs and developed databases that reflect inventory movement, store and territory results, and the performance of each sales representative. In the current implementation, managers can review each store's results, by product, for the previous five weeks. They can also perform "what if" analyses on this data.

"Our idea was to produce results geographically, with a color-coded map," Thompson said, adding that the application required placing PCs on the managers' desktops. Prior to the EIS, fewer than 15% had PCs in their offices. Thompson expanded the reach of the EIS platform by bundling spreadsheet and word-processing software into the EIS application. He said the EIS, which cumulatively contains gigabytes of inventory and POS data, is only as good as the data fed into it. "We're fortunate in that we already had a pretty solid POS system," he said.

Source: Booker, E., "Pushing decision support beyond the executive suite," Computerworld, Vol. 27 No. 51, December 20, 1993, p. 65.

Questions

1. What is the information that the area vice presidents need weekly, and how did they receive the data before the implementation of the new system?

2. What do the senior executives use the EIS for?

3. The data from which the executives extract their information are still collected in the same way as before the implementation of the new EIS. What is their origin?

Decision making is a major component of a manager's job. Whenever there is more than a single way to solve a problem, a **decision** must be made. The decision-making process comprises three major phases: **intelligence, design**, and **choice**. In the first phase, the data are collected from which relevant information will be gleaned. In the design phase, the manager organizes the data into useful information, and uses models to analyze it and produce potential courses of action. In the final stage, the manager selects an alternative, that is, makes the decision.

Problems span a continuum between two extremes: **structured** and **unstructured**. A structured problem is one for whose solution there is a proven **algorithm**. An unstructured problem is one for which there are multiple potential solutions. Between the two extremes we find **semistructured problems**, which are often what executives deal with. Finding solutions to unstructured and semistructured problems requires expertise. **Decision support systems** offer help in dealing with semistructured and unstructured problems.

DSSs have three components. The **data management module** gives the user access to databases from which relevant information can be retrieved. The **model management module** selects, or lets the user select, an appropriate **model** through which the data are analyzed. The **dialog management module** serves as an interface between the user and the other two modules. It allows the user to enter queries and **parameters**, and then presents the result in an appropriate or selected form, such as tablular or graphical.

Personal DSSs serve individual users in their daily decision making. **Intelligent DSS**s are more sophisticated, in that the model management module is programmed to make the model selection for the user. **Group DSS**s are installed in special conference rooms. They promote **brainstorming** and decision making by groups of managers.

DSSs provide a quick way to perform **sensitivity tests**. The user can change one or several parameters in the model and answer "what if" questions.

Executive information systems are a special type of DSS that alleviate the information overload with which high-ranking executives are burdened. EISs select the most relevant data for analysis, and present the results as ratios and charts that are easy to comprehend and decide upon.

Since the development of a new DSS may be expensive, management should consider several factors before making a commitment. To what extent is the problem structured? Are the relevant data available in electronic form? How often do managers encounter the problem? How many employees will use the system? And, can the prospective users spare enough time to participate in the development effort? The involvement of the users in the development of the DSS is essential.

Powerful software tools like electronic spreadsheets let users with little expertise in systems development create their own DSSs. They develop the systems on their own PCs and use them for their individual specific daily job, to save time and effort in decision making.

When decisions are to be made relative to locations and routes, managers can use **geographic information systems (GISs)**. GISs provide maps with icons and colors to represent population concentrations, potential natural resources, and other factors that have to do with locations and routes. A typical decision that a GIS could help make is where to build the new store of a retail chain.

The use of personal data for decision making has raised important ethical questions. Some members of the European Community (EC) forbid organizations, both government agencies and private businesses, to use private data in computer-based DSSs. Thus, banks cannot determine the credit worthiness of an individual, and universities cannot decide whether to admit or reject applicants, on the basis of DSS output. The problem will most likely be solved in the rounds of talks among the EC members.

REVIEW, DISCUSS, AND EXPLORE

REVIEW AND DISCUSSION QUESTIONS

1. What is a decision? When does one have to make a decision?

2. What is an unstructured problem? Which domains pose unstructured problems? Give three examples of unstructured problems that are not mentioned in this chapter.

3. Give an example of a problem that calls for a decision. Describe how a decision is reached through the three phases: intelligence, design, and choice.

4. Give an example of a problem solved with an algorithm.

5. Among the three components of a DSS, which has changed the most in recent years?

6. What is a GIS? What purpose does it serve?

7. What are the differences between GDSSs and personal DSSs?

8. What is a sensitivity test? Give three examples of sensitivity tests in business decision making.

9. What is an EIS? Some people claim that EISs are not really DSSs. Why?

10. People at which management levels are likely to use a DSS?

11. Why is the involvement of users in the development of a DSS so important?

12. *Ethics and Society:* Do you agree or disagree with those who claim that DSSs should not be used to analyze personal data by organizations? Give at least one example that shows how the practice may adversely impact the life of an innocent individual.

CONCEPT ACTIVITY

Find an organization that has implemented an EIS. Interview an executive who uses the EIS about the information that he or she receives from the system. Summarize the benefits: Which decisions does the executive now make that he or she could not make before the implementation of the system? What are the time savings in decision making gained with the system?

HANDS-ON ACTIVITY

You are the marketing manager of a mid-sized company that uses commissioned regional sales representatives. You also regularly place advertisements in the broadcast and print media. Over the years, you have tried to allocate the advertising budget in different combinations to create the best results. Recently, you concluded the following:

◆ Advertising in national magazines: every dollar in addition to current spending increases sales by .005% the following quarter (relative to the previous quarter); every dollar reduced decreases sales by .005%.

◆ A half-page ad in major cities' Yellow Pages increases sales by 1% for the entire year. Sales then return to their original volume. Cost: $2,000 per half-page.

◆ Thirty seconds of a national TV commercial increase annual sales by 2%. Cost: $250,000 per 30 seconds.

◆ Sales representatives can be hired for a period of at least five years. Commission paid to sales representatives: 10% on sales up to $100,000 per calendar year. An additional 3% on any additional sale in the same calendar year.

- The sales volume of this quarter: $2,300,000. Sales volume of the entire year: $10,100,000.

  This year you have used the following combination:

- Advertising in national magazines: $200,000

- Major cities' Yellow Pages: $14,000

- National TV commercials: Two 30-second airings at $400,000

- Sales representatives: 15. They made $3,260,000 in sales.

  Use your spreadsheet software to perform the following sensitivity tests. Do each test independently of the other tests.

a. By how much will the dollar sales volume increase/decrease (for the entire next year) if you add three sales representatives?

b. By how much will the dollar sales volume increase/decrease (for the entire next year) if you (1) increase advertising in national magazines by 30%, (2) air only one 30-second commercial on national TV, (3) do not place ads in Yellow Pages, and (4) hire an additional five sales representatives?

c. For next year, you have received an additional budget of $500,000 (on top of this year's budget). What is the best combination on which to spend it? (Note: you want to consider the ratio of *sales increase ($)/advertising increase ($)*.)

  Turn in: (1) A printout showing your spreadsheet, the results of your calculations, and text conclusions, and (2) a printout showing the formulas that you used, where applicable.

TEAM ACTIVITY

Contact a local stockbroker. Ask the broker to give you a list of the most important points he or she takes into consideration when predicting appreciation of a stock. Ask how each point (such as last year's earning per share, percentage of appreciation/depreciation over the past six months, and the like) affects the net result as a percentage. Use the input to formalize the model in a spreadsheet application. Select a portfolio of 100 units of ten traded stocks. Use the model to predict the increase in the price of each stock and the value of the entire portfolio a year into the future. If you know how to use macros, embellish your new DSS with a friendly dialog management module.

EXPLORE THE WEB

Many vendors use the term DSS to market products that do not fulfill the requirements of this type of application. Use the keywords *decision support system* to "shop" for a DSS on the Web. Prepare a list of the first ten applications you found offered. According to the description the site provides, which of the products are really DSSs, and which are something else (such as a relational DBMS)? Explain your evaluation.

Chapter 13

Artificial Intelligence and
Expert Systems

Genetic Scheduling

John Deere & Co. is a $10.3 billion maker of heavy farm machinery and construction equipment in Moline, Illinois. At its row crop machinery manufacturing facility the company produces 84 different models with some 1.6 million combinations of parts and materials. This huge number of combinations results in difficulties when scheduling purchasing of manufacturing resources, the starting point of what is referred to as the "supply chain": the production and delivery process from the purchase of raw goods from the suppliers to the delivery of products to distributors. Therefore, the company is constantly looking for methods to resolve supply chain issues.

Bill Fulkerson, an analyst for technology integration at the Moline plant, felt that the plant's supply chain issues were complex enough to justify the use of artificial intelligence. After placing an inquiry on the Internet, the firm was approached by a small start-up company that offered to resolve the company's supply chain issues using genetic algorithms, and asked Deere to become its first client. Genetic algorithms? What has genetics got to do with business issues?

Optimax Systems Corp. in Cambridge, Massachusetts, suggested applying its innovative artificial intelligence method to optimize Deere's schedules. These so-called genetic algorithms are modeled on the way species evolve; modules of the systems that are successful at solving problems "prosper" (that is, they are used more and more), and modules of these systems that are not successful are deleted or modified.

Deere now uses Optimax Systems' OptiFlex scheduling software at several plants to synchronize the flow of materials. The system uses as its input the customer orders, supply lead times of potential suppliers, and the capacity of the plants. The genetic algorithms generate schedules that satisfy specified conditions. The programs that create successful schedules are recombined to try to create even better schedules, while those that are unable to generate schedules that work within the specified limits are abandoned: Thus, the fittest survive. The software actually "breeds" hundreds of thousands of schedules, each improved from the last. "The sequence of activities is very important," Fulkerson observed, adding that, "this new system is one of the reasons we have been able to produce and meet our schedule more easily."

Source: Wilder, C., "Start with the Best, Then Build on It," *InformationWeek*, September 9, 1996, pp. 158–166.

Many business opportunities could not be seized without using artificial intelligence applications. The technology has taken on many varied forms and is quickly moving from university laboratories to everyday operations in management, engineering, medicine, and other fields and activities.

When you finish this chapter, you will:

- Understand the basic concepts of artificial intelligence

- Realize how the technology has been used in business, and how it can be further used in the future

- Understand expertise, the purpose of expert systems in business and other professional domains, and why expert systems are so helpful in solving unstructured problems

- Be familiar with the major methods of representing knowledge in software

- Appreciate the challenges involved in garnering knowledge for the construction of knowledge bases

- Understand the concept of knowledge engineering

ARTIFICIAL INTELLIGENCE IN BUSINESS

A narrow definition of the term "intelligence" is "the ability to learn." The better equipped a person is with mental tools to learn and apply new ideas, the higher his or her intelligence. But intelligence actually includes many things: making associations between a previous experience and a new situation, drawing conclusions in a systematic manner, quickly adopting new ways to solve problems, being able to separate what is important from what is not important in solving a problem, and determining what tools can or cannot help in handling complex situations. In short, intelligence is the ability to learn and also to think.

The term "artificial intelligence" was coined in a seminar in 1956, at Dartmouth College. The participants projected that in 25 years, "intelligent" machines would be able to do all the physical and intellectual work for human beings, and people would devote all their time to recreational activity. Obviously, the prophesy has not materialized (yet), but **artificial intelligence (AI)** has become a field of research for computer scientists, cognitive scientists, and business scholars. Efforts by nonacademic organizations have yielded many commercial products. One of the areas where AI has had a positive impact is in business. Combined with information systems and database management systems (DBMSs), programs that use the principles of artificial intelligence can provide outstanding support for high-level decision making in business. The ability of these systems to take into account a wide variety of business conditions and possibilities and to incorporate programs that suggest different relationships among business factors, has made some considerations in business possible for the first time. In this chapter, we will describe the concepts involved in artificial intelligence and the way it has enhanced business.

INTRODUCING ARTIFICIAL INTELLIGENCE

AI efforts may be classified into several categories, as illustrated in Figure 13.1. While the research and development in some areas, such as robotics and artificial vision, involve hardware and software, the research and development of others involve only software.

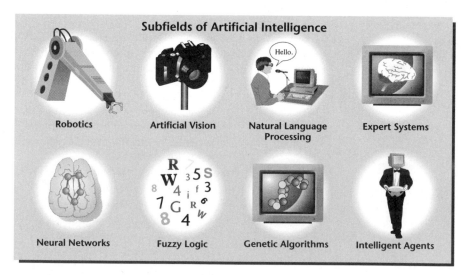

Figure 13.1 *The various research efforts in artificial intelligence*

ROBOTICS

Used by permission from Toyota Motor Manufacturing, Kentucky, Inc.

Robots revolutionized the auto and other manufacturing industries.

Robotics engineers build machines designed to perform useful work. Contrary to popular belief, the majority of **robots** (from Czech: "to work") in industrial use do not look like human beings. However, many are designed to do what the human body does, but more efficiently and effectively. In the auto industry, robots are used to weld, paint, and screw nuts. Much of the automotive and other manufacturing work done manually until the early 1980s is now being done by robots.

Robots are also extremely useful in environments where people can be easily and seriously injured. For example, police forces use remote control units and television monitors to guide robots to defuse bombs. Some sophisticated robots are even capable of detecting explosives by "smelling" objects suspected as bombs (that is, sensing the molecular structure of certain elements in the air). Similar robots are used in nuclear plants to perform duties that pose health hazards.

Some companies have developed robots that carry out household chores such as vacuuming, sweeping, and even removing dishes from tables and turning on appliances. The products have yet to achieve commercial status, that is, the ability to be sold widely to the public for affordable prices.

All robots either contain a computer, or are connected to one. In general, they need to sense their position and their surroundings, execute the functions they are programmed to perform, and provide feedback as needed. With the advancement of voice recognition, some robots are programmed to recognize and execute vocal commands.

Engineers who specialize in robotics are working on improving robot operation and the mode of interaction. They program specially built machines with mechanical limbs to move, recognize their position in space, grab objects, lay them down, and so on.

Robots are highly useful in situations that pose health hazards or risks of injury. Here, a robot is used to defuse a bomb.

Used by permission from AP/Wide World Photos

Used by permission from United States Postal Service

Artificial vision helps sort mail. The intelligent vision device recognizes the address by scanning and recognizing the characters.

ARTIFICIAL VISION

Another important feature needed for robots to function successfully in their environments is **artificial vision**. Artificial vision tries to mimic human vision. Artificial vision is the ability of a machine to "see" its environment, to make choices about its actions based on what it sees, and to recognize visual input (such as handwriting) according to general patterns. For instance, robots must recognize their position in space so they do not bump into obstacles; and they must recognize their position relative to an object they must act on, pick up, or push. Currently, trial devices are being used in the U.S. Postal Service to recognize handwriting and other written forms.

NATURAL LANGUAGE PROCESSING

Natural language processors (NLPs) are programs that are designed to take human language as input and translate it into a standard set of statements that a computer can execute. The programs work by parsing sentences and trying to eliminate ambiguity in a given context. The purpose of these sophisticated programs is to allow human beings to use their own language when interacting with programs such as DBMSs or decision support systems (DSSs), ridding the users of the necessity to learn a programming language.

To illustrate the problem that a natural language application is faced with, suppose you wish to create a list of clients from the Midwest Region who have placed year-to-date orders of less than $50,000. In human language, there are many ways to make the request, including:

◆ "List the names and addresses of clients from the Midwest whose year-to-date order total is less than $50,000."

◆ "Show me the names and addresses of our midwestern clients whose year-to-date balance is less than $50,000."

◆ "List names and addresses of clients with a year-to-date balance of less than $50,000 who are headquartered in the Midwest."

A natural language application will take any of these sentences, parse it, and rephrase it as the following structured query language (SQL) statement:

Robots that move independently must include artificial eyes.

```
SELECT NAME ADDRESS FROM CLIENT
        WHERE REGION="MIDWEST"
        AND Y-T-D_ORD<5000
```

The goal of natural language processors is to eventually eliminate the need for people to learn programming languages or customized commands for computers to understand them. Their great advantage is in the way they can be used in combination with voice-recognition devices to allow the user to command computers to perform tasks, without touching a keyboard or any other input device.

One of the greatest challenges in natural language processing is the fact that the same combination of words may take on completely different meanings depending upon the context in which it is used. The challenge is to teach the machine to interpret the words correctly, according to their context.

Used by permission from Lockheed Martin Corporation

Used by permission from Tim Thompson/Tony Stone Images

Naval officers use verbal commands that are interpreted through natural language processors. The commands are then executed by computer-based weapons systems to hit a target.

Expert Systems

In the late 1950s and early 1960s, computer scientists tried to build computers that would be able to perform intelligent tasks. The efforts at that time were aimed at developing a **general problem solver**, a machine that would be able to mimic human thought processes, to solve any given problem that a human being can solve. These efforts failed because the programs needed for the task would have to be unrealistically huge. Scientists realized that they had to concentrate on designing systems to solve much more specialized types of problems. The efforts were then directed toward the design of programs to solve problems in specific areas by utilizing experts' knowledge and reasoning. These programs are referred to as **expert systems (ESs)**.

The development of early ESs took place in academic research centers. For instance, DENDRAL, a program that identifies molecules from spectroscopic data, was developed at Stanford University in 1965; MACSYMA, a solver of complex mathematical problems, was developed at MIT in 1969; and MYCIN, a system for the diagnosis of bacterial diseases, was developed at Stanford University in 1973.

PROSPECTOR, a software package developed by SRI International, Inc. to target sites for molybdenum exploration based on geological data input, marked the beginning of the large-scale vending of commercial AI applications, starting in 1980. Many other systems followed, developed by commercial designers for commercial applications. ESs now are designed to help in various domains: medicine, engineering, financial analysis, insurance, and numerous other areas of business and industry.

The purpose of ESs is to replicate the unstructured and undocumented knowledge of the few, the experts, and put it at the disposal of others. Because of the way ESs are formulated (based on the experience of experts) ESs cannot help deal with events that are not taken into consideration by the experts during development. However, more advanced programs that include what are called neural networks (discussed below) can learn from new situations and formulate new rules in their knowledge bases beyond events originally considered in their development.

To build an ES, a specialist called a "knowledge engineer" questions experts and translates their knowledge into code. In most systems, the knowledge is represented in one of several forms. The most popular form is **IF-THEN** rules. For example: "If the patient is female, and if the patient's temperature is over 100°F, and if the patient has a rash (and so on), then the patient has disease X."

Two other methods to represent knowledge in a computer program are **semantic frames**, which are tables that list entities and their attributes, and **semantic networks**, which are maps of entities and their related attributes, both of which are discussed below.

ES shells—programs designed to facilitate development of ESs with minimum programming—have facilitated the building of ESs. Some of the more popular shells are VP-EXPERT, NEXPERT, and EXSYS.

ES researchers continue to look for ways to better capture knowledge and represent it. They test the results of such efforts in highly unstructured problem-solving domains, including games. One such game, which has intrigued both

Used by permission from AP/Wide Worlds Photos

Since chess playing requires expertise, scientists have used the game to experiment with artificial chess players. Here, Deep Blue beats the human world champion in 1997.

researchers and laypeople, is chess. The game is a highly unstructured environment in which the number of possible moves is enormous, and hence, the player must be an expert to select the best move for every board configuration. In 1993, a computer program named Mephisto beat a former world champion, Anatoly Karpov. In 1996, a program named Deep Blue beat the world champion, Gary Kasparov in one game, but lost to the human champion in the overall set of games. In 1997, however, an enhanced version of the program lost some games to Kasparov but won the overall match by one game.

The 1980s saw a lot of enthusiasm about ESs and with it several corporations specializing in the development of expert systems for specific uses. While interest has subsided (probably because ESs were oversold), top IS managers still rate ESs as a highly promising emerging technology[1]. It is expected that ESs will eventually be the predominant type of information system in use.

Neural Networks

Rather than containing a set of production rules, more sophisticated ESs use programs called **neural networks** that are designed to mimic the way the human brain thinks—the way it links facts, draws conclusions, and uses experience to learn to understand how new facts relate to each other. Neural networks enable **machine learning**, the ability of a system to update its knowledge dynamically from its own experiences and apply them to future sessions.

Neural networks are software applications programmed to simulate the "wiring" style of a human brain, whose software "cells," or nodes, are connected to other software "cells," or nodes, to form a network. The network consists of several layers of nodes, as shown in Figure 13.2 (where each layer is represented by a different color). The network of software nodes is programmed to mimic the physical network of neurons in our own, human brains. The software nodes are linked logically rather than physically, and simulate brain activity by having different processes take place in different locations and having them assimilated to create the output.

When we cogitate, neurons in our brains communicate by way of electric pulses, generating associations among different pieces of facts and ideas. In neural network applications, software nodes are built to represent neurons. Nodes at the system's boundaries receive signals or input that are passed on to the next layer. After processing takes place in the internal layers, the system produces output, which is a solution to a problem, such as the recognition of someone's handwriting or speech. For example, consider a neural network application whose function is to determine from an x-ray picture whether or not a patient has a tumor. The first layer of nodes in the neural network forms the boundary between the system and the input (the x-ray) when the neural

---

[1] "Leading Trends in Information Services," Sixth Annual Survey of North American CIOs 1994, Deloitte & Touche, 1994.

Smart cards, which have been used in Europe for a number of years, are being updated. Smart cards look like credit cards, but actually store many megabytes of information in an embedded silicon chip, instead of the usual magnetic strip. Developers are planning on incorporating neural networks into the chip, increasing their capabilities significantly. The goal is to have the card conduct security functions immune to fraud, using the increased memory and neural networks embedded in the chip to check various biological characteristics of a card user, known as **biometric checks**.

For instance, biometric checks could be used to verify a unique human characteristic, such as a voice, face, or fingerprint. The neural network's intelligence would enable the chip to identify its owner's voice even if he or she has a cold, or a fingerprint even if it has been scarred.

These security measures could also be applied to credit card purchases over the phone, where a vendor's terminal could generate a real-time speech profile of a person calling by running a signal processing algorithm when the person says a requested word out loud. The profile could then be transmitted back in encrypted form to the user, whose card, with its integral neural network, would then confirm or deny the profile.

Source: Blanchard, D., "Smart Cards Thwart Fraud," *OR/MS Today*, August 1994, p. 16.

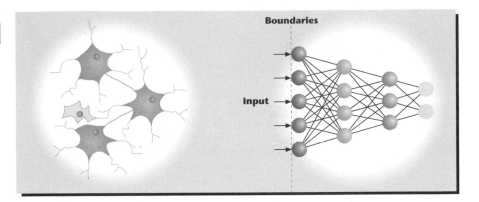

Figure 13.2 *Neural nets simulate the association and inference that take place in a network of neurons in the human brain. Instead of a network of neurons, a network of nodes is developed.*

network system examines the x-ray, much as a doctor's eyes form the "first layer" or boundary between the doctor's brain and the visual input, when the doctor examines the x-ray.

Unlike expert systems, a neural net system learns through trial and error. The knowledge engineer provides feedback, which the system records. As the number of trials and amount of feedback increase, the system becomes more and more accurate in its evaluation and output. Many systems let the user view the connections between the nodes, sometimes called the "wires," graphically on the computer monitor. As the system learns, one can see the favored path to a solution in the form of a color-coded series of nodes.

The uncanny ability of neural networks to learn by themselves without the benefit of explicit software instructions has been enticing scientists for several years. But implementation of the technology in the business world is progressing slowly, mainly because it is difficult to understand and use.

FUZZY LOGIC

Fuzzy logic is a system of rules that are not restricted to "either/or" choices, thus enabling a system to better deal with ambiguity. Since people tend to think in relative, not absolute, terms, fuzzy logic allows computer applications to solve problems in a manner that is more humanlike. When fuzzy logic is incorporated into an ES, the result is a system that closely mimics the natural manner in which a human expert would solve a problem.

Fuzzy logic is a theory of classification of concepts that do not have discrete boundaries, but lie along a continuum. A concept that plays a central role in the application of fuzzy logic is that of a **linguistic variable**, which is the linguistic equivalent of a mathematical variable; the value of the linguistic variable is described by a word rather than a number. For instance, consider the use of the linguistic variable *age*. Its linguistic values are *young, middle-aged* and *old*, with *young* defined by a membership function such as the one in Figure 13.3 on the next page. While in a sharp rule-based system only those up to age 20 would be considered young and all others would not, this graph indicates that a person between the ages of 20 and 40 is still considered young, although to a lesser extent. Thus, the system refers to the probability that a person is young; it does not determine that the person definitely is or is not young.

Too Sophisticated Technology

A major purpose of developing "intelligent" software is to disseminate expertise and rid human beings of the constant need to turn to human experts: doctors, lawyers, accountants, engineers, and other knowledge workers on whose expertise we rely for our health, finances, and general well-being. With the integration of knowledge into software, more and more of the tasks for which we were dependent on specialists we can now carry out by ourselves. For instance, many people use software to write their own wills rather than go to a lawyer; a growing number of citizens use tax expert systems to plan their finances and prepare tax returns; and some people use medical expert systems to diagnose diseases.

Ostensibly, increasing availability of expert programs is progress. However, this increasing dependence on machine intelligence raises new legal and ethical issues for society: Who is legally responsible for advice provided by a program? Is expert judgment needed to interpret program output? Does machine expertise replace or only complement the "real thing"? In fact, how do we know if the "experts" behind expert systems are expert at all?

These legal issues are largely not addressed by current laws. Although it is illegal for people to represent themselves as licensed professionals if they are not, anyone is allowed to use any ES he or she wishes to use, and give advice based on the output of the system. In fact, anyone, regardless of his or her qualifications, can actually create an expert system, even on medical topics. And the law does not prevent people from using medical ESs to diagnose themselves, or legal ESs to defend themselves. The results may be serious injury or financial loss. Increasing self-reliance may pose a problem. The expertise literally at the tips of our fingers can give a false impression that whatever decision the computer outputs is the one we should adopt. While the output may be the optimal decision in the majority of cases, even one mistake may be detrimental.

(continued)

Figure 13.4 adds *middle-aged* and *old* to complete the description of the *age* variable. Members of the set aged 50–65 are always considered middle-aged, and those over age 80 are always considered old. But there is room for interpretation in the other age groups.

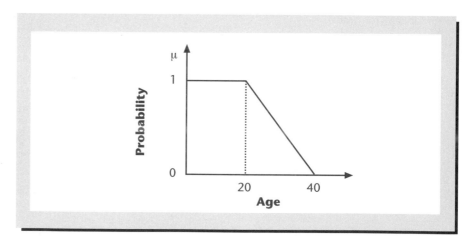

Figure 13.3 *The function* young

Consider the case of the "smart stretcher," a program contracted for development in the early 1990s by the U.S. Army from a company that specializes in medical artificial intelligence. The system used expert physicians and other medical personnel to produce an ES that was to be installed in a small computer that would be attached to stretchers used in combat. The ES was supposed to help the medics of fighting units quickly diagnose wounded soldiers in the battlefield, by entering data describing a soldier's medical profile and wounds into the system, which would then diagnose the soldier and recommend treatment.

The reason you haven't heard of the "smart stretcher" is that shortly before the device was to be launched, the company decided to give up the lucrative contract for fear of lawsuits. Executives said the small company could not afford long and expensive litigation if a soldier or his family sued the developers with a claim that the system misdiagnosed, and therefore harmed the patient.

Who could potentially be at fault when a wrong decision is reached as a result of using an ES? There are four parties that are involved in the development and use of ESs: the experts who contribute the knowledge, the knowledge engineers who build the system, the professional who uses it, and the person who is affected by the decision. Malfunction can be caused by any one of these: the experts might have provided bad knowledge, the knowledge engineer might have constructed the ES poorly, the user might have used it inappropriately, and the affected person, who provided some of the data, might have provided wrong data.

As with other new technologies, the legal profession has not yet considered all these issues. For the time being, an individual or an organization adversely affected through use of an ES may sue the developer and is likely to win the case in court, because courts have so far held the developers of faulty computer programs liable. Furthermore, since ESs contain expertise, the developers may be sued not simply for negligence, but for malpractice, much as a human expert

When categorizing someone in an age group, placing the person according to a mathematical function (as shown in Figure 13.4) is more practical than saying that 18 is young but 30 is not, because the function can be applied in a programmed decision-making environment. A 38-year-old person may be categorized as young or middle-aged, each with a less than 100% probability.

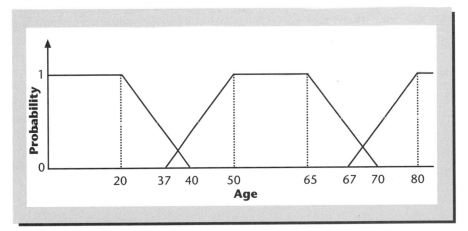

Figure 13.4 *The functions* young, middle-aged *and* old

Command the Computer with Your Thoughts

We have said several times in this book that the ultimate programming language will be natural language, and that the most convenient interaction with computers will be talking to them. Well, why talk to them if you can think to them?

Let us add another "ware" to your computer vocabulary: wetware. "Wet" refers to the brain. **Wetware** is a term used to refer to the knowledge your brain holds. Scientists are now trying to find ways to connect our brains to computers, so that we can directly interact with them. For example: If you need the telephone number of a friend from a computerized directory, a simple thought could activate a microprocessor implanted in your brain to send a signal to the computer, and *voilà*, a seamless operation. The record is now in your brain. And if you wish, you can have the record displayed on the computer's monitor.

While remote interaction with computers through thought alone is years away, scientists are seriously looking for ways to connect our brains to computers. In the future, our heads and hands may be connected directly to computers so that we can send commands to the computers by merely moving our body, rather than by pressing keys on a keyboard. Electrodes will be attached to our skulls that can capture electrical impulses from clusters of neurons in the visual centers of our brains. The signals may then be transferred to the computer, and an image reconstructed on the monitor. We may be able to use our facial or other muscles to send commands to the computer. The results of this research may make it easier for disabled people to use computers.

(continued)

Suppose we are considering a targeted marketing plan, and the potential customer is a person who is considered young. If the definition of *young* is *younger than 38*, then a database query of "get all customers who are young" will not retrieve candidates whose age is just above the threshold, such as 38. This problem can be solved by using fuzzy logic. If the concept "young" is defined using an appropriate fuzzy set, a query like "get all young candidates" will now retrieve all candidates whose age qualifies as "young" to any degree, that is all candidates the system is 100% sure are young and also candidates the system is less than 100% sure are young. This facilitates the retrieval of "intelligent" information from the databases.

This query would now retrieve the records of all candidates whose age has a possibility of 1 or less than 1 to be "young." The records selected would, therefore, include highly qualified 38-year-old candidates. The difference between the two approaches is sometimes referred to as the difference between *probability* and *possibility*. The contribution of fuzzy logic is including some candidates of ages 37–40 in a "young" or "middle-aged" set, and some of 67–70 in "middle-aged" or "old." While its name suggests imprecision, fuzzy logic is not fuzzy at all. It applies precise mathematical functions to problem solving.

Some private firms have entered the arena with innovative ideas. BioControl Systems, a company in Palo Alto, California, is developing armbands and headbands (which look like sweatbands used for sports) to sense electrical impulses in our body and transform them into commands for computers to which the bands are connected through wires. It is hoped that eventually our "thoughts," in the form of electric signals, can be translated into digital instructions and data. This "translation" of electrical signals from the brain into computer signals is among the most challenging aspects of this work.

Another company, IBVA Technologies, Inc., in New York, is developing similar equipment called the Interactive Brainwave visual analyzer. Here, too, a headband collects brain waves and transforms them into pictorial and aural input. And another company, Monsoon Software, in Baltimore, has developed software that draws a map of a person's brain waves on a computer screen. The company calls the program MindSet. The developer hopes that someday there will be no "barriers" between a user and a computer, such as keyboards and mice. The interaction between human beings and computers will then be "transparent," accomplished through thoughts only.

It is doubtful that any machine will be able to contain our entire wetware, that is, the volume of images and information that our brains can store and process. However, even a little wetware in computers, and the ability to interact with machines through our thoughts, would be quite helpful.

Sources: Kantrowitz, B., "Computers as Mind Readers," *Newsweek*, May 30, 1994, p. 68. www.IBVA.com, July 28, 1997.

THINK CRITICALLY

Who will benefit from the use of the above technology? Who will not? Which human activities do you think will diminish when the technology becomes reality? Will the overall effect of ubiquitous use of the technology be good or bad for society?

For instance, consider a bank trying to decide whether to extend a person a loan. A loan officer perceives the person as low, moderate, or high risk. But credit bureaus that provide information to loan officers use ESs that generally use two categories (for example, good/bad) for each characteristic (age, income, or credit history) or, at best, attach several points to each category. The decision-making process, then, is binary because there are only two options for each characteristic. However, under a fuzzy logic system, the loan officer would not decide that the potential debtor is either a bad risk or a good risk, but would consider the possibility that the applicant belongs to one of several "continuous" groups, such as low risk, medium risk, high risk. In the process of deciding this, the system takes into account the probability that a person may belong to any of these groups. So, for example, it could assess that the applicant has a 20% chance of being a low risk, and an 80% chance of being a moderate risk.

Japanese manufacturers have incorporated fuzzy logic into microprocessors that help run everything from refrigerators and washing machines to camcorders, automobiles, and subway trains. Fuzzy logic has improved these devices by making it possible for them to treat the conditions of the consumer environment as flexible. Since fuzzy logic can support decisions in imprecise data environments, it also has applicability in more information-oriented industries such as finance, insurance, and pharmaceuticals.

A good example in the finance field is a hybrid neuro-fuzzy system used to forecast convertible bond ratings. The system has been used by Nikko Securities Co. since 1992, and the company says its advice has been on the mark in 92% of the cases.

GENETIC ALGORITHMS

Genetic algorithms are mathematical functions that use Darwinian principles or random mutation to improve an application. The functions are designed to simulate in the software environment, in minutes or seconds, what happens in the natural environments over millions of years. In nature, living organisms improve through natural selection and mutation based on their success or failure surviving in the physical environment; with genetic algorithms, software mimics this process within a very short time to produce the "fittest," that is the optimal, product. Special algorithms dictate how combinations are to be formed, and the threshold that decides whether the combinations will be left in a select group that will continue to break and combine, or be discarded (see Figure 13.5).

Genetic algorithms break the application's elements into segments called **chromosomes**, which link with each other in a random fashion to form programs. The programs are constantly improved to produce better combinations of

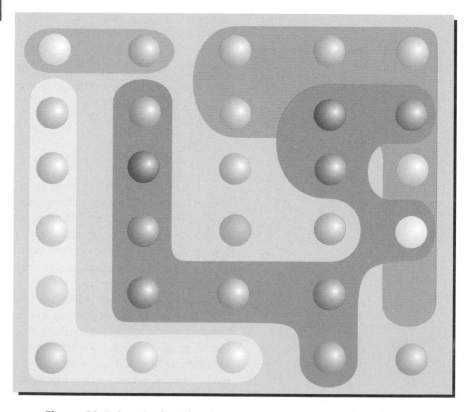

Figure 13.5 *Genetic algorithms are used to produce a combination of factors that combine to provide an optimal result. In this figure, spheres represent factors and their weights, and the combination with the darkest shading is the fittest solution.*

factors that are important in creating an output, and to refine the attributes of these factors. The majority of these programs are discarded, but a few that prove to do the desired job well combine with other survivors and generate offspring programs. The process may produce results that are superior to anything created by human beings, thanks to the ability of the computer to match and discard so many elements in so little time.

Unlike neural nets, which start work with a clean slate and learn patterns through analysis of feedback, genetic algorithms start their work with a large number of building blocks. Through an enormous number of trials and errors, they produce viable solutions that could take human beings years to reach.

For example, when General Electric's engineers were designing a more efficient fan blade for the Boeing 777 jet engine, they faced a huge task. The number of factors affecting a jet fan's performance and cost is a figure with 381 digits. A supercomputer performing a million calculations per second would take billions of years to test every possible combination. GE used a system that is a hybrid of a rule-based expert system supplemented by genetic algorithms, and came up with the optimal solution in less than a week. The system, Engeneous, starts with a pool of combinations of different factors, leaves in the process only the "fittest" (which it defines with a set of rules that are programmed into the system), recombines factors, culls out the unfit, and repeats the process until it reaches a combination that is the best in performance and cost.

INTELLIGENT AGENTS

The latest development in AI is **intelligent agents**, computer programs that automatically wade through massive amounts of data and select and deliver the most suitable information for the user, according to contextual or specific requirements. Advanced intelligent agents are also expected to execute some operations on networked computers, such as placing purchase orders. The most common use of these agents is on the Internet, where they are programmed, or taught, to travel through the Net and carry out tasks, such as retrieving price lists of specified consumer goods, copying articles related to certain subjects, paying outstanding debts electronically, and purchasing goods and services. Note that intelligent agents are not expert systems, which are programmed to provide expert advice in a narrow field of expertise. Agents are not programmed in a narrowly defined area, but are in fact expected to perform a vast array of tasks. The main purpose of intelligent agents is to carry out their assignments significantly faster, more frequently, and more effectively than human beings.

As in the case of expert systems, one of the most difficult problems that intelligent agent researchers must overcome is how to install common sense in these programs. In the future, the research, which began only a few years ago, is expected to address not only the technical challenges of developing agents, but the social and ethical issues as well, such as who should have control (the human owner or the program) in which situations, and other concerns.

DEVELOPMENT OF EXPERT SYSTEMS

Expert systems are the predominant type of AI to have caught the attention of knowledge workers. Because they are designed for use in highly unstructured settings, such as internal medicine, investment in securities, tax planning, and mathematical approximation, engineers, physicians, financial

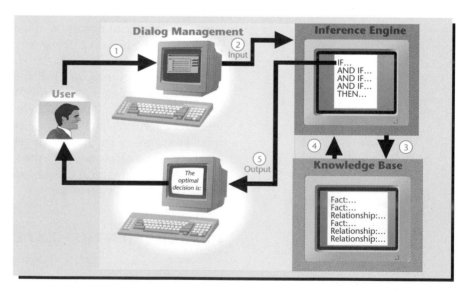

POINT OF INTEREST

AI to the Rescue

Processes in chemical manufacturing plants can be organized in many different ways, but very few yield the maximum output. For many years, managers used their own expertise to decide on the best timing and sequence of these complex processes. In 1990, engineers at Microelectronics & Computer Technology Corp. (MCC) in Austin, Texas, developed special software, a combination of fuzzy logic and neural nets, to do the work for them. The neural net analyzes past operations data and output to determine the best process arrangement. When a plant introduces a new chemical process to the manufacturing operation, fuzzy logic is applied to optimize the production in the real plant. When the software was first used at a plant of Eastman Chemical Co., it improved operations by 30%.

Source: Port, O., "Computers that think are almost here," *BusinessWeek*, July 17, 1995, pp. 68–73.

analysts, accountants, and other professionals have recognized the potential of ESs to provide professionals with expert advice without the need for a human expert. Development of ESs is usually a major undertaking. Thus, you should be familiar with the concept of expertise and how it is translated into an ES.

WHAT IS EXPERTISE?

Expertise is the skill and knowledge, primarily gained from experience, whose input into a process results in performance that is far above the norm. Expertise often consists of massive amounts of factual information, coupled with rules of thumb, simplifications, rare facts, and wise procedures, all compiled in a way that allows the expert to analyze specific types of problems in an efficient manner. To a large extent, expertise is gained through experienced trials and errors. Such experience allows experts to skip options they know will not be fruitful, and choose those that will. Most of the rules that experts accumulate over time are **heuristics** (from the Greek word *Heuristikein*: "to find"): rules that cannot be formulated as a result of ordinary, proven knowledge, but only through experience. Heuristics are compiled hindsight, and draw their power from the various kinds of regularity and continuity in the world: they arise through specialization, generalization, and analogy.

For example, consider what happens when your car malfunctions and emits a strange sound. When you take it to a repair shop, the mechanic listens to the noise, looks at something under the hood, and decides that the water pump is broken. Through years of dealing with this problem and this noise, the expert mechanic knows what is *not* the right diagnosis, and through many trials and errors, she has formulated heuristics in her mind that lead her to decide the diagnosis.

COMPONENTS OF EXPERT SYSTEMS

An ES consists of three components (see Figure 13.6): (1) The "interface" or **dialog management** program facilitates interaction between the user and

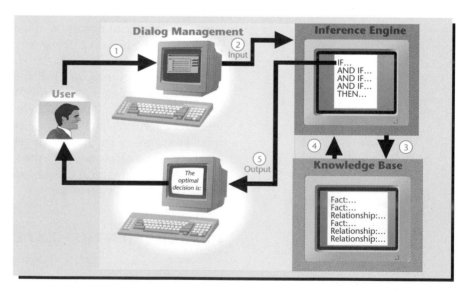

Figure 13.6 *Components of an expert system; numbers indicate the order of the processes*

the system. It is similar to the dialog management program in a DSS. The dialog management module prompts the user to enter parameters required to make a decision in an orderly manner. (2) The **knowledge base** is a set of facts and the relationships among the facts, provided as input to the system. The various methods used to represent knowledge in a knowledge base are discussed below. (3) The **inference engine** is a program that associates the user-supplied data with a set of rules to deduce solutions and explain how they were reached. The inference engine takes the input supplied by the user through the dialog component and combines it with knowledge in the knowledge base to produce a solution to a problem: a decision or a diagnosis.

KNOWLEDGE REPRESENTATION METHODS

While decision support systems use databases, ESs use knowledge bases. A knowledge base contains, in a computer-readable form, the facts, associations, relationships, and beliefs supplied by an expert. There are several methods to organize knowledge in a knowledge base.

IF-THEN RULES IF-THEN **rules**, also called **production rules**, are by far the most popular method of knowledge representation, found in about 70% of all ESs. As a simple example, consider a knowledge base for classifying animals. The system holds the facts in the form of IF-THEN statements like: "If it has *4 legs*, and if it has *a tail*, and if it *barks*, then it is *a dog*." The knowledge base may contain hundreds or thousands of such rules.

Now let's consider the use of an ES to help identify an animal (see Figure 13.7). First, the dialog management module will ask the user to enter the number of legs; then, it will ask whether the animal has a tail; then it may provide a list of animal

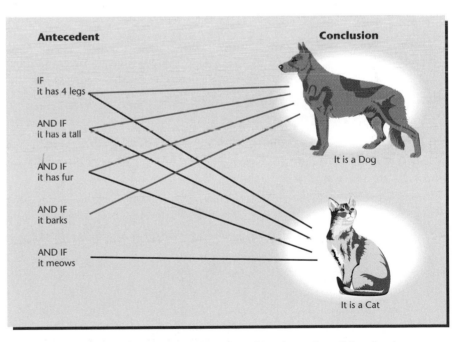

Figure 13.7 *In IF-THEN rules different combinations of conditions lead to different conclusions.*

sounds from which the user must select one, or it may ask the user to enter the word that best describes the animal's sound (barks, meows, chirps, and the like). Once the user answers all of the system's questions, the inference engine is triggered. If the entries were: *4*, *yes*, and *barks*, then the inference engine combines the IFs and reaches the appropriate THEN, and the dialog will output the sentence: "The animal is a *dog*."

Of course, the user may enter: *4*, *yes*, and *meows*. In this case, the first and second IFs are the same, but the third is different. The inference engine will combine the IFs, and find in the knowledge base that this combination yields another THEN: *cat*. The IFs are referred to as *antecedents*, while the result is called a *conclusion*.

FRAMES Knowledge can also be organized as facts in tables, referred to as **frames**, where each table is devoted to one entity or occurrence and its attributes (see Figure 13.8). For instance, the frame for the entity *dog* would include the facts that it is a mammal, has fur, has four legs, barks, and so on. When queried, the inference engine searches the tables. Conditions are satisfied if the information is found in the frame relating to the event or entity.

SEMANTIC NETS When knowledge is stored in the form of objects and the relationships among them, it is said to be stored in **semantic nets** because, when graphed, the knowledge base looks like a network where the boxes contain objects (or attributes), and the lines represent attributes and relationships. To reach a solution to a problem, the system navigates along the network according to the parameters supplied by the user until it finds a unique object that satisfies the parameters.

Consider the example shown in Figure 13.9. If the user provides the facts that the animal is a mammal, has fur, is four-legged, and barks, there is only one choice the system can reach: only a dog satisfies all these facts and relationships.

KNOWLEDGE ENGINEERING

A **knowledge engineer** is a programmer who specializes in developing ESs. He or she is skilled in asking experts the appropriate questions and translating the

ATTRIBUTE	VALUE
Mammal	Yes
Fur	Yes
Sound	Barks
Legs	Four
Tail	Yes

Figure 13.8 *A frame describing a dog*

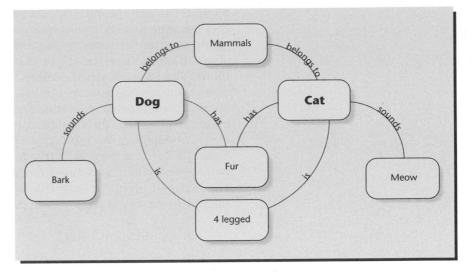

Figure 13.9 *Semantic nets*

answers into a knowledge base that follows one of the above approaches (see Figure 13.10). Interestingly, but not surprisingly, many successful knowledge engineers have a formal education in psychology. This background enables knowledge

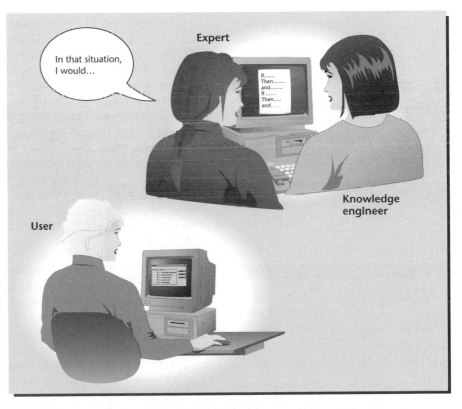

Figure 13.10 *A knowledge engineer must know what to ask, how to ask, and how to organize the answers into a knowledge base.*

engineers to help people work cooperatively to provide all the information they can, which can be a process requiring excellent communications skills and great patience. For instance, imagine trying to get the mechanic described above to explain how she knows what is wrong with a car by listening to the motor. She may tell you she knows "from experience." But what does that mean? Is there a certain irregular sound coming from the motor? Is it always associated with the same malfunction? Clearly, it is not easy to receive a step-by-step explanation of facts and link them.

Considering that, it should not be surprising that some ESs take years to build. Caduceus, a medical ES that diagnoses internal diseases, is the fruit of two people's effort: a nationally acclaimed internist, and a world-renowned knowledge engineer. The system's knowledge base contains over 5,000 IF-THEN rules that took several years to compile and organize.

EXPERT SYSTEM SHELLS

Early ESs were developed using programming languages that were invented especially for AI applications: LISP (LISt Processing), KEE (Knowledge Engineering Environment), Prolog, and others. While some ESs are still constructed using these languages, most knowledge engineers now use **expert system shells**, which are programs that provide an interface to assist the developer in creating an ES. The shell queries the developer for facts and the links among them, and enters the information into a knowledge base. Vendors now offer expert system shells that enable novices to develop their own ESs.

The majority of ES shells represent knowledge as IF-THEN rules. The shell displays the word IF on the screen and lets the developer enter the condition. The developer can go on and enter as many conditions as necessary. When done, the developer so indicates, and the shell displays the word THEN, prompting the developer to supply the consequence. As the developer supplies the conditions and consequences (the THEN statement), the program builds a knowledge base and an inference engine.

Shells are not suitable for large and complex ESs. Usually they are used by experts to build small-scale systems for training or for use by novices, without the participation of a professional knowledge engineer. Three of the most widely used ES shell programs are VP-Expert, NEXPERT, and EXSYS Professional.

FORWARD CHAINING AND BACKWARD CHAINING

An ES that takes certain values of parameters as input, runs them through an inference engine, and outputs the solution to the problem is said to be carrying out **forward chaining**. That is, the system starts the process with facts and works its way to a result. Therefore, forward chaining is also referred to as a **result-driven** process. If the system is given a goal and asked to state the conditions that would bring about the desired outcome, then the process is **backward chaining**, or **goal-driven**. If an investor decides to invest $100,000 for one year in municipal bonds, forward chaining will predict an annual return of 3%. If the investor wants to earn at least a 20% annual

EXSYS Professional, an ES shell, prompts the ES builder to enter IF antecedents and THEN conclusions. The ES shell then combines these entries into a knowledge base.

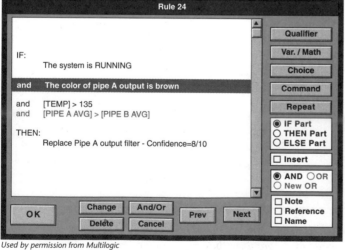

Used by permission from Multilogic

return, backward chaining will lead to recommending an investment in technology stock for more than two years (see Figure 13.11).

While it may sound as if the system must be developed to do either forward chaining or backward chaining, this is not the case. Think of decision making as traversing a decision tree, where at each junction you must find the best path. The same decision tree can serve you to move from a set of givens to a result (forward chaining), or from a goal to the givens (backward chaining). Indeed, many ES shell programs accommodate the usage of the ES they help to build both in forward and backward chaining modes.

While a person can use an ES blindly, providing information as asked and letting the ES do the work, most people want to understand how the system is approaching a problem. So, if an ES requests certain data, in the process of considering a problem, a user may ask to see the reasoning behind the request. In backward chaining, the system simply goes one step back, fetches the previous step's set of conditions, and presents them as an explanation.

FACTORS JUSTIFYING THE ACQUISITION OF EXPERT SYSTEMS

Studies have shown that expert systems can significantly improve decision making in organizations. One of their strengths is the fact that they can serve many professionals in one company and can be used to train newcomers. One study even demonstrated that novices who use an ES on the job internalize some of the knowledge base, and expedite their own learning.

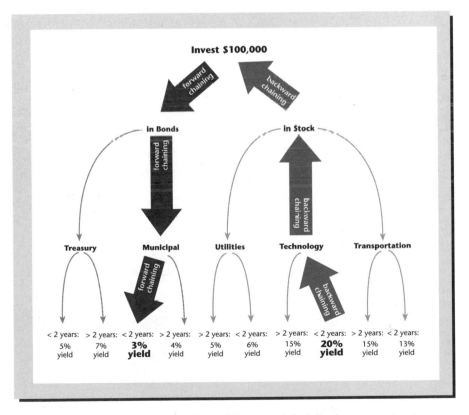

Figure 13.11 *Forward chaining and backward chaining in an expert system*

Net Notes

The Pacific Northwest National Laboratory (PNNL) is an artificial intelligence laboratory whose research projects are sponsored by the U.S Department of Energy. Its Web site (*http://www.emsl.pnl.gov:2080/docs/cie*) is a colorful and friendly resource for all who wish to learn more about the subject. You will find there clear explanations of the latest developments in each of AI's areas, and descriptions of the laboratory's ongoing projects.

- The problem must be nontrivial.
- The problem must occur in a highly unstructured setting.
- The problem must occur frequently.
- An expert must be available to develop the system.

Figure 13.12 *What justifies the acquisition of an ES?*

There are certain factors that should be considered before deciding to develop an ES, however (see Figure 13.12). First, the problem to be solved should not be trivial. Trivial problems can be solved by novices without any aid. Second, the problem must be in a highly-unstructured domain that requires the wisdom of an expert. Third, the problem should occur frequently. Fourth, an expert must be available for building the expert system. The development of an ES requires that an expert contribute much of his or her time in long sessions with a knowledge engineer. This time is expensive and not always available.

CONTRIBUTION OF EXPERT SYSTEMS

ESs offer valuable contributions to organizations. Although the cost of developing some systems can reach seven figures or more, the benefits can outweigh the expense. The greatest benefit of ESs is their contribution to productivity by conducting tasks that free employees to focus on work only human beings can do. Figure 13.13 shows the results of a survey in which 55 companies whose IS annual budget is at least $250,000 gave reasons for using ESs.

Reasons for Using Expert Systems	Percent of Organizations Giving the Reason
To ehance product/service quality	52%
To enforce consistent reasoning	48%
To gain more insight of decision-making process	42%
To better control complex systems	35%
To distribute scarce expertise	35%
To preserve expertise	35%
To train less-experienced employees	29%
To reduce costs	29%
To monitor vast amounts of information	19%

Note: Percentages do not add up to 100 because organizations could indicate multiple reasons.

Source: Tsai, N., Necco, C.R., Wei, G., "Implementing an Expert System: A Report on Benefits Realized," *Journal of Systems Management*, Vol 45 No 10 Iss 400, October 1994, pp. 26–30.

Figure 13.13 *Major reasons for using expert systems*

Recognize the Potential of Artificial Intelligence?

Your company used John Brayne as an expert consultant for over 30 years. John has accumulated an enormous amount of knowledge on the behavior of commodities. For example, to predict the prices of coffee for the next 12 months, he takes into consideration such seemingly disparate input as weather conditions in south-east Asia and new government regulations in Brazil. His advice was invaluable for the firm. But several months ago he retired and moved; he is unreachable, and you no longer have access to his expertise. But things would be different had your firm captured his expertise in an expert system.

Senior managers can run successful companies without knowing much about AI. Yet, in business, if others embrace new technologies that improve performance while you do not, you will soon find that they can sell their goods and services for less than you can. And soon, the competition will capture a growing market share, while yours will shrink. AI is one of those advanced technologies that leading corporations must study, consider, and adopt in order to stay on the leading edge of their industries.

Managers do not have to know all the technical details of AI techniques. However, they would do well to know how AI can be used in complex decision-making situations. If they know what the technology can do for them, they may be able to harness it to their organizations' benefit. AI techniques have been a tremendous resource in solving highly unstructured problems. They can provide an optimal solution to a problem with millions of possible solutions within a fraction of the time it would take a human being. And expert systems, an important segment of AI, have provided an excellent tool for capturing expertise and disseminating it to managers so that they can act using software instead of highly paid human experts.

The areas where ESs can help in business are discussed below.

Planning. ESs can use information from previous projects to improve subsequent plans, by cautioning the planner against pitfalls that may cause budget and time overruns, for example.

Decision Making. ESs can support decision making by bringing input from several experts, rather than from a single expert, thereby providing the organization with a true strategic weapon.

Monitoring. ESs can be used to monitor industrial processes, cash management, and employee activities, easily providing security against fraud by identifying aberrations in cash disbursement.

Diagnosis. ESs can provide valuable support in diagnosing different conditions: human diseases in medicine; malfunctioning equipment, products, or processes in industry; or hardware problems and their solutions in business. Major Swedish corporations such as Volvo, Saab, Asea Brown Bovery, and Televerket have developed ESs to solve control and processing problems in their plants. The British steel industry developed ESs that help in the production of stainless steel slabs.

Training. Many ESs contain an explanation facility that describes the logic being used to address the problem at hand. This makes AI techniques handy in producing ESs that are devoted to training. Training ESs teach users decision rules, which the user can then bring to his or her own work.

Incidental Learning. Studies have shown that while using an ES in the regular course of their work, people internalize how the system reaches decisions. This increases their own expertise and makes them better decision makers even in times when an ES is not available.

Replication of Expertise. Once the expertise is captured in the system, it can easily and inexpensively be replicated and disseminated. Thus, many employees in various divisions and sites can enjoy the knowledge of the same experts.

Timely Response. Unlike human expert consultants, ESs are on call at all times to provide immediate support and to perform processes, in moments, that would be prohibitively time-consuming for human beings.

Consistent Solutions. Many organizations want their managers and employees to be consistent in their decision making. For example, a bank would not like its credit officers to evaluate credit worthiness following different guidelines. Since ESs are programmed to solve a certain problem in the same way every time they are queried, they provide the desired consistency.

EXPERT SYSTEMS IN ACTION

ESs have been implemented to help professionals in many different industries, such as telecommunications, agriculture, manufacturing, and medicine. The following is a small sample of examples.

TELEPHONE NETWORK MAINTENANCE

Pacific Bell uses an ES to diagnose network failures and fix them. The system consists of three parts: Monitor, Consultant, and Forecaster. Monitor constantly monitors Pacific Bell's telephone network, checking for errors. When a problem is detected, the system uses a synthesized voice to warn network specialists, who can then use Consultant to walk them through recommended troubleshooting and repair procedures to correct the problem. Before the company started using the ES, a small number of highly trained specialists did the troubleshooting, which is now done by employees with less training. Forecaster, the third part of the ES, checks system files and notifies personnel of problems likely to occur, based on previous experience, allowing the staff to prevent problems from occurring.

CREDIT EVALUATION

Holders of American Express (AmEx) charge cards can potentially charge the card for hundreds of thousands of dollars per purchase. Obviously, most retailers and restaurateurs will not approve a charge before they contact AmEx for approval. The AmEx clerk who considers the request uses an ES. The system requests data such as account number, location of the establishment, and amount of the purchase. Coupled with information from a database that contains previous

Used by permission from Citicorp

Many banks use expert systems to determine credit worthiness of clients.

data on the account, and a knowledge base with criteria for approving or denying credit, the ES provides a response.

TAX PLANNING

Because federal and state tax laws are so complex, choosing business strategies to minimize tax payments requires expertise. Several tax ESs have been developed for this purpose. For instance, Taxadvisor solves problems dealing with income and transfer tax planning for individuals. The system makes recommendations based upon projected events for tax-related actions that would maximize the wealth that an individual transferred at death.

Financial Advisor is used by tax consultants to get advice on projects, products, mergers, and acquisitions. A consultant provides information about a company, and the system evaluates how proposed transactions, changes in the tax law, or other factors impact the tax owed.

TaxIQ, developed by Coopers and Lybrand, gives advice and guidance to auditors and tax specialists in preparing tax accruals for financial statements. It also identifies important issues for tax planning, tax compliance, and tax services.

DETECTION OF INSIDER SECURITIES TRADING

Like other similar institutions, the American Stock Exchange (AMEX) has a special department to prevent insider trading of the securities under its supervision. **Insider trading** is the trading of stocks based on information available only to those affiliated with a company, not to the general public. This practice is a serious breach of U.S. federal law. To detect insider trading, the department receives information, from several sources, on unusual trading activity, and uses this information to identify a stock it may want to investigate. Using an ES, the department's analysts access a large database of the stock's history and choose the time period of interest. The system provides questions that the analysts can answer with the information they received from the database. The questions are formulated to reflect the experience of expert investigators. After the analysts finish answering all the questions, the system provides two numbers: the probability that a further investigation is warranted, and the probability that it is not.

Expert systems, such as Tax IQ help perform tax planning.

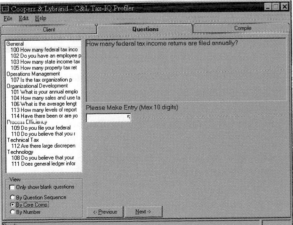

Used by permission from Coopers & Lybrand L. L. P., National Tax Technology

MINERAL EXPLORATION

As mentioned in the discussion of PROSPECTOR, above, another common application of ESs is in identifying whether drilling should continue during a mineral exploration. For instance, when prospecting for molybdenum, the composition of mud samples is considered to determine whether the likelihood of finding deposits is high enough to warrant continued drilling. Assessing the chances of hitting deposits requires the input of a highly experienced and expensive engineer. PROSPECTOR takes mud composition as input and provides the likelihood of finding deposits based on the knowledge base of experts. Using the program, less experienced and less expensive engineers analyze the mud samples, and the ES does the expensive work.

Used by permission from Corel Corporation

Expert systems help predict where to find economically viable quantities of minerals.

IRRIGATION AND PEST MANAGEMENT

Knowing the quantities of water and pesticides to use at different stages of peanut growing can save farmers millions of dollars. After much research, the U.S. Department of Agriculture developed an ES called EXNUT to help peanut growers make these decisions. Scientists produced a large knowledge base on plants, weather, soil, and other factors that affect the yield of peanut fields. Farmers feed EXNUT with data about the field throughout the growing season, and the program provides recommendations on irrigation, the application of fungicide, and the likelihood of pest conditions. It recommends that farmers withhold water during certain stages, and that they use highest and lowest soil temperatures as indicators of soil moisture and plant health.

By 1997, the system had been used by more than 50 farms in Georgia that cultivate about 10,000 acres. Farmers who are not considered experts were able to increase their yield to quantities greater than those harvested by expert farmers, while using less water and fungicide. Versions of EXNUT have been developed for many other states.

PREDICTING FAILURE OF DIESEL ENGINES

A reliable way to predict the failure of diesel locomotive engines is to examine the oil from the engine. Experienced technicians at Canadian Pacific Railroad took many years to develop this expertise, which involves a technician analyzing a sample of lubrication oil for metal impurities, and a mechanic analyzing the data. The process not only takes years to learn, but is difficult to teach to novices, so Canadian Pacific decided to develop an ES for this purpose.

The system takes the spectrum data as input and uses the rules provided by the experts. A technician can use the output report, which details which components require service and which are likely to fail soon. The success of the system has been great. Analysis of over 10,000 samples has yielded accurate predictions 98% of the time. The company saved by replacing components before they failed. In some cases, the replacement of a single component saved more money than was spent on the development of the ES.

MEDICAL DIAGNOSIS

Since medicine is one of the most unstructured domains, it is not surprising that many of the early ESs were developed to help doctors with the diagnosis of symptoms and treatment advice, as mentioned above. MYCIN, CADUCEUS, and PUFF are only a few of these systems. The latter system includes instrumentation that connects to the patient's body and feeds various data about the patient's condition into the ES to be analyzed for pulmonary diseases.

More recent systems involve the integration of neural networks. In a strange twist, a military system that was constructed to recognize enemy weapons, such as tanks and artillery, by imaging land forms is now used by Cornell Medical College to analyze tumors by imaging tissue. Part of the knowledge base is x-rays of cancerous and benign lung growths, which are input to teach the neural network computers how to distinguish between the two. The systems will not replace medical experts, but will enhance their ability to diagnose cancerous conditions. Since radiologists are inundated with

Net Notes

If you wish to learn more about the terminology and history of artificial intelligence, log on to the pages established by the University of Saskatchewan in Canada: *http://alf.usask.ca/spec_int/swaps/ regina_projects/AI/project.html.*

tons of data from x-rays and other machines, such as magnetic resonance imagers, they encounter cases that are extremely difficult to assess. This is where the ES can help.

CLASS SELECTION FOR STUDENTS

Experience shows that having a good advisory system and providing accurate information about classes help retain undergraduate students. But providing good college advice is labor-intensive and expensive, especially in colleges that have a lot of transfer students and students who work and need advising during off-hours. California State University developed an ES to help provide the needed advice.

The ES, run by students, tracks students' interests, their schedules, and the courses they have already taken, both within and outside the university. By analyzing this information, accessing departmental and university databases, and taking into consideration student availability and individual interests, the system can suggest a sequence of courses to help students plan schedules that will allow them to graduate in the shortest time possible. The system considers prerequisites for the largest number of other courses, so the student has maximum flexibility in selection of later courses. The system has saved the university human resources while offering additional service to the students.

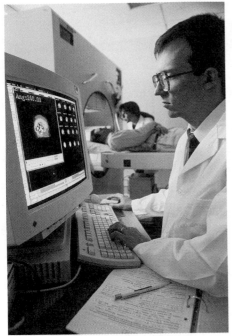

Used by permission from Roger Tully/Tony Stone Images

Medical expert systems help diagnose patients and suggest treatments.

LIMITATIONS OF EXPERT SYSTEMS

While the use of ESs can save resources, the systems have their limitations. Time and research efforts will be needed to overcome the limitations that ESs still have, including the following:

ESs can handle only narrow domains. Early attempts to create general problem solvers failed miserably. Current ESs perform well if the domain they handle is narrowly defined. For instance, it is doubtful that you will find a general medical ES. MYCIN, the first successful medical ES, deals only with bacterial diseases. CADUCEUS, another medical ES, diagnoses only internal diseases.

ESs do not possess common sense. With all their sophistication, ESs cannot recognize problems that require common sense. The system will be able to solve only those problems it was specifically programmed to solve.

ESs have limited ability to learn. While neural networks technology made great strides in the area of machine learning, the ability of computer-based programs to learn remains limited. Knowledge engineers must coach the systems and provide continual feedback for the systems to learn. It may take many years for scientists to produce an ES that can quickly learn and apply self-learned knowledge.

The limitations of ESs caused venture capitalists to get cold feet after several years of enthusiasm, slowing the rate at which innovative ESs were developed during the early 1990s. However, the great potential of these systems for business, medicine, and science has again been recognized. With a more mature and sober outlook in the business community, ESs face a great future.

Lockheed's Expert System Automates Procurement

Lockheed Missiles and Space Co. (now a division of Lockheed-Martin) is a major defense contractor that has to provide the U.S. government with products that are built to exact specifications. The quality of the products is heavily dependent on the quality of the purchased raw materials, whether they are pallets of industrial lubricants or sophisticated satellite components. But until 1993, the purchasing process suffered from a high rate of errors that could potentially affect the quality of the products, so the company built an expert system that would automate and streamline the process.

Before the introduction of an ES, whenever the Palo Alto, California, company's research laboratory needed materials, procurement officers had to fill out a 104-question Procurement Request (PR) form that was a thorn in the sides of Lockheed's scientists and research engineers, with its cryptic abbreviations, arcane jargon, and scores of Lockheed and governmental procurement regulations. As a result, only about 25% of PRs could be processed as submitted.

The erroneous 75% had to be redone, a process that sometimes took six weeks. This high error rate caused more than just a cost problem. The company had to employ "PR checkers," people whose job was to check PRs for errors after they had been filled out by engineers. The delays could also have caused Lockheed to lose its right to purchase materials independently, in which case it would have had to purchase all the materials from U.S. government agencies. To remove this threat, a new system, Fastbuy, combined e-mail with a database system that generates PRs and automatically routes them to everyone who has to approve them.

However, Fastbuy only helped to move documents; it could not help overcome the inaccuracies in the PRs. Filling out a PR for materials still required engineers and procurement officers to answer all the questions. Engineers, who did not have the time to decipher the abbreviations and procurement jargon, created a bottleneck in the process. Management decided to create an expert system that would work with Fastbuy and do much of the work for the engineers.

The project manager acquired a development program from Neuron Data Inc. in Palo Alto. The program is an ES shell. The project manager studied thousands of pages of procurement regulations and held interviews with in-house experts. Once he understood the procurement process, he sat down at his Mac and used the rules editor module of Smart Elements, which prompt the developer to fill in the blanks to specify IF-THEN rules. For example: If gas is bought under a government contract, then the purchase must meet certain requirements, such as delivery to the customer, or it is illegal.

As the project manager was developing the knowledge base, other members of the development team were developing a text analyzer that would let the program understand the free-form text typed into some of the fields. This component interprets some of the text through contextual clues. For example, the word "argon" can be a gas, a street name, or even a person's name. However, if it is near the word "cylinder," it's probably a gas.

Once the development was complete, the new ES was transported to the company's minicomputer. The new system was named the Advisory System for Automated Procurement (ASAP). It automatically checks online procurement forms for errors and helps researchers correct them. It runs on Lockheed's mini-computer system and is available to any of the 1,000 users on a variety of terminals and microcomputers.

With the ES, the time between request and receipt of materials was reduced from six weeks to three days. All of the PR checkers have been reassigned to other areas of the corporation. All the PR originators, including the engineers, have found it easier to fill out PRs with the help of the ES.

Users now complete the Fastbuy screens by keying in answers to questions in a normal way. When the input is complete (or at any time the user requests), Fastbuy calls ASAP. The ES analyzes the answers for simple errors (such as a product name listed where a product number should be) as well as conflicts with regulations (such as purchasing a product from an incorrect fund). The system may also ask follow-up questions, just as the human PR checkers used to do. Finally, ASAP displays the incorrect items along with instructions on how to correct the problems. By explaining its reasoning to the requesters, ASAP teaches the users, and can help reduce the number of mistakes in the future.

The reduced turnaround time was the system's most important benefit, but the financial gains, too, have been significant. The company estimates that ASAP saves $600,000–800,000 annually.

Source: Stevens, L., "Complicated process puts procurement in peril," MacWEEK, Vol 8 No 39, October 3, 1994, p. 42, and Blanchard, D., "Lockheed's Expert System Automates Procurement," OR/MS Today, Vol 21 No 5, October 1994, p. 8.

Questions

1. Was the development of ASAP planned? Explain.

2. Who was the knowledge engineer for ASAP?

3. What makes the filling out of a PR so appropriate for automation?

4. One of the advantages of ESs is the ability to distribute their help. How is that done at Lockheed?

Intelligent Quality Tools

One of the major problems in journalism is how to separate authentic news items from erroneous ones. The Intelligent Quality Toolkit (IQT) is a sophisticated computer system that uses artificial intelligence to detect, in real time, errors in market data supplied to Reuters from exchanges in Ireland and the United Kingdom. The program, which took five years to create, was developed for Reuters to provide real-time, cost-effective, quality management of the financial information distributed to its clients. It checks market data based on a wide range of rules encompassing financial knowledge that has been built up over the years by leading experts. The program reviews several hundred thousand data updates a day, of which approximately 400 items are suspect, 200 are real errors, and 60 are significant errors. It is estimated that to perform the same task without IQT, using existing PC-based utilities, would require a staff of 1,000 to 2,000 people, each with two PCs, at an estimated annual cost of at least £30 million (about U.S. $48 million).

Used properly, the large-scale knowledge-based program, developed by PA Consulting Group in close collaboration with Reuters using object-oriented techniques, finds errors not found by the stock exchange's supervision sections. Since the system is knowledge-based, and since the detailed knowledge of market behavior encapsulated in the rule base is difficult to come by, IQT has provided the added benefit to Reuters of ensuring that this knowledge will not be lost. The goal is to allow Reuters' clients (major mass media) to make decisions based on Reuters data with increased confidence.

Source: "Intelligent Quality Toolkit," in Computer Bulletin, February 1994, Vol 6, Part 1, P. V. Reprinted by permission of Oxford University Press.

Questions

1. What expertise is needed to do what the IQT system does? How structured is the problem at hand?

2. Estimating the cost of financial analysis personnel, do your own calculation and show whether the investment in this expert system was economically justified.

Neural Networks Train on the Job

Once dismissed as more futuristic than practical in their business applications, neural networks are nonetheless hard at work in the Tavenswood Aluminum Corp.'s West Virginia mill, ferreting out imperfections in processed aluminum. The neural network is a key enhancement to the mill's quality assurance application. As the mill's engineers react to on-screen displays of flaws in sheets, their responses are fed into the neural network to train it to identify and classify flaws and to prevent low-quality aluminum from reaching customers' can-making machinery.

That continuous, on-the-job training of the software itself is what makes a neural network different from other types of expert systems. The "usual" expert system requires human specialists to define the set of rules on which decisions are based. Neural networks eliminate the middleman, starting off with no established rules, and instead learning by example.

In the West Virginia mill, the flaw data pass in real time from a specialized memory board in the scanning computer into the companion board installed in a PC outfitted with neural-networking software. Commercial software running on the dedicated PC converts the flaws into groups of flaws that have a set of features associated with them. The neural network reads each cluster's features and associates them with a specific defect it has learned from a previous processing.

Once its kinks are worked out, the neural network serves as a partner to the quality engineers. "The trick is to come up with the right set of features that distinguishes among objects," says Mohammad Waseen, senior software engineer, who was involved in the implementation of the system.

Source: Asbrand, D., "Unlike Expert System, Neural Network Trains on the Job," InfoWorld, October 24, 1993. Reprinted by permission.

Questions

1. Tavenswood Aluminum Corp. could use a "traditional" ES. Why did it choose to employ one that uses a neural network?

2. In the context of *person-machine synergy*, how does a neural network help improve quality? What can the system do that human beings cannot? What can it do better than human beings can? What can the engineers do that the system cannot? What can they do better than the system?

SUMMARY

Artificial intelligence (AI) scientists study methods to develop computer programs that mimic the human mind and behavior. The field consists of several subfields. **Robotics** engineers build **robots** that replace human laborers. In manufacturing, robots are used to carry out routine tasks like assembly and painting of cars. Both in manufacturing and police work, the computer-controlled machines replace human beings in dangerous assignments.

Robots that move in space must have vision. **Artificial vision** allows them to sense walls and obstacles, and to recognize an object that they are to operate on. Artificial vision is also used in machines other than robots, for sorting and identification.

Natural language processors (NLPs) are programs that recognize human commands. They rid computer-based systems users of the need to learn programming or other rigid interfaces. Natural language processors must be able to recognize that one sentence may have different meanings in different contexts. Some natural language processors have been put to use in military and database management systems.

Expert systems are programs that simulate human expertise. Early attempts to create a program that would be a **general problem solver** failed. Over the past two decades, numerous ESs have been developed for use in engineering, medicine, chemistry, mineral exploration, and business.

Neural networks are programs built to solve problems while learning and refining their knowledge, mimicking what scientists believe is the way our own brains learn and act. The programs start with a base model. As the programs solve problems, human operators input the results of the programs' analysis in terms of "hits" or "misses." The program incorporates this new input into its knowledge base, thereby continually improving its performance.

The latest development in AI is **intelligent agents**, programs that carry out daily tasks (involving sifting through and selecting data from massive amounts of information) that otherwise would be performed by human beings. For instance, intelligent agents can move inside a network and find desired literature or the best price of a product, answer electronic messages, pay debts through a credit charge, and carry out, electronically, many other mundane tasks. These "electronic butlers" will save human beings time and serve us more efficiently than we can now serve ourselves in many respects.

Of these subfields of AI, ESs have played the most important role in business. An ES comprises three parts: The **knowledge base** is a compilation of facts and beliefs, and the connections between them, garnered from one or more experts. The **inference engine** is code that combines user input with information in the knowledge base to find a solution to a problem. The **dialog management component** allows the user to interact with the inference engine in a convenient manner.

Although the majority of ESs have their knowledge base organized in the form of **IF-THEN rules**, there are other methods of representing knowledge. In one method, the knowledge is organized in **frames** that store attributes and values. There is a table for each object in the domain. In **semantic nets**, objects are represented as nodes, and relationships are the lines that connect the nodes. The relationships may be: "has," "belongs to," "is," and so on.

Fuzzy logic is a relatively new theory that takes a completely different approach to knowledge representation. The theory recognizes that many of an expert's decisions are based on subjective linguistic variables, such as "low" risk, "moderate" risk, and "high" risk. A function is constructed to represent the possibility that an event, or entity, will fall into a category. The same event, or entity, may have a certain probability of falling into one category, while having another probability of falling into an adjacent category. Therefore, the boundaries of the categories, or sets, are "fuzzy." Fuzzy logic has been incorporated in expert systems that have been applied in appliances, locomotives, managerial decision making, and many other areas.

Two parties are involved in the construction of an ES: the **expert** and the **knowledge engineer**. The knowledge engineer possesses questioning techniques and experience in translating the knowledge garnered from the expert into a computer program.

Early ESs were developed using special AI programming languages, such as LISP, PROLOG, and KEE.

Nowadays, **ES shells** are used to construct new ESs. An ES shell may be thought of as an ES that has been emptied of its knowledge. The shell prompts the builder to enter the **antecedents** (conditions or IF statements) and **conclusions** (THEN statements) of conditions. It transparently builds the knowledge base and the inference engine according to the information supplied by the builder.

ESs reach a solution in one of two ways, **forward chaining** or **backward chaining**. In forward chaining, the user inputs parameters of the problem at hand, and the system uses the rules to produce the best outcome. Thus, this process is also called **result-driven**. Often, the user wishes to specify a desired goal and receive as output the conditions that would produce the result. The ES then performs backward chaining, which is referred to as **goal-driven**.

Like decision support systems, ESs help make decisions in unstructured domains. But the investment is often great, because it involves the time of both highly-paid domain experts and knowledge engineers. Therefore, certain conditions must exist to justify the investment in a new ES: the problems must not be trivial; the domain in which the ES operates should be highly unstructured; the problems should occur frequently; and an expert must be available for questioning.

ESs support managerial activities: planning, decision making, and diagnosis. Organizations use the systems to replace human trainers. An ES may provide knowledge that exceeds the expertise of a single expert. Once the expertise is captured in software, it may be cheaply replicated and disseminated throughout an organization. Unlike human experts, ESs can be made available at all times. All members of an organization using an ES reach the same decisions under given conditions, so management achieves consistency in operations.

However, there are some limitations to the systems. Effective ESs can handle only narrow domains. They do not yet possess common sense. And despite some progress in neural nets, they are limited in their ability to learn.

ESs and other AI applications put expertise at the tips of our fingers, and thus add to our quality of life. They make us more independent of human experts, but, at the same time, they make us more dependent on software. When the software is defective, the damage done by the systems may be considerable. ESs pose a challenge to the legal system, because individuals and organizations may be adversely affected by decisions provided by the systems.

REVIEW, DISCUSS, AND EXPLORE

REVIEW AND DISCUSSION QUESTIONS

1. Explain the term "artificial intelligence."
2. Some experts argue that there is no such thing as artificial intelligence, and that there never will be. What do they mean?
3. What are the reasons for failing to build a "general problem solver" in the 1950s?
4. Give three examples (not mentioned in this book) of how artificial intelligence can be used to improve customer service, manufacturing, or decision making.
5. What is expertise? What differentiates the expert from the novice?
6. What are heuristics? How are they acquired?
7. What is an expert system?
8. What are the advantages of expert systems?
9. What are the disadvantages of expert systems?
10. What are the business conditions that would justify the development of an expert system?
11. What are neural nets, and what is their most important characteristic?
12. How can expert systems be used to reduce fraud in financial institutions?
13. *Ethics and Society*: Several months after a young physician used an expert system to diagnose a patient and prescribe a treatment, the patient dies. An investigation reveals that the patient was misdiagnosed. Whose fault *could* this be? What precautions would you suggest for the use of expert systems?

CONCEPT ACTIVITY

Ask a manager to give you an example of a decision-making process he or she uses. Use Figure 13.12 to determine if the process would justify the construction of an ES.

HANDS-ON ACTIVITY

Use a programming language to build a simple ES that determines the eligibility of an applicant for a bank loan of $20,000 for 30 years. The eligibility is determined by the number of points the applicant accumulates in several risk categories, based on the following:

Risk Category	Points
Age	
20 < age < 25	0
25 < age < 60	10
60 < age	0
Income (annual $) per household member	
income < 20,000	0
20,000 < income < 40,000	10
40,000 < income < 60,000	20
60,000 < income < 85,000	30
85,000 < income	40
Employment at current place	
self-employed	10
> two years	5
< two years	10
Net Worth	
NW < 30,000	0
30,000 < NW < 50,000	10
50,000 < NW < 70,000	20

If the applicant's total number of points is equal to or exceeds 60, grant the loan.

TEAM ACTIVITY

Ask a bank loan officer what factors he or she considers when evaluating the credit worthiness of a prospective debtor. Formulate a set of IF-THEN rules based on the answers to your questions.

EXPLORE THE WEB

Use the keywords *expert system* to search the Web for vendors offering expert systems for sale. Choose one product and determine whether the product is really an expert system. Report: (1) the URL, (2) what domain the ES is supposed to operate in, (3) if the problems in the domain are really unstructured and frequent enough to justify the purchase of the ES, (4) which experts were used to build the system, and (5) if professional knowledge engineers developed the system.

PART 5

Planning, Acquisitions, and Controls

Chapter 14

Planning
Information Systems

Streamlining Software

In 1993, General Motors was using 27 different e-mail systems, ten different word-processing programs, five spreadsheet applications, and seven business graphics packages. Few IS managers knew which user used which application. Nobody could control the cost of maintaining many of the applications. And no one had a clear vision of what the company's portfolio of applications was going to be in the future. GM did not want a situation like the one that another company discovered: the accounts payable department was still writing checks for maintenance agreements supporting software that had been discarded long ago. Office software at General Motors was out of control. To stay competitive, some serious planning had to be done.

Although standardization is only one aspect of many IS planning, the company decided it was important enough to address first. The IS organization took inventory and decided on a standard set of hardware, systems software, and applications. By 1996, every GM employee who used a PC worked on a standard configuration: the same operating system, the same suite of office software, and the same e-mail software, all running on the same PCs served by the same make and model of servers. The company donated most of the old hardware and software to charities. Now no software outside the standard configuration gets into a PC without special approval.

"Employees cannot bring software from home, and they can't download it from the Internet," says GM's Fred Craig, who claims these policies have kept the GM computer network virtually virus-free. Better yet, they have helped GM attain its cost-control goals: The auto maker spent no more on its desktop PCs in 1995 than it did in 1993.

Source: Losee, S., "Burned by Technology," *Fortune*, September 9, 1996, p. 105–112.

LEARNING OBJECTIVES

Investment in most ISs is usually high, involving millions of dollars and years of work. In addition, the way information is gathered and used affects many aspects of many business activities. Thus, careful planning of ISs and their management is of utmost importance to successful business operations.

When you finish this chapter, you will:

◆ Be familiar with different approaches to business planning in general and IS planning in particular

◆ Know how IS planning methods evolved

◆ Understand how IS planning should be carried out

◆ Realize the importance of integrating IS planning into overall organizational planning

◆ Appreciate the many complex factors faced by IS planners

WHY PLAN?

Billions of dollars are spent every year creating, maintaining, and using information systems in business. In fact, many organizations rise or fall on the successful—or unsuccessful—creation and implementation of information systems. Good **planning**, planning that focuses on shaping the future as well as monitoring and controlling processes, is the key to the successful business, and lack of planning or poor planning is often the major reason for failure. Your role in helping an organization succeed will rest partly on your ability to help it plan ISs, which requires tools for assessing processes, creating and articulating a business vision, and applying your knowledge about ISs to recommend what technology is needed to reach the stated goals.

WHAT IS PLANNING?

Any type of planning starts with a general idea or an explicit statement of where an organization wishes to be a year, or three, or five years, from now. Thus, an IS plan is a statement of how management foresees its ISs in the future. An IS plan includes activities that the planner believes will help achieve these goals, a program for monitoring real-world progress against the plan, and means for implementing changes in the plan. While planning may not fully control an organization's business, or dictate what will happen, it is a tool to help shape the future and anticipate and prepare for whatever may occur. Since IS plans should be an integral part of an organization's overall business plan, in this chapter we discuss both business planning as it relates to ISs, and the process of planning ISs themselves.

BUSINESS PLANNING

Successful business managers must have a clear idea about what position their organization currently holds in the market, where they want it to be, and how they want it to get there. These ideas all form the background for **business planning**, which is the process of defining an organization's goals and objectives, determining the resources needed to attain those objectives, creating the policies that will govern the acquisition, use, and distribution of those resources, and providing for any changes in objectives that may be needed along the way (see Figure 14.1).

APPROACHES TO PLANNING

There are many different approaches to business planning, all of which fall along a spectrum. Perhaps the three most common are described here: When top managers believe in the adage "if it ain't broke, don't fix it" (and its corollary "if it is broke, then do fix it"), then the approach to planning is usually based on an organization's response to needs and problems. Because these are usually first experienced and articulated in lower levels of management, this approach is called **bottom-up planning**. On the other hand, a belief that operations can always be improved, even if all is well now, usually has top managers setting goals and objectives that filter down through the entire organization; this philosophy is called **top-down planning**. In general, top-down planning is proactive, while bottom-up planning is reactive. Thus, the former method is more effective in creating strategies for overall business success.

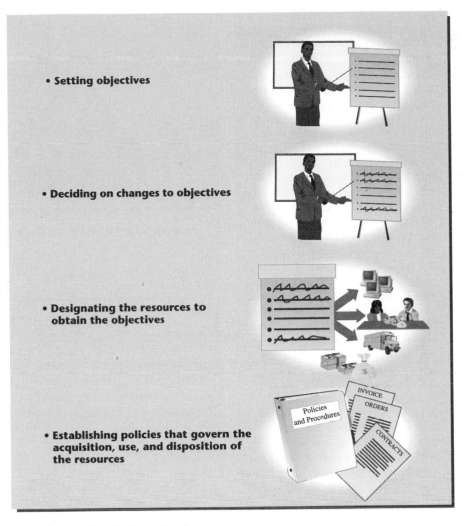

- **Setting objectives**

- **Deciding on changes to objectives**

- **Designating the resources to obtain the objectives**

- **Establishing policies that govern the acquisition, use, and disposition of the resources**

Figure 14.1 *Business planning*

Used by permission from Yellow Freight System

Another popular planning process is to define the critical factors that facilitate an organization's success, and then operate to achieve those factors.

TOP-DOWN PLANNING

Managers who espouse top-down planning start the process by stating clear objectives for the entire organization, usually for the long term; then, they break up the objectives into subobjectives for various divisions and groups in the organization and decide on the allocation of resources for the various units. The assumption in top-down planning, which is more likely to be found in large corporations than in small businesses, is that solving the "big" long-term problems will also satisfy the "little" short-term problems. Even isolated short-term problems are addressed in the context of a larger process. Top-down planning (sometimes called **holistic planning**, because it focuses on the "big picture") is also considered **goal-driven** because it is based on objectives or goals (see Figure 14.2 on the next page).

The case of a large Scandinavian construction materials supplier indicates how important it is to plan new information systems in the context of the business environment, rather than simply consider technical issues. The company expanded its operations throughout the 1970s, and by 1990 had a comprehensive IS for budgeting and control. The corporate financial controller was satisfied with the system, but the investments in material and equipment were growing with the market, and some divisional controllers wanted a new IS that would help them analyze their increasingly large financial decisions in a more structured fashion. Unfortunately for them, no one considered whether the market's growth—and therefore the need for the new systems—would continue. Planning of the system was casual, and was not included in any corporate strategic plan. Soon after the system's initial tests in 1990, a recession started. Construction industry growth slowed and quickly eliminated the need for the investment analysis system. The project was canceled. The corporate financial controller observed that if the company had focused on the business environment instead of the financial details of the system, it could have avoided investing in a new system altogether. "We analyzed it too much as a problem in our financial reporting systems. Had we better understood the significance of the project for our business, we would certainly have organized it in a different way."

Source: Salmela, H., Lederer, A.L., Reponen, T., "Prescriptions for Information Systems Planning in a Turbulent Environment," *Proceedings of the Seventh International Conference on Information Systems*, DeGross, J.I., Jarvenpaa, S., Srinivasan, A. (eds.), 1996.

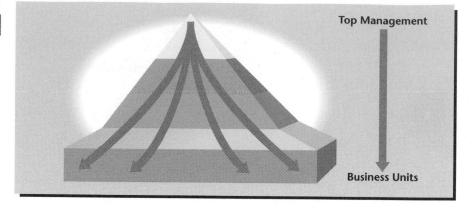

Figure 14.2 *Top-down planning considers the organization as a whole.*

BOTTOM-UP PLANNING

In bottom-up planning, managers focus on the needs of the various business functions. In their planning, they aim to respond to concerns by integrating several subobjectives into larger objectives. The assumption here is that organizational problems are, essentially, aggregates of individual problems; thus, solutions to the individual problems will also satisfy organizational needs.

In contrast to the top-down approach, this approach (1) does not allow a broad view of organizational needs and opportunities, and (2) is reactive rather that proactive; management is waiting for problems to occur rather than taking preventive measures, and seizing business opportunities (see Figure 14.3).

CRITICAL SUCCESS FACTORS

Another approach to planning is to define the factors that are critical for success as the basis for a plan. **Critical success factors (CSF)** are issues identified by executives as critically important to the success of their business units. In the realm of ISs, the planners interview executives to see how information technology can promote their goals. The executives are asked to pinpoint the most critical factors

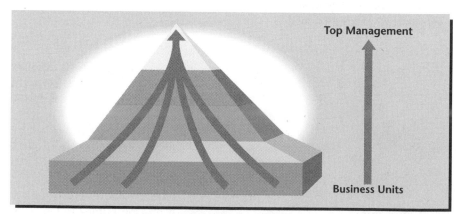

Figure 14.3 *In bottom-up planning, the process starts with consideration of individual concerns.*

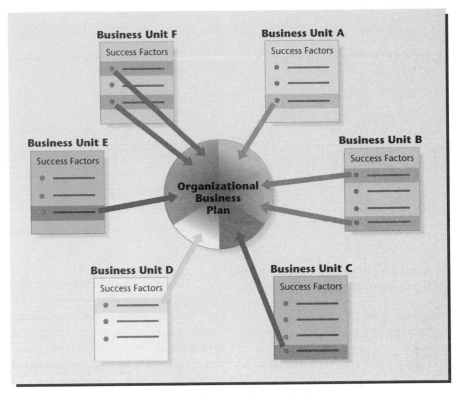

Figure 14.4 *Business planning by critical success factors*

to their success, such as delivery time of manufactured items, length of time to prepare certain reports, availability of information combined from several disparate sources, and online availability of external information.

The underlying thought is that the whole is the sum of the individual parts: The success of the organization is the sum of the successes of individual business units. For instance, a new or improved IS may help one business unit become more successful by shortening product delivery time. A new or improved IS may help another business unit become more successful by reducing the time needed to produce reports. If each unit improves its performance, this philosophy says that the organization will improve (see Figure 14.4.)

INFORMATION SYSTEMS PLANNING

Until the late 1970s, organizations planned without considering either the role IS professionals could take in the planning process, or the planning that is necessary to create a productive IS department. Most companies called their IS units data processing departments, where data processing professionals were considered technicians who concentrated on automating processes, rather than professionals who could help the organization achieve its goals. As indicated in several studies of the proliferation of IS use in corporate America in the 1970s, top management didn't realize for several years that the ISs themselves had to be planned, lest expenditures balloon uncontrollably and get out of hand. The recognition of the large amounts of time and money organizations spent on ISs

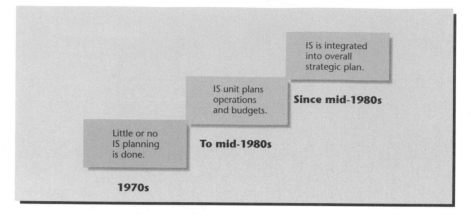

Figure 14.5 *Advancement in IS planning over the past three decades*

Within the figure:
- IS is integrated into overall strategic plan.
- **Since mid-1980s**
- IS unit plans operations and budgets.
- **To mid-1980s**
- Little or no IS planning is done.
- **1970s**

led companies to start planning for their deployment and for the resources needed for timely development and maintenance of the systems. The modern approach to systems development is no longer one of reaction to emerging business needs, as it was early on. In the past, ISs evolved from need, but today IS managers are involved with short-range and long-range IS planning. Like other business managers, they must submit both a budget and a schedule for the operations of their departments.

Not only do IS managers have to plan their activities, but now many organizations integrate their IS planning into their overall organizational strategic planning. Top management acknowledges that IT plays a role in generating business, not just in improving it in small increments. Reaction to needs only satisfies the needs, while planning can create opportunities. As Figure 14.5 indicates, IS planning has evolved over the past three decades to become fully integrated into organizations' strategic planning.

IS planning includes a few key steps that are a part of any successful planning process: creating a corporate and IS mission statement, articulating the vision for IT within the organization, creating IS strategic and tactical plans, creating a plan for operations to achieve the mission and vision, and creating a budget to assure that resources are available to achieve the mission and vision (see Figure 14.6). Note that the broadest, most overarching statement of an organization's purpose is sometimes referred to as its "mission" and sometimes as its "vision," terms that are used interchangeably in this book. Some people differentiate mission and vision by saying that the mission is a declared overall long-term purpose of the organization, and the vision is the general manner in which the mission will be accomplished.

PREREQUISITES FOR INFORMATION SYSTEMS PLANNING

Several conditions must exist before effective IS planning takes place (see Figure 14.7).

First, top management must recognize that IT is an indispensable resource in all business activities. It must see that the impact IT has on an organization is at least as great as the impact of new manufacturing machinery, and that it may significantly change the way an organization conducts its business.

Second, top management must understand that the development and use of ISs must be planned like any other complex resources. Executives must be aware that

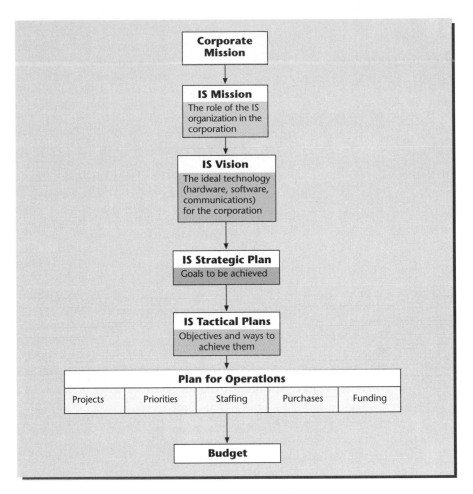

Figure 14.6 *The steps of information systems planning*

ISs are more than just computers; they are hardware, software, people, procedures, and data. The interplay among these components must be planned to avoid waste.

Third, top management must see IT as a resource owned by all members of the organization, not only by the IS unit. Its development and use should be planned like human resources, manufacturing machinery, and finances.

Top management must:

◆ Recognize IT as an indispensable resource

◆ Understand that IT is a complex resource

◆ Regard IT as owned by the entire organization

◆ Regard ISs as a source for gaining strategic goals

◆ View ISs as a tool to control power

Figure 14.7 *Top management support is essential for successful IS planning.*

Code of Ethics for IS Professionals

Like other professionals, IS professionals must protect the interests of different constituencies: society at large, their employers, the employers' clients, and their own colleagues. Often, IS professionals find themselves in situations where the interests of two, or even three, of these constituencies collide. While some organizations have professional codes of conduct addressing many aspects of the IS profession, they do not provide guidelines for resolving conflicts of interest.

Consider this conflict. A programmer working for a consulting firm is involved in a large project for a client. The programmer comes to realize that some of the code she has developed will not be compatible with other systems that the client uses. When she approaches her supervisor at the consulting firm, her boss demands that she follow his instructions because "we are doing everything according to the contract." Her obligation to her employer is to obey his instructions. However, her obligation to the client is to inform him about the incompatibility. The programmer is faced with an ethical dilemma.

Or, what would you do in the following situation? You are an independent database expert involved in the upgrading of a database for a large bank. Your contact at the bank is one of its senior vice presidents, who hired you and approved the payment of your consulting fees. While analyzing the database, you discover that the vice president has been involved in embezzlement. The victims are some bank clients (that is, the public) and, of course, the bank. What should you do? Is it your obligation to inform the bank's management? Should you inform the public by contacting a reporter? Or should you simply go on with the work for which you were hired, and for which you are paid?

While ethical conflicts are not less frequent in other professions, the ethical codes of other professions provide clearer decision rules than those of

(continued)

Fourth, top management must realize that ISs are a source for gaining strategic goals, rather than merely for solving problems.

Fifth, since information is power, ISs impact the distribution of power. Top management should be aware of how this power is granted or denied, and integrate that understanding into planning ISs.

When top managers recognize these realities, they ensure that ISs are planned, and that IS plans become an integral part of the organizational plan.

THE CORPORATE AND IS MISSION STATEMENTS

As we discussed in Chapter 2, "Strategic Uses of Information Systems," strategic planning starts with a **corporate mission statement** that details the purpose of the organization and its overall goals. These general goals provide a framework within which the organization's strategic goals will be formulated. For example, such a goal may be to become the nation's largest car-rental company. Once the corporate mission has been articulated, then each business function formulates its own mission, to be consistent with the organization's mission.

Although the organization's mission statement will usually not mention the IS function specifically, the **IS mission statement** reflects how the IS management sees its place in the organization and its responsibilities. The statement

IT professionals. For example, a lawyer's first obligation is always to his client. The same principle applies to physicians. The ethical code of journalism is to strictly obey the rule of not exposing a source without the source's consent. Journalists have protected their sources to the point of obstructing justice; that is, they have honored the source's interests over the public's interests. An architect who learns that a building may not meet safety standards is expected to halt his work in order to protect the public, even though this may conflict with his obligations to an employer or client.

Several organizations of IS professionals have developed codes of ethics and professional conduct: the Association for Computing Machinery (ACM), the Data Processing Management Association (DPMA), the International Federation for Information Processing (IFIP), the British Computer Society (BCS), the Canadian Information Processing Society (CIPS), and the Institute for Certification of Computer Professionals (ICCP) are the largest and most influential of these organizations. However, each of these and each other IS organization has a different code, and the codes do not necessarily promote the same ideals. Only IT professionals who are members of a professional organization that has a code of ethics are bound by such a code. And even then, unfortunately, the codes do not provide clear guidelines as to which party is to be protected when an ethical dilemma occurs.

For example, which party's interests should the programmer prefer in the first example? She has an obligation to her employer, because the employer pays her salary and counts on her to carry out instructions and work loyally for the company; however, she also has an obligation to the client, because the client counts on her to develop a system that will serve his business well. Unlike attorneys, who must protect the interests of their clients over the interests of any other party, and unlike certified public accountants, who must always disclose facts to shareholders of a client company and to the public, IT professionals do not have a code that guides them in such dilemmas. They must resolve the situation by themselves.

outlines the purpose of ISs in the organization. As an example, Figure 14.8 on the next page is the real mission statement of the IS organization of a large university.

THE IT VISION

As part of the mission statement, or as a separate document, the IS managers draft their vision paper. This is a wish list of what these professionals would like to see in terms of hardware, software, and communications, to contribute to the overall goals of the organization. For example, it may detail the following: (1) Every knowledge worker who needs access to databases and/or business applications will have a desktop computer from which to access the resources, (2) All desktop computers will be connected in a network that will provide e-mail and client/server resources, and so on. Obviously, the list may be changed as business needs change, or as new technology emerges.

STRATEGIC AND TACTICAL INFORMATION SYSTEMS PLANNING

The **IS strategic plan**, a part of the overall organizational strategic plan, is a more detailed extension of the IS vision paper, detailing *what* is to be achieved, with a list of specific goals. The **IS tactical plan** breaks down strategic goals into objectives that together describe *how* the strategic goals will be achieved, and by

> ### Mission Statement of Computing & Information Technology, Wayne State University
>
> *Computing & Information Technology's* mission is to support and enhance the academic and administrative activities of Wayne State University and to enable the University to be a major force in revitalizing the Detroit metropolitan area.
>
> To fulfill its mission, Computing & Information Technology (C&IT) provides computing, information processing, and communications resources to satisfy the needs of students, faculty, and staff, and offers comprehensive support services to help them use technology effectively and creatively. C&IT also makes its resources and services available to individuals and organizations striving to improve the quality of life in the metropolitan area.
>
> C&IT is dedicated to actively seeking input from its customers, understanding their needs and challenges, and working with them to implement appropriate solutions. In its leadership role, C&IT is committed to creating and nurturing the vital information technology environment required for Wayne State University to achieve its vision of excellence in teaching, national prominence in research, and success in revitalizing and redeveloping the community it serves.
>
> Source: Mission Statement of Computing & Information Technology Division, Wayne State University, Detroit, Michigan. Reprinted with permission.

Figure 14.8 *The mission statement of a university IS organization*

when. The strategic plan is established for the long run, such as three to five years, while the tactical plan usually covers one to three years. All tactical plans are subsections of the strategic plan.

For example, a strategic *goal* may be the desire to provide end users more flexible access to databases and tools to develop their own database applications. This would be translated into the tactical plan of advancing toward a client/server architecture. Of course, there are different levels of client/server architecture, and different ways to achieve this goal, which would have to be itemized in the plan for operations (which is covered in detail in Chapter 15, "Systems Development.")

Each objective has a **plan for operations**, detailing the tasks involved, who will carry out the assignment or assignments, and by when they will be accomplished. For each objective, the plan also provides a list of means: personnel, hardware, software, and purchased services.

What happens after the strategic plan is in place? Although strategic plans are made for the long run, they are usually not **rigid** (that is, unchanged for a long period of time). Most strategic plans are **dynamic**, which means that they are examined and revised relatively frequently (see Figure 14.9). Many organizations, especially in industries characterized by frequent change, review their plans annually or biannually, and change them if necessary.

To translate the objectives into action, a plan for operations is created from the tactical plan. At this stage, projects are defined and assigned staff and funds for execution. As the personnel and funds are allocated, the IS budget is developed. The budget is a financial expression of the projects. Often, management lets the new project managers select their own staff.

Large-scale projects are often lengthy and may take several years to complete. In such cases the organization often refers to the project as an organizational unit, and the project manager is considered the head of that unit. Once

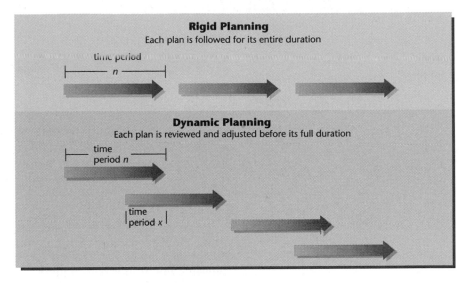

Rigid Planning
Each plan is followed for its entire duration

time period

|—— *n* ——|

Dynamic Planning
Each plan is reviewed and adjusted before its full duration

|—— time period *n* ——|

|time period *x*|

Figure 14.9 *Rigid and dynamic planning*

the project is completed, the staff is disbanded and assigned to other projects. Realize, however, that many IS projects are not over when a new system is installed. The maintenance of a system may be an ongoing effort for which dedicated professionals, working full-time, are required. It is not unusual for a project to last five or ten years.

IMPORTANT FACTORS IN IS TACTICAL PLANNING

Many issues are decided upon as part of the systems analysis and design phase of IS development, but some issues are not specific to any individual system, and these should be considered at the planning stage:

◆ *Flexibility*. Flexibility is the degree to which an organization can use the same hardware or software for different business functions, in different physical and logical environments over time. Careful analysis enables IS planners to designate equipment and software that may be used throughout the organization. Planning also allows for the selection of hardware and software that are the best choice in the long run, even if they may not be used at their optimal levels in the short run. Many companies that fail to consider the flexibility of IS resources and their long-term implications find their resources obsolete after a short period of service. They then incur the extra costs involved in the acquisition of additional resources.

◆ *Compatibility*. Computers and peripheral equipment are not always compatible. Although business units may prefer computers from different vendors, buying the same product for the entire enterprise may be necessary to ensure software, hardware, and telecommunications compatibility. Similarly, the planners must consider how compatible software packages are, so that workers from different departments can import and share data. For example, if the organization is already committed to a certain DBMS and is looking for a new electronic spreadsheet program, the planner should develop a list of spreadsheet programs that are compatible with the DBMS. This way, workers will be able to import data from the database to their own spreadsheet, and vice versa.

A LOOK INTO THE FUTURE ▶

Planning Made Easy

Ostensibly, the planning of ISs in organizations is becoming more and more complex and complicated. As the variety of hardware and software grows, so does the difficulty of selecting portfolios that are best for businesses today but will also meet business opportunities in the years ahead. At least for the near future, the lives of IS planners are getting more difficult. But if some trends continue, their lives may become easier in the more remote future. On what do we base our hopes? Here is what the trends are:

Increasing Use of Software Suites. Sets of integrated programs called suites, which use the same basic functions and allow for the seamless exchange of information unheard of only a few years ago, will make IS planning easier. Typical suites include a word processor, an electronic spreadsheet program, a database management system, data communications software, presentation software, project planning software, and sometimes e-mail, collaborative work software, and Web authoring tools. It is expected that suites will grow to include many other applications.

By adopting suites, businesses eliminate the planning time usually spent addressing the problem of software incompatability.

Open Systems Software. Developers of systems software, or support software as it is sometimes called, try to churn out "platforms" that can support a large number of applications. For example, the UNIX operating system is becoming independent of the hardware on which it runs. This increases portability, the ability to import an application from one machine to another, and gives planners more options.

Platform Independent Software. Because most software is designed to run on only one computer platform, choosing a systems software standard is a major challenge in IS planning. That issue may eventually be eliminated by the growing popularity of platform-independent software—which is written on any computer to run on any computer—and it's easy availability over the Internet. Network computers support that trend as well: designed to depend on the resources of a network to which they are always connected, they download and run software only as needed. The popularity of Java, the first platform-independent programming language, may have marked the beginning of a significant shift in software development.

THINK CRITICALLY

Will IS planning become more, or less, difficult in the future? Why? What do you foresee that makes you think so?

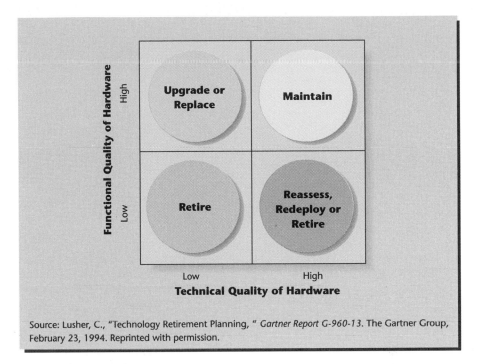

Source: Lusher, C., "Technology Retirement Planning, " *Gartner Report G-960-13*. The Gartner Group, February 23, 1994. Reprinted with permission.

Figure 14.10 *Hardware planning*

◆ *Connectivity*. The planners, particularly those concerned with planning communications networks, should participate in the decision-making process for hardware and software, to allow maximum connectivity among the organization's computers.

◆ *Scalability*. The ability to run the same software on different types of computers, both mainframes and PCs (sometimes referred to as different **platforms**) is known as **scalability**. A growing number of operating systems (including UNIX) and application programs can run on several classes of computers: mainframe, midrange, and PCs. Many IS managers need the flexibility that scalability affords.

◆ *Standardization*. Many organizations have set standards committing all business units to certain hardware and software. IS managers must periodically evaluate the appropriateness of the standards and whether they should be changed, maintained, or updated. A grid of factors can be used to consider replacement or continuing maintenance of resources, according to the level of functional and technical quality of the resource (see Figure 14.10).

IS PLANNING INITIATIVES

Where do IS planners get information about new needs, problems, and opportunities? There are four groups of people who initiate consideration of new or improved ISs from different perspectives: top management, line managers, users, and IS professionals (see Figure 14.11).

Members of top management, such as a CIO or another senior executive, consider new strategic ISs that have a significant impact on the entire organization.

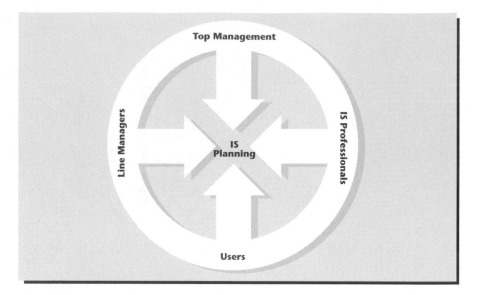

Figure 14.11 *IS planning drives*

By comparison, line managers, who observe their staff daily, are in a position to recommend ISs that would improve business processes and staff performance. Users are most familiar with the strengths and weaknesses of existing systems, and therefore are best qualified to recommend ways in which IS performance could be made more efficient and effective. Through discussions with their peers from competing organizations, these users also often bring ideas about better ISs to their own organizations.

Although modern IS planning and development holds that initiatives for change should come from business managers, IS managers who are familiar with business processes can often see how a new technology could create a business opportunity. Thus, the initiative for IS planning and systems development may come from several sources (see Figure 14.12).

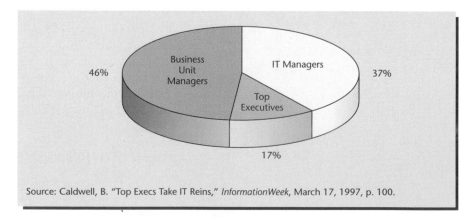

Source: Caldwell, B. "Top Execs Take IT Reins," *InformationWeek*, March 17, 1997, p. 100.

Figure 14.12 *A survey of 100 CEOs and other executives shows that IT projects are initiated by business unit managers and IT managers, but also by top executives.*

THE CHAMPION

Although the realization that a new system must be developed is usually the result of a true business need, there may not be universal support from all members of the organization. For political or rational reasons, some managers may object to the development. In addition, top management is always wary of proposals to commit resources, and usually requests substantive justification for the expense. A sound business and technical proposal for a new system is usually not enough for top management to endorse the new effort. The project needs a **champion**: a high-ranking officer who commands sufficient political clout to promote the idea that a new system is needed, and—when the "go-ahead" signal is granted—to remove obstacles as the project progresses. The champion represents the top management interest in the new system. The most effective champions are executives who are not IS professionals. The fact that they come from other business functions lends credence to their argument that the organization needs the system for a business operation, rather than just for the "glory" of the IS staff. It also conveys the impression that the champion is not influenced by narrow self-centered considerations.

A successful champion is a true leader who can:

◆ Promote the vision of information technology in the organization

◆ Inspire top management and subordinates alike

◆ Remove barriers to realizing the vision

◆ Focus upon both short-term and long-term objectives

◆ Be a torch-bearer for making change happen

◆ Drive accountability to the lowest organizational level so that all who are involved in the development of the new IS (1) feel responsible and therefore committed to succeeding in their roles and (2) are ready to report their progress at any time

IS professionals recognize the power of the involvement of an effective champion. A survey conducted at GroupWare '94 (Boston), a national conference on groupware technologies, reflected the importance of the champion to the success of an IS development initiative. To the question "Who champions groupware in your company?" 59% of the attendees replied that a technology group took the lead. But to the question "Who should be championing groupware to enable its success?" 69% replied: "top management."

Sometimes, the ideal champion is actually a pair of people: an IT manager as technical champion paired with a management champion. The technical manager takes responsibility for product evaluation, planning, and implementation, while the management champion helps deal with corporate culture, political issues, convincing top management of the return on investment (ROI), and the application of the new system to specific business problems.

Although champions often do not come from the ranks of IS professionals, practice shows that overall leadership skills coupled with IT knowledge create champions who drive their organizations to the forefront of business utilization of technology. One of Citicorp's CEOs was the main reason the company became a leader in the use of ATMs and other advanced systems, which gave the corporation strategic advantages. The CEO of Circuit City, a former IS officer, championed the development and implementation of the most advanced IS in that company's market. Executives from competing electronic appliances chains admit that Circuit City's integrated inventory and customer service system is superior to theirs.

Be Involved in IS Planning?

As a manager of a disbursement department you find a note on your desk telling you that the new electronic data interchange (EDI) system will be implemented in two weeks. Part of its function is to automate disbursement for suppliers. You quickly move your eyes down to the section detailing how the system will support your operations. When you reach one of the bullets, your heart almost skips a beat. "No!" you almost shout. "This is not what we needed!" Apparently, in planning the new enterprise-wide system, the features your staff needed were not taken into consideration.

Unlike the old school that did not involve non-IS managers in the planning of ISs, the new approach is to involve business managers to the greatest extent possible. Managers should involve themselves in the planning process so that the resulting systems fit their needs within the greater context of the entire organization.

IS planning is an important component of organizational planning, whose purpose is to achieve strategic goals. Nobody knows the business of a unit better than the unit's manager. Therefore, the manager must be involved in the planning of ISs that are to improve the work of the unit. If managers are not involved in the planning process, they may end up forced to operate systems that either do not improve work, or actually hinder it. In some cases, the results can be disastrous. To be involved in IS planning, you must understand the fundamentals of planning in general and the more specific concerns of IS planning.

THE SYSTEMS ANALYST AS AN AGENT OF CHANGE

Planning almost always deals with change: changing methods; changing the structure of business units; changing the way workers receive, process, and communicate information. However, the physical law of inertia also applies to people. As objects will continue to move in the same direction unless their course is changed, so do people wish to continue to act in the same manner, unless they have to change. The changes involved with new ISs force people to learn new procedures and use new technologies, which many people dislike, particularly if they have performed their jobs in the same way for many years. This is especially true if the changes reward the organization but not the individual employee. As this is often the case, the employee may perceive no tangible incentive for change.

When the change being addressed relates to developing or implementing a new IS, the systems analyst is often the agent of change who must not only explain how the system will improve business performance, but also train individuals in the use of the new system (see Figure 14.13). In order to gain cooperation, the analyst must convince users that the new system will help them in their work. For instance, to clerical staff, the benefits of the new system may be a more relaxed working environment, the satisfaction of creating greater output with less effort, and, often, the satisfaction of learning how to operate a more sophisticated system and enhance one's skills.

In the past, the popular view held that the implementation of a new IS was handled almost exclusively by the systems analyst, who communicated almost no information until the time came to train personnel to use the system. It is now recognized that (1) the changes involved in a new IS must be communicated to employees well before the new system is delivered to them, and (2) education, not just training, is a key success factor. Much of this burden is on the shoulders of the systems analyst.

Figure 14.13 *Systems analysts are agents of change by motivating, educating, and training.*

Mobil Mobilizes a New Plan

One of the world's largest oil companies, Mobil Oil, produced 1.6 million barrels of oil daily in 1995, refined it at more than 20 facilities, and delivered the oil to 19,000 gas stations all over the world. Mobil explores oil deposits and refines oil in 125 countries. Its sales amounted to $80.8 billion in 1996. In spite of the enormity of its operation, until 1996 most of Mobil Oil's operations—including its information systems—were quite decentralized. In 1994, its computers ran several different operating systems: Windows, OS/2, and MacOS. There were nine different e-mail systems, and several different Internet access systems. There were more than 39,000 electronic addresses and more than 40,000 desktop computers in more than 100 countries. But there was no grand plan for the entire enterprise: The headquarters in Fairfax, Virginia, let each business unit run the system that best fit its needs. In spite of a corporate-wide expense of close to $1 billion on IT, local executives made IT decisions that were independent of the decisions made in other business units. Global collaboration among the business units was difficult at best, and impossible at worst. Money was being spent unnecessarily, and Lucio Noto, Mobil's CEO, saw an opportunity to improve his company's performance: redesign the corporation's ISs.

By early 1995, the planning team (working closely with consultants from a notable management and IT consulting firm) prepared a detailed diagnosis of Mobil's IT processes. It reported islands of expertise which the entire organization could enjoy, but didn't. It also found that decentralization caused tremendous duplication and redundancy. The team suggested that the company centralize the administration of IS operations under a single global executive, move to using only one operating system and a standard set of applications, and ensure that all hardware and software in use were compatible across the organization. The team estimated that in such an environment the company could use 60% of its original IS staff, and easily update hardware and software. In addition, it could save money by buying large quantities of the same hardware and software.

Ellen McCoy, the manager of one of Mobil's divisions, was selected to head the new effort, called Standard Managed Environment (SME). Not only was she a savvy business executive, but she also had plenty of IT experience. The effort was painful, however. In 1995, all IT projects were discontinued. All of the IS personnel were evaluated to identify the most qualified to work in the new environment. Those who didn't fit were let go with severance pay. The company cut its IS staff from 4,400 in 1994 to 2,400 in 1997, and Mobil consolidated six mainframe data centers into two.

As the first corporate CIO for Mobil, McCoy established new rules. As long as the hardware and software that a business unit requests are standard, the global IT center approves the purchase with relatively short negotiations. But if the request is for nonstandard equipment and applications, the unit's managers must provide a satisfactory rationale and pay for the purchase out of their own budgets. McCoy has made a special effort to educate both unit managers and IS personnel in IS issues. The former now have a better understanding of what their units really need, and of how to use IT;

the latter now render better service, as they regard the units as customers.

Source: Gross, D., "Getting the Lead Out," CIO, April 15, 1997, pp. 62–70.

Questions

1. What were the moves that saved Mobil IT costs?

2. Was IT planning possible before SME? Explain. Why is a centralized management of IT so important to planning?

KISS: Keep It Standard, Stupid

Lack of IS planning often results in a company running a hodgepodge of incompatible hardware purchased at unnecessarily high costs. Such was the case for Chase Manhattan Bank, especially when faced with its merger with Chemical Bank. Until the early 1990s, the company had a portfolio of many different types of systems. The incompatibility of hardware and software caused islands of expertise, leaving customers to deal with the frustration of consulting multiple lines of business to get information on the status of all their accounts, or to execute transactions. The company's drive to provide better services had a direct and profound impact on Chase's view of IT standards.

"When you start to change focus, you realize what the lack of standardization can do when you're trying to integrate your information and integrate your technology," said Craig Goldman,

CIO and senior vice president at the New York City-based bank. Chase has 60 different business units, many of which operate globally. In the mid- and late 1980s, Chase granted broad power and autonomy to individual business units. "At one time, we had 12 word-processing systems at Chase. We couldn't communicate across the hall, much less across the world," Goldman said.

Soon after taking charge as CIO, Goldman decided to enhance IT planning at the bank. Until this initiative, Chase, like many companies, relied primarily on a standing committee in the centralized corporate technology and information services organization to select Chase's IT standard products and technologies where applicable, which they did without much involvement from business units and their IT groups. These standards were supposed to filter to the business unit IS departments for implementation, but often never got there.

Goldman first mustered upper management backing for IT standards by forming the Technology Service Group Executive Council, made up of senior executives, which he used to promote and continually reinforce the need for a standard IT architecture. He overtly linked architecture and standards to Chase's new core "business drivers." These were a set of principles such as "customers should be able to call any Chase service point and get information on all their accounts." These principles are translated into IT standards at three levels:

products, technologies, and procedures.

Meeting with senior executives, Goldman received agreement on the IT implications that each of the core business drivers would have. From those he produced formal, high-level architecture principle statements. The business principle that all Chase customers should be able to get all account information from any Chase office led management to agree that all of Chase's businesses needed access to consistent account information. That, in turn, led to the architectural principle that Chase would support a single local area network operating system across the company.

Goldman, his chief IS architect, and a full-time IT standards staff have replaced the standards committee with a system of ad hoc groups made up of IS people from the business units, as well as from the central IS unit. The groups propose a specific product or technology as a potential Chase standard. If interest is broad enough, an ad hoc group is formed of six to twelve IS people and an "owner" of the standard, usually an IS person from a business unit with a strong interest in the product or technology under review.

The ad hoc team first produces an informal report and recommendation. Usually, the teams rely on a variety of research sources: presentations from vendors, reports from consulting companies, and help from Chase's internal advanced technology group. The information recommendation is published over e-mail to a community of influential

IS people across the bank, which Goldman calls "The Gang of 60." That group consists of one representative from each Chase business unit. Gang members are expected to respond to the recommendation of the ad hoc team.

Although there is often contention among the business units, the team doesn't let the contention paralyze its process. Eventually it reaches a consensus based on the majority view and the original recommendation. In the end, it becomes a management decision, as Goldman and Technical Services Group Senior Vice President Doug Williams sign off on the final standard report.

Not all ad hoc team recommendations lead to official IT standards. Sometimes a product or technology category hasn't developed enough for Chase to put its stake in the ground. In such cases, the team issues a "guideline" recommendation, which usually includes the option for business units to select from two products or technologies. Later, the team issues a standard recommendation when a vendor satisfies expectations.

Information about the bank's specific standards is widely published throughout the company. Nine thousand employees both in and out of IS receive monthly updates of a standards document that lists all official standards and guidelines, standard sponsors, new technologies under review, and references to supporting research. This reduces unforeseen problems.

The policy is an important ingredient in the company's IS planning. Before and after

implementation, large and high-risk IT projects are examined by an independent audit group that reports through the finance organization. If a project manager is found to have knowingly ignored Chase's IT standards, he or she is disciplined and may be fired.

Good planning and standard enforcement also have a great impact on costs. Chase negotiates licensing, support cost, and other items with vendors after its ad hoc standards teams circulate their initial proposed standard document within Chase, but before a final recommendation is developed and approved by Goldman and other senior managers. A final contract with the vendor is executed after the standard is formally put into place. Since the standards leave only a small number of different technologies in use at Chase, the bank can leverage its negotiation power because it now purchases more units of the same item from a single vendor. This has helped Chase receive discounts of up to 50% off list prices.

Source: Moad, J., "At Last! Standards That Stick," Datamation, October 1, 1994, pp. 60–62.

Questions

1. What was the Bank's problem (with regard to its IS) before Goldman arrived?

2. What did Goldman do to guarantee the success of his IS plan?

3. In all, how many employees are involved in the process of IS standardization?

4. What is the impact of standardization on cost?

Physician, Heal Thyself

When we think of re-engineering, we tend to think of manufacturing organizations, but the massive changes that lead to dramatic improvements in business do sometimes take place in other industries. In 1992, Robert Gibson, President of Beaver County, Pennsylvania's, Medical Center, felt that the hospital was facing competitive pressure. He called in Andersen Consulting to revamp his 470-bed, $130 million hospital, and IS planning was a significant part of this activity.

Before the re-engineering, the hospital's goal was not necessarily overall efficiency, but an attempt to avoid operating below capacity within a given department. For example, since the lab processed tests in batches to save money, patients could wait up to eight hours for test results that could actually have been available in a fraction of that time.

Gibson took doctors, nurses, and administrators on tours of a reorganized Westinghouse Electric plant to show them how re-engineering worked. Now, there are quite a few changes in the Center's wings: tiny antennae hang from the ceilings, infrared sensors blink above each bed, and computer terminals hum in each room. Cellular phones and pagers link doctors and nurses to the hospital's brand-new computer and communications system. And throughout the hospital, there has been a fundamental rethinking about how various jobs are done. Information is no longer accumulated in batches and then processed; it is processed in real time.

Beaver's Medical Center abandoned the assembly-line approach and moved toward multiskilled teams. The assumption is that the more quickly such teams deal with patients' problems, the sooner they will have them out the door. "We want to cut down the turnaround time," said Francine Hixenbaugh, assistant patient-center leader in the orthoneurology unit, which has cut stays by an average 15%.

A communications system is responsible for most of the changes in the hospital. When patients need attention, they press buttons that trigger signals in pagers in doctors' and nurses' pockets. When a member of the medical staff arrives in the room, an infrared eye detects the doctor or nurse. Color-coded lights outside the door indicate to other members of the staff whether there's a nurse or technician inside, in case they need to find one quickly. Procedures rendered to patients are immediately recorded in an IS, through computer terminals placed in each room. When staff members need new medications, they go to an automatic drug dispenser that resembles a bank ATM. The new plan has resulted in improved productivity.

Source: Baker, S., "How one medical center is healing itself," Business Week, February 21, 1994, p. 106.

Questions

1. What were the hospital's problems?

2. The reorganization of the hospital's IS necessitated other, nontechnical, changes. Identify them and explain why they were needed for the reorganization to be successful.

SUMMARY

Planning is an attempt to control the development of future events. **Business planning** is the process of setting **goals** and **objectives**, making decisions pertaining to resources required to obtain the objectives, and determining the policies that are to govern the acquisition, use, and distribution of the resources.

There are several planning methods. The **top-down approach** focuses on organizational goals first, and then on the needs of business units. The **bottom-up approach** assumes that the well-being of the organization depends on the well-being of the individual business units, and therefore concentrates on planning at the business unit level first. The **critical success factors (CSF) approach** lets executives define their critical success factors first, so that planning can be carried out to address the resources to support these factors. The top-down approach is **goal-driven**, while the bottom-up and CSF approaches are problem-driven.

The rapid proliferation of computers in the 1980s and 1990s convinced a growing number of organizations that they must plan their information systems to achieve success. Modern IS planning is integrated into the overall organizational strategic plan. There are several prerequisites for organizational IS planning. Top management must (1) recognize IT as an indispensable resource, (2) understand that IT is a complex resource that must be planned and controlled, (3) regard IT as owned by the entire organization, and not only by the IT unit, (4) regard IT as a source for gaining strategic goals, and (5) view IT as a tool to control power.

The **IS plan** starts with a **mission statement** and a long-term **vision**. The planners then set goals and objectives. They outline the **strategic plan** for IS resources, and the **tactical** steps to attain the strategic goals. Then they get down to the more specific details of **operations**: projects, priorities, staffing, purchasing of hardware and software, and funding. In the latter effort, the planners consider several factors: flexibility of the hardware and software in supporting a variety of business needs, compatibility of hardware and software, connectivity of equipment, and scalability.

Planning initiatives do not necessarily come only from IS managers, but also from top management, line managers, and users. All may trigger discussions of needs that may result in the addition of new elements to the IS plan.

Experience shows that it often takes a **champion** to promote the approval and building of an IS. The champion is a high-ranking officer who commands sufficient political clout to include the IS in the planning, and see to it that adequate resources are secured for its development. Often, it is not top management that needs to be convinced of the merits of a new IS, but the users. They must accept the changes that will come with the new system. Systems analysts play an important role as **agents of change**, in addition to their technical performance as system developers.

REVIEW, DISCUSS, AND EXPLORE

REVIEW AND DISCUSSION QUESTIONS

1. What is business planning? What do planners do?

2. Explain the difference in focus between the top-down approach and the bottom-up approach to planning.

3. Explain the Critical Success Factors approach to planning. What are its advantages? Can you think of disadvantages?

4. Why was there little or no IS planning in the 1970s? Why do many organizations integrate IS planning into their overall plan now?

5. The Point of Interest "No Plan = Waste" depicts a grim picture of what may happen when ISs are not planned. What would you do in this organization to avoid these outcomes?

6. Figure 14.7 gives five conditions for successful IS planning. Can you think of additional prerequisites?

7. What is a champion? What does the champion do to promote a new IS? Should the champion be technically savvy? Why, or why not?

8. What is an agent of change? Why are systems analysts considered agents of change, and how do they promote change in organizations?

9. *Ethics and Society*: Several codes of professional conduct entreat IT professionals not to use professional jargon. Why? What negative results may happen when an IT consultant uses professional jargon with a client?

CONCEPT ACTIVITY

You are invited to prepare an information systems plan for a small sheet metal manufacturer. All you know about the firm is that a small number of personal computers are used for word processing and for spreadsheet work. You must glean as much information as possible in a series of interviews with top management. Prepare a list of questions you will ask in your first interview with the firm's president and other top managers.

HANDS-ON ACTIVITY

Use a library search database (such as ABI/Inform) or peruse the IS trade journals mentioned throughout this book to find two stories on IS planning: one should be a success story, the other a failure. Summarize the elements that contributed to the success, then summarize the elements that contributed to the failure.

TEAM ACTIVITY

You are a management consultant who specializes in information systems. You have been approached by an entrepreneur who is about to start a new pizza delivery chain. The entrepreneur is willing to spend almost unlimited funds on information systems to make operations efficient. She asks you to prepare a preliminary proposal (without dollar amounts) of your vision of IT at the new chain, so that it can compete with existing pizza delivery chains. Keep in mind two important elements:

(1) The chain needs to optimize purchasing of raw materials (flour, cheese, pepperoni, vegetables, and so on) some of which are perishable.

(2) The chain must deliver orders promptly and at minimum total cost (including gas, maintenance, and the like).

Use all your knowledge of telecommunications and information technology to plan the information systems for the new chain. Use your word-processing program to prepare the conceptual proposal.

EXPLORE THE WEB

Use *information systems planning*, IT *planning*, and other appropriate keywords to find information on IS planning on the Web. Review the Web sites and prepare a list of considerations (not already mentioned in this chapter) that would help in the IS planning process. Prepare a separate list of services that consulting groups offer as part of helping organizations plan their ISs. Would all these services really help, or would some just be a source of revenue for the service company? Explain your reasoning.

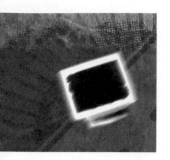

Chapter **15**
Systems Development

Lean, Mean, and Successful

BDM International, Inc. in McLean, Virginia, is well known in the industry as a small but excellent high-tech government contractor. Until the mid-1980s, the company developed applications costing around $500,000. The annual sales volume was $191 million. Then, in 1984, BDM competed with a well-known software development giant, Computer Science Corp., for a $210 million contract from the U.S. Air Force. Managers will remember those times for a long while. BDM won by submitting a small working prototype of the system. A senior vice president at BDM explained that BDM won the competition by harnessing many employees to work around the clock to complete the prototype.

Once it had won the contract, management realized that this was not the kind of job its software developers were used to. The company's experience was with relatively small-scale projects, but this time it had to deliver some 4.2 million lines of code. The system specifications alone filled 7,000 pages. The error rates of the software that was delivered were high and the documentation poor. Neither the Air Force nor BDM was happy. BDM's management decided to try a new approach.

In 1986 BDM adopted four principles. First, it started to rigorously use computer-aided software engineering (CASE) tools and started to adhere strictly to design and development methods. Second, it abandoned the culture of letting brilliant but eccentric professionals become leading players; those who were not team players were let go. Third, the large project team was reorganized into six smaller teams of 10–12 people, each responsible for a distinct product that was a piece of software of about 100,000 lines of code. Fourth, the work flow was changed. Until then, the practice had been to have an analysis group pass on directions to a design team, which in turn passed on its specifications to a programming team. From then on, each team member was in charge of his or her part of the product from concept through delivery. In the process, BDM cut its staff from 280 to 150 people.

The product teams were one of the three main groups of the new organization. The second was a systems integration group whose responsibility it was to ensure the functionality of the developed database and the common user interface, and also to test the systems before delivery. The third was the financial management group, which monitored cost, but also configuration management and quality assurance.

The results were impressive. Productivity increased 30%. Documentation errors decreased by 94% from 8 to .5 errors per 1,000 lines of code. The company ended the year of 1990 under budget.

Source: Anthes, G.H., "Marathon Mind-Set Wins Race," Computerworld, July 9, 1994, p. 97.

LEARNING OBJECTIVES

Developing a new IS is often a complex process. Those involved in it have to translate a business opportunity, a solution to a problem, or a directive into a working set of hardware and software. Once a development project is on its way, many people from different disciplines are involved in the effort. Project management and communications skills are extremely important for successful results.

When you finish this chapter, you will:

◆ Understand the systems development life cycle, which is the traditional approach to systems development

◆ Understand the pros and cons of prototyping

◆ Know what software tools facilitate the monitoring and controlling of systems development

◆ Appreciate the difficulties involved in systems development

◆ Understand the advantages and disadvantages of different system conversion strategies

◆ Understand systems integration

WHY DEVELOP AN IS?

As we have discussed, while some organizations develop their enterprise-wide information systems by combining many different smaller division or department systems, others create their ISs from the ground up. The process of developing ISs within a planned framework, which is the topic of this chapter, often creates the best systems and helps organizations avoid the necessity of patching together a collection of incompatible ISs. Companies usually embark on a systematic development of ISs when they find they are losing competitive ground because they have inefficient ISs, or no ISs at all. Developing an IS is not a trivial matter. It requires a thorough understanding of existing processes, a vision of how an organization should operate, discipline, knowledge, and excellent communications skills.

There are three phenomena that can trigger the development of a new IS: an opportunity, a problem, or a directive. In this context, an **opportunity** means a potential increase in revenue, reduction of costs, or gain in competitive advantage that can be achieved using an IS. A **problem** is any undesired situation. Many problems can be resolved by using an IS. For instance, an organization may realize that certain processes are too slow, cost too much, or produce products or services of inferior quality, and that a new IS could solve the problem. Seeking an opportunity is considered **proactive**, while solving a problem is considered **reactive**. A **directive** is an order to take a certain action. In this context, an organization may need an IS to comply with a law or regulation. For example, a law may require that patient records be recorded and maintained in a certain manner that can only be implemented with an IS.

Planning an IS (discussed in Chapter 14, "Planning of Information Systems") should always be regarded as the first phase of systems development. Then begins the systems development life cycle, which is the subject of this chapter.

THE SYSTEMS DEVELOPMENT LIFE CYCLE

Large ISs that address structured problems, such as accounting and payroll systems, are usually conceived, planned, developed, and maintained within a framework called the **systems development life cycle (SDLC)**. The SDLC consists of several distinct phases that are followed methodically. Although different textbooks may refer to the different phases and subphases by different names, or group two or three phases into one phase, or break another phase into two or three phases, in general, the same steps are followed. While the SDLC is a powerful methodology for systems development, organizations are sometimes forced to take shortcuts, skipping a step here or there. Sometimes, time pressures or other factors lead developers to use other types of systems development, which are discussed in Chapter 16, "Alternative Avenues for Systems Acquisition."

The SDLC approach assumes that the life of an IS starts with a need followed by an assessment of the functions that the system will fulfill, and ends when the benefits of the system no longer outweigh its maintenance costs, at which point the life of a new system begins (see Figure 15.1). Hence, the process is called a "life cycle." After the planning phase, the SDLC includes four major phases: analysis, design, implementation, and support. Figure 15.1 depicts the cycle and the conditions that may trigger the return to a previous phase. The analysis and design phases are broken down into several steps, as described in the following discussion.

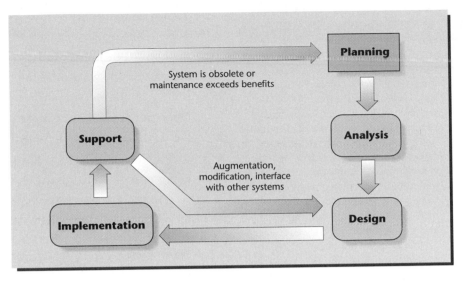

Figure 15.1 *The systems development life cycle*

ANALYSIS

The **systems analysis** phase is a five-step process (summarized in Figure 15.2) that is designed to answer these questions:

Investigation:

◆ How does the existing system work?

◆ What business opportunity do we want the system to seize, or what problems do we want it to solve, or what directive must we fulfill?

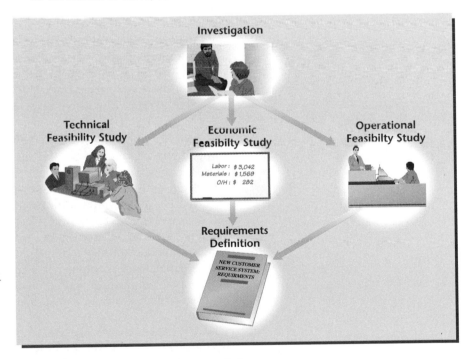
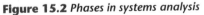

Figure 15.2 *Phases in systems analysis*

Technical Feasibility Study:

◆ Is there technology to create the system we want?

Economic Feasibility Study:

◆ What resources do we need to implement the system?

◆ Will the system's benefits outweigh its costs?

Operational Feasibility Study:

◆ Will the system be used appropriately by its intended users?

◆ Will the system be used to its full capacity?

Requirements Definition:

◆ What features do we want the system to have?

◆ What interfaces will the system have with other systems?

INVESTIGATION The first step in systems analysis is **investigation** to determine whether or not there is a real need for the system, and if the system is feasible. Usually, a small ad hoc team—consisting of a representative of the sponsoring executive, one or two systems analysts, and representatives of business units that would use the new system or be impacted by it—is put together to perform a quick preliminary investigation.

The team interviews staff, spends time with employees at their work stations to learn firsthand about the way they currently carry out their duties, and interviews the workers about problems with the current system. This gives workers the opportunity to express their ideas about the way they would like a new IS to function, to improve their work. The investigative team prepares a written report summarizing the information gathered. The team members also forward their own opinion on the need for a new system. They may or may not agree with the requesting business unit, that a new system is justified.

If the preliminary report concludes that the business situation warrants the investment in a new IS, a more comprehensive investigation is authorized. The sponsoring executive selects members for a larger analysis team. Usually, members of the original team are included in this augmented group. The charge of the investigation team is to determine whether the proposed system is feasible technically, economically, and operationally.

THE TECHNICAL FEASIBILITY STUDY A new IS is **technically feasible** if its components exist or can be developed with available tools. As we know by now, ISs consist of hardware and software. The investigators use their own knowledge and information from trade journals and from hardware and software vendors to determine if the proposed system can be built. Quite often, the prospective users ask for technical features that cannot be developed.

The team must also consider the organization's existing commitments to hardware and software. For example, if the company recently purchased hundreds of a certain model of computer, it is unlikely that management will approve the purchase of computers of another model for a single new application. Thus, the investigators must find out if the proposed system can run on existing hardware.

THE ECONOMIC FEASIBILITY STUDY Like any project, the development of a new IS must be **economically justified**. That is, over the life of the system, the benefits must outweigh the costs. To this end, the analysts prepare a **cost/benefit** analysis, which can be a spreadsheet showing all the costs incurred by the system and all the benefits that are expected from its operation (see Figure 15.3).

The most accurate method of economic analysis is **return on investment (ROI)**, which is the difference between the stream of benefits and the stream of costs over the life of the system, discounted by the applicable interest rate. To find the ROI, the **net present value** of the system is calculated by combining the net present value of the costs of the system with the net present value of the benefits of the system, using calculations based on annual costs and benefits and using the appropriate interest rate. If the ROI is positive, the system is economically feasible, or cost-justified. Remember that during the time the system is developed, which may be several years, there are no benefits, only development costs. Operational costs during the system's life include maintenance personnel, telecommunications, computer-related supplies (such as replacement of hardware during breakdowns, upgrading of software, as well as paper and toner), and power.

Figure 15.3 presents an example of a cost/benefit spreadsheet and analysis. Since the net present value of the system is positive ($43,152), and therefore the benefits exceed the investment, the development effort is economically justified. In 2003, the costs outweigh the benefits of the system, and the net present value starts to diminish. At this point, the organization should be considering creating a new system. If the system is not replaced or significantly upgraded, the existing system will become a drain on the organization over time.

YEAR	1997	1998	1999	2000	2001	2002
Benefits						
Increase in sales			56,000	45,000	30,000	10,000
Reduction in clerical staff			20,000	20,000	20,000	20,000
Total Benefits	0	0	76,000	65,000	50,000	30,000
Costs						
Analysis	15,000					
Design	37,500					
Implementation	0	56,000				
Hardware	0	20,000				
Operation and maintenance	0	0	5,000	5,000	5,000	5,000
Total Costs	52,000	76,000	5,000	5,000	5,000	5,000
Difference	(-52,000)	(-76,000)	71,000	60,000	45,000	25,000
Discounted at 5%	(-49,524)	(-68,934)	61,332	49,362	32,259	18,657
Net Present Value for Six Years	43,152					

Figure 15.3 *Estimated benefits and costs of an IS ($)*

Often, it is difficult to justify the cost of a new IS because too many of the benefits are **intangible**, that is, they cannot be quantified in dollar terms. Improved customer service, better decision making, and the creation of a more enjoyable workplace are all benefits that eventually increase profit, but are very difficult to estimate in dollar amounts. Other benefits not as intangible can also be overlooked.

Savings from staff reductions are probably the most common tangible benefit of new information systems such as client/server applications or sales force automation. But other tangible benefits from new technologies often go unrecognized in standard ROI analyses used in most corporations, such as the one in Figure 15.3. These may include:

◆ A new IS may help to turn over accounts receivable faster. If a new system can send invoices out just one day faster, then annual cash flow may increase by 1/365. For a company with $365 million in sales, that translates into $1 million in increased cash flow per year. If the interest cost on $1 million is 5%, that translates into savings of $50,000 per year.

◆ A new IS may help shorten the monthly general ledger closing cycle. This allows managers to make decisions based on the analysis of more timely financial information.

◆ A new IS may allow managers to perform "what if" analyses in real time during the financial planning cycle.

◆ A new IS may reduce system support costs for existing mainframe-based, in-house accounting systems.

◆ A new IS may improve billing efficiencies by issuing invoices sooner and by reducing errors in billings.

◆ A new IS may reduce the time (and cost) of preparing budgets, business plans, and proposals by making business data increasingly available in real time.

◆ A new IS may make it possible to track, and therefore control, costs more closely.

These are extremely important improvements in business that must be considered, even if they are not quantifiable. To convince management that a new IS is needed, the system's champion and systems analysts must take all the benefits into consideration and present them in a compelling manner.

THE OPERATIONAL FEASIBILITY STUDY The purpose of the **operational feasibility study** is to determine if the new system will be used as intended. More specifically, this analysis answers the following questions:

◆ Will the system fit into the culture of this organization?

◆ Will all the intended users use the system to its full capacity?

◆ Will the system interfere with company policies or statutory laws?

Organizational culture is an umbrella term referring to the general tone of the corporate environment. It takes into account issues such as whether relationships between supervisors and subordinates are usually casual or formal; the existence or lack of dress code; acceptance or rejection of flex time (which allows employees to start and stop work within a range of time, rather than at fixed hours); and acceptance or rejection of telecommuting, which allows employees to work at home. The team must take these points into consideration. For example, if the system will be used by telecommuters, it must be open to telecommunications from external telephone lines. The analysts must find out if this would compromise information security and confidentiality.

Other points the team considers include compliance with statutory regulations and company policy. For example, the staff may want to use a record-keeping system that would violate customer privacy, or risk the confidentiality of government contracts with the company. If these issues cannot be overcome at the outset, then the proposed system is not **operationally** feasible.

REQUIREMENTS DEFINITION When the analysts determine that the proposed system is feasible, the project team is formalized. Management nominates a project leader who puts together a project team that will develop the system until it is ready for delivery. The team includes systems analysts, programmers, and often, representatives from the prospective group of users.

One of the first pieces of information the analysts need to know is the system requirements. **System requirements** are the functions that the system is expected to fulfill and the features through which it will perform its tasks. In other words, system requirements are what the system should be able to do and the means by which it will fulfill its stated goal. This part of the analysis process is often also called **fact finding**. There are several ways to collect information for this purpose:

◆ *Interviews*. The analysts meet with prospective users and ask questions. The users are given an opportunity to discuss problems with the existing system and how they would like these problems solved.

◆ *Questionnaires*. Employees involved in the business processes for which the system is developed fill out questionnaires.

◆ *Examination of documents*. The employees give the analysts documents containing input data and output information involved in their work.

◆ *On-the-job observation*. The analysts spend time with the employees while the latter carry out their normal work. The analysts follow the business process firsthand.

The facts gathered are organized into a document detailing the system requirements. The analysts present the list to the users and their managers to confirm that these are the features they need. In many organizations, to secure agreement, the project leader requests that the prospective owners of the system sign a requirements report. This is a crucial milestone in the analysis process; if the requirements are not well defined, resources will be wasted or underbudgeted, and the completion of the project will be delayed.

It is important to understand that the requirements report does not detail any specific details of the hardware and software that will be used. For example, there is no mention, at this point, of the specific models of the computers that will be used, or the programming languages in which the software will be written. In fact, at this early stage, the analysts have not yet decided whether to develop the application in-house or purchase a ready-made software package.

DESIGN

With a comprehensive list of requirements, the project team can begin the next step in systems development, designing the new system. **Systems design** is the evaluation of alternative solutions to a business problem and the specification of hardware, software, and communications technology for the selected solution. As indicated in Figure 15.4 on the next page, systems design comprises four steps, one that describes how the system will work logically, one that describes the physical layout, and others that deal with the construction and testing of the system.

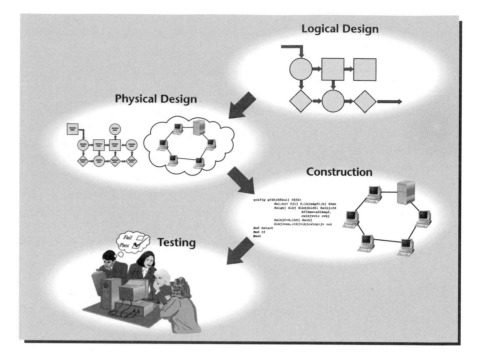

Figure 15.4 *Phases in systems design*

LOGICAL DESIGN The **logical design**, which immediately precedes the physical design of the system, is a translation of the user requirements into detailed functions of the system. During the logical design phase, the designers determine the following components:

◆ *Input files*: the files that will be used to capture the input data.

◆ *Procedures*: the logical algorithms used to process the input. The procedures will later be transformed into code written in a programming language.

◆ *Output files*: the files that will be used to capture information that is the result of processing data, and the files that will record parameters input by customers, employees, applicants, and/or other parties.

◆ *User dialog*: the manner in which the users will interact with the system (this includes menus, icons, and/or provisions for query by example).

◆ *Interfaces*: how the system will interact with other systems. This includes provisions for input of data and information from the files of other systems, lookups in other systems for decision making, retrieval of data from other systems, and output of data to other systems.

Neither the logical nor physical design steps include any construction of real code. At this point, the analysts have not yet chosen the tools with which the application will be built, the programming languages that will be used, the DBMS that will be used to construct the databases, or any similar tools.

Designing and constructing a new IS may be a very complex, if not complicated, task. The approach used most often by managers is "divide and conquer," that is, break the assignment down into small, hierarchical modules, and assign one or several modules to each team. This way, modules are isolated from each other, and problems met in the development of one module will not hamper the progress of other modules.

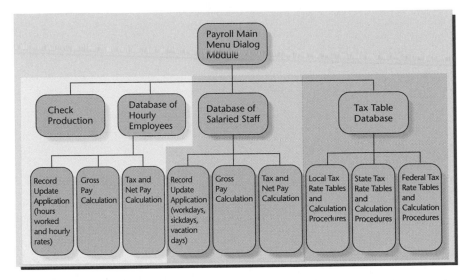

Figure 15.5 *Payroll system development. Using the divide and conquer approach, the planned system is broken into hierarchical modules.*

Let us consider how the system development of a payroll system might be managed in modules, as shown in Figure 15.5. One module would be the database of hourly employees, which includes the processes of collecting data about the number of hours worked and maintaining the correct hourly rates. Another module maintains the database of salaried staff. The third module, the tax table database, would be accessed by the first two modules for tax calculation. It includes tax rates tables and procedures for calculating tax amounts. The check production module receives the gross and net amounts to be paid from either of the first two modules for an employee, and the total tax from the tax table module, and then prints out the pay check. The first three modules are further broken into smaller modules. The four major modules are linked to a dialog module, the payroll main menu, which provides the main menu for selection of the desired operation.

Flowcharts. Flowcharts use graphical symbols to illustrate a system's logical operations as well as the physical parts involved. For instance, there are symbols that represent different pieces of hardware, such as terminals, disks, and communications lines, and also logical operations such as the beginning and ending points of a process and points of decision making. Flowcharts used to be one of the most important tools in systems development, but they have largely been replaced with other tools, which are discussed below.

An example of a flowchart is shown in Figure 15.6 on the next page, which represents the following logic for giving salespeople bonuses: a salesperson with sales over $1 million will get a bonus of $1,000 plus .5% of sales; a salesperson with less than $1 million in sales will receive a bonus of .4% of the sales volume.

For over 40 years, flowcharts have been used by systems analysts and programmers as a language-independent means of describing a system's logical sequence. After detailing the logic of a process in a flowchart, programmers translate the logic into a computer program. There are more than 30 different symbols, each representing an event, a process, a hardware device, or a report type. While

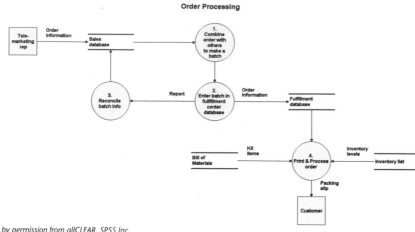

Order Processing

Used by permission from allCLEAR, SPSS Inc.

some symbols have been standardized by the American National Standards Institute (ANSI), others remain non-standard. Occasionally, analysts may use the same symbol to represent different things. The multitude of symbols, the use of nonstandard symbols, and the use of symbols to represent too many things in the same chart (processes, hardware, and so on) have rendered flowcharting less and less popular in recent years. A simpler alternative to graphically representing ISs was developed. The method is called data flow diagrams.

Data Flow Diagrams. **Data flow diagrams (DFDs)** are used to describe the flow of data in a business operation, using only four symbols or elements: external entities, processes, data stores, and the direction in which data flows (see Figure 15.7). **External entities** include individuals and groups of people that are external to the system, such as customers, employees, other departments in the organization, or other organizations. A **process** is any event or sequence of events in which data are either changed or acted upon, such as the processing of data into information, or the application of data to decision making. A **data store** is any form of data at rest, such as a filing cabinet or a computer file. **Data flow** from an entity to a process, from a process to a data store, from a data store to a process, and so on. Thus, a carefully drawn DFD can provide a useful representation of a system, whether existing or planned.

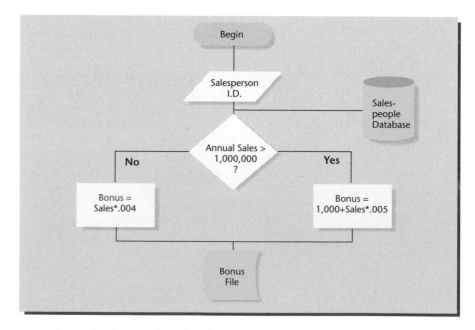

Figure 15.6 *A flowchart describing a sales bonus system*

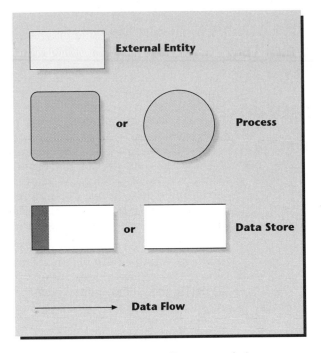

Figure 15.7 *Data flow diagram symbols*

It is important to understand that DFDs describe only entities, processes, data stores, and data flows—nothing else. They are not meant to represent hardware devices or types of reports, nor are they meant to detail the logic of processes. The use of only four symbols and the simplicity of DFDs are their great advantage. They are easy to learn and use.

Figure 15.8 uses a DFD to show the same process of calculating a sales bonus that Figure 15.6 showed using a flowchart. A sales clerk is an external entity entering data (in this case, salespeople's ID numbers), which flow into a process, namely the bonus calculation, which also receives data from the salespeople database (in this case, the dollar amount each salesperson sold over the past year). The result of the process is the bonus amount for each salesperson, information that flows into a bonus file. Later, the company's comptroller will use the information to generate bonus checks.

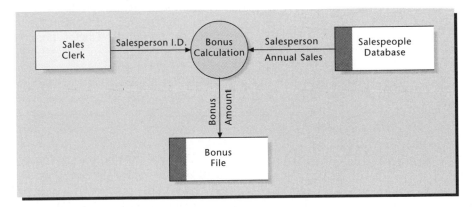

Figure 15.8 *The sales bonus system: A data flow diagram*

Should IS Professionals be Certified?

In Chapter 14, "Planning Information Systems," we discussed the issue of IS professionalism and the ethical obligations of IS professionals. A related issue is how to determine whether or not IS specialists are in fact qualified to build and maintain ISs. The investment in these systems is huge. When organizations commit millions of dollars to developing systems, they count on IS professionals to provide high-quality systems that will fulfill their intended purposes without harming business, employees, or consumers. But the products of IS professionals often fail and cause serious damage. Some people argue that because of the high investment and high risk usually associated with systems development and operation, IS professionals, like other professionals, should be certified. We expect the government or authorized bodies to license experts, people whose knowledge and skills in a certain domain are significantly greater that those of a layperson. Certification is meant to guarantee that the experts have passed tests that ensure their skills.

Malfunctioning ISs. According to a U.S. Congressional report, software failures cost America a billion dollars annually. Consider some failures that have been documented over the years, in the U.S. and elsewhere.

◆ In Florida, a fifth-grade student took a computerized sixth-grade placement test. His grade was zero. Despite protest, he was forced to repeat the fifth grade. Six weeks after the beginning of the new academic year, manual rescoring revealed an extra space between his first and last names on the answer sheet, which caused the zero score.

◆ A 40-year-old woman in Vancouver, Canada, was denied a refund by the Canadian tax authority, which insisted that she was dead. It was later discovered that the social insurance number of her deceased mother had been inadvertently reported as hers.

◆ The U.S. Internal Revenue Service found a Connecticut woman in arrears for $67,714. She was sent a bill for more than $1 billion, including penalties. The IRS found an error in the interest computation.

◆ A system malfunction forced the Bank of New York to borrow $24 billion to cover accounts that showed low balances. The interest on this money was $5 million.

◆ Another programming error allowed ATM card holders in Washington, D.C., to withdraw as much cash as they could carry regardless of their available account balances.

◆ A police computer in Paris, France, misread magnetic labels on 41,000 traffic-violation files and incorrectly charged motorists with crimes ranging from prostitution to murder and drug trafficking.

Certification Pros. Some observers say that there is a way to minimize malfunctioning ISs: certification. Civil engineers must be certified to build buildings and bridges. Doctors pass rigorous exams before they receive their licenses and begin to practice without supervision. Public accountants must

(continued)

DFDs are used both in the analysis and design phases of systems development. In the analysis phase, they are used to describe and illustrate how the existing system operates. DFD symbols are suitable for describing any IS, even if it is not computer-based. A DFD of the existing system helps pinpoint its weaknesses, by describing data flow graphically and allowing analysts to pinpoint

be licensed to perform audits. Lawyers must pass the bar exams to practice. Why, these observers ask, should IS professionals be allowed to practice without licensing?

It seems that software experts do possess all the characteristics of professionals. They work in a field that requires expertise, and the public and their clients usually are not qualified to evaluate their skills. Certification could provide the following benefits to the following groups:

◆ *Employers* often hire software professionals without knowing what they are getting. They count on the information included in the candidate's resume and, sometimes, on letters of recommendation. Mandatory certification might protect potential employers against charlatans. Also, certification would provide potential employers with information on a candidate's suitability for different levels of performance. For example, a professional may be qualified to participate in a systems development team, but not to head the project team.

◆ *Clients* could benefit from mandatory certification even more. While employers can learn, in time, of the real capabilities of their personnel, businesses that hire consultants have no previous employment experience on which to rely.

◆ *Society* might enjoy fewer software-related failures. Only those who are qualified would be allowed to engage in development and maintenance of information systems, thereby improving the overall integrity of ISs. Certification is especially needed for those holding key development positions for systems whose impact on society is significant.

Certification Cons. However, there are two arguments against mandatory certification:

◆ It is difficult, if not impossible, to devise a way to measure software competence. For instance, there are many different methods for developing applications, and there is no proven advantage of one over the others. A computer professional may be well experienced in one method, but not in other methods. It would be unfair to disqualify that individual merely on this basis.

◆ Some argue that mandatory certification may create a "closed shop" by using a single entry exam designed to admit very few people. In such a scenario, the status and income of those admitted would be enhanced at the expense of those excluded. With little fear of competition within the closed group, there is often little incentive to improve skills.

Currently, there is no mandatory certification of IS professionals. In fact, there isn't even agreement about who should be considered an IS professional. Some organizations, such as The Institute for Certification of Computer Professionals (ICCP), test and certify people who voluntarily take the tests. Some software companies certify analysts and programmers who use those companies' tools. However, there are no certification regulations for IS professionals in the U.S. or anywhere else, as there are for many other professions.

which processes and databases can be automated, shared by different processes, or otherwise changed to strengthen the IS. If it is found that a new IS is needed, a DFD of the conceptualized new system is drawn to provide the logical blueprint for its construction.

PHYSICAL DESIGN Once the logical blueprint for the new system is ready, the physical design begins. A system's **physical design** process includes specifying the necessary software and hardware needed to support it. Many organizations have hardware that is not being used to full capacity, in which case the project team designs software to fit the hardware. Of course, organizations usually look first for packaged software, and only if the appropriate system cannot be purchased off the shelf do companies develop systems from scratch.

If a program has to be developed in-house, the project leader will choose development tools (which the organization may already have) such as programming languages, database management systems for building databases, and special software tools to facilitate the development effort. As with hardware, if certain software development tools are the standard at the organization, only these tools will be used.

To make the new code maintainable, the programmers practice **structured programming**, in which the logical process is divided into small functional units, such as the modules described in the payroll system above, which are programmed independently. Then each program unit is designed to be triggered from a controlling module. Such programs are often referred to as "**GOTO-less**" programs. The programs do not use GOTO statements. It is best to avoid too many GOTO commands because they create code that logically resembles spaghetti, and is difficult to follow. In structured programs in general, each logical unit starts with a comment, or nonexecutable remark in plain English, explaining each part of the code to any person who needs to debug or modify it.

CONSTRUCTION Once the software development tools are chosen, the construction of the system begins. **System construction** is predominantly programming. Professional programmers translate input, output, and processes, as described in flowcharts and data flow diagrams, into programs. When a program module is completed, it is tested. Testing is performed by way of walk-through and simulation.

In a **walk-through**, the systems analysts and programmers follow the logic of the program, conduct processes the system is programmed to execute when running, produce output, and compare it to what they know the results should be. In **simulation**, the team actually runs the program with these data. When all the modules of the application are completed and successfully tested, the modules are integrated into one coherent program.

SYSTEM TESTING Although simulation with each module provides some testing, it is important to test the entire integrated system. The system is checked against the system requirements originally defined in the analysis phase, by running typical data through the system. Quality of the output is examined, and processing times are measured to ensure that the original requirements are met.

Testing should include attempts to get the system to fail, by violating processing and security controls. The testers should try to "outsmart" the system, entering unreasonable data and trying to access files that should not be accessed directly by some users or under certain circumstances. This is a crucial step in the development effort, as many unforeseen snags can be discovered and fixed before the system is introduced for daily use. If the new system passes the tests, it is ready for introduction in the business units that will use it.

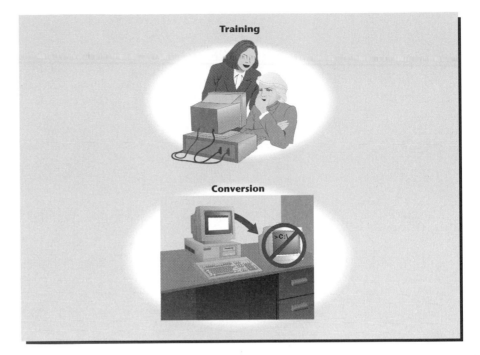

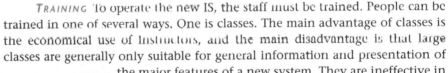

Figure 15.9 *Activities in systems implementation*

IMPLEMENTATION

The **implementation** of a new IS, also called delivery, consists of two steps: training and conversion (see Figure 15.9). Although training usually precedes conversion, if training is done on the job it may succeed conversion.

TRAINING To operate the new IS, the staff must be trained. People can be trained in one of several ways. One is classes. The main advantage of classes is the economical use of instructors, and the main disadvantage is that large classes are generally only suitable for general information and presentation of the major features of a new system. They are ineffective in teaching the detailed features and modes of operation. Because people learn by doing, **on-the-job training**, in which a trainer coaches a new user or a small group of users as they perform their jobs with the new system, is much more effective in teaching the day-to-day uses of a new system. **Multimedia technology** and other training software can also be used. This approach frees systems analysts to attend to other business, while employees train themselves, and also allows each trainee to learn the system at his or her own pace.

Several vendors of widely sold packaged programs such as word processors and spreadsheets now offer training software that employees can use individually for self-training. Large companies often develop their own multimedia programs to train employees to use tailor-made ISs.

Multimedia applications help train employees to use new software. Shown here is the main menu of a training program for a popular presentation application.

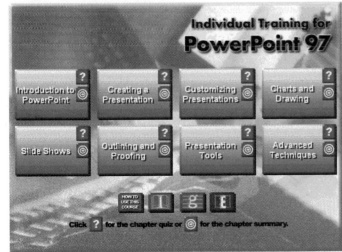

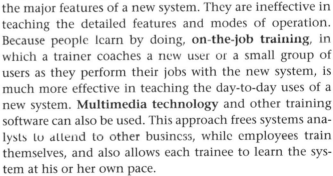

Used by permission from Individual Software, Inc.

CONVERSION **Conversion** takes place when an operation switches from using the old system to using the new system. This can be a difficult time for an organization. Operators need time to get used to new systems, and, while every effort may be made to thoroughly test systems, conversion can hold some unpleasant surprises if certain bugs or problems were not discovered earlier. Services to other departments and to customers may be delayed, and data may be lost. There are four basic conversion strategies designed to manage the transition (see Figure 15.10).

Parallel Conversion. In **parallel conversion**, the old system is used along with the new system for a predetermined period of time. This minimizes risk because if the new system fails, operations are not stopped, and no damage is caused to the organization. However, parallel conversion is costly because of the expenses associated with running two systems, especially labor costs.

Phased Conversion. ISs, especially large ones, can often be broken up into functional modules that can be phased into operation one at a time. Conversion of an accounting IS, for example, can be phased with the accounts receivable module converted first, then the accounts payable, the general ledger, and so on. This approach also keeps risk fairly low, although the benefits of using the entire integrated system are delayed. Also, users can learn how to use one module at a time much more easily than the entire system.

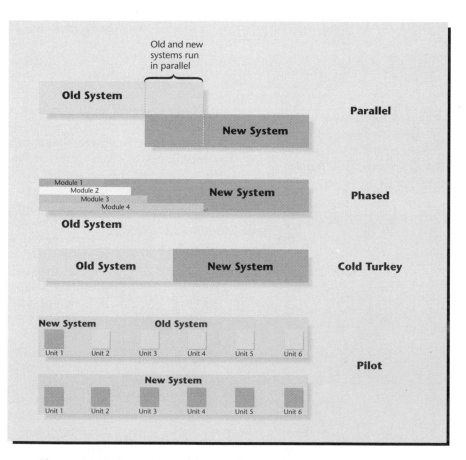

Figure 15.10 *Strategies used to convert from one IS to another*

Cold Turkey Conversion. In a "cold turkey" or "cut over" conversion, the old system is discarded, and the new one takes over the entire business operation for which it was developed. This strategy is highly risky, but can be inexpensive, if successful, because no resources are spent on running two systems in parallel, and the benefits of the entire new system are immediately enjoyed.

Pilot Conversion. If the new system is to be used in more than one business unit, it may first be introduced in a single unit for a predetermined period of time, where problems can be addressed and the system can be polished before being implemented in the other business units. Obviously, piloting reduces risks. It is especially useful for determining how comfortable staff members are with a new system, a lesson that can be applied to the later units. As with the parallel strategy, the pilot strategy means that benefits of the full implementation of the system are delayed.

SUPPORT

The role of IS professionals does not end with the delivery of the new system. They must support it and ensure that it can be operated to the satisfaction of the users. Support includes two main responsibilities: maintenance and user help (see Figure 15.11).

Maintenance consists of two major activities: debugging and updating. **Debugging** is the correction in programs of bugs or problems that were not discovered during tests. **Updating** is revising the system to comply with changes in business needs that occur after the implementation phase. For example, if a company collects personal data for market analysis, managers may want to use the new IS to collect more data, which may require that new fields be added to the databases.

Although maintenance is viewed by IS professionals as glamorless, it should not be taken lightly or left to the less-experienced professionals. While the distribution of costs varies widely from system to system, surveys of companies show that an average of about 20% of the overall IS budget is spent on systems development, and about 80% is expended on maintenance. The major reason for this is the fact

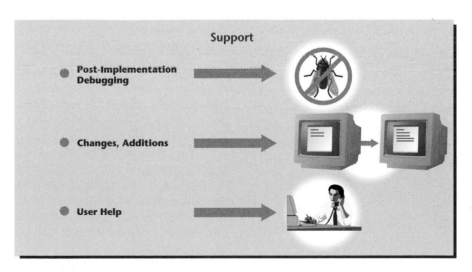

Figure 15.11 *Activities in systems support*

Understand the Principles of Systems Development?

Once the overall plan for an IS has been laid down by an organization, other activities start: budgeting, systems analysis and design, project management, testing, and introduction of the new system in the business units that will use it for several years. By and large, organizations have recognized the need to let non-IS managers play major roles in systems development. You may be called on to participate in this process, not just sporadically, but as a member of a development team. The IS professionals on the team will need your insight into the business activities you run. They will need your advice on ways to improve these activities through use of new or improved ISs.

To be a productive team member, you need to understand the different phases of systems development. You must understand what systems analysts and project managers try to do from the very beginning to the end of the process. Your understanding of their effort, and their understanding of yours as well, are important ingredients for successful development. In summary, this is going to be *your* system. Make sure it is built to satisfy your business needs. In addition, the new practice in many organizations, to let non-IS managers actually *lead* IS development projects, only emphasizes why it is important that you understand the principles of systems development.

that support is the longest phase in the system life cycle. While development takes several months to about three years, the system is expected to yield benefits over many years. Efficient and effective system maintenance is possible only if good documentation is written while the system is developed, and if the code is written in a structured manner.

Support also includes **user help**. The people who work at the organization's help desk (discussed in Chapter 8, "Managers and Their Information Needs") must be familiar with the new system so that they can provide advice and guidance to users.

PROTOTYPING

While the SDLC has its advantages, it is a lengthy process and requires a rather inflexible and formal series of steps. To overcome these detriments, an increasing number of ISs are being developed under a looser approach called prototyping. A **prototype** is an original machine or system that serves as a model for production of more machines or systems. In manufacturing, a prototype refers to an actual physical product that is later mass-produced for marketing. **IS prototyping**, however, has a slightly different meaning, whereby systems are developed through an iterative rather than a systematic process: the developers and users are constantly interacting, revising, and testing the prototype system until it evolves into an acceptable application (see Figure 15.12). This is a contrast with the traditional step-by-step analysis and development process used by the SDLC.

The purpose of prototyping is to develop a working model as quickly as possible, which can then be revised and tweaked as developers and users work

Used by permission from IBM Corporation

In prototyping, prospective users of an IS are involved in every step of the development process.

together. Developers construct a "quick and dirty" model; the model is tested by the prospective users, who provide feedback; using the feedback, developers add some features, delete others, enhance input, output, and processes, and then submit the revised system for the users to test again. This iterative process goes on until the users are satisfied with the product. Then, the productive life of the system starts. While a prototype IS can be duplicated and introduced in many business units, the process is still called "prototyping" even if only one copy of the system will be used. A developer once described this as a "two steps forward, one step back" procedure.

Several studies have shown that prototyping has become a popular approach to systems development, mainly because it requires fewer staff hours and usually leads to a new system more quickly than the SDLC. These studies have shown that the greatest cost component of systems development is personnel time, and that prototyping can translate into cost savings of up to 85%, compared to the SDLC. Prototyping also significantly shortens **systems development backlog**, the time users have to wait for a response to their system requests because IS departments cannot respond to them in a timely enough fashion.

The benefits of prototyping do not come without risks. First, the analysis phase is reduced to a minimum, or is sometimes eliminated completely. This

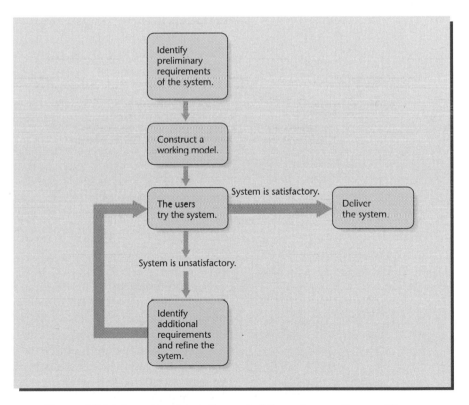

Figure 15.12 *In prototyping, refinement of the system continues until users are satisfied.*

WHEN TO PROTOTYPE	WHEN NOT TO PROTOTYPE
Small-scale systems	Large-scale systems
Systems solving unstructured problems	Complex systems
When it's difficult for users to specify system requirements	Systems with interfaces to other systems

Figure 15.13 *When to prototype and when not to prototype*

increases the risk of incompatibilities and other unforeseen mishaps. The developers devote all of their time to construction and hardly any time to documentation, so modification at a later date can be extremely time-consuming, if not impossible. There are times when prototyping is appropriate and others when it is not (see Figure 15.13).

WHEN TO PROTOTYPE

Prototyping is an efficient approach to development when the system is small, when the system deals with unstructured problems, and when the users cannot specify all the requirements at the start of the project.

When the system to be developed is small in scale, the risk involved in the lack of thorough analysis is minimal, partly because the investment of resources is small. If the development takes longer than planned, the overall cost is still likely to be smaller than if a full SDLC were performed.

Even if the IS is large, it is impractical to carry out a formal SDLC when the system is to help in an unstructured environment. This is the case with many decision support systems (DSSs) and expert systems (ESs), in which developers must hold frequent sessions with the experts who provide the sequences of problem solving. This leads to de facto prototyping. The developer interviews the experts, builds a crude system or part thereof, lets the experts try it, improves it, and so on until the system performs satisfactorily. Then it is delivered to its intended users.

When users cannot communicate their requirements, either because they are not familiar with technological developments, or because they find it hard to conceptualize the system in terms of input and output files, processes, and the user interface, developers have no choice but to prototype. In this case the users are often able to communicate their requirements as the development proceeds.

WHEN NOT TO PROTOTYPE

Prototyping is not indiscriminately recommended. If a system is large or complex, or if it is designed to interface with other systems, prototyping may pose too great a risk because it skips some major phases of systems development, including the feasibility studies.

Prototyping is not recommended for large systems because they require a significant investment of resources, and therefore system failure could entail great financial loss. The systematic approach of the SDLC is also recommended if the system is complex and consists of many modules, because extra care must be applied in documenting requirements and the manner in which components will be integrated, in order to ensure smooth and successful development.

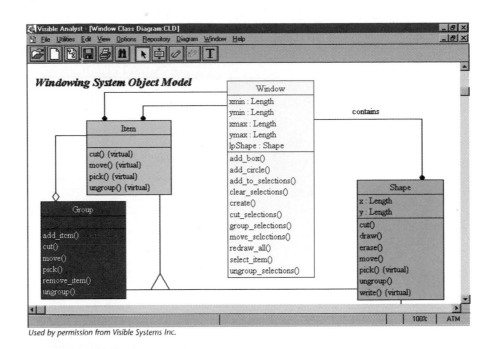

Used by permission from Visible Systems Inc.

Integrated CASE tools let developers use graphical user interfaces to quickly develop working applications

For the same reasons, prototyping should be avoided when the system is to be interfaced with other systems. The requirements and integration must be analyzed carefully, documented, and carried out according to a plan agreed upon by the users and developers before the design and construction phases start. This reduces the risk of incompatibility and damage to the existing system. Therefore, accounting ISs, large order-entry systems, and payroll systems are rarely prototyped.

Developers can use a combination of prototyping and SDLC, in which parts of the system are prototyped, while the SDLC is used to manage the overall integrated system development. For instance, prototyping is often used effectively during the construction step. Fourth-generation languages, system development software (such as CASE, discussed below), and application generators are often used to prototype input and output files, and user interface features. The availability and continual progress of these software tools have been a major factor in making prototyping so popular.

COMPUTER-AIDED SOFTWARE ENGINEERING

Special software called **computer-aided software engineering** or **CASE** tools are system development programs that ease and speed both the design and construction of new ISs. Systems analysts can build data flow diagrams of a new IS, and flowcharts for the different program modules. They can use CASE tools to plan data dictionaries and database schemas for the IS, which, once found to satisfy the users' needs, become the basis of a DBMS.

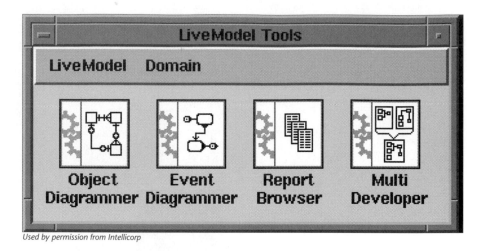

Sophisticated CASE tools provide easy to use graphical user interfaces and expedite the logical design of applications.

Application generators are a special type of CASE tool used to facilitate programming by taking over from analysts and programmers the task of generating code for input and output screen forms. Programmers use the generator's **graphical user interface (GUI)** to create forms, and the code is automatically written by the tool. The programmers can access the code whenever they wish. Similarly, entire databases and processes can be developed with minimum writing of code.

Some CASE tools are limited to only one or two of the above functions. Those that integrate many capabilities, such as diagramming, screen developing, and so on are often called **I-CASE tools**, or integrated CASE tools. The proliferation of easy-to-use CASE tools spawned the concept of **rapid application development (RAD)**. RAD eliminates the need for formal requirements analysis and saves much development time. The term is often used instead of the older term, prototyping.

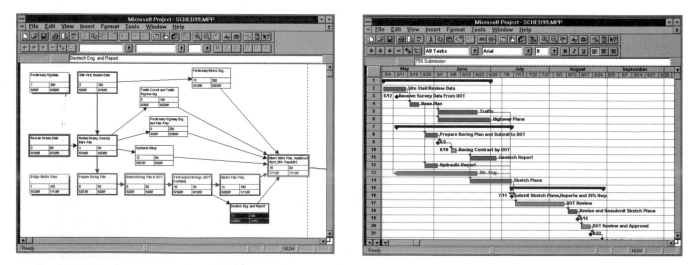

Project management software allows managers to use both PERT charts (left) and Gantt charts (right) to control projects.

The spreadsheet window titled "Microsoft Project - SCHED99.MPP" shows the following table:

ID	Task Name	Fixed Cost	Total Cost	Baseline	Variance	Actual	Remaining
1	**Preliminary Highway**	$0.00	$16,000.00	$0.00	$16,000.00	$0.00	$16,000.00
2	Site Visit, Review Data	$1,200.00	$1,200.00	$0.00	$1,200.00	$0.00	$1,200.00
3	Receive Survey Data	$0.00	$0.00	$0.00	$0.00	$0.00	$0.00
4	Review Survey, Develop E	$400.00	$400.00	$0.00	$400.00	$0.00	$400.00
5	Traffic Counts and Traffic	$6,000.00	$6,000.00	$0.00	$6,000.00	$0.00	$6,000.00
6	Preliminary Highway Eng.	$8,400.00	$8,400.00	$0.00	$8,400.00	$0.00	$8,400.00
7	**Bridge Sketch Plans**	$0.00	$29,800.00	$0.00	$29,800.00	$0.00	$29,800.00
8	Prepare Boring Plan	$2,100.00	$2,100.00	$0.00	$2,100.00	$0.00	$2,100.00
9	Submit Boring Plan to DOT	$0.00	$0.00	$0.00	$0.00	$0.00	$0.00
10	Field Inspect Borings (DOT	$1,750.00	$1,750.00	$0.00	$1,750.00	$0.00	$1,750.00
11	Geotech Eng. and Report	$2,700.00	$2,700.00	$0.00	$2,700.00	$0.00	$2,700.00
12	Hydraulic Study	$3,750.00	$3,750.00	$0.00	$3,750.00	$0.00	$3,750.00
13	Preliminary Struct. Eng.	$12,000.00	$12,000.00	$0.00	$12,000.00	$0.00	$12,000.00
14	Sketch Plan Prep.	$7,500.00	$7,500.00	$0.00	$7,500.00	$0.00	$7,500.00
15	**Sketch Plan and 25% Subm**	$0.00	$3,000.00	$0.00	$3,000.00	$0.00	$3,000.00
16	Sbmt. Sktch Plan, Hyd&Ge	$0.00	$0.00	$0.00	$0.00	$0.00	$0.00
17	DOT Review	$0.00	$0.00	$0.00	$0.00	$0.00	$0.00
18	Revise Sketch Plans	$1,800.00	$1,800.00	$0.00	$1,800.00	$0.00	$1,800.00
19	Submit Revised Sketch Pla	$0.00	$0.00	$0.00	$0.00	$0.00	$0.00
20	DOT Review	$0.00	$0.00	$0.00	$0.00	$0.00	$0.00
21	DOT Approval	$0.00	$0.00	$0.00	$0.00	$0.00	$0.00
22	Public Hearing	$1,200.00	$1,200.00	$0.00	$1,200.00	$0.00	$1,200.00
23	**Final Design**	$0.00	$79,500.00	$0.00	$79,500.00	$0.00	$79,500.00
24	Highway Design and Plan	$22,500.00	$22,500.00	$0.00	$22,500.00	$0.00	$22,500.00
25	Bridge Design and Plan Pr	$57,000.00	$57,000.00	$0.00	$57,000.00	$0.00	$57,000.00
26	75% Submission	$0.00	$0.00	$0.00	$0.00	$0.00	$0.00

Project management software aids project managers in monitoring the expenditure of resources and the progress of projects.

The biggest challenge to those who develop CASE tools is to introduce tools that turn ideas into code. Recently, experts in the field have made great strides in their attempts to realize this dream, and object orientation has played a major role in the effort. Virtually all the new RAD tools are developed to design and build object-oriented applications.

For example, Live Model is used to create business processes and business rules, diagram their relationships, and then allow the user to run them by clicking on the diagrams. The Live Model tool creates objects from the relationships and executes the program on the spot, either in continuous or single-step mode. When the application is ready for production, Live Model users can transfer the resulting objects to a development system for delivery. Live Model combines CASE's ability to diagram business relationships with artificial intelligence to help developers figure out which prepackaged objects to use to generate the executable code on the fly.

PROJECT MANAGEMENT

Like any other organizational efforts, systems development projects must be managed. When management decides to develop a system, it places the responsibility for the effort with a senior executive, often a vice president. The executive nominates a project manager, sometimes referred to as the project leader, who is responsible for the timely execution of the project.

The project manager must first ensure that the necessary resources are available: personnel, funds, and equipment. To do so, he or she selects qualified professionals from the IS department, and sequesters computers and software for the development effort. The project manager then outlines a **project plan** detailing primary and secondary milestones, the personnel dedicated to the different activities, the amount of person-time each activity will consume, and the calendar time by which each milestone should be completed. If software tools and hardware must be purchased, this is incorporated into the plan.

There are several project management methods, the better-known being the Gantt and Project Evaluation and Review Technique (PERT) approaches. A **Gantt chart** represents activities and their start and completion times, but not the relationships among different activities. A **PERT chart** shows events, the activities required to reach the events, and the interdependencies among activities. The events are usually completion milestones.

The advantages of Gantt charts are their simplicity and their linearity. The reviewer can visually sense the length of each activity. The advantage of PERT charts is the communication of interdependencies among activities, so that possible bottlenecks and alternative paths to a complex activity can easily be visualized. Like Gantt charts, PERT charts clearly show parallel processes. However, PERT charts can also show a critical path that must be completed before the project can proceed.

Many project management software packages let planners enter defined activities, events, and times only once, and then present either a Gantt or a PERT chart or both on the computer's monitor. The project manager can then see how changing parameters will alter the charts and completion times. Some

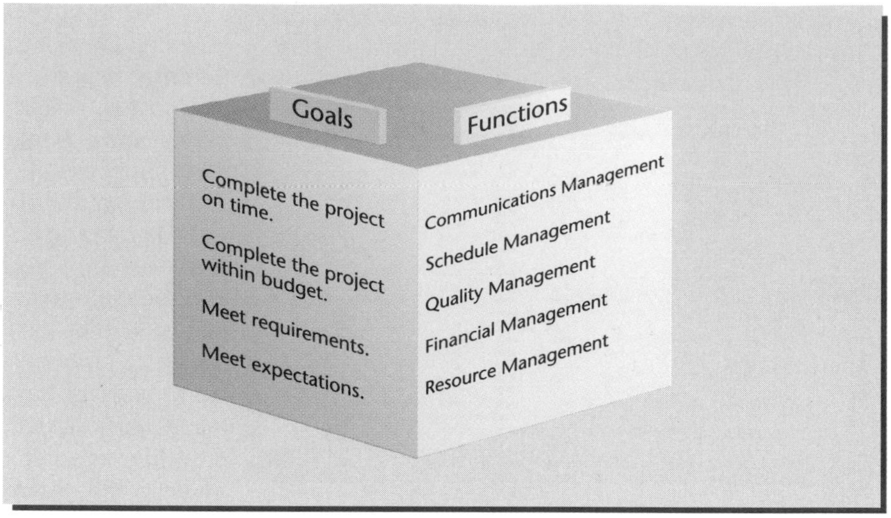

Figure 15.14 *Dimensions of project management*

managers prefer using Gantt charts, some prefer PERT charts, and others use both, for the same projects. The preference depends on the personality of the manager and on presentation needs, rather than on the nature of the project.

It is also the project manager's responsibility to create a budget, keep track of expenses, report to management on budget and time overruns, foresee and forestall mishaps, and ask for additional monies and time well in advance of actual need. Large project teams are often considered a separate reporting unit, similar to profit centers. While they do not expect any income, they must be conscientious about their expenses.

As discussed before, a project is more manageable when broken into smaller modules. Therefore, the project manager defines logical modules and assigns them to small groups of systems analysts and programmers, as was described in Figure 15.5. **Modular project management** is similar to modular systems development. It allows each group to concentrate on its assignments, often in parallel with other groups' tasks, and if a problem occurs in one of the modules, it is isolated and dealt with immediately without impacting other modules.

While project planning is done top-down, systems components are built bottom-up. When the different submodules are completed, they are integrated into one whole module; and when the modules are completed, they are integrated into a whole IS.

The project manager monitors the progress of each group through periodic meetings and reports. To ensure compatibility and coordination, the manager gathers all the group leaders periodically to report on the group's accomplishments, so all the leaders are aware of the overall progress of the project.

PROJECT MANAGEMENT GOALS

As Figure 15.14 indicates, the project manager is responsible to the customer, whether an internal department or an external client, for the following goals:

◆ *Complete the project on time.* The customer expects to receive the system within a predetermined period of time. If time overruns are expected, the project manager should notify the customer ahead of time and explain the reasons.

| Project Bridge Modeler - EXAMPLE.PBM - [Evaluate] |
| File Edit View Setup Operations Method Window Help |

| | What-If | Cost Benefit | Adjustments |

Apply What-If

Technique		Experience		Project Assumptions		Choice	
Project Size (Hours)		10,000		Cost Per Hour		50.00	
Selected Percentages		What-If		Hours Per Day		8.00	

Current WBS	Planning Stage	Std %	User %	Calc %	What If %	Work Effort (Hours)	Cost	Duration
PROJECT PLANNING A	Started	2	2	2	5	500	31,250	40
BUSINESS SYSTEM DE	Detail	34	34	34	40	4,000	250,000	313
TECHNICAL DESIGN A	Summary	50	50	50	40	4,000	250,000	313
INSTALLATION	Summary	14	14	14	15	1,500	93,750	118
Total For Project						10,000	625,000	784

Calculating work effort, cost, and duration estimates.

Used by permission from ABT Corporation

Cost estimation is an important element in project planning and management.

◆ *Complete the project within the budget.* Managing the project budget is as important as managing the technical aspects of systems development. As with time overruns, budget overruns must be communicated and immediately explained to top management. If budget overruns entail a request for changing the price to the client, the new estimate and its consequences must be explained.

◆ *Meet requirements.* The developers must ensure that the new system complies with the requirements specified at the beginning of the project.

◆ *Meet expectations.* Beyond the mere compliance with stated requirements and technical specifications, the new system must meet the users' expectations, even if those expectations exceed the work agreed upon. If the users' expectations are not met, they will tend not to use the system. Even the best system is a failure when not used.

PROJECT MANAGEMENT FUNCTIONS

To achieve these goals, project management should consist of the following functions:

◆ *Communication management.* The project manager must ensure that plans, techniques, resources, and objectives are well communicated to all team members. This is done through periodic meetings, circulars, and briefings. Communication should also be maintained with the client. Communicating with the client will achieve an important goal: making the client a participating owner of the project. **Project ownership** allows the client to give the developers feedback on parts of the project that have been completed, and reduces the gap between expectations and reality.

A LOOK INTO THE FUTURE ▶

The Future of Programming

How will the work of systems analysts and programmers change in the near and distant future? The trend of increasingly efficient systems development will continue, but how far can it go? In the past, with each new generation of programming language, coding became more efficient and easier to learn. Looking to the future, the use of increasingly powerful CASE tools, object-oriented programming (OOP), and virtual reality (VR) in systems development will continue to improve coding efficiency by further automating the coding process. OOP and VR may also create a new market: objects for sale. As more and more programmers use OOP, the reusable modules that are created will represent an ever-growing library of objects, which many companies can then offer for sale, mainly through the Internet.

Here is how the system might work. Software companies will file their objects with a master virtual library on the Internet with a VR interface that allows programmers to travel through the library and view the collection. A software house will connect its code generators to these libraries. Programmers would wear goggles and VR gloves to travel the "stacks," picking and reassembling previously written code modules into new systems. Perhaps they'll see a large console with buttons identifying different objects. "Pressing" a button will bring up a full description of how the object functions and a short history of how it has been used in other applications. Other buttons might appear on the console, allowing the programmer to view the object code, and to integrate it into code already developed or assembled. Another option might allow the programmer to run the code on a sample of data. Special software will track the downloading of objects, and charge the user's accounts electronically.

(continued)

◆ *Schedule management.* The project manager ensures that milestones are met on time, to avoid time overruns. Schedule management is carried out by using Gantt, PERT, and other techniques, as explained above.

◆ *Quality management.* Tests and re-tests must be performed to guarantee quality. For instance, in the system's construction phase, programmers should look for every possible bug in the code, which must be robust and meet client expectations. A good approach is for the code to be tested twice: once by the developers, and again by the prospective users. The latter tests also support client project ownership.

◆ *Financial management.* When the project is large, there is a special person or group of people who manage the project's budget and report to the project manager. Members of the project team should be allowed to incur only those costs (labor, materials, and overhead expenses) that are pertinent to the project, all of which should be recorded.

◆ *Resource management.* The project manager must allocate resources, including personnel, hardware, and software tools, in an optimal manner. Qualified personnel are matched with the best hardware and software for their assigned jobs.

More sophisticated VR systems might allow a systems analyst to use the VR glove to select data flow diagram (DFD) symbols from a menu, and create a DFD specifying processes and possibly structures of databases in virtual reality. When the most detailed level of a DFD or a portion of it is ready, the analyst might select the "generate code" option from a menu, to instruct the system to generate code.

This type of VR system will further blur the lines—already quite blurred—between systems analysts and programmers. Systems analysts will no longer hand down specifications for programmers to use to develop code, because systems will generate the code for them.

Development time is not the only savings offered by the combination of OOP and VR. Maintenance will become significantly easier and less time-consuming as well. Analysts might wear VR gear to modify the code, bringing up the DFD of an application from a library, pointing and clicking symbols (for process, data store, and the like) to be modified. When the analyst finished changing the specifications, the old code could be automatically replaced with new system-generated code. Again, the analyst would be able to test the modified application on a sample of data. In addition to saving time, we should expect applications of better quality.

Some observers do not expect the future of systems development to be so rosy. Regardless of what happens, there will always be work for programmers.

THINK CRITICALLY

If the writing of code is expected to be so easy, why is it also expected that we will need the services of systems analysts and programmers?

To fulfill these functions, managers support their work with project management software packages. Some of the more popular packages include Estimacs, Spectrum/Estimator, Project Workbench, Project Manager, and Microsoft Project. The packages help outline activities and help estimate the resources required. The latter function is especially useful because of the tendency of many projects to overrun the budget.

SYSTEMS DEVELOPMENT LED BY END USERS

Before 1980, the users' role in systems development ended in the formulation of requirements, at which point they were practically disconnected from the development effort, which was carried out by IS professionals. In the 1980s, prototyping promised more user involvement because users were polled for their input throughout the project. But they still did not lead IS development projects.

In the 1990s, a new phenomenon started to take root: users assuming a greater role in *leading* organizational IS development projects. These are not small systems developed by the users for their own use, but large organizational systems for use across business units. **Systems development led by users (SDLU)**

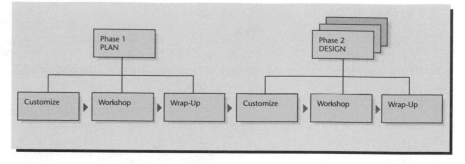

Figure 15.15 *The six steps of JAD*

reflects the view that users, not systems analysts, programmers, or information service organizations are responsible for their ISs. The concept reinforces the users' ownership of their new systems. SDLU's benefits are (1) better design, (2) an increased willingness by business units to use the system, and (3) a more favorable attitude toward computer-based systems in general. But SDLU requires that business leaders have at the very least a basic understanding of ISs.

Users as Leaders

A survey of IS managers and executives of 77 companies was conducted at Drake and Auburn Universities, and reported in the August 1994 *Journal of Systems Management.* The results indicated that 59% of the companies studied granted users voting or leadership responsibilities during program development; one company in seven placed users in positions of leadership on the requirement team; and one in 11 placed users in positions of leadership on the program development team. The researchers were surprised by the high rate of SDLU[1]. It is doubtful that users will be leaders of many large-scale systems development projects, because they lack the technical expertise. But we may see a greater number of users on the leadership team.

JAD: An Example of User-Led Systems Development

In the 1980s, IBM developed **joint application development (JAD)**, a method to be used in SDLU. The method is an alternative to the SDLC, but doesn't skip thorough analysis, as prototyping often does. While the traditional SDLC is sequential and lengthy, JAD facilitates analysis and design by involving representatives of the prospective users in all of the phases (not only in the requirements definition step, as does the SDLC) and by using prototyping wherever possible. (It is, however, more systematic than applying prototyping alone.)

As shown in Figure 15.15, JAD uses a six-step process to take the team through the project's two phases: planning and design. Each of the two phases consists of three steps: customize, workshop, and wrap-up.

In the first phase of JAD, management appoints a team to determine what the new system must do, what business process to use in managing the new system, how big the new system should be, and the overall time frame for the project.

---

[1] Dodd, J.L., Houston, H.C., "Systems Development Led by End-users: An Assessment of End-user Involvement in Information Systems Development," *Journal of Systems Management*, August 1994, p. 34.

The customer-led team creates specifications in a workshop setting, in a facilitated manner. The team includes an executive sponsor, a team leader, IS team members, customer team members who are usually cross-functional, experts who are part-time members as needed, a facilitator who is not necessarily an IS person, and a recording secretary, referred to as a scribe. Usually, this phase involves members of senior management who do not participate in subsequent phases.

The second phase, JAD design, determines how the system will work. The results of these team sessions are: business flow diagrams, data groups, data dictionaries, screens and reports, edit and validation criteria, interfaces, and processing routines. Since many members of the team are people who will actually use the new system, a strong emphasis is placed on developing a design that satisfies the specific requirements of the users. Prototyping is heavily used in designing the system, especially screens, forms, files, and the like, to provide the customer with an idea of how the system will "feel."

Individual executives for Chrysler Corporation, an enthusiastic adopter of the JAD method, have explained that the workshops are usually well structured, that they facilitate meetings, and that they are conducted for two or three full days, off-site, with participants in casual dress. The participants have found these sessions interesting. The following factors have been identified as critical to successful use of JAD:

◆ All participants must be committed to the JAD process.

◆ The customer and IS people must mutually agree on the project's scope.

◆ The sponsor must be supportive and involved.

◆ JAD team members must be empowered decision makers.

◆ Business objectives must be clearly defined.

◆ Business processes must be understood.

◆ Team members must be able to meet two or more days per week.

◆ Members must be committed to the team.

Proponents of the JAD method cite the following advantages:

◆ JAD speeds up the development process by shortening the time required to gather requirements and resolve business issues.

◆ JAD increases customer commitment, confidence, and involvement, while improving communication and design quality.

◆ There is increased commitment to the process because the IS unit and the customers are partners, each with a vested interest in the project.

◆ The resulting system costs less than one developed in a traditional SDLC.

While the system has few disadvantages, it does require the ability of participants to dedicate significant amounts of time, which is often challenging to schedule.

SYSTEMS INTEGRATION

Firms now must wrestle with highly distributed, heterogeneous environments populated with applications for special tasks which cannot be accessed by systems used for other tasks. Often, the disparate systems cannot "talk to each other" because they run on different operating systems (or, as IS professionals say, on "different platforms").

Much of what systems analysts do is systems integration, rather than the more traditional analysis and development of a standalone IS. **Systems integration** takes a look at the information needs of an entire organization or, at least, of a major division of it. The analysts consider the existing, but often disparate, ISs, and then produce a plan to integrate them so that (1) data can flow more easily among different units of the organization, and (2) users can access different types of data via a single interface. Consequently, many IS service companies call themselves "systems integrators."

Systems integration is far more difficult than systems development. In fact, systems development is regarded as a subspecialty of systems integration. This is because the integrator must also be a developer of systems with an understanding of how data maintained in disparate systems can be efficiently retrieved and used for effective business processes.

For example, marketing managers can have richer information for decision making if they have easy access to accounting and financial data through their own marketing IS. The better the integration, the better they can incorporate accounting and financial information into their marketing information.

Systems integrators must also be highly versed in hardware and software issues, because different ISs often use hardware and software that are incompatible with each other. Often, overcoming incompatibility issues is one of the most difficult aspects of integration.

For instance, consider the failure of the CONFIRM system. The system was meant to integrate several ISs, to enable airlines, hotel chains, and rental car firms to record reservations and use a decision support system (DSS) that would analyze the data collected from customers in a large database. The integrator was AMR/IS, American Airlines IS services' sister company. The clients (in addition to American, which would also use the system) were Hilton, Marriott, and Budget Rent-A-Car. AMR/IS's personnel were working to integrate the large databases with a DSS for a comprehensive travel and lodging IS, but the integrators failed to detect problems that made the two components incompatible. When the problem was identified, it was too late to repair the system unless much of it was scrapped. At that point, after spending $125 million and three and a half years, the clients decided to cancel the project.

Not surprisingly, the parties in the consortium established for the project accused each other of miscommunicating their ideas. This emphasizes the need for excellent communications skills on the part of the system integrator, and for a good understanding of the client's business needs now and in the future.

Inland Steel: On Time and Within Budget

Is development projects often overrun their budgets and timetables. This is certainly true of large-scale projects involving millions of dollars. But Inland Steel, a Chicago company that is the sixth largest steel maker in the U.S., with $4.6 billion revenue in 1996, showed that with careful planning and skillful management, even such major projects can be completed on time and within budget.

In 1992, management decided to develop a new order fulfillment system to achieve several objectives: reduced headcount, improved customer service, higher product quality, and more manufacturing and customer information. Inland embarked on an extensive re-engineering effort to redesign 18 business processes. The new system was intended to integrate ISs more tightly with business processes, giving managers better and more timely information for several purposes: market forecasting, tracking shipping, and handling more customer orders.

One problem with the old system was what is referred to as "islands of automation." For example, manufacturing units did what they could to optimize their functions, and so did sales, but manufacturing and sales did not share information. This caused discrepancies in order requests and delayed deliveries. The new order fulfillment system (OFS) was designed to solve these problems.

This was not Inland's first attempt to develop such a system. Previous attempts failed because (1) top management was not committed to the effort, (2) the effort focused on technology rather than on business needs, and (3) proper funding was not provided. This time, the failures served as good lessons. Management supported the project fully.

Vice president of IT William Howard was very methodical with his plans. He first invited one of the leading management consulting firms, McKinsey & Co., to map Inland's management and organization and pinpoint the weak points. A year later, in 1993, he called in Andersen Consulting, another leading management consulting firm, to help manage the project. Another firm, USX Engineers and Consultants, was hired to bring in its experience of a similar, successful project at Inland's sister company, U.S. Steel Group.

Howard assembled a team of business and IT managers to monitor the project, from analysis, through design, to implementation. He carefully divided the effort into discrete business processes. He planned three implementation phases: sales, operations planning, and manufacturing. The purpose was to minimize risk by proceeding one step at a time. The team members were each assigned to one of 18 business processes. Their charge was to review the processes with a theme of "plan, do, check, and act." They met and submitted progress reports regularly. This kept both the business units and the IT professionals on budget and on time. System features such as order cycle time were measured whenever a module was complete, to ensure compliance with requirements.

One of the greatest threats to large-scale development projects like this is scope creep. **Scope creep** happens when original requirements change often, until the original budget and timetable can no longer be met. Indeed, Inland's business units submitted more than 500 change requests. But the team considered each request carefully, and approved only two dozen of them. These few requests had to be accommodated because otherwise the developed system would have failed. As a result of this strict policy, the original budget and timetable were kept (except for one module, which was completed three months later than planned).

The development of the new system was a formidable task. A full year, 1993, was devoted to feasibility studies and design. From January 1994 to November 1996, seven million lines of code were written, and a sum of $37 million was expended. In all, the project team involved 200 specialists who worked 400 staff-years. The developers created a data warehouse to store customer information, and built 27 integrated applications that supported the 18 re-engineered processes.

The results were impressive. The cycle time of customer order entry was reduced by 84%; manufacturing cycle time was reduced by 24%; production recording errors were reduced by 7.1%; and the invoice cycle time (shipping to invoice time) was reduced from 3.9 days to 1.2 days. All this resulted in (1) a one-time saving of $25 million through revenue enhancement, cost savings, and working capital reduction, and (2) an annual benefit of $9 million.

Source: Caldwell, B. "Taming the Beast," InformationWeek, March 10, 1997, pp. 38–48.

Questions:

1. What were the elements that helped this project to succeed? List and explain them.

2. Was the project carried out in a sequential or parallel manner?

Explain. How did this help the project to succeed?

3. Did the execution of this project follow the SDLC approach or prototyping? Why was that so crucial for the success of this type of system?

Hold Your Breath and Flick the Switch

Quantum Corp. is one of the world's largest manufacturers of hard disks, with $4.4 billion in annual sales. The company took an approach that few companies are willing to try, when moving to a new IS. On April 26, 1996, the company literally stopped all its operations. Every business system at its headquarters in Milpitas, California, and its branches throughout the world, was down. For eight consecutive days, the company could not accept a customer order, could not receive raw materials, could not bill a customer, and could not post a cash receipt. Why? Quantum was switching from an old IS to a new one in all of its operations in 25 locations around the globe.

The company realized it needed a new global IS as early as 1992, but this need became even more apparent in 1994, when Quantum purchased Digital Equipment Corp.'s storage devices business. With the purchase, Quantum inherited Digital's financial and Manufacturing Resources Planning (MRP) ISs, and other systems that could not communicate with each other. The company's sales representatives and business managers were not able to use real-time

financial data across the company. Quantum's sales representatives had to collect information manually, using phone, fax, and e-mail, which usually took up to four days. The result was inferior performance, according to Mark Jackson, an executive vice president for the company.

The company wanted to become a leader in customer service, but could not do so as long as its personnel could not figure out how many units of an ordered product were available. This problem was exacerbated by the fact that the company operates in the Americas, Europe, and Asia. If a customer in Asia was promised so many units of a certain product, sales representatives in North America might have promised the same units to a customer in the U.S. The company needed an IS that would guarantee a situation of available-to-promise (ATP). With ATP, a salesperson anywhere could secure promised products so that other representatives would know the units were committed, and would not promise them to another customer.

Most companies avoid a cutover approach to converting from an existing IS to a new one, because the approach is regarded as too risky. But Jackson said that it would be risky for his company *not* to do it this way. "We *had* to do a big bang," he said. Considering what the new system does for the company, he might be right. The system takes an order, schedules it to be delivered anywhere in the world, and confirms delivery immediately. Since it involves several business areas, such as materials ordering, inventory management, and product delivery, Quantum's management felt that the entire application had to run, for the system to fulfill its mission.

The company's CIO, Hank Delavati, feels that a cold turkey approach is actually less risky than the phased approach. He reasons that when a company installs one module at a time, it must build each module with an appropriate interface and test it with the other components of the old system. Only then can the module go live. When all the new modules are developed and implemented, the interface software is discarded, and the company finds itself having expended resources on software that it does not use, creating a waste of time and money. In addition, in phased conversion, not all of the prospective users are involved in a coordinated effort.

In a phased conversion, he said, an organization has to shut down every department and site where a new module is implemented for a day or two. With so many departments and sites, the cumulative shutdown time would exceed a week. There was also the fear that with a prolonged conversion process, individual departments might be impatient and resort to their own locally adopted applications. An IS management consultant observed that Quantum was a rather flat organization that was not tightly controlled. In such an environment, he said, it would be difficult for top management to secure commitment to a new enterprise-wide IS, and therefore, a do-it-all-at-once conversion was required.

But it was not only the conversion method that contributed to the project's success. In the summer of 1994, top management nominated a steering committee chaired by a person who later became the CEO. The committee comprised managers from different functional areas: sales, manufacturing, purchasing, finance, logistics, and ISs, and consultants from a large management consulting firm. A project management team with representatives from 16 business units was assembled to monitor the development project. The project team consisted of 100 key employees from different departments, and of IS professionals.

After the new system was tested, a massive training effort started. Employees were taken off their jobs for two to four weeks to be trained. They had to pass tests before returning to their jobs. Managers could not receive their employees back for any reason before training was over. Management conducted a large awareness campaign. It informed all of the employees about the soon-to-be-implemented system through meetings, presentations, posters, brochures, and an intranet, and emphasized the importance of the system.

On May 3, 1996, after all the old data were converted for the new system, a few programmers ran samples of transactions. There were no mishaps. On May 5, 1996, the new system was up and running without a glitch. About 750 users use the new system in 25 locations around the globe. Now, Quantum representatives can give customers information on delivery dates within minutes instead of days.

Source: Radosevich, L. "Quantum's Leap," CIO, February 15, 1997, pp. 40–46.

Questions:

1. List and explain all the reasons that justified a cold turkey conversion.

2. What were the factors contributing to the successful implementation of the new IS? List them and explain.

Petroleum Firm Relies on CASE

When your business grows a thousandfold in 20 years, you do not have much time to mess around with COBOL. That is why Global Petroleum Corp. has made a major commitment to computer-aided software engineering (CASE) tools and high-level languages. Global, a closely held energy distributor, has grown from a $3 million regional company in 1973 to a $3 billion giant. Yet Global has an information systems staff of only four people.

The secret? Use productivity tools, contract out for expertise, and do not reinvent the wheel. "We automate the stuff that ought to be automated," said data processing director Jim Shelton. "And," he said, "we're good."

Global employs its staff sparingly. The data center manager who supports a Unisys Corp. A6 mainframe and Micro A workstation also supports the 80 local area network users at headquarters. There are just two programmers, and Shelton doubles as database administrator and occasional programmer.

Key to Global's productivity is a commitment to buying what it can and developing new systems entirely in high-level languages. One of its bread-and-butter applications, an inventory system that gets the bulk of new development work, was built in Unysis's Linc 4GL. The system turns out more than 150 reports and 100 screens, and accesses two external databases for real-time reporting.

Accounts payable and general ledger packages were purchased off the shelf. Global's only major homegrown COBOL application is a 20-year-old accounts receivable system that is maintained using an ad hoc report writer called EZSpec. The product provides a checkoff approach for specifying data fields, criteria, and sort orders. "I can probably do in five minutes using EZSpec what used to take two to three hours in COBOL," said Martha Thayer, Global's manager of technical support. "If it's not what I want, I can easily change it and generate the report again."

Under its best-of-breed philosophy, the IS department also chose Progress Software Corp.'s Progress 4GL in 1990 to build a Unisys CTOS application for its traders. As the size of the application grew, Global migrated it to UNIX, a conversion made easier by Progress's portability.

For most of Global's projects, the tools of choice are Linc and the Linc Systems Approach, a methodology designed around the Linc tool set. "We looked at several alternatives to Unisys but found that the other CASE tools aren't as well integrated," Shelton said.

Global's processing load is not very transaction-oriented, but it involves a steady stream of report requests from users. Using a joint application development approach and the Linc tool set, the department's two programmers can turn around most reports in a day or two, Shelton said. IS staff members can produce mock-up reports using Linc screen painters to give users a quick preview of the applications they request.

The Unisys environment is particularly well adapted to quick artistry, Shelton explained. For example, he handled a recent change request that required adding several database fields and application screens by dialing in from home and making the change over the weekend. When the company expanded a product code from three to four digits last year, the staff first ran an impact report to identify the more than 80 reports and 50 screens that would have to change, and then made all the changes in ten days. Shelton estimated that the process would have taken six weeks or more using conventional programming.

"Our primary focus is to make the application do what it's supposed to do," he said. "The Linc system generates code as efficiently as an average programmer. Maybe I could write code more efficiently, but I couldn't do it anywhere nearly as quickly."

Source: Gillin. P., "Petroleum Firm Relies on CASE," Computerworld, November 23, 1992, p. 63.

Questions:

1. Summarize Global's IS policy. What enables the company to employ only four IS professionals, yet successfully receive all the necessary IS services its staff needs?

2. The company adopted a "best-of-breed" approach to software. Explain it.

3. Global is "committed to productivity." What does this mean in the context of systems development?

4. Why were the Accounts Payable and General Ledger packages not developed, but purchased? What makes this type of system more suitable for purchasing than for developing, in many organizations?

SUMMARY

The development of a new IS is triggered by an opportunity, a problem, or a directive. Modern **systems development** is regarded as a continuation of IS planning. Once a decision to develop is reached, a process begins that consists of **analysis**, **design**, **implementation**, and **support**. Sometimes, the effort is carried out, not to create a new system, but to integrate several existing systems. Such activity is referred to as **systems integration**.

The purpose of **systems analysis** is to determine what need the system will satisfy. Developers interview managers and prospective users to determine business needs. Three **feasibility studies** are performed: technical, economic, and operational. The **technical feasibility study** examines the technical state-of-the-art to ensure that the hardware and software exist to build the system. In the **economic feasibility study**, the benefits of the system are weighed against its cost. The process will continue only if the benefits are expected to outweigh the costs. The **operational feasibility study** determines if the system will fit the organizational culture and be used to full capacity. After these studies comes the **requirements definition**, in which the specific requirements of the systems are defined.

The **system design** consists of **physical** and **logical** arrangements of the system. Tools such as **flowcharts** and **data flow diagrams** are used to create a model of the system. Construction is the actual building of the system, consisting mainly of code writing. **Walk-through** and **simulations** are performed to ensure that the code will work well.

When the system is completed, it is implemented. **Implementation** includes training and conversion from the old system to the new system. **Conversion** can take place by one of several strategies: **parallel**, **phased**, **cold turkey**, or **pilot**. The system cycle does not end here, but continues in the form of **support**. The system is maintained to ensure operability without fault, and satisfaction of changing business needs.

Prototyping is a popular alternative to the traditional system development approach. The developer performs a quick needs assessment and develops a working model that is turned over to the user for evaluation. The users express their criticism, and the developers implement the additional requirements. This process of refinement continues until the users are satisfied. Prototyping saves up to 85% of the development time, and thus much of the cost, but it should be practiced only with relatively small, uncomplicated, unstructured, and uninterfaced ISs.

Systems developers often use **CASE tools** to ease and expedite both design and construction of applications. CASE tools are special programs that help developers build data flow diagrams and flow charts, and plan data dictionaries and database schemas. The availability of increasingly sophisticated and user-friendly CASE tools has increased the popularity of prototyping.

Development of an IS is an effort that requires management of resources and activities. This undertaking is called **project management**. Effective project managers divide the effort into smaller modules that can be handled without interfering with the development of other modules. Project management staffs use tools such as **Gantt** and **PERT** to keep track of resources spent and milestones to be met. The goals of project management are: to complete the project on time and within budget, and to meet the requirements and expectations.

In recent years, a growing portion of the systems development effort has been assigned to users. In some cases, the effort is actually led by users. This increases their feeling of responsibility and ownership. However, the complexity of large projects makes it doubtful that the phenomenon will spread to large-scale ISs.

The importance of meticulous IS development is accentuated when we examine mishaps caused by faulty systems. Utility companies, banks, and many other institutions rely heavily on ISs for their daily operations. Bugs that were unnoticed in the development process may wreak havoc, cause financial damage, and in some cases cause death. Because of the great responsibility of IS professionals, the question of whether certification is needed has come up. If doctors, civil engineers, lawyers, and public accountants are subject to mandatory certification, many people argue, IS professionals should be too.

REVIEW AND DISCUSSION QUESTIONS

1. One of the three reasons for developing a new IS usually comes from outside the organization. What is it? Give three examples.

2. Why is systems development referred to as a "cycle?" What happens when the cycle ends?

3. The modern view of systems development starts with planning. Why?

4. Consider a new chain of shoe stores. The marketing department of the corporation would like to know the customers and their preferences. What questions would you ask before developing an IS for data collection and analysis?

5. The analysis phase of systems development includes fact finding. Suggest ways to find facts, other than the ways mentioned in this chapter.

6. What is the difference between the logical design and physical design of an IS?

7. Systems developers often use the term "application development" rather than "systems development." Why?

8. What is meant by "modular project management?" What are the advantages of the modular approach? Give an example that is not mentioned in this chapter of an IS project and how you would break it down into modules.

9. What are the advantages of data flow diagrams over flowcharting? Can you think of any advantages of flowcharting over data flow diagrams?

10. Of the following professionals, who does the majority of the systems construction job: the CIO, systems analysts, the database administrator (DBA), or the programmer? Why?

11. You are asked to recommend a conversion strategy for a new accounts receivable system. The system will be used only by the comptroller's office. Which strategy will you recommend, and why?

12. What are the advantages of prototyping? What is the main disadvantage?

13. Is management of IS development different from management of other projects? If so, in what sense?

14. What is meant by "user-led systems development?" In what sense is it different from the traditional approach to systems development?

15. An increasing number of IS professionals prefer to call the end users of their creations "customers." Why?

16. *Ethics and Society*: Do you support mandatory certification of IS professionals? Why, or why not? If you do, which IS professionals (analysts, programmers, DBAs) would you require to pass tests? Why?

CONCEPT ACTIVITY

You were hired as an IS consultant by a small chain of stores that rent domestic appliances. Partly because operations are run with paper records, one store does not know what is going on in the other stores. The president of this small company feels that the chain doesn't utilize its inventory efficiently. For example, if a customer needs a lawn mower, and the appliance is not available in store A, the people who serve at the store cannot tell the customer that the mower is available at another outlet, or offer to bring it for the customer from another outlet where it is available. The president would like an IS that would allow the chain to serve the customers better, and to help with tracking and billing too.

List the questions you would ask in your fact-finding effort and indicate who in the organization would be asked each question.

HANDS-ON ACTIVITY

1. Prepare a data flow diagram that communicates the following business scenario:

When a customer approaches the counter at Buggy Car Rental, a serviceperson asks the customer for the details of the desired car. She then checks in a computerized database to see if a car with these features is available. If a car is available, the serviceperson collects pertinent information from the customer (including an imprint of the customer's credit card) fills out a contract, and has the customer sign the contract. The customer is then given a key and is told where to find the car in the parking lot. The serviceperson indicates in the database that the car is no longer available.

If a car with the desired specifications is not available, the serviceperson offers another, available car. The customer either rents it or refuses to rent it.

When the car is returned, the customer pays by check or by charging the credit card, and returns the keys. The serviceperson gives the customer a copy of the signed contract, indicates in the database that the car is now available, and records its new mileage.

2. Prepare a flowchart that describes the following application:

Gadgets, Inc. sells its items through traveling salespeople. When a salesman receives a signed contract from a client, he enters the details into a notebook computer. He later transmits the record to the company's mainframe computer at its headquarters.

The program records the details in four files: Sales, Shipping, Accounts Receivable, and Commission. If the buyer is a new customer (one who is not yet in the customers' database), the program enters the customer's record into the customers' database and generates a thank you letter. The program also calculates the 5% commission, which is recorded in the commission file with the salesman's code.

At the end of the month, the program produces a paper report with the records of all the new customers. In addition, if the total monthly sales of the salesman exceed $100,000, the program generates a congratulatory letter showing that total. If the total is less than $5,000, the program produces a letter showing the total and the sentence: "Try harder next month."

TEAM ACTIVITY

Systems analysts should possess good presentation skills. With the other members of your team, prepare a ten-minute presentation of the information system that the team would design and develop for Buggy Car Rental (see above). Use PowerPoint or other presentation software to prepare the presentation, including data flow diagrams. Each team member should contribute an equitable share of the preparation and the presentation before the class.

EXPLORE THE WEB

Search the Web for CASE tools promoted by commercial organizations, and choose three tools. List the features provided in each of the tools. Assume that the vendors' claims are true. Which would you prefer to use in systems development? Why?

Chapter 16
Alternative Avenues for Systems Acquisition

Not Your Specialty? Outsource!

The move of the health care industry to managed care finds insurance companies setting the rates that doctors, pharmacies, hospitals, and laboratories can charge for services, creating great pressures on hospitals and medical providers to contain costs to remain competitive. One of the primary ways health providers are facing this challenge is through the increased use of information technology. Tenet Healthcare faced just such a challenge when it was created from the merger of two hospital systems comprising 75 acute-care hospitals that together generate $5.5 billion in annual revenue. Tenet would increasingly have to abide by the industry rates, and the only way to do that was to become more efficient. Tenet's challenge was the integration of the original hospitals' systems, each with its own telecommunications network with suppliers and insurance companies, and its own array of information systems. How could Tenet create a system that would contain costs while it successfully merged two systems and managed a huge amount of historical and new data?

"The growth of managed care means the primary decision maker for patients is not the patient or even the doctor. Increasingly, it's the company with whom a patient has signed up for insurance… The ability to provide cost-effective health care is what's most attractive to these insurance providers,"

said Steven Brown, Chief Information Officer for Tenet.

Brown had a good idea of what needed to be done, but Tenet Healthcare Corp. did not have sufficient personnel and the other wherewithal to embark on a new streamlining and systems integration project. Management would not even consider hiring new employees or purchasing the necessary systems development hardware and software, because information systems are not in the company's core of competence. How could Brown revamp the company's information systems without adequate personnel? Outsourcing.

Tenet signed a $250 million outsourcing contract with Perot Systems, which combined the separate computer operations of the two hospitals into a single unified system run from a Dallas center. As an outsourcing vendor, Perot Systems had the expertise, tools, and personnel to do the job immediately. The outsourcing contract covers all nonstrategic projects such as administration, billing, insurance claims, and communications. The health-care provider did not have to increase its IS personnel or invest in any new tools for the integration of its ISs. That left Tenet's 30 IS professionals free to concentrate on areas of strategic importance to the health-care provider.

Source: DePompa, B., "Sharing the Cost of Recovery," *InformationWeek*, September 9, 1996, pp. 146–150.

In-house development of systems using the organization's own staff is only one way to obtain an IS. In this chapter you will learn of other alternatives whereby organizations turn to resources outside their own walls. Some of the concepts have been mentioned in previous chapters, but they are discussed in more depth here and will provide a deeper understanding of systems acquisition.

When you finish this chapter, you will:

♦ Understand the alternatives to in-house system development, including outsourcing, maintaining an IS subsidiary, purchasing ready-made

software, and encouraging users to develop their own applications

♦ Understand the trade-offs inherent in the various methods of acquiring systems

♦ Understand why the alternatives to in-house development have become so popular

♦ Understand what circumstances are best for using each approach

♦ Understand how to evaluate what approach is best for your organization

SOURCES FOR INFORMATION

The past decade has seen several alternatives to the traditional in-house development of custom-made information systems: **Outsourcing**—trusting all or part of an organization's IS operation to an outside company—has become a popular way to manage IT. The IS units of some companies have grown so much that top management has turned them into **IS subsidiaries**, independent corporations that offer services not only to the parent company, but also to other companies. In addition, the proliferation of **prepackaged software** that satisfies increasingly specific business needs offers immediately available suitable applications for many situations. And the ever more sophisticated and easy-to-use **development tools** allow many computer-literate users to develop their own applications.

How do IS managers learn about these alternatives, find out who offers them, and determine which is best suited to their particular needs? The best initial source is trade journals (see Figure 16.1). Articles and advertisements provide huge amounts of information that managers use to start exploring options for acquiring ISs. It is essential that you have some familiarity with these publications to keep up with a constantly changing environment. If your company has decided to develop an IS, how should it choose what development course to take: in-house or outsourced, custom-made or prepackaged? First, it's important to understand the pluses and minuses of each approach and then analyze the needs specific to your company.

OUTSOURCING

In the past, many companies had to develop their own information systems because there was no other way to obtain them. But this is no longer the case. A multitude of companies specializing in IS services provide expertise and economies of scale that no single organization can achieve. In considering whether to develop systems in-house or to outsource their development, top managers should ask the following questions:

1. What are our core business competencies? Of the business we conduct, what are the specialties that we should continue to do by ourselves?

Magazine	Focus	Magazine	Focus
Byte	Hardware	PC World	IBM microcomputers and clones
CIO	IS management issues	MacUser	Macintosh hardware and software
Communications Week	Data communications	Mac WEEK	Macintosh hardware and software
ComputerWorld	General IT, news	MacWorld	Macintosh hardware and software
Computer Shopper	Microcomputer hardware and software tips	Network World	Data communications, news-oriented
InfoWorld	The IT industry, general IT	PC Computing	IBM and compatible software, PC software
Datamation	General IT, management issues	PC Magazine	IBM microcomputers and clones, PC software
DBMS	Database management tools	PC Week	IBM microcomputers and clones, PC software
InformationWeek	General IT, news		

Figure 16.1 *Major information systems magazines*

2. What do we do outside of our specialty that could be done better for us by organizations that do specialize in that area?

3. Which of our activities could be improved if we created an alliance with other organizations?

4. Which of our activities should we work to improve internally?

Many companies have come to realize that IT is not their core competence, and should not be a focus of their efforts. In addition, the fast developments in IS technology require more and more expertise unavailable within many organizations. A growing number of businesses turn to IS companies not just for specific hardware or software purchases, but for long-term IS services: purchasing and maintenance of hardware; development, purchasing, and maintenance of software; installation and maintenance of communications networks; help-desks, and so on.

A growing portion of corporate IS budgets is allocated for purchased service. It is estimated that some $36 billion, constituting 4% of the IS budget of corporate America, was spent on outsourcing in 1997. Even companies that made their reputation by providing hardware and software, such as IBM, Digital, and Unisys, have seen their service sales grow dramatically. The largest IS service providers are IBM, EDS, Andersen Consulting, Computer Sciences Corp., DEC, Unisys, First Data, AT&T, Cap Gemini, and Perot Systems.

Many consulting firms are referred to as **systems integrators**. That is because they possess the expertise to integrate the client's various systems into one enterprise-wide system. Often, these consultants develop some of the interfaced system themselves, or subcontract parts of the project, such as code writing, to other firms.

With this change in business operations, outsourcing has come to mean two different things: (1) a short-term contractual relationship with a service firm to develop a specific application for the organization, and (2) a long-term contractual relationship with a service firm to take over all or some of the IS functions (see Figure 16.2). Here, we will use the term to mean the latter—that is, subcontracting all or major segments of IT services. Sometimes, an organization hires the services of a consulting firm to satisfy its needs only in one specialized segment of IT, such as telecommunications. In other cases, a company outsources distinct segments of its IS needs to different providers, each specializing in its own segment. It is not uncommon for an organization to outsource help-desk services to one company and its hardware support to another.

ADVANTAGES OF OUTSOURCING

Users have started to view outsourcing as a means to offload and better manage risks. But there are additional advantages that make the option attractive:

◆ *Improved cost clarity.* The client knows exactly what the cost of the IS functions will be over the period of the contract, usually several years. This allows for better financial planning.

◆ Application development and software maintenance
◆ Hardware purchasing and hardware maintenance
◆ Telecommunications installation and maintenance
◆ Help-desk services
◆ Web site design and maintenance
◆ Staff training

Figure 16.2 *Outsourced IS services*

◆ *Reduced license and maintenance fees.* Professional IS firms often pay discounted prices for CASE tools and other resources based on volume purchases; they can pass on these savings to their clients.

◆ *User concentration on core business.* Letting outside experts manage IT frees executives from managing an IS business. They can thus concentrate on the company's core business—including developing and marketing new products—which only they can attend to.

◆ *Shorter implementation cycles.* IS firms can usually complete a new application project in less time than an in-house development team, thanks to their experience with development projects of similar systems for other clients.

◆ *Reduction of personnel and fixed costs.* In-house IS salaries and benefits are paid whether or not IS staff is being productive. Capital expenditures include expensive CASE tools. IS firms, on the other hand, spread their fixed and overhead costs (office space, furnishings, and the like) over many projects and many clients.

◆ *Access to highly qualified know-how.* Outsourcing allows clients to tap one of the greatest assets of an outside IS firm: experience through work with many clients in different environments.

◆ *Ongoing consulting as part of standard support.* Most outsourcing contracts allow client companies to consult them for all types of IS advice that would otherwise be unavailable (or only available from a highly paid consultant).

◆ *Increased security.* An experienced IS service firm is more highly qualified to implement control and security measures than the client company.

One might expect that the less information-intensive businesses would be most likely to outsource their information needs. But a growing chunk of the service sector does so as well. A 1994 survey by Mentis Corp. revealed that 42% of America's banks use an outside party to run their primary applications, such as deposit and loan accounting and general ledger processing. Not surprisingly, the smaller the bank, the more likely it is to outsource its operations, as Figure 16.3 indicates.

Net Notes

The Outsourcing Institute, a professional association and executive network for independent information and expertise on the strategic use of outside resources, maintains a Web site at *http://www.outsourcing.com.* You may find information there on strategic outsourcing of IS services and products as well as other services.

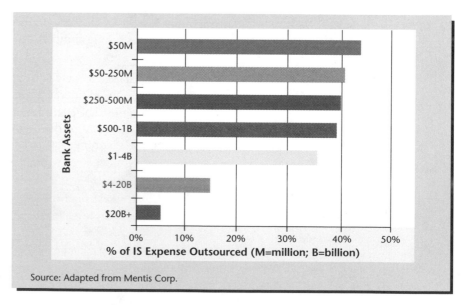

Source: Adapted from Mentis Corp.

Figure 16.3 *Percentage of outsourcing as a function of bank size*

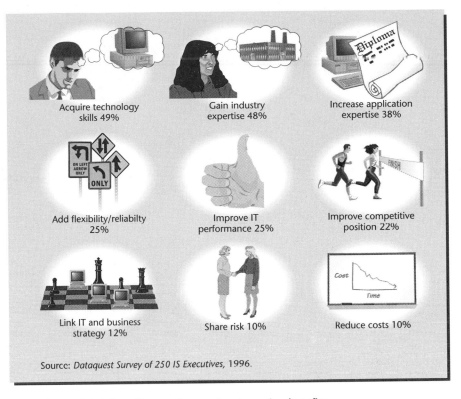

Acquire technology skills 49%

Gain industry expertise 48%

Increase application expertise 38%

Add flexibility/reliabilty 25%

Improve IT performance 25%

Improve competitive position 22%

Link IT and business strategy 12%

Share risk 10%

Reduce costs 10%

Source: *Dataquest Survey of 250 IS Executives*, 1996.

Figure 16.4 *How IS executives rank outsourcing benefits*

Adopting a ready-made business application may work for one company, but that does not mean that it will work for every company. It's all a matter of context, as the Perrier Group, the bottled water subsidiary company of Nestlé, learned the hard way in 1997. Perrier's parent company, Nestlé, uses a popular client/server application called R/3. A large and intricate package sold by a German company, SAP, R/3 is used by Nestlé to address business processes, from sales, through manufacturing, to inventory management, to billing. So the Perrier subsidiary tried to adopt the same software into its operation, spending one year to modify the software to deal with some problems very specific to Perrier that the software does not address—all to no avail. The CIO was let go. An executive said: "Our IT department has been decimated by our attempt at instituting [the system] and our failure to do so."

Source: Stein, T., "IT Stalls at Xerox, Perrier," *Information Week*, March 31, 1997, p. 20.

You may have noticed that cost savings is only one reason for outsourcing. In fact, studies show that saving money is not the most common reason for seeking other companies' services. As Figure 16.4 shows, other benefits, such as access to technological skills and industry expertise, are more important to IS executives than cost savings.

DISADVANTAGES AND RISKS OF OUTSOURCING

Despite its popularity, outsourcing is not a panacea and should be considered carefully before it is adopted. There are conditions under which organizations should avoid this option. For instance, while offering many advantages, outsourcing arrangements contain some risks that must be managed. In addition, some relatively simple issues are frequently ignored or forgotten when arranging for outsourcing, resulting in inflated costs, reduced availability, and unpleasant surprises. Other disadvantages that must be considered include the following:

◆ *Loss of control.* Most importantly, a company that outsources a major part of its IS operations must realize that it will probably be unable to regain control for a long time. The organization must evaluate the nature of the industry in which it operates. While outsourcing may be a good option in a relatively stable industry, it is highly risky in one that is fast-changing. Although the personnel of the service company may have the necessary IS technical skills, they may jeopardize the business in the long run if they don't know how to adapt to constantly changing business realities.

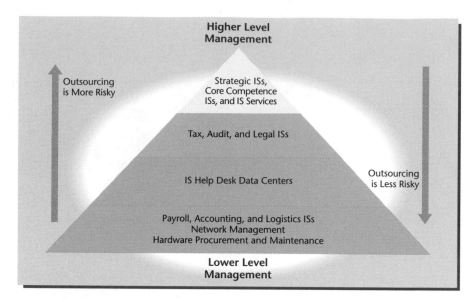

Figure 16.5 *Risks of outsourcing are higher at higher levels of management*

◆ *Loss of experienced employees.* Outsourcing often involves transferring hundreds, or even thousands, of the organization's employees to the IS service company. For example, when Xerox outsourced many of its IS functions to EDS in 1994, about 2,000 of Xerox's employees became EDS employees. As part of Total Petroleum's agreement with Cap Gemini, an IS service company, 53 employees of Total's 55-person IS department became employees of Cap Gemini. The organization that absorbs the workers can usually employ them with lower overhead expenses than their former employer, and use their skills more productively. The outsourcing party gets rid of this overhead cost, but also gives up well-trained personnel. Some people feel that this transfer compromises the company's ability to gain new expertise from outsourcing.

◆ *Risks of losing a competitive advantage.* Innovative ISs, especially those planned to give their owners a competitive advantage, should not be outsourced. Outsourcing the development of strategic systems is a way of disclosing trade secrets. Although confidentiality agreements can reduce the risk, risk remains nonetheless. A competitor may hire the service company to build an IS for the same purpose, thereby potentially eliminating the organization's advantage. In addition, assuming that these systems incorporate new business or technical concepts, IS service firms will bring less than their usual level of experience—and therefore fewer benefits—to the project. Viewed in one way, outsourcing strategic or core business ISs is more risky than outsourcing the routine tasks of operational ISs (see Figure 16.5).

THE INFORMATION SYSTEMS SUBSIDIARY

Some large companies—such as Boeing, Dun & Bradstreet, and AMR (American Airlines' parent company)—own IS subsidiaries, so they have IS services at their disposal while avoiding the direct burden of maintaining an in-house IS

When organizations outsource their IS function, they almost always transfer all (or many of the) IS staff to the IS service firm, except for a skeletal contingent that remains with the company. Now, the IS firm employs the staff, which often still uses the same offices. Thus, the only thing that changes is the company logo that appears on the employees' pay checks. In one case, the employees came full circle. When Mutual of New York (MONY) signed an outsourcing contract with Computer Sciences Corp. (CSC) in 1994, CSC absorbed MONY's 250 IS professionals. But when the seven-year $210 million contract was terminated in 1997, all 250 employees returned to MONY.

Source: Caldwell, B., "MONY Pulls out of CSC Outsourcing Deal," *InformationWeek Online News*, May 15, 1997.

organization. IS subsidiaries are IS service companies like any other IT consulting firms, except that they almost always have a primary client: the company that owns them. The creation of an IS subsidiary occurs in one of two ways.

Corporations that make heavy use of IT often see their IS organization grow to a level where it can render services not only to the corporation, but to outside parties as well. To optimize the utilization of overcapacity, management then incorporates the IS organization as an independent subsidiary authorized to render services to any organization. Examples of such evolution are AMR's AMR Information Services, Dun & Bradstreet's Dun & Bradstreet Software Services, and the spin-off of Baxter International's IS division as a separate corporation providing IS consulting services to the health-care industry.

The other option is to purchase an existing firm. Instead of developing a large IS organization that would advance the company into new technologies, General Motors bought EDS, an already thriving consulting company. (In 1996, EDS became an independent corporation, no longer under GM's control.) The larger part of EDS's revenue comes from non-GM clients.

The main advantage to a parent company of having an IS subsidiary is that the parent company has priority over other clients, without having to carry all the overhead costs during its times of low IS demand. The other advantage is the subsidiary's potential to generate more revenue for the parent.

PURCHASED APPLICATIONS

The major part of an investment in a new IS is usually software rather than hardware, so purchasing prepackaged IS software should be the first alternative to consider, long before huge sums of money are spent to develop a system from the ground up.

Unless an IS must be tailored to the uncommon needs of an organization, purchasing a prepackaged system may well be the best option. Software vendors now offer a huge variety of IS applications in business, often including software that can serve even highly specialized businesses. An organization usually already possesses hardware that supports a software infrastructure, thus purchasing a packaged IS is just like purchasing a new business application.

WHY PURCHASE?

When purchasing a software package, the buyer gains several benefits: immediate system availability, high quality, low price, and available support. Immediate availability helps shorten the software **development backlog**, the name for the long list of applications waiting to be developed for a company's various business units. Purchasing software frees the company's IS professionals to develop the systems that must be specifically tailored to its business needs.

High quality is guaranteed partly because the software developing company specializes in this type of products, and partly because the product would not survive the market if it weren't strong enough. Often, large developers distribute prerelease versions of software to be used at companies (referred to in the development process as **beta sites**) that agree to use the application with actual data for several months, then report problems and propose improvements in return for the free software. (The **alpha site** is the developer's facility.) By the time the software is released to the general market, it has been well tested.

Companies that outsource systems development projects take the risks of late completion and ISs that do not fulfill their intended purpose of added productivity. To entice such companies, a systems developer named Cambridge Technology Partners offers the "80-20-20" program. If the new IS is delivered late or does not accomplish measurable, agreed upon productivity gains, the ordering organization receives a discount of 20% off the agreed fixed price. However, if the system is delivered on time and achieves more than the expected productivity gains, the organization pays Cambridge up to 20% above the price, depending on the extent of the extra productivity. Cambridge executives say the most likely candidates for this program are ISs in the areas of sales force automation, logistics, supply chain management, and customer service, where return on investment and business benefits can be measured.

Source: McGee, M.K., "Shared Risks and Rewards," *InformationWeek*, May 19, 1997, p. 122.

Because software companies spread product development costs over many units, the price to a single customer is a fraction of what it would cost to develop a similar application in-house or to hire an outside company to develop it. Also, instead of tying up its own personnel to maintain the software, the buyer can usually purchase long-term service and be notified of new, advanced versions of the application. The majority of software companies provide a telephone number that users can call when they encounter a problem. Often, buyers enjoy a period of three to twelve months of free service.

There are many sources for packaged software, which is available for almost any imaginable application. The largest software vendors in North America include Microsoft, IBM, Computer Associates, Oracle, Novell, Lockheed-Martin, Digital Equipment Corp. (DEC), and Unisys. Although the relative places of some companies have changed in terms of market share, the members of this group remain the main players in the packaged software market.

STEPS IN PURCHASING READY-MADE SOFTWARE

We tend to think of ready-made software in terms of $200 word-processing or spreadsheet applications, but vendors also offer business software packages that cost thousands and hundreds of thousands of dollars. For example, a package may be installed to deal with all the accounting processes of a company, or an MRP II application may be used to run all the inventory and manufacturing processes of the firm, along with its accounts payable and receivable.

When they select a particular software package, companies invest a lot of money and make a long-term commitment to conducting their business in a particular manner. Factors such as difficulty of installation, cost of training, and quality and cost of after-sale service must be considered in addition to the demonstrable quality of the software. Once a company decides that it will purchase a ready-made application, a project management team is formed to oversee system implementation and handle all vendor contact. The project management team has the following responsibilities (see Figure 16.6):

◆ *Problem identification.* This step is similar to the initial inquiry and fact finding step in the systems development life cycle (SDLC), discussed in Chapter 15, "Systems Development." The inquiry results in the identification of gross functional requirements and key integration points with other systems. The report generated often serves as a basis for a **request for information (RFI)** from potential vendors.

◆ *Identifying potential vendors.* On the basis of information in trade journals and previously received promotional material, as well as client references, vendors are identified who offer applications in the domain at hand. In addition to the above sources, the IS people may gather information at trade shows and from other organizations that have used similar technology.

◆ *RFI.* The project manager sends a request for information (RFI) to the vendors identified, requesting general, somewhat informal, information about the product.

◆ *Requirement definition.* The project manager lists a set of functional and technical requirements, and identifies the functional and technical capabilities of all vendors, highlighting the items that are common to both lists, as well as those that are not. The project management team involves the users to ensure that the chosen application will integrate with existing and planned systems.

◆ *RFP.* The team prepares a **request for proposal (RFP)**, a document specifying all the system requirements and soliciting a proposal from each vendor contacted. The response should include not only technical requirements, but a detailed description of the implementation process as well as a timeline and budget that can be easily transformed into a contractual agreement. The team should strive to provide enough detail and vision to limit the amount of precontract clarification and negotiation.

◆ *Proposal review and vendor screening.* The team reviews the RFPs and identifies the most qualified vendors. Vendor selection criteria include functionality, architectural fit, price, services, and support.

◆ *Site visits.* The complexity of the RFP responses may make evaluation impossible without a visit to a client site where a copy of the application is in use. The team should discuss with other clients the pros and cons of the application.

◆ *Vendor selection.* The team ranks the remaining vendors. The selection factors are weighted, and the vendor with the highest total of points is chosen for contract negotiation. Sometimes there are make-or-break factors that must be identified as early as possible in the process, to eliminate vendors that cannot provide the essential service. By now, the team has gathered enough information on the functionality of the various systems. Conceptually, the evaluation can be described as two circles: one for the team's requirements, and the other for the proposed system, as Figure 16.7 on the next page illustrates.

◆ *Benchmarking:* Before finalizing the purchasing decision, the system should be tested using **benchmarking**, which is a codified system of comparing actual performance against specific quantifiable criteria. (Benchmarking is discussed in more detail below).

◆ *Contract negotiation.* The contract should clearly define performance expectations and include penalties if requirements are not met. Special attention should be given to scheduling, budgeting, responsibility for system support, and support response times. Some clients include a clause on keeping the source code in

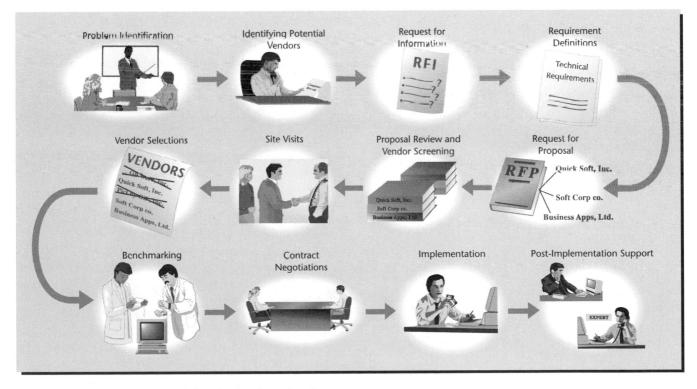

Figure 16.6 *The process of choosing ready-made software*

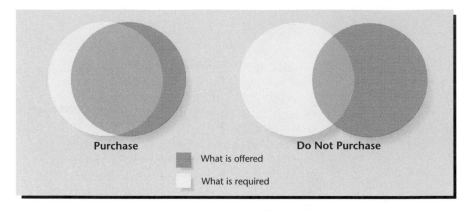

Figure 16.7 *A system should be purchased only if all or most needs are met.*

escrow. If the vendor goes out of business, the client will receive the source code without which the system cannot be maintained. All payments should be tied to completion by the vendor and acceptance of deliverables by the client.

◆ *Implementation*. The new system is introduced in the business units it will serve. Training takes place.

◆ *Post-implementation support*. Vendors expect buyers of their large applications to request extensive on-site **post-implementation support**. Unexpected lapses or unfamiliarity with the system may require fine-tuning, additional training, and/or modification of the software. It is best to develop an ongoing relationship with the vendor. A solid relationship will foster timely service and support.

When choosing a vendor, organizations look for the quality and reliability of the product, but there are additional factors, such as quality of service and support, vendor's support for industry standards, and vendor financial soundness, that are extremely important. A *Datamation* survey lists the priorities of more than 300 polled IS managers and staff (see Figure 16.8). The absolute product quality and reliability stood well ahead of the price/performance ratio.

FACTOR	*RANK* (Scale: 1–10)
Quality and reliability	9.6
Product performance	9.2
Quality of after-sale service and support	8.8
Trustworthiness of vendor	8.2
Price/performance ratio	8.1
Ease of doing business with vendor	7.7
Vendor's support for industry standards	7.6
Openness of future strategies and plans	7.4
Vendor financial stability	7.0

Source: *Datamation*, June 15, 1994, p. 39.

Figure 16.8 *How IS managers rank product purchase factors*

Net Notes

Need to find out in which country a certain Web site resides? The following Web page provides a list of all Internet country codes: *http://www.ics.uci.edu/pub/ websoft/wwwstat/country-codes.txt.*

BENCHMARKING

In addition to being used in the evaluation process, benchmarking is a powerful testing tool used as an ongoing check after a new system is implemented. This codified system of comparing one system's performance to another's uses general performance measurements that are not specific to a particular system. For instance, one benchmark might be the average time required to train someone; another might be a more technical performance measurement, such as the rate of transactions per second, the speed of locating a record in a database, the speed of transferring a file from one computer to another, and the like.

During the purchasing decision-making process, IS professionals in the purchasing organization set certain minimum measurable levels for each performance criterion that the software must meet. The software should be temporarily installed in the organization's computers to be tested against the benchmark before finalizing the purchase, then retested continually after the purchase.

The key to meaningful benchmarking is to measure the identified criteria during typical daily operations, in different combinations and under a wide range of circumstances. This will demonstrate how the system runs in extreme cases of load and pressure. For example, a new client/server system should be tested with the maximum number of users to determine if response time decreases.

There are many methods of benchmarking. But since applications are different, and organizations may use even the same application differently, the best benchmark is one that is tailored by the organization considering the software. Figure 16.9 lists important guidelines for benchmarking.

1. The best benchmark is your own application.

2. If you have standardized on a particular operating system or database management system, write the application first and then use it as a benchmark.

3. If you have an older but similar application you can use as a benchmark, it is the next best thing to testing with the real application.

4. Talk to other users who have tried specific products. Try to find users with applications similar to yours, and see how well these products met their performance requirements.

5. Use standardized benchmarking methods for comparison, not as absolute measures of performance.

6. Keep an eye on your benchmarking budget. An expensive benchmark process may not be worth the cost as hardware prices drop.

7. Compare real systems (the kind you're likely to buy), and not "benchmark specials," which are specially configured to produce the best benchmark results.

8. Keep in mind that performance problems can show up in many parts of a system. For example: in a client/server system, the server's CPU may work satisfactorily fast, but the "clients," may be too slow.

Source: Hayes, F., "More Bang for the Benchmark Buck," *Computerworld Client/Server Journal*, Vol 2 No 1, February 1994, p. 79.

Figure 16.9 *The eight commandments of effective benchmarking*

Computer Use Policies for Employees

Until the early 1980s only professional computer operators had access to information systems, but since then, the increasing numbers of PCs being used in businesses expose more and more people to ISs. U.S. Census Bureau data show that in 1990, 37% of American adults used computers at work. Of people working in the financial, insurance, and real estate fields, 71% used computers (41% were women, and 30% were men). End-user computing encourages workers to use computers to increase productivity, but computers are often used for unproductive, or even destructive, activities. If an employee uses a company car without permission, the act is considered wrong. But if an employee uses a company computer to store private files, is that wrong? Accessing a company's intranet is legitimate and often encouraged. Accessing another employee's file may be wrong. However, some employees may not be aware of the differences. What are the appropriate personal uses of company computers, or are there any? Is the answer to this question already covered in existing laws? Should companies have policies that define the appropriate uses of their IT resources? Do we need new laws to assure a law-abiding workforce? The answers to these questions vary.

The Price of End-User Computing. Risks of increased end-user computing include "futzing," which is discussed in this chapter, as well as more serious undesirable activity. As explained, **futzing** is any unproductive use of computing resources in the work environment, which is a widespread phenomenon in corporate America. Although unauthorized use of computers may be considered theft, authorities usually do not deal with it as such. Perhaps this is why most state statutes usually do not specifically address unauthorized use of computers. There is, however, one exception: California law states that an employee may use an employer's computer services for his or her own purpose without permission if no damage is caused, and if the value of supplies and computer services does not exceed $100.

(continued)

LEARNING FROM EXPERIENCE

It is important to learn from others' experience. After a large company purchased software that had been successfully implemented, its evaluation leader was asked what improvements he would make the next time. He said he would do the following:

◆ Double the number of users on the evaluation team

◆ Obtain more raw information from suppliers early in the process, and force the vendors to give more details about their products, training, consulting services, financing options, and discounts

◆ Hold all vendor demonstrations on the same day, at specific sites, for better comparison

◆ Insist that vendors use scenarios and data supplied by the purchasing company, not by the vendors

◆ Use consultants to help narrow the field to a list of finalist vendors in less time

If someone from outside a company accessed one of the company's computers without authorization and used it for any purpose whatsoever, the act would clearly be criminal under the laws of many countries and of almost every state in the U.S. However, if an *employee* used the same company computer after hours to prepare a homework assignment for a college class, the act may not be considered unethical, let alone criminal, unless the organization has a clear policy against such activity. What about creating a resume or writing a letter, as part of a job search? Without a company policy, the answer to this question is not clear.

Company Policies Work. To avoid misunderstanding, employers should provide clear guidelines stating that any computer use not for the company's direct benefit, without the prior approval of the company, is forbidden. One simple measure that some organizations have taken is to have a written policy that is conspicuously posted, signed by employees upon hiring, or both. The notice could read as follows:

> Company policy forbids any employee, without prior authorization of the employee's supervisor, to (a) access or use any equipment or data unless such access is work-related and required to fulfill that employee's duties, or (b) alter, damage, or destroy any company computer resource or property, including any computer equipment, system, terminal, network, program, software, data, or documentation, including individual employee computer files. Any such act by an employee may result in civil and criminal liability under federal, state, and local laws.

Many companies do not object to recreational or educational use of their computers by employees outside of company time. If this is the case, the policy should say so. Without a policy, companies should not be surprised when their employees' interpretation of reasonable personal use differs from their employers'.

◆ Not divulge to users which product has been selected before the contract is signed, because this undermines the negotiations for better price and terms

◆ Use more multiple-choice questions in the original customer survey, to get more user responses and to make evaluating the responses easier

◆ Ascertain that vendors know that their representatives will meet with real end users

◆ Leverage existing relationships with vendors

Purchasing Risks

Although purchasing a ready-made application is attractive, it has its risks:

◆ *Loose fit between needs and features.* Ready-made software is developed for the widest common denominator of potential user organizations. It may be useful to many, but it will be optimal for few. Companies must take extra care to ensure that ready-made software truly complies with company needs, including organizational culture. Obtaining input from many potential users in the selection process reduces this risk.

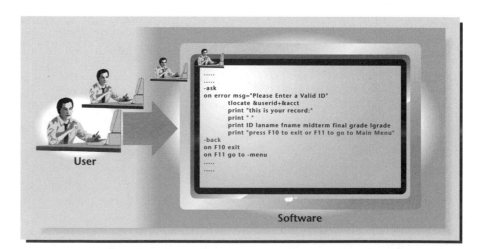

•• POINT OF INTEREST

Long Engagements

Some outsourcing contracts obligate the parties for long times and involve huge amounts of money. In 1996, Swiss Bank Corp. signed a contract with Perot Systems Corp. for 25 years and $6.25 billion. In 1997, the deal was cut down to ten years and $2.5 billion.

Source: "Bank Tweaks Perot Deal," *InformationWeek*, May 19, 1997, p. 122.

◆ *Bankruptcy of the vendor.* If the vendor goes out of business, the purchaser is left without support, maintenance service, and the opportunity to purchase upgrades to an application to which it is committed. Except for checking the financial strength of potential vendors, there is not much the purchaser can do to reduce this risk.

◆ *High turnover of vendor personnel.* Turnover among IS professionals is significantly higher than in other occupations. If a significant number of employees involved in application development and upgrading leave the vendor, support is likely to deteriorate, and upgrades will be of poor quality. Purchasers can do little to reduce this risk.

USER APPLICATION DEVELOPMENT

If an adequate application is not available on the market, or if an organization does not wish to take the risks discussed above, there is another alternative: **user application development**, in which lay users of information systems take part in the effort to write their own business applications. As we discussed in previous chapters, until the early 1980s, computer programs were always developed by professional systems analysts and programmers, but now an increasing number of applications in organizations are developed by their own users. Usually, these are small-scale programs that fit the immediate needs of the individual user, or those of small groups of users.

Figure 16.10 shows how the boundary between users and their software shifts with user application development: whereas users used to know little about the structure of the software underlying a program they interacted with, user application development allows users to do the actual programming.

FACTORS ENCOURAGING USER APPLICATION DEVELOPMENT

As discussed in a number of chapters, several factors led to the shift of development efforts from specialized programmers to users themselves.

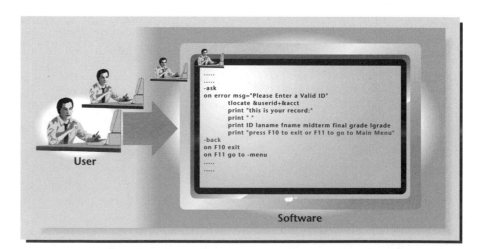

Figure 16.10 *The user has an increasing part in IS development, in user-developed applications*

Used by permission from IBM Corporation

The proliferation of desktop computers in the workplace is a major stimulus in user application development.

THE PROGRAMMING BACKLOG Until the early 1980s, virtually all scientific and business applications were created by professional programmers. The increasing need for ISs caused a great backlog of programming assignments. In some companies, systems that had been approved for development had to wait two or more years until the professional staff started writing code.

As higher-level programming languages emerged, some business units in many organizations decided to allow their own staff to develop applications. Managers encouraged this self-reliance and secured better and better software tools for those employees who welcomed the challenge.

Graphical 4GLs, such as PowerBuilder 5.0 shown here, provide friendly tools for end users to develop their own applications.

THE ADVENT OF PCs Highly centralized mainframe architectures did not offer easy distributed access to business units. At best, procedures dictated a rigid schedule of use by business units other than the data processing department. The data processing staff did not encourage direct access to computing resources.

All this changed with the proliferation of PCs in businesses. Users were no longer dependent on a mainframe, but owned their own computing resource. This, coupled with friendlier software development tools, encouraged many lay users to experiment with application development.

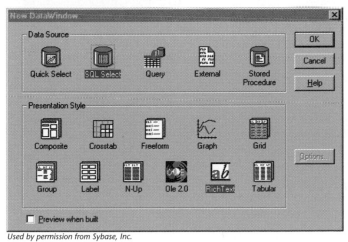

Used by permission from Sybase, Inc.

THE EMERGENCE OF 4GLs PCs alone could not solve the programming backlog problem. Easy-to-use programs like electronic spreadsheets encouraged users to do a little programming through the use of macros. Friendly versions of third-generation languages like BASIC also contributed to self-reliance. But the greatest encouragement came from 4GLs and application generators. These tools are easy to learn, and the new knowledge can be put to use within days.

A LOOK INTO THE FUTURE ▶

Announcements of our Demise have been Greatly Exaggerated

Some 20 years ago, an IS expert predicted: "In less than a decade there will be very little demand for programmers. The market will be flooded with packaged software. No business will need to have its applications specially developed. Everybody, both organizations and individuals, will simply purchase their software in supermarkets. Only a small number of software houses will employ programmers, to develop all the packaged applications. Therefore, I don't recommend young people go into the programming profession."

This prophesy materialized only partially. The number of programmers since then has increased to over a million in the U.S. alone. Packaged software lives side by side with tailored software. However, the ratio of custom-tailored software to ready-made software in organizational applications portfolios has, indeed, decreased, and will most probably continue to do so. Many small businesses already use only packaged software. A decade from now, we will see few organizations that maintain their own software development personnel.

Will there be a sharp decrease in the number of programmers? No. On the contrary, there will be more of them. Where will they be? In the prospering software industry, developing packaged software.

Will custom-tailored software die altogether? No. As more and more advanced GUI 4GLs and application generators become available on the market for lower and lower prices, the phenomenon of application development by users will increase. In many organizations, the function of the IS unit will be reduced to research and development, connectivity, standardization, vendor analysis, software selection, and "help-desking."

Every year, a greater number of computer-literate young people take the place of retiring employees. These new employees are more aware than their predecessors of how IT can help them in their daily work. They are also more aware of which tools they can use, and how to develop their own applications. The combination of familiarity with the power of IT and experience with using it will result in floods of user-developed applications.

Will the outsourcing stampede continue? Not necessarily. Experts have shown that organizations can achieve almost all the benefits of outsourcing by "insourcing." **Insourcing** means letting the IS unit do the job for a cost that competes with that of outside IT service companies. Some large corporations are already taking a second look at outsourcing. The main factor that will determine the future of outsourcing will be whether it provides significant enough cuts in costs.

In general, the need for new software will continue to grow. Improved technology makes a one- or two-year-old technology obsolete. The length of a "technology generation" may shorten to six to twelve months, and corporations will look for additional alternative avenues for acquiring ISs.

THINK CRITICALLY

Will ready-made software applications ever meet all the needs of all businesses? Explain.

Product	*Firm*
Axient	Cognos
Visualage 2.0	IBM
Focus for Windows	Information Builders
Visual Works 2.0	Parcplace Systems
Build Momentum	Sybase
Parts Workbench	Digitalk
Magic 5.0	Magic
Visual Basic for Windows 3.0	Microsoft
Powerbuilder 3.0	Sybase

Figure 16.11 *Graphical 4GLs*

Graphical 4GLs, some of which are cited in Figure 16.11, may further augment the circle of end users who develop their own applications. With a graphical 4GL, the programmer uses icons rather than commands to create code. The program contains prebuilt modules and forms. It offers comprehensive data-modeling capabilities.

Many of these programs are 4GLs that were adapted to a graphical user interface (GUI) operating system, such as Windows. The combination of a 4GL and a GUI provides an easy-to-use powerful tool for developing applications.

Increasing Popularity of Prototyping The increasing use of prototyping (with software tools that support the approach), as well as the availability of graphical development tools and support from information centers, creates a convenient environment for the lay developer to become more self-sufficient. The new software eliminates much of the need to master any code-writing skills, and the end user requires less of the IS professionals' time, leaving information center staff free to assist more users in their systems development efforts.

Increasing Popularity of the Client/Server Architecture A major purpose of the adoption of client/server systems is to empower end users in their daily data processing. Therefore, most client/server environments make additional tools available to users for development of applications on their own desktop computers.

Net Notes

Do you need a zip code for an address? Are you trying to figure out how much postage to use for an overseas letter? Are you moving but don't want to wait in line to fill out a form? Go to the United State Postal Service Web site at *http://www.usps.gov.* This is a good example of how the Net can really save us time.

Managing User-Developed Applications

Development of applications by users poses challenges to IS managers, which can be met by following the basic rules outlined in Figure 16.12 (on the next page) and discussed in general below.

- *Managing the reaction of IS professionals.* IS professionals often react negatively to user development because they perceive it as undermining their own duties and authority. To solve this problem, management must set clear guidelines delineating what types of applications end users may and may not develop.

> End users *should* develop:
>
> ◆ Small-scale programs
>
> ◆ Programs that satisfy immediate business needs
>
> ◆ Programs that can be easily maintained by the end user
>
> End users *should not* develop:
>
> ◆ Programs that affect the work of other workers
>
> ◆ Programs that interface with other organizational systems
>
> ◆ Programs that are designed to collect and maintain large amounts of data

Figure 16.12 *DO's and DON'Ts in user application development*

◆ *Providing IS training and support.* It is difficult to provide IS support for user-developed applications. Training by IS staff, who are usually completely unfamiliar with the newly developed application, is a challenge. However, IS staff must ensure that the user has appropriate software and hardware for development, and must be able to provide IS professionals for support on demand.

◆ *Compatibility.* To ensure compatibility with other applications, standard development tools should be adopted and provided to interested users. Users should not be allowed to use nonstandard tools.

◆ *Development support.* To encourage user development of applications, the IS manager must designate a single technical contact for users. Usually, this is a function of the help desk in the information center (discussed in Chapter 9, "Organization of Information Systems and Services").

◆ *Managing access.* Special care should be taken with regard to access to organizational databases during user development. Access should be granted on a "need to know" basis and with appropriate limits: read-only, or read and update.

ADVANTAGES AND RISKS

There are several important advantages to user development of applications:

◆ *Shortened lead times.* Users almost always develop applications more quickly than IS personnel, because they are highly motivated (they will benefit from the new system); their systems are usually simpler in design, and they have a head start by being totally familiar with the business domain for which they are developing the application.

◆ *Good fit to needs.* Nobody knows the users' specific business needs better than the users themselves. Thus, they are apt to develop an application that will satisfy all needs.

◆ *Compliance with culture.* User-developed software closely conforms to individual units' subcultures, which will make the transition to a new system easier for employees.

◆ *Efficient utilization of resources.* Developing software on computers that are already being used for many other purposes is an efficient use of IT resources.

•• **POINT OF INTEREST**

Joint-Sourcing

Apparently, we could add an additional way to acquire IT services and products, which is a hybrid of the IS subsidiary and outsourcing. In 1997, Farmland Industries, a large cooperative of farmers and ranchers, and Ernst & Young, a big-six accounting firm and a management consulting firm, established a joint venture: OneSystem Group LLC. The new firm will satisfy all of Farmland Industries' IS needs. The deal was signed for 15 years. Farmland Industries was to pay $300–500 million to the new firm for the first five years of operations. The new firm employs 500 former Farmland employees and 40 Ernst & Young consultants.

Source: Caldwell, B., "E&Y, Farmland Form Outsourcing Venture," *InformationWeek* [online], Issue 626, April 14, 1997.

Understand Alternative Avenues for Acquisition of Information Systems?

The representatives of the software company from which your organization purchased an enterprise-wide IS were supposed to finish the modification of the inventory control module several months ago, but they have not. They still come daily to your office to ask questions and try to iron out problems. A year ago, when management decided to purchase and implement the new system, you hoped it would serve you well. The alternatives were either to have the system custom-tailored, or to purchase a ready-made application that would have to be somewhat modified for the Inventory Control unit, of which you are in charge. You were too busy, and hoped that a purchased package would rid you of long sessions with systems analysts. Well, you were wrong. You did not consider the alternatives wisely.

As an increasing number of business activities are supported and enhanced by ISs, it is extremely important for organizations to (1) acquire systems that best fit their needs, and (2) minimize the cost of system acquisition and maintenance of the systems. As we explained in Chapters 14, "Planning of Information Systems" and 15, "Systems Development," it is important that managers involve themselves in the process of deciding which ISs will be introduced in their business units and what features they will have. Since there are several ways in which to obtain ISs, managers must understand the advantages and disadvantages of each.

Managers' input into the process of deciding whether to develop a system in-house, purchase it off the shelf, or outsource the development or perhaps all of IS services and products, may have a tremendous effect on how managers and their subordinates will work for many years. Issues such as incompatibility of purchased software with existing applications, disclosure of strategic positioning when outsourcing, and possible poor performance of user-developed applications are not the business only of IS professionals, but of every manager.

◆ *Acquisition of skills.* The more employees who know how to develop applications, the greater an organization's skills inventory.

◆ *Free IS staff time.* User-developers free IS staff to develop and maintain the more complex and sophisticated systems.

However, with all the pros, there are also cons to application development by users. They must be considered seriously. The risks are:

◆ *Poorly developed applications.* User-developers are not as skilled as IS personnel. On the average, the applications they develop are of lower quality than systems developed by professionals. Users are often tempted to develop applications that are too complex for their ability and tools, resulting in systems that are difficult to maintain and use.

◆ *Islands of information.* An organization that relies on user development runs the risk of creating islands of information and "private" databases not under the control of the organization's IS managers. This may make it difficult to achieve the benefits of an integrated IS.

◆ *Duplication.* User-developers often waste resources developing applications that are identical or similar to systems that already exist within the organization.

◆ *Security problems.* Giving end users access to organizational databases for the purpose of creating systems may result in violation of security policies. This is especially true in client/server environments. The creation of "private databases" known only to the individual user is risky. The user may not be aware that the information he or she produces from the data is classified under an organization's policy.

◆ *Poor documentation.* Practically speaking, "poor documentation" may be a misnomer. Usually, users do not create any documentation at all because (1) they do not know how to write documentation, and (2) they develop the application on their own so as to have it ready as soon as possible, so they don't want to take the time to document it. Lack of documentation makes system maintenance difficult at best, and impossible at worst. Often, applications are patched together by new users, and pretty soon nobody knows how to iron out bugs or modify the program.

◆ *Futz factor.* One expert compared managing user-development of applications to "herding cats." You may try to lead them in one direction, but they will go anywhere they please. End-user development is part of the overall phenomenon of end-user computing, that is, the independent use and learning of IT by end users. Thus, the "futz factor" prevails here, too. **Futz** is any unproductive activity with computers in the workplace. This includes: the use of IT resources for personal gain; the use of entertainment software (such as games) on company time; the use of company-owned software for personal use on company time; the use of company networks, storage, paper, and/or magnetic media for personal entertainment or personal business; and the costs involved in personal use of company services. In a study by the Gartner Group, futz was estimated to incur 30% of the total cost of end-user computing (see Figure 16.13). A case has been reported of an employee who ran a private dietary sales program on his employer's mainframe computer, and in another case an employee developed computerized music sheets on a company PC.

ACTIVITY	PERCENTAGE
Futz Factor	30%
Peer Support	4%
Application Development	14%
Data Management	15%
Supplies	7%
Formal Learning	18%
Informal Learning	12%
Total	100%

Source: The Gartner Group, 1994.

Figure 16.13 *The costs of end user computing*

User-Developers Rewire an IBM Division

A dramatic decrease in staffing of a sales support and analysis unit at IBM's World Trade America/Far East division in 1985 turned into the first massive test of the concept of systems development led by users (SDLU). A reorganization reduced the unit's head count from 62 to 27 through attrition and reassignment, but the unit's responsibilities weren't commensurably reduced. Prior to the re-engineering, the unit received approximately one billion pieces of data per year, which it processed into reports based on specific requests from the field. There was ongoing applications development, and additional functions were being added to systems to respond to every request. Clearly, maintaining organizational manageability, without the time needed for traditional applications development, required a new approach.

Without programmers on staff, and without budget to outsource what used to be done in-house, the group had no choice but to turn to user-led development. Five employees from within the unit were trained in user-led development procedures and returned to rework existing systems and procedures to enhance the productivity of the remaining staff. One of the most important changes the employees made was integrating all the group's systems so that all information was shared by everyone, there was no duplication of effort, and communication was greatly streamlined. This required them to integrate different mainframe-based systems, including a commercial data collection and distribution package, internal multidimensional planning and modeling software, and an executive information system.

Even with the added efficiencies gained by merging the systems, the group could only manage its workload by reducing the shear volume of processing it was handling. It did so by reducing the frequency with which various reports and requests were processed. In fact, incoming data flow from field units was reduced by about 30% by selectively reducing certain report cycles that would not affect the company's overall performance.

At the same time that the unit was working to make its operation more efficient, it also started enhancing the services offered. Instead of providing a lot of reports of unprocessed data, computer-generated reports incorporated processing, included tentative forecasts, and highlighted out-of-line conditions. The impact of the user-developers' efforts exceeded expectations. The time between the arrival of monthly performance data and their use in the decision process dropped from three weeks to 24 hours. As a result, division management made better and more timely decisions. In fact, the unit won internal awards for most accurate forecasts for several years.

Source: Lichtenthal, S., "Connectors Rewire an IBM Division," Datamation, November 15, 1994, p. 62.

Questions:

1. What was the problem with IBM's World Trade America/Far East division?

2. Is the amount of information required now smaller than before the reorganization?

3. Much of the job that systems analysts used to do is now carried out by other people. Who are they?

4. What was the most important result of the new approach to data processing?

To Each His Share

Ryder Systems Inc. is one of America's largest moving companies. It manages the moving of parts and products for Ford Motor company, General Motors, Whirlpool, and Xerox. Because Ryder is a logistics organization, ISs are extremely important for its success. In 1997, the company decided to expand its services so that its customers could use Ryder services for everything that needs to be moved: raw materials, work-in-progress among plants, and shipments to customers. Until 1997, the company was spending $170 million per year on IS equipment and services. However, Ryder specializes in transportation, not in ISs, and therefore management decided to outsource its IS services.

Ryder decided to split the outsource deal between two companies: Andersen Consulting and IBM Global Services, the IBM subsidiary that provides IS outsourcing services. Andersen Consulting was designated the prime contractor with responsibility for software development and maintenance. IBM Global Services was designated to manage Ryder's 110 midrange computers, 12,000 PCs, and the communications network. In addition, an IBM facility in Raleigh, North Carolina, provides Ryder with mainframe processing. The arrangement practically makes Andersen a subcontractor to Ryder, and IBM a subcontractor to Andersen. IBM agreed to this arrangement because Andersen specializes in logistics, an area in which IBM wanted to acquire more expertise.

The majority of Ryder's 610 IS staff were offered jobs with Andersen and IBM. A small group (about 30) remained in the employ of Ryder to manage the outsourcing contract. Another group of 50 remained to support the company's 200 logistics experts. The deal will cost Ryder $1.4 billion over the contract's life of ten years. Executives said the deal would help them acquire much-needed new ISs, one of which is a system to track and trace goods in transit. It was expected to save the moving giant $160 million over this ten-year period. However, an observer said that the deal was an example of not only saving money, but of gaining strategic advantage as well.

Source: Caldwell, B., "Ryder enlists Andersen and IBM to Run IT: $1.4 billion deal will help logistics firm manage customers' entire supply chain," InformationWeek [online], Issue 622, March 17, 1997.

Questions:

1. Ryder retained about 30 IS professionals to manage the outsourcing contract. What does contract management mean? What are these people responsible for?

2. Why did the observer say Ryder would gain a strategic advantage by outsourcing its IS services to the two companies?

Healing the Help-Desk Headaches

United Wisconsin Services is a health insurance company with headquarters in Milwaukee. It manages operations for Blue Cross and Blue Shield in Wisconsin and provides health-care management services to more than 70,000 people in 30 states. It ended 1995 with revenue of $1.8 billion. Over the past decade, United Wisconsin has experienced an increase in the number of claims and a 10%–15% increase in medical costs that it must cover. Like other firms in this industry, the company is constantly under pressure to cut costs, and, like other companies, it targeted its IS maintenance as an area where new economies could be achieved.

To do their jobs well, 3,500 of the company's employees in a multitude of branches use PCs, which must be fixed when they malfunction. Until 1996, a user seeking help had to make a long-distance call to a technical support center staffed with an inadequate number of overworked IS professionals who answered 750 help calls per month. Service was slow and unsatisfactory. It took up to six weeks to install new PCs and other hardware, and up to five days to respond to help calls. Often, the staff of a branch had to stop work while a help-desk person drove hundreds of miles to fix the problem. The problems caused by the inadequate size of the help-desk staff were compounded by high staff turnover and a freeze on hiring imposed by management. Only junior personnel were being hired, and they had to be trained before they could serve others. And often, once these people were trained, they left.

All of this was happening while the demand for help was growing because the number of PCs had doubled from 600 to 1,200 during the period of 1992–1995. The support staff could not cope with the increasing work.

Tom Knapp, United Wisconsin's CIO decided to outsource the help-desk services. He and his staff identified a set of needs and sent requests for proposals to 15 outsourcing vendors, including Andersen consulting, EDS, and IBM, as well as several small, local firms. They chose Entex Information Services, a company headquartered in Rye Brook, New York, for several reasons.

Entext agreed to limit its annual charge to $750,000. Because IS services are charged back to United Wisconsin's departments, the company liked the fact that Entex offered three flexible support options, from which each department could choose its own. One option offered an unlimited number of support calls during a ten-hour day for a monthly fee of $45 per PC. Another option was to offer special business applications that required more attention and speedier response at irregular hours, which cost the company an additional $10 per PC. A third option was to pay only when support is used, with charges including hourly labor as well as materials and any other expenses incurred. The first option was selected by the majority of the departments and covered 90% of the 1,200 PCs. However, the company's government services and disabilities units elected the fee-for-service option, and pay only for service rendered, on a time and materials basis (time: $60/hour).

The second option was not used by anyone in the company.

Entex uses software that was developed by United Wisconsin to track calls reaching the insurer's Entex-staffed help center. Problems that cannot be resolved immediately are forwarded to Entex's corporate response center in New York. If an on-site visit is required, Entex dispatches a specialist from New York.

Knapp estimated that since the outsourcing contract was signed, his company's PC support costs have decreased by at least 10%. Users have reported a 50% improvement in the time it takes to respond to questions and in the time between placing a call and receiving the service. One manager said that 95% of her staff's calls are now answered immediately, whereas in the past the calls were answered after two hours.

Source: Fryer, B., "PC Service Outsourcing: No More Support Headaches, Insurer United Wisconsin improves PC support with flexible help-desk options from Entex," InformationWeek [online], Issue 574, April 8, 1996.

Questions:

1. List and explain the benefits of the outsourcing deal to United Wisconsin.

2. How can a firm like Entex do good business with such deals, while United Wisconsin and similar companies cannot provide adequate help-desk services?

•••• There are several alternatives to having applications developed in-house: **outsourcing**, maintaining an **IS subsidiary**, purchasing **ready-made software**, and **development by users**. Outsourcing, which is the use by an organization of a separate company to handle all or part of its IS resources, has been a very popular option since the early 1990s. Its advantages include improving cost clarity and reducing license and maintenance fees, freeing organizations to concentrate on their core businesses, shortening the number of implementation cycles, reducing personnel and fixed costs, gaining access to highly qualified know-how, receiving ongoing consulting as part of standard support, decreasing investments in software tools and training, and improving security.

The main disadvantage of outsourcing is the long-term loss of control over IS development and operations. When outsourcing, organizations that operate in a fast-changing environment can lose the flexibility to adapt their ISs to new business needs and opportunities.

Large companies whose information needs are substantial have established large IS organizations. Some have turned these units into independent **ISs service subsidiaries** that offer their services to the market at large. This allows the parent company to have access to readily available IS resources while not having to absorb the cost of overhead and fluctuations in demand for IS services.

The first option organizations should explore before investing in a new IS is **purchasing packaged software**. Purchasing ready-to-use applications is significantly less expensive than developing software in-house.

Benchmarking, the codified comparison of performance measures between systems, is an important step in software selection as well as for ongoing evaluation after implementation. It ensures that the adopted application satisfies the organization's minimum requirements, such as access time to data and processing speed.

Several factors have encouraged organizations to let their users develop their own applications: the **programming backlog** (the build-up of programming requests awaiting attention by the IS department), the increasing use of PCs, the emergence of 4GLs and GUI tools, the popularity of prototyping, and the adoption of client/server systems. There are several advantages to **user application development**: a short lead time, good fit of application capabilities to business needs, good compliance with organizational culture, efficient utilization of computing resources, acquisition of skills by users, and the freeing of IS staff to deal with the more complex systems challenges. But there are also risks: poorly developed applications, undesirable islands of information and "private databases," duplications of effort, security problems, and poor documentation. Thus, end-user development of applications needs to be managed. IS managers should determine the applications that users should and should not develop, and dictate the tools that should be used as well.

Well over half of America's office workers now have rich computer resources at the tips of their fingers. However, much of their computing time is not spent for the benefit of the organization. This is called the **futz factor** and, according to recent studies, it may account for 30% of the company's IS spending. Often, employees do not know which activity is welcomed and which is not. If the organization lacks a clear policy, employees are not discouraged from abusing computers. Lack of clear guidelines may cause damage.

REVIEW, DISCUSS, AND EXPLORE

REVIEW AND DISCUSSION QUESTIONS

1. Why is outsourcing so popular?

2. The major hardware and software makers derive an increasing portion of their revenue from outsourcing contracts. Try to analyze why they direct more of their efforts in this direction.

3. What are the sources of information about hardware and software? Where would you turn to glean information if you were an IS manager? Think of sources not mentioned in the chapter.

4. How does an IS subsidiary evolve? What are the advantages of holding an IS subsidiary?

5. You are the CIO of a large manufacturing company. A software vendor approaches you with an offer to have your company serve as a beta site for a new human resources application. What would you do before making a decision?

6. What is an RFI? What is the difference between an RFI and an RFP?

7. The ideal response to an RFP is one that can be easily transformed into a contract. Why?

8. When purchasing an off-the-shelf application, to which phase of SDLC is the post-implementation support and service equivalent?

9. What is the "programming backlog"?

10. Why don't users document the applications they develop? Why is poor documentation a problem?

11. *Ethics and Society*: Do you agree or disagree with the following statement: Employees are smart enough to know what they should and should not do with their computers. A conduct policy will not prevent wrongdoing. Why, or why not?

CONCEPT ACTIVITY

Prepare an RFI for an application to assist in the analysis of market performance of a particular product. Assume that the application must run on underutilized networked PCs. You may make any other assumptions.

HANDS-ON ACTIVITY

Find an organization that has purchased a software application three to six months ago. The application may be in any business area: accounting, payroll, inventory control, financial management, manufacturing, human resources, and so on. Interview the person who recommended the purchase, and summarize the reasoning behind his or her decision. Then interview one or two daily users and summarize the pros and cons they discuss. What, if anything, would you do differently before deciding to purchase this application?

TEAM ACTIVITY

Approach an organization (a start-up company, an established company, your university, or any other organization) that is considering the implementation of a new IS for any business activity, including marketing, accounting, or human resources management. Prepare a document with recommendations: Which part of the systems acquisition should IS professionals carry out? What can end users contribute to the process? List a general plan of work, and list the responsibilities of specific end users. For help, refer to the "Systems Development Life Cycle" section discussed in Chapter 15.

EXPLORE THE WEB

Throughout this book, we have mentioned the Web sites of many organizations that provide information and advice on IT. Explore the Web sites of these organizations and the Web sites of IT-related magazines to find the latest statistics on the different alternatives for obtaining ISs. Try to answer the following questions:

1. What was the dollar amount spent on IT in each of the past three years?

2. How was this amount distributed among in-house development, purchased ready software, and outsourced systems?

Chapter **17**
Controls and Security Measures

Fast Recovery is Good Business

While some organizations can continue serving their customers for several days or even weeks without the aid of IT, information-rich industries are totally dependent on the technology. Imagine a utility company that cannot bill its customers; imagine an insurance company that has no access to its customers' computerized policies; or imagine a bank that cannot provide you with your balance. NationsBank Corp, America's fourth largest bank, would not even consider such a situation.

NationsBank Corp.'s management in Charlotte, North Carolina, knows the bank must have the data on their information systems available 24 hours a day, seven days a week and cannot afford to lose even a small amount of data. When a disaster occurs, the bank must recover immediately to resume business, or it may lose customers. While working over a period of 48–72 hours to recover from a disaster that brings systems down may be tolerable for a local bank, it is not sufficiently quick for NationsBank. "We can't survive if we're down that long," said Bill Douglas, a senior vice president with the bank's IT services arm. He estimates that the bank could lose up to $50 million for every 24 hours of down time. The long-term damage to the bank's reputation could entail even greater financial losses. He needs measures that would allow recovery within 12–18 hours.

The solution? Starting in fall 1997, the bank plans to send all its transaction data to an IBM disaster recovery site in Gaithersburg, Maryland, using special software called Remote Dual Copy, supplied by IBM Business Recovery Services. The software automatically creates an exact copy (called a "mirror copy") of the bank's most critical databases. In case of disasters such as floods, fires, tornadoes, or malicious destruction of original databases, the bank will be able to use the mirror database to continue operations. Most bank employees will hardly notice the transition, and customers will not be affected.

To enhance its ability to recover fast, NationsBank agreed, in March 1997, to become a test site for compression technology. High capacity memory circuits of 45 Mbps each are used to compress data before they are sent to the mirror site via communications lines. After the new devices are implemented, the bank will be able to operate using only half of its high-capacity communication lines, creating a savings of $240,000 per month.

NationsBank spends 10% of its IT budget on disaster recovery. The average for the banking industry is only 5%. It is the only bank that backs up all of its databases. With so much at stake, management has determined that peace of mind is worth the cost of the precaution.

Source: Thyfault, M.E., "Squeezing out Savings: NationsBank saves on disaster recovery," *InformationWeek*, June 2, 1997, Issue 633.

LEARNING OBJECTIVES

As the use of computer-based information systems spreads, so does the threat to the integrity of data and the reliability of information in organizations. Natural and "man-made" menaces have become risks that organizations can no longer dismiss. A computer expert noted: "The only truly secure system is powered off, cast in a block of concrete, and sealed in a lead room with armed guards. And even then I have my doubts." Indeed, there is no way to fully secure an information system against every potential mishap, but there are ways to significantly reduce the risks and recover the losses.

When you finish this chapter, you will:

- ◆ Be aware of the main types of risks to information systems
- ◆ Understand how a system is vulnerable from development, through construction, implementation, and operation
- ◆ Recognize the types of controls required to ensure the integrity of data entry and processing
- ◆ Appreciate the importance of integrating security measures into systems development
- ◆ Understand how organizations develop recovery plans
- ◆ Comprehend the economic aspect of pursuing information security

A 1997 survey by the IT staffing firm RHI Consulting revealed an interesting discrepancy: Although 98% of the CIOs surveyed agreed that it was important to have a disaster recovery plan for catastrophes such as hurricanes, earthquakes, and floods, only 25% of them had one. The survey polled 1,400 CIOs of U.S. companies with more than 100 employees. The most prepared companies were those in the finance, insurance, and real estate industries: 95% of these companies had disaster recovery plans.

Source: "Flirting with Disaster," *InformationWeek*, May 5, 1997, p. 160.

GOALS OF INFORMATION SECURITY

As you have already seen, the development, implementation, and maintenance of ISs constitute a large and growing part of the cost of doing business; protecting those resources is a primary concern of most organizations. The increasing reliance on ISs, combined with their connection to the "outside world" in the form of the Internet, makes securing corporate ISs increasingly challenging. What would happen if an enterprise-wide system were infected with a virus and ceased operating? What would happen if an errant employee accessed confidential data and sold them? What if criminals become adept at breaching security over the Internet? Needless to say, the answer to these questions is: potential catastrophe. The role of computer controls and security is to protect systems against these and many other mishaps, as well as to help organizations ensure that their IS operation complies with the law and with expectations of employees and customers for privacy. The major goals of information security are:

◆ To lower the risk that systems and organizations may cease operating

◆ To maintain information confidentiality

◆ To ensure the integrity and reliability of data resources

◆ To ensure the availability of data resources

◆ To ensure compliance with national security laws and privacy laws

These goals can be jeopardized in the ways indicated above, perhaps most of all by the explosion of online activity over the Internet and the increasing use of intranets. To plan measures to support these goals, organizations first must be aware of the possible risks to their information resources (which include hardware, applications and data, and networks) and then they must execute security measures to defend against those risks.

RISKS TO INFORMATION SYSTEMS

In October 1990, a major earthquake hit the San Francisco area. The immediate concern of the management of one international corporation headquartered in the southwest was to obtain information concerning the status of their San Francisco-based operations. They needed the locations of company facilities, office phone numbers, and names and home addresses of all employees located in the area. However, in this company's case, the information was not computerized. There was a paper file containing all the desired information, but no one knew who had it or where it could be found. Furthermore, all corporate executives were meeting off-site and couldn't have accessed it even if it were in their offices. After more than five hours of frantic phone calls, the file was found in an employee's briefcase in a small Pennsylvania town. Five precious hours of response time were lost because critical resources were dispersed across the country without the appropriate backup and recovery mechanisms in place.[1] This case demonstrates one risk facing ISs: natural disasters, which can result in blackouts and brownouts, vandalism, theft of information, data alteration and data destruction, computer viruses, and nonmalicious mishaps, all of which are discussed below.

---

[1]Hurd, J.E., "Do you know where the briefcase is?," *Journal of Systems Management*, August 1994, p. 16.

Computer Losses		
CAUSE	NUMBER OF REPORTS	LOSS IN MILLIONS
	1993	*1993*
Theft	275,000	$1,011
Power Failure	389,000	$318
Accidents	276,000	$246
Miscellaneous Causes	269,000	$157
Lightening	91,000	$86
Fire	19,000	$72
Transit	54,000	$53
Water	34,000	$51
Total	**1,407,000**	**$1,994**

Source: Safeware, The Insurance Agency, Inc., quoted in "1993 Computer Losses," *MacWeek*, Vol 8 No 36, September 12, 1994, p. 28.

(a)

Desktops & Laptops Computer Losses				
CAUSE	NUMBER INCIDENTS	DOLLAR LOSS	NUMBER INCIDENTS	DOLLAR LOSS
	1994	*1994*	*1995*	*1995*
Power Surge	378,000	$240,980,000	322,000	$217,619,000
Accidents	360,000	$261,617,000	338,000	$246,189,000
Theft	291,000	$978,807,000	342,000	$1,160,444,000
Other	260,000	$126,286,000	230,000	$123,420,000
Lightning	88,000	$74,067,000	77,000	$65,957,000
Transit	50,000	$80,935,000	45,000	$878,251,000
Earthquake	44,000	$80,579,000	1,000	$3,000,000
Water/Flood	44,000	$67,547,000	39,000	$70,865,000
Fire	15,000	$70,958,000	15,000	$9,550,000
	1,535,000	$1,983,626,000	1,409,000	$1,984,295,000

Source: Safeware, The Insurance Agency, Inc. Columbus Ohio, 1800-800-1492

(b)

Figure 17.1 *Estimates of total computer-related losses and losses of desktops and laptops*

A company by the name of Safeware, The Insurance Agency, Inc. estimates that, according to reported cases, losses related to computers surged from $1.3 billion in 1992 to $2 billion in 1993, more than half of them being attributed to theft and power surges. Figure 17.1 presents the major causes of loss, the amount lost, and the number of cases reported for each cause in the U.S. The data underscore the need for reliable measures to prevent such mishaps.

RISKS TO HARDWARE

Risks to hardware involve physical damage to computers, peripheral equipment, and communications media. As illustrated in Figure 17.2, the major causes of such damage are natural disasters, blackouts and brownouts, and vandalism.

◆ Natural Disasters: Hurricanes, Floods, Tornados and Earthquakes

◆ Blackouts and Brownouts

◆ Vandalism

Figure 17.2 *Risks to hardware*

NATURAL DISASTERS **Natural disasters** that pose a risk to ISs include fires, floods, earthquakes, tornadoes, and lightning, which can destroy hardware, software, or both, causing total or partial paralysis of systems or communications lines. Flood water short-circuits and burns delicate components such as microchips. Lightning and voltage surges cause tiny wires to melt and destroy circuitry. Obviously, all data and programs stored in memory chips in the computer are lost when this happens. Water from floods and the heat created when circuits are shorted may also ruin the surface of storage media such as magnetic disks and tapes, thereby destroying the data. In addition, wildlife and human error occasionally destroy communication lines; animals gnaw cables, and farmers occasionally cut wires inadvertently while tending their crops.

Probably the easiest way to protect against loss of data caused by natural disasters is to automatically duplicate all data periodically, a process referred to as **backing up** data. Many systems have built-in programs that conduct this operation automatically. The data may be duplicated on inexpensive storage devices such as magnetic tapes. In recent years, makers of storage devices have offered **redundant arrays of inexpensive disks (RAID)** for this purpose. A RAID is any set of disks that is programmed to redundantly store data in order to provide a higher degree of reliability. The disks are inexpensive because they may not provide the same fast storage and retrieval time as the "original" disks, but they fulfill the backup task well.

Of course, backing up data is not enough. The disks or tapes with backed-up data must be routinely transported to an **off-site location**, so that if a business site is damaged by a disaster, the remote storage location is likely to be spared. Many companies have a truck haul back-up disks and tapes to an off-site location at the end of every business day. For additional protection, the tapes or disks are locked in safes that can withstand fire and floods.

Communications media are among the most vulnerable parts of a system, where natural damage is concerned, because they run outside the confines of an organization's operation. Although they add significantly to the cost of communications hardware, thick protective sheaths made of special plastics can be used to protect communication cables and wires.

Natural disasters are a serious threat to hardware.

Used by permission from AP/Wide World Photos

Used by permission from AP/Wide World Photos

A Growing Problem

The results of a 1997 survey by the National Computer Security Association (NCSA) indicate that the computer virus problem in North America continues to grow. A staggering 99.33% of all medium-sized and large organizations in North America have experienced at least one computer virus infection. The survey showed that despite the 13% increase in the use of antivirus software from 1996 to 1997, the infection rate was still growing. Of the computers these companies employed in 1997, 40.6% were infected at least once.

Source: *http://www.ncsa.com/pressrelease/pr5.html*, visited on May 8, 1997.

BLACKOUTS AND BROWNOUTS Computers run on electricity. If power is disrupted, the computer and its peripheral devices cannot function, and the change in power supply can have very damaging effects on computer processes and storage. **Blackouts** are incidents of a total loss of electrical power. In **brownouts**, the voltage of the power decreases, or there are very short interruptions in the flow of power. Power failure may not only disrupt operations but also cause irreparable damage to hardware. Occasional surges in voltage are equally harmful, because their impact on equipment is similar to that of lightning.

The popular way of handling brownouts is to connect a voltage regulator between computers and the electric network. A **voltage regulator** boosts or decreases voltage to smooth out drops or surges, and guarantees a maintenance of voltage within an acceptable tolerance.

To ensure against interruptions in power supply, organizations use **Uninterrupted Power Supply (UPS)** systems, which provide an alternative power supply for a short time, as soon as a power net fails. The only practical measure against prolonged blackouts is the maintenance of a separate generator that uses gasoline or another fuel, and thus is independent of electricity. Once the general power stops, the generator can kick in and produce the power needed for the computer system.

VANDALISM **Vandalism** occurs when human beings deliberately destroy computer systems. Bitter customers may damage ATMs, or disgruntled employees may destroy computer equipment out of fear that it will eliminate their jobs, or simply to get even with their superiors. For instance, several years ago, postal service employees stuck paper clips in a new computer that sorted mail, because they feared the new system would eliminate jobs.

It is difficult to defend computers against vandalism. ATMs and other equipment that are accessible to the public are often encased in metal boxes, but someone with persistence can still cause severe damage. In the workplace, the best measure against vandalism is to allow access only to those who have a real need for the system. Sensitive equipment, such as servers, should be locked in a special room.

Used by permission from AP/Wide World Photos

Used by permission from J. Messerschmidt/The Stock Market

Used by permission from Storage Computer Corporation.

Redundant Arrays of Inexpensive Disks (RAID) automatically back up transactions onto disks that can be removed and stored in a safe place.

Surge protectors are an inexpensive solution to extreme changes in voltage, which could damage a computer.

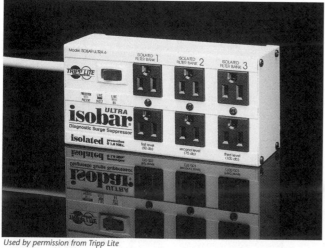

Used by permission from Tripp Lite

All computer systems are susceptible to disruption and damage. While the culprit in the destruction of hardware is often some natural disaster or power spike, the culprit in damage to software is almost always human. As illustrated in Figure 17.3, the major risks to software applications and data are theft of information, data alteration and destruction, computer viruses, and nonmalicious mishaps.

THEFT OF INFORMATION Before the advent of electronic computers, most businesses kept secret information in a safe. A thief had to physically tear the locking mechanism out, or illegally obtain a key to the safe. Now even the most sensitive information is usually stored electronically somewhere on a company's information system. Today's electronic equivalent of the physical key is a **code**, a combination of characters that is needed to access secured data. Before the computer age, large amounts of data meant a lot of paper, which was awkward to steal and awkward to hide when stolen. These days, thousands of pages filled with information can be stored on a small magnetic disk, making information easier to steal (as the following story shows), and also easier to hide.

A young man worked in the research and development department of an international food company that had over one hundred microcomputers in its headquarters. In 1985 he inserted his own disk into a computer that held the formulas for flavoring products of a successful food line; he made a copy of the information, and sent the disk to a former manager who worked for a competitor. Since the manager did not know how to print out the information from the disk, he gave it to a service company to do it for him. The serviceperson noticed that the name of the manager's company was different from the company name appearing on the printout, and notified the victim company. The company had been wondering how the competitor kept introducing similar products so soon after their own new products came on the market; now they understood.[2]

DATA ALTERATION AND DATA DESTRUCTION **Alteration** or **destruction of data** is often an act of mischief (in which case it is called **data diddling**). In San Francisco, United States Leasing International, Inc., found one morning that data in its files were replaced with curses and friends' names. In this case, the damage was financial. In other cases, however, computer pranks such as these can put people's lives at risk.

In 1983, a group of Milwaukee teenagers accessed a computer system at Sloan-Kettering Cancer Research Institute in New York via a modem and altered patients' records just for "fun." An alert nurse noticed a double—and lethal—dose of a medication in a patient's record and called a doctor. She saved the patient's life.[3]

---

[2]Davies, D., "The Nature of Computer Crimes," *Computer and Law*, 2 July 1991, pp. 8–13.

[3]Yee, H.W., "Juvenile Computer Crime-Hacking: Criminal and Civil Liability," *Comm/Ent Law Journal*, 7, No. 2, 1985, pp. 355–358.

◆ Theft of Information

◆ Data Alteration and Data Destruction

◆ Computer Viruses

◆ Nonmalicious Mishaps

Figure 17.3 *Risks to applications data*

In a survey conducted by the American Bar Association's Task Force on Computer Crime, the respondents ranked "destruction or alteration of data" as the most significant type of computer crime. A related crime, "destruction or alteration of software," was ranked second. These two crimes are the dreaded nightmares of chief information officers and database administrators.

It is not only the effort to reinstate missing or altered records that causes financial damage. Even if the actual damage is not great, IS staff must spend a lot of time scanning the data pools to ascertain the integrity of the entire resource, and they must also figure out how the perpetrator managed to circumvent security controls. This activity itself wastes the time of highly salaried employees.

COMPUTER VIRUSES A biological virus is a microorganism that attacks the living cells of a host, a human being or another animal. It penetrates the cells, multiplies, and then causes the cell to burst, thereby destroying it. It is rapidly transmitted from one living creature to another. A **computer virus** is a few lines of programming language that are usually inserted in a legitimate program that is later copied by unwary users. Computer viruses are so named because they act on programs and data in the same way that biological viruses act on living tissue: the virus code is self-replicating and easily spread from computer to computer. Viruses are spread by sharing disks, inserting a disk into an infected computer, or executing an infected program. The worst viruses are those that attach themselves to operating systems. As you already know, the operating system is the large program that manages and controls all basic computer resources. Since the operating system interacts with every program and data file that is used in the computer, a virus in an operating system can damage every file used.

What the public refers to as a computer virus may be one of three kinds of programs whose purpose is to cause panic, damage legitimate computer programs, destroy data files, disrupt data communication, and harm hardware. A virus may be a worm, a logic bomb, or a time bomb.

A **worm** is a program independent of any other program. It is written with the intention that other users will copy it unknowingly, and that it will then damage their files. Worms are launched into computer networks and infect the computers that make up the network.

A **logic bomb**, is a virus program that attaches itself to operating systems or to other programs. It is programmed to cause real damage, or to produce some output, at a specified future time. The output is usually a message on the computer screen, or some audio message broadcast through a computer loudspeaker. A destructive logic bomb attaches itself to legitimate programs and is dormant until a certain event takes place in the computer, or until the inner clock of the computer indicates a prespecified time; then it starts causing damage. In the latter case, the code is called a **time bomb**.

No Smooth Sailing for the Clipper

As previously discussed, one of the most effective ways to prevent eves-dropping on electronic communications devices is to encrypt the information before it is sent, and provide decoding information only to those who are authorized to receive the communication. However, the use of encryption can make surveillance by law enforcement agencies ineffective. In 1991, Congress considered a measure—subsequently put on hold—to make it easier for law enforcement agencies to gain access to encoded communication. The proposed bill would require providers of communications equipment to "design and engineer such equipment in a manner that allows law enforcement agencies to obtain the plain text [meaning the decrypted message] of voice, data, and other communications when appropriately authorized by law." The purpose of the bill was to prevent criminals from concealing illegal activity by encrypting their communications when planning criminal activities, including terrorism and espionage.

To this end, the National Security Agency developed Clipper, a microprocessor that holds a complex encryption formula. The government wanted every U.S. manufacturer of computers to install the chip in every computer and microprocessor—including cell phones—so that law enforcement agencies could decipher encrypted communication. Any information, even encrypted information, would be processed by the Clipper encryption, so that the key to the formula could decipher any communication. The NSA claimed that the chip could generate codes that would not be decipherable without special keys, which would, of course, be held by the government.

Two federal agencies would hold decrypting codes, the combination of which could decipher any scrambled communication. Law enforcement officials would require a court warrant to have communications suspected of being criminal intercepted and deciphered by the two agencies.

Privacy advocates cried foul because they were afraid of potential misuses of the method by unscrupulous law enforcement officers. They claimed that Clipper put too much power to monitor private communication in the government's hands. Manufacturers, too, have emphatically resisted the idea. They are afraid that foreign clients will shun American computers. It is all right if America wants its citizens to be subject to the measure, they say, but we cannot force our non-American clients to agree to it. The computer industry has strongly lobbied against Clipper for fear of losing markets.

As mentioned above, the enactment of the measure was put on hold, and it is still under debate. The government's explanation that the measure would be used with strict checks and balances, especially in the form of a joint key held by two different agencies, has not pacified privacy advocates. However, protest has not discouraged the U.S. government and other governments (predominantly the British government) from trying to find ways to intercept and decipher digital information. When cellular phone companies first introduced the new technology, they wanted to install a special encryption microchip in each phone, which would encrypt conversation so that no third party could intercept and decipher the communication. The U.S. government and many other governments forbade it. Now, once again, computer technology has created a struggle between the government's effort to harness technology to help it preserve law and order, and the privacy champions who strive to protect a basic human right.

••• *POINT OF INTEREST*

Gnawing Problems

Animals have a funny habit of bringing computers and telephone networks to a grinding halt.

- In August 1994, a squirrel picked the wrong piece of cable to gnaw on while scampering about outside the NASDAQ stock exchange's computer center in Trumbull, Connecticut. The sudden blackout caused trade reconciliation algorithms to fail, sending the system into overload. A supposedly fail-safe backup power supply didn't switch on. The NASDAQ computerized stock-trading system was down for 34 minutes.
- In December 1991, MCI customers calling from Washington, D.C., to the southern USA found phone service disrupted for an hour when a beaver near Woodford, Va., gnawed through a fiber-optic cable.
- On May 4, 1991, four of the FAA's 20 major air traffic control centers shut down for 5 hours and 22 minutes. The cause, according to the FAA: "fiber cable cut by farmer burying dead cow. Lost 27 circuits. Massive operational impact."

The increasing complexity of telephone technology—as much as its vulnerability to beavers, backhoes, and dead cows—is a problem drawing increasing attention. "The impact of individual outages has become far more significant and far more severe," says Richard Firestone, the FCC chief telephone regulator.

Source: Bott, E., "Risky Business: Risks Digest on Internet," *PC-Computing*, Vol 7 No 11, November 1994, p. 43, and Schneidawind, J., "Gnawing Problems: Toothy Critters Tackle Technology," *USA Today*, December 18, 1991.

To illustrate the damage that a virus can cause, consider this famous case. On the evening of November 2, 1988, a computer science graduate student at Cornell University named Robert Tappan Morris sneaked five thousand lines of code onto the Internet. He only meant to program the code to copy itself once onto every computer it encountered; his goal was to prove that his genius could overcome the safeguards of the network. He did not mean to infect the system with a malicious, destructive virus, but unfortunately, he made a mistake while writing the code, a mistake that evolved and created a chain of harmful consequences.

Because Morris failed to include code that prevented the virus from attacking computers that were already infected, a computer could be infected many times over. Since an infection takes only a few milliseconds, the same computer could be hit many times within minutes. That hectic action caused the infected computers to devote almost all of their resources to the virus, significantly slowing down legitimate productive work. As a result, the users of many computers disconnected from the network. About 6,200 computers were infected. Potentially, 60,000 could have been attacked. A Cornell University report on the case concluded that the virus could have been developed by any reasonably competent computer science student, and the event triggered increasing attention to computer security.

How can the damage caused by such a virus be estimated? Many institutions pay a few hundred dollars for every hour of computer use—whether it be productive or wasted on processing a virus. Experts who try to eradicate viruses also charge hundreds of dollars per hour, and at the same time, productive work is suspended. Morris's virus caused an estimated $10–$98 million in damage. Two years later, Morris was convicted in court under the Federal Computer Fraud and Abuse Act of 1986. The maximum penalty for his mischief was five years imprisonment and a $250,000 fine. He was sentenced to three years probation, fined $10,000, and ordered to perform 400 hours of community service, pay the cost of his probation supervision, and pay attorney fees estimated to be at least $150,000. Ironically, Morris's father is an expert in computer security, and worked as chief scientist at the National Computer Security Center, an arm of the National Security Agency at the time of the incident.

One way to protect against viruses is to use virus detection software, which is readily available on the market. The problem with virus detection software, however, is that it is usually designed to intercept only known viruses. If a new virus is designed to operate in a way not yet known, the software is unlikely to detect it. The better detection software tries to detect any files that "do not belong" in the running of system software. This generic approach warns the user of suspected files of any kind before applications are retrieved for use. Virus detection applications allow the user to automatically, or selectively, destroy suspected programs.

NONMALICIOUS MISHAPS Unintentional damage to software occurs because of (1) poor training, (2) lack of adherence to simple backup procedures, or (3) quite simply, human error. Although this rarely occurs in robust applications, poor training may result in inappropriate use of an application so that it ruins data, unbeknownst to the user. When faced with an instruction that may change or delete data, a robust application will pose a question such as: "Are you sure you want to delete the record?" or issue a warning like "This may destroy the file."

More common is destruction of data due to the failure to save all work and create a backup copy. This often happens when using a word-processing program to create text files, and when updating databases. As Figure 17.4 on the next page shows, human errors cause the greatest damage to software.

Security doesn't get much respect from senior management, according to a survey by *Ernst & Young* and *InformationWeek*. According to 42% of the respondents, senior managers just don't care about security. More than 50% of respondents running mission-critical applications on local area networks (LANs) say that their LAN security is less than adequate for this sort of work. More than 40% of respondents who have vital applications on departmental minicomputers say that security on those computers is unsatisfactory. Fifty-four percent of the respondents reported a loss due to inadequate security during 1993 and 1994; 13% reported more than one loss. Several individual losses exceeded one million dollars.

Source: "Security: Who Cares?" *Datamation*, February 1, 1995, p. 18.

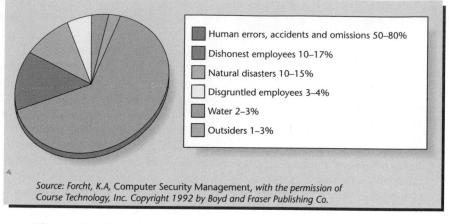

- Human errors, accidents and omissions 50–80%
- Dishonest employees 10–17%
- Natural disasters 10–15%
- Disgruntled employees 3–4%
- Water 2–3%
- Outsiders 1–3%

Source: Forcht, K.A, Computer Security Management, with the permission of Course Technology, Inc. Copyright 1992 by Boyd and Fraser Publishing Co.

Figure 17.4 *What causes damage to ISs?*

CONTROLS

Controls are constraints imposed on a user or a system, and can be used to secure systems against the risks discussed above. For instance, user controls allow access only to those who need to know, and system controls ensure that processes are carried out in accordance with business policies and standards. As is evident from Figure 17.4, the largest part of IS mishaps is caused by human beings: the greatest number from errors and omissions, and the second greatest number from dishonest employees. There are several ways to impose controls to minimize the number of these cases (see Figure 17.5).

ACCESS CONTROLS

Access controls are measures taken to ensure that only those authorized have access to a computer or network or to certain applications or data. One way to block access to a computer is by physically locking it in a facility to which only authorized users have a key, or by locking the computer with a physical key. However, in the age of computer networks, this is often an impractical solution.

The most common way to control access is through the combination of an **access code** (also called **user ID**) and a **password**. While access codes usually are not secret, passwords are. IS managers encourage users to change their passwords frequently, which most systems easily allow, so that others do

- ◆ Program Robustness
- ◆ Access Controls
- ◆ Atomic Transactions
- ◆ Audit Trail

Figure 17.5 *A system needs many controls to protect it from risk.*

not have time to figure them out. Some organizations have systems that force users to change their passwords at preset time intervals, such as once per month.

Access codes and their related passwords are either maintained in a special list that becomes part of the operating system, or are maintained in a database that the system searches before allowing access, to determine if a user is authorized to access the desired resource. In many business situations, an employee or customer may have "read" access but not "write" or "update" access, which can be controlled by a similar type of look-up system.

PROGRAM ROBUSTNESS AND DATA ENTRY CONTROLS

Much of the **robustness** of a computer program is measured by the degree to which the program can resist inappropriate usage, such as incorrect data entry or processing. The same type of application can be written with different levels of robustness, depending on the expectations of the developers. The least robust program assumes that the user will enter only parameters that are expected of him or her, and will not try to outmaneuver the system. The most robust program takes into consideration every possible abuse.

For example, a system may be programmed to accept telephone numbers as input only in a certain format, such as 10 digits (3-digit area code followed by 3-digit exchange and 4-digit phone number). In this case, if the user enters a 7- or 11-digit number, the data entry controls of the system will display an error message, such as "You must enter a 10-digit number." If a record is not to be entered into a file unless the telephone number is supplied, the system will not accept any of the record and will produce an appropriate message when the user leaves the displayed field empty or enters an invalid number. A highly robust program includes code that promptly produces a clear message if a user either errs or tries to circumvent a process.

Controls are also a means of translating business policies into system features. For example, Blockbuster Video used its IS to implement a policy not to carry more than a certain level of debt for each customer. When a renter who has reached the debt limit tries to rent another tape, a message appears on the cash register screen: "Do not rent!" Thus, the policy is implemented at the point of sale.

Menus are an easy tool to use to implement controls. Systems can be programmed so that the menu options that are displayed depend upon a user's access authorization. By varying available menus, the system forces users to limit what they do on the system.

Limits are an important data entry control.

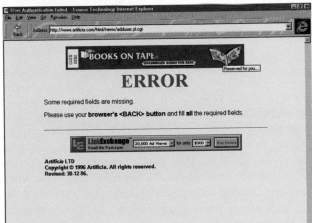

Programming **limits** on the numerical values that can be either entered into quantitative fields or output through processing is another effective way to control system use, especially when dealing with a Transaction Processing System (TPS). Upper limits are often set on quantities such as payments, salaries, number of units ordered, and lengths of time (such as the number of hours spent on a task). Systems often establish both a minimum and maximum that are reasonable in that type of transaction. For example, an organization may set a minimum for the sum paid for a purchase at zero and a maximum at $50,000, if that is the most expensive item the organization purchases. Upper and lower limits for a field recording the daily number of hours worked by an individual would be zero and 24 respectively.

The Ultimate IS Nightmare

With all the sophisticated antivirus software available to us, ISs are still highly vulnerable to virus attacks. About 3,000 new computer viruses are released every year. National security agencies are afraid that the future war will not take place on the battlefield, but on computer networks, and they are hard at work to prevent massive attacks. What do they fear? Consider the following scenario.

It is May 15, 2003, 10:36 a.m. on the east coast of the United States. Shares worth millions of dollars are traded on the floor of the New York Stock Exchange (NYSE). Suddenly, the electronic board showing stock information blanks out. The electronic ticker tape, here and in thousands of brokerage houses that broadcast it, stops moving. A NYSE manager hits an emergency button on a small console to alert a standby maintenance crew, hoping that this is a power failure. But the problem seems to be different. The technicians cannot fix it. Brokers throughout the country are cut off from their main source of information. Systems experts for the NYSE switch the board to an alternative computer program, but this one, too, fails after a few minutes. Thousands of brokerage house managers try to call in, but cannot get through. Apparently, telephone exchanges are malfunctioning. Some people try to log on to the Internet for information, but by 10:51 a.m., many servers stop functioning.

Banks in Boston and New York experience difficulties using their electronic funds transfer (EFT) systems. Money transfers become slower and slower. After several minutes, banks on the west coast start experiencing similar difficulties. At 11:26 a.m. no bank on the east coast can transfer a single dollar to another bank. By noon, the entire banking system is paralyzed. Customers are told that only the most important transactions can be executed, and even these transactions must be handled manually. Fortunately, most television networks have not experienced serious problems, and keep their regular programming schedules. At 11:45 a.m., CNN interrupts its regular program to report a major collapse of thousands of computer programs in the stock exchanges and banks.

(continued)

AUDIT TRAIL

In spite of the many steps taken to prevent system abuse, it nonetheless occurs. Consequently, further steps are needed to keep track of transactions, so that (1) when abuses are found, they can be traced, and (2) fear of detection will indirectly discourage abuse. One popular tracking tool is the **audit trail**: a series of documented facts that help detect who recorded what transactions, at what time, and under whose approval. Whenever an employee records a transaction, such a system prompts the employee to provide certain information: an invoice number, account number, salesperson ID number, or the like. Sometimes data about an operation, such as the date and time of the transaction, or the name or

Soon, it is apparent that financial institutions are not the only victims. Utility companies throughout the U.S. receive an increasing number of calls from citizens whose power and gas are out. Telephone companies realize that large parts of their networks are out of service. They try to use their computers to fix the problems, but they soon discover that the computers *are* the source of the problems. The computers in air traffic control towers display gibberish on the monitors. The controllers try to direct pilots "in the blind." After four fatal crashes, a repetitive radio announcement warns all aircraft and urges pilots to land their planes in Canada or Mexico.

Toward the end of the day, the Department of Defense and four large software companies replace major telephone and utility programs with secretly kept backup software, after disconnecting the systems from all external communications. In a special television and radio broadcast, national security experts instruct all computer users to disconnect from telephone networks until further notice, and reload their computer systems with fresh software. Permission to reconnect is given only hours later.

The nation is informed that it has been a victim of a computer virus attack. A few hours later, it is discovered that there were actually several viruses, undetected by the vast array of screening programs because all the viruses were new and sophisticated enough to avoid detection. All were released at the same time. It is discovered that the viruses were first introduced five years earlier, and were unknowingly copied millions of times over, as individuals and organizations transferred data, programs, and other telecommunications through millions of transactions over the years. The viruses are identified. A special program is quickly written by an emergency team at the Pentagon to destroy them in the networks. The total damage is estimated to be billions of dollars.

Three weeks later, after a thorough investigation, the directors of the FBI, and the Secret Service, report that the viruses were planted by a terrorist group that wanted to cause damage in a nonviolent, yet very effective, manner.

Currently, significant human and computing resources within the government are working to prevent such a scenario from actually taking place.

THINK CRITICALLY

What measures would you take if the federal government asked you to develop a plan that would prevent what is described in this scenario? Remember: your plan must be cost-effective.

password of the user, are recorded directly from the computer—often unbeknownst to the user—and attached to the record of the transaction.

Such a trail of information helps uncover undesirable conduct, from innocent mistakes to premeditated fraud. The information helps determine who made and authorized the entries, the date and time of the transactions, and other identifying data that are essential in correcting mistakes or recovering losses. The audit trail is the most important tool of the **electronic data processing (EDP) auditor**, the professional whose job it is to find such cases and investigate them, as discussed in Chapter 10, "Information Systems in Business Functions."

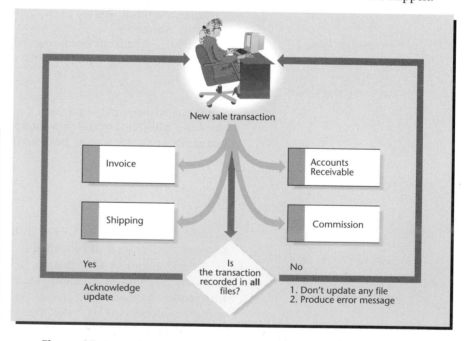
ATOMIC TRANSACTIONS

As you know, in an efficient IS, a user enters data only once, and the data are recorded in different files for different purposes, according to the system's programmed instructions. For instance, in a typical order system, a sale is recorded in several files: the shipping file (so that the warehouse knows what to pack and ship), the invoice file (to produce an invoice and keep a copy in the system), the accounts receivable file (for accounting purposes), and the commission file (so that the salesperson can be compensated with the appropriate commission fee at the end of the month). As indicated in Figure 17.6, a system supports **atomic transactions** when its code will only allow the recording of data if they successfully reach all their many destinations. So atomic transactions will ensure that only full entry in all the appropriate files occurs.

For instance, suppose the different files mentioned above reside on more than one disk, one of which is malfunctioning. When the clerk enters the sales transaction, a transparent process tries to record the appropriate data from the entry into each of the files. The shipping, accounts receivable, and invoice files are updated, but the malfunctioning commission file cannot accept the data. Without controls, the sale would be recorded, but, unknown to anyone, the commission would not be updated, and the salesperson would be deprived of the commission on this deal. The control mechanism detects that not all of the four files have been updated with the transaction, and doesn't update any of the files. The system may try to update again later, but if the update does not go through, the application will produce an appropriate error message for the clerk, and remedial action can be taken.

Note that this is not only a control against a malfunction, but also against fraud. Suppose the salesperson collaborates with the clerk to enter the sale only in the commission file, so she can be rewarded for a sale that has never taken place, and split the fee with the clerk. The above control would not let this happen.

Figure 17.6 *Atomic transactions ensure updating of all appropriate files. Either all files are updated, or none is updated and the control produces an error message.*

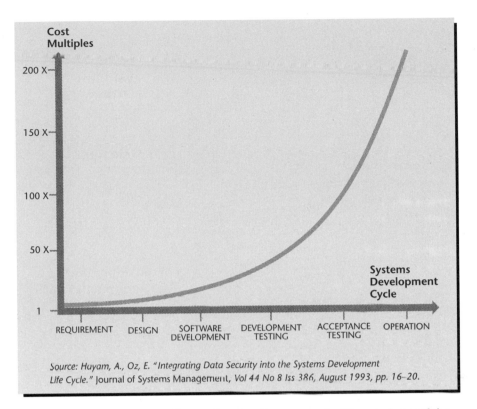

Source: Huyam, A., Oz, E. "Integrating Data Security into the Systems Development Life Cycle." Journal of Systems Management, Vol 44 No 8 Iss 386, August 1993, pp. 16–20.

Figure 17.7 *The cost of integrating security measures in different phases of the system's life cycle*

INTEGRATING SECURITY MEASURES INTO SYSTEMS DEVELOPMENT

Experience shows that it is much less expensive to incorporate security measures into a system during development than to impose them onto an existing system. The relative costs of incorporating security measures into a system at different phases of development and operation are shown in Figure 17.7. These data are derived from actual costs of making programming changes at different points of development; they vary by a factor of over 200. Figure 17.8 on the next page outlines the activities required to integrate security into the traditional phases of the system development cycle.

SECURITY STANDARDS

Managers must be aware of the degree to which their ISs are secured against unauthorized access and manipulation of data resources. One of the ways to judge that degree of security is by considering established **standards**. Perhaps the best known of these standards are the ones detailed in *Trusted Computer System Evaluation Criteria*, a book published by the federal government and popularly known as The Orange Book because of the color of its cover. While the book was originally written for military ISs, it is now used by the IT industry as a guide. In it, the National Computer Security Center (NCSC), which is an agency of the U.S. Department of Defense, defines four security levels, ranging from the minimal protection called Decision D to ultra-security called Decision A:

1. A: Verify Protection
2. B: Mandatory Protection
3. C: Discretionary Protection
4. D: Minimal Protection or No Protection

Net Notes

The *Disaster Recovery Journal* has a Web site that addresses the topics discussed here. Use the URL *http://www.drj.com* to explore it.

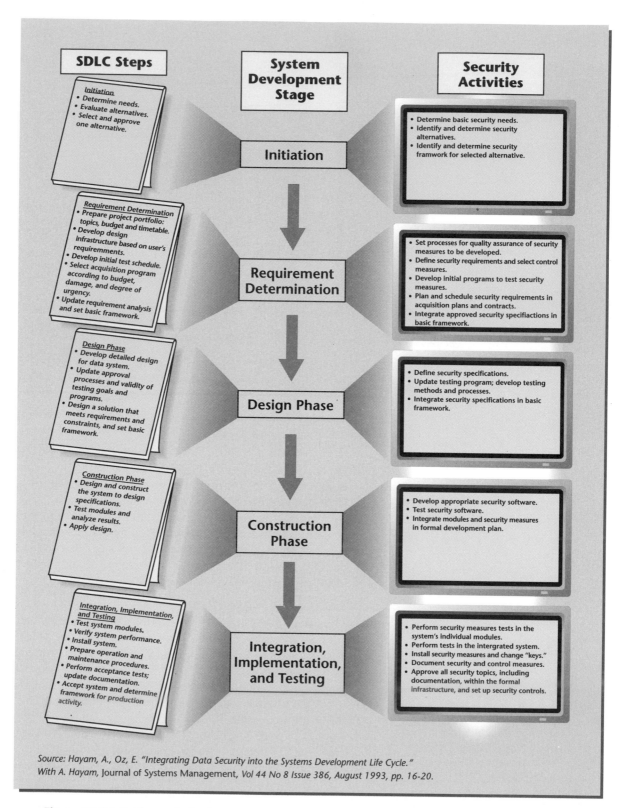

SDLC Steps

Initiation
- Determine needs.
- Evaluate alternatives.
- Select and approve one alternative.

Requirement Determination
- Prepare project portfolio: topics, budget and timetable.
- Develop design infrastructure based on user's requirements.
- Develop initial test schedule.
- Select acquisition program according to budget, damage, and degree of urgency.
- Update requirement analysis and set basic framework.

Design Phase
- Develop detailed design for data system.
- Update approval processes and validity of testing goals and programs.
- Design a solution that meets requirements and constraints, and set basic framework.

Construction Phase
- Design and construct the system to design specifications.
- Test modules and analyze results.
- Apply design.

Integration, Implementation, and Testing
- Test system modules.
- Verify system performance.
- Install system.
- Prepare operation and maintenance procedures.
- Perform acceptance tests; update documentation.
- Accept system and determine framework for production activity.

System Development Stage

Initiation

Requirement Determination

Design Phase

Construction Phase

Integration, Implementation, and Testing

Security Activities

- Determine basic security needs.
- Identify and determine security alternatives.
- Identify and determine security framwork for selected alternative.

- Set processes for quality assurance of security measures to be developed.
- Define security requirements and select control measures.
- Develop initial programs to test security measures.
- Plan and schedule security requirements in acquisition plans and contracts.
- Integrate approved security specifiactions in basic framework.

- Define security specifications.
- Update testing program; develop testing methods and processes.
- Integrate security specifications in basic framework.

- Develop appropriate security software.
- Test security software.
- Integrate modules and security measures in formal development plan.

- Perform security measures tests in the system's individual modules.
- Perform tests in the intergrated system.
- Install security measures and change "keys."
- Document security and control measures.
- Approve all security topics, including documentation, within the formal infrastructure, and set up security controls.

Source: Hayam, A., Oz, E. "Integrating Data Security into the Systems Development Life Cycle."
With A. Hayam, Journal of Systems Management, Vol 44 No 8 Issue 386, August 1993, pp. 16-20.

Figure 17.8 *Activities required to integrate data security in the systems development life cycle*

Understand Controls and Security Measures in Information Systems?

You are working on a marketing plan for a new product. The work is exciting but involves many figures and formulas, and you stayed late last night to complete your presentation for 10 a.m. this morning. Just as you are finishing, you notice that certain totals have disappeared from one of the spreadsheets. You check the underlying formulas of a sample of the cells. Some of the formulas are there, some are not. Apparently your computer has been attacked by a virus. You instinctively reach to the bottom drawer of your desk for the backup disk, but freeze when you remember that you didn't back up the last update. You have a major problem on your hands.

As explained and demonstrated throughout this book, information is the lifeblood of any modern organization. Practically every aspect of business is dependent on the currency of processed data and the timely provision of information. This can be achieved only if information systems are protected against threats. As a manager, you must be aware of what may happen to the ISs you and your subordinates depend upon. You must protect the systems against events that threaten their operation and make it impossible to carry out critical business activities. When a new system is developed, you should ask that the developers provide a system that not only supports the functions of your business unit, but also incorporates controls that will minimize any compromising of the system. And to be prepared for a disaster, you should know how to implement your part of the disaster recovery plan to help restore operations as soon as possible.

The four categories are further broken down into subclasses (seven in all) that represent, as the book itself puts it, "increasing desirability from a computer security point of view."

Essentially, a D level classification means that the system is unrated, or that it has no inherent security. An example would be an out-of-the-box plain PC. Systems that merit a B3 or an A1 level rating—the top two levels assigned by the NCSC—are assumed to be "bullet-proof" since they are designed from scratch to protect classified military information and government secrets.

Most commercial-grade systems, both hardware and software, fall into either the C1 or C2 rating. The Orange Book says that a C1 system "satisfies discretionary security requirements" by providing separation of users and data. Essentially, C1 systems let users protect their data from the roaming hands of other users.

The more robust C2 rating "makes users individually accountable for their actions through log-in procedures, auditing of security relevant events, and resources isolations," The Orange Book states. Many commercial systems, such as Microsoft Corp.'s Windows NT, Apple Computer Inc.'s A/UX, and IBM's OS/2, meet, or will meet, the C2 requirement.

Experience shows that once a set of standards is established, it becomes a reference for many players in the industry, and manufacturers start incorporating the standards into their products. It is expected that makers of hardware and developers of software will take notice and soon adhere to The Orange Book recommendations for higher-level security measures. Once the public is aware of the standards, buyers of computer systems will inquire about the security of the systems offered them. Competition may prod the industry to incorporate better security features.

Critics of The Orange Book claim that it is fine for protection of secrecy but not for protection from other types of damages, such as monetary fraud. Because the emphasis is on secrecy, the only aspect considered is access. Also, they claim, the book does not address networking issues.

SEPARATION OF DUTIES

One of the most important measures used to prevent abuse of ISs and criminal "inside jobs" is the **separation of duties**. Separation of duties establishes an environment in which people are in charge of different activities, to allow checks and balances and minimize the possibility of criminal behavior. As with all other controls, for separation of duties to succeed, policies must be established during systems development and maintenance, as well as during its operation.

SEPARATION OF DUTIES IN SYSTEMS DEVELOPMENT AND MAINTENANCE The breaking up of the development task into several subtasks serves not only an important principle of modularity (discussed in Chapter 15, "Systems Development"), but also the security interests of the enterprise. As indicated in Figure 17.9, during the construction of the application, menus, access codes, passwords, and other security measures are incorporated. A security-conscious project manager will let programmers write code, but will ensure that access methods can be easily changed by end users after a system is delivered. This way, the programmers will not be able to control the security mechanism of the system; once users have established their access codes, the original programmers will need those codes to access secured areas.

Remember that all systems are tested to make sure they will operate successfully, but they are also scrutinized to be sure there are no **trapdoors**—that is, points in the code where the program could allow an intruder to circumvent security measures in the application. Ideally, a team of specialists completely separate from the development team tests the system for security measures, tries to attack the system in every possible way, and fixes the weak points before the system is introduced for use.

SEPARATION OF DUTIES WHILE USING THE SYSTEM Separation of duties by system users is also desirable, especially when ISs involve financial or accounting activities that may be subject to fraud or theft. Separation of duties was practiced by many firms well before the days of computer-based systems, but it is now a more sensitive issue because of the ease with which money can be manipulated. Millions of dollars can be transferred from one account to another in a legitimate transaction, with a few keystrokes, and it's just as easy for a dishonest employee to illicitly transfer money from a corporate account to his or her own account.

Security Responsibilities

SYSTEM BUILDER	SYSTEM OWNER
◆ Create menu system that can be used to conrol access by providing different menus depending upon authorization.	◆ Establish access codes.
	◆ Establish passwords.
	◆ Establish access procedures.
◆ Include program modules that allow users to create access codes and passwords.	

Figure 17.9 *Separation of duties between developers and users*

Separation works best when a process can be broken into a sequence of easily distinguishable steps, each handled by different people. For example, many companies have systems for the transfer of large sums of money, such that transfer is initiated by one person, authorized by another person, and executed by a third person. In many financial institutions, the electronic transfer of funds cannot be executed unless two employees join their passwords to trigger the transaction.

Though simple, the principle of separation of duties is an extremely powerful control on a system's security. A survey by KPMG Peat Marwick revealed that "normal system control" (which includes the separation of duties that relate to the operation of the computer systems) can detect 59% of computer fraud; internal audit functions can detect 47%; 32% is discovered by accident; and 3% is uncovered by external auditors.[4]

NETWORK CONTROLS

As use of networked systems increases, fewer and fewer computers are standalone machines. Many are permanently connected directly to other computers via dedicated lines ("hardwired"), or are equipped with modems or other communication devices that allow users to connect to other computers. This means that any resource on a networked computer can technically be used by the user of another computer connected to the network. While extending access and increasing operational flexibility, networked systems have their own special security needs, because they are designed to be accessed by parties whose identity and intentions are unknown to the organization. In general, once a user enters a network, security measures using access codes and passwords are similar to those applied to any computer system: ascertaining that users access only authorized parts of databases and ensuring that the proper access privileges are exercised. However, callback procedures, encryption, and firewalls are additional precautions against unauthorized use specifically on networks.

CALLBACK Sadly, the more organizations open their systems for employees to work from home or while traveling, the more prone they are to security breaches. A popular measure against unauthorized remote access is called **callback**. When a modem dials into a system, a special application asks for the telephone number from which the call has been made; if the number is authorized, the system disconnects and dials that number. If the number does not match a number on its list of authorized numbers, the system does not allow access. This system sometimes requires temporary authorization to allow people who are traveling to access systems from the road.

ENCRYPTION The sharing of resources over computer networks requires the transfer of data over communication lines, whose monitoring then becomes another major security concern. Both LAN and WAN managers try to shield networks against unauthorized interception of signals to protect privacy or the secrecy of the communicated information. **Encryption** programs are used to scramble information transmitted over the network, so that an interceptor will receive unintelligible data. As indicated in Figure 17.10 on the next page, the receiving computer uses a key, which is a special combination of bytes, to activate a **descrambler**

---

[4] Quoted in Messina, F.M., Tanju, D.W., and Eaton-Hammers, S.L., "Welcome to the World of Internal Auditing: Lessons from the Field," *New Accountant*, September 1994.

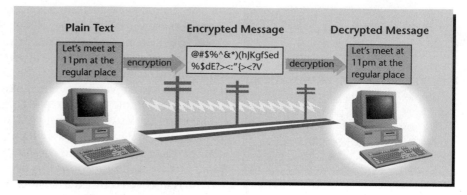

Figure 17.10 *Encrypting communications increases security.*

that translates the signals back into the original message. When these programs run, each transmission is assigned a different decoding key. One such descrambling program, based on the **Data Encryption Standard (DES)**, uses a key that consists of a string of bytes long enough to generate 2^{56} (roughly 72 quadrillion) different possible values; only one of them is the key to any one communication. Only the person with the correct key can read the message. Needless to say, these odds make the encryption difficult for an unauthorized hacker to decipher.

Obviously, experts try to come up with encryption schemes that are difficult for illegitimate interceptors to resolve. Several excellent encryption formulas have been developed for government and commercial use. One that has made headlines is Clipper. Clipper is actually an electronic chip containing an encryption scheme developed by the National Security Agency. The federal government's position is that a court order should allow it to descramble any communication between any two computers, for national security or crime prevention reasons. If Clipper were installed in every computer manufactured in the U.S., government agencies would be able to decipher any communication: two keys held by the government would combine to provide the software required to descramble any communication into plain text. Clipper invoked a heated public debate, as described in the *Ethics and Society* section.

FIREWALLS The great increase in the number of people and organizations using the Internet, and especially running Web sites, has provided fertile ground for unauthorized and destructive activity. In recent years many companies have found their home pages defaced with electronic graffiti, some with offensive material. Some companies have experienced destruction of data in the databases that they opened for service through common gateway interfaces (CGIs).

The best defense against unauthorized access to systems over the Internet is a **firewall**, which is software whose purpose is to separate users from computing resources. (Early firewalls used combinations of hardware and software.) The software screens the activities of a person who logs on to a Web site; it allows retrieval and viewing of certain material, but blocks attempts to make any changes in the information or to access other resources that reside on the same computer.

A safer way to prevent unauthorized access to an IS via a Web site is to use a completely separate server for the resources meant to be accessible to Net surfers. The Web pages on this separate server will be a **mirror** of the pages from the main server. A mirror is a complete, identical copy of software on another server. The mirror on the Internet server is periodically updated, and the computer with the

Net Notes

The Organization for Economic Cooperation and Development (OECD) maintains Web pages with its policy and recommendations on issues such as protection of personal data and privacy, security of information systems, and cryptography. The URL is *http://www.oecd.org/dsti/iccp/legal/top-page.html*.

original copy remains physically disconnected from the Net. This approach is inconvenient when dealing with dynamic, time-dependent information. In such cases, a good firewall must be used.

It is important to note that while firewalls are used to keep unauthorized users out, they are also used to keep unauthorized software away. When an employee uses a company computer to access external Web sites, the firewall screens for viruses and active attempts to invade company resources through the open communication line. It may also be programmed to block employee access to sites that are suspected of launching rogue programs, or to sites that provide no useful resources. The firewall then prohibits the user from logging on to those sites.

RECOVERY MEASURES

Security measures may reduce undesirable mishaps, but nobody can control all disasters. To be prepared for such cases, organizations prepare **recovery measures**. Organizations that depend heavily on ISs for their daily business often use **redundancy**; that is, they run all systems and transactions on two computers in parallel, to protect against loss of data and business. In this setting, if one computer is down, the work will continue on the other computer. This makes the system **fault-tolerant**. However, in distributed systems, doubling every computing resource is extremely expensive, and other measures must be taken.

To prepare for mishaps, either natural or malicious, many organizations have well-thought-out programs in place, called **disaster recovery plans**. The plans detail what should be done and by whom, if critical ISs go down, or if IS operations become untrustworthy. In recent years, many large corporations have taken steps to outline a more holistic scheme that looks at all of the critical business operations. With this approach, the corporation puts in place a **business recovery plan** that considers factors beyond just computers and ISs.

THE DISASTER RECOVERY PLAN

Concern about disaster recovery has spread beyond banks, insurance companies, and data centers, the traditional disaster recovery fanatics. Many customer service and retail firms realize that they can easily lose customers if they don't deliver services and products in a timely manner, which is why the term **business recovery** or **business resumption** has caught on in some circles. In interactive-computing environments, when systems are idle, so are the people who bring in revenue to the business. In addition, companies' reputations can be harmed, and competitive advantage and market share lost.

Experts propose nine steps for development of a **business recovery plan**:[5]

1. *Obtain management's commitment to the plan.* Development of a recovery plan requires substantial resources. Top management must be convinced of the potential damages that paralysis of information systems may cause. Once management is committed, it should appoint a business recovery coordinator who will develop the plan and execute it if disaster occurs.

---

[5] Song, K.W., Monaco, A.M., Sellaro, C.L., "Disaster Recovery Planning: Suggestions to Top Management and Information Systems Managers," Journal of Systems Management, May 1994, pp. 28–33.

A computer that was processing credit card transactions for Banc One Corp. crashed after a software downloading error by an operator, leaving the bank unable to access computer files for some customers. Spokesman John Russell said the crash occurred on a Sunday night, during routine downloading of outside files, when the operator entered the wrong date into the computer. The company had to turn to paper backups for credit card authorizations while the system was being fixed, according to Mr. Russell. While he said that customers should notice no differences, they did report difficulties in getting authorizations. Mr. Russell said the affected area was in the Midwest.

A telephone recording at Banc One's call-in center told callers that the company was experiencing information-processing difficulties and was unable to access computer data for customers. The recording said that the bank holding company expected to be able to access most files within a day, and that credit cards still were usable at merchants and automatic-teller machine locations. But it also urged customers with non-emergency questions to postpone calling in for help until early the following week, due to the heavy volume of calls expected.

2. *Establish a planning committee.* The coordinator establishes a planning committee comprising representatives from all business units that are dependent on computer-based ISs. The members serve as liaisons between the coordinator and their unit managers. The managers are authorized to establish emergency procedures for their own departments.

3. *Perform risk assessment and impact analysis.* The committee assesses which operations would be hurt by disasters, and how long the organization could continue to operate without the damaged resources. This analysis is carried out through interviews with managers of functional business areas. The committee compiles information regarding maximum allowable downtime, required backup information, and the financial, operational, and legal consequences of extended downtime.

4. *Prioritize recovery needs.* The disaster recovery coordinator ranks each IS application according to its effect on an organization's ability to achieve its mission. **Mission-critical** applications, those without which the business cannot conduct its operations, are given the highest priority. The largest or most widely used system may not be the most critical. The application may be categorized into several classes, such as:

   ◆ *Critical*: Applications that cannot be replaced with manual systems under any circumstances

   ◆ *Vital*: Applications that can be replaced with manual systems for a brief period, such as several days

   ◆ *Sensitive*: Applications that can be replaced with acceptable manual systems for an extended period of time, though at great cost

   ◆ *Noncritical*: Applications that can be interrupted for an extended period of time at little or no cost to the organization

5. *Select a recovery plan.* Recovery plan alternatives are evaluated by considering advantages and disadvantages in terms of risk reduction, cost, and the speed at which employees can adjust to the alternate system.

6. *Select vendors.* If it is determined that an external vendor can better respond to a disaster than in-house staff and provide a better alternate system, then the external vendor that will be most cost-effective is selected. Factors considered include the vendor's ability to provide telecommunication alternatives, experience, and capacity to support current applications.

7. *Develop and implement the plan.* The plan includes organizational and vendor responsibilities, and the sequence of events that will take place. Each business unit is informed of its responsibilities, key contacts in each department, and training programs for personnel.

8. *Test the plan.* Testing includes a walk-through with each business unit, simulations as if a real disaster had occurred, and (if no damage will be caused) a deliberate interruption of the system and implementation of the plan. In mock disasters, the coordinator measures the time it takes to implement the plan and how effective it is.

9. *Continually test and evaluate.* The staff must be aware of the plan at all times. Therefore, the plan must be tested periodically. It should be evaluated in light of new business practices and the addition of new applications. If necessary, the plan should be modified to accommodate these changes.

Industry	Process	Sample Resource Requirements
Mortgage lender	Process mortgage application	◆ Financial data ◆ Knowledge of mortgage qualifications standards
Retail store	Deliver customer order	◆ Order data (delivery address, payment requirements, etc.) ◆ Information on products to be delivered ◆ Information on transportation
Consulting firm	Prepare project	◆ Project requirements ◆ Knowledge of experienced consultant ◆ Word processing ◆ Printer

Source: Hurd., J.E., "Do You Know Where the Briefcase Is?" *Journal of Systems Management*, Vol 45, No 8, Issues 398, August 1994, pp. 16–21.

Figure 17.11 *Typical business processes and resource requirements*

Figure 17.11 presents examples of the types of business activities that may be interrupted by the threatening phenomena discussed above, and the resources required to support the activities. These would be the main focus of a business recovery plan.

THE BUSINESS RECOVERY PLAN

Business recovery planning (BRP) focuses on enabling businesses—including their hardware and software applications, communications, and facilities—to continue to function in an emergency. Whereas disaster recovery planning originally focused on getting centralized database computer systems running, BRP also focuses on the client/server or distributed computing environment.

A business recovery plan is a comprehensive statement of consistent actions to be taken before, during, and after a disaster to minimize disruption and ensure an orderly recovery, ongoing availability of critical resources, and continuity of operations. The plan should (1) be well-defined and cover all options, (2) include preventive measures as well as procedures to implement in the event of a disaster, and should minimize the number of decisions that must be made following the disaster. The plan should (3) be set up to address the worst-case scenario, but should permit parts of the plan to be executed when less severe disruptions occur. The plan should address hardware, systems software, applications software, communications, and facilities (such as office workspace). The plan should also include the key personnel and their responsibilities, as well as a procedure to reinstitute interactions with outside business partners and suppliers.

Virtual Reality South, a small maker of virtual reality games in Charleston, South Carolina, got a dose of real life when a disgruntled employee quit in August 1996. It seems that the employee, as a parting shot, password-protected some Microsoft Word documents that are vital to VR South's business. He refused to disclose the passwords unless the company paid him off in cash and stocks.

VR South responded by seeing if it could hack the passwords. "We called Microsoft to find out how we could break into the documents," said Jon Pherigo, the company's general manager, "and they told us there was no way to do it." Undaunted, Pherigo hired a programming expert to surf the Net and find a program that decrypts Word 7.0 documents. VR South ran the program, deciphered the passwords, and gained access to its locked-up data. Pherigo said that the company would pursue the former employee, believed to be in France, and charge him with extortion.

Source: Violino, R. "The Reality of Insecurity Hits Home," *InformationWeek*, September 30, 1996, p. 10.

Planning for business recovery follows the same steps as mentioned above for disaster recovery. Once the plan is in place, it should be tested on a regular basis. The plan must also be updated. The enterprise's priorities and environment will change over time. There will be new business processes or changes in the relative importance of existing processes or tasks, new or different application software, changes in hardware, and new or different IS and end-user personnel. The plan must be changed to reflect the new environment, and the changes must be thoroughly tested. A copy of the plan should be kept off-site, because if a disaster occurs, an on-site copy may not be available.

THE ECONOMIC ASPECT OF SECURITY MEASURES

From a pure cost point of view, how much should an organization spend on data security measures? There are two types of costs that must be considered to answer this question: the cost of the potential damage, and the cost of implementing a preventive measure. The cost of the damage is the aggregate of all the potential damages multiplied by their respective probabilities, as follows:

$$Cost\ of\ Potential\ Damage = \sum_{i=1}^{n} Cost\text{-}of\text{-}disruption_i \times Probability\text{-}of\text{-}disruption_i$$

Where i is a probable event, and n is the number of events.

Experts are usually employed to estimate the cost and probabilities of damages, as well as the cost of security measures.

Obviously, the more extensive the preventive measures, the smaller the damage potential. This means that as the cost of security measures goes up, the cost of potential damage goes down. Ideally, the enterprise will place itself at the optimum point, which is the point where the total of the two costs is minimized, as Figure 17.12 illustrates.

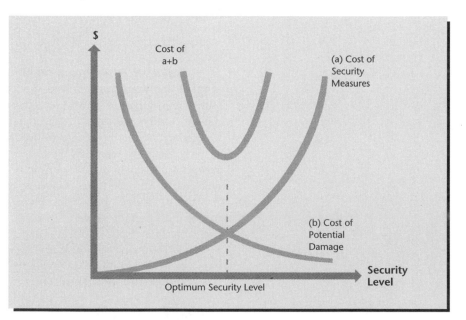

Figure 17.12 *The total cost to the enterprise is lowest at "Optimum." No less, and no more, should be spent on information security measures.*

No Code, No Payroll

Sometimes, security measures can wreak havoc, especially if they are not well documented. Several years ago, a systems analyst compiled a payroll procedure for a large corporation. To ensure that no one could print unauthorized checks, he devised a nine-digit numerical code that had to be entered to enable the payroll program to write checks. Other than the systems analyst, only two computer room operators, who had a need to know, were privy to this code.

A few years after establishing the system, the systems analyst left the company. At the start of the next calendar year, a strange thing happened to the program. It would operate up to the time it came to print the checks, and then operations would shut down. No matter what was tried, checks could not be produced. As the program had been running for several years and no one had made any changes, the systems analysts were mystified. A review of past projects revealed that no documentation was on file, a common failing in many companies.

Finally, in desperation, the company tracked down the systems analyst who wrote the program and asked for his help in debugging the system. After a quick review that refreshed his memory, he found the problem to be very simple. When the analyst had devised the system, he had used his nine-digit social security number as a verification key. This check-printing authorization code was matched against his social security number stored in the personnel file. He initiated this ingenious ploy to prevent theft by a person not knowing the code who would establish a new code, try to run checks, and then re-enter the original code.

After he left his position, his name and, more importantly, his social security number were retained in the active file until the end of the year. This was required so that income tax documents could be issued to all employees who had received salary during the past calendar year. After all the documents were issued, departed employee data were transferred to the inactive employee file. The entered authorization code could no longer approve check printing. It did not match the established verification key because his social security number was no longer in the other file.

Source: Stevens, R., "Cracking the code," Journal of Systems Management, September 1992, p. 17.

Questions:

1. Was it wrong of the programmer to use a code?

2. What would you have done immediately after implementing the system, to avoid such a mishap while still limiting access to protected files?

Taking Some of their own Medication

Jennifer Lawton is a co-founder and the CEO of NetDaemon Associates, a small firm in Boston that provides network support and Internet consulting. The company employs 14 people and has annual revenues of $1.5 million. One day in February 1995, she received a phone call from a man who accused her of invading several Web sites. Lawton was furious, and told the man he was crazy. It was inconceivable that any of her firm's employees would do such a thing. But after she hung up, she and Christopher Caldwell, co-founder and chief technical officer, took a closer look and were shocked to find the unthinkable. Someone had broken into their computer and used it to hack into other people's sites, including those of some of their own clients.

Lawton's first move was to disconnect the computer from the Internet to prevent further attacks. Then she called all of her 50 clients and told them that their systems might have been invaded. Some did not understand what that meant (remember, this was 1995), and she had to explain. To her surprise, some were not dismayed by the news; they felt fortunate to know where the system was vulnerable so they could close the gaps. None of the clients left NetDaemon.

For the next six months, Caldwell and Secret Service agents tried to track down the invaders. They eventually managed to put eight hackers in jail. The criminals had stolen credit card numbers and cellular phone numbers, and then sold them over electronic bulletin boards to other criminals, who used the numbers to run up credit card accounts and telephone bills. NetDaemon turned out to be just one of many victims. The perpetrators invaded its system, stole passwords of NetDaemon's clients, and then broke into the clients' systems.

These unpleasant events cost the firm thousands of dollars' worth of lost labor hours. This time includes the 24 hours they worked on clients' files to detect and restore damaged information, and the hours working with the Secret Service. They spent an average of ten hours per week for several months working with the federal agents. Luckily, Lawton had always insisted that the clients back up all the information on disks. This way, all that was damaged could be restored.

Until this event, NetDaemon used very light precautions against break-ins. It used free security software that its employees downloaded from the Web, and ran it monthly to detect unauthorized access to its computers. Ironically, just before this happened, Caldwell was considering purchasing more sophisticated software. Now, he and Lawton decided to purchase a firewall. It cost them $5,000, but they have never regretted the expense. They now use the incident to explain to their clients why firewalls are so important.

Source: Schafer, S., "Case Study: On-line Crime (Part 1), Inc., May 1996, p. 126; and Schafer, S., "Case Study: On-line Crime (Part 2), Inc., June 1996, p. 123.

Questions:

1. Sometimes, a successful break-in into a single system makes it easy to invade many other systems. Explain.

2. List the lessons one can draw from this case for any organization that maintains a Web site.

Thou Shalt Not Fail

Pitney Bowes Inc., $3.9 billion company in 1996, dominates the postage meter market with an 85% share and 1.3 million postage meters in circulation, mostly at large companies that pay monthly leases and other fees beyond the postage itself. In all, the company provides mail and message management for more than two million clients worldwide. The company delivers technological solutions to its customers' various needs, such as automatic stamping machines, facsimiles, copiers, and mail software. The hardware needed to support the ISs includes a great variety of mainframes and PCs. The company employs a network consisting of a star topology with a server at the data center and 200 point-to-point lines that support multiple sites.

The rapid popularity of the Web prompted Pitney Bowes to embark on a new project: a system that would allow any user of a PC with connection to the Internet to have access to a digital postage meter. The idea is as follows: using special software and the addition of a small added-on hardware piece, customers will be able to run an electronic postage account with Pitney Bowes, who will in turn run an account with the post office. The actual postage will be held electronically in the small hardware piece attached to a PC's printer that functions on the same principle as telephone cards that store a certain dollar-amount on their magnetic strip that is debited when phone calls are made. Using communication over the Internet, the postage can be digitally replenished, and when a user applies postage through their software, which can be printed onto the same label as a mailing address, the account will be electronically debited. To minimize fraud, the small device generates an encrypted bar code for the postage, which incorporates the nine-digit zip code of the customer. Purchasing and processing postage will eliminate activities such as maintaining the meter, visiting the post office to credit the meter, and physically having to print postage and attach it to mail, and also creates an excellent tool for a company to track postage expenses. The primary market for this revolutionary service consists of small businesses, home-based businesses, and individual consumers. The biggest challenges are maintaining security and maintaining service.

The new system uses not only new software but also a lot of hardware: a public telecommunications network, routers (devices to route electronic messages), servers, encryption devices, an internal computer network, a midrange computer, and two mainframe computers. To ensure that the system continues to provide services under any condition, the company had to use redundant computers and put in place a detailed disaster recovery plan. It also had to assure against potential break-ins to a system that is essentially a bank filled with money in the form of digital postage.

A Business Continuity Team was established to identify and develop recovery procedures for all the systems components whose failure could adversely affect the availability of the new service. (The team was composed of representatives from all the potentially affected areas, such as operations, networks, security, technical services, engineering, and marketing). Three phases were laid out to develop the plan: (1) identify all the components, their dependencies on each other, and their respective times of operations; (2) identify the major transactions and their respective process flows; and (3) create

simulated scenarios for the failure of each component of the system to help identify the required recovery procedures.

The recovery procedures for the two mainframe computers had been put in place years ago and are tested at least twice a year. The team had to decide on procedures for the rest of the system. It was decided to use three communications links from the value added network that the company used. Two of them shared the communication load, but the third was fully dedicated for back up, in case one of the other two failed. The servers were split into two groups that were housed in two different locations.

All the servers were up seven days per week 24 hours per day. They were replicated so that if any of them failed, another one would immediately take its place. Using backup servers requires extreme caution because there are small time gaps when switching, and the system cannot afford to lose "in flight" transactions (the ones taking place during the switch). When switching from a primary server to a backup server and back again, both servers must have identical data just before the switch. It was decided that all switching be manual rather than automatic because control of this complex system was extremely important.

The team felt that outlining a business recovery plan for the system while it was in its design phase had benefits. Team members had a full picture "from end to end" of how the system would operate. Their view was not

limited only to their business units' interface with it. Therefore they learned about many different undesirable situations that might occur, and wisely devised many response alternatives. Deciding on recovery plans concurrently with the system design allowed the company to design the system to be "bullet proof" almost under any condition.

Source: Kisslinger, J., "Business Continuity and the Project Life Cycle: A Case Study," Journal of Disaster Recovery, *June 1997, and Zuckerman, L., "New Company Wants to Sell Stamps Via Internet,"* New York Times, April 24, 1997.

Questions:

1. The team was called "Business *Continuity* Team" rather than "disaster recovery team" or "business recovery team." Explain why, in terms of what the team was supposed to ensure.

2. Without preventive measures, in what ways is this IS more prone to failure then other systems?

3. The case mentions some advantages of planning security controls during systems development, rather than afterwards. What other advantages are there?

The purpose of controls and security measures is to maintain the functionality of ISs, the confidentiality of information, the integrity and availability of data and computing resources, and compliance with security and privacy laws.

Risks to hardware include natural disasters, such as earthquakes, fires, floods, and power failures. Risks posed by human beings include theft of information, data alteration and destruction, computer viruses, vandalism, and inadvertent mishaps caused by incorrect commands or procedures. Protective measures run the gamut from surge protectors to the maintenance of duplicate systems, which make ISs **fault-tolerant**.

To minimize disruption, organizations use **controls**. Access controls ensure that only authorized people, can gain access to systems and files. Program **robustness** and data entry controls provide a clear and sound interface with the user. **Menus** and **limits** ensure that the user enters data in a desired sequence, and that the data are reasonable and do not deviate from preset ranges. **Audit trails** are built into an IS so that transactions can be traced to people, times, and authorization information. **Atomic transactions** ensure that transaction data are recorded properly in all the pertinent files, to ensure integrity. **Backup** procedures minimize the risk of losing data if the original data are destroyed or altered.

The sooner security measures are integrated in an IS, the less costly the implementation. Therefore, consideration of security must be a part of the systems development cycle, and appropriate measures must be integrated in all of its phases.

In addition to taking steps to prevent disruption, organizations also need a recovery plan so that they can resume business as soon as possible after a disaster strikes. Many organizations have **disaster recovery plans** and **business recovery plans** that are developed and periodically tested by a special committee. The plans identify **mission-critical** applications and prescribe steps various departments should take in a disaster.

To minimize the possibility of unauthorized access and fraud, **separation of duties** should be exercised both during systems development and in the system's productive phase. Separation of duties during development prevents the installation of **trapdoors**.

Separation of duties while the system is in current use minimizes abuse, especially in the electronic transfer of funds.

As growing numbers of ISs are connected through networks, especially through the Internet, special attention should be given to network controls. **Network controls** are intended to ensure that only authorized people have access to the network, and that after they access it, they use only authorized resources. Controls are also implemented to prevent interception of messages. To this end, **encryption** schemes are developed, which scramble messages at the sending end, and descramble them into plain text at the receiving end.

When considering how much to invest in security measures, organizations should evaluate the dollar amounts of the potential damage on one hand, and the cost of security on the other hand. The more that is spent on security, the smaller the potential loss. Organizations should spend the amount that brings the combined costs to a minimum.

The government's need to protect citizens against crime and terrorism often collides with individuals' right to privacy. Such is the case with Clipper, a microchip the U.S. government wants computer manufacturers to install in every computer made in the U.S. The chip would allow federal agencies to obtain the plain text of any encrypted message sent between computers. However, the fierce objection of IT industry leaders and civil rights advocates has pressured the U.S. government to put the idea on hold.

REVIEW, DISCUSS, AND EXPLORE

REVIEW AND DISCUSSION QUESTIONS

1. What are the goals of security measures for ISs? Explain.

2. Data alteration and destruction are dreaded by many IS managers more than any other mishap. Why?

3. The average damage in a bank robbery is $3,400, and the culprit has an 85% chance of being caught. The average damage in a "usual" white collar fraud is $23,000. The average amount stolen in computer fraud is $600,000, and it is extremely hard to find the culprit. Why is the amount involved in computer fraud so high, and why is it difficult to find the culprit?

4. The majority of computer fraud criminals are insiders, that is, employees. What measures would you take to minimize fraud through ISs?

5. Comment on the following statement: If your computer is connected through an external telephone line, anyone with a computer and a modem has access to it.

6. Assume that you are charged with the development of an application for the recording of baseball performance ratios. What limits would you include to ensure that the information entered is reasonable?

7. What is an audit trail? What audit trail information would you have a shipping IS record?

8. This chapter gives an example of an atomic transaction. Give another example, from any business area.

9. Why is it so important to include security measures in the early phases of the systems development cycle?

10. Why do many organizations prefer to consider a Business Recovery Plan, rather than a Disaster Recovery Plan?

11. What is meant by "network controls"?

12. To prevent unauthorized people from copying data from a database, some companies use installed diskless computers at designated locations. How could a crooked user overcome this obstacle?

13. When organizations establish Web sites, they run the risk that some Internet surfers will change the content of the sites or invade their databases. What measures can they take to prevent such attacks?

14. List and briefly explain the risks to (1) organizations and (2) individuals who are engaged in electronic commerce via the Internet.

15. *Ethics and Society*: What is your opinion of the Clipper issue? Should the public accept the government's demand that manufacturers install the Clipper in all computers? Why, or why not?

CONCEPT ACTIVITY

Use your word-processing application to write a document to the president of a small bank that is planning the implementation of banking via the Internet. Outline the risks of the planned system. Outline your suggestions for protecting the system.

1. Examine the latest application you programmed. How could you make it more robust? Implement all these features in the program.

2. Use a human resources database you prepared that has more than one table (possibly the Hands-On Activity of Chapter 7, "Data Management"). The application should allow read access to any person whose ID or SSN appears in a table. It should allow write access to anyone who knows the password you designated. Test your application to ensure its robustness.

TEAM ACTIVITY

Visit a local business and discuss the various security and BRP strategies that are in place. Prepare a list of strengths and weaknesses of the strategies.

EXPLORE THE WEB

Find five Web sites that require the transmission of private data—that is, any personal information, credit card number, social security number, or investment portfolio information. Evaluate the measures taken to secure the information from prying eyes. Provide the URL of each site and answer the following questions:

1. Is there a warning that the information may be intercepted?

2. Which types of access codes are used?

3. Is any encryption method used? (If you cannot answer this question, send an e-mail message to the Webmaster asking for information.)

4. In general, via which site would you be most comfortable doing business? Why?

GLOSSARY

Access Control - Hardware and software measures used to control access to information systems, such as user IDs and passwords.

Agent (electronic) - A computer program that searches bulletin boards and other resources in a telecommunications network to satisfy a need expressed by the owner of the program.

Agent of Change - Any person, an employee or a consultant, whose work results in significant change in the way workers perform their jobs. Often, systems analysts are agents of change.

Algorithm - A sequence of steps one takes to solve a problem. Often, these steps are mathematical formulas.

Analog Signal - A continuous signal, for example a human voice or the movement of the hands in an analog watch, which represents different degrees of mechanical or electrical power.

Applet - A small software application, usually written in Java or another programming language for the Web.

Application - A computer program that addresses a general or specific business or scientific need. General applications include electronic spreadsheets and word processors. Specific applications are written especially for a business unit to accommodate a special activity.

Application Data Independence - A situation in which an application can be developed to manipulate data without regard to the physical organization of the data in the files. This is achieved in the database approach to data management.

Application Generator - A software tool that expedites the application development process. Often, the term is synonymous with fourth generation language. Modern application generators include graphical user interfaces.

Application Software - Software developed for specific business purposes or for development of business applications. Spreadsheets are an example.

Application-Specific Software - A collective term for all computer programs that are designed specifically to address certain business problems, such as a program specifically written to deal with a company's market research effort.

Arithmetic Logic Unit (ALU) - The electronic circuitry in the central processing unit of a computer responsible for arithmetic and logic operations.

Artificial Intelligence - The study and creation of computer programs that mimic human behavior. This discipline combines the interests of computer science, cognitive science, linguistics, and management information systems. The main subfields of AI are: robotics, artificial vision, natural language processors, and expert systems.

Artificial Vision - A subfield of artificial intelligence devoted to the development of hardware and software that can mimic human vision.

ASCII - (pronounced: ASKee) American Standard Code for Information Interchange, a computer encoding scheme whereby each group of eight bits (a byte) uniquely represents a character.

Assembler - A compiler for an assembly language.

Assembly Languages - Second-generation programming languages that assemble several bytes into groups of characters that are human-readable, to expedite programming tasks.

Asynchronous Communications - Data communications whereby the communications devices must synchronize the transmission and reception after the transmission of each byte. Each byte is accompanied by synchronization bits, such as start and stop bits.

Asynchronous Transmission - Transmission in which each byte is accompanied with start and stop bits to ensure synchronization, at the byte level, between relatively simple communications devices, such as modems.

Atomic Transaction - A transaction whose entry is not completed until all entries into the appropriate files have been successfully completed. A data entry control.

Audit Trails - Names, dates, and other references in computer files that can help an auditor track down the person who used an IS for a transaction, legal or illegal.

Backward Chaining (Backward Reasoning) - The processes in which an expert system searches the conditions that would bring about the achievement of a specified goal. For example, an ES uses backward chaining to determine how long to invest how much money in which stocks to achieve a specified yield.

Bandwidth - The capacity of the communication channel; the number of signal streams the channel can support. A greater bandwidth also supports a greater bit rate, i.e., transmission speed.

Bar Code - A series of wide and narrow lines that represent data. Usually printed on product tags for ease of data entry and recording of shipment and sales by a special machine used to read the code.

Barriers to Entrants - Any and all of the measures that a business can take to prevent potential competitors from entering the market.

Baseband Link - A communications channel that allows only very low bit rate in telecommunications, such as unconditioned telephone twisted pair cables.

Batch Processing - A mode of transaction processing in which all the transactions of the same type for a period of time are collected, and then entered into a computer system together and processed.

Baud - After J.M. Emile Baudot, a French scientist; the number of signals per second that a communications channel can support.

Benchmarking - The measurement of time intervals and other important measurable characteristics of hardware and software, usually when testing them before a decision to purchase or reject.

Beta Site - An organization that agrees to use a new application for a specific period and report errors and unsatisfactory features to the developer in return for free use and support.

Bill of Materials - A list showing an explosion of the materials that go into the production of an item. Used in planning the purchase of raw materials.

Binary Number System - A number system in which 2 is the base (rather than 10, which is the normal base human beings use in everyday counting). Used in computers.

Bit - Binary digit; either a zero or a one. The smallest unit of information used in computing.

Bit Map - The arrangement of bits representing an image for display on a computer monitor or a paper printout.

Blackouts and Brownouts - Periods of power loss or significant fall in power. Such events may cause computers to stop working, or even damage them. They can be protected against these events by using proper equipment, such as UPS (Uninterrupted Power Supply) systems.

Bottom-Up Planning - An approach to planning based on satisfying the needs of individual business units. Reactive in nature.

Bridge - A device connecting two communications networks that use similar hardware.

Broadband Link - A communications channel that supports high-speed communication.

Browsing - Using a special application called a Web browser to move from one Web site to another.

Bug - An error in a computer program. Despite a famous story about a real insect that interrupted the work of a 1940s computer, the word "bug" had been used for "error" a long time before the advent of computers, and has nothing to do with that event.

Bus - The set of wires or soldered conductors in the computer through which the different components (such as the CPU and RAM) communicate. It also refers to a data communications topology whereby communicating devices are connected to a single, open-ended medium.

Business Recovery Plan (BRP) - A set of procedures to be followed by managers and their employees in the event of undesirable stoppage of business processes due to natural or other mishaps. The purpose of the plan is to resume vital processes as soon as possible.

Buzzword - A new or existing word that takes on a very specific meaning when used in a particular context. Buzzwords are usually used to impress someone with new jargon or to promote a product, service, or idea.

Byte - A standard group of bits. In ASCII, a byte comprises seven bits. In ASCII-8 and EBCDIC, a byte comprises eight bits.

Cache - From French, pronounced "cash." A part of RAM made of faster (and more expensive) memory chips. Usually devoted to the most frequently used instructions and data of a program.

Callback - A telecommunications security measure whereby the communications device at the destination end disconnects and calls the user back at the user-provided telephone number, to ensure the authenticity of the caller.

CASE (Computer-Aided Software Engineering) - Software tools that expedite systems development. The tools provide a 4GL or application generator for fast code writing, facilities for flowcharting or data-flow diagramming, data-dictionary facility, word processing, and other features required to develop and document the new software. Modern CASE is often called I-CASE (integrated CASE).

Cash Management Systems - Information systems that help reduce the interest and fees that organizations have to pay when borrowing money, and increase the yield that organizations can receive on unused funds.

Cathode-Ray Tube - A display (for a computer or television set) using an electronic gun to draw and paint on the screen by bombarding pixels on the internal side of the screen.

CD-ROM (Compact Disc Read-Only Memory) - A compact disc whose data were recorded by the manufacturer and cannot be changed.

Central Processing Unit (CPU) - The circuitry of a computer microprocessor which fetches instructions and data from the primary memory and executes the instructions. The CPU is the most important electronic unit of the computer.

Champion - An executive with much clout who supports a project and endeavors to muster support from top management. A champion is important for the success of a project to develop a new information system.

Channel (Link, Path) - The guiding or nonguiding environment in which communications signals are transmitted.

Chargeback - A method to manage the expenses involved in rendering information system services. The greater part of the expense is charged to the budget of the business unit that ordered it.

Chief Learning Officer - See CKO.

Chip - A flat piece of silicon in which electronic circuitry is integrated.

CIO (Chief Information Officer) - The highest-ranking IS officer in the organization, usually a vice-president, who oversees the planning, development, and implementation of IS and serves as leader to all IS professionals in the organization.

CKO (Chief Knowledge Officer) - A relatively new position in some large organizations. The CKO is responsible for garnering knowledge and making it available for future operations in which employees can learn from previous experience. The CKO works closely with the CIO, who is in charge of the technical means for garnering the necessary information. In some firms, the position is called Chief Learning Officer.

Client/Server - An information system arrangement in which one large computer holds large databases that are tapped by the users of smaller local microcomputers, but much discretion and creation of the applications that manipulate the data are in the hands of the users. The larger computer is the server, while the local computers are the clients.

Coaxial Cable - A transmission medium consisting of thick copper wire insulated and shielded by a special sheath of meshed wires to prevent electromagnetic interference. Supports high speed of telecommunications.

Common Gateway Interface - Special software used in Internet servers that allows the capture of data from a form displayed on a page and the storage of the data in a database.

Communications Channel - Any medium that supports transmission and reception of data and information. May be a guided channel, such as wires, or an unguided channel, such as the atmosphere or space. Also called communications link and communications path.

Communications Protocol - The set of rules that govern data communications. When more than two parties participate in the communication, it is also called network protocol.

Compact Disc (CD) - A plastic disk in which pits and flat areas represent bits. A laser beam "reads" the data. Also called "optical disk" and "laser disk." CDs have a storage capacity 100–150 times that of regular magnetic disks. Used as the predominant medium for storing musical works and archival data.

Compiler - A program whose purpose is to translate code written in a high-level programming language into the equivalent code in machine language for execution by the computer.

Composite Key - In a data file, a combination of two fields which can serve as a key to locate specific records.

Compression (Data Compression) - The re-storage or communication of data, using special software techniques, so that the new file takes up significantly less space on the storage medium, or takes less time to communicate over a channel.

Computer-Aided Design (CAD) - Special software used by engineers and designers that facilitates engineering and design work.

Controls - Constraints applied to a system to ensure proper use and security standards.

Control Unit - The circuitry in the CPU that fetches instructions and data from the primary memory, decodes the instructions, passes them to the ALU for execution, and stores the results in the primary memory.

Conversion - The process of abandoning an old information system and implementing a new one.

Critical Success Factors - Processes and their results that are critical to the success of business units. One approach to defining requirements for information systems is the outlining of CSFs by managers.

Customized Application - A computer program designed especially for an organization, to satisfy particular business needs.

Data - Facts about people, other subjects, and events. May be manipulated and processed to produce information.

Database - A collection of shared, interrelated records, usually in more than one file. An approach to data management that facilitates data entry, update, and manipulation.

Data Communications - The transmission and reception of digitized data in the computer, between the computer and its peripheral devices, and between computers. Data communications over a distance is called telecommunications.

Data Definition Language - The part of the database management system that allows the builder of a database to define the characteristics of fields, records, and the relationships among records.

Data Dictionary - The part of the database that contains information about the different sets of records and fields.

Data Entry Control - Software controls whose purpose is to minimize errors in data entry, such as a social security number with more or fewer than nine digits.

Data Flow Diagram - A convention of four symbols used to describe external entities, data stores, processes, and direction of data flow in an information system.

Data Manipulation Language - The part of a database management system that allows the user to enter commands to retrieve, update, and manipulate data in a database.

Data Mining - Using a special application that scours large databases for relationships among business events, such as items typically purchased together on a certain day of the week, or machinery failures that occur along with a specific use mode of a machine. Instead of the user querying the databases, the application dynamically looks for such relationships.

Data Redundancy - The existence of the same data in more than one place in a computer system. Although some data redundancy is unavoidable, efforts should be made to minimize it.

DASD (Direct Access Storage Device) - An external storage medium that allows direct (random) storage and retrieval of records from stored files. Example: magnetic disks and optical discs.

Data Warehousing - Techniques to store very large amounts of data in databases, especially for data mining.

DBA - Database administrator. The IS professional in charge of building and maintaining the organization's databases.

DBMS (Database Management System) - A computer program that allows the user to construct a database, populate it with data, and manipulate the data.

Decision Support Systems - Information systems that aid managers in making decisions based on built-in models. **DSSs** comprise three modules: data management, model management, and dialog management.

DFD (Data Flow Diagram) - A graphical method to communicate the data flow in a business unit. Usually serves as a blueprint for a new information system in the development process. The DFD consists of four symbols, for external entity, process, data store, and data flow.

Digital Signal - An expression of discrete, noncontinuous signals produced by electrical or electromagnetic bursts of different power levels. Only a digital signal can represent bits, and therefore be processed by a computer.

Direct Access - The manner in which a record is retrieved from a storage device, without the need to seek it sequentially. The record's address is calculated from the value in its logical key field.

Disaster Recovery Plan - An organization's list of the activities that will be performed by designated employees when its information systems fail because of natural disaster, or for any other reason.

Downloading - The copying of data or applications from a larger computer to a smaller computer, for example from a mainframe computer to a notebook computer. The term has come to mean the copying from another computer to your own computer, regardless of computer size.

Downsizing - The process of replacing large computers with smaller powerful computers.

EBCDIC - Extended Binary Coded Decimal Interchange Code. A binary computer encoding scheme devised by IBM. Consists of eight bits per byte, each byte uniquely representing a character.

Effectiveness - The measure of how well a job is performed.

Efficiency - The ratio of output to input; the greater the ratio, the greater the efficiency.

Electronic Data Interchange (EDI) - A set of software, standards, and telecommunications technology designed to support the interchange of electronic documents between organizations.

Electronic Data Processing (EDP) Audit - Audit of hardware, software, and procedures to detect errors or fraud in the operations of information systems.

Electronic Superhighway - The Internet. Often called the **information superhighway**.

E-mail (Electronic Mail) - The exchange of messages between computers either in the same building or over great distances.

Encoding Scheme - A convention of representing characters with the use of a small set of characters or special marks. Morse code, EBCDIC, and ASCII are encoding schemes.

Encryption - The conversion of plain text to an unreadable stream of characters, especially to prevent a party that intercepts telecommunicated messages from reading them. Special encryption software is used by the sending party to encrypt messages, and by the receiving party to decipher them.

Enterprise System - A system that supports the activities of many or all of the organization's activities, as opposed to small local systems.

Entity Relationship Diagram - One of several conventions for graphical rendition of the data elements involved in business processes and the logical relationships among the elements.

Ergonomics - The science of designing and modifying machines to better suit people's health and comfort.

Executive Information System - An information systems that extracts high-level organization-wide information from large amounts of data stored in the business' databases. Typically, an EIS presents information graphically as charts and diagrams for a quick grasp of patterns and trends. Also called **executive support system**.

Expert System (ES) - A computer program that mimics the decision process of a human expert in providing a solution to a problem. Current expert systems deal with problems and diagnostics in narrow domains. An ES consists of a knowledge base, an inference engine, and a dialog management module.

Expert System Shell - An expert system without a knowledge base. A tool that eases the building of an expert system by prompting the designer for facts and relationships among the facts that are built into the shell as a knowledge base.

Fault-Tolerant Computer System - A computer system that has extra hardware, software, and power lines that guarantee that the system will continue running even when a mishap occurs.

Feasibility Studies - A series of studies conducted to determine if a proposed information system can be built, and whether or not it will benefit the business: technical feasibility study, economic feasibility study, and operational feasibility study.

Field - A data element in a record, describing one aspect of an entity or event.

File - A collection of records of the same type, for different entities or events.

File Transfer Protocol - Software that allows the transfer of files over communications lines.

Firewall - Hardware and software designed to control access by Internet surfers to an information system, and access to Internet sites by organizational users.

Flowchart - A graphical method to describe an information system, including hardware pieces and logical processes. Over 30 symbols represent various types of operations, processes, input and output devices, and communications.

Foreign Key - In a relational database: a field in a file that is a primary key in another file. Foreign keys allow association of data from the two files.

Forward Chaining (Forward Reasoning) - The process in which an expert system looks for an outcome under the constraints of given conditions. Example: A medical ES accepts the conditions (age, temperature, etc.) of a patient and provides a diagnosis of the patient's disease.

Fourth-Generation Languages (4GLs) - High-level programming languages that allow the programmer to concentrate on what the program should do, rather than on how it should do it. 4GLs contain many preprogrammed functions to expedite code writing. Sometimes called "application generators."

Full-Duplex - Telecommunications whereby a party can transmit and receive data at the same time the other party transmits and receives.

Futz Factor - The time that users of information technology in the workplace spend on activities that do not add value for the organization, such as playing computer games or learning features that are not necessary for their work.

Fuzzy Logic - A rule-based method used in artificial intelligence to solve problems with imprecise conditions. The method uses membership functions to characterize a situation.

Gateway - A device that connects two communications networks, each consisting of a different hardware devices for example, an IBM- and a Macintosh-based network.

Genetic Algorithms - Sets of algorithms used in artificial intelligence to solve complex problems for which the number of models for solution is huge. The algorithms are either eliminated or combined with other algorithms to eventually produce the one that can solve the problem optimally. Called genetic algorithms because the method mimics the evolution of species over millions of years through changes in their genetic codes.

Geographic Information Systems - Information systems that exhibit information visually on a computer monitor with local, regional, national, or international maps, so that the information can easily be related to locations or areas on the map. GISs are used, for example, in the planning of transportation and product distribution, or the examination of government resources distributed over an area.

Global Village - A term referring to our world in the age of information and telecommunications, because people are highly accessible to each other.

Graphical User Interface (GUI) - Icons, frames, scroll bars, and other graphical means to make the use of software easy and intuitive to learn and use.

Group Decision Support System - A set of personal computers and one large screen with special software that facilitates brainstorming, examination of ideas, voting, and reaching a decision by a group of decision makers.

Groupware - Any of several types of software that enable users of computers in remote locations to work together on the same project. The users can create and change documents and graphic designs on the same monitor.

Hacker - A person who accesses a computer system without permission.

Half-Duplex - Telecommunications whereby the receiving party must wait until the transmitting party finishes, before transmitting to that party. A party cannot receive while transmitting or transmit while receiving.

Hierarchical Database - A database model that generally follows an upside-down tree structure, where each record type can have only one parent record type.

HTML Editor - An application that provides a GUI to help generate HTML code. It minimizes the need to know specific HTML commands.

Hypertext - Computer-generated text that allows the reader to click designated words (typically colored or boldfaced) to open a linked file that elaborates on the topic, or to invoke images or sound associated with the topic.

Hypertext Markup Language (HTML) - A programming language for Web pages and Web browsers.

Hypertext Transmission Protocol (HTTP) - Software that allows browsers to log on to Web sites.

IC - Information center. An organization unit that provides IS services to other business units. May have different sets of responsibilities in different organizations.

IC - Integrated circuit. The circuitry condensed in the microchips of modern computers.

I-CASE - Integrated CASE. Another name for computer-aided software engineering.

Imaging - The transformation of text and graphical documents into digitized files. The document can be electronically retrieved and printed to reconstruct a copy of the original. Imaging has saved much space and expense in paper-intensive business areas.

Indexed File - A data file that contains an index, a directory-like table that indicates where each record physically resides on the storage medium by the value of its key field. The records are usually organized sequentially, so that retrieval can be carried out either sequentially, without using the index, or through the index. To retrieve a record, a lookup is performed to find the record's location.

Indexed Sequential Organization - A file organization that allows direct access to specific records in a sequential file by using an index of key fields.

Inference Engine - The part of an expert system that links facts and relationships in the knowledge base to reach a solution to a problem.

Information - The product of processing data so that they can be used in a context by human beings.

Information Overload - A situation in which people have too much information from which to choose for their problem solving and decision making.

Information System - A computer-based set of hardware, software, and telecommunications components, supported by people and procedures, to process data and turn them into useful information.

Ink-Jet Printer - Inexpensive type of printer that sprays ink to create the printed text or pictures of a computer-generated document.

Input - Raw data entered into a computer for processing.

Insourcing - Assigning an IS service function to the organization's own IS unit. The term was invented to emphasize a decision not to outsource.

Intelligence - 1. The ability to learn, think, and deduce; 2. The first phase in the decision-making process: gathering relevant data.

Intelligent Agent - A sophisticated program that can be instructed to perform services for human beings, especially on the Internet.

Interface - The connection of two systems to establish interaction.

Internal Memory - The memory circuitry inside the computer, communicating directly with the CPU. Consists of RAM and ROM.

Internet - An international network of networks providing millions of people with access to rich information resources.

Internet Domain - The part of an Internet address, such as .com, .psu, or .gov, that is shared by many users and indicates the particular community of users to which they belong.

Internet Protocol (IP) Number - A unique number assigned to a server that is connected to the Internet, for identification purposes.

Internet Relay Chat (IRC) - Internet software that allows remote users to correspond in real time.

Internet Service Provider (ISP) - An individual or organization that provides Internet connection, and sometimes other related services, to subscribers.

Interpreter - A programming language translator that translates the source code, one statement at a time, and executes it. If the instruction is erroneous, the interpreter produces an appropriate error message.

Intranet - A network using Web browsing software, serving employees within an organization.

ISDN (Integrated Services Digital Network) - A set of hardware and software standards that support the transmission of text, images, and sounds through the same communications channel. ISDN will result in the combination of the telephone, fax, computer, and television into one device.

Java - Object-oriented programming language that allows Web browsers to download applets that can run on any computer with any operating system.

Key Field - A field in the record that contains a value that is unique to that record in the entire file. Typical keys are part number (in an inventory file) and social security number (in a human resources file).

Knowledge Base - The collection of facts and the relationships among them that mimic the decision-making process in an expert's mind and constitute a major component of an expert system.

Knowledge Engineer - A programmer whose expertise is the extraction of knowledge from a domain expert and the transformation of the knowledge into code, that is, into the knowledge base of an expert system. Knowledge engineers construct expert systems.

Knowledge Worker - Any worker who produces information. The term roughly overlaps with "professional."

LAN (Local Area Network) - A computer network confined to a building or a group of adjacent buildings, as opposed to a wide area network.

Laser Printer - A nonimpact printer that uses laser beams to produce high-quality printouts.

Learning Organization - The concept of an organization that accumulates knowledge through the experiences of its employees. Information systems facilitate learning by organizations.

Legacy System - An old information system still in use. Usually, the term is used when contrasting such a system with a new information system, or a new type of information system.

Logic Bomb - A destructive computer program that is inactive until it is triggered by an event taking place in the computer, such as the deletion of a certain record from a file. When the event is simply a particular time, the logic bomb is referred to as a **Time Bomb**.

Machine Cycle - The four steps that the CPU follows repeatedly: fetch an instruction, decode the instruction, execute the instruction, and store the result.

Machine Language - Binary programming language that is specific to a computer. A computer can execute a program only after its source code is translated to object code expressed in the computer's machine language.

MacOS - The family of Macintosh operating systems.

Magnetic Disk - Disk, or set of disks sharing a spindle, coated with easily magnetized substance to record data in the form of tiny magnetic fields.

Magnetic-Ink Character Recognition (MICR) - A technology that allows a special electronic device to read data printed with special magnetic ink. The data are later processed by a computer. MICR is widely used in banking. The bank code, account number, and the amount of a check are printed on the bottom of checks.

Magneto-Optic Disc - A compact disc whose surface is magnetized to deflect a laser beam in two different angles for binary storage of data. The discs are erasable and can be recorded multiple times. Also called CD/R, (Compact Disc/Recordable).

Mainframe - A computer larger than a midrange computer but smaller than a supercomputer.

Manufacturing Execution System - An information system that helps pinpoint bottlenecks in production lines.

Matrix Organization - An organization in which managers report to both a divisional executive and a functional executive. For instance, the marketing manager of the manufacturing division reports both to the division's president and to the corporate vice president of marketing.

Microcomputer - The smallest type of computer, including desktop, laptop, and hand-held computers. The term is less and less in use. Trade journals now use the terms PC and PDA.

Microprocessor - An electronic chip that contains the circuitry of either a CPU or a processor with devoted and limited purpose, such as a communications processor.

Midrange Computer - A computer larger than a microcomputer but smaller than a mainframe.

Migration - The move from older hardware or software to new hardware or software.

Mirror - An Internet server that holds the same software and data as another server which may be located thousands of miles away.

MIS (Management Information System) - A computer-based system that supports managers and their subordinates in their daily work and strategic planning: transaction processing systems, decision support systems, executive information systems, and any other type of system that supports managerial decisions and daily operations.

Mission-Critical Hardware or Software - Hardware or software without which the business cannot operate and survive.

Modem - Modulator/demodulator. A communications device that transforms digital signals to analog telephone signals, and vice versa, for data communications over voice telephone lines. Almost all of the commercial modems currently offered on the market also serve as **fax** devices, and are, therefore, called **fax/modems**. ("Fax" comes from the Latin words *fac simile*, "make alike" or "copy.")

Multimedia - Computer-based technology that provides information comprising text, images, motion pictures, and sound from the same source.

Multiplexer - A device that allows a single channel to communicate data from multiple sources simultaneously.

Multiprocessing - The mode in which a computer uses more than one processing unit simultaneously to process data.

Multitasking - The ability of a computer to run more than one program seemingly at the same time; it enables the notion of windows in which different programs are represented.

Native Application - A computer program originally written for the specific type of computer that is running it. As opposed to a native application, a **cross-system application** is one that was originally written for one type of machine, but then adapted for a newer computer. Usually, a cross-system application results in slow or poor performance.

Network - A combination of a communications device and a computer, or several computers, or one or several computers and terminals, so that the various devices can send and receive text or audiovisual information.

Network Database - A database model similar to the hierarchical model, but with the ability to establish many-to-many relationships among record types.

Neural Net - An artificial intelligence computer program that emulates the way in which the human brain operates, especially its ability to learn.

Nonvolatile Memory - Storage media that keep data and programs unchanged because they do not need electric power to maintain the stored material. Examples: ROM chips and magnetic disks.

Notebook Computer - A computer as small as a book, yet with computing power similar to that of a desktop microcomputer.

Object Code - Program code in machine language, immediately processable by the computer.

Object Linking and Embedding (OLE) - The linking of different applications to the same software so that it can be addressed and used by any of these applications. The object may be text, graphic, or audio-visual material.

Object-Oriented Technology - An approach to development of software that consists of objects, data, and the procedures that process the data, which can be invoked by different programs.

Online Processing - Using a computer while in current interaction with the CPU, so that the data are processed as they are entered, as opposed to batch processing.

OOP (Object-Oriented Programming) - A programming method that combines data and the procedures that process the data into a single unit called an "object," which can be invoked from different programs.

Open Operating System - An operating system that can run on every computer. Absolute open systems do not exist, but some operating systems, UNIX for example, can run on a large variety of computers, and therefore are often referred to as open operating systems.

Operating System - System software that supports the running of multiple applications developed to utilize its features.

Optical Character Recognition (OCR) - A way of capturing data from source documents in which scanning devices read characters and transform them into digital data processable by the computer.

Optical Fiber - A thin fiberglass filament used as a medium for transmitting bursts of light that represent bits. The most advanced physical communications channel, now in use for data, voice, and image telecommunications.

Optical Tape - A storage device that uses the same principles as a compact disc.

Output - The result of processing data by the computer; usually, information.

Outsourcing - Buying the services of an information service firm that undertakes some or all of the organization's IS operations.

Packet - Several bytes that make up a part of a telecommunicated message.

Packet Switching - A telecommunications method whereby messages are broken into groups of fixed amounts of bytes, and each group (packet) is transmitted through the shortest route available. The packets are assembled at the destination into the original message.

Parallel Transmission - Transmission of more than one bit at a time, usually the transmission of one byte at a time via parallel channels. Such transmission can take place only inside the computer or between the computer and its physically close peripheral equipment, such as a printer.

Parity Check - A method to reduce errors in data communications both inside the computer and among remote communications devices. An extra bit is added to each transmitted byte to ascertain that the number of 1s is odd (in an odd parity check), or even (in an even parity check).

Personal Digital Assistant (PDA) - A small hand-held computer. Many PDAs require the use of a special stylus to enter handwritten information that is recognized by the computer.

Pixel - A phosphor dot on the inside of a cathode-ray tube monitor. In a color monitor a triad of red, green, and blue dots is used. When the pixels are bombarded by electrons shot from the tube's electron gun, they emit light, thereby creating an image on the screen. The larger the number of pixels on the screen, the better the resolution. The term "pixel" is short for "picture element."

Platform - Either the standard hardware or the standard operating system that the organization uses. The term has been used differently in different contexts by IS professionals and trade journals.

Plug-and-Play - Hardware and software that can be installed and used by users with minimal training. Lay users can plug in the new system and use the preloaded software immediately.

Point of Presence (POP) - A telephone number that a user can dial to log onto a server even if the server is many miles away, to save the user long-distance call charges.

Point to Point (PPP) - A protocol for communications between two computers (as opposed to a network).

Primary Key - In a file, a field that holds values that are unique to each record. Only a primary key can be used to uniquely identify and retrieve a record.

Primary Memory (Primary Storage, Main Memory, Main Storage) - The built-in memory chips in the computer, made of transistors. The majority of the memory is of the RAM type, and the rest is of the ROM type.

Privacy - The ability to control information about ourselves. In a larger sense, "the right to be left alone." Information technology has made invasion of privacy a major issue in our society due to its ability to collect, maintain, store, and manipulate huge amounts of personal information.

Private Branch Exchange (PBX) - A computer-based digital switching device that simultaneously handles communications of internal voice telephones, computers, and the external telephone network.

Productivity - Efficiency, when the input is labor. The fewer labor hours needed to perform a job, the greater the productivity.

Program - A set of instructions to a computer.

Project Management - The set of activities that is performed to ensure the timely and successful completion of a project within the budget. Project management includes planning of activities, hiring and managing personnel, budgeting, conducting meetings, and tracking technical and financial performance. Project management software applications facilitate these activities.

Proprietary Operating System - An operating system that runs only on the computers made by a certain manufacturer, as opposed to an open operating system. For example, until 1994, the Macintosh operating system was proprietary.

Protocol - A standard set of rules that governs telecommunications between two communication devices or in a network.

Prototyping - An approach to the development of information systems in which several analysis steps are skipped, to accelerate the development process. A "quick and dirty" model is developed and continually improved until the prospective users are satisfied.

Query - An instruction to a database management system to retrieve records that meet certain conditions.

RAID (Redundant Array of Inexpensive Disks) - A set of magnetic disk packs maintained for backup purposes. Sometimes RAIDs are used for storing large databases.

Random Access Memory (RAM) - The major part of a computer's internal memory. RAM is volatile; that is, software is held in it temporarily and disappears when the machine is unplugged or turned off, or it may disappear when operations are interrupted or new software is installed or activated. RAM is made of microchips containing transistors. Many computers have free sockets that allow the expansion of RAM.

Rapid Application Development (RAD) - Methods using I-CASE tools and 4GLs to quickly prototype an information system. Often, software is reused in RAD.

Read-Only Memory (ROM) - The minor part of a computer's internal memory. ROM is loaded with software by the manufacturer that cannot be changed. Usually, ROM holds very basic system software, but sometimes also applications. Like RAM, ROM consists of microchips containing transistors.

Record - A set of standard field types. All the fields of a record contain data about a certain entity or event.

Re-engineering (also: Business Process Re-engineering) - The process by which the organization takes a fresh look at a business process and reorganizes it to attain efficiency. Almost always, re-engineering includes the integration of a new or improved information system.

Register - A fast memory location in the CPU, made of special semiconductors and circuitry.

Relational Database - A database in which the records are organized in individual tables (called "relations"). In order for data from different tables to be related, tables must contain foreign keys, which are primary keys in other tables in the database. The ease of building and maintaining a relational database has made it more popular than the hierarchical and network models.

Resolution - The degree to which the image on a computer monitor is sharp. Higher resolution means sharper image. Resolution depends on the number of pixels on the screen and the dot pitch.

Ring - A communications network topology in which each computer (or other communications device) is connected to two other computers.

RISC (Reduced Instruction Set Computer) - A computer whose CPU includes only the most commonly used functions. A reduced instruction set makes the computer significantly faster than the same computer with a full instruction set in its CPU.

Robotics - The science and specialty of developing machines that can mimic human movement. Robots are highly automated machines controlled by computers.

Sales Force Automation - Equipping traveling salespeople with notebook computers, PDAs, telecommunications devices, and other devices that allow them to communicate with the home office, retrieve and store information from and to other computers remotely, and fax information.

Scalability - The ability to adapt applications that originally ran on large computers to run on smaller computers.

Scanner - A device that scans pictures and text and transforms them into digitized files.

Schema - The structure of a database, detailing the names and types of fields in each set of records, and the relationships among sets of records.

Semantic Nets - A method of representing knowledge whereby facts are linked by relationships. The links create a "net."

Semistructured Problem - An unstructured problem with which the decision maker may have had some experience. Requires expertise to resolve.

Sensitivity Analysis - Using a model to determine the extent to which a change in a factor affects an outcome. The analysis is done by repeating IF-THEN calculations.

Separation of Duties - Assigning tasks in a way that will minimize the opportunity for fraud. Separation of duties is important when designing security measures during development of an information system.

Sequential Access - A file organization for sequential record entry and retrieval. The records are organized as a list that follows a logical order, such as ascending order of ID numbers, or descending order of part numbers. To retrieve a record, the application must start the search at the first record and retrieve every record, sequentially, until the desired record is encountered.

Serial Transmission - Transmission of streams of bits one after another. This is the only kind of transmission possible in telecommunications.

Server - A computer connected to several less powerful computers that can utilize its databases and applications.

Simplex - Transmission from a transmitter that can only transmit, to receivers that can only receive. Example: radio and television broadcasts.

Snail Mail - Regular mail handled by the postal service (as opposed to e-mail).

Software - Sets of instructions that control the operations of a computer.

Software Piracy - The phenomenon of copying software illegally.

SOHO - Small Office/Home Office. The fastest growing type of business, thanks to the availability of inexpensive microcomputers and fax/modems. Also called TOHO (Tiny office/Home Office).

Source Code - An application's code written in the original high-level programming language.

SQL (Structured Query Language) - A data manipulation language for relational database management systems that has become a de facto business standard.

Star - A network topology in which many computers are linked to a single computer through which all messages must be passed.

Strategic Information System - Any information system that gives its owner a competitive advantage.

Structured Problem - A problem for whose solution there is a known set of steps to follow. Also called a **programmable** problem.

Suite - A group of general software applications that are often used in the same environment. The strengths of the different applications can be used to build a single powerful document. Current suites are usually a combination of a spreadsheet, a word processor, a database management system, and telecommunications software. In the past, suites were called "integrated software."

Supercomputer - The most powerful class of computers, used by large organizations, research institutions, and universities for complex scientific computations and the manipulation of very large databases.

Synchronous Transmission - Transmission in which several bytes are lumped together and transmitted as a packet. Synchronous transmission requires sophisticated synchronization devices.

Synergy - From Greek: to work together. The attainment of output, when two factors work together, that is greater or better than the sum of their products when they work separately.

System Software - Software that executes routine tasks that are not typical for any specific business need. System software includes operating systems, language translators, and communications software. Also called "support software."

Systems Analysis - The early steps in the systems development process, to define the requirements of the proposed system and determine its feasibility.

Systems Development Life Cycle (SDLC) - The oldest method of developing an information system, consisting of several phases of analysis and design, which must be followed sequentially.

Systems Integrator - An individual or an organization that specializes in integrating several different hardware items and software applications for business operations. Often, the system integrator integrates one new information system into the existing information resources of the business. The term has become synonymous with "information systems consulting firm."

Telecommunications - Communications over a long distance, as opposed to communication within a computer, or between adjacent hardware pieces.

Telecommuting - The phenomenon of working from home with the help of information technology, rather than performing the same tasks in the office.

Teleconferencing - The ability to hold conferences with a number of other people who are all geographically remote from one another, via telecommunications devices.

Time Bomb - Rogue code that is installed in a computer system and starts destroying data files and applications at a preset time, or when a specific activity in a file occurs (for example, the deletion of a certain record).

Token Passing - A telecommunications method whereby a computer that needs to send a message captures a "token" consisting of a small group of bytes and attaches the message to the token.

Topology - The physical layout of a network.

Touch Screen - A computer monitor that serves both as input and output device. The user touches the areas of a certain menu item to select options, and the screen senses the selection at the point of touch.

Transaction - A business event. In an IS context, the record of a business event.

Transceiver - A communications device that can receive messages, amplify them, and retransmit them to their destination. Transceivers are used when the distance is long, and the signal may weaken on its way to the destination.

Transparency - A desired environment for the use of applications and telecommunications whereby the user is not exposed to the inner workings of the software or to the fact that information may actually come from different sources.

Trapdoor - Software that programmers leave in an information system without permission. It later allows them to access the system without authorization.

Tree - A network topology in which each computer (or other communications device) is connected to several other computers in a shape that resembles the branches of a tree.

Twisted Pair Cable - Traditional telephone wires, twisted in pairs to reduce electromagnetic interference.

Universal Resource Locator (URL) - The address of a Web site. Always starts with *http://*

UNIX - A popular operating system, versions of which run on machines from different manufacturers, and therefore make the software almost machine-independent.

Unstructured Problem - A problem for whose solution there is no pretested set of steps, and with which the solver is not familiar—or is only slightly familiar—from previous experience.

Uploading - The copying of data or applications from a smaller computer to a larger computer, for example, from a laptop computer to a mainframe computer. The term has come to mean copying from your computer onto another computer, regardless of computer size.

Value-Added Network (VAN) - A telecommunications network owned and managed by a vendor that charges clients periodic fees for network management services.

Very-Large-Scale Integration (VLSI) - Techniques to include a very large number of electric circuits on a small piece of silicon. Thus, many circuits are integrated in the chip.

Virtual Memory - Storage space on a disk which is treated by the operating system as if it were part of the computer's RAM.

Virtual Organization - An organization that requires very little office space. Its employees telecommute, and services to customers are given through telecommunications lines.

Virtual Reality - A set of hardware and software that creates images, sounds, and possibly touch that give the user the feeling of a real environment and experience. In advanced VR systems, the user wears special goggles and gloves.

Virtual Reality Modeling Language (VRML) - A standard programming language that supports three-dimensional presentation on the Web.

Virus (Computer Virus) - A rogue computer program that infects any computers it is entered into. It spreads in computers like a biological virus.

Voice Recognition - Technology that enables computers to recognize human voice, translate it into program code, and act upon the voiced commands.

Volatile Memory - Computer memory that cannot hold the original data when the machine is unplugged. Example: RAM.

WAN (Wide Area Network) - A network of computers and other communications devices that extends over a large area, possibly comprising national territories. Example: the Internet.

Webmaster - The person who is in charge of constructing and maintaining the organization's Web site.

Web Page - A screenful of text, pictures, sounds, and animation that the user encounters when using a Web browser. Web pages are developed using HTML or HTML editors.

Web Site - The electronic presence of an organization or individual on the World Wide Web. The site is composed of Web pages and either shares a server with other sites or has a dedicated server.

Windows - A popular operating system from Microsoft that runs on IBM and IBM-compatible machines and can also be run on Macintoshes equipped with proper intermediary software.

Wireless LAN - A local area network that uses electromagnetic waves (radio or infrared light) as the medium of communication.

Word (Data Word) - The number of bits that the control unit of a computer fetches from the primary memory in one machine cycle. The larger the word, the faster the computer.

Workstation - A powerful microcomputer providing high-speed processing and high-resolution graphics. Used primarily for scientific and engineering assignments.

World Wide Web (Web, WWW) - The section of the Internet that allows the posting and retrieval of text, pictures, sounds, and motion pictures. "Surfing" the Web is done by way of clicking on marked text and pictures to move to other pages at the same site or to a different site.

Worm - A rogue code that spreads in a computer network.

WORM (Write Once, Read Many) - A storage medium that is loaded with software by the manufacturer, and can never be overwritten. Example: CD-ROM.

MEASUREMENT UNITS

Baud - The rate of signals (rather than bits) per second. Named after J.M. Emile Baudot, a French scientist. Baud is equal to *bps* when each signal represents a single bit.

bps - Bits per second. The rate at which bits are transmitted in a communication. Transmission is conducted at thousands, millions, and billions of bps (**Kbps, Mbps**, and **Gbps**, respectively).

Dot Pitch - The distance, in millimeters, between the screen wires in a computer monitor. Typical dot pitches are .23–.28. The smaller the dot pitch, the better the resolution.

DPI - Dots per inch. The number of dots per inch on the paper output of a printer. The greater the DPI, the better the resolution of the output.

Gigabyte (GB) - One billion bytes.

Gigahertz (GHz) - One billion cycles per second.

Hits - The number of times a Web site has been visited.

Megabyte (MB) - One million bytes.

MegaFLOPS - Millions of floating-point operations. A measure of computer speed when executing arithmetic operations.

Megahertz (MHz) - One million cycles per second.

Microsecond (µsec) - One millionth of a second.

Millisecond (msec) - One thousandth of a second. Often, the average data retrieval time of storage devices is indicated as so many µsec.

MIPS - Millions of instructions per second. One measure of computer processing speed.

PPM - Pages per minute. Measure of the speed of printers.

Terabyte (TB) - One thousand billion bytes. Typically, large arrays of storage media have storage capacities of several terabytes.

Internet Protocol, 176
prototyping, 311, 378, 460–463
    applications, 462
    unnecessary, 462–463
    user application development, 499
public-key cryptography, 320
publishing, scientific, 41
PUFF, 410
punched cards/tapes, 82
purchased applications, 488–496
    benchmarking, 491, 493
    learning from experience, 494–495
    reasons to purchase, 488–489
    risks, 495–496
    steps in purchasing, 490–492

Q

Qiagen, 313
Quaker Oats Co., 129
Quantum Corp., 473–474
queries, 213
QWERTY keyboard, 73

R

R/3, 485
RAD (Rapid Application Development), 463
RAID (redundant arrays of inexpensive disks), 510–511
RAM. *See* random access memory (RAM)
RAMIS, 104
random access memory (RAM), 70, 71
    dynamic and static, 71
    running programs, 101
random access storage devices, 86–87
Rapid Application Development (RAD), 463
rational decisions, 262
reactive approach, 444
read-only memory (ROM), 70, 71
    running programs, 101
real estate industry, 345
records, 212
    linking, 220–221
recovery measures, 528–531
    business recovery plan, 530–531
    disaster recovery plan, 528–529

lack of plans, 508
recruitment of employees, 322
reduced instruction set computing (RISC), 90
redundancy, 528
redundant arrays of inexpensive disks (RAID), 510–511
re-engineering, 39–40, 279
    improving, SIS development, 45–47
refresh rate, 78
registers, 70, 102
relational database model, 218
relational operations, 229–230
relevance, information, 6
repeaters, 143
repetitive stress injuries (RSIs), 72
replication, 232
reports
    ad hoc, 17
    exception, 17
request for information (RFI), 491
request for proposal (RFP), 491
requirements definition, systems development, 449
research, multimedia software, 116
resolution, monitors, 78
result-driven chaining, 404, 405
retail, information system applications, 19
return on investment (ROI), 447
RFI (request for information), 491
RFP (request for proposal), 491
RGB monitors, 78
rightsizing, 278–279
rigid plans, 430
ring typology, 154
RISC (reduced instruction set computing), 90
risks, 197–199, 508–516
    applications and data, 512–516
    hardware, 509–512
    insurance policies, 526
    Internet. *See* Internet risks
    purchased applications, 495–496
    purchasing IS applications, 495–496
    user application development, 500–502
Roadway, 293
robot(s), 389
robotics, 389
robustness, 518–520

ROI (return on investment), 447
ROM. *See* read-only memory (ROM)
roots, hierarchical database model, 216
RSIs (repetitive stress injuries), 72
running programs, 100–101
Ryder Systems, 504

S

SABRE, 40, 49, 345
St. Louis Post-Dispatch, 75
sales. *See* marketing/sales
sales force automation, 321–322
SAMM (Software Aided Meeting Management), 374
sampling, 140
satellite microwave, 145
Saturn, 40
Saturn Automobile Corp., 337–338
scalability, IS tactical planning, 432
schema, database management systems, 225–226
Schlage Lock, 299–300
Schneider National, 167
scientific interests, global information systems, 349, 351
scientific publishing, 41
scope creep, 472
ScreenLink, 325
SDLC. *See* systems development life cycle (SDLC)
SDLU (systems development led by users), 467–470
Sears Roebuck and Company, 43
security, 164, 506–535
    controls. *See* control(s)
    databases, 213–214
    documentation, 532
    economics, 531
    global information systems, 349, 351
    goals, 508
    integrating into systems development, 522
    operating systems, 123
    recovery measures. *See* recovery measures
    risks. *See* risks
select operation, 229
semantic frames, 391
semantic nets, 402